BATTLE REPORT

BATTLE REPORT
THE END OF AN EMPIRE

Prepared from Official Sources by
Captain Walter Karig, USNR
Lieutenant Commander Russell L. Harris, USNR
and
Lieutenant Commander Frank A. Manson, USN

RINEHART AND COMPANY, INC. • 1948
New York • Toronto

The authors of this book have been given access to official documents which have been utilized in its preparation. The Navy Department is in no way responsible for its production nor for the accuracy of its statements.

The illustrations for this book were selected and edited by Captain E. John Long, USNR, assisted by Commander John H. Levick, USN, C. Earl Cooley, and the Misses Delia Rinalli and Susan Gibson. Charts and maps were drawn especially by Mr. James T. Rawls' Design and Standards Section of the Navy Department, under the supervision of the authors. All pictures are Official Navy Photographs unless otherwise designated. Official Combat Art work is indicated by the name of the artist.

COPYRIGHT, 1948, BY RINEHART & COMPANY, INC.
PRINTED IN THE UNITED STATES OF AMERICA
BY THE FERRIS PRINTING COMPANY, NEW YORK
ALL RIGHTS RESERVED

Authors' Foreword

THIS, the fourth volume of the BATTLE REPORT series, continues the narrative of the Navy's part in World War II as it was initiated by the late Frank Knox as Secretary of the Navy, and authorized to be completed by Colonel Knox's then Undersecretary, James V. Forrestal, upon his succession to the secretaryship.

In this volume, as in the preceding ones,[1] the major task of the series' editor and his associates has been the selection of material to tell the story of the fighting fleets principally in the words of the men who finally sailed them to triumph over a brave, sagacious, and well-equipped enemy.

The fifth and final volume is being completed as this text goes to press. The gratifying reception of the series, not only by the American public but by thousands in the homelands of our allies, is the compilers' and the publisher's only reward, and none could be greater. Designed to be a public service, sold at a price as close to cost as prudence permitted, the residue of profit and royalties is returned to the public through the Secretary of the Navy by distribution to the Navy's public welfare agencies. All the books were compiled and written as additional duty. The authors performed other routine naval duties, including service at sea, during the series' preparation.

As explained in other BATTLE REPORT prefaces, the series was not initiated as a definitive and analytical history of the Navy in World War II. Its cordial reception by historians in the United States and in the British Commonwealth is a bonus which the authors accept with genuine humility, while pointing to the parallel series of Captain Samuel E. Morison, professor of history at Harvard between wars. Necessarily slower in publication than the BATTLE REPORTS, the Navy's story as prepared by Captain Morison and his associates was authorized at the same time as this parallel

[1] BATTLE REPORT I, *Pearl Harbor to Coral Sea*, 1944; BATTLE REPORT II, *The Atlantic War*, 1946; BATTLE REPORT III, *Pacific War: Middle Phase*, 1947. All published by Rinehart & Co. under original designation by the Council on Books in Wartime, Inc.

series to provide the American public with the detailed analytical history of the naval campaigns.

Against as factually and technically accurate a background of the strategy and tactics of the opposing forces as BATTLE REPORT's authors could devise with the generous help herein acknowledged, this series attempts to relate the narrative of the Navy in terms of human experience. Secretary Knox's directions to "tell the bad along with the good" had consistently been interpreted in those terms. The directive did not impose upon the authors the obviously impossible chore of sitting in judgment on the strategy of the war's management, which a few critics have chosen to deplore as a deficiency. It will take the perspective of years, and expert appraisal of volumes of reports still unstudied, before that sort of history of the war can be objectively issued.

Here, then, is the story of the war as it looked and felt to the men who fought it on the sea, over the sea, under the sea and on the beaches. It is compiled from and as often as possible told in the words of seamen and admirals, Marine privates and officers, Regulars and Reserves, as related by them while the smoke of battle was still bitter in their nostrils, their bandages still wet, their elation at peak and their woes at nadir. Or so the authors have attempted, against the chronology of the movements of ships, the flights of airplanes, the deployment of troops, the decisions of admirals, generals, sergeants, and petty officers.

Thus the thanks of the authors for the help given to them are offered with respect to every person whose name is recorded in these pages, and to the scores of others whose contributions are anonymously merged in the whole narrative. All these are the real authors of the several BATTLE REPORTS.

For particular assistance in providing the writers with good counsel and valuable source material, grateful acknowledgment is due also to others named herewith: To Mrs. Belle B. Scheibla, whose library was always open to us; Captain John W. McElroy and his able assistants, Miss Loretta I. MacCrindle and Miss Catherine MacDonnell, of the Operational Records Division and Microfilm Library; Lieutenant Robert I. Curts, for his valuable information on Japanese planning; Commander Vincent D. Engels, who willed us his source material; Commander Robert J. Bulkley, Jr.; Ensign Raymond Moley, Jr.; Major Theodore F. Van Gestel, AAF (Ret.) for data and pictures of the entire New Guinea campaign; Lieutenant Albert Harkness, Jr., whose administrative history of

AUTHORS' FOREWORD

the Southwest Pacific was an enlightening aid; Vice Admiral Daniel E. Barbey; Commander John R. Leeds; Rear Admiral Ralph A. Ofstie, head of the Naval Analysis Division of United States Strategic Bombing Survey; Captain Arthur H. McCollum; Lieutenant Earl Burton, coauthor of BATTLE REPORT, Vol. II; Rear Admiral Russell S. Berkey; Lieutenant Commander LeRoy W. Vance; Rear Admiral Thomas H. Robbins, Jr.; Commander Harold E. Cross, of the Office of Naval Operations; Lieutenant Colonel E. Hunter Hurst, of the Marine Corps; Admiral Thomas C. Kinkaid; Admiral Raymond A. Spruance; Vice Admiral Forrest Sherman; Vice Admiral Robert B. Carney; Vice Admiral Jesse B. Oldendorf; Rear Admiral Felix L. Johnson, Director of Public Relations; the Misses Philibert, Estelle and Helene, of the Reference Section, Office of Public Information; Miss Margaret Emerson, of the War Department Historical Records Section; Mr. William Adam, of the War Department Bureau of Public Relations; and, of course, Chief Yeoman Elvina J. Sudol, of the skirted Navy, who, without complaint, broke many a tinted fingernail legibilizing the manuscript.

Deep thanks to all these and to many others who made the task of writing this volume easier for

WALTER KARIG
RUSSELL L. HARRIS
FRANK A. MANSON

Table of Contents

Part I · Southwest Cleanup

CHAPTER		PAGE
Prologue	ESTIMATE OF THE SITUATION, 1942–1943	5
One	NEW GUINEA	9
Two	RABAUL	37
Three	TO THE TOP OF THE LADDER	48
Four	GREEN ISLAND AND POINTS NORTH	64

Part II · The Real Offensive Begins

Five	THE MARSHALL-GILBERT-CAROLINE PROBLEM	75
Six	CROMWELL'S LAST DIVE	99
Seven	DEATH BY "FLINTLOCK"	104
Eight	DEJAPITATION CONTINUED	126
Nine	THE BUBBLE THAT LOOKED LIKE A BOMB	138
Ten	OPERATION CHERRY TREE	156

Part III · Southwest Cleanup Completed

Eleven	THE ADMIRALTIES: "CORKING THE BOTTLE"	166
Twelve	KOGA'S LAST STAND	177
Thirteen	HOLLANDIA	188
Fourteen	TRUK REVISITED	193
Fifteen	WAKDE AND BIAK	202
Sixteen	NEW GUINEA ADIEU	212

Part IV · The Marianas

CHAPTER		PAGE
Seventeen	"IF BIG BOMBERS FROM JAPAN ..."	219
Eighteen	SAIPAN: THE MARIANAS' TURKEY SHOOT	228
Nineteen	"WHEN THE LIGHTS GO ON AGAIN ..."	244
Twenty	MARIANAS COMPLETED	255

Part V · The End's Beginning

Twenty-one	CLOSING THE GAP TO THE PHILIPPINES	285
Twenty-two	"I HAVE RETURNED"	306
Twenty-three	HALSEY CUTS THE PIPELINE	322
Twenty-four	TOYODA'S ALL-OR-NOTHING GAMBLE	333
Twenty-five	SURIGAO STRAIT	347
Twenty-six	AND STILL THEY COME	366
Twenty-seven	JEEPS *vs.* GIANTS	384
Twenty-eight	THE GREAT SACRIFICE	402
Twenty-nine	THE END OF A NAVY	413
	APPENDIX	425
	CASUALTY LIST	465
	INDEX	523

List of Illustrations

MAPS

			PAGE
FIGURE	1	The Pacific Battleground	2–3
FIGURE	2	New Guinea	10–11
FIGURE	3	Eastern New Guinea and New Britain	14–15
FIGURE	4	Bismarck Archipelago. "The Top of the Ladder"	49
FIGURE	5	The Central Pacific	74
FIGURE	6	Invasion of Gilbert Islands, Nov. 20, 1943	80
FIGURE	7	Invasion of Kwajalein Atoll, Jan. 31, 1944	105
FIGURE	8	Assault on Eniwetok Atoll, Feb. 17, 1944	130
FIGURE	9	Battle of the Philippine Sea, June 19–20, 1944	164–165
FIGURE	10	Admiralty Islands, Los Negros Landing, Feb. 29, 1944	168
FIGURE	11	Invasion of the Marianas: Saipan, June 15, 1944; Tinian, July 24, 1944	218
FIGURE	12	Invasion of Guam, July 21, 1944	265
FIGURE	13	Invasion of Leyte, Oct. 20, 1944	310
FIGURE	14	Japanese Approach, Oct. 15–25, 1944	334
FIGURE	15	Battle of Surigao Strait, Oct. 25, 1944	348
FIGURE	16	Battle of Samar, Oct. 25, 1944	386
FIGURE	17	Battle for Leyte Gulf. Disposition of Third Fleet, Oct. 24–25, 1944	403

Photographs

Photographs appear in five sections. General classification headings are as follows:

PLATES I TO XVI *between pages*
President Roosevelt at Hawaii; PT boats, New Guinea; Bismarck Sea; Marcus Island; Lae; Wake; Rabaul; Cape Gloucester; Tarawa 52–53

PLATES XVII TO XXXII
Kwajalein Atoll; Hellcat and Jap "Emily"; Truk Atoll; Eniwetok Atoll; fueling at sea; Seabees; Ponape; New Guinea: Hollandia, Sansapor, Biak 116–117

PLATES XXXIII TO XLVIII
Battle of the Eastern Philippines: Saipan; Tinian; Guam; prisoners, American and Jap; US and British attack on Sumatra: Sabang; Soerabaja; Morotai 180–181

PLATES XLIX TO LXIV
Palau: Peleliu, Angaur; *Fury in the Pacific*; Liberators; Underwater Demolition Teams; Leyte; Battle for Leyte Gulf, opening phase: loss of USS PRINCETON 244–245

PLATES LXV TO LXXX
Battle for Leyte Gulf: Sulu Sea; Sibuyan Sea; Surigao Strait; San Bernardino Strait; Cape Engano; loss of USS GAMBIER BAY; Kamikaze attack on USS SUWANNEE; attack on YAMATO; casualties 340–341

PART ONE

Southwest Cleanup

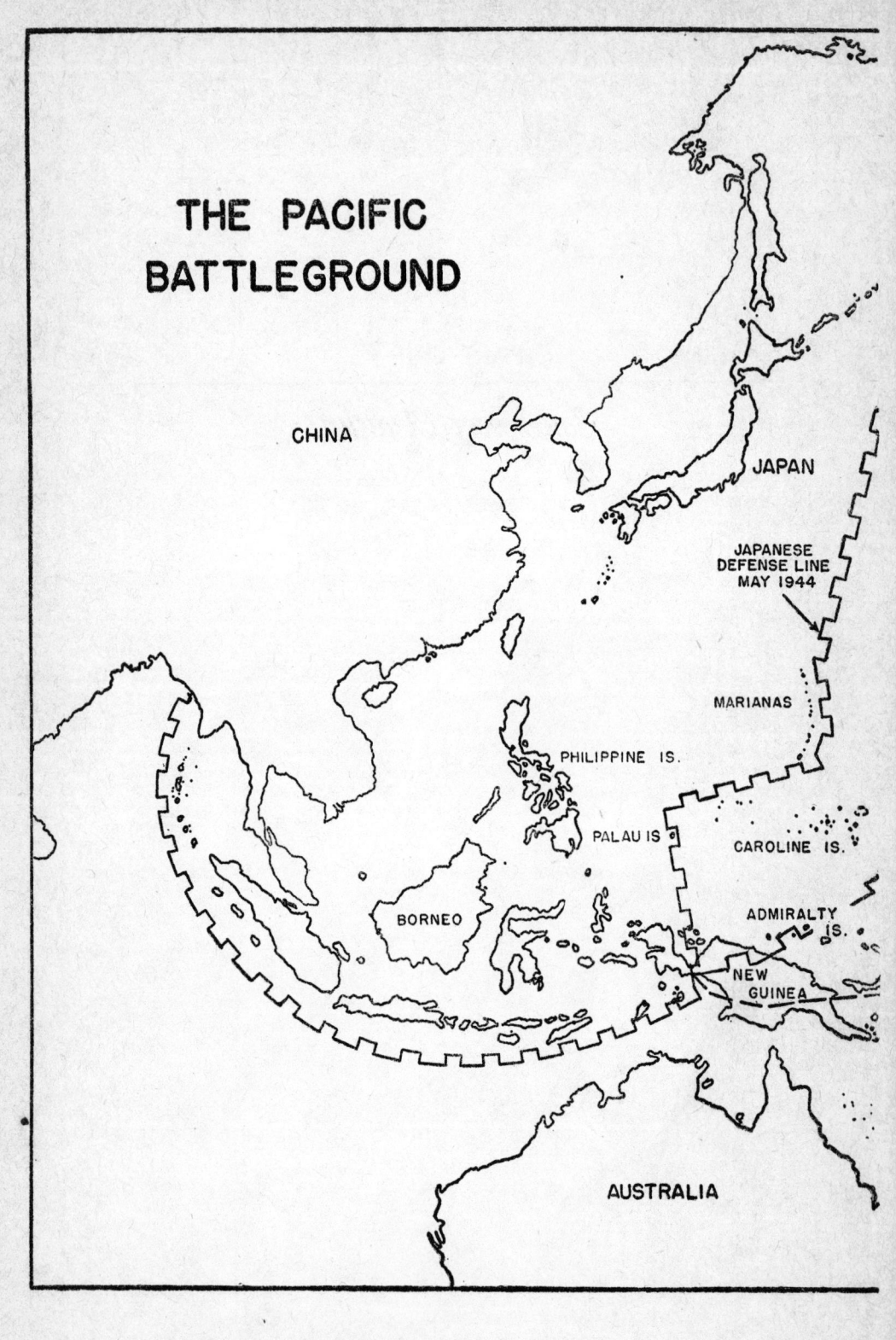

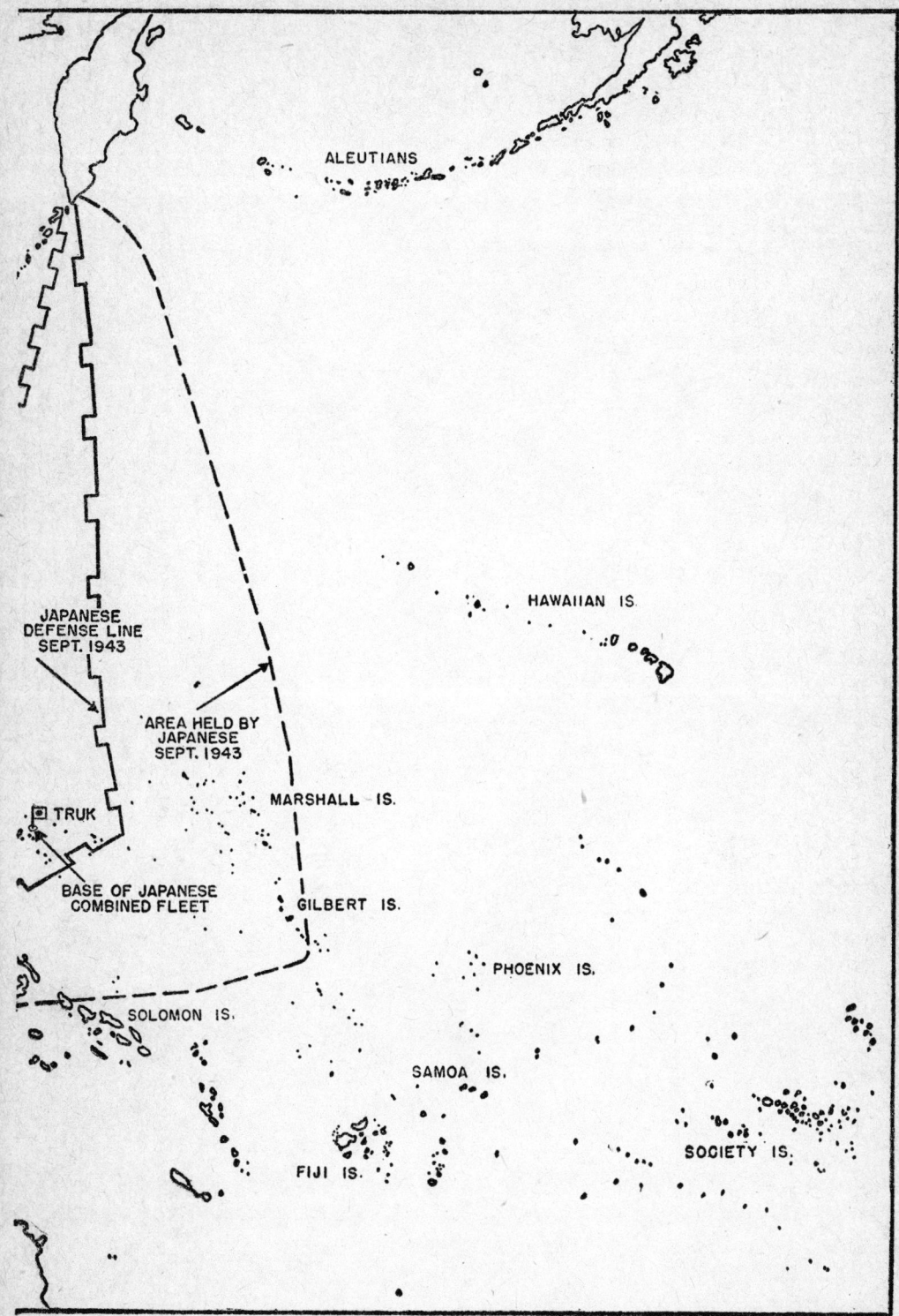

FIGURE I

PROLOGUE: Estimate of the Situation 1942-1943

JAPANESE expansion had been swift and decisive during the first six months of the war. Dai Nippon stretching a long and determined arm south into the so-called Southern Resource Area—French Indo-China, Malaya, the Philippines, the Netherlands East Indies, and most of Burma—had quickly grabbed an empire. Thus the goal of war seemed to be attained. Japan was at last self-sufficient.

This southward lunge was so cheaply successful that the Japanese optimistically pushed their expansion beyond the originally intended limits. Forces nosed into the Indian Ocean occupying the Andaman Islands. The Solomon Islands and the southeastern part of New Guinea were brought within the extended perimeter as space-defense for Rabaul, the strong hub of the Southeastern Area. Eastward, in the lonely atoll world of the Central Pacific, the perimeter was pushed to a line running through Wake, the Marshalls, and the Gilberts.

In Tokyo at the time of this expansion officers of the Imperial Headquarters held divergent views. For the most part the Army favored holding a compact line centered on the Southern Resource Area and the sea lines of communication between the homeland and this raw-material area. The Navy, on the other hand, favored extending the perimeter in order to build a defense in depth to protect this vital zone. In the end the Navy view prevailed.

But Japan with her limited strength could not adequately defend such a huge area. It was a vicious circle: the more the Japanese had the more they had to expand to protect what they had. In more earthy terms, the little sons of a Sun Goddess had bitten off more than they could chew.

Once the territorial aims of the initial offense were attained, the Japanese hoped to dig in behind the perimeter, thumb their noses at the Americans, and stand pat. There were no grandiose delusions of landings on the West Coast and peace treaties in the White House. The best that was hoped for was a compromise peace with the soft, weak-willed Americans who would not be willing to accept the tremendous losses inevitable in blasting the Emperor's men loose from their gangling conquests. The Imperial Navy hoped to make its point clear by striking a crippling blow against the American Fleet from one of the outlying bases.

In addition the Japanese planned various darting raids on advanced Allied bases to prevent their being strengthened as springboards of counterattack. In this category belong the carrier raids on Darwin (February, 1942) and Ceylon (April, 1942) and the midget submarine attacks on Diego Suarez—Madagascar—and Sydney (May, 1942).

Then came Midway.

Admiral Isoroku Yamamoto, wishing to press a decisive engagement with the American Fleet before its strength became too great, decided to occupy Midway as an eastern outpost. If the occupation of Midway didn't precipitate the decisive naval engagement, it was thought that from Midway the Japanese Fleet could force an engagement in Hawaiian waters.

The results of the Battle of Midway are well known (BATTLE REPORT, Vol. III). It was a decisive engagement but not the kind planned by Yamamoto. The Japanese were turned back with heavy losses.

Because of Midway the Japanese invasion of New Caledonia and the Fiji Islands, which would cut the supply lines from the United States to Australia, had to be abandoned. The Aleutian invasion, the purpose of which was to buttress Japan's northern flank, did take place, but within a year it ended in inglorious retreat.

The Japanese war machine was geared for offense, and at a time when the Japanese should have been consolidating their ill-got gains and converting their machine to a defensive and interception instrument, they had plunged headlong across the Pacific and had been slapped down.

This marked the beginning of a new stage of the war. Up to this time the Allies had fought a purely defensive war. There had been many fierce and gallant battles but all had been fought under a cloud of retreat. They now were standing firm and beginning to strike back.

In August, 1942, the Allies began offensive action in the Solomons area. When Guadalcanal was captured after long and violent fighting, many of the Japanese war planners became alarmed and began to think more in terms of defense, of strong points to be held. No great forces were sent into the Solomons in an all-out defense effort. Instead the Japanese trickled their planes and ships into the area over a long period of time at a high rate of attrition.

By the summer of 1943 the Americans had landed on New Georgia in the Central Solomons and gave every indication that they had plans to go on from there. True, the fighting was being done on the outer fringes of the Japanese defense perimeter, but what worried the Japanese was not the location of the fighting but the fact that the United States was able to conduct offensive warfare in growing proportions, each month gaining more strength and a little more ground.

After a year and a half of war the might of American industry was beginning to be felt in the steaming jungles of the Solomons and the blue waste of the Central Pacific. When Japan dropped the first bombs on Pearl Harbor, her leaders realized that the initial advantage gained by this sneak attack would not last indefinitely. Fleet Admiral Osami Nagano estimated that new task forces employing new ships could be organized by the United States within ten months after Pearl Harbor. He realized that the United States could replenish both men and ships with much more speed than Japan. Consequently he estimated that Japan could fight the war successfully for two years. After that there would be difficulties.

The two years were almost up, and he was right—there were difficulties!

Admiral Mineichi Koga, who had become Commander-in-Chief Combined Fleet after Yamamoto had fallen into the American-laid death trap, carefully balanced the facts and decided that the one chance of success for Dai Nippon lay in a decisive naval engagement. Only in that way could Japan bring home to the Americans the high cost, in blood and money, of attempting to challenge Japan's supreme position in Asia.

Furthermore Koga figured that if this fleet engagement took place in 1943, the Japanese would have a 50–50 chance of success. Koga would not accept the concept of a slow, stubborn point-by-point defense. Some strategists thought of the island perimeter only in terms of passive defense, but Koga's idea of the best defense was a hard, quick blow against the American Fleet.

By the fall of 1943 the tide of war had definitely shifted in favor of the Allies—all over the world. In the Ukraine the massed Red Army swept across the scorched plains toward the Dnieper, driving the battered Germans before them. In Italy the British and American armies cracked the Axis wide open and the Badoglio government could do nothing but surrender. By night and by day fleets of British and American bombers roamed freely through the skies of Europe.

The Japanese had never closely planned their war with the Germans, but of course they were delighted at having the war in Europe drain off American resources and manpower. With the continued Allied victories in Europe many Japanese strategists began to think that the main Allied attack would come across the Indian Ocean and be directed against Burma, Malaya, and the western part of the Netherlands East Indies. Koga, however, felt that so long as the main strength of the American Fleet was concentrated in the Central Pacific, the main threat lay to the east.

Koga's views finally prevailed and the central authorities at Imperial Headquarters decided to allow him to keep his strength undiminished in the east, his fleet poised for the coming strike against the Americans.

It was not Koga's plan to take any positive action to draw the American Fleet into a decisive engagement. Instead he intended to keep his fleet concentrated at a central point, Truk, behind his atoll-network of cross-supporting airbases, the "unsinkable carriers." He was sure that sooner or later the Americans would come out and he could engage them in his own territory at his own choosing.

The one all-out battle would leave the Americans bowed and bloody, happy to negotiate a compromise peace.

Things were to be different, however. The Americans had plans of their own. This volume is the story of the execution of those plans. To bring the chronology of the ever-widening area of Pacific conflict into focus, it is necessary to look backward briefly at what General Douglas MacArthur had been doing in New Guinea while the Navy and its Marines were dispossessing the Japanese from the Solomon Islands, as related in the preceding book of this series.

Chapter One

New Guinea

I

IF YOU WILL look at a map of the continents that bound the Pacific Ocean you will notice that they seem to crumble at the edges. Beginning with Vancouver's big chunk off the North American mainland, a great oval of islands interposes between the ocean and the land masses of North America, Asia, and Australia and doubles back upon itself almost to the coast of South America.

It was among those islands, and for those islands, west of the international date line and north of the equator, that the War in the Pacific was waged by the United States.

Some of these islands are scarcely large enough to afford dry footing at high tide. Others are among the most densely populated areas on earth —Java and Japan notably. But the biggest one of all, and next to Greenland the largest island in the world, has been the least known. It was, and is, populated with cannibals and tribes so primitive that they do not understand the use of bow and arrow. Just before the war one hardy explorer emerged from the interior with a blurred snapshot as evidence that dinosaurs still survive in its deepest jungle marshes.

That island of 300,000 largely unexplored square miles is New Guinea. You will see on the map that it is shaped somewhat like a dinosaur itself, with gaping jaws directed at Asia and its long tail trailing in the Coral Sea between Australia and the Solomon Islands. To the tip of that tail the last remnants of the shattered Allied forces clung desperately in the spring of 1942, preparing for a last stand against the so-far overwhelming Japanese.

They held fast, and from that point started the slowly accelerating, painful, and costly journey that was to end in the triumphal parade of fighting ships into ash-strewn Tokyo Bay.

Geography (that science most neglected in our public educational system) largely determined that the parallel drives to the enemy's heartland from the farthest reach of Japan's advance would be predominantly

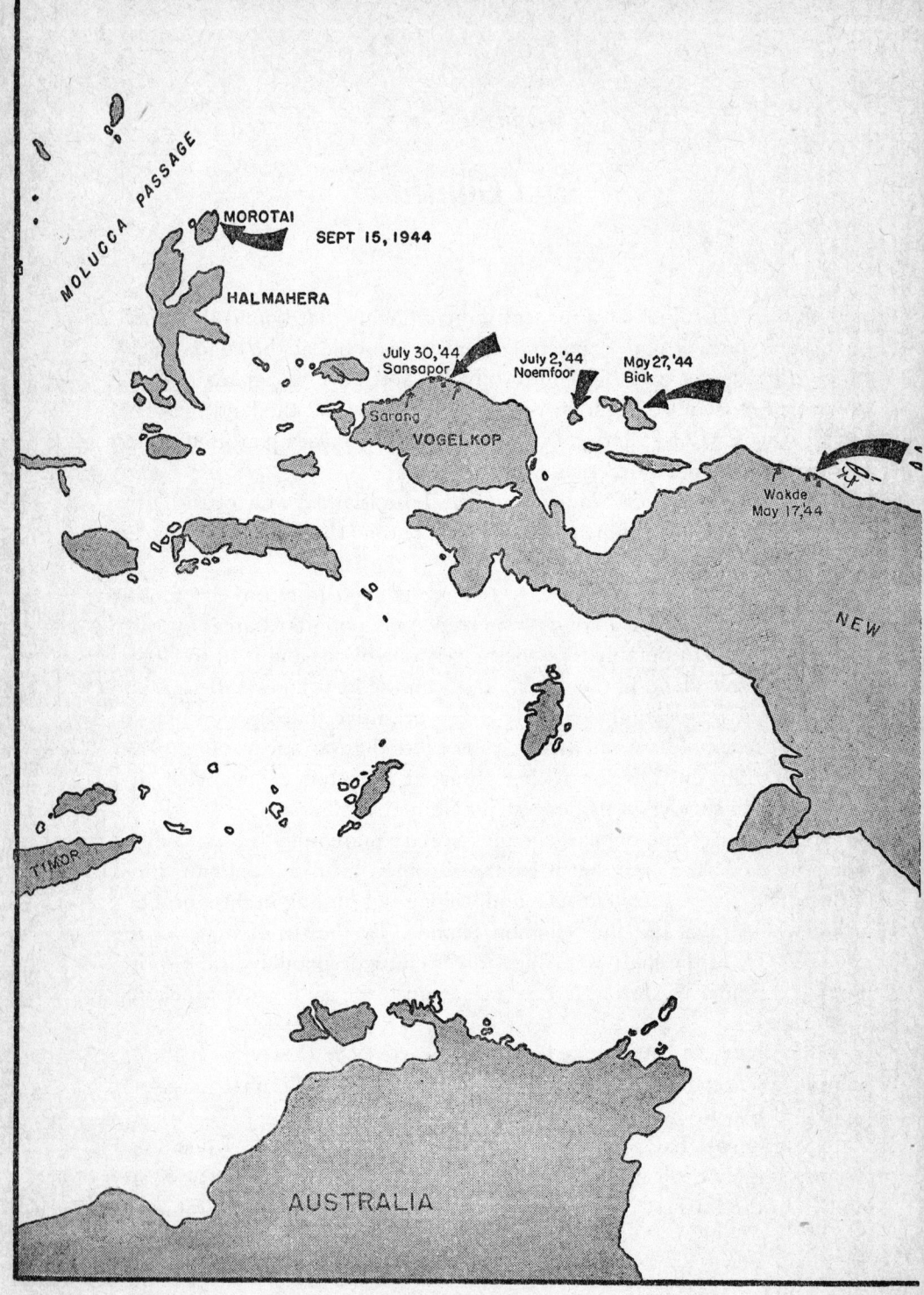

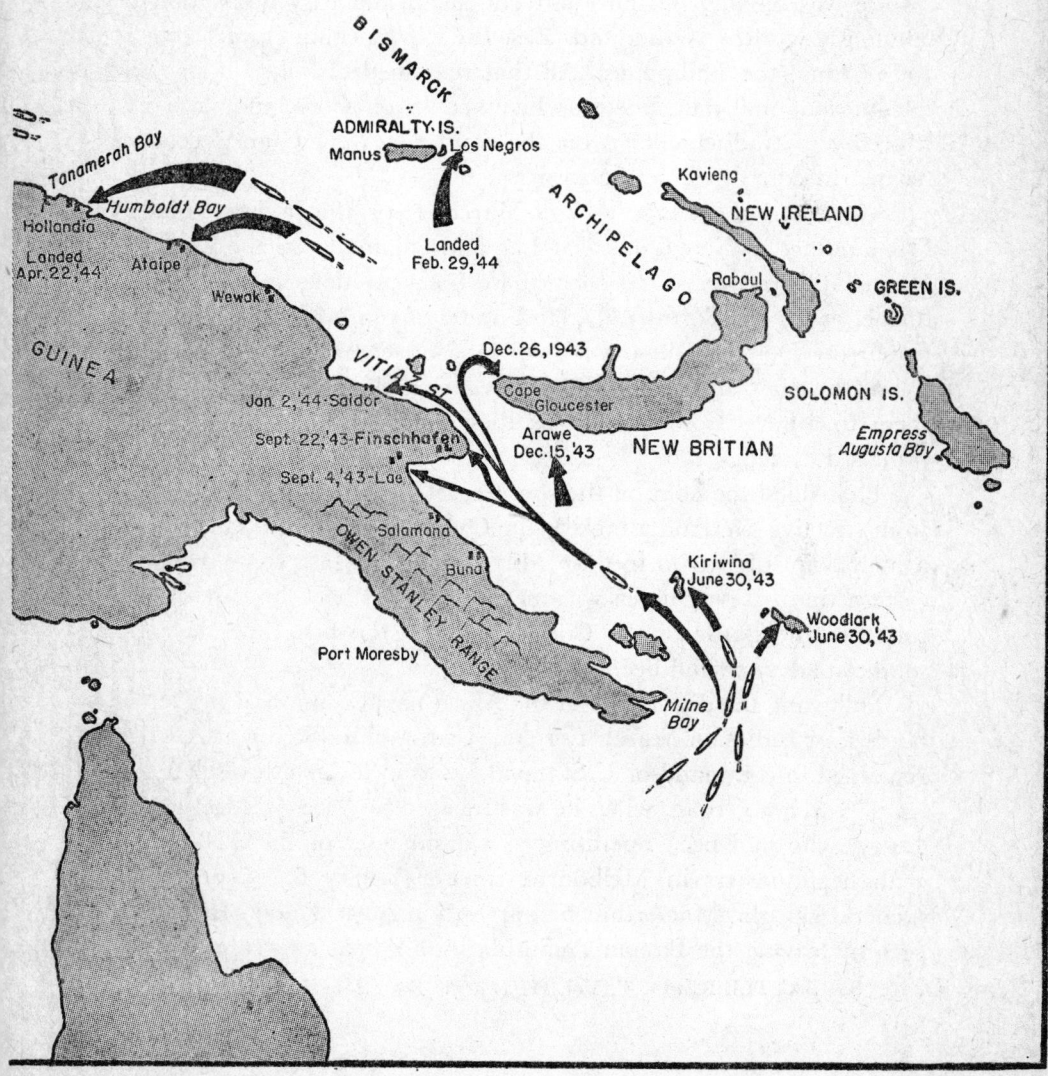

FIGURE 2

a naval operation on the right and center, and the Army's task on the left, or New Guinea, flank. The reconquest of the Solomon Islands has been related in the third volume of this series (*Pacific War: Middle Phase*). But the Navy was an indispensable adjunct to General Douglas MacArthur's expansion of New Guinea from a toe hold to a strangle hold, and it is necessary now to backtrack a little so that the narrative can be all squared away for the recital of the campaigns that cost Japan an empire it took three hundred years to build.

Three months after Japan's explosive entry into World War II, that empire was bloated by the relatively cheap and easy absorption of the fabulously wealthy Netherlands East Indies, "unconquerable" Singapore, Indo-China, the Philippines. All that remained of Allied might west of the international date line was hemmed in on Corregidor and in Port Moresby, a trading village on the southeast New Guinea coast. Both seemed in equally desperate straits.

At the end of the first week of March, 1942, the Japanese made their first landings in New Guinea at Lae and Salamaua on the west coast of Huon Gulf and began to consolidate their positions in preparation for further advances. Fortunately, land routes of communication were limited to narrow foot trails in the rugged interior, compelling the Japanese to follow the coast line, slowing their advance and at the same time exposing them to attacks from the sea as they opened their campaign to Australia's doorstep.

The Allies' toe hold on the south coast of New Guinea was protected from effective overland attack by the Owen Stanley Mountains that touch a high point of 13,200 feet. In May a Japanese task force rounding the eastern tip of New Guinea was met and turned back by American naval forces in the Battle of the Coral Sea.[1] For the first time the Japanese southern advance had been checked.

Following the dissolution of the Allied naval command in the Netherlands East Indies on March 1, 1942, Rear Admiral William A. Glassford remained in command of U.S. naval forces in the Southwest Pacific area until March 30, 1942, when he was relieved by Vice Admiral Herbert F. Leary, who had been operating as Commander of the ANZAC Forces with headquarters in Melbourne since February 6, 1942. Meanwhile General Douglas MacArthur had arrived in Australia on March 17, after secretly leaving the Bataan Peninsula by PT boat and submarine, to as-

---

[1] See BATTLE REPORT, Vol. III (*Pacific War: Middle Phase*) Chap. 1.

sume supreme command of the Allied Forces in the Southwest Pacific area.

As early as June, 1942, the planners in Melbourne and Washington began to think of punching back at the Japanese with an offense of their own.

General MacArthur wanted to go after the Japanese immediately in the New Britain-New Ireland area at the western tip of the Solomons, opposite the butt of New Guinea. For the job he requested a division of amphibious trained troops and a two-carrier task force—extremely rare commodities in those days, and as yet unavailable to the General.

In Washington the Joint Chiefs of Staff issued a directive outlining three tasks for the U.S. naval forces in the South and Southwest Pacific areas: the seizure and occupation of (1) the Santa Cruz Islands, Tulagi and adjacent positions, (2) the remainder of the Solomon Islands and Lae and Salamaua on the northeast coast of New Guinea, (3) Rabaul and adjacent positions in the New Britain-New Ireland area. But this carefully calculated plan had to await the assembly of men, arms, planes, and ships—and there was a war in Europe to fight as well.

The Japanese Empire was now stretched almost to the limit. In July the final effort was begun to dislodge the Allies from the last bit of territory they tenaciously held in southeastern New Guinea. Japanese troops went ashore at Buna, Gona, and Sanananda on the northeast coast of New Guinea and began to push southward across the Papuan peninsula.

The Japanese hoped to clamp a land-sea pincer on Port Moresby, the last Allied outpost north of Australia, for in conjunction with the movement of troops across the Owen Stanley Range an amphibious attack near Port Moresby was planned. To secure staging bases for the amphibious operation, Japanese units were landed at Milne Bay on the extreme southeastern tip of the island during the last week of August. This attack was quickly halted by two Australian brigades, one of which had been moved into the area scarcely more than a week before. After three days of heavy fighting the main body of the attacking force was evacuated by Japanese destroyers.

Japanese naval units remained in the vicinity, however, and on the nights of September 3, 6, and 7 they entered Milne Bay and shelled Australian troop positions. On September 11, Desron 4 (USS SELFRIDGE (F), BAGLEY, HENLEY, and HELM), under the command of Captain Cornelius W. Flynn, received orders from Rear Admiral V. A. C. Crutch-

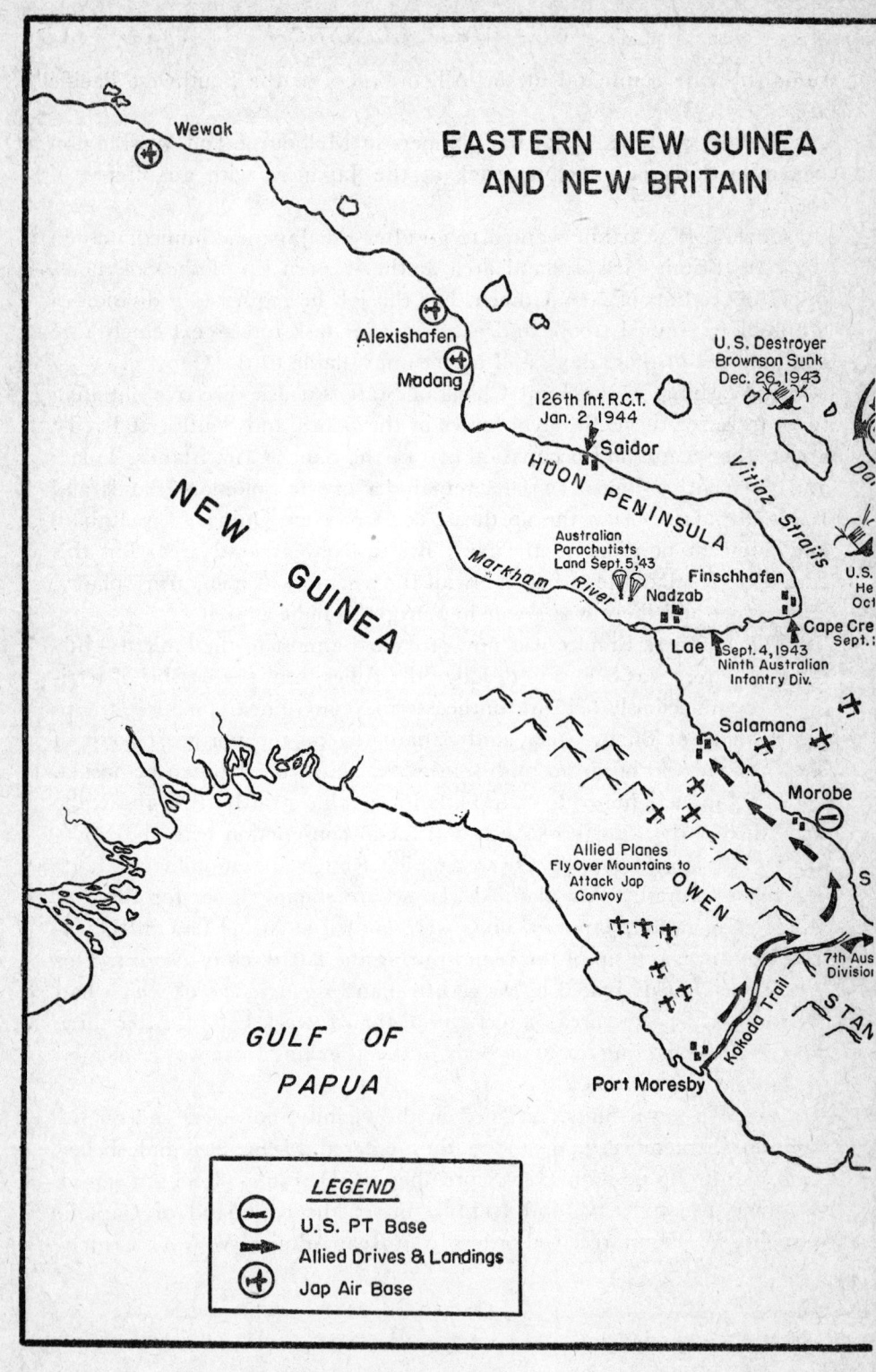

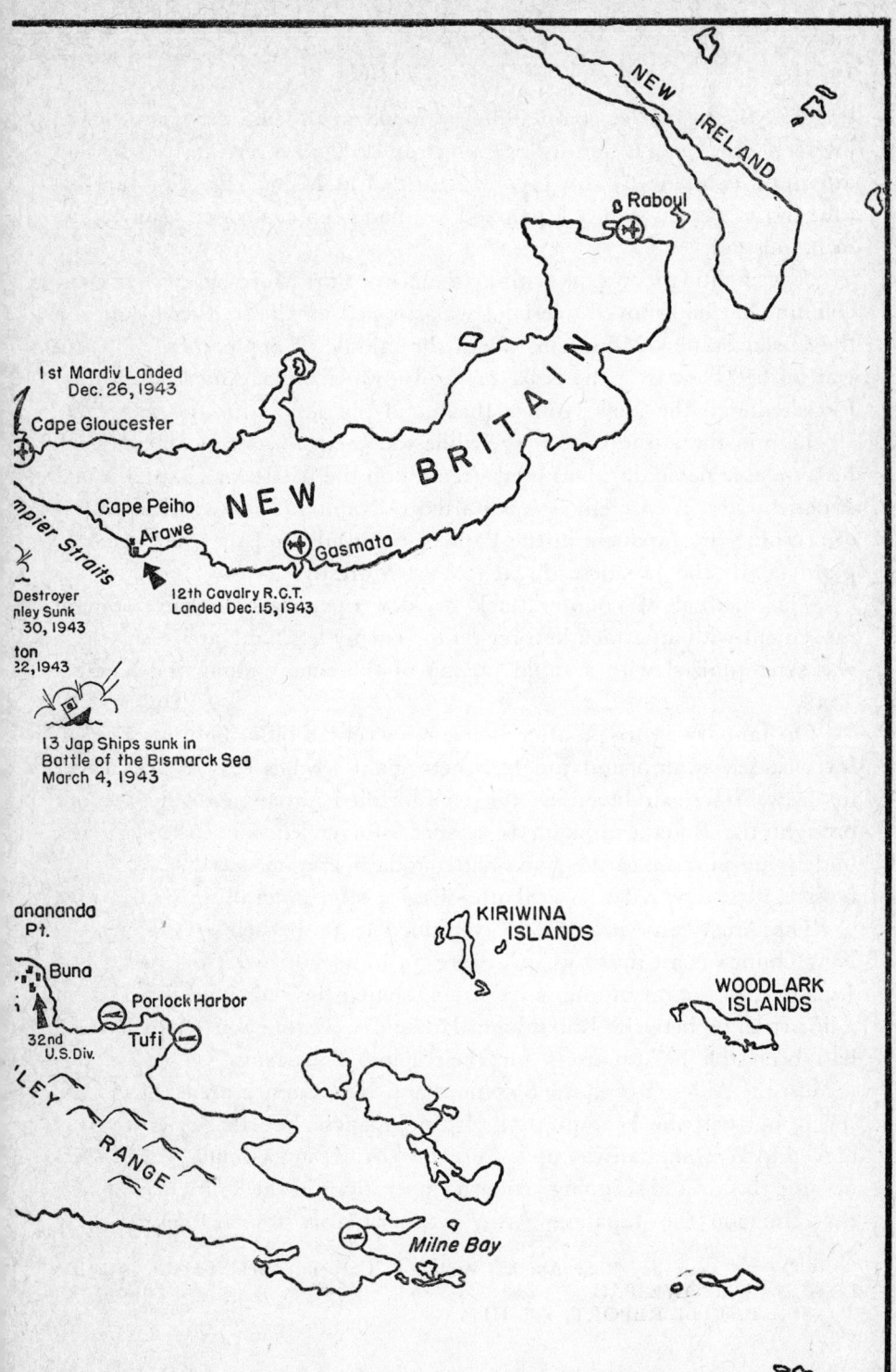

FIGURE 3

ley, RN, the task force commander, to move north from the Coral Sea to intercept the enemy.[1] No interception resulted, however, and no further attempt was made by the Japanese to land at Milne Bay. For the first time in the Pacific War a Japanese force had been evacuated after failing in its mission.

After fighting its way to within 32 miles of Port Moresby, the Japanese column that had moved overland was stopped on the southern slopes of the Owen Stanley Mountains about the middle of September. Slowly it was pushed back over the Kokoda Trail toward Buna. American ground forces entered the New Guinea theater of operations for the first time.

Late in the autumn of 1942, while the enemy was concentrating all his available naval, air, and land strength on the battle for Guadalcanal,[2] American and Australian troops started to counterattack with the object of crushing the Japanese in the Papuan peninsula and thereby removing permanently the Japanese threat to Port Moresby.

The method of counterattack decided upon was an envelopment movement with an attack in force on the enemy left flank at Buna, which was synchronized with a rapid pursuit of the enemy along the Kokoda Trail.

On January 23, 1943, after almost ten weeks of bitter fighting through fever-ridden swamp and jungle, where giant leeches clustered as eager to draw American blood as the well-fortified Japanese, Allied troops brought the Buna campaign to a successful conclusion. Although the underlying purpose of the Buna-Sanananda operation was essentially defensive, it represented a tactical offensive—a forerunner of things to come.

The American-Anzac forces continued to push their way along the New Guinea coast and by April were 75 miles northwest of Buna. The Japanese, in the meantime, were strengthening their air-land defenses on a line running between Rabaul and Hollandia. Throughout 1942 Rabaul had been the headquarters for their joint Army-Navy air operations against the Allies in both the Solomons and New Guinea areas, but in the spring of 1943 the headquarters of the Japanese Fourth Air Army was moved to Wewak, halfway up the north coast of New Guinea, which then became the air and shipping center for operations in the entire area. From that time on the Japanese Army was primarily responsible for New

[1] On the same day Rear Admiral Arthur S. Carpender relieved Vice Admiral Leary as COMSOWESPAC.
[2] See BATTLE REPORT, Vol. III.

Guinea while the Japanese Navy devoted its efforts to turning back the Allied drive in the Solomons. Because of the extensive commitments the Japanese assumed in the early part of the war, they were finding it more and more difficult to maintain simultaneous pressure in both Solomons and New Guinea areas. The American-Australian forces were finding it correspondingly less and less difficult, but they suffered no less than the Japanese.

Allied plans in the Southwest Pacific called for the establishment of a chain of air and naval bases along the north coast of New Guinea. Control of the air was absolutely necessary. The Japanese, too, understood this, for during the first six months of 1943 they took no offensive ground action, now in their turn waiting and preparing for the showdown. Meanwhile they concentrated all efforts on strengthening air facilities and defenses, and in air strikes to harry and disperse Allied forward positions.

Half a world away, in Washington, "things were beginning to roll"—literally so—to crush the Nipponese.

2

On a bright summer day in 1942 a weird and wonderful mechanical contrivance rumbled down 14th Street in Washington. It was indeed a hybrid thing, with the body of a barge and the wheel tracks of a tank. It behaved like an automobile, besides, when it came to traffic lights and stop signs. But then after crossing the Potomac the nightmare thing slid into a lake with the nonchalance of a duck. Immediately a man on the shore began to scream wildly and wave his hands above his head as he ran along the shore parallel to the course of the "thing." When the ugly monster emerged from the water, all the occupants were put under arrest for invading a wild waterfowl sanctuary.

This was the first recorded action taken against an amphibious vehicle.

One of the occupants was a Navy captain named Daniel E. Barbey, who held the unique post of head of the Navy's Amphibious Warfare Section, thus placing himself well on the road to acquiring the nickname he later was tagged with in the Southwest Pacific—"Uncle Dan, the Amphibious Man."

When the Japanese dropped the first bomb on Pearl Harbor, amphibious warfare had not progressed much since the British went ashore in small boats from warships during the Battle of New Orleans. With the convenient use of pierheads denied to us by the enemy in this war it was necessary to devise some method of getting troops and heavy equipment ashore and on the beaches.

One of the prototypes of the strange new family of ships, boats, and small craft that were to confuse even naval officers with their alphabetical designations was the "Alligator." It was in an Alligator that Barbey got into trouble with one of Secretary Ickes's bird watchers.

The Alligator was an invention of Donald Roebling, of the world-famous family of bridge builders. It was not conceived to be a naval craft, but as a carrier of cargoes and hunting parties through the weedy, sand-barred, log-snagged Florida bays and swamps. Something that could travel over land and water, where there were highways or channels or none, and triumph over any mixture of land and water in whatever consistency or viscosity.

It was not even an engineer, but a scholar with a ready hand for tools, who devised the unique propulsion gear of the Alligator, Noyes Collinson, house guest and lifelong friend of Roebling. With tapes, cardboard, rubber bands, and an oblong wooden cream-cheese box he built a model whose caterpillar track was equipped with rubber flanges that would serve as elongated paddle wheels in water, on land as treads pliant to rocks or logs, and as self-cleansing grips in mud or quicksand. The first embryo Alligator triumphantly traversed the Roebling swimming pool, climbed its tiled edge and proceeded to give birth to a huge family of hybrid mechanical saurians at home in surf or jungle.

Into their evolution went the landing ramp, experimented with by our Navy and Marine Corps and used by the Japanese on shallow-draft small boats employed in the invasion of the East Indies, and the half-keeled invasion ships experimentally built by the British from Admiral Lord Keyes's designs. Marine Corps and Navy experts contributed new ideas, or demands for performance which inspired new ideas, and in the midst of it all came General MacArthur's request for an amphibious admiral. The obvious man for the assignment was Dan Barbey, who not only had worked on the construction of the new fleet but had also assisted in training the 1st Marine Division (later to land at Guadalcanal) and the 1st Army Division (used in the North African invasion) in the techniques of amphibious warfare.

On December 15, 1942, Barbey was nominated a rear admiral and ordered to Australia, as Commander Amphibious Force Southwest Pacific. At the time Admiral Barbey had only a paper fleet but it was to grow into the mighty Seventh Amphibious Force, which as part of the Seventh Fleet was to take part in fifty-six amphibious landings, move more than a million men over the Eastern seas, and transport cities of supplies to the malaria-ridden jungles of New Guinea and to the shores of the liberated Philippines.

3

The Seventh Fleet [1] was a far cry from the type of fleet that was later to pound a path across the Central Pacific. Lacking were the large heavy units that men think of as traditionally belonging to a fleet. There were no battleships, no aircraft carriers, and only a few cruisers, some of them Australian. True, these larger units were to be added in the future, but there were many long miles of New Guinea coast to hop up before the mighty landings in the Philippines saw the Seventh Fleet full-blown and strong enough to combat the remains of the Japanese Navy.

[1] The Seventh Fleet was designated as such on February 19, 1943, by COMINCH. Previous to that it had been known as the Southwest Pacific Force. The task organization finally resolved itself into the following:

Task Force 70:	Administrative designation for the Commander Seventh Fleet, under which the only operational units were PTs as Task Group 70.1 and the Guerrilla Supply Group as Task Group 70.4.
Task Force 71:	Submarines (Fremantle).
Task Force 72:	Submarines (Brisbane) under Operational Control of COMSOPAC.
Task Force 73:	Service Force, Seventh Fleet.
Task Force 74:	Australian Cruisers (Rear Adm. V. A. C. Crutchley).
Task Force 75:	Cruisers (Rear Adm. Russell S. Berkey).
Task Force 76:	Amphibious Force (before it became the Seventh Amphibious Force) and later became the administrative designation for the same command.
Task Force 77:	Operational name for Adm. Kinkaid at Leyte and Lingayen and on several occasions as operational designation for Amphibious Forces.
Task Force 78:	At first escort and minecraft but when these were absorbed by the Service Force, used for operational purposes as Amphibious Force designation.

When men of the Pacific spoke of "MacArthur's Navy" they meant the Seventh Fleet. This was true from both an operational and an administrative standpoint. The primary function of the fleet was the support of land operations, and because of this the core of the fleet became the Amphibious Forces. Even the Brisbane-based submarines and Air Forces attached to the fleet were used as support for the land operations. Vice Admiral Carpender (promoted from Rear to Vice on arriving in Australia) as Commander Seventh Fleet was responsible to the boss of all Allied forces in the Southwest Pacific—General MacArthur.

Admiral Barbey arrived in Australia in January, 1943. The organization he proceeded forthwith to create was destined, except for two occasions, to lead all the major combined landing operations of our sweaty advance along the jungled coast of New Guinea and into the heart of the Philippines and Borneo. The story of his Amphibious Force is the history of the Seventh Fleet.

The problems of amphibious warfare were known to Barbey from his Atlantic days,[1] but as this whole conception of warfare was new, rough, original ideas had to be painfully polished up by trial and error methods in the field, or, to be more exact, in the surf. Many lessons were learned from studying the amphibious landings in the Solomons.

Training was the first problem confronting Admiral Barbey. Without ships, however, the problems of amphibious warfare were academic, so Admiral Barbey, with two floors of the staid New Zealand Building in Brisbane as his base of operations, went out in search of shipping. Pickings were lean, to put it mildly, for other theaters of war had a priority on things that floated, but enough was scraped together for a beginning.

The HENRY T. ALLEN, formerly the liner *President Jefferson* converted into an attack transport (APA), was acquired from the South Pacific in March, 1943, for troop training. The Australian Government kicked in with three former passenger ships previously used as merchant cruisers. These, WESTRALIA, MANOORA, and KANIMBLA, were converted into Landing Ships, Infantry (LSIs), the British equivalent of our APAs, and were put to immediate use. These four ships formed the slim beginnings of the Seventh Amphibious Force and were to serve with that force until the end of the war.

At Port Stephens, north of Sydney, the Royal Australian Navy had an amphibious training base known appropriately as HMAS ASSAULT. The

[1] See BATTLE REPORT, Vol. II (*The Atlantic War*), Part IV, Chap. 1.

facilities were offered to Admiral Barbey, who immediately set up the Amphibious Training Command for the purpose of accustoming Australian and American soldiers to flying spray and bouncing boats. Soon after the establishment of the base, Captain John W. Jamison, who was a veteran of Atlantic amphibious training and who acquired much experience as a Beachmaster (an officer who supervises the landing of troops and the unloading of supplies on the beaches) in the North African invasion, took over command. Almost all Army units that later participated in Southwest Pacific landing operations learned their lessons under the critical eye of this veteran naval officer.

Other training centers were set up at Toorbul and Cairns in Queensland. The great pinch was still shipping "bottoms." There was only one thing left to do—improvise, or, in naval lingo, set up some sort of "jury rig."

LSTs (Landing Ship, Tanks) were rigged with debarkation nets and used as transports, carrying as much as a battalion aboard. Ships' sides were built over the water and troops debarked over these into a landing craft, simulating debarkation from transports. Despite handicaps of makeshift, and despite the recurrent malaria that kept some divisions as much as thirty per cent under strength, Admiral Barbey's Amphibious Forces in 1943 trained one Marine division (the 1st), four U.S. Army divisions (32nd Inf., 1st Cav., 24th Inf., and 41st Inf.), and two Australian divisions (6th and 9th, part of the original "Rats of Tobruk" returned from the Middle East).

The Amphibious Forces were ready for their first show in June, 1943. The objectives were two islands in the western Solomon Sea off the coast of New Guinea—Woodlark and Kiriwina.

Admiral Barbey's flagship was the USS RIGEL, a repair ship. The RIGEL was so small that there were bunks for only a fraction of the Admiral's staff, and consequently the wardroom—the officers' dining room, recreation room, and library—became office, wardroom, or sleeping quarters according to the greatest need at the time. Off to Milne Bay she wallowed with an overload of humanity to prepare for the first operation. The Kiriwina invasion force was to stage, as best it could, out of Milne Bay; the Woodlark force used the better facilities of Townsville, Australia, for its preparation.

On June 30, 1943, while amphibious forces of Admiral Halsey's South Pacific Command were going ashore on Rendova and New Georgia,

Admiral Barbey's hybrid craft [1] ground their noses on the sand, and unfortunately sometimes on the coral, of Kiriwina and Woodlark. On Kiriwina an unexpected ally was found in the form of an Australian missionary who had organized the natives to resist the invasion that at first was thought to be Japanese. On discovering the nationality of the landing force, the bushy-haired warriors were converted to enthusiastic stevedores. The Woodlark landing, owing to a more favorable beach, came off fairly smoothly, but Kiriwina, in sailor lingo, was "FUBAR"—"fouled up beyond all repair." Several LCIs scraped their bottoms on uncharted coral heads, others damaged their propellers; LCTs could not land on assigned beaches because of an incorrectly charted sand bar; equipment had to be unloaded forty feet from the beach with much damage by salt water. About all Admiral Barbey could say about Kiriwina was: "After the first two weeks unloadings progressed smoothly!"

The absence of Japanese helped, too.

But the landings had been a good drill, and the Army could now carve out vital airstrips on the two islands. In support of the dress rehearsal Captain James Fife's submarines from Brisbane had covered the northern end of the Solomon Sea with an offensive reconnaissance. Cover had also been furnished by nimble PT boats. The tactical use of submarines and torpedo boats during this first landing forecast the cover-reconnaissance work they were later to perform at the great landing on Leyte.

4

The PT boys with the Seventh Fleet grumbled that their brethren in the Solomons across the way had all the fun. They had big game to shoot at—Japanese cruisers and destroyers charging down the Slot—whereas in the waters of New Guinea there was mainly the drudgery of hunting Nip motor barges, impossible to torpedo, difficult as corks to sink with gunfire.

The New Guinea PT war did not start off that way. Among the first half dozen of the fragile, gun-studded patrol-torpedo craft to arrive in the area in December, 1942, was No. 122, Ensign Robert F. Lynch in command.

[1] To a large extent Adm. Barbey's fleet was borrowed. It consisted of: 4 APDs (from Adm. Halsey's SOPAC Fleet, the Third Fleet), 17 LSTs (6 belonging to the Third Fleet), 20 LCIs, 20 LCTs, 10 DDs, 10 SCs, 4 YMSs, and a civilian-manned salvage tug.

By the calendar it was Christmas night, but as un-Christmas a night as Lynch or Lieutenant Daniel Baughman, in charge of the patrol, had ever experienced. No snow, no sleigh bells, no holly, no eggnog. Just heat and the smell of the sea polluted by the jungle steam of the strangest land on earth. The 122 was coming off patrol and heading southeast across Dyke Acland Bay to the PT base at Tufi, on the far side of Cape Nelson; just the end of another working day.

Suddenly the lookout shouted and pointed to starboard. Lynch couldn't hear the words, but he quickly muffled his engines and headed the boat to the right. Then his eyes made out a shadow against the shadows, the silhouette of a surfaced submarine—and it was obvious even in the gloom that it was no American submarine. Ours didn't come that big.

"A sitting duck," observed the hastily summoned Baughman.

"Good lord, there's two of 'em! See—on the other side?"

The range slowly closed to 1,000 yards: "Fire!"

Twin lines of bubbles streaked out from the 122. The port torpedo missed but the starboard one hit the after part of the submarine. The submarine remained afloat—not damaged enough to sink, too damaged to dive. It was the undamaged ship that lurched forward, nose down.

Quickly the forward torpedoes were made ready, and four minutes later, with the range now point-blank at 500 yards, two more torpedoes were tossed at the black bulk. Again the starboard torpedo hit, this time amidships with a violent explosion. As quick as an echo a second violent explosion shattered the hull. Like a match stick cracked between two strong fingers the submarine broke in half and sank.

By this time the second submarine had submerged. In rage she fired four torpedoes but the little giant killer easily sidestepped and headed back toward her base at Tufi, having sunk the I–18, a 2,180-ton Japanese undersea monster, larger than any of our fleet-type submarines, which had been evacuating troops from Buna.

The motor torpedo boats, the "spitkit" navy, became famous in the first of the war when Lieutenant John Bulkeley rescued the reluctant General MacArthur from Bataan on the first leg of his grueling journey to become the commander-in-chief of all Allied Forces in the Southwest Pacific. Romantic interpretation of the PT's abilities made the little PTs popularly thought of as a match for a cruiser, an obviously lop-sided evaluation. They performed wonders enough, however.

Italy introduced the fast, fragile, heavily armed little craft a few years before the opening of World War II. The British copied and then improved upon them. The United States Navy, without funds to experiment, had a chance to study them when Secretary of the Navy Charles Edison helped arrange for the manufacture of some of the British craft in private American yards. When Congress finally gave the Navy its go-ahead signal and the money with which to proceed, we were thus ready with designs improving upon the prototypes.

Eighty feet or less in length, the PTs carried two officers and a crew of nine. Armed with from two to four torpedo tubes, depth charges, sometimes mine racks and, later, rockets, the little plywood warcraft bristled with guns ranging from twin 50s to 30-caliber machine guns, giving them the hardest punch per ton of any ship in any navy.

The first PT boats moved into the New Guinea area in December, 1942, more than six months before the Seventh Amphibious Force made its amateurish bow in the empty theater of Woodlark and Kiriwina. The beginnings were small, only six boats and a tender, the converted yacht HILO (Lieutenant Commander Frank A. Munroe, Jr.). An advanced base was set up at Porlock Harbor on the west coast of Cape Nelson but by Christmas the base had been moved to the more suitable Tufi on the east coast of the cape. Commander Edgar T. Neale's chief problem as commander of motor torpedo boats in the Southwest Pacific area was to cut off supplies for the Japanese advanced forces, which were shipped down the coast on 80-foot armed wooden power barges. It was a gunboat war, and a night war, the adversaries hiding in jungle-screened bays by day. One of the greatest dangers, besides the intense return fire from the barges, was uncharted reefs. Many of our boats had to be destroyed by our own hands after grounding themselves on some jagged coral peak a few feet under water. This game of hide-and-seek, where to be "it" usually meant to be dead, was carried on during 1943 from Tufi to Vitiaz Strait, 200 miles to the northward.

The first major action against enemy barges took place the night of January 17, 1943. The PT 120 was on the prowl near Douglas Harbor when, across the calm water, she saw three Japanese barges heading south, as usual hugging the coast. Immediately the PT went to full speed and headed in, all guns blazing. Simultaneously the barges opened up with machine guns and 20mms, the long strings of greenish-blue tracer showing the surprised Japanese to be consistently firing too high. At top speed the PT circled the barges, raking them from stern, beam, and stem, from every angle, for twenty-five minutes.

Even ordnance can't work without rest, and the 120's guns were glowing hot as all but two jammed, and the action had to be broken off. But two of the barges had been sunk, and the third was ablaze. The PT had been hit twice; one 20mm shell pierced the wooden bow and exploded in the chain locker and another 20mm hit the after 50-caliber gun mount. Chief Motor Machinist's Mate J. J. Masters, Jr., was badly wounded and died ashore twelve hours later.

Not much of a battle, of course. It will not appear in the history books as the Battle of Douglas Bay, if at all. But Masters is just as dead as any of the thousands who died in the big fleet engagements, his ten shipmates fought as gallantly against odds, and the small victory left some thousands of Japs short of food, ammunition, and medical supplies. A two-bit contribution to a ten-billion-dollar victory, maybe, but the one example of what the PT boys' chore was, night after night, through the years encompassed by this book.

In February two men who had fought with the Asiatic Fleet during the dark days in the Philippines joined Motor Torpedo Boats, Southwest Pacific (on March 15, 1943, to become Motor Torpedo Boats, Seventh Fleet, or Task Force 70.1). One was Commander Morton C. Mumma, Jr., who had been commanding officer of the submarine SAILFISH in the Philippines, the other Commander Bulkeley. Mumma was to command all PTs in the Southwest Pacific, and Bulkeley to command Squadron 7. Later Bulkeley was to add to his reputation when he attacked an enemy barge with his PT boat and, failing to sink it, came alongside and boarded it.

5

By the end of January the Australian 7th Division, after slugging its way across the Owen Stanley Mountains, and the U.S. 32nd Division (plus a regiment of the 41st) had mopped up the last Jap in the Buna-Sanananda area, and, after rest and reorganization, began pushing slowly up the fever-haunted coast.

The Japanese had no choice but to reinforce the Lae-Salamaua area with troops from their great base at Rabaul on New Britain, one of the world's superb but misplaced harbors. On the last day of February a convoy of six transports, ranging from 2,700 to 6,900 tons, two small freighters of about 600 tons apiece, and a special service vessel set out across the Bismarck Sea escorted by eight destroyers. On the evening of the next day, March 1, 1943, the convoy was sighted by a patrolling B-24. Word was flashed back to headquarters at Port Moresby, but it was too late to strike that day.

Great thunderclouds and rainstorms draped the Owen Stanley Range when, at dawn the next day, Australian and American fliers leapt across the three-mile-high mountains to pounce on the convoy in Vitiaz Strait between New Britain and New Guinea. The weather sided with the Japanese, obscuring the target, and the attack had to be broken off.

All that night the convoy was shadowed by those lumbering aerial work horses—the Navy's "Black Cats," black-bodied Catalina Flying Boats whose night patrols became famous throughout the South Pacific. The Navy fliers kept Port Moresby informed of the ships' course and speed. The next morning dawned clear and the bombers came back for the kill, guided by the Black Cats' over-the-spot directions. The convoy was now only 60 miles east of its destination, Salamaua, but it was never to arrive there.

Throughout the day Allied fighters and bombers shuttled over the Owen Stanley Mountains between Port Moresby and the convoy—Beaufighters, Flying Fortresses, Havocs, Mitchells, Lightnings, Kittyhawks, Airacobras—gassing up, rearming, and dumping death and destruction. At one time there were more than 109 planes over the convoy, or what was left of it by then. By nightfall only four destroyers and two cargo ships were reported to be afloat, and both cargo ships were burning.

To finish the work of the bombers eight PTs were sent out that night, and two of them, the 143 (Lieutenant (jg) John S. Baylis) and 150 (Lieutenant (jg) Russell E. Hamachek), polished off the only Japanese ship of the convoy left afloat. The surviving destroyers had fled.

The now-famous Battle of the Bismarck Sea was over and the Japanese had lost all of the eight ships in convoy, four of the escorting destroyers, and the special service vessel. Loss of life was high among the troops of the 51st Japanese Division. About 2,900 men were drowned. Japanese destroyers and submarines picked 2,734 survivors out of the water.

The Battle of the Bismarck Sea convinced the Japanese that sea routes from Rabaul to Lae and Finschhafen were unhealthy for any ship as large as a destroyer. No more could the positions around Lae and Salamaua be reinforced by cargo ships and fast destroyer transports. Supplies had to be muscled overland through the swamps, toted in handfuls by submarine, or brought in on barges sneaking along the coast from Wewak. It was in the strangulation of this barge traffic that the PT boats were toilsomely to demonstrate their hell-raising potentialities. The doughty little giants were not to find heftier game again until the Leyte operation.

6

Two months after the dress rehearsal at Kiriwina and Woodlark, Admiral Barbey's Seventh Amphibious Force was ready for the Japanese. The picked point of contact was on the rugged Huon Peninsula, 14 miles east of Lae. Here it was planned to put the 9th Australian Division ashore for a drive on the Japanese stronghold, 14 miles through mangrove forest and over stinking, miry river deltas. Of the 56,000 enemy troops estimated to be in New Guinea, 12,000 were believed to be in the Lae-Salamaua area.

The Japanese, who had so easily and cheaply swept down to Australia's doorstep, were being pushed back to Rabaul where the Imperial Southeast Area Fleet was an ever-present threat to our operations in the Solomons, New Guinea, and beyond. Someday the Japs were bound to react violently to the pressure.

Two weeks before the Lae landing a group of four destroyers headed out at night from Milne Bay. They were Captain Jesse H. Carter's Desron 5—PERKINS (Lieutenant Commander Gerald L. Ketchum), SMITH (Commander Robert A. Theobald, Jr.), CONYNGHAM (Commander James H. Ward), and MAHAN (Lieutenant Commander James T. Smith). Its mission was to sweep the Huon Gulf clean of Jap shipping between Finschhafen and Salamaua. Nothing was found, so, not to make the foray wholly wasted, the ships swept close in to Finschhafen at 15 knots in column formation and shelled it for ten minutes, catching the invaders completely by surprise. The Seventh Amphibious Force was beginning to flex its muscles.

The Lae Task Force [1] formed up in the Milne Bay area and headed up the coast. At Buna the ships paused and prepared for the overnight leap across Huon Gulf to the two landing beaches east of Lae.

Before dawn on September 4, the destroyer CONYNGHAM eased in toward the dark low coast. The mountains that rise abruptly from the flat,

[1] See Appendix for list of ships participating in this and succeeding operations.

wooded coastal plain could not be seen in the darkness. Landing beaches were hard to identify. Aboard the CONYNGHAM Admiral Barbey studied a chart with an Australian naval lieutenant, who before the war had been part owner of a plantation near the beach area. Before sunrise the two sandy strips had been found, and the APDs, LSTs, and LCIs were drawn up ready to empty their troops.

As the practice was to be in the Pacific theater on an increasing scale, sustained efforts were made to knock out Japanese air power in the vicinity of the landings. For almost three weeks prior to the Lae operation Allied planes hammered at the enemy's airfields in Wewak, Hansa Bay, Alexishafen, and Madang. At Wewak, alone, over 200 planes were destroyed on the ground and 64 in the air by American and Anzac Army fliers. Japanese air support was pushed back 300 miles to Hollandia.

The morning of the landing, however, there was still grave danger of air attack from Rabaul. The destroyer REID (Commander Harry H. McIlhenny) took position off Cape Cretin to sweep the eastern horizon with radar and to direct our fighters to enemy planes that might head from that direction.

The two beaches selected were "Red," just east of the mouth of the Busu River, and "Yellow," three miles farther east. Between them lay the Australian naval reservist's coconut plantation.

As the first waves of boats started in from the APDs, the destroyers LAMSON (Commander Philip H. Fitzgerald) and FLUSSER (Commander Josephus A. Robbins) began to rake Yellow Beach with 5-inch fire while PERKINS, SMITH and MAHAN gave Red Beach the same treatment. But, except for a sniper's rifle shot here and there, the enemy made no response. They were laying for us at Salamaua, southward (and nearer the Allied bases) across the bay. The Japanese may have felt indignant at being bypassed, and certainly disappointed to be miles from where the Aussies were piling safely ashore from bobbing LCPRs, side-ramped LCIs, LST-borne LCTs, and finally LSTs themselves.

But if the Jap was not on hand to greet us from the shore, he was quick to leap on us from the air. At 0705, little over half an hour after the first boat had stumped its nose on the beach, seven Mitsubishi light bombers and three Zeros came diving down from the mountains to the west, where they had sneaked in, undetectable by radar.

At that time the LCI 339 (Lieutenant (jg) James M. Tidball) was approaching the beach, dropping her stern anchor and in no position to maneuver. A shout of warning, a few seconds to swing the AA guns on the target, and then three Zeros ripped her bow to stern with their bullets.

Close behind came the bombers. Two "paint-scrapers" exploded in the water to port and to starboard, staggering the little ship and then, in a perfect bracket, a third bomb bore into the deck amidships, blasting a jagged hole seven feet across, buckling decks, rupturing bulkheads, and riddling the superstructure with large holes. The doctor's quarters were smashed and the pilothouse wrecked beyond recognition. Listing badly to port the LCI made a dying lunge onto the beach and settled in the shallow water.

On the blasted decks Australian and American blood flowed together. Twenty Australian soldiers had been killed and just as many wounded. Eight Americans were wounded, among them the ship's doctor, Lieutenant (jg) Fay B. Begor, who lay with both thighs shattered by shrapnel. He died a few days later aboard the LST 464 (Lieutenant Augustin K. Ridgway), the converted landing ship that had been fitted out as a first-line hospital ship of the Seventh Amphibious Corps. (The LST hospital ship was not protected by the rules of the Geneva convention. She looked the same as her fighting sisters and bristled with as many guns.)

The troop-filled LCI 341 was caught in the same attack. A near miss blasted a gaping hole in her port side, starting numerous fires. Lieutenant (jg) Robert W. Rolf calmly ordered the troops to starboard to counteract the port list, and, like a battle-wise veteran (which he wasn't), skillfully brought his craft into the beach, firmly snubbing her upon the sand. When the troops were unloaded, Rolf personally lead a fire-fighting party and soon the flames were smothered. The craft was so badly hurt that the crew had to be assigned to other duties. But Rolf stayed with his ship, sure that it could be salvaged.

On September 6 he was still checking damage when a flight of Japanese bombers came in over the western mountains. It happened very quickly. One explosion bathed the 341 with a hot shower of shrapnel, and Rolf was deeply wounded in the right thigh. His ship—for which he had risked his life—would fight again, but not he. Forty-five minutes later Rolf died on the operating table. Beside him, tight-lipped, stood the Army colonel whose men he had landed safely on the beach.

On the first day of the Lae landings over 7,800 fully equipped troops had been put ashore, quickly so as not to overexpose the almost defenseless landing craft to avoidable air attacks. When Jap planes struck at the landing beaches the afternoon of September 4 they found only the two injured LCIs and one of those tough little bulldogs of the Navy, the tug SONOMA (Lieutenant (jg) George I. Nelson). But more men and more supplies were on the way. One of the approaching convoys was a group of LSTs [1] under Commander Thomas C. Green.

In the wheelhouse of the LST 473 (Lieutenant Rowland W. Dillard) at five minutes to two on the afternoon of September 4, 1943, stood Johnnie Hutchins, Seaman 1/c. The ship was at General Quarters and his station was lee helmsman. He peered over the shoulder of the man at the wheel, watching the gyro click back and forth to either side of 132, the course being steered. Soon it would be time for him to relieve the man at the helm. Meanwhile he wished he could smoke.

Then—"Bogies on the port bow!"

Nine of them, all enemy, dive bombers and fighters. Simultaneously twin-engined torpedo planes slanted out of the sun on the port beam. The LST 473, under attack for the first time in its career, was blanketed with four bombs, all of which seemed to explode together. Two were near misses, but two hit all too true. One demolished the commanding officer's station and blew up a 20mm gun, including the ammunition, killing six and wounding thirteen. The other ripped through to the bottom of the ship and exploded near the keel amidships, bulging the deck four feet out of true.

In the smoke and debris of the wheelhouse the helmsman lay dead, and beside him lay Johnnie Hutchins, bleeding badly, both feet a pulp of shattered bone and flesh. But he wasn't dead. He could see—and he saw the helm untended. He could hear—and from what seemed to be miles away he heard the order from the officer of the deck: "Right full rudder!"

Torpedo planes were coming in fast at masthead height.

Through the puzzling blackness that fogged his eyes, Johnnie reached for the wheel and twisted it to the right with his last ounce of strength.

As the ship swung right, the straight white wake of a torpedo passed 20 feet astern. Johnnie's turn had saved the ship.

After the attack, the boy's dead fingers had to be pried loose from the wheel. Johnnie David Hutchins, age twenty-one, had given his life

[1] The convoy was in two columns. LSTs 471(F), 474, and 473 to the right, and LSTs 467, 475, and 457 to the left. These were escorted by Motor Minesweepers 49, 50, 51, and two sub-chasers.

for his shipmates, and had earned the Congressional Medal of Honor. The next year, at a shipyard in Orange, Texas, his mother christened a sleek, new destroyer escort—the USS JOHNNIE HUTCHINS.

Other ships of the convoy were being attacked at the same time the LST 473 was absorbing so much punishment. Evidently mistaking the minesweepers for destroyers, several dive bombers peeled off for the attack but succeeded in scoring only near misses. The LST 471 (Lieutenant George L. Cory) also was receiving the one-two punch of dive bomber and torpedo plane, but a damage control party led by Lieutenant Albert E. Craig, the executive officer, kept her afloat.

The casualties were relatively heavy. We counted six of our men dead, one missing, five injured. The Australian dead numbered 45, with two missing and seventeen wounded. The Japanese lost two planes out of the attacking dozen.

The two crippled LSTs were taken in tow to Morobe, where, next day, the dead were buried ashore.

The Japanese in the Lae-Salamaua sector now found themselves caught in a master squeeze play. The day after the landings on Red and Yellow Beaches, units of the 7th Australian Division were dropped by parachute in the Markham River valley near Nadzab up from Lae, the first use of airborne troops in the Southwest Pacific. And, pushing westward across the swollen Busu River, the troops landed by the Seventh Amphibious Force pressed in on Lae along the coast. Southward at Salamaua more of our forces completely routed the enemy, surprised as he turned his back to rush to the defense of Lae.

There was no escape for the trapped Japanese. Retreat overland was cut off. Withdrawal in barges or submarines across the Huon Gulf was made disastrously unhealthy by our PT boats and destroyers. The effectiveness of the PT patrol is attested to by the diary of an officer of the Miyake Regiment, one Kobyashi: "Last night, with the utmost precautions, we were, without incident fortunately, transported safely by barge from Sio to Finschhafen. So far there had not been a time during such trips when barges had not been attacked by enemy torpedo boats. Truly we were lucky. However it was reported that the barge unit which transported us was attacked and sunk on the return trip last night. The barge commanding officer and his men were all lost."

To the Japanese the PT men seemed to be cat-eyed devils. A captured Japanese document described American PT tactics: "Usually two enemy high speed torpedo boats patrol the vicinity of our supply routes, or they communicate with their intelligence system which has infiltrated the area we have taken—They seem to have excellent night binoculars [Ed. note: radar]. Our small craft try to sight the enemy first with seven power binoculars but we rarely sight them first. The enemy usually opens fire . . . The enemy attacks savagely. When our small craft are sunk, they whistle as they fire on the men floating in the water . . ."

The enemy retaliated with air attacks on our convoys that kept the vital supplies pouring onto the beaches east of Lae. The destroyer CONYNGHAM, with Admiral Barbey aboard, fought off a swarm of bombers while returning from the initial landings. On September 12, by which time the Seventh Amphibious had landed over 16,500 troops on Red and Yellow, bombers attacked our advanced base at Morobe and damaged the LST 455 (Lieutenant William E. Peterson), but the fire was put out with the aid of that veteran tug, the SONOMA, who, having undergone three intense air attacks in one week, felt as if she were fighting a single-handed war against the Japanese. Two of her men, unable to stand the strain, broke down with hysteria, as truly wounded as if by bullets.

On the morning of September 16, troops of the 7th Australian Division, after fighting their way down the Markham Valley, entered Lae, still smoldering from the attacks of Allied heavy bombers. The Japanese who remained offered only slight resistance before they fled into the brush.

With the capture of Lae, the last serious threat to southeastern New Guinea and the possible threat to Australia were removed. The Allies now had control of Huon Gulf, with all its strategic advantages, and Vitiaz Strait was now wide open for Allied aerial and surface patrols against enemy barge traffic between New Guinea and New Britain.

7

Things had gone well at Lae. So well, in fact, that the schedule of attack in New Guinea could be stepped up considerably. Originally it had been planned to start operations against the next objective—Finschhafen, on the tip of the Huon Peninsula—a month after the fall of Lae. But the Japanese were so obviously stunned by the crushing speed of our victory that it was decided to take advantage of their dismay. Lae fell on September 16. The assault date for Finschhafen was moved up three and a half weeks to September 22. Plans were literally still being made for the operation as the first echelon moved toward the beaches.

The ships of the Seventh Amphibious Force—LCIs, LSTs, APDs, and destroyers—had the absolute minimum of time for refitting and rest at Milne Bay. PT boats, operating from Morobe, pushed their reconnaissance patrols to Fortification Point, north of Finschhafen, while our aircraft kept a hawk's eye on the Jap airstrips at Cape Gloucester, Hollandia, Wewak, Gasmata, and Rabaul.

Just before midnight on D-minus-2 day, six LSTs pulled away from Buna and headed for George Beach, east of Lae, escorted by four destroyers and the omnipresent tug SONOMA. The following morning sixteen LCIs shoved off from Buna. With them were four destroyers of the bombardment group plus the HENLEY (Lieutenant Commander Carlton R. Adams). Admiral Barbey, his flag again on the CONYNGHAM, preceded the group.

Lae was the first stop. There the 20th Australian Infantry Brigade (Brigadier Windeyet), fresh from battle, was taken aboard. The Japanese were evidently fooled by this maneuver, mistaking this stop at Lae for a reinforcement operation for that area.

The beach selected, "Scarlet," was on a small bay six miles north of Finschhafen, flanked at either end by steep cliffs. Not much was known about the area. Photographic coverage had been inadequate, and the party of ten scouts landed the night of September 11 from PT boats had not obtained all the information they were after because Japanese activity kept them lying low.

The time selected for the landing was a compromise. The Navy, at this stage of the war having in mind the continuous menace of aircraft, preferred night landings. The Army, on the other hand, wanted a dawn landing so that their troops could see what they were doing. The compromise hour was 0445, permitting a landing in darkness and at the same time giving the troops good light shortly after they had hit the beach.

The stage was now set. Before midnight the heterogeneous fleet weighed anchor and headed east, some of the ships trailing canvas in bridal-veil fashion to conceal their phosphorescent wakes from night-flying Japanese.

First blood was drawn by the PTs 133 and 191 on patrol north of

Finschhafen when they sighted a 120-ton coastal trawler scouting near Fortification Point. Like a dog after a thrown stick the two boats went to flank speed and closed, blowing the scout out of the water and breaking its keel.

Precisely on schedule, at 0433, four destroyers, LAMSON, MUGFORD (Commander Howard G. Corey), DRAYTON (Commander Richard S. Craighill), FLUSSER, commenced the beach bombardment. While the destroyers were still sending their whistling 5-inch shells through the darkness, the first wave of boats from the destroyer transports started in toward the beach. Our troops found the beach defenses fully manned—the Japs had probably been waiting there ever since the bombardment of August 22. A machine-gun position, in fact, was located at the exact spot where one of the boats from the destroyer transport BROOKS (Lieutenant Commander Charles V. Allen) landed.

Machine-gun and mortar fire was intense. Sniper fire also was heavy, and in an effort to silence it, several of the ships opened up at the treetops.

Landing in the darkness caused some confusion. Two LCIs, one leaving and one approaching the beach, collided. One LCI had its port ramp carried away when it attempted to land troops in deep water. Operations all along the line were delayed when the LCMs and LCVs carrying units of the 2nd Engineering Special Brigade lost their way—or, euphemistically, "had navigational difficulties."

But in spite of all, by 0935, the last LST had unloaded and another beachhead was firmly established on the Road to Tokyo.

The first air attack—10 torpedo planes—that broke through the tight umbrella that the Army fighters capped over the area, came a little after noon when the last three LSTs, the SONOMA, and the destroyers PERKINS, SMITH, REID, MAHAN, HENLEY, and CONYNGHAM were retiring south. Captain Jesse H. Carter, in command of the escorting destroyers, immediately signaled the prearranged maneuver against aircraft attack. The destroyers rang up full speed and started circling the convoy in a counterclockwise movement while the tug and LSTs kept course and formation, wiggling right and left like agitated polliwogs.

Two of the planes were hit at long range by the destroyers' 5-inch fire and were down before they could loose torpedoes. A third, hit at long range, dropped its torpedo 90 degrees from its proper course.

One of the LSTs, being under fire for the first time, experienced difficulties of an internal nature. Two of her green gun crews became so enthralled watching the fight that they forgot to watch where they were shooting. Nathaniel Rickey, Seaman 2/c, manning the phones for guns one and two, was for a while under fire from four sources before his anguished and unquotable protests brought the absent-minded gunners to their senses and target.

Wakes of seven torpedoes crisscrossed the water, but none hit. By the time the P-38s arrived to take charge of the situation our ships had knocked out eight of the attackers, and the two others were heading for Rabaul. Added to the 37 planes that the Army fighter-cover had knocked down over the beach that day, the total bag left the sky empty of planes marked with the red "meat ball."

After cleaning out Japanese mortar batteries and machine-gun implacements on Scarlet Beach, Allied troops advanced rapidly southward along the coastal plain. Another Allied force moving eastward along the coast from Hopoi cut off the southern escape route of the Japanese. Again the PTs and Allied patrol planes made withdrawal across Vitiaz Strait in barges to New Britain extremely dangerous for the bottled Japanese. On October 2, within ten days following the initial landings, Finschhafen fell after hard fighting to elements of the Australian 9th Division.

But the sweet taste of victory was bittered the next day by the loss of one of the desperately few combatant ships the Seventh Amphibious Force possessed. At six in the evening the destroyers REID, SMITH, and HENLEY, under the tactical command of Commander Harry H. McIlhenny, were in a loose column formation about to commence an antisubmarine sweep off Finschhafen, when suddenly the SMITH sheered out of column to starboard. Four torpedo wakes wrote the reason in the water. As the HENLEY came left, increasing speed to 25 knots in pursuit, the commanding officer, Commander Carlton R. Adams, saw two torpedoes approaching his ship from the port side—one heading for the bow, one for the stern.

"Hard left rudder!"

The slim ship seemed to pivot around her mast, heeling to the turn. One torpedo passed clear of the bow by about 30 yards and another skittered 10 yards astern on the surface. It looked as if the ship had avoided certain death, but five seconds later a third torpedo tore in, heading straight for the ship's belly. It hit the port side amidships and dug into the fire room before exploding, destroying the boilers and snapping the keel. Within three minutes, with the main deck awash, Commander

Adams gave the order that tears at the heart of Navy skippers: "Abandon ship!"

The SMITH and REID immediately jumped after the submarine, but after a number of attacks lost contact and were not able to regain it. That night the seas were carefully combed for HENLEY survivors floating in rafts. When the last oil-coated man was hauled aboard, only one officer and fourteen enlisted men were missing.

With the capture of Finschhafen the first phase of the New Guinea campaign was over. During the next few months the main Allied effort was devoted to the neutralization of the great Japanese bases at Rabaul and Kavieng. Once this was accomplished, "MacArthur's Navy" would be in a position to commence the 1,200 miles of leapfrogging the troops up the northern New Guinea coast to poise for the long jump to the Philippines.

CHAPTER TWO

Rabaul

I

YASUMI DOI, Commander in the Imperial Japanese Navy and Staff Gunnery Officer of the Imperial Southeast Area Fleet, felt hemmed in. Kicking at the small stones in his path, he climbed up the hill to his quarters in Rabaul. Rabaul was still an active base. Yes, but the Americans were closing in from two sides. Only last month they had captured Finschhafen across the straits from New Britain. In spite of the best efforts of the Japanese Imperial Navy they had slowly climbed up through the Slot and were even now attacking Torokina on Bougainville. If they could not be thrown back from there, it would be only a matter of time before Rabaul would be a ghost harbor, unless—

He came to a turn in the path. From there he could look out over Simpson Harbor. His depression lifted a little, to see the harbor filled again. Admiral Kurita's cruisers and destroyers, down from Truk, were lying at anchor, some of them fueling. Tomorrow they would sortie for a strike against the Americans on Bougainville. And Admiral Ozawa's 250 planes overflowed the three Navy fields. They would be able to give the Americans an awful sting, too. But if they didn't succeed—

Well, Rabaul had known tragedy before. He looked up at the slumbering volcanoes that ringed the harbor, which often shook the earth with titanic violence. The Germans had known their violence before the last war, and had seen their beautiful city destroyed. And before the Emperor's Navy came, the Australians had moved the capital of their mandated territories from Rabaul to Lae in New Guinea. The gods of the underworld were too dangerous.

Rabaul was beautiful, very beautiful at sunset. Too beautiful. Doi had a strange sense of impending death even in the midst of all this activity. If only the Army were a little more co-operative. It had sent practically no aircraft to Rabaul, and the two Army fields were so rough that it was an adventure to land a plane on them.

The sky reflected the dropping sun in vivid reds and deep purples. Tomorrow, the 5th of November, would be a fine day. He hoped the big American bombers would not come again that night. It always took at least a day to repair the runways after an attack, and they would be needed tomorrow. Besides, his gun crews were exhausted from fighting off previous attacks.

Staff Gunnery Officer of the Southeast Area Fleet! The title sounded fine but the fleet really wasn't much—three cruisers, a dozen destroyers, seven submarines. And only four minesweepers. Of course, the mines the Americans kept dropping at Rabaul didn't do any harm. The water was too deep. At Kavieng it was a different story. A ship had been sunk there in September, and others damaged. Now the regular harbor could not be used and ships had to anchor outside. That caused delay in unloading and delay in getting the needed supplies down to Rabaul via small boat.

Yes, in spite of the unusual activity today in the harbor, Doi felt hemmed in, as he was endlessly to recall at the Peers' Club in Tokyo after the American flag was hoisted over that sacred city. But low in spirits though he felt that day, the awful possibility that he would live to feel at home beneath that flag never remotely occurred to him.

2

The U.S. Marines were ashore at Empress Augusta Bay in Bougainville all right, but whether they knew it or not they were in a spot. Although their landing November 1, 1943, had been stoutly protected by Rear Admiral Merrill's fast, hard-punching Task Force 39,[1] those cruisers and destroyers had punched so hard and so fast that by November 3 they were practically out of ammunition and fuel, and were unable to fight another surface engagement until they had replenished at Purvis Bay. If the Japs came down again from Rabaul with more ships, the Marines would be stranded on their narrow beachhead at Bougainville for the brief time they survived at all.

Admiral William F. Halsey, Jr., Commander of the South Pacific area, knew that Admiral Kurita's Second Fleet had sortied from Truk heading for Rabaul—and ultimately Bougainville—and a decision had to be made.

[1] See BATTLE REPORT, Vol. III (*Pacific War: Middle Phase*) Chap. 14.

SOUTHWEST CLEANUP

Halsey's aerial reconnaissance and thin submarine line had reported the force as consisting of twelve cruisers and twelve destroyers plus auxiliaries, enough to mean the difference between life and death for General Vandergrift's leathernecks. Halsey figured the Jap fleet would have to stop at Rabaul to refuel, twenty-four hours or less. Then it would move southeast against Bougainville. Merrill's cruisers simply could not be readied in time to meet them.

Most of the naval strength at this time was being concentrated in the Central Pacific for the assault on the Gilberts Archipelago. The only ships available to stop Kurita were two carriers—the aged SARATOGA and the small PRINCETON—plus their escorts, which had been supporting the Bougainville landings with strikes against the guardian twin Buka-Bonis airfields, beyond reach of land-based fighters. Halsey decided upon a bold stroke—to go in after the Japs as they prepared for battle behind Rabaul's defenses.

Admiral Halsey later said it was the hardest decision he ever had to make: "I never expected to see those two carriers again." To make it even tougher, his son, Lieutenant (jg) William F. Halsey, III, was a supply officer on the SARATOGA.

Orders were flashed to Rear Admiral Frederick C. Sherman aboard the "Sara." Famed Rabaul—the tiger's den—was to be attacked for the first time by carrier-based air, an operation which heretofore had been considered much too risky even to think about.

Grouped around SARATOGA and PRINCETON were two cruisers, the antiaircraft cruisers SAN DIEGO and SAN JUAN, and ten destroyers.[1] The success of the Bougainville operation depended on these few ships.

Steaming through the night at 27 knots the Task Force received word that Simpson Harbor, Rabaul, was jammed full of ships refueling—a perfect setup.

On the morning of November 5, the Task Force arrived in the appointed place, in the Solomons Sea. In an operation which was to alter the technique of our carrier warfare, Navy land-based fighters were sent

[1] SARATOGA (F) (Capt. John H. Cassady), Air Group 12; PRINCETON (Capt. George R. Henderson), Air Group 23; SAN DIEGO (Capt. Lester J. Hudson), SAN JUAN (Capt. Guy W. Clark), LARDNER (Lt. Comdr. Otto C. Schatz, Jr.), FARENHOLT (Lt. Comdr. Alcorn G. Beckmann), WOODWORTH (Lt. Comdr. Charles R. Stephan), BUCHANAN (Comdr. Floyd B. T. Myhre), LANSDOWNE (Lt. Comdr. Francis J. Foley), GRAYSON (Comdr. Henry O. Hansen), STERETT (Comdr. Charles J. Gould), STACK (Lt. Comdr. Philip K. Sherman), WILSON (Lt. Comdr. Charles K. Duncan), EDWARDS (Lt. Comdr. Paul G. Osler).

out from the Solomons to fly combat patrol over the ships while all aircraft aboard the carriers were launched against Rabaul.

It was a perfect day for the attack, clear with a 7-knot wind. The planes had been "spotted" on deck during the night and were now loaded and waiting. One by one the engines turned over—coughed, sputtered a bit, and then caught with a whirling roar as blue flame shot out of cold exhaust pipes.

The Sara's planes went in first, followed by PRINCETON's. The Japs were waiting with 100 planes in the air, while cruisers and destroyers in the harbor frantically tried to throw off fuel lines and weigh anchor. Leaving the Jap fighters to their 55 accompanying Hellcats, the dive bombers pushed over and headed down for the ships through intense AA fire, the torpedo planes coming in low behind them.

Simpson Harbor that day was a confused picture of twisting planes and squirming ships. When the last covering Hellcat headed back to its waiting carrier, the Marines of Bougainville could breathe easily again. Admiral Kurita would not sail against them. Nearly half his ships had been hit—the heavy cruisers MAYA, ATAGO, MOGAMI and TAKAO; the light cruisers AGANO and NOSHIRO; and the destroyers FUJINAMI and WAKATSUKI. Although none of the ships were sunk, his fleet would have to scatter from Rabaul to Tokyo for repairs. In addition, over a score of precious fighter planes, some of them on loan from Admiral Ozawa's carriers, had been lost in aerial combat. And against that awful tally could be counted only ten American airplanes destroyed.

Thus ended one of the most decisive engagements of the war—one whose results were not only felt immediately on the narrow beaches of Torokina but one whose impact was to influence the entire Japanese strategy in the Central Pacific, as will soon be seen.

Admiral Halsey was all for hitting the Japs again while they were still hot. He suggested to Admiral Nimitz that Central Pacific cancel a projected carrier strike on the island of Nauru and attack Truk instead to polish off the limping Imperial Fleet. But Nimitz ruled against it.

3

Rabaul got no rest. Less than a week later, on November 11, Task Force 38 was poised, east of Bougainville, for another strike. West of Bougainville Admiral Alfred E. Montgomery's carrier group (TG 50.3), recently arrived from the Central Pacific, stood by to attack. Admiral Sherman's group contained the same ships that had struck on November 5 less four DDs transferred to TG 50.3. Admiral Montgomery had the carriers ESSEX, BUNKER HILL, and INDEPENDENCE plus nine destroyers.[1]

On the morning of this strike, the weather quixotically shifted allegiance to the Japanese. Heavy squalls covered Simpson Harbor, and the vanguard SARATOGA group sighted only one light cruiser and three destroyers, all of which they damaged. Admiral Montgomery's planes, winging in later, found better pickings.

Squalls still covered the eastern half of Simpson Harbor and extended out into St. George's Channel. Outside the harbor a number of cruisers and destroyers were maneuvering excitedly trying to find cover in protecting patches of rain. Some of the bombers peeled off after ships in the harbor, others to go after the ones in the channel.

Lieutenant (jg) William L. Gerner of Bombing Squadron 17 flying from the BUNKER HILL planted a 1,000-pound bomb directly amidships on what appeared to be a light cruiser. After diving he pulled out between two volcanoes on the peninsula flanking the harbor when two Zeke fighters jumped on his tail. The situation was taken well in hand by S. E. Wallace, ARM 3/c, the rear-seat man, who shot down both with his twin 30-caliber guns.

Many Jap fighters buzzed about the attacking squadrons, attempting to pounce on the bombers at the pull-out point of the dives. But the Hellcats were always there to handle the situation. As Commander Paul E. Emrick, commander of Air Group 9, stated: "Teamwork was the keynote. There was no indiscriminate 'burning of the blue' in quest of personal glory."

[1] Task Group 50.3
Carriers:
    ESSEX (F) (Capt. Ralph A. Ofstie), Air Group 9
    BUNKER HILL (Capt. John J. Ballentine), Air Group 17
    INDEPENDENCE (Capt. Rudolph L. Johnson), Air Group 22
Destroyers:
    BULLARD (Lt. Comdr. Bernard W. Freund)
    EDWARDS (Lt. Comdr. Paul G. Osler)
    STACK (Lt. Comdr. Philip K. Sherman)
    CHAUNCEY (Lt. Comdr. Lester C. Conwell)
    STERETT (Comdr. Frank G. Gould)
    WILSON (Lt. Comdr. Charles K. Duncan)
    KIDD (Comdr. Allan B. Roby)
    MCKEE (Comdr. John J. Greytak)
    MURRAY (Comdr. Paul R. Anderson)

A bizarre and somehow typically Japanese tactic was encountered. Jap fighters, darting low above the attacking formations, attempted to knock out the American bomber and torpedo planes by dropping small aerial bombs upon them. As might be expected, the stunt was about as successful as trying to catch trout by dropping rocks on them.

In spite of having to dodge between rain squalls and Zekes that morning, the raiders sank one destroyer—the SUZUNAMI, caught as she tried to sneak out the entrance to the harbor—besides damaging three more (UMIKAZE, NAGANAMI, and URAKAZE) and two cruisers (AGANO and YUBARI). The AGANO had also been hurt in Sherman's raid of the week before. Now she was so badly crippled that she would have to be towed to Truk. In addition thirty-five Jap airplanes were blasted from the sky. Later in the day some forty B-24s, based in the Solomons, hit Rabaul again with a follow-up raid.

While their fighters rode into Rabaul with the bombers and torpedo planes, the carriers were protected with Combat Air Patrol by Navy Corsairs, land based in the Solomons. It was an excellent example of the joint use of naval shore-based and carrier-based air. Carrier fighters performed at their maximum value by protecting squadrons with whom they had been trained to work as a close-knit team. The shore-based air extended the time they could remain in the area protecting the carriers by landing on the empty flat-tops for reservicing and refueling.

Before noon the striking planes had returned from rain-drenched Rabaul. Thirteen planes were missing from Admiral Montgomery's group and only two failed to return to Admiral Sherman's carriers.

Originally it had been planned to strike again that afternoon, but two circumstances prevented.

Admiral Sherman's Task Force 38 was low on fuel. Operating in almost a dead calm, SARATOGA and PRINCETON had been obliged to steam at full speed all morning, launching and landing planes. At such speed the screening destroyers quickly digested their oil, and the force, low in fuel, had to retire at reduced speed toward Espiritu.

Not so handicapped, Admiral Montgomery's carriers were steaming northwest launching planes for the afternoon raid when the TBS circuit gave voice warning to all ships: "Bogies closing in from 336 degrees true, distance 70 miles, altitude 15 and 22 thousand feet."

Sweating men in Combat Information Center on each ship bent low over maneuvering boards as they plotted the course of the planes—"Many bogies bearing 345 true, distance 45 miles, speed 180."

Fighting 17 from the Solomons led by Lieutenant Commander Tom Blackburn, flying protective cover, was quickly vectored out to meet the enemy: "Raid intercepted by our fighters at 345 true, distance 45 miles." Silence. Aboard the ships ears ached to the pressure of radio headsets. Then, startlingly: "Kee-rist! There are millions of 'em. Let's go to work."

CIC, plotting the oncoming attack by radar, announced that the Japanese sky force had broken up into three parts and one was closing rapidly, at 340 true, 27 miles distant. On the bridge binoculars were turned upon a large group of planes in a loose V formation—enemy Vals!

"Man your guns and blast those bastards," boomed orders from Admiral Montgomery.

Five-inch guns roared from the three carriers steaming in line and from the destroyers that plowed a rough ring around them.

"Do not launch any more planes. Send those in air to strike."

"Watch out for dive bombers coming in on you."

"Knock off firing on our own planes."

But the last order was rather difficult to execute. Over two hundred planes, both Jap and American, were scrambled in the sky. Some fighters were even using the ships' own AA fire as an unorthodox method of fighter direction, heading right into the thick of the shell bursts which, they knew, marked elusive enemy bombers.

The sky was a doodle of burst and tracer streaks. The BUNKER HILL, with attacks coming in from dead ahead, dead astern, and on both beams, had several fully loaded SB2Cs warming up on the flight deck. Without orders, rear-seat gunners augmented the ship's fire power with their aircraft machine guns.

If ever there was a melee, this was it.

Lieutenant (jg) George M. Blair of Fighting 9, who later was to be shot down over Truk and sensationally rescued, came in on a Japanese "Kate" for a stern run. After a short burst his guns jammed, so Blair improvised a new form of aerial combat on the spot. He flew up directly over the Japanese plane and released his auxiliary gasoline tank, which hit true, and knocked his adversary flaming into the sea.

Bombs dropped, and missed. Torpedo planes boxed in below the belt —and missed. Suddenly it was all over. The Task Group ships and planes had accounted for 76 enemy aircraft and lost only three.

By sunset the shore-based planes had been landed on the carriers, refueled, and sent on their way. Admiral Montgomery and his ships started home. The two-hour battle had canceled the afternoon strike on Rabaul.

The Japs had stopped it, but at the expense of having had their backs broken in the air.

4

The noose was drawing tighter. Admiral Kurita's attempt to pry the Marines from Bougainville had only resulted in bringing ruin to his fleet and to Rabaul. Following the resounding victory at Empress Augusta Bay,[1] COMSOPAC relentlessly pressed the surface attack. Destroyer Squadron 23, commanded by one of the most dashing figures of the war, Captain Arleigh Burke, was always in the van.

On November 24, after two days of offensive sweeps off Bougainville, the destroyers of the squadron[2] were refueling at Hathorn Sound, New Georgia Island, when an intelligence report was received saying that the Japanese might try to evacuate key aviation personnel from beleaguered Buka Island by destroyer or high-speed transport.

Captain Burke was ordered to get underway and proceed at 30 knots west of Treasury Island and then on to the north. More instructions would come later. As Burke steamed north, he twice reported his position and "making 31 knots." By the time his second progress report had been received COMSOPAC had decided that the best way to nab the Japs was to put Burke's destroyers astride the Buka-Rabaul escape route. Instructions were dispatched to "31-Knot" Burke, the first time this moniker was used.[3]

[1] See BATTLE REPORT, Vol. III (*Pacific War: Middle Phase*), Chap. 14.
[2] Destroyer Squadron 23 ("The Little Beavers") (Capt. Arleigh A. Burke)
  Desdiv 45 (Capt. Arleigh A. Burke)
    CHARLES AUSBURNE (Comdr. Luther K. Reynolds)
    CLAXTON (Comdr. Herald F. Stout)
    DYSON (Comdr. Roy A. Gano)
  Desdiv 46 (Comdr. Bernard L. Austin)
    CONVERSE (Comdr. DeWitt C. E. Hamberger)
    SPENCE (Comdr. Henry J. Armstrong, Jr.)

[3] Applied for posterity by Capt. H. R. ("Ray") Thurber, Operations Officer for COMSOPAC. "That bird has told us he could make only 30 knots formation speed," growled Ray, as he started writing instructions to be sent his old peacetime squadron mate. "Okeh! We'll fix him!" So "31-Knot" Burke it was and Arleigh was tagged for life. Ray was later made an honorary Little Beaver, complete with engraved certificate, by Desron 23.

With his two destroyer divisions in column formation—CHARLES AUSBURNE, CLAXTON, DYSON, CONVERSE, and SPENCE—Burke steamed on through the darkness. His instructions simply were: "If enemy is contacted you know what to do."

At 0130, the morning of November 25, 1943, the squadron arrived in position. The night was dark, with no moon. The sky was overcast and occasionally a squall blew up from the seatheast. The smooth seas were rocked by slight swells; visibility was about 4,000 yards. Dropping speed to 23 knots, the five destroyers started to patrol.

Only eleven minutes later, the DYSON picked up a contact on radar bearing 085 degrees true, range 22,000 yards, and immediately alerted other ships by TBS—the short-range "talk-between-ships" voice radio.

For many months, over countless cups of coffee in the wardrooms, the destroyer skippers and Captain Burke had discussed what should be done in just such a situation as this. Now they were ready. The only order that came over the TBS was a hoarse: "Hold your hats, boys. Here we go!"

Captain Burke's Squadron 45, the CHARLES AUSBURNE (F), DYSON, and CLAXTON, closed for an attack. The two destroyers of Division 46, CONVERSE and SPENCE, trailed in behind.

The range closed rapidly. At first it was thought that there were only two targets present, but as the three destroyers drew closer the radar indicated three enemy ships steaming in column toward St. George's Channel, wholly oblivious of lurking fate.

Desdiv 45 eased slowly right to the attack position. At 0156 the range was 6,000 yards. The torpedo setup was ideal—three unsuspecting enemy ships in column on a steady course and steady speed. It was a destroyer officer's dream. Captain Burke gave the terse order: "Execute William!"

From the starboard side of each destroyer five torpedoes—a half salvo—leaped toward the enemy.

The torpedo watches ticked away the seconds. These moments of waiting, after the launching of a torpedo, always seem like overstretched eternity to destroyer men. Course was changed 90 degrees to the right to avoid possible torpedoes from the enemy. Perhaps he was not as night-blind as he appeared.

The three destroyers had just come about on their new course when the radar spotted another group of three enemy vessels, 12,000 yards on the port quarter of the first trio. If the torpedoes did not connect, an interesting time was certainly going to be had by all. Reversing rudders, Desdiv 45 came about and headed for the new threat.

The second hand of the torpedo watch started the last revolution. Twenty-two seconds before the "mark" the first torpedo exploded, followed in rapid succession by bunched multiple blasts. Flames shot high in the air from all targets, one sending up a lapping tongue 500 feet, which illumined the American destroyers in brilliant relief. When the smoke cleared away only one Japanese ship was visible, crippled and circling slowly.

Now everyone felt better. No matter what lay beyond the radar range, the forces would be somewhat on equal terms.

The explosions had warned the second enemy group of lurking danger. Either not choosing to engage an unseen foe or not wishing to risk their valuable cargoes of evacuated personnel, these three turned north, piling on the steam. Burke's destroyers jumped to the chase, leaving CONVERSE and SPENCE to finish off the wounded enemy.

But the Jap destroyers were fast: 30 knots—31 knots—32 knots. Black-gangs on the American destroyers sweated to get every available revolution out of the whirling shafts. By 0215 the range was slowly closing and Burke's ships were straining through the black waters at an amazing 34 knots.

But in a race that fast, gaining two miles an hour on a homeward-speeding enemy who had a 12-mile head start, trouble can be the prize. The hoped-for torpedo attack had to be abandoned, so at 0221 the three ships came back to the left in echelon and opened fire with their 5-inch batteries.

The Japanese now decided that the best way to stay alive was to scatter. One ship continued in a northerly direction. Another slanted off to the northwest. The third veered sharply to the west. And with that they started firing back. Salvos in groups of four and six shots started dropping uncomfortably close to the pursuit. The port side of CLAXTON's bridge was drenched when several salvos landed less than 100 yards short. No hits were scored by the enemy but, in the words of one officer, "the crack of the burst was more confusing than amusing."

Captain Burke hesitated to break up his orderly formation, so the three destroyers kept hot on the trail of the ship fleeing to the north, which doggedly slugged back, the flash of her guns practically invisible through the heavy smoke screen she was laying down.

The end was near. At about 0300 a vital hit smashed into the Japanese and the wounded destroyer slowed to 10 knots. Several minutes later all steering control was lost and the ship began to turn in tight circles erupting "constant fires, explosions and pyrotechnic effects."

The three destroyers pumped full salvos into the burning carcass as they passed in column. Then Desdiv 45 did a countermarch, and came back within 3,000 yards of its victim. The Jap ship loomed large in the light of her own explosions and by now was down at the bow and well heeled over.

The DYSON was ordered to administer the coup de grace with her torpedoes. But before the torpedoes reached the target, the destroyer sank. The DYSON thus achieved the unique distinction of being the only destroyer in the war to fire her torpedoes *over* an enemy ship.

In the meantime CONVERSE and SPENCE had finished the job of polishing off the remaining destroyer of the first group. Under the combined impact of five torpedoes from CONVERSE and of many rounds of 5-inch fire, she blew up, rolled over, and sank.

During the engagement CONVERSE maintained her reputation as one of the luckiest ships in the Pacific. A torpedo had struck her on the port side aft but failed to explode.

The Japanese forces that night had consisted of five destroyers, not six, and none of them cruisers as at first enthusiastically reported. They were the ONAMI, MAKINAMI, AMAGIRI, YUGIRI, and UZUKI, the three latter loaded with 900 key Army aviation personnel and their equipment. In the first encounter ONAMI and MAKINAMI went down, and in the chase to the north the YUGIRI was sunk, but the other two got through to Rabaul unscratched except for one dud hit on UZUKI.

But it was a good show. Three destroyers of the Emperor's fast-shrinking escort fleet had been sent hissing to the bottom. Our only casualties were a few cases of exhaustion from over-exertion and some ruptured eardrums.

Arleigh Burke would have been flattered to know that the breathless survivors officially reported having been attacked by "a division of cruisers, a destroyer division, and several motor torpedo boats."

Chapter Three

To the Top of the Ladder

I

FOR NEARLY two years Rabaul had been the southeastern sub-capital of Japan's ambitious Greater East Asia Co-Prosperity Sphere, which was slowly growing less great and decidedly unprosperous.

With the capture of Bougainville by Admiral Halsey's South Pacific forces in November, 1943, and the occupation of Finschhafen on New Guinea by General MacArthur's Southwest Pacific forces, Rabaul suddenly found itself on the front line of a war that had so recently been moving in the opposite direction hundreds of miles to the south and east. The huge harbor, where once had lain hundreds of warships and fat-bellied merchantmen loaded with victorious troops and the implements of further success, was now a wreckage-paved desert, timidly crossed by night-faring barges to deliver short rations to the defenders. But as an air base Rabaul still loomed large.

The Allied advance up the New Guinea coast and the slippery ladder of the Solomons had been a tedious and bloody business. Their losses had been heavy, and so had the Japanese', but here was the decisive difference: the Americans could absorb their losses and come back stronger in ships and men and aircraft; the Japanese could not.

Many of Japan's best fleet units, many of her best troops, and certainly her best aviators had been destroyed in the vain effort to push back—hold back—slow down—the relentless march of MacArthur and Halsey. They could not be replaced. But for every American soldier, Marine, or sailor killed, it seemed to the frantic Japs that two better-trained, better-equipped men stepped into place. American airplanes and American ships had been rather inferior to his Imperial Majesty's; now, though, that state of affairs was reversing itself.

Many Japanese, especially the better-traveled professional naval officers, admitted to their more trustworthy colleagues that the Empire was on the skids.

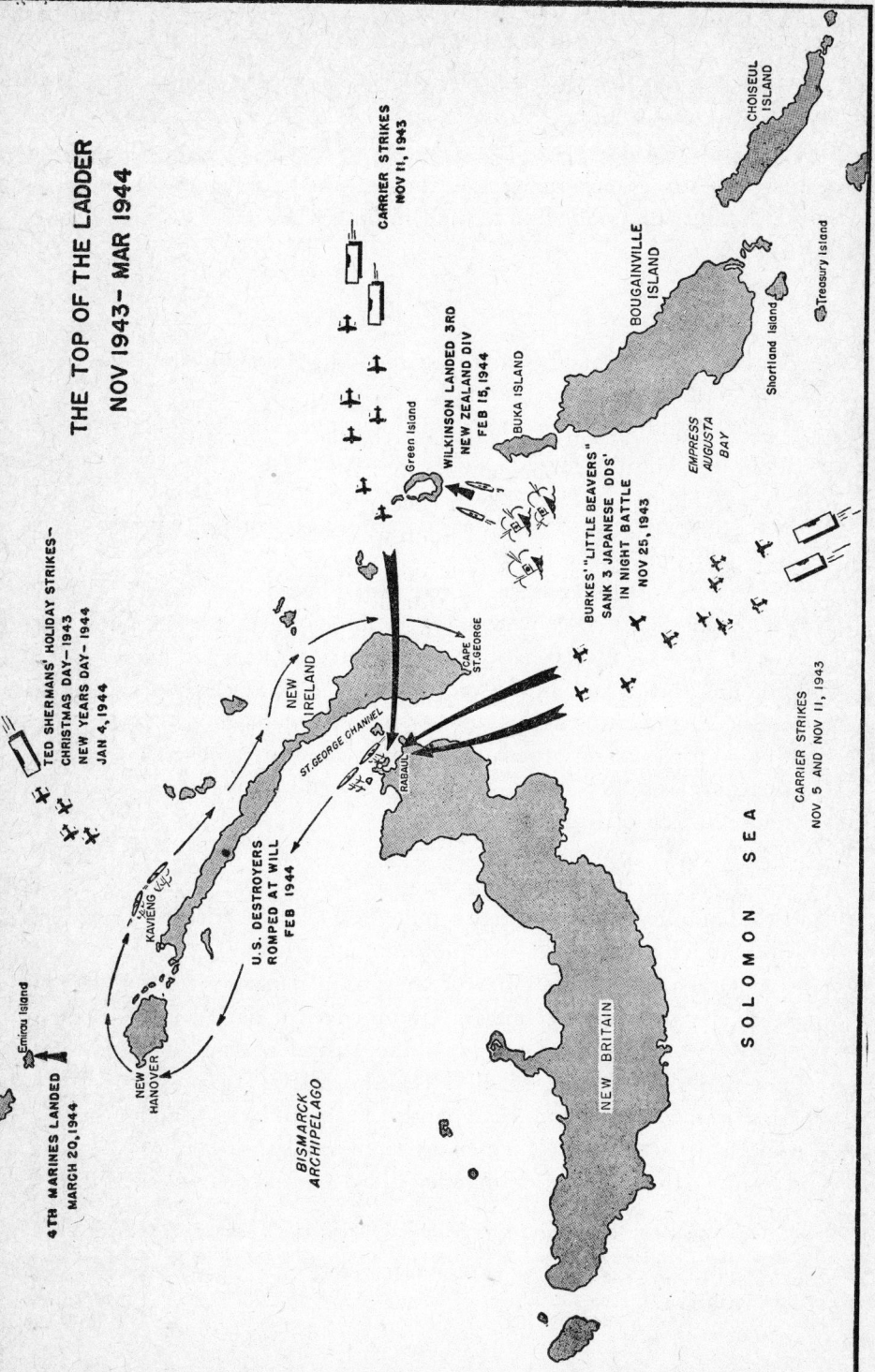

FIGURE 4

Where would the Americans strike next, to give Dai Nippon its next shove? And with what?

The answer was not slow in coming. It arrived on December 15, under a shower of strange new projectiles that fell thick as Paulownia leaves in autumn, but with a noise like all the whistling wind devils of the typhoon.

2

To the Allied strategists, the next move in Rabaul's elimination was obvious—a landing on the island of New Britain.

The tactical details were not so obvious. The most desirable prize was Gasmata on the south coast of the island, where the Japanese had established a powerful air base which was still a constant menace. But the elements that made it so desirable to capture also made that seizure exceedingly difficult.

Well, the Austral-American forces had Finschhafen, on the point of New Guinea closest to New Britain. So the capture of Cape Gloucester on the far shore was reasonably well indicated. And if Gasmata was too tough a nut, then a landing between it and Cape Gloucester was certainly a necessity. Arawe was a likely place. It had a good harbor from which light naval forces could protect shipping in the straits and make forays on Gasmata, if desirable; and in any event it would provide a starting point for the reduction of Rabaul.

The Seventh Amphibious Force,[1] rapidly becoming veterans, prepared to put the 112th U. S. Cavalry Regimental Combat Team (Brigadier General Cunningham) on the beach at Arawe in what was to be the first of three major amphibious operations in eighteen days.

On December 14 the ships of the group departed from Buna and made a feint toward Finschhafen. Under cover of darkness the course of the convoy was changed. The bows of the Australian transport WESTRALIA (Commander A. V. Knight, RANR), the LSD (Landing Ship Dock) CARTER HALL (Lieutenant Commander Francis Harris), and the attack transports HUMPHREYS (Lieutenant Commander Frank D. Schwartz) and SANDS (Lieutenant Commander Lloyd C. Brogger) pointed directly

---

[1] On November 26, 1943, Vice Admiral Thomas C. Kinkaid, veteran of the Battle of the Coral Sea, Battle of Midway, Battle of the Solomon Islands, Battle of Santa Cruz Islands, the Battle of Guadalcanal (Third Savo), and recent commander of the North Pacific Fleet, took over command of the Seventh Fleet.

for Arawe. Around them scurried the escorting destroyers.[1] Leading the procession was the destroyer CONYNGHAM with Admiral Barbey again aboard.

To the east, British Rear Admiral V. A. C. Crutchley's Australian cruisers and destroyers,[2] up from Milne Bay, stood by to intercept anything the Japs might send down from Rabaul. The western approaches in the Vitiaz and Dampier Straits were guarded by vigilant PT boats.

This was to be a night of surprise. Much depended on that. The plan called for two landings to be made by rubber boats from attack transports during darkness, before the main landing forces debarked from WESTRALIA and CARTER HALL at dawn. Nervously, troops on HUMPHREYS and SANDS looked wryly up at a bright moon that threw long silver fingers across the smooth water.

Shortly before 0400 the transports were in position off Arawe when a lone enemy float plane slipped in and dropped a stick of bombs that struck 200 yards off the port quarter of the destroyer REID. It looked as if the enemy had been alerted.

The SANDS moved toward her beach, 5,000 yards to the east of Arawe, where she intended to land 150 men to block off the narrow peninsula on whose western tip the main landing was to be made. Five days before, amphibious scouts had been put ashore on the same beach and had not been heard from since.

The HUMPHREYS under the protecting guns of LAMSON moved toward the tip of Pilelo Island where a radio station was thought to be. As destroyers circled them at 15 knots, the WESTRALIA and CARTER HALL, now hove to, commenced to debark troops into amphibious vehicles (Buffaloes and Alligators) and small landing craft.

A thousand yards off Blue Beach the SANDS started sending her troops toward shore in ten rubber boats. No bombardment had been attempted, for the plan was to preserve the element of surprise. It was one—in reverse.

The boats never reached the beach. As they drew close, the waiting

---

[1] Escort Unit: SHAW (Comdr. Richard H. Phillips), DRAYTON, MUGFORD, BAGLEY (Comdr. Thomas E. Chambers). Bombardment Group: REID, SMITH, LAMSON, FLUSSER, MAHAN.
[2] Heavy cruisers AUSTRALIA (Capt. H. B. Farncomb, RAN) and SHROPSHIRE (Capt. J. A. Collins, RAN); destroyers ARUNTA (Comdr. A. E. Buchanan, RAN) and WARRAMUNGA (Capt. E. F. V. Dechaineaux, RAN).

Japs opened up with a couple of 40mm and three or four machine guns. Tracers skimmed low over the water in intermittent bursts and volleys. The lead boats were all hit and vanished like pricked balloons. So heavy was the fire that the rear boats did not press the attack.

The destroyer SHAW, standing by as gunnery support for the troops, started firing, now that the enemy positions were revealed. After eight rounds of 5-inch probing, all enemy batteries were silenced. But the damage had already been done, and our troops never touched sand at Blue Beach. An hour later SHAW picked up the remnants of the rubber boat flotilla.

Meanwhile the LCVPs and LCMs from WESTRALIA, manned by men of the U.S. Engineer Special Brigade, and the Alligators and Buffaloes from CARTER HALL, manned by Marines, weaved in by moonlight through islands and reefs toward the main landing beach. They were underway an hour and a half, long after the mother ships had withdrawn under escort toward Buna.

For fifteen minutes before the landing at sunrise the destroyers REID, SMITH, LAMSON, FLUSSER, and MAHAN in column lobbed shells over Arawe Island into the beach area. When the shelling stopped, the stoical Japanese, crouching in their foxholes, blinked at the sight of two small, squat, bargelike craft that thrashed into distant view. Suddenly the scows erupted like volcanoes and into the sand and trees of Cape Merkus, in hissing arcs of death, showered explosive symbols of the new age—rockets!

Two ugly DUKWs, fitted with rocket launchers, brought death in its most modern raiment to the jungle world of the South Pacific.

The walking cavalrymen went ashore without heavy opposition. By 0900 the larger ships had left the harbor except for the flagship CONYNGHAM that was seeing the final echelon of LCTs from Cape Cretin safely into the landing area. Troops were still being fished out of the water near the Blue Beach fiasco. The SC 699 lifted 70 dripping soldiers onto her narrow decks. A small boat from the CONYNGHAM recovered more. Of the 150 men who attempted the landing about 60 were killed or wounded. The Pilelo Island rubber boat men were more fortunate and succeeded in exterminating their allotted number of Japanese.

About 0930, enemy planes struck from the east in two waves, in all 36 Vals and Zekes. The CONYNGHAM was in the process of hoisting her boat aboard when the attack came, but by quickly jumping to 20 knots

PLATE 1—The President discusses high strategy with his top Pacific military leaders in Hawaii, midsummer of 1944. (*above*) Aboard the cruiser BALTIMORE, in Pearl Harbor, the President receives General Douglas MacArthur and Admiral Chester W. Nimitz. During this same voyage the President also called at the Aleutians. (*below*) Mapping the drive on Tokyo. The President with his chief of staff, Admiral William D. Leahy, and General MacArthur listen to Admiral Nimitz.

PLATE 11—Rendezvous of the "Green Dragons" in New Guinea. Net camouflage and overhanging jungle conceal the night-faring Navy's PT boats during daytime overhauls and refueling. PT boats operating from such bases as these (*upper left*) proved thorns in the side of the Japanese and played a major role in whittling down the Jap positions along the coast of New Guinea.

(*center*) Looking reptilian in its weird camouflage, a "Green Dragon" blends into the jungle background of its New Guinea base.

(*lower*) "Morning-after rehash" occurred after every night action, when PT-ers "told all" to intelligence officers, describing everything that happened—or failed to happen. Except for the oppressive tropical heat and insects, the men of the torpedo boat squadrons lived in comparative comfort at bases they hewed out of the "gumbo" soil and matted underbrush, with the aid of friendly natives.

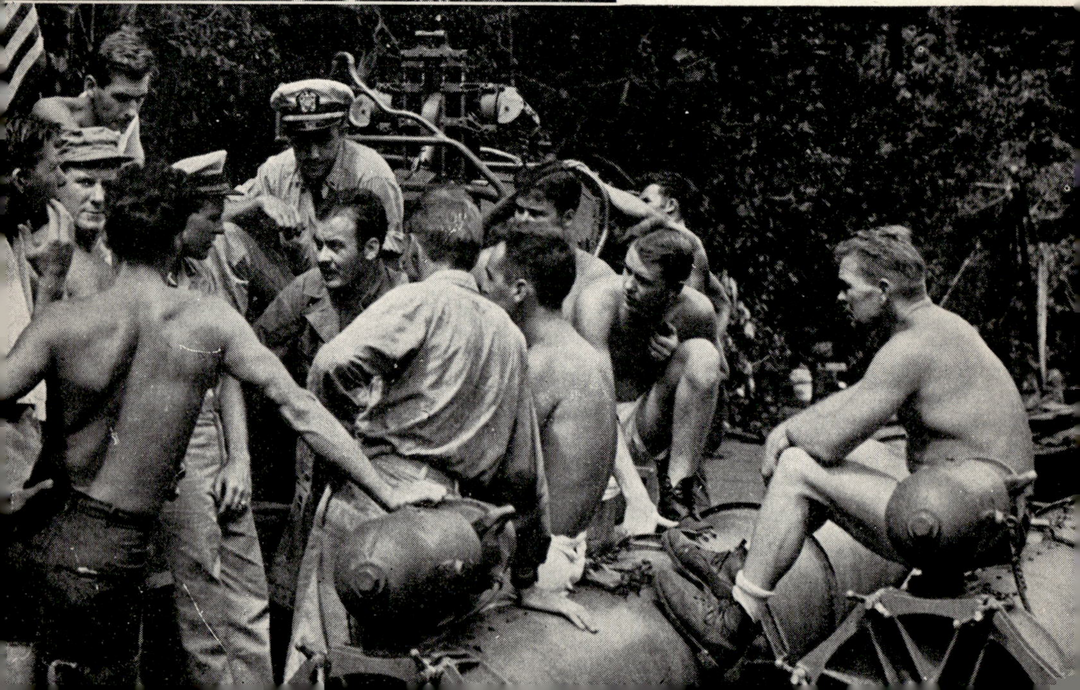

PLATE III—In an attempt to reinforce hard-pressed garrisons in the Lae-Salamaua area the Japs, early in March, 1943, sent a convoy of nine ships, escorted by eight destroyers, from their great base at Rabaul. Spotting B-24s soon picked up the force. On March 3, Allied fighters and bombers pounced on the convoy, sinking all but four ships in daring low-level attacks, and drowning more than 2,900 enemy troops.

(*upper right*) Japanese take cover as an Army plane sweeps in low for a strafing run on an enemy destroyer. (*Army Air Force Photo.*)

(*center*) Burning oil trails behind a stricken Japanese cargo ship during the Battle of the Bismarck Sea. (*Army Air Force Photo.*)

(*lower*) Great black smoke plumes arise from burning Japanese bombers and blazing oil storage tanks on Marcus Island, during a surprise hit-and-run raid upon this important enemy outpost, September 1, 1943. The Hellcat (F6F) Navy fighter plane first saw combat during this attack. In the foreground is an Avenger (TBF), or Navy torpedo bomber.

PLATE IV—The battle for Lae, Japanese New Guinea stronghold, was long and bitter. These photographs afford a striking demonstration of the power and accuracy of Allied bombardment.

(*upper left*) From behind the mountains, where they were undetectable by radar, Japanese light bombers and Zeros struck savagely at the Allied landing force. Here is what happened to one of the LCIs caught in the line of aerial fire. Riddled and listing, its decks running with the blood of both Australian and American troops, it pushed on to complete its mission at the beachhead. Lae fell on September 16, 1943.

(*center*) Caught with their flaps down, the remains of ten Japanese warplanes line the runway at Lae. They were smashed by strafing gunfire, before they could take off, during an Allied air raid.

(*lower*) Japanese outposts, such as Wake, received periodic "treatments." This Douglas Dauntless dive bomber (SBD) is ready to plant its 1,000-pound bomb on Japanese-held Wake Island the morning of October 6, 1943, during the second day of a carrier task force raid under Rear Admiral Alfred E. Montgomery. Sixty-one planes were destroyed, along with shipping, barracks, shops and airfield installations.

PLATE V—"Hell on earth" describes the devastation found by our landing forces following the bombardment of Lae.

(*upper right*) Here two of the Navy's famed combat photographers, Lt. H. Newcomb, of Philadelphia, Pa., and Photographer 1/c V. V. Valenzio, of New York City, survey the steaming ruins of what was once a lush tropical jungle near Lae, New Guinea.

(*center*) A casualty of the carrier air strike on Rabaul being helped out of the turret of an Avenger torpedo plane upon its return to the USS SARATOGA. He is AOM Kenneth Bratton, of Mississippi. Aboard the same plane, piloted by Commander H. W. Caldwell, Photographer's Mate 1/c Paul Barnett, of Corpus Christi, Texas, was killed by machine-gun fire while photographing a head-on attack by a Jap Zero. Teaming with a Hellcat, Caldwell's Avenger fought off eight Zeros, downing three, damaging two, and chasing off the others.

(*lower*) Another Pearl Harbor, in reverse. On November 5, 1943, carrier-based U. S. Navy planes swooped down on the Japanese stronghold of Rabaul and damaged four heavy cruisers, two light cruisers and two destroyers. Of the 70 Jap fighter planes that rose to meet the attack, 24 were shot down and 22 others were listed as "probables." Later the same day Army bombers and fighters made a follow-up raid, and on November 11 the Navy struck again. This aerial view shows Jap shipping frantically running in circles to avoid our bombs and strafing.

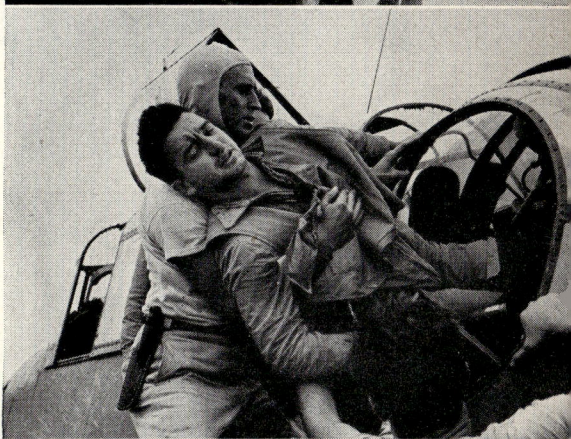

PLATE VI—At the opposite end of strate[gic] New Britain Island from Rabaul sto[od] a lesser Japanese base on Cape Glouc[es]ter. It was attacked the day af[ter] Christmas, 1943, by a well-equipp[ed] Allied expeditionary force.

(*upper left*) Everything, including [the] kitchen sink! The deckload of a Co[ast] Guard manned LST (Landing Sh[ip, Tanks), nearing Cape Gloucester, [re]veals what it takes to capture a bea[ch]head on enemy soil. The troops sho[wn] in the picture are U. S. Marin[es.] (*Coast Guard Photo.*)

(*center*) Green Island, last rung in [the] "Solomons' Ladder," fell on Febru[ary] 15, 1944. Here Admiral William [F.] Halsey, then Commander South [Pa]cific Force, chats with Vice Admi[ral] A. W. Fitch, Commander Aircr[aft] South Pacific, on an inspection tour [of] the small but strategically import[ant] island, which lay only 120 miles fr[om] the Jap bastion of Rabaul. In the r[ear] of the jeep sits Rear Admiral R. [B.] Carney, Admiral Halsey's chief of sta[ff.]

(*lower*) Close-up of an actual landi[ng.] Thanks to heavy preliminary bomba[rd]ment, including the use of rockets, [not] a shot was fired at Marines who wad[ed] ashore at Cape Gloucester. The o[nly] reception committee at the beachhe[ad] consisted of dazed alligators, snak[es] and a few shellshocked wild p[igs.] (*Coast Guard Photo.*)

ATE VII—(*upper right*) The wife of the President inspects Samoa's famed petticoat Marines. Mrs. Roosevelt paused during her South Pacific trip for the American Red Cross to review one of America's most unusual military units, native troops organized as a part of the U. S. Marine Corps. Maj. Gen. C. F. B. Price, commanding general of the area, and Capt. John R. Napton, Jr., accompanied the First Lady. Samoa played an important role as a supply and air base during the Pacific War.

nter) Wherever Americans go they take their sense of humor with them. This purely unofficial document was given to a member of Admiral Halsey's staff by Captain A. A. ("31-knot") Burke, commanding officer of a destroyer squadron known as the "Little Beavers." The origin of the name is a bit obscure, but officers of the squadron admit that the name "Beaver" did call to mind the familiar story of the mountaineer people who also had a rough ride at night!

ver) U. S. Coast Guard gunners fight off a determined Japanese aerial attack during the invasion of Cape Gloucester, New Britain. How nearly successful the Jips were in their attempt to hit the LST can be seen from the bomb splashes. This was the only real resistance offered by the Japanese at Cape Gloucester. (*Coast Guard Photo.*)

PLATE VIII—Napoleon said, "An army travels on its stomach," and the Navy echoes "us, too!" A prime inducement for many to join and to "ship over" with the Navy is good chow, and plenty of it at all times. The story of "How the Navy Is Fed" would require scores of photographs. The next six pictures, however, give a brief cross section of the number one requirement and favorite of men on shipboard.

(*left*) At battle stations men are fed regularly with sandwiches and coffee. Mess cooks in white, kneeling along the edge of the flight deck of the USS INDEPENDENCE (carrier), serve a snack to gun crews on watch.

(*right*) Chow line aboard the "Mighty Mo" (USS MISSOURI). Service cafeteria style, and partitioned aluminum trays (less dishwashing), are popular innovations for enlisted men aboard all the larger ships of the Navy. In line with the food conservation program, Navy men are cautioned, "Take all you want but eat all you take."

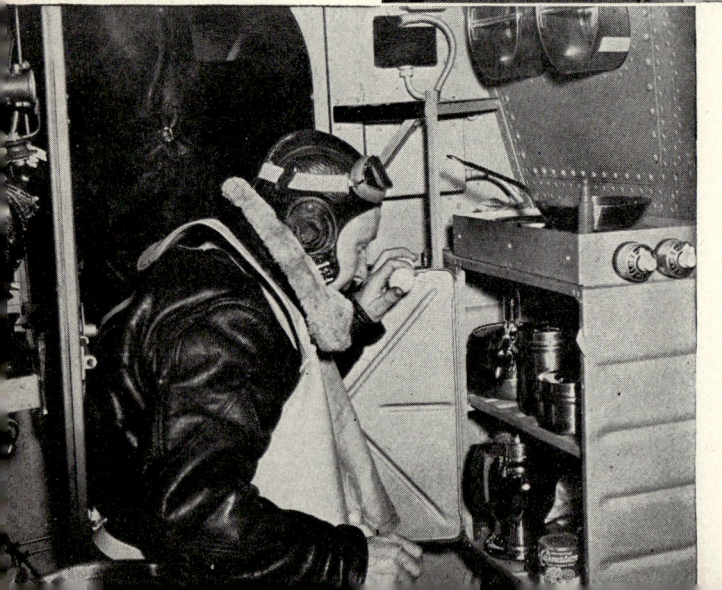

(*left*) Some of the Navy's larger patrol planes have small but amazingly efficient cooking facilities, in order that the crews may have hot meals on long flights in the cold upper atmosphere. A member of the crew of a Catalina (PBY5A) prepares a meal during a wartime patrol flight from the U. S. Naval Air Station, Alameda, California.

PLATE IX—To officers returning from an invasion beachhead, a ship's wardroom is more than a haven, it is heaven! Clean napery, shining silverware, spotless glasses, the refinements of home—a far cry from foxholes, K rations and greasy mess kits. Yet they may be only a mile apart!

(*right*) Typical of thousands of other officers' messes throughout the fleet is this wardroom on the USS ALDERAMIN (AK 116), a Navy cargo ship. The white-jacketed stewards' mates serving the officers have regular battle stations when "General Quarters"

sounds—acting as anti-aircraft gun crews, ammunition passers, damage controllers, etc.

(*left*) A study in contrasts with that above is this wardroom on a PT, or motor torpedo boat, anchored in a New Guinea cove. Informality is the keynote, the clammy heat making near-nudity a must in styles.

(*right*) Getting dessert the hard way! One of the most popular "happy hour" stunts aboard ship, and a good means of relieving the tension for all hands in combat zones, was a good old-fashioned pie-eating contest. Here members of the crew of the heavy cruiser USS CANBERRA dive into the pastry, despite constant threat of enemy attack.

PLATE X—Careful briefing preceded the amphibious operation against Tarawa, an obscure but strategically important Gilbert Island atoll. The cracking of Tarawa was the beginning of the great offensive across the Central Pacific.

(*upper left*) On a transport bound for Tarawa, Marines study a rubber contour map of Betio islet and airstrip. The map was prepared from data and photographs obtained during reconnaissance flights. (*Marine Corps Photo.*)

(*center*) Preceding each amphibious operation, men of every rank, race and creed aboard ship gathered for brief devotional services. These are Marines attending mass aboard a transport nearing Tarawa. Meanwhile their comrades stand guard. (*Marine Corps Photo.*)

(*lower*) "The toughest fighting in Marine Corps history" was the way the Marines, led by Maj. Gen. Holland M. ("Howling Mad") Smith, described the initial attack, November 20, 1943, on the tiny coral atoll. The bitter Japanese resistance and murderous cross fire on Betio provided a laboratory of warfare which was to save uncounted lives in future operations. This artist's sketch is based on combat correspondents' reports of the opening phase of the 76-hour battle. (*Official Coast Guard Drawing by Hunter Wood.*)

PLATE XI—Betio, once a South Pacific paradise, was practically denuded in the fierce naval and aerial bombardment that preceded the landing of the Marines. But we were to learn, at the cost of many lives, a lesson that proved invaluable later: coconut logs and coral make excellent fortifications to withstand abnormal battering. Hiding behind them, and in deep shelters, the enemy, many of them crack Japanese Imperial Marines, waited until the barrage lifted, then mowed down our men with accurate machine-gun and mortar fire.

(*upper right*) U. S. Marines duck for cover as our dive bombers roar in overhead to blast Jap positions. (*Marine Corps Photo.*)

(*center*) Once ashore, the orders were: "Capture the airstrip." As Leathernecks in camouflaged suits and helmets dash across the beach toward their objective, one of them carries a shovel in his hand to dig a slit trench or throw up a hasty barricade if necessary. (*Marine Corps Photo.*)

(*lower*) Two Marines (center), barely visible in their jungle gear, hide behind palm stumps as they blast, with dynamite, a Jap sniper's pillbox. Snipers hid in treetops, in ruined gun emplacements and even under the pier. It was weeks after the battle ended that the last of them surrendered or were eliminated. (*Associated Press Photo.*)

PLATE XII—The stoutest Jap fortification, command headquarters, rose from the center of Betio—a thick mound of coconut logs, banked high with coral rubble and sand. Deep in its recesses last-ditch defenders held out until they were blown to bits by hand grenades or instantly burned to a crisp with flame-throwers. The remnants of the fort later became our own command headquarters.

(*upper left*) Target: pillbox. A Marine gets ready to throw a hand grenade at a Jap pillbox as the smoke of battle rolls back over the hastily thrown-up sandbag entrenchment. (*Marine Corps Photo.*)

(*center*) Over the top go the Marines, as they storm the outer rim of Jap defenses guarding the airstrip. Crouching low, others fire until it is their turn to go through. This photograph was taken from the water's edge, and gives an idea of the small strip of beach—only twenty feet wide at this point—to which the Marines doggedly clung during the first day. (*Marine Corps Photo.*)

(*lower*) Exhausted Marines drop where they stood to take a few minutes' rest when organized fighting ceased on Betio. This photograph shows the beachhead the Marines took and held through more than three days of bitter fighting. The highest point of ground on Betio rises only twelve feet above the sea, and the average height is but six feet. (*Marine Corps Photo.*)

PLATE XIII—The atoll of Tarawa was not the only objective of *Operation Galvanic*—as the Gilbert campaign was known in code. At the same time landings (by the Army's 27th Division) were made on Makin, 100 miles northwest of Tarawa, and at Apemama, the latter described by Stevenson as a "treasure trove of South Sea Island beauty." Admiral Raymond A. Spruance was in overall command.

(*upper right*) Tsk! Tsk! and Tsk! This Marine, struck by a stray piece of shrapnel, gets a little first aid from a buddy—and a lot of kidding from his pals later, when he reported the location of the wound. (*Marine Corps Photo.*)

(*center*) Quiet reigns along the lagoon waterfront of Tarawa, where but a few short hours earlier an inferno raged. As bodies eddy around stranded amphibious tractors, the smell of death is heavy and sickening in the humid tropical air. Lessons learned about the defects of tractors and other equipment on Tarawa proved invaluable during later amphibious operations throughout the Pacific. (*Marine Corps Photo.*)

(*lower*) Of the few prisoners taken on Betio, most were Korean laborers. These prisoners, stooped over so that they will make no surprise attack or dash for freedom, hurry along the beach under Marine guard. (*Marine Corps Photo.*)

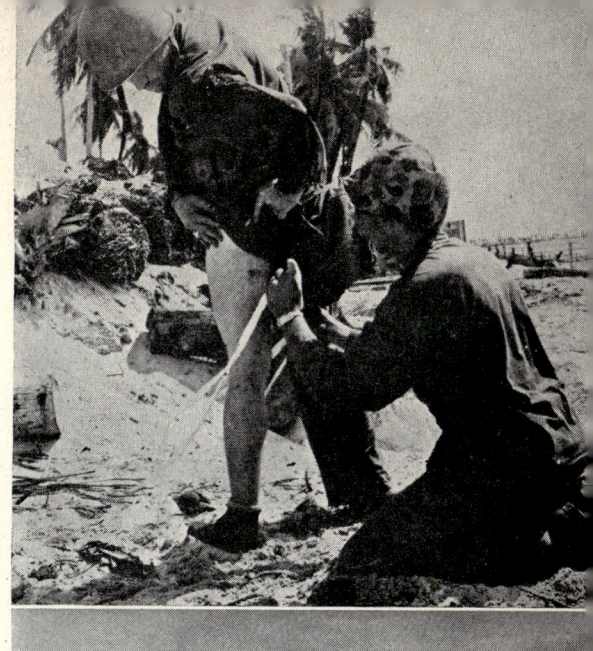

PLATE XIV—(*left*) Two Marines, braving vicious Japanese cross fire, rescue a fallen comrade from under the very noses of snipers. The dust and smoke of battle, and the equatorial heat, aroused such terrific thirsts among both the well and the wounded, that water soon became more scarce than bullets. All of it had to be brought from ships offshore. (*Marine Corps Photo.*)

(*right*) The blood donated by thousands of Americans back home, through their Red Cross, was put to vital use wherever our men suffered from shock or loss of blood on the battlefront. Blood plasma flows from a flask on a rifle that has been up-ended on its bayonet, as a wounded Marine receives a transfusion on the beach at Tarawa. (*Marine Corps Photo.*)

(*left*) When landing craft stuck on the reefs, rubber boats were used to transport the less seriously wounded from the beachhead to larger vessels offshore. At Tarawa a wide expanse of shallow water extended from the shore to the reefs on the lagoon side. Here many casualties occurred, as the slow-moving men offered easy targets for Jap mortar and rifle fire. (*Marine Corps Photo.*)

PLATE XV—The price of victory at Tarawa was high: a total of 1,026 officers and men were killed.

(*right*) As soon as the airstrip could be put into commission, hospital planes were flown in to remove the wounded, eliminating the long, tedious evacuation by litter, landing craft and ship. Jeep ambulances brought the men from field dressing stations to planeside. (*Associated Press Photo.*)

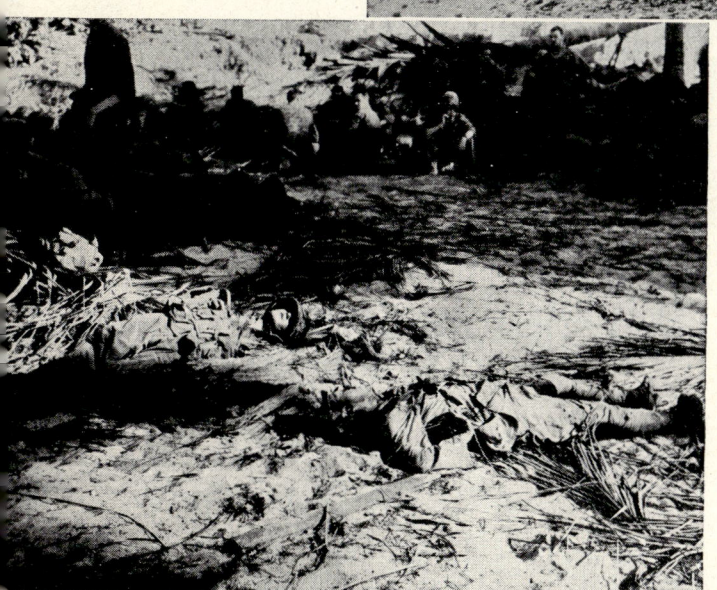

(*left*) Side by side, where they fell, lie the bodies of a U. S. Marine and a Jap on Tarawa. In the background other Marines rest during a lull in the battle—the time being too short to remove the bodies. When the island fell, a few hours later, the Marine was buried at sea. (*Marine Corps Photo.*)

(*right*) The flag-draped body of a Marine killed on Tarawa is given sea-burial from a transport standing off the atoll. Although most of the killed were buried ashore, the wounded who died on shipboard were buried at sea. Appropriate religious ceremonies and a guard of honor (generally close friends) marked each burial. (*Marine Corps Photo.*)

PLATE XVI—Navy planes soon swarmed on Tarawa's rebuilt and greatly enlarged airstrip. (*above*) Admiral Chester W. Nimitz, Commander-in-Chief of the Pacific Fleet, arrives on the first transport plane to land on the newly reconstructed strip. (*below* "Pistol Packing Airedales" of the USS LEXINGTON smile, and no wonder. On November 23, 1943, they intercepted a squadron of Jap planes headed for Tarawa, shooting down 17 out of 20 Zeros in a single action without losing a man.

she managed to slip out from under three bombs with 50 yards to spare. Admiral Barbey was getting his share of close misses.

Luckily none of the small craft in the harbor loaded with men and equipment was hit and only slight damage done to the beach area before covering P-38s sent the Japs scattering.

By the middle of the afternoon CONYNGHAM joined the main body of the force returning to Buna. Twenty-five hundred men were firmly footed on New Britain.

3

To participants most large-scale military operations appear to be "fouled up" in some respect or other. This will happen almost inevitably in spite of detailed and careful planning. There is always some overlooked fact, some streak of freakish luck, some break in the weather—or most often, "someone doesn't get the word." After a battle is over and won the whole experience is neatly wrapped up in a page or two of history with no ragged edges showing. Readers believe that the operation was an easy, logical progression from inception to conclusion. But to get the real story ask the man who has been there.

Cape Gloucester, however, was different. It was most extraordinarily *not* fouled up in the least.

At the northwest end of New Britain, Cape Gloucester spreads in a coastal plain like a sweeping train from the skirts of Mount Talawe, a 6,600-foot—and active—volcano. The area is covered by jungle and scattered kunai patches. On the very tip of the cape, only 50 yards from the sea, the Japs had built a two-strip airdrome.

The shore of this part of New Britain is rock bound and coral fringed, and, as was so often the case in the South Pacific, few accurate charts were available. Sometimes the most recent were pre-World War I German charts bearing observations noted ninety years ago, and warning that the landmarks were sometimes a thousand yards out of line, one way or another. So the Seventh Amphibious Force made their own charts from photographs taken by the Army's Fifth Air Force.

But good charts or not, the fact still remained that off the coast about five miles was a very dangerous reef. The rusting hull of a Japanese destroyer firmly wedged on a shelf of coral stood out as grim warning to those in ships who came near. It served the Allied ships well, as will be seen.

When the destroyers FLUSSER and MAHAN (Lieutenant Commander Earnest G. Campbell) and the minesweeps YMS 51 (Lieutenant Francis P. Allen, Jr.) and YMS 52 (Lieutenant Albert I. Roche) and the "spitkits" SC 742 (Lieutenant Robert H. Blake) and SC 981 (Lieutenant (jg) Robert A. Campbell) swung out from convoy on the dark, overcast night of Christmas, 1943, the importance of their mission was much greater than their relative size. They were to channel-buoy the entrance through the reefs.

Groping underwater by sound with submarine detection apparatus, the destroyers eased in toward the reefs. The sharp "ping" of the sonar gear sounded incessant and monotonous on the blacked-out bridge. Finally an answering "ping" was heard, an echo from an underwater object. Reefs ahead!

The destroyers moved slowly in, carefully noting the ranges as they ran their fingers of sound up and down the coral, feeling for a gap in the reef. An hour and a half before the first landing boat was scheduled to hit the sand, MAHAN found the breach. Five hundred yards off, MAHAN hove to and directed YMS 52, with its big yellow buoy, in toward the planting area. Soon after, the second edge of the entrance was located and YMS 51 moved in with its cargo of red buoys. By the time the main landing force arrived the path to the beaches would be as clearly laid out as a transcontinental highway.

Offshore the cruisers by this time had started shooting. The Aussie cruisers AUSTRALIA and SHROPSHIRE under Rear Admiral Crutchley bombarded the airdrome. The American cruisers PHOENIX (Captain Albert G. Noble) and NASHVILLE (Captain Herman A. Spanagel), with Rear Admiral Russell S. Berkey directing, gave the main landing beaches (Yellow 1 and 2) a working over. And, thanks to the reef-clutched Japanese destroyer, these two cruiser groups kept correct position during the bombardment by taking frequent radar ranges and bearings on the wreck. It was as good as a lighthouse. With the reefs now securely located, FLUSSER and MAHAN moved inside for close-in blows on the same Yellow beaches, as the YMS 49 (Lieutenant John R. Lewis) swept ahead for possible mines.

The spot selected for the 1st Marine Division (Major General William H. Rupertus) to go ashore was about midway between the airdrome and Borgen Bay. A smaller landing was to be made simultaneously about seven miles southwest of Cape Gloucester to prevent enemy reinforcement or escape via the southern coastal route.

By 0727 the bombardment ships had done their job. Now it was the Air Force's turn. Forty B-25s came in low over the Yellow beaches for strafing and bombing runs in a well-integrated attack.

Rockets had worked so well on the small DUKWs at Arawe that now the Seventh Amphibious had LCIs fitted with them. The LCI 31 (Lieutenant (jg) Thomas J. Morrisey) and LCI 34 (Lieutenant (jg) Joseph F. Keefe) moved in ahead of the forty boats from ten APDs and blasted great, gaping holes in the green jungle.

Later when a captured Japanese officer was asked who, of the Allies, were the best jungle fighters, he replied: "The Australians." Indignantly a leatherneck interrogator demanded, "What about the United States Marines?" Meekly the prisoner replied that "when the Marines land there is no jungle left."

Not a shot was fired at the Marines when they touched sand at 0745. Their reception party consisted of dazed alligators, snakes, and a few shell-shocked wild pigs. Some guns, rifles, and documents scattered along the beaches indicated that what few Japs had been there were killed or dispersed by the bombardment. The papers revealed that the Japanese had expected a landing, but not here. They had expected it the day before, on Christmas Day, and farther south in Borgen Bay where they had concentrated most of their 7,500 troops in anticipation. (Later information showed that the only beaches on the north coast not defended in considerable strength by pillboxes and trenches were the two Yellow beaches chosen for the landing. Probably the Japanese had believed themselves adequately defended by the navigational hazards of the reef.)

Following the landing boats in smooth succession came a dozen or so Marine-laden LCIs and then two dozen LSTs with the bulk stores. It was the first time the Marines had landed from LCIs or LSTs. The 4-foot surf drenched them to the chin, but to a Marine that's walking ashore dry-shod.

The 1st Marine Division was made up of the Guadalcanal Marines.[1] After four months of continuous and savage fighting there, they had been evacuated to Melbourne, Australia, for much-deserved rest and rehabilitation. Their presence now at Cape Gloucester did not augur well for the Japanese. Tokyo Rose greeted them with the announcement: "Butchers of Guadalcanal, we welcome you to New Britain."

Previous to the landing the Southwest Pacific Air Forces had made an unprecedented effort against the Cape Gloucester area, using 60 per cent

---

[1] See BATTLE REPORT, Vol. III (*Pacific War: Middle Phase*), Chaps. 3 and 5.

of its available bomber strength to drop 4,500 tons of explosives. Attacks were made 21 out of 31 days. Now on D-day high-level bombing by Army B-24s was excellently co-ordinated with the landings. White phosphorous smoke bombs were dropped on "Target Hill" back of the landing beaches. A gentle breeze blew the smoke down over the beaches and 3,000 yards out to sea, thus covering the movements of our troops in the boat lanes.

It had been expected that the Japanese would send out every plane at Rabaul and Gasmata to oppose the landing but not till midafternoon were two large groups of bogies picked up, one to the north and one to the east. The destroyer SHAW, now fighter director ship since the departure of HMAS SHROPSHIRE, vectored a squadron of Army fighters after each of the groups and kept two more squadrons over the ships and beach, while the destroyers and LSTs not in the process of unloading were ordered out of the harbor, clear of the reefs.

The SHAW led DRAYTON, BAGLEY, and BEALE (Commander Joe B. Cochran) out in column. The LAMSON and MUGFORD also headed north. The HUTCHINS (Commander Edwin W. Herron), BROWNSON, and DALY (Commander Richard G. Visser) formed another group.

Of eighty attacking Vals (Jap Navy dive bomber) and Zekes (Jap Navy fighter) ten got through our covering fighters, and singled out the destroyers for their bombs.

Men on BROWNSON were at their battle stations, grimly watching the sky, when one Val swooped out of the clouds and deposited a bomb 60 feet to starboard.

"Left thirty degrees rudder. Ahead flank!" shouted the captain, Commander Joseph B. Maher, at the instant the gunnery officer bellowed: "Dive bombers astern!"

Two Vals came screaming down in a 40-degree dive as the ship's 20mm guns rattled frantically. One plane wobbled and veered off, smoking, but the other loosed two bombs that hit with a tremendous explosion starboard of number two stack.

Commander Maher "took one look aft and saw that the entire structure above the main deck and the deck plating from the center of number one torpedo mount, aft to the number three five-inch mount, was gone," and the ship, her back broken, collapsing rapidly amidships, the bow and stern canted upward as if in a defiant V-for-victory gesture.

"I saw a group of bluejackets handling wounded, working hard to get their injured shipmates into a raft," Commander Maher recalled later.

"The last man to get aboard the raft was standing in water above his knees, but they got clear. Uranowich, Chief Signalman, and A. H. Andrews, Chief Yeoman, were on the bridge with me and stayed with the ship to the last.

"F. P. Mora, Coxswain, and eight seamen were calmly standing by on the forecastle as a salvage party, in case the stern broke off and the bow section should remain afloat. The bow took a sudden additional list to starboard. I called to the men to jump and they did."

A few seconds later Maher ordered his signalman and yeoman to jump. Then he followed them over the side.

Of 311 officers and men aboard 108 were lost.

The SHAW was severely damaged by the near miss of a 500-pound, and the destroyers LAMSON and MUGFORD were slightly hurt by near misses, as were the LSTs 66 (Lieutenant Howard A. White, USCG) and 202 (Lieutenant Benjamin Ayesa, USCGR). Fifty-five of the 80 enemy planes were claimed destroyed.

And 12,500 Marines were snugly perched on the back doorstep of once mighty Rabaul.

4

Rabaul was now besieged, bereft and groggy, hemmed in by Marines, cruisers, submarines, and pounded from the air. But it was still full of Japanese and their aircraft.

With obvious delight Major General Ralph J. Mitchell, USMC, COMAIRNORSOLS (Commander Aircraft North Solomons) watched his squadrons grind down this Jap airpower until nothing was left but a bloody nub. From Munda, Ondonga, Vella Lavella and Bougainville, Navy and Marine land-based squadrons flew in groups of thirty to fifty planes attacking Rabaul day after day—and occasionally at night. One of these squadrons was the "Black Sheep," Marine Fighter Squadron 214, commanded by Major Gregory Boyington.

On the morning of January 3, Boyington's squadron took off for a "go" at Rabaul. Boyington had 25 "meat balls" to his credit, shot down in aerial combat, when his wheels left the ground. When he was fished out of the water a few hours later he had 28, and an unwelcome ticket into Rabaul.

The sky over the target was hazy that morning, which was a good thing, for the AA fire from Rabaul was still thick and accurate. The Marines, in their cockpits, were alert for the usual fighter reception committee. Then it appeared.

"My wing-man, Captain George Ashmun, and I dove into a flight of four Zekes," relates "Pappy" Boyington. "I got one. The Nip bailed out.

"Then the two of us dove into a fight some 4,000 feet lower, where George and I both got one Zeke apiece, before my partner's Corsair started to smoke and go down. I followed him all the way down to the water, chasing Nips off his tail. In doing this I saw my 28th plane go up in flames, but George crashed into the water and was killed.

"As I tried to get away myself, what seemed to be a dozen Nips shot me full of holes just off the water. My main gas tank caught fire. After bailing out at 100 feet I was strafed in the water by four planes for 15 minutes. It wasn't till half an hour later I got into my raft, bleeding pretty badly.

"About dusk a large Nip sub picked me up, and into Rabaul we went. There I had six weeks of third degree and no medical attention. Outside our target areas of the harbor, docks and flying fields, Rabaul itself was little damaged. The Nips were well dug in, in air raid shelters.

"Later I was flown with five Allied prisoners to Yokohama and kept in an intimidation camp at Ofna for 13 months. The last five months of the war I was in Tokyo Bay in the Camp of Omori (on a sand spit). I was liberated August 29, 1945, by Commander Harold Stassen and party."

5

All supplies for Rabaul, except some submarine-borne, funneled through Kavieng. Large ship convoys from the north came to Kavieng, where their cargoes were transferred to coastal trawlers and barges and then sneaked into Rabaul and distributed to the defending forces in the surrounding area. Rabaul was by now too hot to risk large ships, and Sherman with his two November strikes had helped to make it so.

"Ted" Sherman, Admiral, seemed to be assigned holidays for his big air actions. Not little holidays like Arbor Day, or middle-sized ones like Halloween. COMSOPAC picked Christmas for Ted to blast Kavieng.

The carrier task group that on Christmas Eve, 1943, was making a high-speed run to the launching point 150 miles northeast of Kavieng was unique. It consisted of two carriers, BUNKER HILL (Captain John J. Ballentine) and MONTEREY (Captain Lester T. Hundt), and six destroyers, BRADFORD (Commander Robert L. Morris), BROWN (Commander Thomas H. Copeman), COWELL (Commander Charles W. Parker), BELL (Commander Lynn C. Petross), CHARRETTE (Commander Eugene S. Karpe), and CONNER (Commander William E. Kaitner). Rarely before had carriers gone so lightly escorted.

The harbor was disappointingly empty. All that the 87 planes—fighters, dive bombers, and torpedo—from Air Groups 17 (BUNKER HILL) and 30 (MONTEREY) could claim on returning to their carriers at midmorning were a cargo ship and three barges sunk, and some coastal trawlers, torpedo boats, and another cargo type shot up. Only one of our planes was missing in spite of the heavy antiaircraft barrage.

Sherman stayed at sea and primed his bombs for the Day of Resolutions. In the meantime the Marines were relentlessly pinching off Cape Gloucester. On December 30 Major General William H. Rupertus, Commanding General, 1st Marine Division, sent a dispatch to Lieutenant General Walter Krueger, Commanding General Sixth Army: "First Marine Division presents to you as an early New Year gift the complete airdrome of Cape Gloucester—"

The New Year's Day attack on Kavieng was as disappointing in results as the first. Two cruisers and two destroyers were located west of the harbor but through skilled, high-speed maneuvering they were able to twist out from under our planes. One cruiser was lightly damaged. Fourteen intercepting enemy planes were shot down with a loss of three of our own.

One more try. This time on January 4. But again the fliers found the area bare of juicy targets. Two destroyers were damaged and a dozen planes shot down. The naval aviators dumped their bombs on docks, warehouses, and airstrip. All returned safely but one.

Kavieng was chalked off.

Returning to Espiritu Santo the group made ready for a change of scenery. *Operation Flintlock* against the Marshalls was coming up.

6

While these landings and air strikes were in progress the PT boats were carrying on their own war with the energy of bees. Night after night, in moon or squall, they patrolled, usually in pairs, along the dark coast of New Guinea and New Britain looking for trouble. John Paul Jones had once said: "Give me a fast ship, for I intend to go in harm's way." PT men adopted this as a motto.

By December the PT boats had a death grip on Vitiaz Strait. After the landing at Finschhafen, a base had been established at near-by Dreger Harbor. From here the swift little boats nosed far up the New Guinea coast. Others crossed to New Britain looking for game. Often the PTs operated with "Black Cats," using them as elevated eyes. Frequently, too, they teamed up with the American submarines searching for bigger game.

There was grim proof of the extent to which motor torpedo boats disrupted the enemy barge supply system. Advancing ground forces in New Guinea found many Japanese dead of starvation. During the months of November, December, and January, PTs in this area sank a total of 147 supply-laden barges.

The Japanese were forced more and more to supply their beleaguered troops by submarine. Watertight boxes of foodstuffs were often dumped overboard in hope they would float in to shore. Because of the sub's sound gear, it was very difficult for the PTs to catch one unaware on the surface and have him "sit for a shot," but by keeping the submarines submerged the "splinter fleet" also kept them ineffective as supply ships, to which use they were more often put than combat.

There were other missions, too, for the busybody PTs. Many scouting parties were landed behind enemy lines and later safely evacuated. Enemy shore positions were shelled and, in several instances, shore batteries silenced. The starving Japanese (some resorted to cannibalism to survive) placed more and more guns along the coast to protect their barge supply routes.

One of the most spectacular engagements of the war was fought by two torpedo boats, PT 190 (Lieutenant Edward I. Farley) and PT 191 (Ensign Rumsey Ewing).

On the afternoon of December 26, the day the Marines waded ashore at Cape Gloucester, these two boats with Lieutenant Henry M. S. Swift riding in the 190 as officer in tactical command headed out from Dreger Harbor. Aboard were some Army personnel bound for Arawe as well as mail for troops fighting in that section. Lieutenant E. M. Howitt, RANVR, was riding along as an observer for the Royal Australian Navy. He was to get a bigger eyeful than he expected.

SOUTHWEST CLEANUP

After dropping men and mail at Arawe, the two PTs headed northwest 25 miles to their patrolling station south of Cape Peiho, their mission to sink barges.

All night, back and forth, the two boats cruised at slow speed peering hard into the darkness for any sign of movement. There was none. At daybreak the PTs turned into Marjie Bay for a sweep. But it was empty. As they retraced their wakes and headed for home it looked as if this would be another one of those uneventful patrols which one must endure in order to get an occasional good one.

But they were wrong.

At 0815 the starboard lookout on PT 190 swept the sky to the north.

"Jee-suz. Jap planes!" he shouted, pointing upward.

Almost immediately a dive bomber, Val, peeled off the V formation and came screeching down on the boats. One bomb exploded in the wake of the 191 and another off the bow of the 190.

The two PTs shied apart as suddenly as two startled fillies. Their sterns bit deep into the water as they poured on flank speed and started zigzagging toward low-hanging squall clouds, about 12 miles away.

And then the planes seemed to rain in on all sides; fighters and bombers, strafing and bombing.

"Thirty of them, I said. Goddammit, count 'em yourself!"

"Shut up and keep the ammunition coming. That last bastard came too damn close."

On the second strafing run Ensign Ewing, captain of the 191, got a bullet in the stomach. Ensign Fred Calhoun, although himself painfully wounded in the thigh, took over command.

The bombs were coming close too. One near miss sent fragments splattering off the 20mm magazine on the 191, wounding two more men. On the same boat shrapnel and bullets ate into the engine room. The boat was kept running mainly due to the efforts of V. A. Bloom, Motor Machinist's Mate 1/c, who repaired the leaking water jackets and, when danger of fire was imminent, blanketed the gas tank compartment with carbon dioxide gas.

The two little PTs were under heavier attack than Admiral Sherman's entire task force at Kavieng!

Not that the Japs were doing all the shooting. A reverse hail of fire poured from each wiggling spitkit. The 190 knocked down two Vals in flames. Tracers from the 191 dug into another attacker. Up she spiraled and then went into a steep dive, crashing into the sea. The pilot, no Kamikaze he, bailed out.

Near misses sent geysers shooting up all around the racing boats. The Japs dropped their 100-pound bombs from between 500 and 1,000 feet. Lieutenant Farley and Ensign Calhoun, following the trajectory of the bombs, nimbly sidestepped their boats.

As soon as the attack began, both PTs attempted to call for fighter assistance. But as is often the case in such emergencies the radio circuits were congested with traffic. Finally they got through.

"We'll be with you in five minutes" came back the welcomed promise. And they were.

Nothing on wings ever before looked as good as the P-47s did to the sweating men in the boats. But by the time the air help arrived, 191 had swatted down another enemy, bringing the total to two each for the boats, and both were cozily hidden in the rainstorm. For forty minutes they had fought off thirty determined Jap planes. Forty bombs had been dropped at them. They had been fiercely strafed. They had been wounded. But—they had won the fight.

Two weeks later the high score for a single night's action was made by PT 320 (Ensign Joseph W. Burk) and PT 323 (Ensign James F. Foran) on January 8–9. Between Iris Point and Garagassi Point on the New Guinea side of Vitiaz Strait—and between sunrise and dawn—they destroyed ten armored motor barges, silenced a shore battery, and destroyed fifty boxes of foodstuffs. And don't be deceived by that word "barges." They packed a hefty wallop of guns.

John Paul Jones would have liked PT boats.

7

Pick 'em up and put 'em down. Once more the Seventh Amphibious Force was on the move. This time the outfit picked up was the 126th Regimental Combat Team from the 32nd Division (Brigadier General Clarence Martin). The place they were put down was Saidor, around the corner of Vitiaz Strait on the north coast of New Guinea.

The landing, at sunrise on January 2, 1944, on the three patriotically named beaches—Red, White, and Blue—was not important in a battle sense. It was unopposed. The first real contact with the enemy came at four in the afternoon, four hours after the last amphibious craft had cleared the beaches.

What was significant about the landing was the fact that it was the third major operation by the Seventh Amphibious Force in eighteen days. The ships used were occupied at Cape Gloucester until December 27, leaving little time for New Year's festivities before the Saidor hop.

By the end of D-day 7,200 men had been landed with 3,000 tons of supplies. Total casualties were two wounded. The next day the airstrip was captured and Allied air coverage was advanced another notch.

During the amphibious push up eastern New Guinea and into New Britain the responsibility of the Navy did not end at the beachhead with the troops firmly ashore. Without the fleet, MacArthur's brilliantly effective "leapfrog" advance could not have been accomplished, but the Navy's job was more than blasting beachheads and ferrying troops. The troops had to be supplied, and the amphibious craft were given the job of bringing in the guns and butter past the pinched-off Japanese concentrations, who were ill-tempered indeed. The resupply runs—jokingly referred to as "Milk Runs"—were tough, for besides the vengeful Nipponese on the beaches the Japanese Fourth Air Army at Wewak and the 25th Naval Air Flotilla at Rabaul liked to snap at the convoys.

"Uncle Dan's" 7th Phibfor, as the Navy wrote it, was now a veteran organization. Most of the officers and men of the amphibious craft were reserves who hadn't even rowed a boat up to a year or two ago, but now they were battle-tough and sea-wise. The term "90 day wonder" as far as Uncle Dan was concerned was literally true.

Chapter Four

Green Island and Points North

1

WELL might the Japanese sing their tragic songs in a minor key accompanied by the wail of the classical shakuhachi. Rabaul, once queen of the southeastern seas, had not long to live. Within a month she would be dead. No, worse than dead, for monarchs fear exile and the loss of power more than death. And Rabaul would be exiled, her power broken.

2

One more rung to the top of the Solomons ladder. The long hard climb that had begun at Guadalcanal in August, 1942, was almost over. Only the Green Island, between Buka and New Ireland, remained. From here, Rabaul, only 117 miles away, and Kavieng, 235 miles distant, could be kept wholly neutralized by relatively small forces, and barge traffic supplying the isolated Japanese forces in the Solomons halted for keeps.

Back 125 miles at Cape Torokina on Bougainville the Allies were firmly dug in. Since the landing at Empress Augusta Bay on November 1, 1943, over 78,000 men had been put ashore. In the surrounding area there were still many Japs—thousands of them—on Shortland Island, in the Choiseul Bay area, on Bougainville itself. Since the barges were increasingly well armed, destroyers also began to hunt them. On the night of January 20–21 the ANTHONY (Commander Blinn VanMater) and PRINGLE (Commander George Demetropolis) engaged in a three-hour "rat race" with 20 enemy barges and escorts between Choiseul Bay and the Shortland. Two Black Cats helped the destroyers by dropping flares, spotting gunfire, and strafing the scattered group. Six barges were destroyed and most of the others damaged.

By day and by night our ships moved in close to shore to bombard the by-passed Japanese. Usually the ships were destroyers but sometimes cruisers from Purvis Bay would lend a hand. For example, Task Force 38 — light cruisers HONOLULU (Captain Robert W. Hayler) and ST. LOUIS (Captain Ralph H. Roberts), and destroyers BUCHANAN (Commander Floyd B. T. Myhre), FARENHOLT (Commander Alcorn G. Beckmann), LANSDOWNE (Commander Francis J. Foley), LARDNER (Lieutenant Commander Otto C. Schatz, Jr.), and WOODWORTH (Lieutenant Commander Charles R. Stephan) — under Rear Admiral Walden L. Ainsworth bombarded shore installations on Faisi, Poporang, and Shortland islands on the night of January 8. Concealed behind a smoke screen which baffled the enemy shore batteries, the ships employed radar and air spotting to knock off the Japanese guns with proverbial neatness and dispatch.

On the night of January 31, American naval forces and New Zealand Army units put a tentative toe on the top rung of the ladder. The destroyer transports TALBOT (Lieutenant Commander Charles C. Morgan), WATERS (Lieutenant Commander Charles J. McWhinnie), and DICKERSON (Lieutenant Commander James R. Cain, Jr.) were escorted by the destroyers FULLAM (Commander William D. Kelly), GUEST (Lieutenant Commander Earle K. McLaren), BENNETT (Lieutenant Commander Philip F. Hauck), and HUDSON (Lieutenant Commander Richard R. Pratt). Their mission was to reconnoiter,[1] not to occupy.

From two PTs and twelve landing craft a naval reconnaissance unit of thirty men under Commander J. McD. Smith, and 330 troops of the 30th New Zealand Battalion under Lieutenant Colonel Cornwall, went ashore without opposition near Pokonian Plantation. Twenty-four hours later they re-embarked, having acquired vital information concerning water depths of the lagoon entrances, possible landing beaches, and suitable sites for airstrips. The Japs lay low during the whole operation, and only four of the party were killed by snipers.

Two weeks later, on February 15, the Allies were back, this time geared for a full-scale invasion of the 4-mile-wide island, which is shaped something like a doughnut with a bite taken out of it. Rear Admiral Theodore S. Wilkinson's Third Amphibious Force, veterans of invasions all the way up the Slot, was to put the 3rd New Zealand Division (Major General Barrowclough) on the top rung of the bloody ladder. Because of the shallow lagoon entrances of the atoll no capital ships could be used. The force consisted of 8 high-speed transports (APD), 12 LCIs, 7 LSTs,

---

[1] The Submarine GATO (Comdr. Robert J. Foley) had made a preliminary survey of Green Island for CTF 31 on January 5–6.

and 6 LCTs screened by 17 destroyers. Smaller service craft also went along.

Covering the landing were two cruiser task forces that were well known in the area—Ainsworth's Task Force 38 and "Tip" Merrill's Task Force 39. Ainsworth took his ships, HONOLULU and ST. LOUIS plus the destroyers FARENHOLT, WOODWORTH, BUCHANAN, LANSDOWNE, and LARDNER, to the west of Green Island and placed them between the Third Amphibious Force and St. George's Channel, out of which any surface opposition from Rabaul would come. Merrill took the cruisers MONTPELIER (Captain Harry D. Hoffman), CLEVELAND (Captain Andrew G. Shepard), and COLUMBIA (Captain Frank E. Beatty) plus 31-Knot Burke's rugged Destroyer Squadron 23 (CHARLES AUSBURNE, DYSON, STANLY, CONVERSE, and SPENCE) east of Green Island.

This arrangement was a lure. The plan was to give the Japanese the impression that only Ainsworth's light force was covering the invasion, in hopes that they would come out for a fight. Then Merrill's force would spring the trap.

But the rats didn't take the bait.

The only opposition was from the air. During the night, as the transports moved north over a glassy sea, enemy snoopers dropped float lights and a few bombs, but did no damage. Ainsworth's force to the westward was attacked at dusk by six dive bombers, one of which scored a hit on the ST. LOUIS, killing 23 men and wounding 30. The material damage was slight. Merrill's ships to the east remained unmolested and undetected.

Next morning about 0645, while the LCIs and LSTs, flying barrage balloons to discourage dive bombers, were concentrated off the entrance channel to the lagoon, a group of 15 Japanese Vals came down on them, but were driven off by AA fire and covering fighters. The only damage was to LST 486 (Lieutenant Edward C. Shea) from a near miss, and this was negligible. Because the natives had proved friendly and co-operative, the usual shore bombardment was canceled, the Allied command taking the risk of unlikely Japanese beach defenses in preference to slaughtering the innocent islanders.

Fifty-eight hundred New Zealanders were landed unscratched. Within four days the small Japanese garrison in the southern part of the island had been wiped out. The top rung of the ladder had been infinitely less slippery than the bottom one eighteen months before.

The Solomons campaign had come to an end. With the landings in

New Britain, MacArthur's advance from the southwest through New Guinea had merged with Halsey's advance from the southeast through the Solomon Islands.

"Along the line of advance all Japanese strongholds had either been captured or neutralized. In the Solomons operations Japan had lost a total of 50 combat vessels as well as having a large number of ships damaged and rendered inoperative for periods of several months. In the air she had incurred a loss of 2,935 aircraft and the lack of rescue facilities caused an equal loss in combat crews. The latter losses were keenly felt, for, due to the lack of fuel and training facilities and the pressure of the United States advance, it was never possible to replace these highly trained first line aircrews. The losses suffered in the Solomons weakened all subsequent Japanese defensive efforts and reduced Japanese naval air strength to a point from which it was never able to recover." [1]

3

Now the time had come for the final humiliation of once-fearsome Kavieng and Rabaul—shelling by surface ships. To the north Marc Mitscher's carriers smashed at fabled Truk, as the destroyers of the two cruiser task forces each picked a target.

Captain Rodger W. Simpson's Destroyer Squadron 12 (FARENHOLT, BUCHANAN, LANSDOWNE, LARDNER, and WOODWORTH) under a heavy overcast and through frequent rain squalls moved in toward Rabaul on the night of February 17–18. Steaming in column, the ships poured 3,868 rounds of 5-inch shells into the town and harbor. Fifteen torpedoes were loosed at shipping in Keravia Bay. The panic-frozen Japs did not open with their shore batteries until five minutes after the bombardment started.

Captain Burke's target was Kavieng. Here the Japanese were as ready and angry as hornets, and the destroyers had to fishtail back and forth to dodge the accurate return fire poured from shore batteries. The destroyers made runs for an hour and ten minutes outside the harbor, beginning at 0632 the morning of February 18. An Army B-24 served as eyes for the group, since the firing had to be done over an island. One destroyer shot up the airfield to discourage planes from taking off, while the others

---

[1] *Campaigns of the Pacific War* (United States Strategic Bombing Survey, p. 160).

worked over the ships and installations in the harbor. The 6,681 shells expended accounted for a large tanker, damage to a dozen ships, and havoc on the waterfront.

"After the bombardment," related Captain Burke, "we were to retire to the east and then come south again to Treasury Island to refuel. We had been clear of Kavieng perhaps for half an hour when a B-24 squadron flew over us. We got in communication with them and they knew we were American ships. They were taking photographs.

"About a week later, when we came back into port again, we received copies of these photographs and to our dismay found ourselves labeled as five Fubuki type Japanese destroyers steaming out of Kavieng! We felt very much disappointed in this. We felt that the Army's photo interpreters should know the difference between the old type Japanese Fubuki destroyers and our pride and joy. We wrote them a letter about it, but we never got a reply."

The "Little Beavers"—as Burke's destroyers were called—lived up to their name. They reached Purvis Bay at five in the afternoon of February 19. At six the next morning they were at sea again, after having provisioned and fueled all night.

Their mission this time was to sweep the convoy routes that stretched from Kavieng northword to Truk and northwest to Palau, forbidden territory to American warships since the 1920's. Once this was done, the ships were to move in on Kavieng again and take up the bombardment where they had left off.

No shipping was sighted until "the 22nd about 10:15 when we were up on about the equator quite a bit northwest of New Ireland, STANLY had a radar contact down to the southeast, which we closed at high speed, sighting a single ship, possibly 1,500 tons. We were five ships against one. My conscience hurt a little bit.

"Since we were coming down from the northwest," continued Captain Burke, "the poor devil probably thought we were Japanese. Anyway he didn't turn or run until we got within about 5,000 yards. I decided to give him a chance, so I hoisted the international signal to surrender. Maybe he couldn't read it. Anyhow, he opened up on us with machine guns and started zigzagging radically. I knew if he were not sunk fast he would report our position by radio and that wouldn't be good for us. So we let him have it. In a few minutes it was all over.

"At first it looked as if thousands of people were in the water; possibly there were 150. Some of them were dazed, others wounded. They were quite a distance from land so we decided to rescue them.

"Desdiv 45 stopped while Desdiv 46 circled the whole formation to keep from getting caught by a submarine, and to watch for air attack or surface contact. We had some difficulty with our first prisoner, who swam up to the line that we'd thrown towards him and took hold of it while we pulled him aboard. I guess he expected to be shot or something; anyway, he was a very frightened man. One of the men on the fo'c'sle gave him a cigarette and talked to him a minute or two, reassured him. Soon this Jap lad called and waved to the others in the water. Apparently what he told them was satisfactory because many of them started swimming toward the ship . . .

"However, not all of the Japanese wanted to be taken prisoner. There were many weird methods of committing suicide. Many of them cut their throats. Some of them had no knives and would bump their heads against wreckage. Some of them couldn't hit hard enough to render themselves unconscious and they would try to dive down and drown. It seemed to be quite difficult to drown voluntarily. They would come to the surface, gasp a little bit, try to save themselves instinctively, then realize that they didn't want to be saved and dive down again. Sometimes it took a man four or five dives before he could commit suicide in that way."

About half the survivors were rescued, many in spite of themselves. Most of the prisoners were aviation personnel bound for Truk or Palau. The ship sunk was the Japanese Navy tug NAGAURA. Within twenty-four hours some of the able-bodied Japs, grateful for not being cooked and eaten or tortured, were offering to help pass the ammunition during the bombardment of Duke of York Island.

Division 46 (CONVERSE, SPENCE) broke off and moved in to bombard Kavieng. The rest of the squadron, after having sunk a minesweep southwest of New Hanover Island, placed themselves off the south entrance to Steffen Strait hoping to catch any ships that might be driven out of Kavieng by Division 46's bombardment. The "anvil" operation worked to the extent of one freighter and two barges.

Thereupon the two divisions romped triumphantly down either side of New Ireland Island, and, being so far ahead of schedule, one of them gave Rabaul an unpremeditated bombardment just for luck and full measure.

Like hounds snapping at a wounded bear, destroyers circled Rabaul and Kavieng, biting deep. Occasionally the bear slapped back, as when FARENHOLT and BUCHANAN were hit by the shore batteries off Kavieng. Captain Ralph Earle, Jr.'s Squadron 45 (FULLAM, BENNETT, GUEST, HALFORD, HUDSON, ANTHONY, BRAINE, TERRY, and WADSWORTH) entered the show, as did Captain Wallis F. Petersen's Squadron 22 (WALLER, PHILIP, RENSHAW, SAUFLEY, CONWAY, EATON, PRINGLE, SIGOURNEY).

Rabaul was through. That was certain. No more would her fighters rise to challenge our persistent bombers, for there were no fighters left. On February 16–17 Mitscher's carrier task force had struck hard at mighty Truk, wiping out almost all the aircraft concentrated there. Truk was the key to the Japanese defenses in the Central Pacific and as such had to be kept well planed. The Solomons were an Allied playground. Consequently, the 18th, 19th, and 20th of February saw a mass exodus to Truk of what planes Rabaul had left, 120 of them. The five airdromes looked bare indeed, populated as they now were by ten planes.

Tojo saw the sad sight for himself. On February 22 he visited Rabaul with Admiral Nagano and thoughtful Admiral Shimada, who was soon to succeed Nagano as Chief of the Naval General Staff. For Tojo it was an inaugural visit, for he had just added the duties of Chief of the Army General Staff to his job as premier. But it was a gloomy inaugural.

It was as if he and his party were presiding over the liquidation of his Imperial Majesty's short-lived Empire of the South Pacific.

4

The fighting had been long and hard and exhausting. Arleigh Burke and his destoyer men had been in the middle of it for nine months. They were fighting men, and Burke eloquently tells of their feelings:

"It happens to so many people who have been in battles for a long time. Their ideas of what is important change rapidly. Things that used to be very important were completely unimportant now. Good food was important. A glass of beer was important. What your shipmates thought of you was important. But what was written down on a piece of paper, or what somebody who was not fighting thought about how you were fighting, that was completely unimportant. He didn't know what he was talking about. We knew that. It was obvious from some of the letters, too, although nobody had criticized us. But we could read criticism of other people's action, and we commenced to believe that it took a combat man to analyze another combat man's action. And even then it can't be done because nothing can ever be completely written in action. The reasons why a commander made the decision that he did make is probably obscure.

"I've tried keeping logs on the bridge, keeping yeomen to write down all the reasons why I was going to do a certain thing. But then when the stress came I would probably think of a half dozen reasons very quickly. The yeoman would perhaps be asleep and I would hate to wake him up, and I'd let it go. Or perhaps he didn't even have time to write it down. In any case I made the decision and hoped it was right. But I never recorded all the reasons why I made it or why I did not make some other decision. The same thing is true with everybody. Without the stress and the strain and the limit on time, nobody can actually duplicate the strain that a commander is under in making a decision during combat. Consequently it's a brave man, or an incautious one, who criticizes another man for the action which he took in battle unless it is obviously an error caused by lack of character . . ."

5

Perhaps the most quickly executed invasion of the war was that of Emirau Island.

After pushing triumphantly up the Slot, Halsey thought that the final isolation of Rabaul and Kavieng could be best achieved by taking Emirau, the tiny island to the north of the Bismarck Archipelago. But MacArthur, who passed on South Pacific strategy when it overlapped into his assigned territory, had turned thumbs down on the project and instead had directed that Kavieng, itself, be the invasion target.

On March 14, however, Halsey received a dispatch from the Joint Chiefs of Staff canceling the Kavieng operation in favor of Emirau. Halsey dusted off his old plans, borrowed a regiment of Marines from Lieutenant General Holland M. Smith, and six days later had the island in his hip pocket. Not a man was scratched in the entire operation except the Seabee who fell off his bulldozer and broke his leg.

6

The South Pacific was closing shop. "On the 23rd [March]," continues Captain Burke, "we returned to Purvis where I received orders that I was to be detached from Desron 23 and was to report to Comcardiv 3 (Commander Carrier Division 3—Mitscher) as Chief of Staff. This nearly broke my heart because I knew that I would never again get a command like this destroyer squadron. Never again would there be so many fine captains in one organization. Not only that but I was leaving some of my very best friends.

"However, the whole squadron was going to join Task Force 58. The hunting in the South Pacific was nearly over. There was not much game left for our ships. The Japanese had not sent any surface craft to amount to anything out to Rabaul or Kavieng since our last sweep. Our ships were roaming at will around the Admiralties. There was nothing more for us to do in the Solomons, so we thought that perhaps this new duty would be pretty good."

And it was.

PART TWO

The Real Offensive Begins

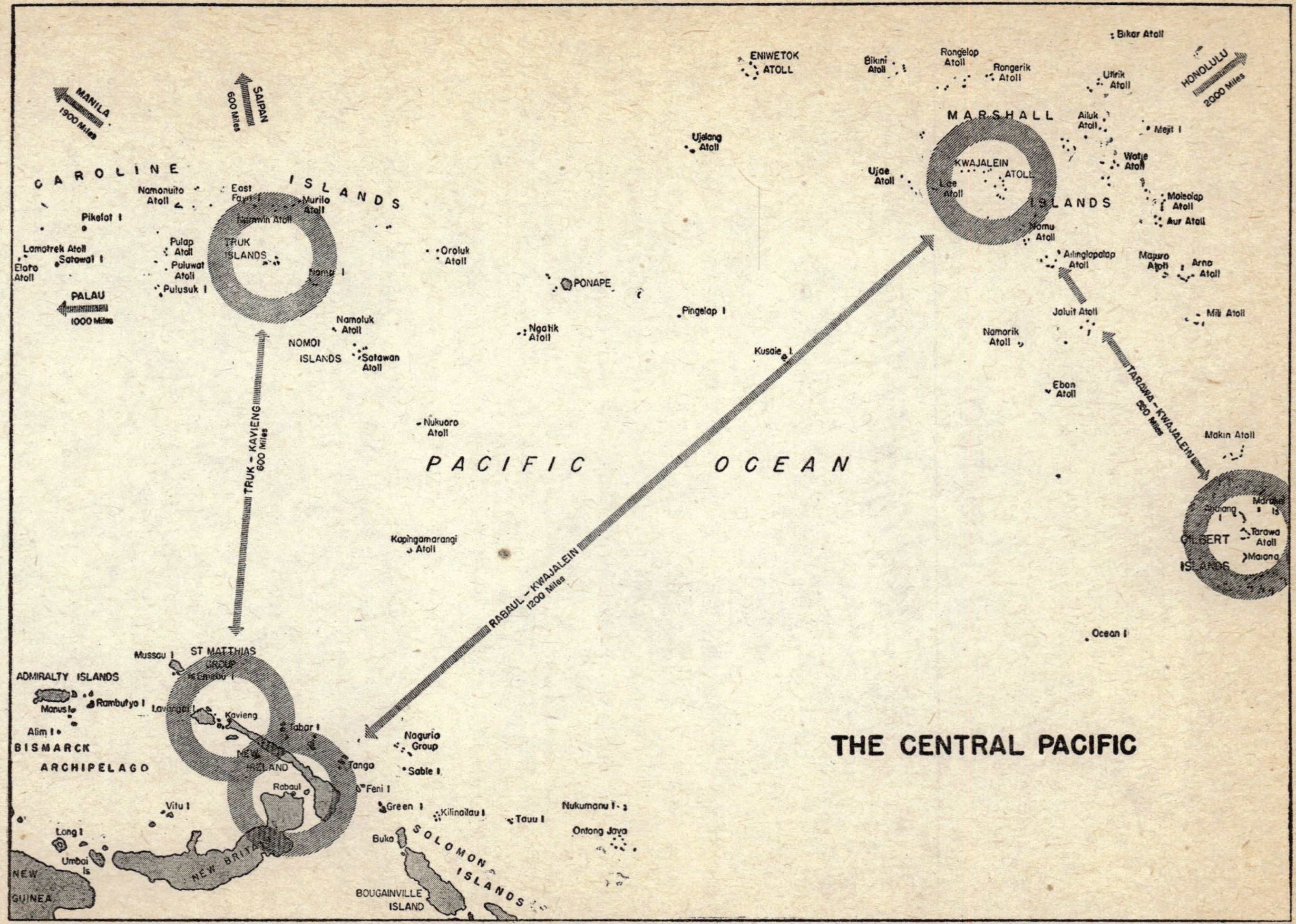
THE CENTRAL PACIFIC
PACIFIC OCEAN
CAROLINE ISLANDS
MARSHALL ISLANDS
GILBERT ISLANDS
SOLOMON ISLANDS
BISMARCK ARCHIPELAGO
ADMIRALTY ISLANDS
MANILA 1900 Miles
SAIPAN 600 Miles
PALAU 1000 Miles
HONOLULU 2000 Miles
TRUK - KAVIENG 600 Miles
RABAUL - KWAJALEIN 1200 Miles
TARAWA - KWAJALEIN 550 Miles
TRUK ISLANDS
KWAJALEIN ATOLL
ENIWETOK ATOLL
PONAPE
Kusaie I
Pingelap I
Ujelang Atoll
Ngatik Atoll
Oroluk Atoll
Nukuoro Atoll
Kapingamarangi Atoll
Namoluk Atoll
Satawan Atoll
NOMOI ISLANDS
Namonuito Atoll
Pikelot I
Lamotrek Atoll
Satawal I
Elato Atoll
Pulap Atoll
Puluwat Atoll
Pulusuk I
East Fayu I
Murilo Atoll
Nama I
Bikini Atoll
Rongelap Atoll
Rongerik Atoll
Bikar Atoll
Utirik Atoll
Ailuk Atoll
Mejit I
Wotje Atoll
Maloelap Atoll
Aur Atoll
Ujae Atoll
Lae Atoll
Namu Atoll
Ailinglapalap Atoll
Majuro Atoll
Arno Atoll
Jaluit Atoll
Mili Atoll
Namorik Atoll
Ebon Atoll
Makin Atoll
Abaiang I
Marakei Is
Tarawa Atoll
Maiana
Ocean I
ST MATTHIAS GROUP
Mussau I
Emirau I
Lavongai I
Kavieng
NEW IRELAND
Tabar I
Tanga
Feni I
Rabaul
NEW BRITAIN
Nugurio Group
Sable I
Green I
Kilinailau I
Tauu I
Nukumanu I
Ontong Java
Buka
BOUGAINVILLE ISLAND
Manus I
Rambutyo I
Alim I
Vitu I
Long I
Umboi Is
NEW GUINEA

FIGURE 5

CHAPTER FIVE

The Marshall-Gilbert-Caroline Problem

I

IN THE second year of the war in the Pacific, the enemy was beginning to regard the map in terms of territory lost. It was a new and distressing experience. No Japanese warrior had felt it for a thousand years.

At the other end of the Axis the picture was just as cheerless. But, while the Allies were indubitably deep in Italy, so far none of the prewar territory of Germany had been lost, and the Japanese could boast the same of their infinitely farther-flung empire. All the ground they had lost amounted to only a fraction of the territory snatched from the United States, the Netherlands, Great Britain, Australia, France, China. And it was the least desirable fraction—coconut country, coral heaps.

That was one way of looking at it, but not the way any naval strategist, Japanese or American, contemplated the charts.

What he could see was a long arm curling up through the Bismarck Sea to gather in the Micronesian islands, a flexing arm that could lash out against the Philippines or Japan itself, in a staggering backhander.

Remember, the American strategy was—and for nearly another year would be—based on the expectation of continuing on the northwestern drive commenced at Buna and Guadalcanal, to enter the Philippines from the south, through Davao.

Part of that strategy, both to straighten out the dog's-leg line of communications from the United States (and Hawaii) and to remove the menace on the right flank, called for the conquest of the Gilbert, Marshall, and Caroline archipelagoes—hundreds of islands commanding many thousands of square miles of ocean between Pearl Harbor and New Guinea and the southern Philippines.

Armchair strategists complained about "island hopping" and other critics, for reasons of their own, called loudly for less emphasis on the European theater and the diversion of the armies to MacArthur. How the armies would be adequately housed, fed, and kept equipped over 6,000 miles or more of hostile ocean in trackless, disease-ridden jungles, and how they were to be deployed in an area more water than ground, were questions ignored—usually out of ignorance, it is to be charitably supposed.

Meanwhile in the farthest corner of the Pacific combat area the military and naval commands went ahead with their plans, which called for (in essence) the capture of key Japanese positions and by-passing their dependencies, leaving them to wither unnourished on the severed vine of supply.

On New Britain the Southwest Pacific Forces (MacArthur-Kinkaid) and the South Pacific Forces (Halsey vice Nimitz) had merged. Now their paths were to separate again, MacArthur's air-land-sea forces to hack their way to the northwest tip of New Guinea and the Philippines' back door, while the sea-air power of the South Pacific Forces was to head northeast and, with the Central Pacific team, range westward in an enveloping sweep of the islands that Japan had readied for twenty-five years against her day of reckoning with the Occident.

But let an expert state the problem: Admiral Raymond A. Spruance, in the words he addressed to the Royal United Service Institution in London, October, 1946.

"In the late spring of 1943 it began to look as if sufficient resources would be available, not only to continue the offensive that was gaining momentum in the Solomons-New Guinea area, but, in addition, to open up a front in the Central Pacific. The purpose of this second front was to wrest from the Japanese the control which they exercised over the great belt of ocean lying approximately west of longitude 180° and north of latitude 5° south. This control was maintained by the main Japanese fleet, based on Truk in the Carolines and supported by a series of air bases strategically located on islands throughout the area. These air bases were, as far as geography would permit, mutually supporting, and they had air pipe lines extending back to Japan, along which reinforcements of all types of aircraft could be flown to them. The Japanese air empire had no such breaks in it as we had in our 2,100 miles between San Francisco and Honolulu.

"So long as the Japanese fleet could operate from Truk, any amphibious operations of ours to the northward of New Guinea-New Britain were exposed to enemy naval attack, unless we ourselves furnished adequate fleet support. Truk would continue as a secure base so long as the surrounding screen of islands remained firmly in Japanese hands. It was therefore decided that our first major objective in the Central Pacific must be to gain control of the Marshall Islands. Six of the Marshall atolls were strongly held by the Japanese, five of them having airfields and the sixth a seaplane base. To the northward, 600 miles distant, they held Wake, well defended and with sea- and land-plane facilities. To the southward they controlled the Gilberts, with their main strength on Tarawa, which had an airstrip, and with less strength on Makin, which had seaplane facilities only. To the westward of the Gilberts they had occupied and fortified Nauru and Ocean Islands, and had built an airstrip on Nauru. These outposts, north and south, were an essential part of the defenses of the Marshall Islands.

"At this time we had never attacked and captured a strongly held atoll. We knew, however, that a thorough and continued photographic reconnaissance would be required to show up the details of the enemy defenses if our attack was to be successful and our losses kept within acceptable limits. Carrier aircraft were not as well suited to obtain the necessary photographs as were the regular land-based photographic aircraft. Unfortunately, we had no airfields then that were in range of the Marshalls, nor could our patrol seaplanes reach them. Our nearest landing fields were at Funafuti in the Ellice Islands, 1,300 miles, and at Canton, nearly 1,600 miles from Kwajalein in the center of the Marshalls.

"After rejecting a proposal to make a simultaneous assault on five of the six Japanese-held atolls in the Marshalls, and after consideration of an approach from the north by first taking Wake, or an approach from the south through the Gilberts, the southern flank was decided upon as our first step toward taking the Marshalls.

"This had many advantages. We would be coming from our main line of communications to the South and Southwest Pacific, with a number of fairly well-established bases along that line. In the Gilberts we could be taking atolls with islands on which excellent airfields could be built quickly. These airfields would be useful as bases from which our land-based aircraft could be operated throughout the Marshalls in connection with our next move. The scope of the operation would, we thought, be kept safely within the capacity of the resources allocated to its accomplishment. We would have an opportunity to test our amphibious equipment and methods against positions on the perimeter before attacking the center.

"As a preliminary to taking the Gilberts, we built additional airstrips suitable for heavy bombers on Nukufetau and Nanomea in the Ellice Islands and on Baker Island, which is 350 miles northwest of Canton. These fields enabled us to operate more aircraft, and they gave us positions closer to the Gilberts and the Marshalls, which extended the range of our aircraft. We also commenced, on a small scale, the formation in the lagoon at Funafuti of a Mobile Service Squadron to furnish our advanced base logistic support.

"The Gilberts operation was important to us in that our plans for it established, basically, the organization and the pattern that were used thereafter as a basis for future operations in the Central Pacific. Our task organization gave us: a Fast Carrier Force; a Joint Expeditionary Force; and a force which had the operational control of the shore-based aircraft and shore bases within the area of operations and of the Mobile Service Squadron which was to furnish our advanced base logistic support."

2

It was early morning of the 19th of November, 1943. In the leading plane of three bombers winging homeward from a 600-mile predawn scouting patrol, Lieutenant Kichi Yoshuyo of the Imperial Japanese Navy nervously tuned his high-frequency transmitter: "Enemy contact report . . . fleet sighted . . . several carriers and other types too numerous to mention . . ."

The rest of the story was told when the Japanese patrol landed at Tarawa, its home base. In hurried conference with Commander Goro Matsuura, seventeen years in the Imperial Japanese Navy, the pilots told how they had visually contacted (for their planes had no radar) a vast armada of American ships on a course that would bring them within point-blank range of where they were standing within twenty-four hours.

Commander Matsuura broadcast the tragic news to Kwajalein, to Truk, and on to Tokyo. The little men from Nippon faced quite a dilemma. According to plans from Tokyo, an invasion of the Gilberts would be repelled as follows: "Long-range aircraft would attack from the Bismarcks." (There were none left.) "Short-range planes would be staged through Truk from the Marianas." (It would take four days for short-range aircraft to get into an attack position.) "Warships would sortie from Truk and destroy surface forces. Submarines operating around Rabaul also would be available."

Those were the plans, but—the Americans had amended them.

The price Japan paid in fruitless defense of the Solomons and the Bismarck Archipelago during the last few weeks had killed her chances of repelling any large-scale invasion in the Central Pacific. The umbrella of aircraft that had existed to protect their surface forces had been blown to tatters in the South Pacific. The carriers were afloat, but with naked decks. The cruisers and destroyers had been badly mauled at Rabaul.

By all information, the Allied naval forces had been hit just as hard. Then what was this fleet of ships "too numerous to mention"?

What those pilots had actually seen was the silky silhouette of a newly formed and powerful Fifth Fleet, steaming at standard speed, outward bound on *Operation Galvanic,* seizure of the key atolls of the Gilbert group: Makin, Tarawa, and Apemama. Its orders were being issued from the cruiser INDIANAPOLIS by Admiral Spruance, who had proved himself as commander of a task force in the Battle of Midway.

Makin was the northernmost target; Tarawa, 100 miles to the southeast, was the central objective; another 100 miles southward, Apemama, (the land Robert Louis Stevenson once described as a "treasure trove of South Sea Island beauty," but strategically only a good lookout post) was the third—and least important.

Although spread out over an area considerably larger than Texas, the combined land mass of the Gilberts is only 166 square miles—less than 1/6 the size of Rhode Island. Despite the limited space, these islands support normally 26,000 copper-colored natives. Not much specific information was had of this group of islands except what geographic description of lagoons, reefs, and channels and data on wind and currents could be remembered by Australian, New Zealand, and Fiji Naval Reserve officers who had either lived in the islands or had sailed among them as shipmasters.

The sea was fairly calm that night of November 19, 1943. A light breeze was whipping a fine spray across the blunt closed bows of the landing ships. In front of the landing ships, the fighting men-of-war were cutting glittering paths through fluorescent water. It was D-minus-1-day. All lookouts had been alerted aboard the destroyer RINGGOLD, on picket duty for Rear Admiral Harry W. Hill's Tarawa attack force, TF 53.

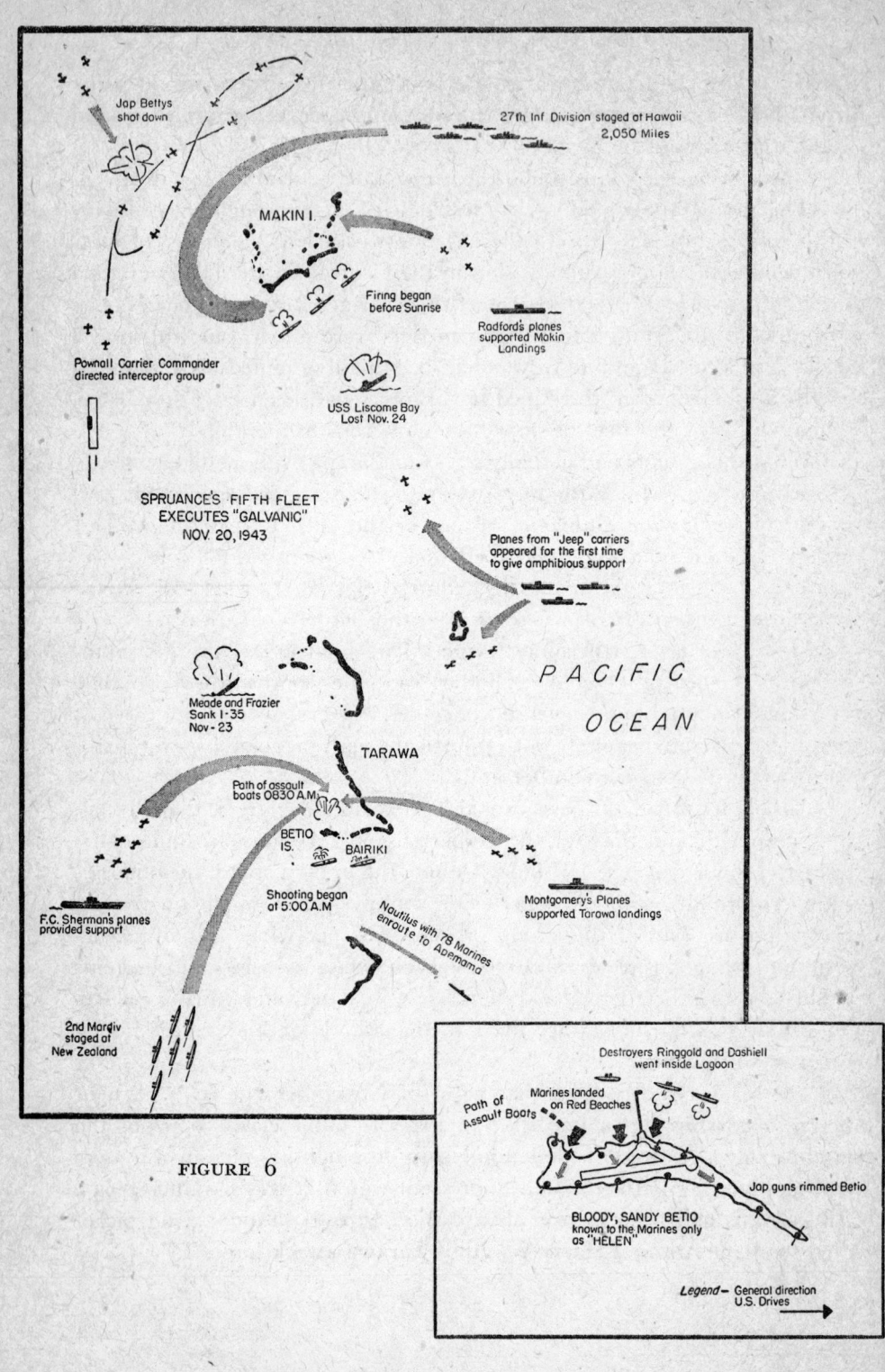

FIGURE 6

THE REAL OFFENSIVE BEGINS 81

"Land dead ahead, sir," shouted the starboard lookout. In code over TBS came the news that all hands had tensely awaited. "CTF 53 FROM RINGGOLD. WE NOW HAVE TARAWA ATOLL IN SIGHT."

But no sooner had their message been acknowledged when RINGGOLD suddenly opened up again over the naval equivalent of walkie-talkie:

2130 CTF 54 FROM RINGGOLD: SKUNK (Unidentified surface target) BEARING 278 DEGREES TRUE—DISTANCE 7 MILES—OVER.

2132 RINGGOLD FROM CTF 53: ROGER—SANTA FE AND GANSEVOORT PROCEED TO INVESTIGATE SKUNK PICKED UP BY RINGGOLD.

2134 RINGGOLD FROM CTF 53: MAINTAIN CONTACT BUT DO NOT FIRE TORPEDOES.

Admiral Hill was in a tough spot. He knew that friendly submarines were in the area, but he had no information of friendly subs in the position of the target. He weighed the odds. An enemy suicide ship could cause ghastly damage, not only to ships and lives but to the mission of the Task Force. Hill decided the risk was too great, and issued the message:

RINGGOLD FROM CTF 53: TORPEDO HIM IF YOU HAVE FAVORABLE OPPORTUNITY BUT AVOID GUNFIRE. SOME OF OUR SMALL BOYS (submarines) MAY BE IN THE VICINITY.

He was advised that the three ships having the target under observation were sure it was a surface vessel, estimating its speed at 20 knots. So, a few seconds later, the postscript was sent:

ALL RESTRICTIONS ON USE OF YOUR OFFENSIVE WEAPONS ARE REMOVED.

The RINGGOLD's skipper, Commander Thomas F. Conley, Jr., was all set to attack. He fired two "fish" at flank speed. One exploded at approximately the correct time to have reached the target. The other went wild, a not infrequent failure in those days, and Commander Conley had to maneuver to avoid being hit by his own crazily circling torpedo. The target appeared to slow down. At 2159—one minute before 10:00 P.M.—the RINGGOLD slowed to 20 knots and came around to a course where all her main battery 5-inch guns would bear on the target, and opened fire. The cruiser SANTA FE joined in, and exactly nine minutes after the action began the target disappeared below the surface.

RINGGOLD FROM CTF 53: WELL DONE.

The excitement was over.

But it wasn't over for 78 Marines and the crew of the U.S. submarine NAUTILUS, on their way to occupy Apemama atoll. For them, all hell had broken loose and had followed them down 50 fathoms deep. Water was gushing through the conning tower where she had been hit by the cruiser and destroyer's shell fire. One Marine yelled, "Foxholes were never like this."

3

According to the log of the NAUTILUS, "at 2154, three surface targets speeded up to approximately 25 knots and headed for us. We were in a bad way. We believed the ships were friendly but they were acting very belligerent. Our batteries were low and without air supply. We were about two miles off a reef toward which the current was setting at about two knots. If we submerged, we would be in for a nasty time. If we didn't we weren't sure we could properly identify ourselves in time.

"2159—We fired our recognition signals [seen by neither RINGGOLD nor SANTA FE]. The ships were closing us and opened fire. Their first salvo landed. Perfect shooting! The Executive Officer, Lieutenant Commander Richard B. Lynch, was just leaving the bridge when one projectile exploded nearby. Our diving was disturbed and we forgot to close the outer voice tube valve. The conning tower was hit and damaged. Sparks spurted from the conning tower bilges. Salvos could be heard landing all around us as we went deeper.

"2200—We went to test depth and went to depth charge battle stations. We had decided they were Japs. Water in torrents streamed down the conning tower hatch. We were 310 feet deep. We felt time was running out fast; we had an important date at Apemama which we were going to keep, even if we had to surface and fight our way through. The 78 Marines were stoic, but unanimous that they would much prefer a rubber boat on a very hostile beach to their predicament."

So, the NAUTILUS labored her way to the surface and went about her business, without casualties, convinced that a Japanese attack had been thwarted, her fast-disappearing adversaries under the same delusion. The Marines seemed anxious to get off the submarine, forever convinced that torpedo rooms made unsatisfactory foxholes. As soon as darkness permitted, next day, the Marines paddled their rubber boats undetected to the coral beach of Apemama.

The primary mission of the NAUTILUS was to land the Marines on that outpost. Its secondary mission was to stand by to observe what happened to them, and to give what help was asked for. Meanwhile, like Br'er Rabbit, NAUTILUS lay low. After considerable shooting ashore, Marine Captain James L. Jones paddled out to the submarine.

"Our weapons are too light to knock out their guns," he told the skipper of the NAUTILUS, Commander William D. Irvin.

"I'll surface at daybreak and we'll shell hell out of them," said the skipper obligingly.

But the Marine objected. The trajectory of the shells would have to be too flat to blast out the entrenched Japs. The natives, who were friendly, might be alienated by the damage. The Marines themselves might be put in jeopardy by stray shots. "You just bring me a chart of the Jap positions," Irvin counseled.

The Marine Captain returned to the submarine with a chart of the exact gun locations. With him he brought some badly wounded Marines, one who was dying. There were more wounded ashore, he reported. The Japs were putting up a tough battle.

The submarine would enter the fight, it was agreed. Irvin selected a position from which the submarine's bombardment would begin with minimum risk of the unpleasant by-products the Marines feared. They would display a wide white banner at the northern extremity of their position. Beyond that would be the Japs, and the gunners would know where to shoot.

During morning twilight of the 24th, the NAUTILUS surfaced. At daybreak, after the body of Pfc Harry J. Marek, USMC, had been committed to the sea, the submarine opened fire. After 75 rounds the Marines radioed, "Cease fire, situation in hand."

4

With the exception of the accidental shelling of the NAUTILUS the entire Fifth Fleet operation was working with stop-watch precision.

Amphibious-minded Rear Admiral R. K. Turner commanded the northern attack force. With him were Marine Major General H. M. ("Howling Mad") Smith, in command of all landing forces in the Gilberts, and Army Major General Ralph Smith, commanding the 27th Division. Their job was to take Makin, the island ring temporarily invaded by Lieutenant Colonel Evans Carlson and his daring "Raiders" in a lightning sweep in August of 1942.[1]

"Air attacks will commence on Makin ten minutes prior to sunrise," read the operation order. Only a few natives and the sentries for the garrison of 900 Japs were awake on the sleepy coral atoll when U.S. Navy bombers came into view. Then everybody was awake. The pilots were prying for targets concealed in the groves of pandanus and coconut.

It was the first time most of the broods of the new escort carriers had tried their wings in warfare. One by one the planes nosed over and plummeted earthward.

The big guns of the battleships MISSISSIPPI (Captain Lunsford L. Hunter) and NEW MEXICO (Captain Ellis M. Zacharias) turned their long snouts toward the objective, and spat forth the first volley. Seconds later the entire firing line was sheeted in flame, and the detonation of shells sounded like Titans endlessly bowling strikes with mile-high tenpins.

At 0830 on D-day, led by Lieutenant Colonel Gerard W. Kelley, troops from the 165th Combat Team of the 27th Infantry, a division made up of National Guard units from upstate New York, waded ashore on the eastern side of Butaritari beach. The troops were lightly opposed by small mortars and machine-gun fire. By evening one-half of the island was captured.

(In the midst of the morning bombardment a powder charge in one of the 16-inch batteries of the USS MISSISSIPPI ignited while being loaded. Although the fire was confined to the gun chamber, it cost the lives of 43 officers and men and wounded 20 others.)

After two days of fighting, Makin was won. A chunk had been bitten out of the Japanese perimeter nearest the United States. But, more impor-

[1] See BATTLE REPORT, Vol. III, Chap. 6.

tant, there was now available a lagoon where seaplanes could replenish, refuel, and rest between searches for the Jap fleet.

5

Spearheaded by the doughty destroyer RINGGOLD, Admiral Hill's southern forces moved in on Tarawa, in whose circlet of reef-connected islands Betio was the stronghold. The Marine Corps' Major General Julian Smith with his famed Chief of Staff, Congressional Medal of Honor-wearing Colonel Merritt A. Edson and Lieutenant Colonel David Shoup, the operations officer, had carefully laid plans for their 2nd Marine Division to take Betio.

From the time the first U.S. Navy reconnaissance raider had droned over the blue triangular lagoon enclosed by 25 coral-built islands, strung like beads on a thread of reef, it was known that Tarawa would be "tough going." Betio was the biggest and most heavily fortified islet in the atoll. It was there that Japanese Imperial Marines had dug in, determined to stay.

Only after the Task Force got underway had Betio been singled out as the feature attraction of the aerial blitz that had been pressed against the Gilberts, or two days out of the preceding ten. Army Air Force Liberators had been flying from Funafuti every day, and Rear Admiral John H. Hoover, commander of shore-based aircraft, reported to Admiral Spruance on D-minus-1-day that 19 B-24s had planted 21 tons of bombs on Betio.

Up to this time the bombers had not concentrated on any one island or atoll in the group, because the plan was both to neutralize air power in all the Gilbert area and to avoid identifying invasion points by special attention. The tempo of the aerial onslaught mounted against the two major atoll-targets, carrier air groups joining in the attack two days before the invasion when it was too late for the Japanese to reinforce any particular spot.

The aviators reported Betio to be completely devastated. They couldn't even find a Jap to strafe above the sandy ground. What they also could not see were the numerous elaborately camouflaged pillboxes; the 8-inch naval guns brought in from Singapore and artfully concealed, or the 5-inch guns and blockhouses all hidden and especially bolstered against bombing. The Japanese had discovered that palm logs, layered with coral sand, not only defied detection from the air but heavy bombing as well. But regardless of reconnaissance, Betio was obviously "it."

The curtain was about to rise on one of the bloodiest assaults in Marine history.

Captain Earl J. Wilson, Marine Public Relations Officer for General Julian Smith, tells the story:

"I was awakened at 0200 in the morning of November 20, 1943 by bells that told me it was General Quarters and D-day. In our wardroom everyone was griping about the coffee not being prepared and the water not being on. There was no excitement or tension. The moon was at quarter with a faint golden ring surrounding it and one lone star. By the dim moonlight I could see the black shapes of other ships, all now laying off to the island, a faint strip not very far away.

"The word came over the public address system for all boats away, and the thin pipings of the boatswain's whistles sounded over the ship in the darkness. I could see the dark outlines of boats and hear the whining of their motors, as they splashed into the water and began circling off the stern."

Shortly after 0500 a Jap signalman sighted the invasion fleet. He challenged one of our ships with blinker light. Receiving no answer, Japanese shore batteries opened fire at 0507. Admiral Hill ordered Captain William Granat's COLORADO to open counterbattery fire. Seconds later Captain Carl H. Jones, skipper of the MARYLAND, ordered his ship to commence firing.

"First you would see a big flash at sea, then a graceful slow-moving arc of twin balls with bright flashes where they hit. Then would came a rumble like distant thunder. It was beautiful—to watch.

"The sun rose now in a brilliant display of red. There was only one planet and it was Mars—bright and significant, I thought at the time. Smoke poured up from the island, the billowing clouds rivaling the mist which was lifting over the island. I stood beside the rail and watched the scene. Suddenly about 100 yards off from where I was standing, I saw a huge geyser of water, and I was very surprised. At first it occurred to me, that one of our ships had misjudged and her shot had fallen short. Then, I realized that the Japs were using their coastal guns and were shooting back at us."

Captain Wilson was learning that war is a two-way affair.

"Behind, our boats strung out in a long chain and I thought what would happen if one of those shells should hit in the middle of them. Another whine and a whispering note, and again we hit the deck, for we were learning fast. The shell passed through our rigging and landed a hundred yards off our port side. We all began to ask, Where are our planes? For Christ's sake, why don't they get here? Why don't they get here? Why don't they get in there and knock out those big guns? One lieutenant remarked that today was his seventh wedding anniversary and he couldn't decide when he was most frightened. The ship opposite us, steaming along at full speed with a wide "bone" of foam at the bow, had a string of landing craft following her. It reminded me of a string of black beads against a wide strip of lace. The island became clothed in clouds of smoke and licking flames leaped toward the base of these clouds. The warships came in closer and closer, pouring shells from their guns."

At 0642 the RINGGOLD hoisted battle colors and headed inside the lagoon, followed closely astern by the destroyer DASHIELL (Commander John B. McLean). They were steering in the path of the minesweepers REQUISITE (Lieutenant Herbert R. Pierce, Jr.) and PURSUIT (Lieutenant Roman F. Good). All four ships were under heavy fire. Lieutenant Gordon J. Webster, Royal New Zealand Naval Reserve, coolly gave orders to the helmsman in the wheelhouse of the RINGGOLD. He had lived on the shores of the lagoon before the Japs came. Lieutenant Lyttleton B. Ensey, gun boss on the RINGGOLD, cut loose at a pillbox.

Suddenly the Japs found the range. The RINGGOLD was hit twice before she silenced the straight-shooting Jap. Luckily the shells did not explode, but one hit was below the waterline and an arc of black water poured into the ship. Lieutenant Wayne A. Parker, the Chief Engineer, perhaps remembering boyhood tales of the Dutch boy and the leak in the dike, plugged the hole with his body until material was brought up to plug it. Then he directed the removal of the unexploded shell, and threw it overboard. The men on the RINGGOLD were under heavy fire all day, but her gunnery department consistently outclassed the shore batteries.

Captain Wilson continues: "The sky was red, and it reminded me of the old saying, 'Red in the morning, sailors take warning.' Then it began turning gray, as the fleet moved in closer, pounding the island with its guns. Waves of landing craft sped toward the beaches, and flights of our planes, finally arrived, streaked through the smoke columns over the island."

At 0830 a scout and sniper platoon led by Lieutenant William D.

Hawkins darted for Betio. The name of Hawkins has become legend to all those of the great 2nd Marine Division and to all who have read about his heroic efforts to capture the airfield that now bears his name.

Commanded by Colonel David Shoup (promoted en route from Wellington, New Zealand, the staging area), Marine assault waves followed closely behind Lieutenant Hawkins. Major William C. Chamberlin, former professor at Northwestern University and Executive Officer for Major Jim Crowe's 8th Marines, recalls that "the first two waves landed with few casualties aboard LVTs. The third wave came in LCVPs, and got stuck on the reef. We knew in advance the reef would be a 'touch and go proposition.' I was in that third wave. I could swear that it took me twenty-four hours to walk across that reef. Men were dropping all around me. That is when our casualties started mounting. Any man who had to walk across that reef during the first two days suffered.

"We were being hit by a Jap twin 5-inch mount. The RINGGOLD's radio crackled, 'We have seen those gun flashes, can we fire?' All I answered was: 'Hell yes'!

"At one time Commander John B. McLean had his DASHIELL so close to the beach her crew could have hit the Japs with rocks, if they had had any. Once she beamed over the radio: 'How are we shooting?' I reported, 'Fine, but don't get any closer.' Their last shell had landed just twenty-five yards in front of our line. That is what I call close fire support."

One of the toughest aspects of war, better known to Marines and infantrymen, is being shot at while you can't shoot back.

"The Battle for Betio was won in the first three hours," Sergeant Jim Lucas, Marine combat correspondent and now Washington Scripps-Howard correspondent, recalls. He landed late the first day, after being turned back a few times because boats had been successively machine-gunned and shelled from the beach. "The issue was decided by the assault waves; had these troops faltered, we would not have taken the Gilberts. Most of the heroic efforts of the first three hours will never be written because most of the principals and witnesses are dead."

Progress on Betio was slow. The Japanese were setting a higher value on it than had been guessed—and guesses were all there was to go by. Then the warships were authorized to use their full ammunition allowance.

"We could see the task force as it fired," Lucas reports. "We could see the shells as they hit. Every now and then ammunition and fuel dumps went up with a roar that could be felt. We could watch the dive bombers begin their runs; we could see the explosions, and, seconds later, hear and count the blasts.

"Betio was burning from end to end. Dock buildings, wrecked in the first bombardment, were now charred embers. Only the center of the atoll, where our beachhead was established, was clear. As our shells found their mark, Japanese resistance faded. Toward the end of the day the Japs were replying only with machine guns and rifles."

At sunset, while recovering aircraft, Admiral Montgomery's Task Group 50.3 was attacked by 15 Bettys. The planes, flying from airfields in the Marshalls, came in so low that they were in sight before they were picked up by radar. The Jap pilots pressed home the attack through intense AA and our own fighter planes. A direct torpedo hit was scored on the USS INDEPENDENCE. Captain Joseph W. Fowler's ship was put of action. Her engine rooms were flooded. Seventeen of her crew were dead and thirty-four were burned or torn by flying shrapnel.

The next morning, after a night of vigilance ashore and afloat, the ship buried its dead. Rich organ music poured through the public address system, not quite drowning the deep throaty rumble and sharp explosions of combat on the island, and the roar of planes skimming past to deliver their bombs. The shipmates of the victims removed their helmets; bare to the waist, unshaved, uncombed, they wearily came to attention as the bodies, wrapped in canvas and covered with huge flags, were carried in by officers. The Chaplain took a deep breath and pitched his voice high to carry through the tempest of bomb and gunfire: "O death, where is thy sting? O grave, where is thy victory?"

On the island, catnapping Marines began the painful labor of routing out the surviving Japanese. They marveled, as they tossed grenades and hosed liquid fire into dugouts, at the quantities of steel and concrete reinforced with anchor chains that had sheltered the Japanese Marines so ineffectively.

Captain Wilson recalls being awakened, half buried by sand in his foxhole, by a sound from another world—the clear-sung reveille of a barnyard rooster.

"Snipers were everywhere," he wrote. "And everywhere there were bodies. Many were Marines. So many seemed to be merely asleep."

There was a shortage of drinking water, for it all had to be brought in from the ships offshore. Frank Filan, AP photographer, and Wilson decided to forget thirst by taking a sightseeing tour. The snipers would help dispel dreams of dewy steins of cold beer. "We moved on and came to a dugout which I glanced into briefly and sat down to examine a lot of blueprints near-by, thinking probably it was an engineering shack. Frank jumped and said that someone was in the dugout. I had the only weapon. We moved around to investigate. Two other Marines joined us, and we leveled our weapons, all tense. Finally an unmistakably Brooklynese voice was heard: 'Shay, I found some sha-sha-sake down here.' A Construction Battalion bluejacket crawled out, blinked at the muzzles of the rifles. 'Holy cats, fellas, don't shoot! I'm a Sheebee.'"

Although Japanese officers had told their men that our Marines could not take Tarawa in a hundred years, General Julian Smith reported Betio secure after 76 hours of what Colonel Edson termed "the most bitter fighting in all Marine Corps history."

The actual number of Japanese killed is not known, but it is estimated that a total of 4,800 troops were on the island, and only 146 prisoners were taken. One method which had been used to calculate the strength of Tarawa, which led to earlier exaggerated estimates, was the large number of privies which were always built out over the water. The estimate was exaggerated because, as it turned out, Tarawa was defended by Imperial Marines, hand-picked from husky, oversized Japs who naturally utilized more space.

The land once described by Robert Louis Stevenson as a paradise possessing "a superb ocean climate, days of blinding sun and bracing wind and nights of heavenly brightness" serves as a resting place for 1,026 gallant Marines who proved they could outfight the best Marines the Japanese could send against them, and they could capture the best island fortress that Japanese engineers could devise.

Tarawa served as a laboratory and proving ground for future Pacific island assaults. When Marine Colonel Shoup ordered an LCVP to lay off the reef and help guide the landing forces to the most favorable landing spot, he established the advantages of the control boat, which would save many lives in future operations. The need for destroying underwater obstacles was revealed, and underwater demolition teams were created as a result. Flat-trajectory fire support proved less effective against heavy emplacements than high-trajectory fire, and was thereafter abandoned for the higher arc and more deadly impact.

6

The Japanese fleet was not in position to interfere with our amphibious operations. The urgent warnings of our approaching task force flashed to Japan by Commander Matsuura made little difference; the heart of Japan was willing, but the pulse was weak. No Japanese fleet sortie in strength could be made against us. There was a plan in existence to reinforce the garrison strength of Makin by transporting about 1,500 army troops to the island from Truk. The troops were loaded on Fourth Fleet's NAGARA, ISUZU, and two destroyers which departed from Truk on November 19, one day prior to the American invasion, but the force of ships was prudently diverted to Mille in the Marshalls.

Another small Japanese naval force consisting of the cruiser NOSHIRO and Destroyer Squadron 2 sortied from Truk on November 24, proceeded to Kwajalein, and remained in the Western Marshalls until December 4. This force, apparently knowing when it was well off, made no move to interfere with our landings.

Roi, on Kwajalein atoll, and Maloelap, both in the Marshalls, were the bases from which occasional Japanese air attacks were thrown against our forces. On November 24 the Japanese logged: "Rescue plane from Roi finds no evidence of friendly forces left on Tarawa. Great activity by enemy on building of airstrips."

Six large Japanese submarines that had been operating in the Rabaul area moved into the Gilberts and were crawling around beneath the surface in search of our shipping. Lookouts kept close watch on the surface, often seeing for a heart-stopping second a periscope that on second look proved only to be a broom, mop, palm log, or some other deceiving bit of the flotsam of war.

Destroyers' soundmen hopefully listened for the vibrant echo that would send their ships into action.

While searching in a smooth sea about 9 miles northwest of Betio, the destroyer MEADE (Commander John Munholland) picked up a probable submarine contact. The FRAZIER was ordered to assist in the hunt.

"Sound contact, bearing three-two-zero, range two-oh-double-oh," shouted Soundman George A. Lewis through a brass voice tube to FRAZIER's skipper, Lieutenant Commander Ellis M. Brown, who was standing on the bridge. Since the echo was clear and sharp, Sound Officer Ensign Thomas P. Higgins said he was sure the "pinging" was a Jap submarine. Brown ordered his ship to a collision course with the submarine.

"Stand by for depth charge attack," came the voice of the Quartermaster of the watch over the ship's speakers.

"Target bearing three-two-two, range one-four-double-oh. Target appears to be moving to the right," piped Soundman Lewis.

"Change course to three-three-two," from the Captain.

A minute later depth charges started to roll. Then the sea shook with cracking explosions and mushrooms of water sprouted violently into the air.

Lieutenant Gilbert H. Scribner, Jr., the executive officer, and Lieutenant (jg) Thomas E. Anderson, the main battery control officer, yelled that the sea stank of oil.

In verification of their keen noses, a large batch of oil bubbled to the surface. Four more charges were dropped on the leading edge of the oil slick, and the water became so befouled with diesel fuel that a brown bow wave was kicked up as the "tin can" cut through the sea.

Now the submarine had taken all she could and came to the surface to fight it out. Forty-millimeter gunners on the FRAZIER opened fire immediately, as the destroyer stepped up speed and headed for the submarine. Hits by 5-inch guns ripped the conning tower and riddled the forward part of the sub. Japanese sailors were hurled into the sea or dropped in their tracks as they tried to man the gun forward of the conning tower. The FRAZIER closed for the kill, and with a crash like a moving van plowing through a plate-glass store window the destroyer's bow struck just aft of the conning tower.

As FRAZIER backed down to free her bow the sub began to sink rapidly by the stern. The Imperial Japanese Navy's I-35, bow lifted and pointing symbolically toward the crimson sunset, hung there for a moment, and then slid beneath the surface. Two Japanese sailors were rescued and taken prisoner; the rest of the complement of seven officers and thirty-five men perished with their submarine.

But that was only one of the six, and of the five that eluded the hunters one was to get more than ample revenge.

7

As the sun dipped below the horizon, a string of gaily colored flags fluttered "at the dip" of Admiral Mullinnix's flagship, LISCOME BAY,

THE REAL OFFENSIVE BEGINS

farther to the south. The signalmen of the other ships scanned the hoist and sprang to display the flagship's signal in recognition.

"Two-block it," said the Admiral, watching his signalmen to see how well they handled the hoists. All ships in the task group stood by for the "execute," ready to fall into night cruising disposition, forming a circular screen around the precious carriers.

As the signalmen smartly hauled down the colored bunting, each ship put on steam to maneuver into its assigned position. Into the first circle surrounding LISCOME BAY, at a distance of 2,000 yards, moved NEW MEXICO and MISSISSIPPI, the cruiser BALTIMORE (Captain Walter C. Calhoun). The carriers CORAL SEA (Captain Herbert Watson Taylor, Jr.) and CORREGIDOR (Captain Roscoe L. Bowman) took position, as the outer circle was formed by the destroyers HOEL (Commander William D. Thomas), FRANKS (Commander Nicholas A. Lidstone), HUGHES (Lieutenant Commander Ellis Rittenhouse), MORRIS (Commander Gordon L. Caswell), MAURY (Lieutenant Commander Joseph W. Koenig), GRIDLEY (Lieutenant Commander Jesse Motes), and HULL (Lieutenant Commander Andrew L. Young, Jr.). The formation was not zigzagging. Makin Island was only about 20 miles distant to the north. The swift tropic night concealed the ships, but the invisible antennae of sound gear probed under the black water without rest.

It was a short night, and an uneventful one. The LISCOME BAY planes were scheduled for their first combat flight operations at dawn, November 24. Flight quarters sounded at 0450. Thirteen planes had been spotted on the flight deck of the "jeep" carrier. In the hangar an additional seven planes had been armed but not yet fueled. There were on board at least nine 2,000-pound bombs, seventy-eight 1,000-pound bombs, and ninety-six 500-pound bombs.

Fifteen minutes later the crew of the flagship went to general quarters. It was still dark with little wind and sea. The LISCOME BAY, as a guide of the carrier formation, started to turn right. One destroyer darted out of the formation, its TBS reporting a possible target. The remaining "cans" moved up to close the gap left in the screen. With all the excitement of a football team running out on the field for its first game, the pilots and air-crew men manned their planes.

"Torpedo sighted!" One of the flight control officers bellowed the dread words from the flight deck. The torpedo's foaming wake was drawing a chalk line at right angles to LISCOME BAY's hull. Before those who had heard the alarm could make a voluntary move, a violent explosion scattered them like bundles of rags. Captain Irving D. Wiltsie had no chance even to order a maneuver.

The senior surviving officer, Lieutenant Commander Oliver Ames, later described the explosion as a huge column of bright orange-colored flames, with incandescent spots streaking through it, like white-hot metal. Ships in the formation reported the column of flame to have flared a thousand feet high. Some saw only a single explosion, others reported two explosions almost simultaneously. The decks of NEW MEXICO, 1,500 yards away, clattered under the impact of a shower of debris.

Instantly the stricken ship began to settle in a sea of blazing oil. The gunnery officer, Lieutenant Commander John R. Bodler, and the navigator, Lieutenant Commander Delancey Nicoll, seeing the situation to be hopeless, passed the word to "abandon ship." Fires belched from the hangar deck and engulfed the superstructure. The few planes remaining on the part of the flight deck that hadn't been blown off were blazing, their exploding ammunition spreading further death.

Typical of the acts of heroism performed that day in the blazing, exploding inferno was that of Lieutenant Commander Wells W. Carroll, the ship's first lieutenant. Refusing medical aid although badly wounded he led a damage-control party in a vain effort to restore pressure in the ruptured fire main.

Five men were in sick bay, a doctor, Lieutenant Commander John B. Rowe, three hospital corpsmen, and one patient. The first blast threw the men to the deck. They picked themselves up only to be knocked down again a second later. But all, seared and bruised, managed to grope through darkness to topside and leap from the canting deck.

Only twenty-three minutes after the first explosion, LISCOME BAY listed to starboard and sank. The loss of life aboard the "baby flat-top" was almost as great as the number killed in the fighting at Tarawa. Fifty-four officers and 648 men were lost, including Admiral Mullinnix, Captain Wiltsie, and the executive officer, Commander Finley E. Hall. They were last seen sliding down a line into flame-covered water.

A sister submarine to the I-35 had fired a spread of torpedoes at the guide ship and scored a lucky hit. But two, three, or four torpedoes could not have caused all the damage. Investigators concluded that the mass detonation of aircraft bombs—135,000 pounds of them—had completed the demolition.

8

While the land battle raged on Betio, fast carrier task forces under Rear Admiral Charles A. Pownall cruised near the southern end of the Marshalls, neutralizing enemy air power in this area. During this period the Admiral's forces, with the loss of three fighters and one bomber, destroyed forty-six enemy planes that would undoubtedly have caused serious damage to the amphibious forces.

Rear Admiral Pownall's group of carriers—the COWPENS (Captain Robert P. McConnell), the new YORKTOWN (Captain Joseph J. Clark), named after the carrier sunk at Midway, and the new LEXINGTON (Captain Malcolm F. Schoeffel), which kept alive the name of the carrier lost in the Battle of the Coral Sea—were among the group that had been striking Mille atoll, southernmost Japanese stronghold in the Marshalls.

An account of the action is found in penciled notes scribbled by Lieutenant Frederick Gwynn, who piloted a torpedo bomber of Air Group 16 aboard the "Lex."

> *November 19*—Attacked Mille atoll and really wrecked it . . No enemy planes . . No AA . . It was a picnic. I put four 500 pound delayed action bombs on the runway although it already looked like a piece of cheese. Mille is a beautiful atoll, but it is a Jap cemetery tonight. Lieutenant (jg) Norman White disappeared in a cloud on the way to Mille and never came back.
>
> *November 20*—Went after Mille again. Plenty of AA today and pretty accurate. Lieutenant Commander Robert H. Isley, Jr. (everybody affectionately calls him Capt. Bob) led the attack. I was right behind him. Took a good look at the ruins and they still had plenty of guns.
>
> *November 23*—A big day. The Japs were on the prowl. General Quarters and battle stations were manned in nothing flat. The radar picked up large group of Japanese fighters and dive-bombers closing us. We immediately launched our combat air patrol and twelve additional fighters. What happened was one of the best interception jobs of the war. Air Group Sixteen's fighters swooped in on a twenty plane attack of Zekes and Haps (old Jap fighters) and simply shot down all of them. Lieutenant (jg) Ralph Hanks accounted for five in five minutes. First he had ever shot down. Actually ten Hellcats shot down twenty Japs in ten minutes without losing a pilot. If any Jap escaped, his report to the Emperor should be interesting.
>
> *November 24*—General Quarters again and many bogies. Heard the tragic news about the LISCOME BAY. God be with them.

November 25—Thanksgiving Day. Snow 24 inches deep in New England. Now we have the Gilberts, with only 30 more battles to go until the end of the war—What a life for a would be scholar!

Frederick W. Gwynn, Ph.D. (Harvard had granted him military leave to fly for the Navy), resumed his teaching career at Harvard in the fall of 1946.

"Big-butt Betty," Japan's most versatile airplane, heckled Admiral Radford's Task Group 50.2 on three consecutive nights, November 25, 26, and 27. "Heckled" is the word. Ordinarily used day and night for reconnaissance, patrol, high- and low-level bombing, this time the fat-fuselaged twin-engine planes were being used for night torpedo attack, but for the first two nights they stayed irritatingly out of range save for one dash which cost them two of their number, dropping flares and making bigger (and no more dangerous) nuisances of themselves than a night-yapping dog in a suburban community.

Anticipating a third attack on the 27th, ENTERPRISE (Captain Grover B. H. Hall) launched at sundown its first "bat" team of two fighters and one torpedo plane, equipped with radar to act as night eyes for the F6Fs. Lieutenant Commander Edward H. ("Butch") O'Hare, Commander of Air Group 6 and holder of the Congressional Medal of Honor for saving the old LEXINGTON off Bougainville in February, 1942, and Ensign W. A. ("Andy") Skon piloted the Hellcats. Lieutenant Commander John L. Phillips, Jr., Torpedo 6's skipper, had the TBF.

As "Raddy" had figured, that was the night the Japanese decided to stop fooling around; they sent over thirty Bettys from airfields in the Marshalls to attack Radford's three carriers, three battleships, and six destroyers.

Sickly-looking yellow flares were dropped about 5 miles on the starboard bow of the task group's screening destroyers, and pale-orange float lights were parachuted by the Japanese vanguard as rendezvous points for later arrivals. The three American naval fliers kept the rendezvous.

The radar specialist in Phillips's plane picked up the enemy formation and sent the two Hellcats on collision courses with the enemy. But O'Hare and Skon, depending on quick glimpses of exhaust flames to spot the Japanese planes, could spot no targets in the enveloping blackness. At one point ENTERPRISE, watching by radar, radioed O'Hare that he was in the midst of many bogies.

"No contact," replied O'Hare.

Phillips, equipped with electronic night vision, was having better luck. He shot down two planes, effecting such complete surprise and bewilderment to the Japanese that they started shooting among themselves. Finally, convinced that they were outnumbered, they fled.

With the sky clear of the enemy, the three American pilots spoke to each other and decided to return to ENTERPRISE. For mutual identification and to avoid colliding, they momentarily switched on their running lights, whereupon a lost and bewildered Japanese maverick joined the formation, mistaking it for his own.

Phillips's gunner, A. B. Kernan, promptly opened fire on the newcomer. The startled Nipponese promptly returned it.

"My God, I'm hit," flashed O'Hare.

His plane, caught in the crossfire, banked steeply and fell, streaming fire, into the sea.

That was the price paid to defeat one of the biggest night torpedo attacks of the war against the Pacific Fleet.

9

Air-sea power in the Pacific was well established at the conclusion of the Gilberts operation. The air groups demonstrated that they could strike the island fortresses, knock out all the airfields, and remain indefinitely to neutralize enemy air power while amphibious forces effected the occupation. Seizure of the Gilberts proved that the fast carriers could interpose themselves between our landing forces and the areas of greatest mobile enemy power. The Gilbert Islands became the first proving ground of the present-day fast carrier force.

10

Admiral Spruance officially reported to Admiral Chester W. Nimitz, Commander in Chief of the Pacific: "Galvanic was executed according to plans. At the close of the month all Galvanic objectives had been secured. The garrison forces were established ashore and fighters were operating from Hawkins field."

For the initial thrust into the Central Pacific, Admiral Nimitz's staff had provided more than a joint operation. It had prepared one integrated plan for all participating services: naval, air and land superiority at the objective (achieved not in numbers alone, but in organization, equipment, and tactics) was Nimitz's prerequisite to the attack. It was teamwork in the essence, and power to the maximum.

Upon completion of the assault phase of Galvanic, the task forces divided and withdrew to Hawaii, and to the Ellice and Samoan areas. Carrier task groups under the command of Rear Admirals Pownall and Montgomery made a fast hit-and-run strike against the Japanese-mandated Marshalls on December 4. The prize target was to be shipping around Kwajalein, largest atoll in the world. The box score, as figured after the war when Rear Admiral Shunsaku Nabseshima, IJN, disclosed the damage done, was not outstanding. The light cruiser ISUZU received two bomb hits, putting the rudder out of commission and making her temporarily unnavigable; the light cruiser NAGARA received several near misses, but could still navigate. Three freighters were sunk and approximately ten aircraft were destroyed. Personnel losses were "slight."

Since the primary target had been designated as shipping, the American fliers by-passed Roi Island in the Kwajalein ring, where at least thirty torpedo-laden Bettys were all set to take off. That night, as the carrier forces were retiring from the strike, the Bettys poured in on them low above the waves to avoid radar detection. The LEXINGTON was hit on the starboard quarter with a torpedo. She lost steering control. For twenty minutes she circled helplessly until a specially designed hydraulic unit, invention of Lieutenant P. M. MacDonald, brought the rudder amidships and, steering by engines, the Lex headed for the Pearl Harbor "garage" at 20 knots. One man was killed by the explosion.

Another task force under Rear Admiral Willis A. Lee, Jr., proceeding 350 miles westward from the Gilberts, attacked the isolated island of Nauru. Aerial and surface bombardments were delivered constantly against the Marshall Islands, first fleet penetration of prewar Japanese territory, during December and January, both from newly won air bases in the Gilberts and by roving task forces. The United States Navy was paving the way for the next all-out invasion.

CHAPTER SIX

Cromwell's Last Dive

I

WITHIN A WEEK after the landings in the Gilberts orders were flashed from Naval Radio at Pearl Harbor instructing the submarines SCULPIN, SEARAVEN (Lieutenant George C. Cook), and APOGON (Commander Walter P. Schoeni), to form the first wolfpack in U.S. submarine history. Captain John P. Cromwell, riding in SCULPIN, was to command the group.

But acknowledgment of orders was never received from Captain Cromwell.

The SCULPIN, commanded by Commander Fred Connaway, was on picket patrol near Truk. Her job was to warn Admiral Spruance's surface ships of any movements of the Japanese Fleet, and, of course, to attack any enemy ship that might cross her path.

Here is the simple, matter-of-fact narrative of one of the war's most inspiring stories of supreme self-sacrifice. "It was the 19th of November, the second night of our patrol," Fireman 1/c J. N. Baker starts the saga. "We spotted a convoy one hundred miles off Truk. Because it was beginning to get light we were forced to submerge. We dove the boat; got a trim, and came back to periscope depth. As we were looking over the convoy, we figured by their actions that they spotted us. The depth charge bell sounded and down we went to about 108 feet to stand by to get worked on.

"Everything was quiet—no depth charges. Up went the periscope, and we saw the convoy sailing over the horizon. The word was passed to stand by to surface. The time was about 7:10 A.M. Up we went, the hatch opened, the engines started, and off we went chasing the convoy on the surface.

"We were only on the surface about five minutes when a ship came over the horizon behind us. Again we dived to periscope depth, and Captain Connaway took a look at the oncoming ship which turned out to be a destroyer, chasing right down the course we dove on. It was evident that he had seen us and was about to give it to us. Word passed for battle stations submerged. The depth charge alarm was sounded and water tight doors were secured. We stood by for that same old story, 'ash cans.'

"On the first run he dropped sixteen 600-pound depth charges, which jarred holy hell out of us. After the second run we were leaking, our lighting system was gone, and every man was knocked all over the deck. We couldn't get a trim on the boat. Next run he knocked out all of our sound gear. All this time the air was getting worse and the heat was terrific. Still they don't let up on us. At one time we could hear his screws going right over our heads, and all we could do was just sweat it out."

By now SCULPIN's hull was distorted, outboard valves were leaking badly, torpedo tube doors were jammed, and so much water had been flooded into the sub that in order to maintain depth control at all it was necessary to run at high speed, which made tracking an easy matter for the Jap destroyer. To top everything off, SCULPIN's batteries were almost exhausted and the depth was too great to permit lying on the bottom.

Seven hours of this!

"Things were looking damned rugged for the SCULPIN. They had dropped fifty-two 600-pound depth charges, which is a lot of TNT. But the crew wasn't about to give up without a hard fight first.

"Up we went, the hatches opened and we dashed quickly out on the deck to man our 3-inch gun and our two 20mm. Once and for all we were going to fight it out. The day was a pretty one, with whitecaps coming up over the decks. At first we couldn't find the enemy ship and then we spotted him about three thousand yards off. We got the first shot in which went over him. The second fell short. We got in about eight shots but our men were being killed as they came out of the hatches. The Japs got some good hits in the conning tower. And soon the topside was pretty much reduced to a shambles. Finally the skipper passed the word to 'abandon ship.'"

Pharmacist's Mate Paul A. Todd interrupts: "Captain Cromwell asked the skipper to keep the boat down. However, he spoke too late because the boat was then on the surface. The skipper wanted as many men as possible to escape. He ordered all hands over the side. When we were in the water we found out that he hadn't followed us. He had been cut down by Jap bullets."

Motor Machinist's Mate 2/c Edward F. Rickets continues the story:

"The boat was making 17 knots when she went down with the hatches wide open. Ensign Wendell Max Fiedler, the commissary officer, grabbed himself a deck of cards and went into the wardroom to play solitaire. He went down with the boat, too.

"Her last dive was really a nice one," Rickets gulps.

Captain Cromwell had good reason for wanting to keep the submarine down. He had been carefully briefed on all the plans for the Marshall-Gilberts operations, and he was afraid that, if captured, he might talk under torture. After a course of burning splinters under the fingernails, the most resolute man is liable to lose self-control.

"Go ahead," he said to Lieutenant George E. Brown, the last person ordered off SCULPIN, "I know too much to go with you."

We don't put up statues to men like these any more. Although for this deliberate self-sacrifice Captain John Cromwell was posthumously awarded the Congressional Medal of Honor, how many remember him by name or deed besides his shipmates and family?

Rickets continues: "After strafing us in the water and killing several men, the Nips pulled us aboard the destroyer YOKAHOMA. One sailor was wounded in the arm and above the eye. He could have been saved, but the Japs tossed him overboard. John Paul Rourke was about to be thrown over because he was vomiting, but he kicked free just in time. Torpedoman Thomas spread the bum dope, upon questioning by the Japanese, that American subs were refueling at a secret island between the Gilberts and Truk. Thomas gave us the word and we repeated the same story. The Japs dragged out charts from as far back as 1820, but we just couldn't locate the secret island. There were 41 of us left after the one had been thrown overboard. At Truk, they split us in two groups when we started for Japan. Each group was on a different carrier."

Wait. The story is only half told.

On the night of December 3, 1943, against a background of lashing typhoon weather, was enacted a drama of Fate that rivals the best in Greek tragedy.

The submarine SAILFISH, Lieutenant Commander R. E. M. Ward in command, was on patrol 300 miles southeast of Tokyo when she surfaced in tremendous seas and in rain driven by a 50-knot wind.

At twelve minutes before midnight SAILFISH got a radar contact. The small "pips" on the radar scope were electronic reflections from a Jap convoy bound from Truk to Tokyo: two escort carriers, CHUYO and

UNYO, one carrier, ZUIHO, one cruiser, MAYA, and two destroyers, SAZANAMI and URAKAZE. (Before another twelve-month all were to perish; the ZUIHO by carrier planes, the rest by U.S. submarines.)

But at the time Ward could not identify them. As he logged it at the time, "the seas are mountainous with a driving rain. Can't see a thing but blackness and water, with the water mostly in my face."

The convoy had been warned that a submarine was in the area. With the seas churned by the typhoon, and the convoy making 18 knots, its commander took the chance to stop zigzagging.

The SAILFISH closed for the attack and dived to 40 feet, coming right for a bow shot on the biggest pip. The four forward tubes were fired with the range at 2,100 yards.

The first evidence the Japs had of a sub contact was the torpedo exploding against the hull of the escort carrier CHUYO.

"We are torpedoed," radioed the crippled CHUYO. But at this point the Jap communications broke down completely. Only the cruiser MAYA got the message. The destroyer URAKAZE noticed from maneuvers that a ship had been hit, but lacking instructions she continued on. This failure of communications foreshadowed the disaster to befall the Japanese Fleet in the Battle of Leyte Gulf.

The SAILFISH went deep after the attack. Twenty-one depth charge explosions were counted.

At two minutes to two SAILFISH surfaced again and set out on the trail of the cripple, although leaking herself. At dawn, with the CHUYO in sight, Ward noted: "With visibility improving so rapidly must fire soon. Have decided to fire three bow tubes on the surface and then attack again in daylight by periscope, making reload during approach."

Two minutes later three torpedoes leapt toward the limping CHUYO. Then Ward logged: "Observed and heard two torpedo hits. First hit looked like a momentary puff of fire; second hit looked like and sounded [on the bridge] like a battleship firing a broadside."

The CHUYO immediately sent out a message telling of her second torpedoing but only ZUIHO and URAKAZE got it, and by this time URAKAZE was out of sight. Orders were relayed to the destroyers SAZANAMI and URAKAZE "to join the CHUYO immediately and attempt to neutralize the enemy sub with concerted efforts."

In the meantime, with the persistence of a seasoned hunter, SAILFISH was closing for the kill.

At twelve minutes after nine Ward logged: "Depth control is extremely difficult due to mountainous seas. When we are at 60 feet there is nothing but green waves with the scope looking into or under a wave most of the time. At 55 feet we damn near broach and still can only see about twenty percent of the time."

He swung the submarine for a coup-de-grace. The SAILFISH cut loose with her stern tube torpedoes, two of which dug into their mark. The URAKAZE came up over the horizon to the rescue of her sister ship just in time to see CHUYO go under the waves at 0948.

Thus went down the first enemy carrier sunk by an unaided U.S. submarine.[1] The CHUYO had been converted from the MITA MARU in 1941 and was used primarily to ferry planes from the Empire to Truk. She was a veteran of many sub attacks and had been one of a carrier formation that was attacked by Commander J. A. Scott in the TUNNY off Truk the previous April.

But Fate, with an ironic grin, rode the winds of the typhoon. Aboard CHUYO were 21 survivors of SCULPIN! Coincidence enough? There is more to come.

The SAILFISH had been launched originally in 1939 as the SQUALUS. In May of that year she foundered off the Isle of Shoals near Portsmouth, N.H. While she lay on the bottom with the crew trapped in her half-flooded hull, SCULPIN had stood by during rescue operations.

2

The remaining 20 survivors of SCULPIN were taken to Japan to work in the copper mines, Baker, Rickets, and Todd among them. They had not heard of CHUYO's loss as they were booted into line for their first meal in Japan. Just then a new prisoner was shoved into the enclosure. "He was all black and burned as if he had been in a fire," Baker reports the drama's epilogue. "His clothes were all ripped and his eyes were sticking out of his head as though he had seen a ghost. It was George Rocek of the SCULPIN. Then we learned that he had been on the other carrier, with the other 21 of us, that he had been hit and sunk and was the only one still alive."

The twenty-one lived as prisoners in Japan until the end of the war. Then, on their return to the States, they told this story.

[1] The SORYU had been sunk at the Battle of Midway by carrier planes and submarine. See BATTLE REPORT, Vol III (*Pacific War: Middle Phase*).

CHAPTER SEVEN

Death by "Flintlock"

I

January 1: Welcome the New Year at my ready station beside the gun. This will be a year of decisive battles. I suppose the enemy, after taking Tarawa and Makin, will continue on to the Marshalls but the Kwajalein defenses are very strong. Roosevelt is going to counterattack furiously as an apology to his people.

From a Japanese diary found on Kwajalein.

1944 coming up. The Allied scheme still is to drive the Japanese forces in upon themselves, and to spear them with a belly thrust through the southernmost Philippines. General MacArthur's forces are gathering strength and position in the New Guinea area for that effort, but first the flanks have to be protected. There is feared and fabled Truk to be reduced, behind its many bastions of fortified islands.

The pattern of war in the Pacific was set, as it was to be followed with minor variations and elaborations until there was no more Japanese Navy left to fight.

Carrier task forces: the marriage of sea power with air power, slashing and boring and overleaping the contracting perimeters of Japan's stolen empire.

Far-faring submarines, cruising impudently closer and closer to Japan itself for the ever-rarer prey of enemy ships or lying awash on sentry duty to warn the American task forces of enemy sorties.

With the Navy sailed the Army, to join the Marines in the occupation, depopulation, and conversion of enemy real estate. Behind came the Army Air Forces, after airstrips and fuel storage had been provided them.

Landing craft with names as weird as their contours. Amphibious vehicles that could swim through deep water, wade through the shallows, climb the beaches, and change from gunboats to tanks in a twinkling.

Army, Navy, Marines, AAF, Coast Guard: boring in, slashing, chop-

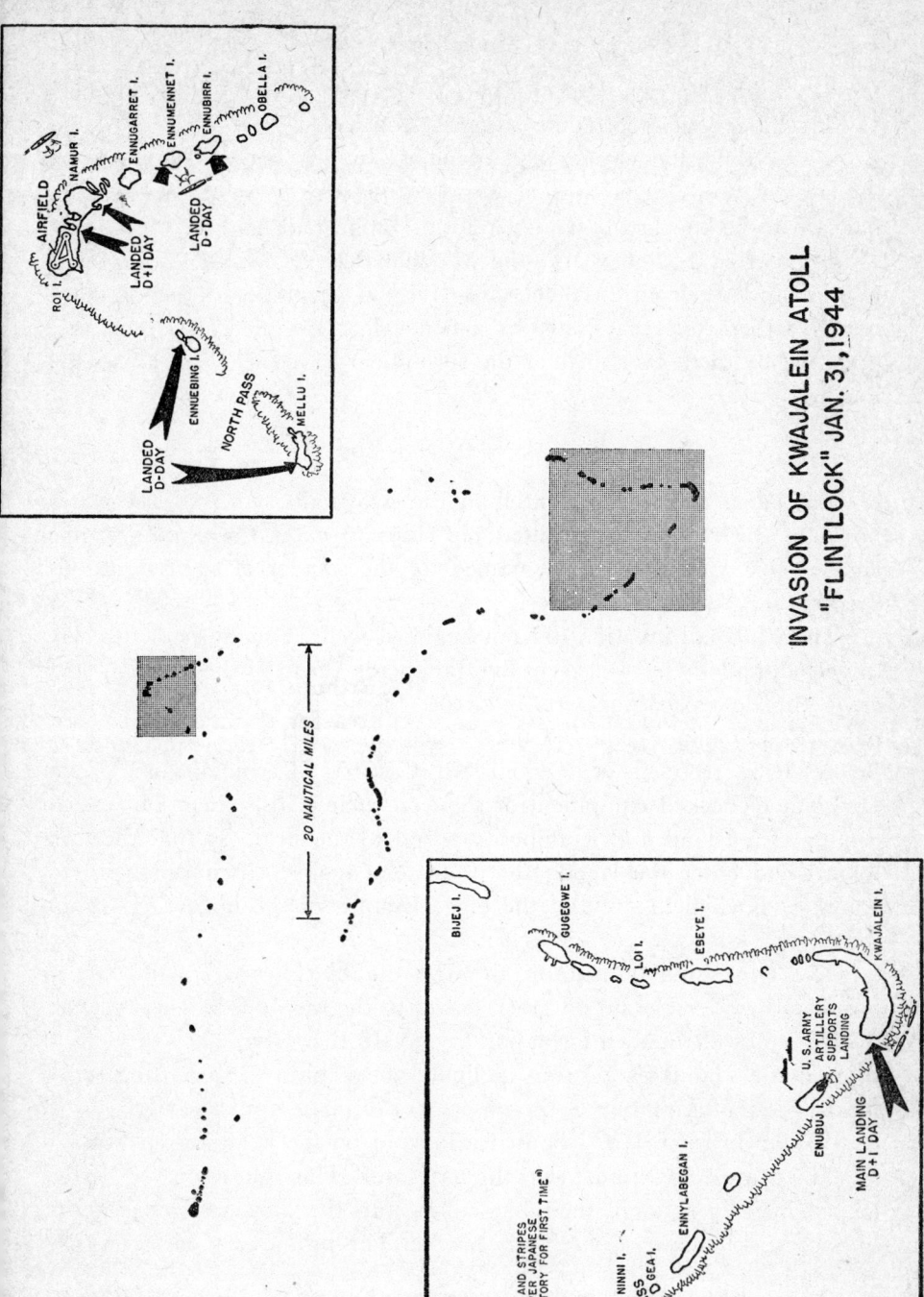

FIGURE 5

ping, blasting, knocking askew the eight mystic pillars of the All-The-World-Under-One-Roof edifice conceived in Tokyo.

So far the Allied forces had managed to regain only fragments of the territory lost to Dai Nippon in 1941 and 1942. Now the Rising Sun flag was to be knocked down on soil that Japan had held for the first 25 of an expected 10,000 years: the Marshall Islands, painlessly captured by the Japanese from the defenseless German proprietors in 1915, mandated to them five years later by a benevolent League of Nations, and prepared by them ever since as the springboard for their leap across the Pacific.

2

Kwajalein first—biggest atoll in the Marshalls, with a deep-water break in the reef that permitted big ships to enter the almost sealike lagoon. Gea Pass, it is called, named for the smaller of the two islands marking it.

The Marshall invasion did not begin so well. A slight error, quickly corrected, nobody hurt—except five Japanese. Ahead of the invasion fleet came the destroyer-transports OVERTON (Lieutenant Commander Desmond K. O'Connor) and MANLEY (Lieutenant Robert T. Newell, Jr.). Below decks troopers of the old 7th Cavalry (Reconnaissance), 7th Division, rechecked equipment or slept on their arms. Their job was to occupy Gea Island and its opposite portal to the strait, so that the task force could enter the lagoon for protection against submarines and to bombard Kwajalein—one of the bigger islands of the huge ring—from their rear.

The two ships pushed on through the blackness. A light breeze brought the odor of rain on green leaves to the men on deck—a strange smell to most of the men for a January 30. In the radar shack the screen showed the islands as a string of light spots, "pips." It was their only means of identifying one of the unseen coral heaps from another.

"Island bearing 340," shouted a lookout on the leading OVERTON.

"That must be Ninni," said the navigator. The officers on the bridge looked intently through their binoculars into the darkness. Vague outlines of an island were barely discernible. The profile seemed to be that of Ninni.

The skipper gave the order to commence loading the wooden Higgins boats, LCP(R)s. The plan was for the LCP(R)s to tow rubber boats with the Reconnaissance troops aboard to within a thousand yards of the beach and release them on radio signal from the APDs. Later additional troops were to be brought into the beaches by the LCP (R)s.

The MANLEY split off and headed to Gea, where her troops would be led ashore by Lieutenant Emmett L. Tiner. On OVERTON, Army Captain Paul B. Gritta gave his men last-minute instructions as the rubber boats splashed over the side. The quartermaster logged the local time: 0423. The LCP(R)s, their engines throttled down to a purr, hauled the loaded rubber boats in train toward the splotch of blacker darkness. When the boats reached a point where radar ranges showed them to be a thousand yards off the beach, a radio message was sent from the transports instructing them to cast off the rubber boats. Time: 0508.

Thirty yards offshore the rubber boats bumped the reefs. The cavalrymen, jumping into three feet of water, waded the remaining distance. No opposition was encountered on the beaches, and red guide lights were soon set up to guide in Higgins boats carrying the support troops. Patrols spread out. There was one sharp skirmish: four dead Japs, two prisoners—one hysterical with fear, the other dying. Good going! This wasn't as tough a job as may have been feared.

But with the predawn twilight came an urgent message from OVERTON, ordering the troops back. They had captured the wrong island. They had taken Gehh—just one palm grove too far to the north.

Before climbing back into his rubber boat, Captain Gritta walked up to the tallest palm tree he could find. Folded under his arm he carried an American flag, a contribution from USS OVERTON. A few minutes later the first Stars and Stripes to fly over captured Japanese territory flapped damply in the morning air.

Ninni was occupied without resistance. Gea, after some skirmishing, was captured by Lieutenant Tiner's Reconnaissance troops. By afternoon minesweeps could move through Gea Pass into the lagoon.

The securing of Gea Pass was a small facet in gigantic and intricate *Operation Flintlock,* the invasion of the Marshall Islands.

The United States, long noted for its mass production techniques in industry, was bringing mass-produced war to the palm-topped atolls of the Central Pacific.

3

The possibility that the Marshalls would be the next objective after the Gilberts had been anticipated by the Japanese, but exactly where the blow would fall was not clear. In the Gilberts, the atolls of Tarawa, Apemama, and Makin were the only logical points of attack, wherefore the Japanese could invest a heavy defense in Tarawa, certain it would be attacked. The Marshalls, on the other hand, contained many islands suitable for bases spread over a large area, some well fortified by the Japanese, others as suitable only lightly garrisoned. As a result the Japanese defenses were spread thin.

As one Japanese staff officer said when recalling discussions among the members of the Combined Fleet Staff: "There was divided opinion as to whether you would land at Jaluit or Mille. Some thought you would land at Wotje, but few thought you would go right to the heart of the Marshalls and take Kwajalein." As a consequence Mille, Wotje, and Maloelap were reinforced with additional troops.

The strategy decided on by Admiral Nimitz and his planners was one of surprise and saturation. The surprise was the directing of the assault against the biggest, strongest target—Kwajalein; the saturation was with explosives, in an unprecedented and systematic bombardment of all Japanese air and naval bases in the Marshall group.

Through the month of January land-based aircraft flying from our new-won bases in the Gilberts had kept Japanese airstrips throughout the Marshalls under constant attack, with emphasis on the atolls Mille, Maleolap, and Wotje. Rear Admiral John H. Hoover, in charge of this preinvasion phase, commanded Army, Navy, and Marine Corps units totaling some 1,200 aircraft known as Task Force 57.

In charge of *Operation Flintlock* was a frosty-eyed, taciturn Hoosier, a man who had ably thrown his weight around the Pacific before—Vice Admiral Spruance.

Admiral Spruance had visited the Marshalls two years before, almost to the day. At that time he had commanded a cruiser-destroyer bombardment group that had given the Allies a morale booster in those early, dark days of the war. His weight in combat vessels this time was 15 battleships, 12 heavy cruisers, 6 light cruisers, 19 carriers, 92 destroyers, and 21 minesweepers and destroyer escorts. Besides these there were the auxiliary ships, the troop carriers, the transports, the cargo carriers, and miscellaneous small craft, in all over 300 ships, centered upon the carrier task force (TF 58) under Rear Admiral Marc A. Mitscher. On D-day-minus-2 (January 29) his four carrier groups [1] sent in their 700 planes ahead of the fleet to strike so hard at the remaining enemy air power that not one Japanese aircraft rose to attack our surface forces on the day of invasion.

Japan's "unsinkable carriers" —the island bases—had been reduced to "unsinkable hulks." In the Gilberts the strategy had been to attack and seize some airbases and assume a defensive role toward the others. At Kwajalein the tempo was stepped up to attack and destroy as simultaneously as possible all the enemy airbases within reach.

That atoll, administrative seat of the Marshalls, presented three major targets: the causeway-connected islands of Roi and Namur in the north and, 45 miles across the giant lagoon, the island of Kwajalein itself, for which the whole sprawling circle of reef-bound islands is named. At the same time, Majuro Atoll, 250 miles southeast, was to be taken. Recon-

CARRIER TASK FORCE 58
The organization of this task force was as follows:
CARRIER FORCE (TF 58), Rear Admiral Mitscher
  Task Group 58.1, Rear Admiral John W. Reeves, Jr.
    Carriers: YORKTOWN (FF), ENTERPRISE (F), BELLEAU WOOD
    Battleships: WASHINGTON, MASSACHUSETTS, INDIANA
    Light Cruiser: OAKLAND
    Destroyers: C. K. BRONSON, COTTEN, DORTCH, GATLING, HEALY, COGSWELL, CAPERTON, KNAPP, INGERSOLL
  Task Group 58.2, Rear Admiral A. E. Montgomery
    Carriers: INTREPID (F), ESSEX, CABOT
    Battleships: SOUTH DAKOTA, ALABAMA, NORTH CAROLINA
    Light Cruiser
      (Anti-aircraft): SAN DIEGO
    Destroyers: OWEN, MILLER, THE SULLIVANS, STEPHEN POTTER, HICKOX, HUNT, LEWIS HANCOCK, LANG, STERETT, STACK
  Task Group 58.3, Rear Admiral Frederick C. Sherman
    Carriers: BUNKER HILL (F), MONTEREY, COWPENS
    Battleships: IOWA, NEW JERSEY
    Heavy Cruiser: WICHITA
    Destroyers: IZARD, CHARRETTE, CONNER, BELL, BURNS, BRADFORD, BROWN, COWELL, WILSON
  Task Group 58.4, Rear Admiral Samuel P. Ginder
    Carriers: SARATOGA (F), PRINCETON, LANGLEY
    Heavy Cruisers: BOSTON, BALTIMORE
    Light Cruiser
      (Anti-aircraft): SAN JUAN
    Destroyers: MAURY, CRAVEN, GRIDLEY, MC CALL, DUNLAP, FANNING, CASE, CUMMINGS

naissance had shown its excellent harbor to be lightly defended. With these key positions in grasp, the whole Marshall group could be dominated, leaving only Eniwetok on the western perimeter to be taken and with it to secure the upper hand over all the Micronesian Pacific.

To protect the assault against enemy fleet attack from sinister Truk, 950 miles away, Admiral Mitscher's fast carriers, battleships, and cruisers, including the newest elements in the Pacific Fleet, were drawn across the invasion area in a great arc.

At Truk Admiral Koga, IJN, had a well-mailed fist—but he prudently kept it in his pocket. It included three battleships, eight carriers, eleven cruisers, plus supporting destroyers and lesser ships.

Had Koga, however, decided to send his fleet to try to break through Mitscher's line and oppose the landings, it would have met with resistance in its own dooryard. American submarines, as always, kept close watch at the focal points of Japanese power for any sign of movement. At Truk PERMIT (Lieutenant Commander Carter L. Bennett), SKIPJACK (Commander George G. Molumphy), and GUARDFISH (Lieutenant Commander Norwell G. Ward) up from Brisbane guarded all exits. Ponape, Kusaie, and Eniwetok were patrolled by SEAL (Lieutenant Commander Harry B. Dodge), SUNFISH (Lieutenant Commander Edward E. Shelby), and SEARAVEN (Lieutenant Commander Melvin H. Dry).

But Koga had no intention of sortieing, and so the pickings for the submarines were lean. On the night of January 25 SKIPJACK sank the Japanese destroyer SUZUKAZE. The GUARDFISH followed this up on February 1 by getting another destroyer, UMIKAZE.

The Joint Expeditionary Force, whose task it was to make the actual assault, was commanded by Rear Admiral Richmond K. Turner. The troops themselves, including both Army and Marines, were under the over-all command of Major General Holland M. Smith.

They had been assembled on the Pacific Coast and in the Hawaiian Islands with a few elements having been brought up from the Ellice and Samoan areas. The 4th Marine Division was lifted from the West Coast and staged through points in Hawaii, where it was joined by the 7th Infantry Division of the Army.

Integrated with the troop transports and cargo ships of this force were the old battleships (IDAHO, PENNSYLVANIA, NEW MEXICO, MISSISSIPPI, TENNESSEE, MARYLAND, COLORADO), which still could hit so hard, escort carriers, light and heavy cruisers, and destroyers.

THE REAL OFFENSIVE BEGINS

The islands of Wotje in the atoll of the same name and Taroa in Maleolap Atoll were particularly formidable as enemy airbases. To make triply sure of their being neutralized on D-day, they were first pounded by Admiral Hoover's land-based planes, then by Admiral Mitscher's carrier pilots, and during the invasion bombarded by a special surface neutralization group [1] of cruisers and destroyers under Rear Admiral Ernest G. Small.

In the early morning of January 30, just after daybreak, Wotje was also bombarded by a group of cruisers and destroyers under Rear Admiral Laurence T. DuBose. The cruisers LOUISVILLE (Captain Samuel H. Hurt), SANTA FE (Captain Jerauld Wright), MOBILE (Captain Charles J. Wheeler), BILOXI (Captain Daniel Michael McGurl), and the destroyers MORRIS (Commander Gordon L. Caswell), HUGHES (Lieutenant Commander Ellis Brooks Rittenhouse), FLETCHER (Commander Robert D. McGinnis), MUSTIN (Commander Monro M. Riker), RUSSELL (Lieutenant Commander Lewis R. Miller), and ANDERSON (Commander John G. Tennent, III) took part.

But the Japanese still had a lot of fight left in them. Three minutes after ANDERSON had opened up, she was hit by a 5-inch Jap shell fired from a shore battery 6,000 yards away. The shell hit the superstructure and exploded. The Captain, John Tennent, standing on the port wing of the bridge, was killed instantly. Two more officers and three men in Combat Information Center were killed, and fourteen were wounded.

4

This is the stuff of which history is made, and then forgotten by all except those whose duty it is to delve into it—or to be recalled in peacetime bull sessions by those who took part.

Admiral Montgomery's task group, moving into position through

---

[1] NEUTRALIZATION GROUP (TG 50.15), Rear Admiral Small
TAROA Neutralization Unit (TU 50.15.1)
    Heavy Cruisers: CHESTER (F), PENSACOLA
    Destroyers: ERBEN, HALE, BLACK
WOTJE Neutralization Unit (TU 50.15.2), Captain Leroy W. Busbey, Jr.
    Heavy Cruiser: SALT LAKE CITY (F)
    Destroyers: ABBOTT, WALKER, KIDD
Carrier Unit (TU 50.15.3), Captain Stanley J. Michael
    Carriers: NASSAU (F), NATOMA BAY
    Destroyers: Desdiv 96 (BULLARD, CHAUNCEY)
    Minelayers: PREBLE, RAMSAY

storm-lashed darkness, picked up a radar pip, a pinprick of light on the screen that meant there was something over yonder that might or might not have business being there. And with that, a hoarse gabble erupted from the TBS receivers—the pip was speaking by radio, and it spoke the acceptable recognition signal, identifying itself as the U.S. destroyer BURNS. Said BURNS:

"We have you bearing 220 true, distance 10 miles."

"Roger," replied the Task Group laconically.

"We are in an enemy convoy and have set three or four ships on fire."

The Task Group commander was interested. "Need any help?" he spoke.

"Negative," BURNS answered, with terse nonchalance. "We have set four ships on fire. Two have lifeboats in the water."

"Is there anything left we can clean up?"

"We have cleaned all ships up," BURNS said politely, but firmly. "Do not believe another ship in area would help."

The Task Group relaxed and headed for its date at Roi Island. The BURNS took a last look at the carnage it had caused and headed back to rejoin Admiral Sherman's carrier brood.

What had happened was this:

While engaged in the dull business of screening Sherman's carriers as their planes neutralized Kwajalein's air power, BURNS's skipper, Lieutenant Commander Donald T. Eller, had welcomed the errand to locate and rescue three downed aviators reported adrift in a rubber boat 35 miles south. The destroyer located the trio with the help of passing airplanes, and transferred one badly wounded aviator to the battleship SOUTH DAKOTA by breeches buoy.

Before leaving on his rescue mission Eller had been told the Task Group would have finished with Kwajalein before he could return, and to go on to Eniwetok where Sherman's ships had another task to initiate. So BURNS headed northwest under a heavy overcast from which black clouds bellied to mast height from time to time and spewed rain squalls, and when night came it brought total darkness.

Traveling through unknown, almost uncharted, seas, in enemy territory and on a stormy night is nobody's idea of pleasure cruising, but the invention of radar has contributed no little toward the prevention of prematurely gray heads among those whose duties take them on such journeys.

THE REAL OFFENSIVE BEGINS

Radar's far-roving, night-seeing eye registered a blob of light for BURNS at 11:00 P.M.

"That's Ujae Island," the radar officer said. "Bearing 063 true, 20 miles off. Check."

An hour. And nearly another half. Then radar winked again.

"A particularly heavy rain squall" was the interpretation. The pip was drooling along at 7 knots, with the wind. But then, suddenly, it split into four, and it was four ships in line or BURNS was the Staten Island ferry!

Abruptly the hoarse bray of the call to quarters sounded throughout the lone-faring destroyer. The range was closed at 25 knots, all guns trained on the quadruplet target. Were they friend or foe?

Commander Eller sped his challenge across the miles of black water. No answer.

At 0107—67 minutes after midnight, three-quarters of an hour after the radar's warning, the destroyer's 5-inch guns spoke a more peremptory challenge. It was answered with gunfire.

The range closed from 9,000 yards to 6,000, four ships banging away at one. Then came the first ocular glimpse of the enemy, a storm-haloed pillar of fire. One down.

Still groping by radar, the destroyer's guns pointed a second ship. Four minutes of firing, and a second column of fire. The third enemy vessel was close enough, now, for BURNS's 40mm and 20mm to add their sting to the 5-inchers.

Twenty-five minutes to two—and three fires burning. (She was well-named, was the BURNS.) Number four target on the screen. The destroyer poured a cone of gunfire into the unseen enemy. This one did not burn. It blew up.

Score: two Japanese escorts, one Japanese tanker, one medium cargo ship, totaling 13,500 tons. Time: 30 minutes.

The BURNS came in to see what she had bagged, saw that there were lifeboats afloat, and shoved for Eniwetok. There was a moment's excitement when radar produced evidence of a whole big fleet approaching, but it was just some friends passing by.

5

On D-minus-1-day, all the intricate parts of *Operation Flintlock* began to mesh. Fast ships catching up with slow ships. Ships that had left California converging upon ships that had departed Hawaii, the Ellice Islands, from here and yon. The mass movement was as delicately and precisely timed as the works of the finest chronometer, now clicking into place to sound the hour for the Japanese calloused grip on the Marshalls.

The comparatively small Majuro attack group [1] (Task Group 51.2) under Rear Admiral Harry W. Hill peeled off from the main force and headed south. The other two groups continued on a southwesterly course, toward the twin objectives at either end of Kwajalein Atoll. Japanese searches in this direction were known to be weak. The northern force under Rear Admiral Richard L. Conolly was to put the 4th Marine Division, commanded by Major General Harry Schmidt, USMC, ashore at Roi-Namur islands. The southern force was to attack Kwajalein Island itself. Rear Admiral R. K. Turner, who was in command of the over-all expeditionary force, was also in direct command of this group. The troops to be used were the Army 7th Division, veterans of the fog-bound fighting of Attu.

The air-sea bombardment of the selected islands continued with rising crescendo. Neutralization was achieved on D-minus-2-day. On D-minus-1-day the objective was pulverization. To the westward the last enemy power was squashed at Eniwetok by Admiral Sherman's carriers. Kwajalein, Roi, Wotje, and Taroa again caught holy hell. The whole operation began to split into well-planned complexities of destruction. Carrier aircraft and land-based planes from the Gilberts alternated their aerial haymakers. Two cruiser divisions split off from the carrier task groups and began pumping salvos into Wotje and Taroa, already left ragged by Admiral Small's Neutralization Group of cruisers and destroyers. Eight of the new fast battleships, detached from the carrier groups, proceeded systematically to plow up Kwajalein and Roi-Namur. War had become a massive, death-dealing engineering project, an assembly-line delivery of destruction that had its origin in the mills and mines, farms and factories of the United States.

But war remained a very personal thing to the troops crowded into

---

[1] MAJURO Task Group (51.2), Rear Admiral Harry W. Hill

Heavy Cruiser: PORTLAND
Escort Cruisers: NASSAU, NATOMA BAY
Destroyers: BULLARD, BLACK, KIDD, CHAUNCEY
Minesweeps: CHANDLER (DMS), SAGE (AM), ORACLE (AM)
Transports: CAMBRIA (F) (APA), KANE (APD), LST 482

the transports making last-minute checks of equipment. The whine of the sniper's bullet always makes the bowels of the bravest men go weak. In spite of the sky-high clouds of dust and smoke rising from the flat, scarred islands, they knew there would be some Japs left holed up in the rubble pointing very personal rifle muzzles in their direction. Marines thought of their brothers at Tarawa and slipped another grenade into their pockets.

6

Advance intelligence indicated three or four hundred Japanese garrisoned on Majuro, 270 miles to the southeast of Kwajalein. Admiral Hill's attack group was correspondingly small. The largest ship was his one heavy cruiser, PORTLAND (Captain Arthur D. Burhans). About 1,600 men, both Army and Marines, constituted the landing force.

The night of D-minus-1-day a Marine Reconnaissance company commanded by Captain James L. Jones, USMC, slipped ashore in rubber boats from USS KANE (Lieutenant Frank M. Christiansen) (APD 18), but found no enemy. At daybreak Captain Jones had his first human encounter—with an amiable English-speaking native—who told him there were only four Japanese on the whole atoll.

Scouts spread out and quickly confirmed this with the capture of the four Japanese, who had been left to janitor the extensive (and usable) installations. All the rest of the island garrison had been moved to Mille to construct an airfield.

Majuro, one of the best and most strategically located harbors in the Pacific, was put to immediate use as an advanced base and fleet anchorage. Channel and lagoon were quickly swept for mines, soundings taken, and by D-plus-2-day anchorage charts were available. Much of the credit for this fine work was due to Lieutenant Commander John C. Tribble, Jr., U.S. Coast and Geodetic Survey.

On D-plus-3-day when Admiral Hill left for other duties more than thirty ships were already in the anchorage, including two battleships damaged in collision.

The occupation of Majuro was not a glorious feat of arms, but a piece of sweaty work well done—the major part of any war. Admiral Nimitz in his report commented: "This part of the three-prong operation was executed with skill and precision and was a great help to the operation as a whole."

7

The dot of light was first spotted about 0330 the morning of D-day. At first some of the officers aboard the ROCKY MOUNT (Captain Stanley F. Patten) thought that the Japs on Kwajalein, working under lights, were trying to repair the bomb damage of the preceding day. But as the blacked-out ship stood in closer the light grew into the flaming hull of a vessel hit during the bombardment.

The ROCKY MOUNT, a converted destroyer tender, was the control ship of the Southern Attack Force. Aboard her, Admiral Turner and his staff were putting the last polishing touches to the invasion plans. Kwajalein itself was not to be attacked until D-plus-1-day. The smaller islands of Ennylabegan and Enubuj flanking to the northwest, plus Ninni and Gea controlling Gea Pass, were to be the D-day objectives. Army heavy artillery was to be landed on Enubuj and used to support the D-plus-1-day landings on Kwajalein, firing across the intervening two miles of water. By 0530 the ROCKY MOUNT had gathered her brood of transports around her and was lying to off the southern reefs.

Dawn came up with a thunder Kipling had never dreamed of. The old battleships, cruisers, and destroyers attached to Admiral Turner's force threw their shells into Kwajalein and adjacent islands at point-blank range. Carrier aircraft from YORKTOWN (Captain Joseph J. Clark), ENTERPRISE (Captain Matthias B. Gardner), and BELLEAU WOOD (Captain Alfred M. Pride) hit at everything above ground—ammunition and gasoline dumps, gun emplacements, barracks, pillboxes. Dozens of smoke plumes rose lazily toward the broken clouds.

"I do recall one incident which was most interesting to us," said Lieutenant (jg) Sheldon Briggs, Executive Officer of LCI 82. "Just previous to the landing on the Marshalls—we happened to be about two days out at sea and tuned in our ship's radio to an aircraft that was spotting for a battleship. We heard the directions given by the aircraft spotter, 'Right Ten, Up Five,' etc. until finally he called for 'Salvo,' and at the end of the period of time which would take the shells to land we heard the aircraft spotter over his radio whistle very loudly and say, 'Hot damn, I'm glad I'm on your side.'"

Enubuj Island housed the main radio station for the Marshall Islands. One of the radio towers had been knocked down by the previous bombardments, leaving the other one looking rather lonely against the sky.

PLATE XVII—*Operation Flintlock*, the attack on the Marshalls, may be considered a classic in invasions. It was preceded by many weeks of preliminary air strikes, during one of which (*above*) gunners on a carrier scored a direct hit on a Jap bomber. (*below*) Under Secretary of the Navy James Forrestal lands with Marines on Namur, Kwajalein Atoll. Mr. Forrestal (center, left) confers with Vice Adm. R. A. Spruance, USN, and Maj. Gen. Harry Schmidt, USMC, as other Navy and Marine officers look on. (*Marine Corps Photo.*)

PLATE XVIII—Less than three months after Tarawa and the Gilberts fell, a gigantic and complex task force struck Kwajalein, the "solar plexus" of the Marshalls. Although stronger than Tarawa, Kwajalein, thanks to lessons learned in the Gilberts, cost us fewer casualties—our losses were 286 killed, 82 missing and 1,148 wounded. For hours, preceding the landing, Kwajalein was subjected to a merciless pounding from air and sea.

(*above, left and right*) Long clouds of smoke sweep over the beachhead as U. S. Navy warships, on a "bombardment assembly line," pound Kwajalein on the second day of the invasion, February 1, 1944.

(*left center*) Marine gunners, still wearing life belts, set up a machine gun position on Namur Island, Kwajalein Atoll. (*Marine Corps Photo.*)

(*lower left*) Death for the enemy, whether it came in battle or by hara-kiri, seemed more honorable than surrender. Here, in a Namur Island trench, lie a row of Japanese troops who did not choose to surrender. (*Marine Corps Photo.*)

PLATE XIX—Choice of Kwajalein as the initial Allied objective in the Marshalls came as a surprise to the Japanese, who thought we would first attack the eastern fringe of atolls. Preliminary air strikes, carefully dispersed, added to the enemy's confusion. Kwajalein, incidentally, was the first Japanese-controlled territory to be captured after the attack on Pearl Harbor.

(*center right*) As Marine infantrymen and a light tank move up on Namur Island, Kwajalein, communications men (right) set up their equipment to keep in touch with beach headquarters. (*Marine Corps Photo.*)

(*lower right*) Thirty-six hours after Namur was "secured" a supposedly silenced Japanese blockhouse blew up. This is a survivor of the twenty inside before the explosion. He is trying to warn the Leathernecks of an aerial bomb cache, but the Marine sentries, fearing a booby trap, turned him and the job over to a special bomb-disposal squad. (*Marine Corps Photo.*)

PLATE XX—The invasion of Kwajalein served as pattern for most of the remaining Allied amphibious operations in the Central and Western Pacific. Ship and air bombardments were augmented, in the opening stages of the landing, by enfilading fire from field artillery landed on flanking islets. At Kwajalein, replacements promptly took over mop-up operations, and Seabees and Army engineers soon had damaged Japanese airstrips and other facilities in working order.

(*upper left*) The destructive power of our preliminary bombardment speaks for itself in the wreckage of this twin British gun (removed from Singapore) at the eastern end of Kwajalein Island.

(*center*) "Bomb bay" at Kwajalein occupied a crater blasted by one of our own bombs during the preliminary attack. Most of the missiles shown here were dropped by Army planes attached to the Seventh Air Force during air raids on Truk, Ponape, Jaluit, and on neighboring Japanese-held Marshall islands.

(*lower*) This, and the photograph on the page opposite, graphically illustrate the "before" and "after" of an atoll subjected to the merciless air and ship pounding that preceded a Pacific landing. From the air the southern end of Kwajalein appeared to be a typical South Seas paradise early on the morning of D-day, January 31, 1944.

PLATE XXI—War took its toll, too, of war correspondents. This outdoor theater (*upper right*) on Kwajalein memorializes a gifted American journalist, Raymond Clapper, who was killed in a plane crash while observing pre-invasion bombing of Eniwetok, westernmost atoll of the Marshalls.

(*center*) Yankee ingenuity and a little foraging among the debris resulted in this crude, but very effective, washing machine. A windmill made of boards and tin operates a crank and plunger in a garbage can, giving clothes a rugged but thorough cleansing. The GI Joe wringing out a shirt is Corporal Duvall Stevens, of Las Vegas, Nevada, attached to the Seventh Army Air Force, Kwajalein.

(*lower*) "The Spruance haircut," as a Navy flyer described one of the most terrific air-sea bombardments in history. This scene of utter desolation is Kwajalein, after the three days and nights of unceasing bomb and shell "softening up."

Hellcat stalks Emily, starboard quarter, altitude 8,000 feet.

Lt. Thad T. Coleman, Jr., pilot of Hellcat which shot down Jap.

"First Blood"—thin smoke trails from hit on starboard engine.

Cockpit an inferno, Emily is nearly down to the water.

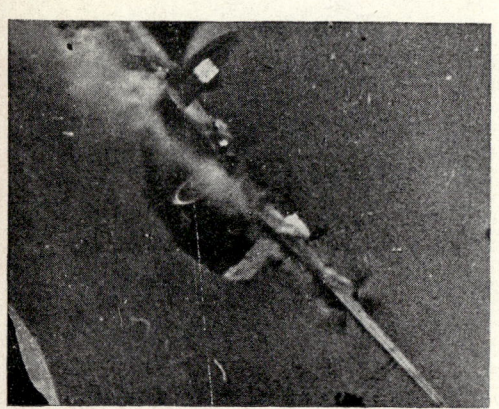

As Hellcat rakes huge flying boat, flames burst from inboard engine.

A few seconds after Emily hit the surface and exploded.

PLATE XXII—This series of photographs is remarkable for two reasons: the Japanese plane, a four-engined "Emily" flying boat, made its first combat appearance before the gun camera of a U. S. Navy plane; and the Navy plane, a Hellcat (F6F), scored one of its first victims, having just gone into service. Just five minutes elapsed between sighting the big Japanese plane, on patrol east of the Gilberts, and the black funeral pyre marking its end.

PLATE XXIII—(*above*) They were the first Americans to fly over the almost mythical fortress of Truk, taking photographs that proved invaluable during later attacks. Posing in front of their two Liberator bombers, after the 2,000-mile trip, are the following Marines: Pvt. 1/c W. J. Butuad; Sgt. J. A. Martin; Corp. T. J. Humphrey; Sgt. E. P. Troy; Corp. E. A. N. Prokasky; Sgt. P. P. Kawalski; Staff Sgt. A. J. Chambers; Staff Sgt. J. R. Perry. *Second row:* Sgt. Dale A. Kerwin; Tech. Sgt. Max L. Winters; Tech. Sgt. Albert S. Mezinis; Staff Sgt. Edmund H. Turner; Staff Sgt. Geo. S. Kneitz; Sgt. Chas. H. Keck; Staff Sgt. John A. Perdue; Tech. Sgt. Bernerd W. Payne. *Third row:* 2nd Lt. Richard W. Starnes; Capt. Donald D. Kennedy; Maj. Jas. R. Christensen; Capt. Jas. Q. Yawn; Capt. Edward J. Sanders; and 2nd Lt. W. Paul Dean. (*Marine Corps Photo.*) (*below*) One reason why the Japanese could not keep their island outposts supplied and garrisoned. An enemy freighter off Jaluit Atoll, the Marshalls, is strafed and sunk by U. S. Navy carrier-based planes.

PLATE XXIV—Truk, the "mystery island" which the Japanese propagandized as an impregnable fortress both from the sea and the air, felt the sting of U. S. Navy carrier-based dive bombers and torpedo planes during the first attack on Japan's chief Pacific base, February 16–17, 1944. Neither anti-aircraft fire nor enemy fighter opposition was as heavy as expected, and our planes were not only able to bomb their assigned targets but even rescued flyers downed within the lagoon.

(*upper left*) Despite fire from hillside batteries, the Japanese Navy Yard on Dublon Island, Truk, received heavy punishment from our bombers.

(*center*) Happy ending of a daring rescue mission. This cruiser scout plane, returning from Truk, rescued the pilot of a Hellcat (downed in the lagoon) despite heavy enemy anti-aircraft fire. Lt. (jg) D. F. Baxter, of Summertown, Tenn. (in front cockpit) flew the rescue plane with ACR Reuben F. Hickman, Waverly, Tenn. (on wing). The rescued flyer, Lt. (jg) G. M. Blair, sits in the rear cockpit.

(*lower*) Plumes of dense smoke testify to the accuracy of U. S. Navy bombers during the raid on Truk. The falling bombs trail predecessors into the target area.

PLATE XXV—Airmen get an assist from the undersea service. The USS TANG was among the U. S. Fleet submarines spotted along the routes followed by Navy carrier-based flyers to Truk, to pick up crews forced down.

(*right*) Aboard the TANG, as she stood in at Pearl Harbor, were the following survivors of the Truk raid, April 29–30, 1944. *Bottom row:* H. B. Gammell, J. Branek, J. L. Livingston, and J. D. Gendroa. *Second row:* Robert William Gruebel, Robert Edwin Hill, Richard H. O'Kane (Captain of the TANG), H. A. Thompson, Aubrey James Gill. *Third row:* Carroll L. Farrell, James G. Gole, John Joseph Dowdle, J. A. Burns, Robert T. Barber, Harry Edwin Hill, Scott Scammell II. *Top row:* Owen Fred Tabrum, Robert F. Karson, Donald Kirkpatrick, James J. Lenahan, A. R. Matter, Richard L. Bentley, Robert S. Nelson.

(*left*) After surfacing, TANG crewmen help the fliers aboard, a dramatic rescue deep in enemy territory. During the two-day operation, the TANG, commanded by Lt. Comdr. Richard H. O'Kane, rescued a total of 22 fliers adrift in rubber life-rafts.

(*below*) Its after section seemingly severed as a white comber roars over its scuppers, a damaged Japanese destroyer of the ASASIO class vainly maneuvers in an attempt to escape the attack of a U. S. Navy Grumman Avenger, during the raid on Truk, February 16, 1944.

PLATE XXVI—Eniwetok, westernmost atoll of the Marshalls, was captured February 17-19, 1944, by a combined force (22nd Marines and 106th Infantry, plus reinforcing units). Despite sharp Japanese opposition *Operation Catchpole* was carried out with train-schedule precision.

(*left*) Partially concealed by plane-dropped smoke bombs, the first, second and third waves of landing craft approach Engebi Island, Eniwetok. The pockmarked, well-bombed Japanese airstrip lies useless, so there was no enemy air opposition.

(*right*) Clustered like ants around the rim of a giant bomb crater, U. S. Marines cover with machine guns the advance of comrades, inching across the Eniwetok airstrip to the last strongholds of the beleaguered enemy. Outlined in its own ashes, at the left, lies the wreckage of a two-motored Japanese plane. (If the picture is held upside down the shell-hole appears to be a black-capped mound.)

(*left*) For several months in 1944 Majuro atoll, central Marshalls, was staging point and springboard for most of the Central Pacific Fleet operations. This aerial view of the famed Task Force 58 at anchor, June 1944, reveals how well these once-ignored atolls serve both air and sea units. The central lagoon affords a sheltered harbor for both seaplanes and ships, and the encircling islets can easily be converted into airstrips for land or carrier planes. Within such a lagoon a fleet is comparatively safe from storms or submarine attack.

PLATE XXVII—So fierce was the preliminary air-sea bombardment of Eniwetok, and so thorough the investment, that few of its defenders survived. Total Japanese casualties were 3,334 (of 3,400 that garrisoned the atoll); American casualties totaled 716. (*right*) One of those wounded during the landing on Eniwetok was Captain Waldo Drake, Pacific Fleet Public Relations Officer. While awaiting transfer to a transport he confers with Harold Smith, Chicago *Tribune* war correspondent. (*Coast Guard Photo.*)

(*left*) Coffee for the conquerors. Marines, begrimed and weary from two days and nights of fighting, sip a cup of "Joe" aboard their transport. Sniper fire on Eniwetok was intense, but the Marines, profiting by costly experience on Tarawa and Kwajalein, took no chances. Each new wave re-dynamited every pillbox. Engebi was taken in six hours; in less than ten days U.S. fighters were operating from its rebuilt airstrip (*Coast Guard Photo.*)

right) Marines and Coast Guardsmen display a captured Japanese battle flag picked up by one of them during the invasion of Engebi Island. Note bullet holes through the flag. From a diary found on the body of a Japanese defender of Engebi the story of the Japanese First Amphibious Brigade was pieced together, giving our intelligence officers valuable military information. Our forces were not permitted to keep diaries.

PLATE XXVIII—One of our best "secret operational weapons" was refueling at sea. Thus our ships could steam for weeks and months, deep in enemy-held waters, without returning to base. The operation called for a special rig for lines and hose and the smartest seamanship.

(*upper left*) Not all fueling was done from tankers. Here a carrier fuels one of her destroyer escorts, during a heavy blow in the China Sea.

(*center*) Holding to the railing to keep from being swept overboard, men on a U. S. Navy tanker strive valiantly to bring in a line from the aircraft carrier YORKTOWN. Water has swept clear across the deck of the tanker.

(*lower*) Vast stockpiles of materials of war—tanks, trucks, jeeps, fuel and ammunition—were built up on various Pacific islands, awaiting the call for amphibious operations. One of the largest "pools" was the ABCD (Advance Base Construction Depot) at Los Negros, the Admiralties, where Seabee R. A. Lynch, of Peoria, Illinois, puts a new jeep through a road test. Most of these vehicles were used in the Philippine invasion.

PLATE XXIX—(*upper right*) Aerial "aureole." Poised for a take-off from its carrier, this Grumman Hellcat gathers about itself a strange "aura." Rapid change in pressure and consequent drop in temperature, most pronounced at the tips of the propeller, sometimes created a condensation of moisture in the humid Pacific tropics. As the "halo" moved aft, it rotated in accord with the blades.

(*center*) Not a fantastic dance militaire, merely Marines, tacking into the wind, as they exercise on the flight deck of a carrier in a heavy Pacific gale.

(*lower*) One of the most strategically located Japanese mid-Pacific bases was on the rugged island of Ponape, with its fine sheltered harbor. Its value as an enemy air-base, however, was neutralized through frequent attacks by Navy carrier planes and the long-range bombers of the Seventh Air Force. This photograph was made during a Navy raid on February 20, 1944.

PLATE XXX—Skipping over the strongly-held Japanese bases at Wewak and Madang, MacArthur's forces made three surprise landings 400 miles up the New Guinea coast near Hollandia, April 22, 1944. (*above*) Troops pour ashore at Humboldt Bay. Other landings were made at Aitape and Tanah Merah Bay (*below*). The town of Hollandia, which gave its name to the operation, lies west and inland from Humboldt Bay. Not a life was lost in the landings, because Japanese defenders fled to the hills.

PLATE XXXI—(*above*) General MacArthur goes ashore (from the USS NASHVILLE) in a landing craft at Hollandia. With him are Colonel Lloyd Lehrbas, his aide, and (facing camera) Admiral Halsey's liaison officer, Captain Felix Johnson. (*below*) Bombs from U. S. Navy carrier planes rip one of Hollandia's airstrips. This was the first time carrier planes had been used as close air support in landings by Southwest Pacific forces.

PLATE XXXII—Moving up the New Guinea coast, MacArthur's forces continued their successful leap-frog tactics, by-passing strongholds and thereby isolating thousands of Japanese. Those stranded behind the Allied lines either surrendered or starved.

(*upper left*) Only the jungles faced American soldiers landing at Sansapor, New Guinea, July 30, 1944. A green wall of foliage confronted the troops as they stepped ashore, unopposed.

(*center*) In support of the Hollandia landings Navy carrier planes bombed every adjacent Japanese airfield. Here a Curtis Wright Helldiver flies over burning Wakde Island, one of the Japanese aerial "stepping stones" along the Dutch New Guinea coast.

(*lower*) Climax of the long, hard campaign up the New Guinea coast was the landing at Biak, strategic island lying on the equator at the northwest end of New Guinea. Moving along the beach, ahead of advancing landing craft, a U. S. Navy destroyer shoots up a Japanese ammunition dump, shown flaming from direct hits by 40-mm. machine guns, May 27, 1944.

The artillery General whose howitzers were to be put ashore on Enubuj requested that this last tower be left standing to serve as an observation post. In spite of the intense shelling and bombing that practically shook the little island from its coral bed the Navy was able that day to offer the General the highest chair in the Marshalls.

Much of the destruction this D-day was caused by the heavy infighting of a pair of rejuvenated battleships—MISSISSIPPI (Captain Lunsford L. Hunter), repaired after her Makin Island turret explosion, and PENNSYLVANIA (Captain William A. Corn), flagship of the Pacific Fleet at the time of Pearl Harbor.

Their major mission was the quick destruction of the coast and antiaircraft defense guns on the west side of Kwajalein, to prevent shelling of the clustered transports unloading for the assault on Enubuj. Later MISSISSIPPI moved in to cover a beach reconnaissance party.

Through the gray predawn, PENNSYLVANIA's first salvo shrieked toward the target and erupted a black pall of debris-hailing smoke. Aboard ship there was a moment of silence, suddenly broken by one clear, loud, exulting yell:

"Reveille, you slant-eyed sons of bitches!"

Nothing was spared. First the gun emplacements were smashed. Then the pillboxes, ammunition dumps, gasoline stowage areas, the sea wall that was supposed to serve as a tank barricade. The small spotter plane circling slowly over the target brought the salvos down to sniper accuracy.

Minesweeps nosed into the lagoon. An anchorage was needed for the transports lying exposed to submarine attack beyond the reefs. Admiral Turner wanted no repetition of the LISCOME BAY calamity. Nor did he want little matchbox ships cluttering the anchorage area.

Troops transferred from the large transports (APAs) to the LSTs, whose long corridorlike holds were lined with amphibious vehicles (LVTs or Amtracs). They rocked in the water while reconnaissance units paddled ashore for a preliminary look-see at Enubuj, having in mind the mines found on the beaches at Tarawa. The MISSISSIPPI closed in to cover the joint reconnaissance units as they paddled their rubber boats close to the teeth-sharp reefs. Although not an enemy shot had been fired from the crushed defenses, PENNSYLVANIA swung around to guard MISSISSIPPI, few of whose guns could be brought to bear on the beach while heading directly for the target.

"0904—Resumed fire all batteries. Range 2,500 yards."

"Old Miss" was making dead sure that the men in the rubber boats would not be bothered even by a stray sniper bullet.

"0925—Troops land on Enubuj Island," she signaled.

The men went ashore dry. Opposition was negligible. Enubuj Island was secured before noon, and by six that evening the Army's 105mm and 155mm howitzers had been landed and were adding to the uproar on Kwajalein. Ennylabegan also fell like a ripe coconut. These islands, plus Gea and Ninni, were the total D-day objectives. Gehh had unwittingly been thrown in for good measure.

Meanwhile, from an average range of 3,000 yards, the battleships were methodically destroying Kwajalein Island's blockhouses, pillboxes, barricades, and trench systems. Naval reconnaissance units probed the reefs for mines, Lieutenant William K. Rummel leading his men in two surveys, one at morning high tide and another at low tide. Many landing craft had hung on the reefs at Tarawa. Here LVTs would crawl the reefs, but first they must be made safe by eliminating all mines.

The MISSISSIPPI had done her job well. The men wading and probing on the reefs were not molested by Jap fire. No mines or other obstructions were found. The investigators worked behind a screen of gunfire from the sea that rocked the beach defenses with 14-inch main batteries and 5-inch secondary batteries, and raked the jumping ruins with 40mm and 20mm.

Half an hour before noon:

"Main battery ceased firing. Morning fire support mission completed. All firing apparently entirely effective. No casualties."

After a morning of sweat and smoke the battleship men left their stations. Five hours of steady fire had left most of them temporarily deaf, but a greater physical discomfort was hunger. When "chow down" sounded from the mess hall, no one was too deafened to hear it.

8

Late that afternoon the transports eased through narrow Gea Pass into the lagoon. Troops of Regimental Combat Team 184 (Colonel Curtis D. O'Sullivan, USA) and Regimental Combat Team 32 (Colonel Marc J. Logie, USA), who were to assault Kwajalein Island the next morning, were transferred to the LSTs and smaller vessels. During the night the troop-laden craft were harassed by an inaccurate bombardment from light field artillery that had managed to survive the day's terrific bombardment.

Next morning the science of co-ordinated destruction reached new heights.

The MISSISSIPPI carefully maneuvering through uncharted waters close to the reef drew up at a point 1,500 yards off the landing beaches, Red Beaches 1 and 2. At 0615 she cut loose with her 14-inch broadside.

Promptly at 0800 the 7th Division artillery, massed across the coral-studded water on Enubuj Island, started laying down its barrage.

From 0830 to 0839 nine bombers of Admiral Hoover's land-based air up from the Gilberts saturated the area with 2,000-pound bombs.

From 0845 to 0900 all artillery fire was stopped while Navy dive bombers and torpedo bombers came in low, followed by strafing fighters.

At 0900 the maximum possible gunfire from battleships, cruisers, and destroyers was poured into the beach area. By this time the first waves of LVTs had crossed the line of departure and were churning toward the beach. Leading them in were rocket-launching LCIs, fitted to carry rockets instead of infantry, but now pouring a steady hail of machine-gun fire. Then, like a fighter taking the measure of his opponent before the knock-out blow, the LCI rocket boats fired a few ranging shots from their racks. Two minutes later, at 0920, with a hissing rush of flame and smoke the whole cargo of rockets was let loose in an arc of death.

Eight minutes later artillery fire was lifted 200 yards inland. At 0930 the first waves hit the beach standing up. What they saw was well described in the report of a naval gunfire officer: "The effect of naval gunfire on the island of Kwajalein was devastating. The entire island looked as if it had been picked up to 20,000 feet and then dropped. The ground was so torn up that it made even movement by foot difficult. It was impossible to tell where the sea wall had stood. All beach defenses were completely destroyed. Practically every defense installation above ground had been hit by gunfire, due to the ships closing the range to where they could see the target and use direct fire. Prisoners of war testified that the terrific blasting effect of the heavy and continuous bombardment terrorized the defending forces. . . ."

The bombardment had made it tough even for our own tanks, which landed with the initial waves; they could not maneuver on the rubble-strewn shell-pocked beaches. As the troops advanced, the terrain inland proved less churned but at no time could the tanks move freely.

With the pedestrian advance sniper resistance increased. Occasional mortar and howitzer fire came from the twisted steel and concrete remains of half-destroyed emplacements. When a particularly strong position was encountered, ships were called on to eliminate it. Specially trained naval officers, ashore with the troops, directed such fire from grid-maps, duplicates of which were aboard the ships, with portable voice radios.

Here is an example of how shore-directed naval bombardment is managed, as logged by the destroyer HAGGARD (Commander David A. Harris).

The HAGGARD, anchored in Kwajalein lagoon, is leisurely lobbing 5-inch shells into ammunition dumps and pillbox areas within view when her radio crackles and the voice of the Shore Fire Control Officer comes through:

Shore: "Come in, please."
Ship: "Go ahead."
Shore: "At present time I cannot give you the front lines but will do so as soon as possible. I have no targets for you but you may fire at targets of opportunity that you can see in Zone T."
Ship: "Roger. We have a possible blockhouse in Zone T and will fire a few salvos at it."
Shore: "Are you firing now?"
Ship: "Affirmative. We are firing at a possible blockhouse in Zone T."
Shore: "I would now like to fire on a real blockhouse in Square 105. I will give you co-ordinates of this point. Fire at Emplacement 486474 in Square 105. I will adjust fire."
Ship: "Firing ship ready."
Shore: "Commence firing."
Ship: "Wilco."
                    (Salvo, Salvo!)
Shore: "No change in elevation. Left 200."
                    (Salvo, Salvo!)
Shore: "No change. No change. Rapid fire. Three salvos."
                    (Salvo, Salvo, Salvo!)
Shore: "Up 50. No change. Rapid fire. Three salvos."
                    (Salvo, Salvo, Salvo!)
Shore: "Down 25. No change. Three salvos."
                    (Salvo, Salvo, SALVO!)
Shore: "Cease firing. Target neutralized. Good shooting."
Ship: "Wilco."

It was like ordering six cans of soup from the grocery.

Four days later, at 1530 on February 4, when all organized resistance had ceased, the only usable Japanese articles left on the island were a few anchors and some large buoys.

Machine-age war, indeed. It wasn't all going to be like that, though, from here on in.

9

To the north, at the other end of Kwajalein Atoll, the pattern of destruction was simultaneously being repeated against Roi and Namur. The instruments used were the ships of Admiral's Conolly's Northern Attack Force and the Marines of Major General Harry Schmidt's 4th Division.

The pulverization with shell and bomb had been every bit as intense as on Kwajalein Island. The plan of attack was the same: on D-day to capture flanking islands, set up artillery, and bring the transports into the lagoon; on D-plus-1-day to land on the main objectives, Roi and Namur.

H-hour was set at 0900 on January 31. First stop on the schedule were Ennuebing and Mellu islands (Anglicized in the operation orders to Jacob and Ivan) flanking North Pass to the lagoon. A 19-knot wind scattered the slow LVTs at the line of departure. Short choppy seas smacked the treaded vehicles, sending salt spray down the backs of the huddled Marines. But soon they were steamed dry by the hot sun. The control officers aboard the destroyer PHELPS (Lieutenant Commander David L. Martineau) saw that a concession would have to be made to the elements. H-hour was pushed back about 30 minutes.

In the whole Marshall campaign this was the only change in the planned schedule.

When the much-pounded LVTs waddled ashore through the heavy surf, only light opposition was encountered. Marines sitting on top of their vehicles waved to the pilots, affectionately known as the Rover Boys, zooming low over them. Over the TBS came the report: "Everything looks Jake on Jacob." By noon the two islands were reported secured, and the minesweeps moved in.

Scene II of Act One came that afternoon when the landing craft crossed the lagoon and went ashore on three islands with mouth-filling names: Ennubirr, Ennumennet, and Ennugarret. Again opposition was negligible. Before dark all the Northern Attack Force was anchored in the lagoon as protection against possible submarine attack.

Next morning, in the deep darkness before dawn, the upper decks of USS APPALACHIAN (Captain James M. Fernald), Admiral Conolly's flagship, were a grandstand from which to watch battleships, cruisers, and destroyers work on Roi-Namur. Orange-yellow flame from the muzzles of the guns glowed against the low clouds like sheet lightning. The first faint dawn revealed the island as a seaborne fragment of the Inferno. Leaping up to low-rolling masses of black smoke gushed fountains of earth, sand, and water, all spouting flame. Even five miles from the target, the spectators' eyes ached with each flash, and the concussions sucked at eardrums and lungs.

Then came the planes, swarm after swarm—from an infinite hive, it seemed—scattering their hundreds of bombs until the island was eclipsed by one huge pall of smoke. The ships took no recess. Salvo continued to follow salvo relentlessly, doggedly, mercilessly, until noon.

In describing the scene Commander Anthony Kimmins, RN, British naval observer at the operation, said, "No matter how strong the defenses, nothing could have lived through that sea and air bombardment. I was on the very first ship in, and I can't tell you how much impressed I was by the way this thing was run. No indiscriminate shelling or bombing anywhere. You saw the shells relentlessly and systematically taking on each little bit of the island until the whole area had been cleared. Automatically, the aircraft appeared on the screen all by prearranged plan. As I saw it, they didn't seem to be hanging around waiting their opportunity. They just came right bang on the moment."

From the bridge of the old battleship TENNESSEE (Captain Robert S. Haggart) a slim, alert little man in unadorned khakis watched the entire spectacle. He was James V. Forrestal, Undersecretary of the Navy.

The landings came from the south, from the lagoon. The Japanese had not expected an attack through the back door. Like the British defenses at Singapore, all their guns and fortifications pointed seaward. They had laughed at the British for that—laughed and did likewise. And, to add to the irony, the guns on Roi and Namur had been loot from Singapore.

At high noon Regimental Combat Team 23 (Colonel Louis R. Jones) attacked Roi. Regimental Combat Team 24 (Colonel Franklin A. Hart) attacked Namur, which was connected by an umbilical causeway to its sister island. In a huge arc outlined against the clouded horizon the landing craft moved in slowly, determinedly toward the beaches. Then the scene was blotted out by one of those huge tropical cloudbursts that leave a man wetter than if he had fallen overboard. A half hour later the curtain of rain was blown aside for the last act.

Lieutenant (jg) Sheldon Briggs described his feelings: "I was very much impressed as we went into Roi Island with the apparently carefree attitude with which we practically walked up to the Japanese back yard and with impudence sat there and got our troops and ships ready just to walk right in and take their island. I was also very much impressed with what seemed to me was a stopping of time, time just seemed to stand perfectly still as we all formed up and prepared to go into the beach. I have noticed this on other occasions afterwards, the fact that time just seems to stand absolutely still for just a few seconds before men actually go in to do or die, and many die, you know. . . ."

Commander Kimmins could not believe that "anything could really live after that terrific bombardment. As you got ashore the beach was a mass of highly colored fish that had been thrown up by nearby explosions. There didn't seem to be a square yard of ground that hadn't been either hit or hadn't been covered with debris from a nearby hit. The shore was just a mass of any number of dead Japs all over the place. Some of them were short a leg here, a head there. Our bombardment at Salerno in comparison to this did absolutely nothing, absolutely nothing. It wasn't the same proposition at all."

The Marines quickly pushed across treeless Roi, capturing the excellent airfield and seventy skeletons of Jap planes. By the middle of the afternoon the island was secured except for some isolated groups of diehards holed up in the drainage system under the airstrip. The next morning these were sprayed out with bullet and flame.

Namur was harder to crack, for the remains of what had been an intricate system of blockhouses had to be overcome. Resistance was isolated, for, as Secretary Forrestal's aide, Captain John E. Gingrich, said, "the bombardment and bombing of the island disrupted any possibility of organized resistance. At the time of the landing on D-day-plus-1 the opposition was scattered with no opportunity for the Japanese to organize. The operation then consisted of destroying the isolated groups of Japanese in their pillboxes and cement blockhouses—which incidentally were two feet thick and reinforced with railroad iron and heavy steel, so that you had to get a direct hit on them with a major caliber shell or bomb to put them out of business. The Marines used flame throwers to dislodge the Japs, who crept all the way back into the underground ammunition stowages. The flame-throwers blew up the ammunition and blew up the Japs inside. But that also blew up a number of our own Marines so the use of flame throwers had to be forbidden in places where ammunition might be stowed, so the Marines just went in with a flashlight and Tommy gun and simply dug the Japs out."

On D-plus-2-day, February 2, James V. Forrestal explored the islands with Admiral Spruance, General "Howling Mad" Smith, Admiral Conolly, and General Schmidt. Quite an impressive surrender ceremony could have been arranged except for the absence of the party of the second part. Lying with sightless eyes beneath the smoldering rubble was Rear Admiral Yamata, Imperial Japanese Navy, late commander of Namur.

Shortly after noon of D-plus-2-day the island was declared secured. Garrison troops were landed. The assault troops were withdrawn to rest and be refitted for the capture of Eniwetok to the westward, nearly three months earlier than originally planned.

"Originally the Pacific Fleet forces involved in the capture of Kwajalein were to have gone to the South Pacific for the support of an operation Northwest of the Solomons. This operation was to have been followed by the capture of Eniwetok, the westermost atoll in the Marshalls and the key position in the Japanese air pipe line between Truk and the by-passed atolls in the Marshalls. It was decided to proceed as soon as possible with the capture of Eniwetok. With Eniwetok in our hands we would have complete control of the Marshalls and we would have the base needed for future operations in the Central Pacific, whether these operations were against Truk or the Marianas, which was as yet undecided. The Japanese would be given the minimum of time in which to build up their defenses with the additional troops they had recently put into Eniwetok." (Lecture by Admiral Spruance, October 30, 1946, to the Royal United Service Institution at London.)

The world had never before seen naval power used so devastatingly. Admiral Nimitz in his report said: "It must be appreciated that these assaults and seizures could not possibly have been accomplished so expeditiously with such minor losses without the bombardment preparation exceeding in duration and intensity anything previously known to warfare except possibly that at Verdun in World War I. It had been estimated that 50% of the Japanese were killed by the air, naval, and artillery bombardment prior to the assault, not to mention destruction of defenses and equipment and the stunning effect on the morale and fighting capacity of the survivors. In the Red Beach area at Kwajalein everything was reduced to rubble so that it was impossible to even visualize what 90 per cent of the installation originally consisted of. . . ."

The score in blood was as impressive as the material destruction. The enemy dead totaled 8,122 for Kwajalein and Roi-Namur against 318 Americans killed and missing. Of the 437 prisoners taken, 290 were Korean. Most of our 42,546 troops were unscratched.

10

The lesson of Tarawa had been well learned, and the first strategic objective of the United States' Central Pacific offensive was achieved. The Gilbert-Marshall archipelagoes were in hand, and the Navy was a thousand miles nearer Japan in consequence.

Eniwetok next—and then, maybe, fearsome, fabulous Truk?

Chapter Eight

Dejapitation Continued

I

ON Truk, Admiral Mineichi Koga, Commander-in-Chief of the Japanese Combined Fleet (Nimitz's counterpart) was thinking in almost identical terms, and pondering a Secondary Defense Line through the Marianas, Truk, Palau, and northern New Guinea.

Eniwetok, most western atoll of the Marshalls, was not within the indrawn defense line that Koga thoughtfully traced on his chart. During the middle of February, Eniwetok must indeed have felt like the orphan of the Pacific. Eniwetok never really had a chance.

But Eniwetok was to prove no cinch, either.

When Admiral Harry Hill left Majuro Atoll on February 3, after directing its occupation, he headed for Kwajalein and for a bigger job—command of the Eniwetok Expeditionary Group. There, while the sweet stench of enemy dead was still heavy in the air, he began to put final details on the basic plans. His ships were ready. So were the reserve attack troops (22nd Marine Regiment and 106th Infantry Regiment, USA, plus reinforcing units all under Brigadier General T. E. Watson, USMC), unused at Kwajalein.

After a St. Valentine's Day conference of commanding officers and flag officers, the old battleships, cruisers, destroyers, escort carriers, transports, minesweeps, and landing craft sortied from Kwajalein lagoon on February 15 and headed northwest in two groups. Admiral Ginder's carrier-cruiser group (Task Group 58.4), which had been slapping at the Japs on Eniwetok since early in the month, topped off with fuel and headed back to the now-familiar territory to cover the operation. To the westward Admirals Spruance and Mitscher were about to bloody the Japs in their own back yard—Truk, Saipan, Tinian, Guam—thus ensuring freedom from Japanese air attack during the Eniwetok operation.

Land-based bombers continued hitting Ponape, Kusaie, and Wake. The stronger of the by-passed Marshall atolls were kept impotent by intermittent shellings and bombings. Eniwetok was completely isolated.

THE REAL OFFENSIVE BEGINS

That atoll looks like a slightly lopsided hoop on the chart. Its 70 miles of coral reef are strung with over 30 small islands, the principal ones being Engebi, in the north, and Eniwetok and Parry, in the south. The two southern islands each flank the breaks in the reef through which ships can enter. Thus, to get at Number One Target, Engebi, the invasion forces had to steam past Parry and Eniwetok Island.

2

D-day was February 17. In spite of the Japanese attempts to isolate their islands from Western eyes, Eniwetok would look familiar to some of the men who were to enter her lagoon. Between January 26 and February 13 the submarine SEARAVEN had made a thorough photographic reconnaissance of the atoll. By sunup that morning Captain Ephraim R. McLean, Jr., in charge of the southern section of the Expeditionary Group, could make out one of the two usable entrances to the huge lagoon, Wide Passage. From the bridge of the destroyer PHELPS he ordered his heterogeneous group of LSTs, LCIs, tugs, oilers, and destroyers into line. Preceded by the minesweeps ORACLE (Lieutenant Commander John R. Fels) and SAGE (Lieutenant Franklyn K. Zinn) they headed through Wide Passage, Eniwetok Island on their right, and into the lagoon where no American ship had entered since 1923 when USS MILWAUKEE entered through the same strait. The whole operation seemed so casual that it might just as well have been a convoy entrance through the narrows into New York harbor.

At 0820 the SAGE reported she had swept a moored mine. The column was called to a halt until the SAGE machine-gunned the horned red ball. When it had been sunk, the ships continued to ease forward. Nice going.

Hours later it was learned that the entire group had passed over a minefield! Captain McLean in his report stated: "The fact that the entire Southern Group, including two deep-draft oilers [GAZELLE and GEMSBOK], entered by Wide Passage and through a mine field from which twenty-nine mines were subsequently swept, attests either to ineffectiveness of enemy mines or to a large amount of very good luck on our part."

In the meantime the Northern Group, consisting of the major combatant ships and the transports, including CAMBRIA (Captain C. W. Dean, USCG) with both Admiral Hill and General Watson aboard, arrived off the second breach in the reef, Deep Entrance. At 0700 the cruisers INDIANAPOLIS (Captain Einar R. Johnson) and PORTLAND (Captain Thomas G. W. Settle) sounded the starting gun with salvos at Eniwetok and Parry islands. The densely wooded islands swallowed the explosives without response.

3

Up until the day of departure from Kwajalein it was thought that the only island strongly garrisoned was Engebi. Then had come a dispatch from Admiral Nimitz saying that a prisoner of war had declared Parry and Eniwetok also strongly held. But aerial reconnaissance had shown no large installations on either of these islands. Maybe they were craftily camouflaged under the dense foliage. But why were the Japs holding back their fire? Were there any Japs at all?

But the first matter to be taken care of was at the other end of the lagoon—Engebi, whose airstrip now lay dead and full of holes. Perhaps during the next couple of days Admiral Hill could learn more about these silent green islands of by-passed Parry and Eniwetok.

The sweeps CHANDLER (Lieutenant Commander Harry L. Thompson, Jr.) and ZANE (Lieutenant Commander William T. Powell, Jr.) cautiously slid through Deep Entrance. Following them the destroyers MCCORD (Commander William T. Kenny) and HEERMAN (Commander Dwight M. Agnew) threw abrupt 40mm fire into the flanking islands of Parry and Japtan. Still no answer from the coconut palms. The PENNSYLVANIA (Captain William A. Corn) and TENNESSEE (Captain Robert S. Haggart) also raked the beaches and fringes of the mangrove groves with red tracers without provoking a return fire. By 1034 the last of the transports were in the lagoon and heading north.

For the next two days triangular Engebi took a three-dimensional pounding. Out of the north from beyond the horizon came storms of planes from Admiral Ginder's SARATOGA (Captain John H. Cassady), PRINCETON (Captain William H. Buracker), and LANGLEY (Captain Wallace M. Dillon). From the east came the pilots based on Admiral Van H. Ragsdale's jeep-carriers, SANGAMON (Captain Maurice E. Browder), SUWANNEE (Captain William D. Johnson, Jr.), and CHENANGO (Captain Dixwell Ketcham). From the sea the gray old battleship COLORADO (Captain William Granat) and the heavy cruiser LOUISVILLE

(Captain Samuel H. Hurt) kept up a "slow deliberate destructive" fire. This was paralleled inside the lagoon by TENNESSEE and PENNSYLVANIA.

On D-day the little odd jobs necessary before the attack were accomplished. Small islands to right and left of Engebi were occupied without resistance and artillery set up. The LCI 365 (later in the operation to meet tragedy from an unexpected source) went within 450 yards of Engebi's beach spitting 40mm and 20mm fire at Jap positions that were hindering the Joint Beach Reconnaissance Unit marking reefs and looking for mines. Tanned troops of the 22nd Marine Regiment (Colonel John T. Walker) shifted from the transports ARTHUR MIDDLETON (Captain S. A. Olsen, USCG) and HEYWOOD (Captain Paul F. Dugan) to LSTs where the sturdy LVTs were already lined up ready to go down the ramp.

D-plus-1-day, February 18, before sunrise battleships and destroyers started their accepted pattern of pulverization, bombing, strafing, invasion. With the first daylight the planes came. (At the same time to the west Mitscher's boys were hitting the enemy hub of the South Seas—Truk.) Then, bouncing through the choppy water, the LVTs headed toward the beach. Some of the Marines were seasick. Some of the boat drivers were to be sick before the day was over from pure exhaustion. Plane-dropped clusters of parachute flares signaled the warships to cease firing, the boats were close to shore.

Three minutes ahead of schedule, 18 minutes before 9:00 A.M., the Marines touched ground. Sniper fire was intense, but the Marines, supported by tanks, knew their job. Each new wave, taking no chances, redynamited every pillbox. Within six hours, what was left of the three-sided island was American.

4

Aboard the CAMBRIA a JICPOA (Joint Intelligence) team was piecing together the answer to the puzzle of where were the Japs and how many. "Dog-tags" from the necks of dead Japs and documents discovered unburned in the debris of Engebi were sent to CAMBRIA and translated. Native islanders were brought aboard to tell what they knew. All evidence pointed toward the same thing. Sometime in January the Japanese 1st Amphibious Brigade had landed on Eniwetok and Parry. Six hundred troops were estimated to be on Eniwetok and twice that number on Parry; considerably more than Admiral Hill had expected. Admiral

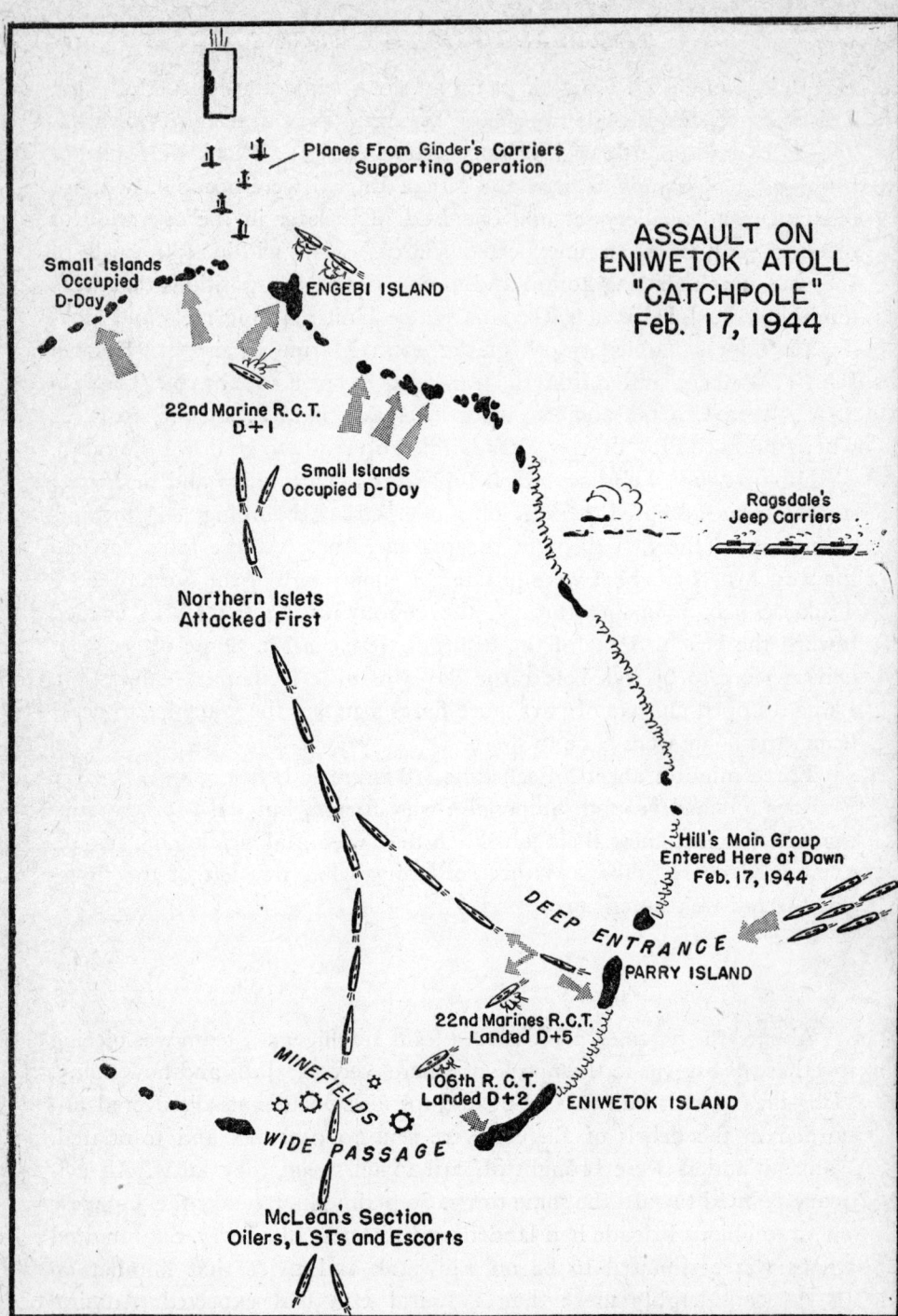

FIGURE 8

THE REAL OFFENSIVE BEGINS

Nimitz had been more than well informed. Plans would have to be modified. Two Battalion Landing Teams of the Army's 106th Infantry, Colonel Russell G. Ayers, instead of the previously planned one, would go ashore simultaneously on two beaches. Ship bombardment would be stepped up. The revised plans were distributed before midnight. The next morning would witness H-hour for Eniwetok.

Since the D-day entrance into the lagoon four ships had been taking turns shelling Eniwetok and Parry—the heavy cruisers PORTLAND and INDIANAPOLIS and their accompanying destroyers TRATHEN (Commander Fondville L. Tedder) and HOEL (Commander William D. Thomas). On the afternoon of the first day HOEL had caught sight of several Japs moving about the pier on Parry. She had been given permission to take them under fire.

From then on there had been no peace for Major General Nishida's industrious little men. There was no letup. The nights were the most terrifying. Balls of galloping fire screamed into the darkness. Great mushrooms of brilliant white light exploded over the islands. Far-reaching white fingers of searchlights swept along the beaches and groped deep into the vine-tangled groves, and if a man moved bullets rained. There was nothing the bravest soldier of the Emperor could do but lie low in his foxhole—and wait.

The destroyers were making certain that the Japanese did not unite their forces by crossing the reef between Parry and Eniwetok by literally turning the night into day with searchlights and bursts of white phosphorus.

From early dawn of February 19 the four southern veterans hit hard at the lagoon beach area of slim Eniwetok. To even up the shock the destroyer HAILEY (Commander Parke H. Brady) left the lagoon to shell from the seaward side. The HAGGARD added her 5-inch shells north of the landing beaches.

Aboard the CAMBRIA, now within two miles of the beaches, Captain Richard F. Whitehead, commander of support aircraft, watched tiny flyspecks on the horizon grow into roaring bombers and fighters. As the planes came out of the north toward the atoll they were told where to put their bombs and spray their bullets.

The troops ground up to the beach 22 minutes late that morning, but the taking of Eniwetok Island was to be delayed all the way around. Japs and jungle growth were thicker than had been expected. That night the Japs at both ends of the island were pinned low by the level rays of powerful searchlights. Like red-eyed meteors the tracers slid down the beams and exploded against the low coral beaches. A Japanese order had been found which stated: "In the event that the enemy succeeds in making a landing annihilate him by means of night attacks." A very good idea, if only the Americans had not decided that there should be no night.

Not until February 21 could the Stars and Stripes be raised to the frazzled top of a decapitated palm, to mark possession of Eniwetok.

Washington's Birthday all the spots of islands along the reef of the atoll had been occupied with negligible resistance by the Fifth Amphibious Corps Reconnaissance Company and the Scout Company "D." Now it was Parry's turn.

5

All the strength of the expeditionary force was converged on this one remaining island where 1,800 Japanese were dug in, fully aware of what was going to happen to them. Battleships (COLORADO, PENNSYLVANIA, TENNESSEE), cruisers (INDIANAPOLIS, LOUISVILLE, PORTLAND), and destroyers (HALL, AYLWIN, MACDONOUGH, MONAGHAN, JOHNSTON, MCCORD) probed deep at their trench systems with flat trajectory fire from a range sometimes as close as 850 yards. Planes added their bombs to the destruction. The steady wind from the northeast whirled smoke and coral dust into the eyes of the attackers as the LVTs foamed toward the beaches. Leading the first wave as usual were the LCIs, groping through the thick haze to find position before loosing their avalanches of rockets. The men in the assault waves cursed the gritty, dust-laden fog more viciously than they did the Japanese.

One of the three rocket boats was LCI 365 (Lieutenant Commander Theodore Blanchard). Precisely at 0856, as scheduled, its first flight of rockets was sent hissing to the beach. A minute later a hot blast of fire and metal shook the little ship from keel to masthead. Smoke rolled from the burning deckhouse. Nobody knew what had struck the boat, but orders were given to keep on with the rockets while the wounded were cared for and damage patched up.

A small spotter plane from the LOUISVILLE, peering through gaps in the smoke pall, sent forth a frantic warning. Shell fire from the haze-blinded HAILEY was falling in our boat lanes.

THE REAL OFFENSIVE BEGINS

All three LCIs were hit, the 365, 440 and 442. Thirteen men had been killed and 46 wounded by our own shell fire. But before clearing the area, the battered boats emptied their racks of rockets onto the enemy positions, with "gallantry and contemptuous disregard of dangers," as Admiral Hill praised them, that had "been an inspiration to us all." And still should be, it might be added even now.

When the sun went down that evening in red and purple splendor, Parry Island was ours. But there was always a time lag between declaring an island secure and killing the last holed-up enemy. That night the Marines requested the destroyer MC CORD to illuminate the island with star shells. One shell revealed a group of eleven Japanese sneaking in with grenades and machine guns. A few quick bursts of fire and that last threat to the Americans in the Marshalls was stamped out.

Parry had been won by 1,280 tons of explosives plus 73 American lives.

By February 27 United States fighters were operating from the airfield on Engebi Island. Of the 3,400 Japanese that had garrisoned Eniwetok Atoll 3,334 had been killed. Total American casualties were 716.

6

Kicking at the broken, swollen body of a late defender of Parry a grease-smeared Marine noticed a small notebook half-protruding from the Jap's pocket. Bending down, rifle in hand, he picked it up wondering how the Nips could read that funny writing of theirs. Thumbing through the little book he debated whether to keep it or not. Good souvenir but maybe it had some hot dope in it for the guys who could read this lingo. He slipped it into his blouse and walked down toward the beach.

From diaries like this thrown up by the backwash of war the fatal story of the life and death of the 1st Amphibious Brigade was pieced together.

Warrant Officer Shionoya begins the story in Manchuria the preceding December:

"6 Dec. At Paichengtze. I finished all my preparations for leaving and for sending my family back to Japan. I had supper with my family at the house of the Commander of my unit. I drank so much sake there that I became intoxicated and stupidly left my wife and child without saying anything.

"13 Dec. We arrived in Fusan [Korea] this morning, transferred our baggage, and boarded ship.

"14 Dec. We worked all night on the ship. At 1600 finally our ship left. It was my farewell to the continent. Our ship headed for Japan. We felt fine when the people aboard the Shimonoseki-Fusan ferry, which we met up with, waved flags and handkerchiefs at us.

"15 Dec. From 1305 continued explosions were heard. It was reported that we were being attacked by a submarine, and we prepared to abandon ship. According to what I heard, the enemy fired some twenty torpedoes at our convoy, and it barely escaped, thanks to the depth charge attacks launched by our escorting destroyers. We went through the Shimonoseki Straits into the Inland Sea, and then between Kyushu and Shikoku. According to reports, there were submarines around.

"18 Dec. Today we continued southward. For three days we have seen no land. The only objects we have seen besides the sea have been the ships of our convoy—four transports and two destroyers.

"24 Dec. Today we took a southwest course toward our destination—Truk. One battleship and two destroyers passed the convoy headed in the direction of Truk.

"25 Dec. Our convoy is headed east and we are scheduled to reach Truk tomorrow. According to a report, the battleship that left us yesterday was attacked by submarine.[1] We took precautions against submarines at once. I am praying that we reach Truk without mishap.

"26 Dec. Today we finally reached Truk.

"27 Dec. Last night we stayed at the entrance of the harbor, but this morning we went into it. There were convoys and warships of all types in port. At 0820 we had an air-raid alert. It was a great number of our own Navy planes, however, and we had no reason to worry. Tonight we have no blackout.

"28 Dec. Today we are to get supplies from here and load them on our ship. This evening the mission of our unit was revealed. We are destined for Eniwetok in the Marshall Islands, which is about three or four days by ship from here. Things are scarce. We got a pamphlet about the conditions on the islands and studied it.

"30 Dec. Our unit left Truk with the TAJIMA MARU at 1500 heading for Eniwetok. The area between Truk and Eniwetok is dangerous and I hope we get through without trouble.

"4 Jan. At 1130 we entered the East Channel [Deep Entrance] and

---

[1] On December 25, 1943, the new 73,000-ton YAMATO was torpedoed by the submarine SKATE (Commander Eugene B. McKinney).

THE REAL OFFENSIVE BEGINS

at 1300 we reached Engebi. I placed my feet on the soil of the South Sea Islands for the first time. After doing a little sightseeing all hands were put to work.

"6 Jan. After landing on Engebi we were scheduled to go the next day to Parry Island on the HIYOSHI MARU.

"23 Jan. Today we studied new weapons. We were lectured on anti-personnel mines and bangalore torpedoes."

Second Lieutenant Kakino also went to Parry Island. So far, war for the 1st Amphibious Brigade had been nothing but a Cook's tour geared to Army routine. The South Sea Islands had at first been a fascinating contrast to the frozen land of Manchuria. Kakino liked it. But then—

"28 Jan. Tracer bullets suddenly came flying from the direction of headquarters. I didn't know which company was carrying on live ammunition firing but thought that to make a mistake on direction was serious. The soldiers dived into foxholes and lay down under mosquito nets. Overhead a huge four-motored plane appeared. 'My God, it's an enemy plane!' I thought. I immediately rushed to the AA defense, but they had already made a second attack and left.

"31 Jan. AA warnings were sent to the whole island. It seems that the enemy aimed only at buildings. Tracer bullets rained down. We fired machine guns until their barrels were burning hot. At that time I was with Sergeant Major Nonomura under the floor of the office. Kudo who was on telephone watch was killed. For lack of time we couldn't cremate him or stand vigil, but taking advantage of a pause in the bombing we burned incense.

"8 Feb. The time of the daytime air raids is so uncertain that we couldn't even go out to repair the coast defense positions, and in the end we repaired only individual shelters near the tents. Afterwards there was nothing to do but take a nap or attend to personal matters. Every day from 1800 to about 2000 we have regular bombing, but somehow today when I went outside there was no noise of bombs . . .

"9 Feb. This morning was perfectly clear. When we returned from our defense positions to our tents at 0300 we could see the full moon. The enemy bombers finally withdrew and the soldiers could be heard singing Army and popular songs. Half of the brigade's food supply has been destroyed by fire. Each company will therefore have to get along on two-thirds of its present supply. What will the soldiers have to look forward to? There is nothing more important than eating.

"11 Feb. We celebrated the anniversary of the coronation of the Emperor Jimmu, this fourth year of our holy war, under an enemy air attack. There must be some meaning for us in that—we couldn't settle down to work during the day, so we worked at night. Tomorrow we are going to begin constructing fortified positions, so I am going to sleep early tonight. We had red-bean soup, so I've been suffering from an attack of diarrhea.

"13 Feb. At 0610 when the soldiers, sleepy from working all night, were rubbing their eyes, we had another raid. They were early today; no sooner had we dived from our foxholes than bombing started. The sky was completely dark. The bombs seemed to drop near by. I was concerned about the safety of the soldiers, but the firing was so intense that I couldn't go out.

"15 Feb. They didn't come to bomb yesterday morning. I can't understand what has happened to the enemy. The soldiers are exhausted from their nightly work, yet when they try to sleep during the day there is always the threat of an air raid and so they don't sleep soundly.

"16 Feb. We have finally finished our night work, and it is morning. The soldiers worked extremely hard. Because things are as they were yesterday they are resting during the day. It was hard to sleep above because of the heat and the flies, so I crawled into a foxhole and went to sleep. It would be impossible in Japan to conceive of so many flies.

"17 Feb. I was tired from yesterday's work and was sleeping when the enemy planes came over at 0530. They came four times during the morning. The first time about fifty-eight planes came over the East Channel [Deep Entrance]. Fragments flew in the vicinity of the platoon, and you couldn't stick your head out of the foxhole. They came in the afternoon making a total of five bombings. They have been resting the last four days, so it is certain that something will happen before long. The soldiers are exhausted from the night work, so tonight we did not work. Everyone slept.

"18 Feb. The soldiers who went to work at 0300 returned. At 0350 the East Pass lookout shot off three red star flares. An enemy fleet was passing by. We had just made preparations and reached our battle positions when the enemy ships started shelling. Some men were buried by the shells from the ships. About twenty transports had come and all were heading for the island. I was wounded slightly in the shoulder by the shelling. One couldn't get any food, so I took along some dried bread.

In the evening the enemy moved within three hundred meters of the island. The transports offshore seemed to be ready. When evening came, we had been at our positions all day and remained there as it grew dark. I did not want the farewell sake which the commanding officer gave me, so I divided it among the platoon personnel.

"19 Feb. Everyone from the top-ranking officers down was sleepy as a result of the continuous bombardment last night, but we will hold out until we die in honor . . ."

Over a thousand soldiers of the 1st Amphibious Brigade, some with photographs of Manchuria still in their pockets, were buried on Parry.

CHAPTER NINE

The Bubble That Looked like a Bomb

I

FOR YEARS the name had been whispered with awe. For years military men of the West had stroked their chins and wondered what gun emplacements, what airfields, what fleet facilities the busy little men of Nippon had built among the high-cliffed islands. For years the word had been a synonym for rock-tough strength, no less than Gibraltar on the other side of the world.

During the first months of World War I the Japanese rushed down into the South Seas occupying all German-owned islands, among them the strategic Truk. A naval garrison and a military government moved in, establishing the first toe hold of empire. The Japanese stayed on after the war with a League of Nations mandate in their pockets. As a phrase "iron curtain" was yet to be coined, but as a policy the Japanese created it there and then, double riveted and case hardened. Anxious glances from the West were met only with polite smiles and assurances of peaceful intentions.

During the between-war period perhaps the only white man to see Truk—certainly the only one to tell what he saw—was the explorer-author Willard Price who described it as the most beautiful place on earth. Unlike the older atolls in the Marshalls to the east the Truk islands, some 245 in all, rise abruptly mountainous from inside a lagoon. Palm trees stretch from the highlands down to the water's edge. Ringed by a protective reef some 40 miles in diameter, the lagoon forms one of the best deep-water anchorages in the Carolines. A half dozen round-the-compass passes through the reef make ship movement easy. Beyond the lazy breakers the ocean depth falls precipitously to 4,000 fathoms. In fact, Truk is a sort of sample case of all Pacific geology and geography; a composite of highland and lowland, coral and igneous rock, all wrapped up in tropic beauty.

THE REAL OFFENSIVE BEGINS

But the natural beauties of Truk were of no concern to the U.S. Navy, either before the war or during the first three-fourths of it. The Navy knew Truk much more objectively as the Japanese hub of empire in the South Seas, as the staging point for ship and plane movements to the Solomons-New Guinea area, as the base for Admiral Koga's Combined Japanese Imperial Fleet.

This knowledge, however, was all general. The answer to the specific question of how-much-and-where was hidden behind the screen of twenty years' isolation. An editorial in one of the leading American newspapers suggested in 1943 that an up-to-date set of photographs of Truk would be worth nearly as much as one of our old battleships. Many who saw the MISSISSIPPI in action at Kwajalein would dispute that, but the fact remained that Navy planners were literally in need of "the inside dope" on Truk.

On February 3, while destroyers were still knocking out reluctant pillboxes on Kwajalein, the screen over Truk was partially pierced. A lone Marine Liberator of Marine Photographic Squadron 254, flying from the Solomons 1,000 miles away, sneaked in at an extreme height of 24,000 feet, which inevitably put a lot of clouds between the plane and the islands. After a jittery twenty minutes the plane banked away and headed home. The photographs presented a picture far from complete, but they were a lot more than the nothing previously possessed by the Navy's tacticians.

The Marine spotters had not gone undetected, and this fact was to prove more important than the pictures. The plane had given Admiral Koga a headache.

The Americans had already cracked his first line of defense in the Gilberts and Marshalls, he pondered. His carriers were bare of aircraft. He could not risk a fleet engagement, either with the powerful American task groups steaming unmolested to the east or with a force assaulting Truk itself. And the reconnaissance plane was as fair a gage of battle as was ever thrown. Truk would be next.

Koga looked out over the blue-green lagoon at his fleet. Strength, yes; but blind strength, at close quarters, without the carrier planes' long vision and reach. A decisive fleet engagement would have to wait, and the line of defense would have to be drawn back to the Marianas and western Carolines until the planes and pilots being assembled in Japan arrived to replenish Admiral Ozawa's carriers. Land-based aviation would have to be strengthened in men and machines, too. If Koga did not curse American marksmanship at that moment, it must have been because he was too desperately busy with plans to spare the time. Those plans would have to be laid persuasively before the Central Authorities in Japan. Somehow, Tokyo didn't seem to understand the gravity of the situation.

No, Admiral Koga did not at all enjoy the portents of American planes flying over Truk.

2

Fuel lines had just been passed over from the oiler. The boatswain on the main deck shouted at two seamen to bear a hand and get the coupling secured. On the bridge the captain, feeling the ship jump slightly in toward the oiler, eased her back into position with orders to the helm for slight course changes. Red "Baker" flapped conspicuously at the starboard yardarm.

Spread around the five oilers—over the whole ocean, it seemed—were Admiral Mitscher's carriers with "accompanying fast battleships, cruisers, and destroyers." Having sortied from the newly won base of Majuro two days before, they were now "topping off" with fuel before slipping in to slap the Jap in his own back yard. All the men aboard the ships had heard of Truk and had a healthy respect for it. If the force could ease in undetected and start the whole show with a surprise punch, it would help a lot. Alert eyes carefully scanned sky and water.

While fuel lines still sagged heavy between the ships, radar picked up a distant wayfaring "bogie." A Hellcat from the BELLEAU WOOD sped to the target and pounced. "Scratch one Betty." Everyone hoped that our fighter had made the kill before the task force had been sighted.

Turning southwest from the Eniwetok area the carriers pointed their bows toward Truk. Admiral Spruance, with his flag on the new 45,000-ton battleship NEW JERSEY, was in over-all command of the striking force.[1]

[1] The following Truk Striking Force (Task Force 50) under Vice Admiral R. A. Spruance was organized:
TRUK STRIKING FORCE (TF 50), Vice Admiral Spruance
   Force Flagship (TG 50.2), Captain Carl F. Holden
      Battleship: NEW JERSEY (FFF)
   Carrier Force (TF 58), Rear Admiral Mitscher
   Group 1—(TG 58.1), Rear Admiral J. W. Reeves, Jr.
      Carriers: ENTERPRISE (F), YORKTOWN (FF), BELLEAU WOOD
      Light Cruisers: SANTA FE, BILOXI, MOBILE
      Light Cruiser
        (Anti-aircraft): OAKLAND

The striking force itself was composed of three of the four carrier task groups that had been stomping pitilessly up and down the Marshalls. Admiral Reeves's ENTERPRISE, YORKTOWN, and BELLEAU WOOD, Admiral Montgomery's ESSEX, INTREPID, and CABOT, and Admiral Sherman's BUNKER HILL, MONTEREY, and COWPENS were ready to drop the first bombs of the war on terrible Truk.

By now everyone knew the objective, and the news was not greeted with wild enthusiasm, Truk being what it was—or believed to be. Lieutenant Commander Arthur Decker, commanding Bomber Squadron 9 of the ESSEX, said: "We were all set to come home after the Marshalls operations but after about a week in Majuro they told us we were going to hit Truk. We had heard a lot about Truk; it had quite a reputation and we weren't too happy, but there wasn't much we could do about it."

The strike at Truk was timed to coincide with the assault on Eniwetok, thereby cutting off all chances of outside aid to that doomed atoll. The first blow, an all-out fighter sweep, was to fall at dawn on February 16.

At 0635 the task force was about 90 miles northeast of Truk; sunrise would not be until 0810 by the West Longitude time on which the ships' clocks had been retained.

The night was squally. Dark clouds sped low over the sullen water, parting occasionally to let the moon cast pale slivers of light on the ghostly fleet.

Men stood at their battle stations waiting, wondering: When would

---

Destroyers:	C. K. BRONSON, COTTEN, DORTCH, GATLING, HEALY, COGSWELL, CAPERTON, INGERSOLL, KNAPP
Group 2—(T.G. 58.2), Rear Admiral A. E. Montgomery	
Carriers:	ESSEX (F), INTREPID, CABOT
Heavy Cruisers:	SAN FRANCISCO, WICHITA, BALTIMORE
Heavy Cruiser (Anti-aircraft):	SAN DIEGO
Destroyers:	OWEN, STEMBEL, THE SULLIVANS, STEPHEN POTTER, HICKOX, HUNT, LEWIS HANCOCK, STACK
Group 3—(TG 58.3), Rear Admiral F. C. Sherman	
Carriers:	BUNKER HILL (F), MONTEREY, COWPENS
Battleships:	SOUTH DAKOTA, ALABAMA, MASSACHUSETTS, NORTH CAROLINA, IOWA, NEW JERSEY (FFF), (When not acting as independent flagship)
Heavy Cruisers:	MINNEAPOLIS, NEW ORLEANS
Destroyers:	IZARD, CHARRETTE, CONNOR, BELL, BURNS, BRADFORD, BROWN, COWELL, STERETT, LANG, WILSON

the Jap planes come? When would the Jap submarines cut loose with their deadly "fish"? So far no contact had been made with enemy search planes or picket boats except the lone Betty off Eniwetok. That was strange, sinisterly so. Waiting can be more painful than desperate battle.

Over the scratchy-voiced TBS came orders from YORKTOWN for the carriers to drop out of tight formation and to turn into the wind. One by one small white lights flashed on, bright across the dark sea—masthead lights on the destroyers to guide the aviators. A pair of red and green wingtip lights rolled down the flight deck of a carrier, dipped and then rose skyward. The first Hellcat was airborne. Time: 0650. Within a few minutes seventy fighters had circled their carriers and were headed in toward Truk, the unknown. A slight drizzle began to fall as the men left behind looked at their watches and waited. Surely now the Japanese powerhouse would loose its voltage.

It was estimated two hundred planes were based on Truk. The fighters of the first sweep were to destroy these wherever found, on the ground or in the air. Then the bombing and torpedo squadrons would get their chance. They hoped to crack the back of the Jap fleet that the Marine photographs had shown anchored in the lagoon.

At 0714 the Truk radio went off the air.

Lieutenant Commander Sam L. Silber, commander BUNKER HILL's Fighter Squadron 18, tells of going in: "Our particular squadron was assigned to high cover. We were to stay up there most of the time and make sure there was no aerial opposition. I thought the Japs would be doing just about what they had been doing at Rabaul, taking off as soon as they learned something was coming in, getting 40 or 50 miles away, climbing to about 30,000 feet and coming back in again. As it turned out they evidently didn't have even enough time to do that.

"We streamed into Truk undisturbed. We took off about an hour before dawn and hadn't been gone more than 20 minutes when we found ourselves on the outskirts of the lagoon at Truk. We were down pretty low at that time, not more than 2,000 feet. We skirted the lagoon and climbed up to 2,000–2,500 feet. The other fighter squadrons came in a few minutes later and managed to catch most of the planes on the ground or as they took off. Of all the Japanese planes destroyed, I would say 75 per cent were shot down between zero and 1,000 feet. The Japs were completely disorganized and didn't know what to do. Few of them made any real concentrated attacks. We were able to maintain air superiority after the first hour and a half."

The planes assigned to medium and low altitudes did not find things serene when they arrived. Superiority had to be violently fought for. The sky in the half-light of dawn became a scramble of diving, twisting planes, as the Japanese flew in helter-skelter, every man for himself. The squadrons of American fighters broke up and engaged in individual dogfights. The Jap fliers were not good, but there were a lot of them. Tracers whipped across the sky in eccentric patterns of death, and in the first minutes of confusion a Hellcat was shot down by cross fire from its squadron mates.

The results of the fighter sweep were not only impressive, they were astounding. In the air the Japanese had lost 56 planes, and 72 more had been destroyed on the ground. We lost only four planes from all causes.

3

When the clouds began to break up over Truk with the coming of sunrise, the target observer (a pilot who does not enter into combat but who directs attacking aircraft to specific targets and observes the results) made ready to guide the dive bombers and torpedo planes to the fattest targets in the Japanese Fleet.

He looked—and looked again. *There was no Japanese Fleet!* True, the harbor held a good half hundred ships in the anchorages, but most of them were cargo types. The only warships in sight were two light cruisers and four destroyers.

Nevertheless, with the air fairly well cleared of enemy fighters, the torpedo planes and dive bombers started pouring in. Shipping was the primary target, with only enough attention given to the airstrips to keep them neutralized. "When I went in on the second bomber strike," said Lieutenant Commander Decker, "I saw only one enemy plane, and I think he was lost."

The ships were hit with everything from 2,000-pound bombs to torpedoes. Lieutenant James E. Bridges of Torpedo 6 (INTREPID) dived his plane toward an anchored ship. At exactly the right moment he released his bomb and saw it hit the target squarely.

He had no way of knowing that his target was an ammunition ship.

A devastating explosion shook the 1,000-foot cliffs of Dublon Island, as a flame-slashed mushroom of black smoke soared high above them, enveloping Bridges's plane. Ship and attacker were consumed together.

Some of the ships weighed anchor and made a dash for the open sea. A BUNKER HILL plane radioed that several large ships, among them a cruiser and two destroyers, were escaping via North Pass. On receiving this news Admiral Mitscher gave orders that strike leaders should give these ships preferential attention. Other planes flashed back quick warnings of the fleeing Japanese, giving split-second estimates of types, course, and speed, so that at one time the flagship was given the belief that five cruisers were leaving the lagoon.

Admiral Spruance, who had been waiting with ready-made plans for an attempted escape, hoped that it was so. He had the power to annihilate any combination of ships the Japs could float. Now there were only a few cruisers walking into his trap. So much the worse for them.

Orders were radioed to the task force from the flagship NEW JERSEY. The battleship IOWA and the heavy cruisers MINNEAPOLIS and NEW ORLEANS in that order would form up in column behind the NEW JERSEY for a sweep of the areas around Truk. The destroyers BURNS, BRADFORD, IZARD, and CHARRETTE would screen to port and starboard.

An atmosphere of picnic prevaded the heavy-gunned surface ships despite the grim externals of men in battle dress standing to their stations. Action at last; something to do besides standing by as potential antiaircraft defense for the carriers. Too long had the men abroad these ships fought a vicarious sort of war, watching the planes from the carriers fly over the horizon and then return from the same direction, sometimes crippled, more often unscratched. Sketchy and disjointed reports of what went on beyond the horizon would trickle back to the waiting ships and then would be expanded by scuttlebutt to unrecognizable dimensions. But never was there real relief from the drum-taut anticipation of attack.

An hour before noon the eight ships separated from the task force and headed toward Truk's northern reefs at 25 knots. Although all hands had been at general quarters stations since dawn, the excitement of cruising in the Jap's back yard dispelled all weariness. Munching sandwiches and fruit, the men beside the antiaircraft guns intently watched the low cumulus clouds that might contain wrathful enemy bombers. On the bridges of three of the ships, admirals also watched as eagerly as the greenest "boot"—Rear Admiral Olaf M. Hustvedt, Commander of

THE REAL OFFENSIVE BEGINS

Battleship Division 7 in the IOWA (Captain John L. McCrea), Rear Admiral Robert C. Giffen, Commander of Cruiser Division 6 in the MINNEAPOLIS (Captain Richard W. Bates), and Vice Admiral Spruance, wearing his flag in NEW JERSEY (Captain Carl F. Holden) in charge of the whole show.

For nearly two hours the group steamed unmolested, on a westward track now to intercept the Japanese ships leaving North Pass. Some of the youngsters grumbled. Where were the damn Japs, anyhow? The answer came in the sharp whine of a diving plane. A lone Japanese Zeke plummeted from a low cloud to starboard of IOWA, where he had hidden undetected by eye or radar, and loosed a bomb. It missed the ship by 50 yards, but if the belated antiaircraft fire from IOWA and MINNEAPOLIS spoiled the pilot's aim it did not frighten him, for the Zeke came back and strafed the IOWA while crossing from port to starboard. Unscathed, the Japanese bomber sped back to its cloud and escaped. The men were silent now, angry and a little ashamed, standing tense at their stations, wishing the Zeke—no, a whole flock of them—would nose through the clouds just once more.

The navigator aboard NEW JERSEY peered intently through his binoculars at the hazy horizon to port. Faintly he could see two small, dark dots—part of the outlying reef. Truk sighted for the first time by an American surface ship since the beginning of the war.

And now, for as many eyes as searched the sky, others watched the water apprehensively. Thus close to the Japanese citadel, the ships were in a submarine sanctuary. That meant that any submarine detected by United States ships would not be attacked except in retaliation for a hostile move, because the submarine SEARAVEN was standing by in the area on a mercy mission to pick up downed American aviators.

What the task group might expect in the way of enemy ships became clearer when a BUNKER HILL plane established radio contact with NEW JERSEY on VHF (very high frequency) radio, reporting that it had been assigned as air spotter for the group and was now on station. The pilot then gave a general description of the situation: directly ahead of the task group, about 30 miles distant, were a KATORI-class light cruiser apparently dead in the water, a destroyer motionless and burning, and another cruiser or large destroyer circling. What appeared to be a "small tug" was directly ahead about 20 miles, apparently approaching Truk from the north completely unaware that war had overtaken the atoll.

The carrier aviators had been working this group of enemy ships over ever since early morning. All the way up the lagoon they had caught hell, and now in the open sea they were still catching it in bombs and torpedoes. Twisting violently at flank speed, the destroyers sought to get out from under the dive bombers, and for the most part did. The cruiser was neither as agile nor as lucky, and lay crippled in the water, but still slapping vigorously at the pestering planes with heavy AA fire. One of the destroyers, finally hit, was smoldering near-by.

Winging out from the carriers ESSEX (Captain Ralph A. Ofstie) and INTREPID (Captain Thomas L. Sprague) torpedo planes, dive bombers, and fighters were rapidly approaching the last-reported enemy position. Lieutenant Commander Philip Torrey, Jr., Commander Air Group 9 (ESSEX), peered from his Hellcat through rolling clouds, and caught a glimpse of a large force of combatant ships. He dropped down to investigate and was greeted with a "tremendous volume of AA fire." Torrey had not been told, previous to his take-off, of the foray by Admiral Spruance's group. ("There's always somebody who doesn't get the word.") Pulling out of the black puffs of 5-inch flak, Torrey recognized the ships as our own. After the exchange of a number of messages on VHF he succeeded in persuading the NEW JERSEY that they were fighting on the same side and that he and his planes were after the same Japs.

"Having identified these ships as our own," he reported, "I proceeded further west and located one KATORI-class light cruiser and one destroyer maneuvering violently at high speed, the cruiser being some six to eight miles west of the destroyer. I ordered the INTREPID group to attack the ship to the west and the ESSEX group to attack the ship to the east."

If the carrier boys were trying hard to finish off the Japs before Admiral Spruance got within gun range they didn't quite do it. Crippled though they were, the enemy ships were as tough and dangerous as wounded tigers.

4

The smoke of the air-sea battle could be seen clearly from the lookout stations of the fast-approaching task group. Aboard the NEW JERSEY the CIC (Combat Information Center), where all radar positions are plotted, sent the picture of the situation to the bridge—approaching dead ahead at a range of 28,000 yards was the "light tug"; a destroyer, apparently undamaged, by the evidence of its speedy retreat, was on the port bow at a range of about 32,000 yards; beyond that at 42,000 yards was the half-dead cruiser; 48,000 yards in the same direction another destroyer lay burning.

Three destroyers—IZARD, BURNS, and CHARRETTE—were detached to take care of the tug, or whatever it might be. It looked more like a trawler when the destroyers brought the ship into view, and it looked like nothing much but a floating bonfire after a few rounds of 5-inch shells had been wafted aboard. The destroyers went about on other business, and the blazing hulk drifted into the path of the big battlewagons, so the NEW JERSEY, just to tidy up the area, dropped a few shells on the craft.

Its identity as a minelayer was made very clear in the detonation that followed. As IOWA swept past in JERSEY's wake, all that remained of the Japanese vessel was an acre of charred trash and one man clinging to a swamped dory. As the pride of the U.S. Navy swept past, the lone Japanese survivor defiantly shook an oily fist.

Meanwhile Admiral Spruance sent the cruisers to polish off the two crippled Japanese warships. They, too, died gamely. Dead in the water, they went down shooting although the battleships added their big guns to effect the coup de grâce. As a final futile gesture, the sinking Japanese cruiser and destroyer fired a fan of torpedoes at the American task group.

The destroyer was his Imperial Japanese Majesty's Ship MAIKAZE. Aboard her were the survivors of the new light cruiser AGANO, which had been sunk the day before at sunset north of Truk by the submarine SKATE [1] (Lieutenant Commander William P. Gruner, Jr.) in a superbly executed submerged attack. The cruiser was the KATORI.

The fourth enemy ship, reported as a large destroyer-leader type, displayed none of the gallantry of the others. Utilizing every second of the American ships' occupation with her damaged companions, the destroyer high-tailed it at better than 31 knots for the horizon. The NEW JERSEY and IOWA sent five salvos after her at a range exceeding 17 miles, but if the tons of pelting explosives had any effect it was only to add speed to the vanishing Jap.

The victory, minor as it was compared to the over-all destruction

---

[1] The SKATE was one of a group of submarines fanned out to the northwest of Truk patrolling the approaches. The others were SUNFISH (Lt. Comdr. Edward E. Shelby), TANG (Lt. Comdr. Richard H. O'Kane), which sank a large freighter February 17, ASPRO (Lt. Comdr. William A. Stevenson), BURRFISH (Comdr. William B. Perkins), DACE (Lt. Comdr. Bladen D. Clagget), and GATO (Comdr. Robert J. Foley).

hammered out at Truk, provides a good example of co-operation between air and surface forces. The planes pinned down the enemy ships and the task group sent them under. Triumphantly Admiral Spruance ordered all ships to fly "Prep Four," the largest American flag in the locker. With that symbol of victory waving from the gaff, the ships fell into formation and proudly, exultingly, paraded around the atoll in full view of the battered enemy stronghold.

Victory, however, was marred by one of those unfortunate tragedies of war.

A group of four or five enemy ships, some of which were thought to be cruisers, had been reported west of Truk. Bombing Squadron 6 of the INTREPID, with Lieutenant Paul E. TePas as strike leader, was ordered to attack this group. En route the squadron passed over our own task group without being challenged. Ninety miles west of Truk the enemy was sighted, but instead of cruisers the ships turned out to be two cargo types, an oiler and a destroyer escort. Dive-bombing attacks were made through heavy AA fire resulting in one large cargo ship being sunk and the oiler damaged.

Returning from the strike Lieutenant (jg) Willis G. Laney asked Lieutenant TePas over his radio whether he intended to inform our own group of the location of the enemy.

"Yes, I do," replied TePas, "I have one of the messages completed now."

Breaking away from the bomber formation TePas went down low and approached the IOWA from the port quarter for a message drop. He was recognized and the machine-gun officer on the IOWA directed: "Friendly plane. Track but do not fire." Mutely the lifted muzzles of the AA guns followed the airplane's approach, and then, with TePas only a hundred yards away, one gun section, which had misunderstood the order, started firing. The plane passed over the bow of the IOWA in a slanting glide toward the sea, the port wing drooping. Then the wingtip hit the water. The plane spun in a crazy cartwheel, wing over wing, and sank almost instantly. When the BRADFORD closed to investigate, there was no trace of survivors.

5

A destroyer from the task group was to chalk up one more enemy ship before nightfall. At 1805 a ship was sighted on the horizon. A lookout officer reported it as a cruiser, but as had happened so often it was an over-optimistic identification and the target proved this time a small submarine chaser of about 300 tons. The BURNS, the same ship that had cleaned up the Jap convoy in the Marshalls, was ordered in for the slaughter. After fifteen minutes of fire, during which time the Japanese popped back ineffectively with a lone 3-inch gun, the subchaser, the PC 24, sank stern first. The BURNS, reporting to the task group that "60 well-dressed Japanese" were floundering in the water, put over her boat to rescue them. In spite of the most compelling persuasion, only six Japanese would allow themselves to be picked up. The others fought off rescue, swimming out of reach and diving to elude the boatmen.

The BURNS wrote them a brief obituary: "In view of probable rescue of survivors by the Japanese and their return to further action and of their refusal to be rescued by ship's boat or lines from USS BURNS, three depth charges set on depth 50 feet were dropped to destroy them."

6

During the Truk attack only twenty-five of our aircraft were lost, and eight of these were due to operational accidents. More than half the crews of the destroyed planes were rescued by recovery teams, of which the previously mentioned submarine SEARAVEN was but one unit. It added to the confidence of the youngsters in the air, who had to compete with death at the shortest of odds, to realize that even if they were shot down they still had better than a 50-50 chance of climbing into a dry bunk that night.

Typical was the experience of Lieutenant (jg) Relly I. Raffman.

Flying a Hellcat, he took off from COWPENS with five other planes of his fighter squadron—their mission, to bomb and strafe the airfield on Eten Island. As he emerged from the clouds over Eten, he felt a jar, reminiscent of driving a car over a cobblestone. His engine immediately started missing. Flak fragments had perforated it. Doggedly, Raffman completed his run and scored a good hit on the target, although the engine was smoking and his speed had fallen to 90 knots. Raffman called his companions and told them he did not think he could make it back to the ship. Three other fighters joined up with him and they started home.

Forty miles east of Truk Raffman began losing altitude at the rate of 300 feet a minute. He told his companions he was going to water-land and methodically began the oft-practiced routine of "abandoning ship." He detached his parachute harness, unbuckled his life raft from the chute harness, inflated the outboard section of his "Mae West," and tightened his shoulder straps to the limit. He headed into the wind, and as his plane slid belly-whoppers on the water he unbuckled his safety belt and climbed out onto the right wing. Then he reached into the cockpit, grabbed his life raft, pulled the other toggle of his "Mae West," threw out a dye marker and jumped clear. Ten seconds after striking the water the F6F sank, nose first. Raffman was pulled under momentarily by the horizontal stabilizer, and swallowed some green-dyed water before he bobbed back to the surface, mechanically inflated his rubber boat, and climbed aboard.

His plight had already been reported to the task force some 35 miles away. Within a half hour a "Bug" (catapult plane) from the battleship MASSACHUSETTS (Captain Theodore D. Ruddock), piloted by Lieutenant Charles G. Ainsworth, landed on the water near-by, picked him up, and carried him back to a cup of hot coffee and dry clothes.

Truk lagoon itself was the scene of another sensational snatch. Lieutenant (jg) George M. Blair of the ESSEX was shot down by heavy AA during a strafing attack on shipping and found himself floating in the lagoon with only his Mae West to keep him company. A Japanese destroyer saw his plane hit the water and headed over to investigate, but Blair's nine flight companions formed a strafing circle which drove back the destroyer to a respectful distance, but still watching the proceedings. Several times, like a hesitant hound dog itching for trouble, she tried to ease in only to be turned back by the sharp sting of the circling fighters' 50-calibers. Four of the fighters, being low on gas, had to return to their carriers. They were soon followed by three more. Finally, just as the last two protective Hellcats reluctantly left the scene with just enough gas to reach their ships safely, the destroyer steamed away to the westward, probably convinced the show was over. It was, in fact, just reaching its dramatic climax.

The BALTIMORE had catapulted her plane for the rescue pickup, and Lieutenant (jg) Denver Baxter, the pilot, had no trouble finding Blair surrounded by the green dye of his marker. When Baxter put his Bug down on the lagoon, he became the first American deliberately to land at Truk. Blair was hauled aboard, and rode uncomfortably but happily in Chief Radioman R. F. Hickman's lap on the return trip to the cruiser.

When the plane was hauled back aboard only one pint of gasoline remained in the tank.

Not only were the fallen fliers helped by their buddies of the air, but even men from under the sea came up to lend a hand. The submarine SEARAVEN on lifeguard station north of Truk rescued three men from one of YORKTOWN's downed torpedo planes within sight of the lagoon. The DARTER (Commander William S. Stovall, Jr.) to the south of the island was standing by but got no business.

7

The second Jap cruiser to slip out of Truk lagoon when things began to get hot headed south. She was the light cruiser NAKA, and for half an hour or so her crew felt pretty sure she would "live to fight another day," the reward—or excuse—of those who run. Thirty miles from Truk the refugee was spotted from the air and reported to BUNKER HILL. Immediately torpedo planes and dive bombers took to the air and streaked the 100 miles to the target. This sinking was to be an "all airedale" show.

When the NAKA sighted the planes approaching she put on flank speed of 25 knots, shoved her rudders over hard, and went into a tight clockwise circle, putting up her best AA fire. The BUNKER HILL boys circled the frantic cruiser in the opposite direction, a halo of death. One by one they peeled off to meet the ship head on at 200 knots. The NAKA quaked from truck to keel as the magazines went up with a volcanic gush under bomb blast and torpedo impact. When the BUNKER HILL boys headed back toward the task force, her turrets were already awash. She could go in only one direction—down.

That night, February 16–17, both sides traded punches, the Japanese getting theirs in first.

Task Force 58, composed of the three task groups, was maneuvering about a hundred miles to the east of Truk. Aboard the INTREPID radarmen intently watched the light spots on their screens. At 2111 an unidentified pip appeared:

"Bogie [unidentified airplane] bearing two-three-five, range four-two-oh-double-oh," reported the watch-stander as he turned the little black knobs of his machine, measuring distance, accurate to the yard, with the silent unseen electrons.

The plane did not close the task force but it proved that the enemy had planes on the prowl that night, fresh Bettys from Saipan.

Every radar in the task force glowed its warnings as the hours passed, but only one enemy plane came close enough to be fired upon. A night fighter was launched from YORKTOWN to drive off the pests, the ENTERPRISE as force fighting director vectoring the black-bodied fighter to the single enemy plane still within radar range. But the Hellcat lost contact with the Jap at about midnight and as it groped in the black sky for its opponent INTREPID's radar showed the raider boring in on the task force. In the ESSEX, Admiral Montgomery ordered the ships into an emergency turn to course 240, the speed goosed to 25 knots.

Still the plane bore in. No guns fired, for fear of hitting one of our own fliers. Then, at eight minutes past midnight, the pip on INTREPID's radar winked out. The bogie seemed to have vanished, four miles to the north.

One minute later another order from the Task Group Commander was executed—an emergency turn to the left.

"Left fifteen degrees rudder," ordered the Officer-of-the-Deck on INTREPID.

"Left fifteen degrees rudder, sir," echoed the helmsman as he spun the wheel. The stern of the gray ship skidded into a turn leaving a smooth slick of water to port.

"Passing one-eight-zero," reported the helmsman, watching the gyro click off the degrees. And as if that were a signal, a small low-winged plane whined out of the darkness and sped over the ship. There was a muffled explosion, aft somewhere. The helmsman gulped hard before he made his next observation.

"Rudder appears to be stuck, sir. No response to the helm."

Smoke poured from a 20-foot hole in the carrier's stern, and the sea rushed in upon her shattered steering gear compartment. The torpedo had been well placed.

By steering with the engines, and using the North Star as anachronistic substitute for the disabled compasses, the wounded ship was finally brought to a steady course. Still making 20 knots, she headed to put the newly conquered Marshalls between herself and Truk. Below-decks, aft, men scrambled through ruptured, half-flooded compartments looking for wounded—and dead. Machinist George St. Schlemmer put on a diving outfit for the first time in his life and went into the flooded steering room.

Six bodies were recovered, five men were missing, and seventeen were brought to sickbay injured.

Our fliers now punched back hard. Torpedo 10 on ENTERPRISE had been waiting for this opportunity for a long time. The idea of utilizing radar for a low-altitude, night attack on enemy ships was originated by the squadron's commander, Lieutenant Commander William I. Martin, and for months Torpedo 10 had been making "dry runs" at night on friendly ships. Now they were ready for the real thing, a surprise revisit to Truk.

Twelve Avengers were unleashed from the carrier, each loaded with four 500-pound bombs. Martin, his arm broken, was unable to lead the group on the first test of his idea.

The planes flew in low, at 500 feet, thereby avoiding radar detection. As they passed the outer reefs, a hospital ship in the lagoon suddenly illuminated itself and sent up flares. With that, antiaircraft fire sprouted from ships and shore through the night, all of it aimed too high to harm the sea-skimming planes headed for the anchorage areas, and following the unerring finger their radar pointed at a row of blacked-out ships. Not until the bombs began to fall on carefully selected targets did the Japanese get the range on the Avengers. Lieutenant Lloyd Nicholas's plane went down. Others reported holes in wings and tail, but for thirty minutes Torpedo 10 sped back and forth across the lagoon loosing bombs into selected targets from altitudes impossible in daylight.

In the drab half-light of dawn, when the eleventh riddled Avenger jerked to a stop on the flight deck, Martin's theory was declared proved: thirteen direct hits had destroyed eight merchant ships and damaged five, 4.6 times the daylight average of success for ammunition expended. Seven of the squadron's planes had been hit, and one lost. The skipper of the ENTERPRISE, Captain Mathias B. Gardner, said in his report to COMINCH, Admiral Ernest J. King, that it had been proved possible to maintain "round-the-clock air operations against shore objectives and/or ships in harbor. No sleep for the enemy—somewhat more for us."

8

The raid on Truk cost the Japanese two light cruisers, four destroyers, twenty-six cargo ships, and 340 airplanes, besides the less-mourned and more replaceable lives lost. Additionally, four destroyers and fifteen cargo ships were damaged beyond immediate usefulness.[1] One lone destroyer was the only ship to escape.

The raid had cost the Japanese more than that. The U.S. Navy had invaded the dragon's lair and found it to be a rat's nest.

No one knew that better than Admiral Koga, whose flagship MUSASHI dropped anchor in Toyko Bay on the day the United States task force turned its collective backs on Truk. Koga had timed his departure well, and the departure of Admiral Kurita's Second Fleet even better. The Japanese warships spotted by the Marine fliers on February 3 had gone to Palau, in the western Carolines, just a week later, Admiral Ozawa's pilotless carrier force continuing still farther west, to Singapore.

Admiral Koga, himself, left Truk on February 4 aboard his flagship and headed for Japan to lay before the Central Authorities his revised plans for redistribution of strength in the Pacific. Vice Admiral Fukudome, his chief of staff, in an interview after the war said: "By the time that your landing around the Marshalls commenced, we were able to estimate fairly well the strategic situation in that region. There was no change in Admiral Koga's fundamental policy, which was the need of one decisive engagement, but the new situation forced the decision to make the Marianas and the Western Carolines the last line of defense. . . .

"The decision of primary importance made at that conference was the adoption in principle of Admiral Koga's plan, namely, that we must absolutely hold the line of defense between the Marianas and the Western Carolines. If we were to hold that line, it would be necessary to concentrate in that area not only the whole of the Navy's strength but also the full air force of the Army. Unfortunately, my contention was not accepted by the Army. They agreed that they would hold themselves ready to give their support when subsequently developments should make such support necessary. I left Toyko with the request that the Army's full air strength should also be concentrated in that area."

[1] Sunk: Light Cruisers: NAKA, KATORI
Destroyers: OIKAZE, TACHIKAZE, FUMITUKI, MAIKAZE
Severely damaged: Destroyers: SHIGURE, HARUSAME, AKIKAZE, NOWAKE
Rescue Tug: AKASHI
Target Ship: HAKACHI
Cargo ships sunk: HOKI, AIKOKU, SHOJIN, REIYO, HEIAN, RIYO, SEIKO, HOYO, SEICHO, HOKUYO, TEIKICHI, SOKO, NAGAMO, AMAGISAN, TATSUHAMA, FUJISAN, ZUIKAI, RIO DE JANEIRO, ADI SAN TONAN, YAMASHIMO and AKAGI, plus 5 other unidentified ships

After the war, Vice Admiral Hara, the commander of Truk, said: "I heard many radio broadcasts from the United States describing Truk as an impregnable bastion. We could not help but laugh at this knowing how weak we really were. I had the South Sea blues for fear that you would find out the truth."

Truk had been a bubble that looked like a bomb.

Chapter Ten

Operation Cherry Tree

I

AFTER the quick, hard punch at Truk, Admiral Spruance's force had split up. The crippled INTREPID (now dubbed by the wags the DECREPIT) rigged a huge sail on her forecastle to cut down excessive vibration, and, steering with her engines, limped at 20 knots toward the Pearl Harbor Navy Yard. Escorting her were a half dozen cruisers and destroyers and the light cruiser CABOT.

Led by the convoy-destroying BURNS, the NEW JERSEY, flying Admiral Spruance's three-star flag, headed for still-smoldering Kwajalein. A task group, under Admiral J. W. Reeves, built around the carrier ENTERPRISE peeled off for a go at by-passed Jaluit in the Marshalls, which was hit hard on February 20 without loss to our own forces.

After a fueling rendezvous with fleet tankers, the two remaining carrier groups headed north. With the departure of Admiral Spruance for Kwajalein small wind-wrinkled Mitscher was on his own. For the first time he was in top command of a task force; for the first time an attack deep into Japland was to be entirely his show.

Originally the plan had been to hit Ponape on the way back from Truk. But the war in the Pacific was now swinging into high gear. The Japs at Truk had been relatively soft, so, instead of the routine retirement raid on Ponape, it was decided to keep the Empire off balance with a quick thrust at the Marianas, of which American-owned Guam is the southernmost island. To some of the battle-tired fliers this shift in plans seemed like the old Navy game. As one of them described it: "We retired to the east and sailed back and forth between Eniwetok and Ponape. 'They' said we were going to hit Ponape, and then 'they' said we weren't. We were ready to go home and then 'they' said 'just one more.' So we headed for the Marianas . . ."

One of the main reasons for sending our carriers against the Marianas was to obtain information as to the nature of the Japanese installations there. Little was known about these strategic islands, squarely athwart the east-west ocean approaches to the Philippines. One flier remarked: "When we hit Tinian-Saipan, we didn't have the faintest idea where the airfields were, or how many, and so on. We were pretty sure they had some because our submarines had seen planes land but they didn't know in what part of the island. We knew the general geography of the islands, and the National Geographic Society supplied us with a lot more information."

The date of the strike was a happy patriotic coincidence. "I cannot tell a lie," Mitscher messaged to his ships. "D-day is Washington's Birthday. Let's chop down a few Nip cherry trees." But Mitscher, unlike the Father of his Country, was armed with considerably more than a hatchet.

2

Mitscher had hoped to slip in undetected and catch the Japanese with their planes down. But a snooping Betty, which escaped Lieutenant Clarence F. Avery during the afternoon of the 21st when the guns of his Dauntless jammed, gave the game away, and the Admiral knew his force would have to fight its way in. If the Japanese followed their usual routine they would start attacking about an hour after sunset, so Mitscher immediately regrouped his ships and prepared for the most dreaded enemy offensive tactic—the night torpedo attack.

The Japs were right on schedule. At 2100, an hour after sunset almost to the minute, the first "bogie" was picked up on ship's radar.

"Alert! Alert! Raid Able. Emergency turn 9," crackled the sharp orders over the TBS radio.

Simultaneously all the ships of the two task groups spun their helms and heeled over in an abrupt turn to the right presenting only their sterns and foamy, phosphorescent wakes to the rapidly closing enemy. With the unfortunate experience of the INTREPID in mind Mitscher had ordered all his ships to open up on any targets as soon as they were within range. Soon the bright, quick 5-inch muzzle flashes from the fringing cruisers and destroyers lit up the dark, moonless night. Some of the Japs turned away, some pressed on, still unseen by eye, until just one suddenly became visible as it burst into flame from a direct hit. Another darted low over the cruiser MOBILE and strafed her starboard side through red strings of

20mm AA fire. As always, the Japanese were after the carriers, but they didn't get through.

"Raid Dog! Raid Dog! Emergency turn to two-seven-oh."

Through the long night the ships twisted violently over the dark sea. Admiral Montgomery's Task Group 58.2 took the brunt of the attack, shooting down eight twin-engined Bettys, while to the south Admiral Sherman's group bagged two. Although enemy aircraft were hovering near our forces continuously during the night, none of them was able to land a bomb or torpedo. The task force was able to either shake them off by slippery maneuvers or knock them down with extremely accurate AA fire.

Knowing what damage a single enemy plane could do, the carrier men were more than grateful for their plane-tight ring of antiaircraft fire. Captain L. T. Hundt, commanding officer of the light carrier MONTEREY, stated in his report of the action: "The MONTEREY is proud to have been with the escort and screen who fight them off these dark nights when 'they aren't seen until they burn.'"

The screen did leak a couple of times, but only to afford the carrier gunners some target practice, too.

The ships still being on West Longitude time, dawn was not until 0800. On the hour, the Japs made their last effort and the BELLEAU WOOD had a couple of close calls.

As Captain A. M. Pride described it: "Shortly after sunrise a Betty was seen low on the horizon off the starboard quarter and heading for the Task Group. It continued flying at an altitude of 25 to 50 feet on a course directly for this ship and penetrated the heavy barrage of gunfire from the screening ships. After the Betty was within the screen, this ship's starboard automatic weapons opened fire and the plane, its port engine flaming, spun into the water about 200 feet off the port beam and sank immediately.

"About 0910 another Betty was seen approaching the formation low on the horizon off the port bow. It also penetrated the screen and pressed home its attack on a direct course for the BELLEAU WOOD, flying about 50 feet above the water. After the plane had survived the barrage laid down by the screening ships, the port automatic weapons [40mm and 20mm] of this ship opened fire. When about 500 yards away the Betty burst into flames and crashed in the water dead ahead of the ship, which had been turned to head for the attack . . ."

The fighters of the CAP (Combat Air Patrol) entered into the morning melee by shooting down two dive bombers streaking for ESSEX and YORKTOWN. The gunners of the ESSEX knocked down another while fire from the screening ships got three more. The only fatality among the American fliers was the pilot of a fighter plane who darted in to attack a Japanese bomber at the instant the sky was ripped by concentrated AA fire from the ships of the screen.

3

Now for the first time in twelve hours the radar screen was clear of bogies and Mitscher's men took to the air for the Washington's Birthday celebration. But, as with many outdoor parties, the weather interfered. Lieutenant Commander Sam Silber tells of leading Fighting 18 to Saipan from the BUNKER HILL. But Saipan was blotted out by clouds, so "the twelve of us flew southward until we were able to see the ocean again, and when we did we sighted Rota Island, so I decided we might just as well go down to Guam." On that island, first American territory to be captured by the Japanese, the fliers spotted a big airstrip on what had formerly been the golf course.

"We saw a couple of fighters just ready to land. They apparently hadn't seen us and we waited until both of them had their wheels and flaps down before we strafed them; they had just about hit the ground when we polished them off. . . . After our third run we found two other Bettys about a half mile away who looked as if they were coming in to land, and shot them down before they put their wheels and flaps down. At that point we were getting pretty low on ammunition, so we decided to head back to our ship."

Bombing Squadron 9 of the ESSEX, with luck and electronics, was able to get through to Saipan although Lieutenant Commander Decker also found the target blanketed under a solid overcast 12,000 feet thick.

"We weren't sure where the island was, but one of the TBF pilots picked it up on his radar, gave me a correction, and I headed in that general direction. We first knew we were near the island when we saw one of our fighters shoot down a Jap. We circled for about 20 minutes before we could see a hole large enough to warrant going through it. We had a general idea where the airfield was and Phil Torrey, the group commander, said, 'Go ahead and attack.' We couldn't dive; we couldn't split our flaps and really push over as we like to, so we went through in a glide. We hit the airfield very thoroughly, and the hangar and installations around it, although the weather was so bad around the island we were very lucky to get everybody together in a rendezvous. It was solid right down to the water with visibility about 20 yards in spots."

Then they found another hole in the clouds, climbed up through it, and went home to the Big E.

Again the undersea men were standing by either to pick up aviators who fell in the "drink" or to slide a few fish into any ships driven from the harbors by the attack. Within 30 miles of Saipan were the APOGON, SEARAVEN, SUNFISH, and SKIPJACK. The SUNFISH in the early morning hours of February 23 sank a large cargo ship that was erroneously thought to be a carrier. The TANG, which held down the safety position some 60 miles from the island, sank four large ships between the 22nd and the 25th.

When the weather cleared in the afternoon, some of the most important work of the day was done by Lieutenant Commander Edgar E. Stebbins in a torpedo plane rigged with cameras. Escorted by four fighters he took an aerial tour around the islands, recording impressions in silver nitrate. The camera, having the same basic devotion to truth as George Washington and Marc Mitscher, was performing an errand important to the planners in Pearl Harbor. Admiral Nimitz already had his eye on Guam, and not only as a pleasant site for his afternoon game of horseshoes.

Other flights chopped at everything from freighters to sugar mills. Two cargo ships and a small sub-chaser were left sinking west of Saipan, in the area where the submarine SUNFISH lurked on lifeguard duty. Tanapag harbor on Saipan was almost empty, so the birdman had to be content with herding a freighter onto a reef. Another freighter with two escorts was caught near Tinian.

"That afternoon," said Silber, "there were seventy planes parked on Tinian, most of them bombers and twin-engine fighters. We strafed practically all of them with the help of a couple of other squadrons. Practically every plane we destroyed that day was on the ground. It was pretty hard to figure out why they were on the ground; they had had all night and practically all day to get them out, but they had made no attempt to do anything. We decided that since Tinian was a training station, the boys weren't ready for their final check."

He was right. After the carrier strike on Truk the Japanese decided to shift the First Air Fleet, which at the time was training in the home islands, to the Marianas. The advance echelon arrived on February 20, "just in time to have its protruding nose flattened," as one Jap put it. Of the forty torpedo pilots at Tinian thirty were students. Of the twenty bomber and torpedo planes sent out to attack the American forces on the night of February 21–22, only five returned. The Japanese had not expected the Americans so soon.

Admiral Mitscher, not knowing what the Japs might bring in for another night attack from the Japanese mainland, decided to cut the operation short. Before dark the task force was rapidly retiring to the east.

4

Like slacked violin strings, everyone from admirals to mess cooks relaxed. Below-decks on the blacked-out ships laughter came a little more easily; the after-dinner cigar tasted a little better; the acey-deucey games were a little livelier; the cooks received a little less abuse. Life in the Navy wasn't so bad after all! A week before, steaming toward Truk, the men had felt vaguely akin to the Light Brigade going "into the jaws of death, into the valley of hell." Never since the attack on Pearl Harbor had American combat ships pushed so deep into the Empire's South Sea area. The cost had been amazingly light. The birthday party losses were partly self-inflicted—four planes lost in combat, two operationally; injuries on the MOBILE from the straying fragments of a 5-inch shell; casualties on the ALABAMA when one gun mount shot up another. Perhaps the most important result of the raid, exceeding even the material damage done to the Japanese, was the boost in morale given all hands by the successful beating off of the dreaded night torpedo attacks. That is no belittlement of the raid's accomplishment. With the destruction of the entire strength, 95 planes, of the advance echelon of the Imperial First Air Fleet a severe blow was dealt to the organization upon which Japan was depending heavily for the defense of the Marianas and Western Carolines.

Mitscher was justly proud of his men when he sent them the following message: "The task force commander will not attempt to enumerate results obtained during the Truk and Marianas episode of this cruise. His heart is too full for verbal expression of pride for his force . . . After the Nips' loss of face at Truk we expected a fight, we had a fight, we won a fight. I am proud to state that I firmly believe this force can knock hell out of the Japs anywhere, any time. Your standard is high; I can only congratulate all hands on an outstanding performance and give you a stupendous 'Well done!' "

5

Preparation and execution of the Gilbert-Marshalls campaign covered the period between August, 1943, and the end of February, 1944. In that time the United States air-amphibious team, spearheaded by carrier task forces, shattered the Japanese defensive perimeter and brought under United States control an ocean area of 800,000 square miles containing strategically situated islands which provided at least three large fleet anchorages and a score of airfields on the enemy flank and center. United States carrier task forces and land-based aircraft had destroyed or rendered impotent all Japanese air power east of the Marianas, and had forced the Japanese Fleet to the extreme western Pacific Ocean. Truk had been eliminated and was not worth the effort of invasion, and the eastern Caroline Islands were no longer an effective part of the Japanese Pacific defense system. Before the debris was cool, work was underway converting the Japanese bases to American use in support vital to the Southwest Pacific Forces in New Guinea. And, of more immediately decisive value, the road block on the way to Guam's recapture had been removed.

PART THREE

Southwest Cleanup Completed

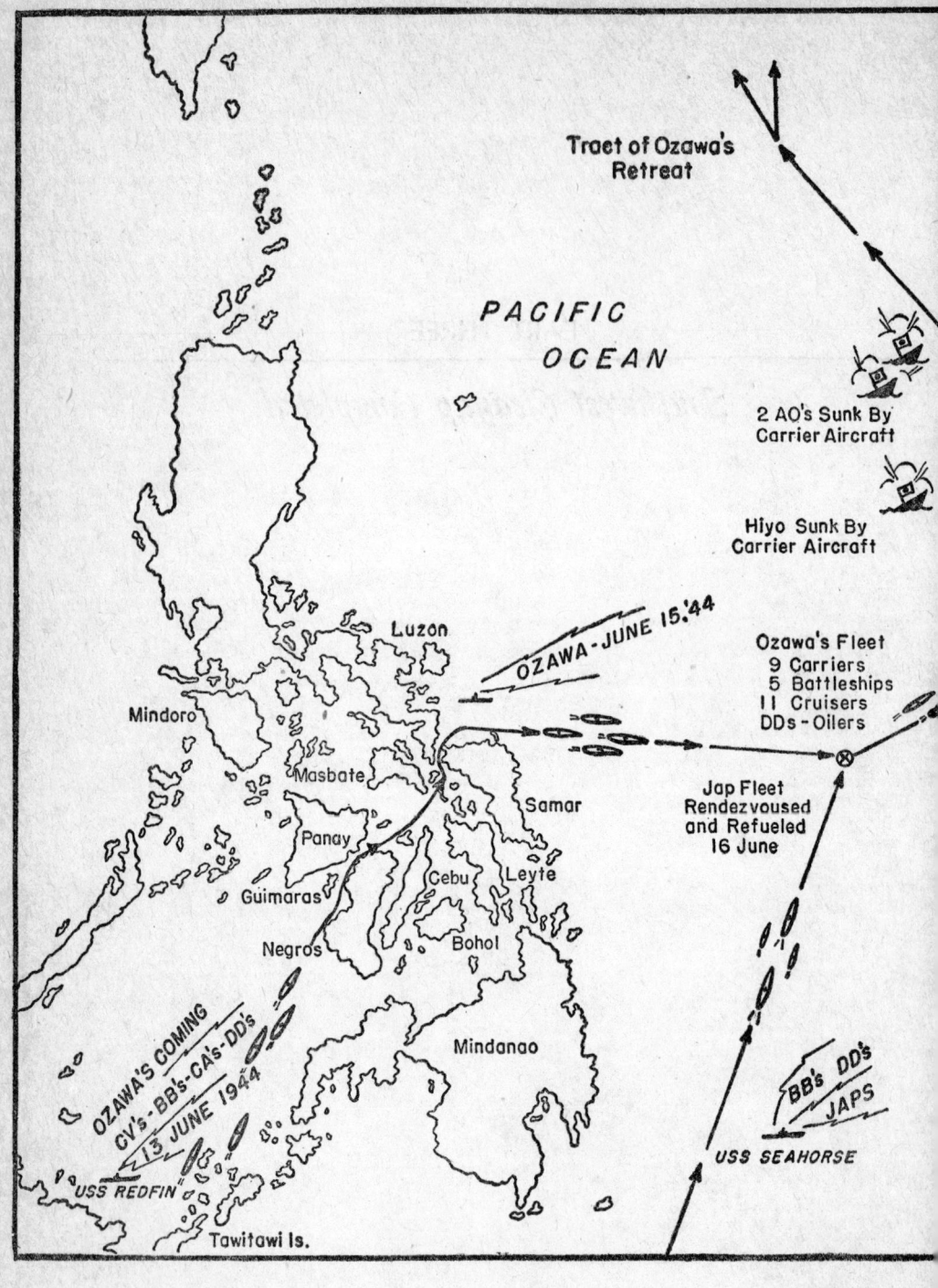

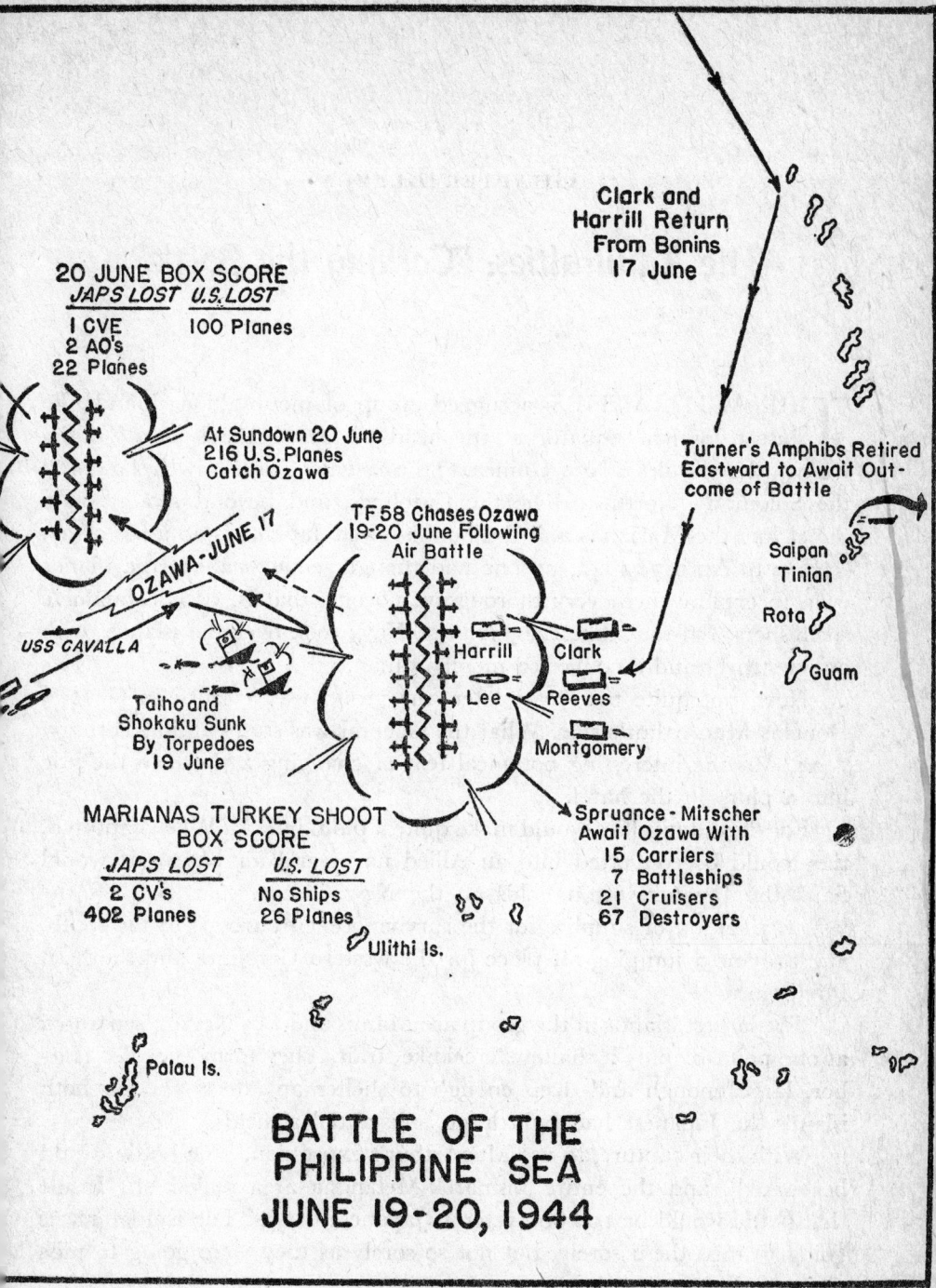

CHAPTER ELEVEN

The Admiralties: "Corking the Bottle"

I

THE ADMIRALTIES, a rugged group of mountainous islands, lie just below the equator at the head of the Bismarck Sea. To the westward 200 miles is New Guinea, to the east and south New Ireland and the Solomons. Northward lie the Carolines, and beyond almost on a direct line the Marianas and the Bonins—and Japan, 2,500 miles away.

Up to April 7, 1942, no one had thought enough about the islands even to explore them very thoroughly; no one, that is, except Japanese shellfishers. On that date the Japanese Navy took over the islands, with one destroyer and a converted merchantman.

Now, not quite two years later, the group was a thorn in General Douglas MacArthur's side. What the General was studying in February, 1944, was the interesting botanical feat of changing a thorn in the side into a plum in the hand.

For the Admiralties would make quite a plum indeed. When captured, they could be converted into an Allied naval and air base that would flank the Japanese strongholds on the New Guinea coast, cut off the last way station of supplies for the surviving enemy troops to the south, and provide a jumping-off place for the western Carolines and southern Philippines.

The largest islands in the group are Manus and Los Negros, separated at one point by only a shallow, creeklike strait. They form Seeadler Harbor, large enough and deep enough to shelter any fleet, and on both islands the Japanese had built large, substantial airfields.

With their capture, to use MacArthur's expression, "the bottle would be corked" and the entire Bismarck-Melanesia area sealed off. Inside that bottle would be 100,000 veteran Japanese troops. The Emperor was going to miss them sorely, but not so sorely as they were going to miss their meals.

2

Jap air strength was already ebbing fast in the Bismarck area. Enemy fighters now would not attack Allied bombers if they were escorted by fighters. On February 15 a group of enemy fighters fled to seaward upon sighting an equal number of Allied fighters. Destroyer sweeps around New Britain and New Ireland failed to flush up Jap planes in the same waters that a year before had been blanketed by enemy aircraft.

"After the Gloucester operation," Admiral Kinkaid recalls, "we headed up the New Guinea coast, taking our bases and our airfields with us. But we had to keep an eye on the Admiralties. Every day the Fifth Air Force put planes over the Admiralties without much opposition and one day they flew low over the islands without getting shot at, at all. They thought there were no Japs around . . ."

Originally it had been planned to attack the Admiralties on April 1, but on the basis of reports MacArthur decided that a coup de main might stand a good chance of being successful.

"MacArthur called a conference," continues Kinkaid, who was top naval man in the Southwest Pacific, "and in just four days we organized the operation."

The operation was to take the form of a reconnaissance in force on Los Negros Island, not later than February 29. If the opposition got too tough, and it looked as though the small force could not hold the cork in the bottle the troops could be withdrawn. The 1st Cavalry Division, turned pedestrian for Pacific operations, was nominated by Lieutenant General Walter Krueger, boss of the Sixth Army, to spearhead the attack.

The 1st Cavalry was a division proud of its military exploits—both ancient and modern. Its oldest regiment had been organized in 1855 by Jefferson Davis. Among its commanders had been Robert E. Lee and Jeb Stuart. Its present commander was Major General Innis P. Swift.

"MacArthur's Deputy Chief of Staff, Major General Stephen Chamberlin, came to me one day," mused Admiral Kinkaid after the war, "and said that MacArthur wanted to see the operation at first hand and wanted to go to the Admiralties on one of the destroyers. I said I didn't think it was such a good idea because MacArthur would be too uncomfortable on a destroyer.

"Chamberlin came back later and said MacArthur was insistent. 'All right,' I said, 'if he insists on going, he can go up on a cruiser'—although

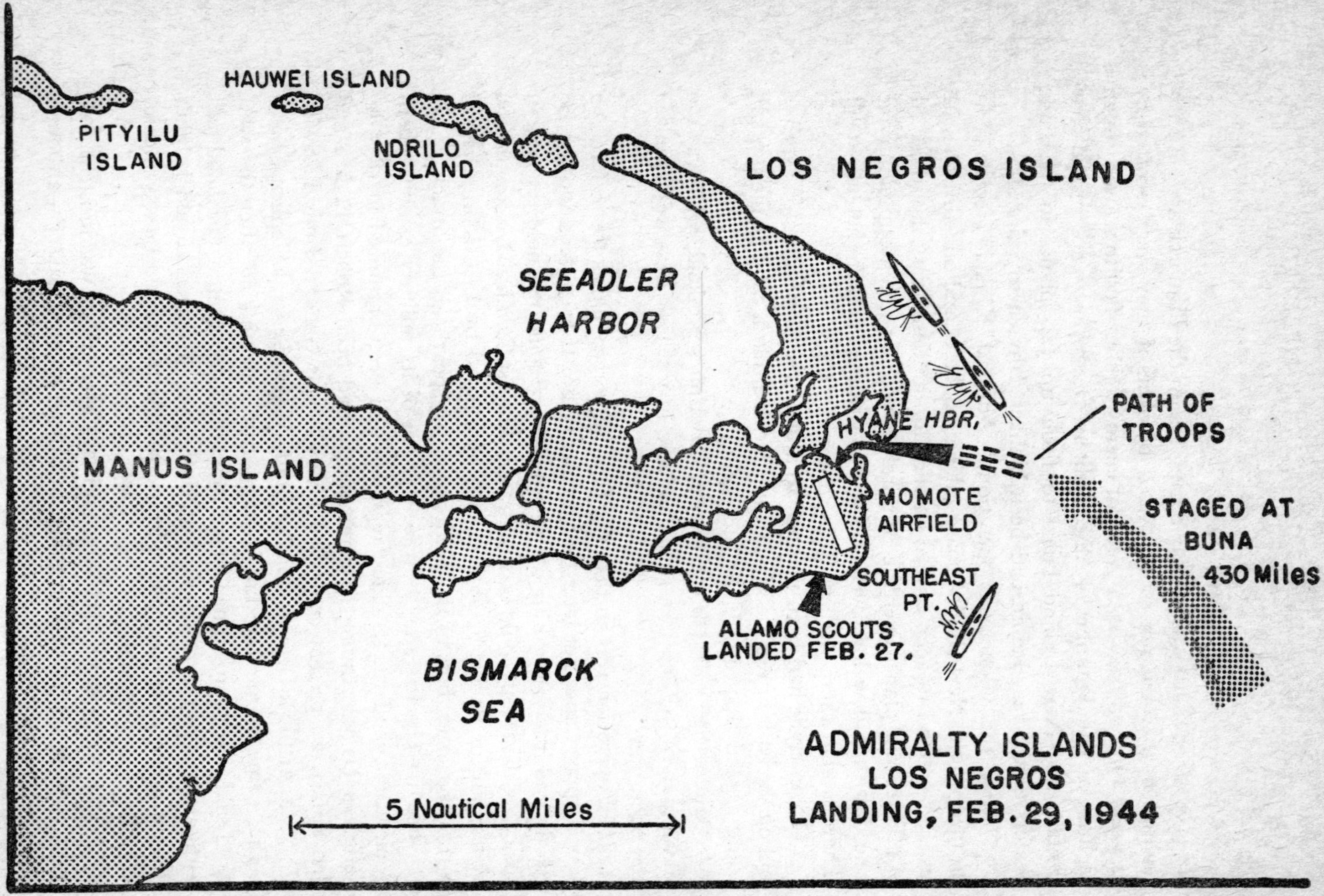
HAUWEI ISLAND
PITYILU ISLAND
NDRILO ISLAND
LOS NEGROS ISLAND
SEEADLER HARBOR
MANUS ISLAND
HYANE HBR.
PATH OF TROOPS
MOMOTE AIRFIELD
STAGED AT BUNA 430 Miles
SOUTHEAST PT.
ALAMO SCOUTS LANDED FEB. 27.
BISMARCK SEA
ADMIRALTY ISLANDS
LOS NEGROS
LANDING, FEB. 29, 1944
5 Nautical Miles

FIGURE 10

I hadn't intended to use any cruisers in the operation. I have a basic rule never to send one ship to do something. I always send another of the same kind along just in case something goes wrong. So two cruisers—PHOENIX and NASHVILLE—went up on the operation, and I accompanied MacArthur at his request."

Exactly how much opposition, if any, would be encountered on Los Negros was still not known. Pictures taken by aviators who had flown low over the little islands revealed little Jap activity.

But on the evening of D-minus-2-day some startlingly contradictory news was received. Army scouts who had gone ashore that day on Los Negros from a Catalina flying boat reported that the area southwest of the Momote airstrip was "lousy with Japs!"

All gunfire support from the ships, it seemed, would be welcomed and needed.

"Embark, transport, and land the landing force on Beach White at the south end of Hyane Harbor, Los Negros. Support the landing by gunfire!" These were the orders handed Rear Admiral William M. Fechteler, the Attack Group commander, by Rear Admiral Daniel E. Barbey as the destroyer attack force with 1,026 1st Cavalry troops aboard, assembled in Oro Bay. In the group were three destroyer-transports—HUMPHREYS (Lieutenant Commander Frank D. Schwartz), BROOKS (Lieutenant Commander Charles V. Allen), and SANDS (Lieutenant Jerome M. Samuels)—under command of Lieutenant Commander Schwartz, each carrying 170 men, and three destroyers—STOCKTON (Lieutenant Commander William W. Stark), STEVENSON (Commander Edmond F. Wilson), and REID (Commander Samuel A. McCornock)—each carrying 57 men. The last-named ship wore the flag of Rear Admiral Fechteler.

At quarter to seven the morning of the 28th the group weighed anchor and headed north—before Barbey had time to complete his operation order. An hour later six more destroyers led by Captain Jesse H. Carter, riding in FLUSSER (Lieutenant Commander Theodore R. Vogeley), and including MAHAN (Lieutenant Commander Earnest G. Campbell), DRAYTON (Lieutenant Commander Richard S. Craighill), SMITH (Lieutenant Commander Robert A. Theobald), BUSH (Commander Thurmond A. Smith), and WELLES (Commander Doyle M. Coffee), followed.

Preceding the attack group and carrying MacArthur and Kinkaid was

Rear Admiral Russell S. Berkey's covering force: the cruisers PHOENIX and NASHVILLE screened by destroyers BEALE (Commander Joe B. Cochran), BACHE (Lieutenant Commander Robert C. Morton), DALY (Commander Richard G. Visser), and HUTCHINS (Commander Caleb B. Laning). Besides carrying the gold braid of the Southwest Pacific this force was given the function of supporting the troops by bombardment, and preventing interference with our landings in case the Japs sent some ships or planes down from Truk.

The beach selected by General MacArthur was not on the spacious but presumably heavily mined Seeadler Harbor but the small palm-rimmed Hyane Harbor on the east side of Los Negros. At that, forcing the entrance to Hyane presented a ticklish problem, for the arms of the bay, only 1,700 yards apart, permitted the enemy to lay down a heavy cross fire against landing craft maneuvering through the 50-foot break in the reef. The troops were to land on the southern and southwest part of the bay, the other shores being swampy, at a point only 150 coconut-jungled yards from the Momote airdrome, which was the real objective of the expedition—to hold if possible, to destroy if withdrawal was forced.

H-hour was 0815. At 0723, on the signal "Deploy," the destroyers and cruisers nosed into position for fire support and APDs swung their twelve landing craft outboard on the davits and lowered them into the sea. The coxswains of the LCPRs, which carried 37 men each, faced most of the responsibility for a successful landing. The boats proceeded in waves of four.

Japanese gunners rimmed Hyane Harbor, and their machine guns began spitting at the radically maneuvering LCPRs as they stood through the entrance, turned left and headed toward the beach. Heavier shore batteries opened up on the destroyers and cruisers standing offshore lobbing over the support fire. The Japanese shooting was inaccurate, but it revealed the targets for the ships' guns.

The aerial bombardment that the Fifth Air Force had lined up was washed out by bad weather. Of the forty B-24s scheduled to arrive, three turned up; heavy overcast and low ceiling baffled the rest. The planned missions of four groups of B-25s fared little better; only nine of the bombers appearing and these somewhat behind schedule. The timetable called for a halt in naval gunfire at H-minus-20 minutes (five minutes to eight) to permit low-level strafing and bombing. The ships kept up the shelling for fifteen minutes past schedule, when it was halted to try to fetch the bombers in by visual signal, radio communication having been impossible to achieve. Streaming star shells were fired by the flagship REID as a guide to any B-25s in the area. Shortly afterwards the nine B-25s, in units of three, slipped through the cloud cover and bombed and strafed the beach area.

Nevertheless, the first waves of boats hit the beach only two minutes late. First ashore were soldiers of Troop G commanded by Lieutenant Marvin J. Henshaw, who led his men on a run across the narrow beach to the coconut grove where fallen trees and kunai grass offered cover. The troopers landed unopposed, but when the landing craft tried to return to their destroyers for new loads, heavy cross fire broke loose again. The MAHAN, maneuvering 1,000 yards off the southern beach, silenced the Jap battery on her side of the area with 5-inch guns.

Landlocked Hyane made naval fire support difficult while the landing craft were crossing the bay or on the beach. It was necessary to hold fire to avoid hitting the boats. The situation was further aggravated after the third wave was ashore because communications with the scattering troops broke down, and there was no way of telling where the front lines were. The Japanese took every advantage of the situation, hiding in their dugouts during the shelling and leaping out to man their guns when the ships had to hold their fire.

In three round trips between ships and shore, four of the ferrying landing craft were sunk. Three boat coxswains were dead, and two more were seriously wounded. Without the twelve landing boats, the reconnaissance force could not be evacuated in case things took a turn for the worse on the beach.

The situation looked grim. It *was* grim! Jap batteries that could not be reached from outside the harbor were raising hell with boats and troopers, and with no aerial support to knock them off, it looked as if it was up to the destroyers. Admiral Fechteler told one destroyer to go in. If it went aground, he would take the blame and the consequences. Then, at the crucial moment, fickle Nature decided she had been partial to the Japanese long enough and shifted her allegiance. A blinding rainstorm, in full tropic fury, gushed down upon Hyane and although it short-circuited the radios on the landing boats, it screened the rest of the landing operation with a magic cloak of invisibility.

One hour and thirty-five minutes after the first landing, Momote airdrome was captured—overgrown with weeds and littered with rusting fuselages. Pools of water filled the bomb craters that made the runways look like a close-up of the moon.

"MacArthur," said Admiral Kinkaid, "was extremely impressed by the naval gunfire—maybe too much so. He saw our cruiser knock out a Jap shore battery by putting a salvo under the Jap position, then one over it, and then one right on. From that time on I had to emphasize to MacArthur the things naval gunfire could *not* do.

"I went ashore with the General in a landing boat that afternoon, after the rain let up. We examined the airstrip which was intended to be ready for operation in 24 hours. It took longer. The commanding General was nervous about MacArthur and told him he should go back, for a Jap had been killed a short time before near where we were . . ."

But as usual, General MacArthur scorned personal danger. He would not leave until he had done all that he had come to do.

Among the pleasant duties he had set himself was to decorate the first man to land, Lieutenant Henshaw, with a Distinguished Service Cross. He commended the commander of the reconnaissance force, Brigadier General William C. Chase: "You have all performed marvelously. Hold what you have taken, no matter against what odds. You have your teeth in him now—don't let go."

"Our original intention," Kinkaid comments, "was to land the troops and then take the ships out. But I didn't like the looks of things. When I went ashore with MacArthur, I told Berkey to ease over towards Fechteler's ship and tell him by megaphone I would be happy if he left some DDs there. He did and soon after we got back aboard, I read the dispatch ordering the BUSH and STOCKTON to remain."

It was a good hunch. After the operation the commanding General said that he would have been pushed into the sea had it not been for the destroyers. For, although the cavalrymen had their "teeth in" now, they did not know that they had bitten into a garrison of over 4,000 enemy troops. As it was, they felt lonely enough as they watched the fire-support ships carrying MacArthur and Kinkaid disappear over the horizon, leaving only a couple of destroyers as floating artillery.

Although so far the Japs had offered negligible resistance, General Chase could smell trouble, too. Captured documents indicated that there were many more Japs on the island than had either been anticipated or revealed, and if they decided to attack during the night, the airstrip would be too large to defend. General Chase and Lieutenant Colonel W. E. Lobit, commander of the 2nd Squadron, 5th Cavalry, agreed that before digging in they should pull their lines back to the jungle perimeter east of the airstrip toward the bay. There was no barbed wire to string around the beachhead, so men and weapons had to be closely spaced and every man available had to stand alert in case the Japanese wanted to fight.

They did.

It was a bloody fight. With the steaming darkness, the enemy—equipped with knives, guns, swords, hand grenades, and sake—began infiltrating. The BUSH and STOCKTON gave everything they had, but nothing could prevent the Japs from sneaking in. The fighting was all hand to hand, but when morning came the only Japanese in sight were dead ones.

All the assault troops could do was to hang on, their backs to the coconut grove, the open terrain of the airstrip before them. On the morning of the third day the first reinforcement echelon of LSTs 171, 454, 458, 466, 22, and 202 arrived, screened by destroyers HMAS WARRAMUNGA and USS AMMEN and MULLANY, the minesweepers HAMILTON (Commander Robert R. Sampson) and LONG (Lieutenant Commander Rexford V. Wheeler, Jr.)

The convoy of reinforcements pushed through the entrance of Hyane Harbor at 1000 with their "noses almost on the ground." Many enemy guns were still in shooting condition and the big LSTs had to fight their way in. When the big boats grounded to a stop and their doors swung open, 1,500 combat troops splashed through the shallows and behind them came 534 of the Navy's Construction Battalion, the Seabees. They had come along to rebuild the airbase and make the islands habitable by American standards of shelter and sanitation, but besides the tools of that trade they each carried another useful gadget just in case of interference by the locals—a Browning automatic rifle.

Although the area was still under enemy fire, the 40th Naval Construction Battalion immediately started clearing the airstrip while the ditchdigger, a complicated machine that only one man in the unit had the patience and skill to run, scooped out a trench 300 yards long. (The cavalrymen looked on enviously from the foxholes they had chipped in the coral-cemented earth. This was war de luxe.) The Seabees not immediately engaged in their primary specialty took their positions in the trench, rifles in hand, and turned their one truck-mounted 20mm gun on a grove across the airstrip to rout snipers.

Some profanely wistful remarks from the soldiers about the density of the jungle were overheard by the Seabees. What was it the troopers wanted? Alleys cut through the jungle growth—what-you-may-call-'ems? Fire lanes?

The obliging bluejackets wheeled their snarling, clanking bulldozers toward the enemy-infested boon docks and charged like a tank assault. Down went trees and brush, as the shares of the machines sliced into the enemy cover, and the soldiers had what they wanted—clear lanes of fire for their automatic weapons.

But more orthodox fighting was required of the Seabees, too. One night they stood off a frontal assault after Army troops ran out of ammunition. Some of the enemy, themselves without bullets, used bayonets attached to 5-foot poles like medieval spearmen. Many of the Japanese had bandages tied around their arms at pressure points, to enable them to continue fighting even if only for an extra few minutes, if an artery was severed.

The Presidential Unit Citation, presented to the 40th Battalion by the War Department in the name of the President, said of the Seabees: "They worked by day and fought by night."

Having gained admittance to the Admiralties by the back door, the American forces now decided to kick the front door in, and the minesweepers HAMILTON and LONG were sent around Los Negros island to sweep a path through Seeadler Harbor for the LSTs. Not only were enemy mines bound to be there, but a second crop had been sown by Fifth Air Force bombers.

Seeadler being the better harbor and logically the main objective, the Japs had protected it with coastal guns on the small seaward fringe of islands. These batteries, fit for the biggest game, promptly made it too hot for the minesweepers.

Colonel Yoshio Ezaki, commander of the Admiralty Islands garrison, played a canny game. When the cruisers PHOENIX and NASHVILLE were sent back to the area on D-plus-4-day, to destroy the harbor guns, Ezaki's forces withheld their fire and lay low, giving the cruisers no targets and no means of determining whether their bombardment had been effective.

The indicated strategy was to trap Ezaki into showing his strength.

Commander Alvord J. Greenacre's Desdiv 26 drew the assignment, and the destroyer NICHOLSON (Commander William W. Vanous) was elected to be the bait. Vanous steamed to the entrance of Seeadler Harbor, with orders to draw enemy fire, and, if successful, to destroy the enemy guns thus spotted.

Through unswept waters, silently and cautiously, NICHOLSON started on her first hazardous run past Hauwei Island, 1,500 yards from the beach. No response from the enemy. Reversing course, the destroyer came in closer. Finally binoculars weren't necessary to search the beach for gun emplacements. The range was now under 1,000 yards. One gunner said he could see sand crabs scampering on the beach.

Suddenly a sailor yelled, "There's a gun, sir, and it's looking right at us." The range was 850 yards. The gun, a 5-incher with heavy shield, was knocked out before it could fire a shot. One down, and NICHOLSON hadn't been touched.

On the next run, just 100 yards off the reef, gun flashes were seen 50 yards to the left of the emplacement that had just been knocked out. The gun itself was obscured by heavy jungle but NICHOLSON's 5-inch batteries aimed for the orange muzzle blasts. Two salvos blew away the surrounding foliage, the enemy gun snapping back defiantly.

The last exchange drew blood on both sides. It obliterated the enemy gun just as it loosed its final round, which struck the NICHOLSON in number two handling-room, knocking out one main battery gun. Three of the five men in the handling-room were instantly killed, the other two seriously wounded. As shipmates rushed to the rescue, the two badly wounded sailors were trying to pull their dead comrades from the flames.

The NICHOLSON continued the fight, only there was nothing left to fight against. The two enemy guns were all that had survived the cruisers' blind shooting.

To make certainty doubly sure, PHOENIX and NASHVILLE, accompanied overhead by bombers from the Fifth Air Force, worked the area over once again before the minesweepers were ordered to sweep for a second time, while the troops jumped the narrow strait to Manus to seize the shore side of the harbor. It was jungle fighting all the way, and a battle of wits besides. The Japanese, to whom English is a second language and its idiomatic use frequently perfected by American residence, tapped the troopers' telephone lines, and not only to listen. Once a voice over the wire pleaded, to the accompaniment of much groaning, "For God's sake, lift that mortar fire." The Americans complied.

Again, a Japanese who had thus learned the names of the American platoon leaders, yelled to one lieutenant: "Retreat! The whole regiment's falling back to another line." Obediently, the platoon left its position, losing three men to the well-posted Japanese snipers, and was forced out of the advance for the rest of the night.

The final mopping-up operations saw jungle fighting at its worst. With field telephones rendered unreliable, communications were sent by friendly native runners, by pigeons, and by portable radio. Runners and pigeons proved to be more reliable, although the birds would not fly when rain-soaked. But the Army had a trick of its own, when somebody remembered that there were six Sioux Indians in the cavalry detachment. They became the troopers' communicators forthwith, chattering radio messages in their own tongue without fear of interception. "If it isn't in Sioux it's Jap" was the rule, and the baffled enemy's bluff was called.

Mopping-up operations were concluded on May 12. Patrols and quickly armed natives stalked the estimated 150 surviving Japanese. Days later, many of them were found in their cave retreats, dead of starvation.

In writing to Admiral Nimitz following the close of the Admiralty campaign, Rear Admiral Barbey accurately described the Navy's role in the fighting. He wrote: "The part played by the Navy in this operation was not confined to the actual landing operation, but extended to the continued full co-operation of cruisers, destroyers, PT boats, and amphibious craft in actively supporting the land forces throughout the occupation. Excellent combat service was rendered by the personnel of the 40th Naval Construction Battalion."

General MacArthur's decision to send a small force of 1,026 men and 10 ships against an unknown number [1] of men had proved worth the risks involved. The capture of the Admiralties coupled with the occupation of Emirau by South Pacific forces made the difficult ground assault on Kavieng unnecessary. With Rabaul that enemy stronghold was helpless "inside the bottle." From the Admiralties and Emirau our air attacks could drench western New Guinea, the entire Caroline chain, and threaten enemy sealanes for a wide radius.

But overshadowing all of this, a tremendous fleet anchorage from which to stage an invasion of the Philippines was in American hands.

---

[1] Later estimated to be 4,300 troops.

Chapter Twelve

Koga's Last Stand

I

SURROUNDED BY dangerous reefs which in peaceful years had caused steamers to give them a wide margin, the jungle-covered western Carolines were considered by the Japanese to be out of range of Admiral Mitscher's dreaded and deadly Task Force 58.

That was before March 30, 1944.

A glance at the chart will show that the eastern Carolines flank New Guinea from the north. Before MacArthur could make his scheduled assault on Hollandia in April, the stinger in the Carolines' tail would have to be drawn. Palau was that stinger.

The astonishing thing about the raid on Palau and the other island groups on the westernmost perimeter of Carolines was not so much the conquest of the enemy as it was the conquest of geography. Palau was 1,176 miles west of Truk. It was much farther west than Tokyo itself, and from Palau the Japanese had staged their original assaults on the Philippines and New Guinea.

If it had always been a stronghold, the keystone of Japan's inner defense zone, Palau was now headquarters for the Combined Imperial Fleet, Admiral Mineichi Koga commanding. After the invasion of the Marshalls, it will be recalled, Admiral Koga decided that Truk was no longer either a safe fleet anchorage or a desirable headquarters for himself. So he ordered Admiral Kurita to take the Second Fleet to the fancied security of Palau, and sent Admiral Ozawa's carrier fleet to Singapore.

Koga, having visited Tokyo on February 17 to convince the Imperial Command that the Marianas and the western Carolines were the last possible barrier to defeat, went to Palau aboard his flagship MUSASHI to die there if necessary, in holding the line. The battleship and Admiral Kurita's shrunken fleet of one cruiser and four destroyers nestled in the lagoon, surrounded by some fifty auxiliaries, while the Japanese debated means of making a debacle of any Allied attempt to pierce the stronghold that summer.

Koga's plan was founded on the hope that the Allied forces would have to spend a few months consolidating their phenomenal gains. By that time Ozawa's carriers would be re-equipped with new planes and trained crews and Kurita's surface forces would be augmented for what the Japanese naval leader planned to be the showdown. His fleets would be fighting in familiar waters, close to their bases of supply and reinforcement. The Americans would not only be at the end of their logistical tether, but would be forced to operate in treacherous seas of whose reefs and shoals they knew nothing.

The cogitations of the Japanese were disturbed, and that violently, by MacArthur's B-24s. During March the land-based high-level bombers cost the defenders of Palau, Yap, Truk, and Woleai many a sleepless night, besides costly damage to airfields and stabled aircraft.

When, however, a lone Liberator soared over Palau on March 28 on what was most obviously a photographic mission, Koga's unmerry men wondered acutely whether the visit might not mean more than curiosity about damage done—might not, instead, be an evangel of worse to come, in the shape of a naval raid.

They did not know that Admiral Mitscher knew nothing of the Army's snapshotter, but before noon on the 28th they knew that Mitscher was headed in their direction. For the sake of either confirming or allaying their worst fears, the Japanese sent forth their reconnaissance planes with orders to come back fast if they saw anything, and never mind dying for the Emperor just yet. Time for that later, and plenty of opportunity, no doubt.

The news laid before Commander Chikataka Nakajima, intelligence and planning officer on Koga's staff, was sickening.

The Americans were indeed on their way, and in force such as no aerial scout had seen before. By Jimmu, the ocean was solid with aircraft carriers!

2

Admiral Mitscher knew what ships his adversary had up his kimono sleeve, and Admiral Mitscher was determined that Koga wouldn't even have the sleeve, presently.

So he led his task force along the equator, well south of Truk, on as deceptive a course as could be devised. Mitscher wanted to wipe out Kurita's impoverished little fleet, and he knew that, now that ships were more precious to the Nipponese than prestige, Kurita would run rather than fight.

Task Force 58 was built around 11 carriers: the tireless veteran ENTERPRISE and the BELLEAU WOOD, COWPENS, BUNKER HILL, CABOT, HORNET, MONTEREY, YORKTOWN, LEXINGTON, PRINCETON, and LANGLEY, with customary battleship, cruiser, and destroyer support. For maximum success, everything depended on surprise—but because the Japanese misunderstood the Liberator's visit, the surprise party was spoiled. Koga peeked, and saw the uninvited guests arriving, and saw what they were bringing with them.

The plan was similar to the one executed at Truk: first the carrier fighters would go in at dawn to gain control of the air and clear the way for the dive bombers and torpedo planes. Their targets would be, in order of priority, enemy warships, cargo shipping, aviation facilities and installations, and fleet-servicing facilities. The objective—to immobilize Palau for at least a month, so that MacArthur's Hollandia operation would not be hampered unduly by reinforcements for the enemy. To make the raid effective beyond the time the task force could linger—two days was the limit—the harbor was to be heavily mined. That operation had never before been tried with carrier-based planes, although the Navy had mined Truk with bombers land-based on Eniwetok. Lugging a mine off a carrier's deck was not considered to be a holiday chore, especially if the Japanese fliers and submarines were trying to hamper the experiment.

3

Admiral Koga blinked his small black eyes at his hastily summoned staff while Commander Nakajima tersely interpreted the data collected by the reconnaissance.

"Very well," said the Admiral. "We will fight, of course."

Without subscribing in their hearts to the "of course," everybody nodded impassive agreement.

"This is the way I believe we should meet the enemy . . ."

The conference droned on, as the dead-pan officers bent over charts and tables. Then came an interruption, a most welcome one, an interception to be toasted later with sake or good Kirin beer for the lower echelons.

"The Yankees are retiring. It was all a big bluff!"

No doubt about it. The reports checked from all sources. A bluff, indeed. Banzai!

"In that case," said Koga, turning to Kurita, "it will be well to retire with the fleet northward, and to disperse the merchant shipping." In short, let's get the hell out of here while we have the time.

Palau has only three deep-draft channels from the lagoon to the sea, and all are narrow. The exiting ships had to negotiate them in single column, and that slowly and cautiously. The precious warships and the larger, speedier cargo ships went first.

(Next day, as Task Force 58 once more bore down on Palau, this time not fooling, Admiral Mitscher received a message from Commander J. A. Scott, skipper of the submarine TUNNY. A 19-ship enemy convoy of warships and merchantmen had been seen high-tailing it to the north, too far and too fast to attack. In that flotilla were the MUSASHI, the cruiser, and two of the four destroyers.)

When Admiral Koga heard that the American task force was again headed his way, he knew—as he probably had really believed all the time—that the enemy was not bluffing. Anyhow, the better elements of his combat ships were out of harm's way. Two destroyers remained, for antiaircraft defense and whatever else they could offer. It was too great a risk to send any more cargo ships to sea; if one or more were sunk in the reef's channels, the lagoon would be a dead sea.

On Palau, the jungle comes down to the water's edge, so as many vessels as could be brought close to shore were moored and camouflaged with palm-tops spread on netting. Others were moved into shallow water. They would probably be hit, but they could sink only a few feet and thus remain salvageable.

All that night the Japanese toiled. Before they could see the dawn to which the high-flying American aviators had their backs turned, Task Force 58's harbingers were upon them.

4

The combat results of the Palau strike can be summed up quickly. In two days, with nearly 1,000 U.S. Navy aircraft shuttling between

PLATE XXXIII—On February 22, 1944, a U. S. Navy task force struck a daring blow, within range of land-based planes, at Saipan and Tinian in the Marianas. *Operation Cherry Tree* netted 135 enemy planes and 5 Japanese ships. Six U. S. Navy planes were lost. (*above*) Crew of a U. S. Navy carrier cheer as a Japanese plane meets a blazing finish. (*below*) Almost hidden by a sheet of flame, a Japanese "Betty" sinks off Saipan in the same raid.

PLATE XXXIV—(*top left and right*) Under the protection of the 6-inch guns of the USS BIRMINGHAM (foreground) and other cruisers, the first waves of Marines advance on Saipan, Japanese headquarters in West-Central Pacific. The fighting was bitter and continued for almost a month.

(*left center*) Roaring shoreward at Saipan, Marines hold their fingers aloft with the "V for Victory" sign. The ramp of the LCVP bears the insignia of the Coast Guard, whose crews manned many of the landing craft at Saipan. (*Coast Guard Photo.*)

(*lower left*) Heavy enemy gunfire kept the Marines close to the ground during the first few minutes of the landing at Saipan. This is an actual photograph of the first wave taking cover until additional troops could be landed by amphibious tractors. (*Marine Corps Photo.*)

PLATE XXXV — (*below center*) A hand grenade, tossed by the Marine (center) sails through the air toward a nest of Japanese snipers on Saipan. Another Marine gets set to heave his grenade in the same direction.

(*lower right*) Aftermath of a suicide charge. Wholesale slaughter marked the last desperate Japanese attempt, July 6, to drive the American forces back on Saipan. Of the estimated 1,500 enemy killed in the attack, many fell on the beach.

PLATE XXXVI—A feint on the northwest beaches of Saipan drew the attention of the Japanese from the real objective—the town of Charan-Kanoa. Thus we were able to put ashore 8,000 men in less than 30 minutes. By nightfall this had been swelled to 20,000 men. (*above*) The burning sugar mill at Charan-Kanoa, set afire by naval air and ship bombardment. (*Painting by Official Navy Combat Artist, Lt. Comdr. William F. Draper.*) (*below*) American units unload vital supplies into the ruins of the town of Charan-Kanoa for the troops pushing inland on Saipan. (*Marine Corps Photo.*)

PLATE XXXVII—(*above*) Four men in a jeep. A rare photograph, showing a trio of the Navy-Marine high command. *Left to right:* Admiral Ernest J. King, Commander-in-Chief, U. S. Fleet; an unidentified Marine driver; Lieutenant General Holland M. Smith, Marine commanding general of amphibious assault troops; and Admiral C. W. Nimitz, Commander-in-Chief, U. S. Pacific Fleet and Pacific Ocean Areas. The three were on an inspection tour of Saipan, July 17, 1944. (*Marine Corps Photo.*) (*below*) Three large-caliber enemy guns which never fired. It might have been different, had not the Americans arrived so soon.

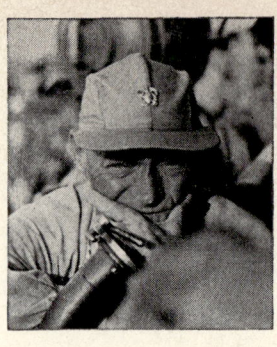

PLATE XXXVIII—(*above*) Close-up of a tactician—Vice Admiral Marc A. Mitscher, of famed Task Force 58.

(*upper left*) Over the barrels of 40-mm. anti-aircraft guns, a Navy Grumman Avenger takes off from a U. S. carrier to bomb enemy strongholds in Saipan.

(*center*) June 19, during the First Battle of the Philippines, is known as the "Marianas Turkey Shoot." One of the 402 Jap planes destroyed that day heads for a fiery doom.

(*lower*) Carrier planes from Task Force 58 trap Ozawa's Japanese fleet, June 20, 1944. Running in circles are a battleship of the KONGO class (center), after receiving hits, and a large carrier (right rear). The wakes of other ships in the enemy fleet also may be seen.

PLATE XXXIX—(*above*) Admiral Richmond K. Turner, who passed the word "land the landing force" at the Marianas.

(*upper right*) Navy pilot Lt. Donald P. ("Rip") Gift, of Marlette, Michigan, after helping to carry out the instructions written on the blackboard behind him—Battle of the Philippine Sea, June 18–19, 1944.

(*center*) An ace's scoreboard. Lt. (jg) Alexander Vraciu, USNR, of Chicago, Ill., signifies he shot down six Japs on one mission.

(*lower*) Maneuvering futilely to avoid Navy carrier-plane bombs, a Japanese carrier of the SHOKAKU class (upper center) wallows in distress. Two carriers and two other ships were sunk, and a dozen other Jap warcraft were damaged during the Battle of the Philippine Sea.

PLATE XL—(*left*) Like scurrying water bugs, amphibious tractors and other landing craft leave streaming white wakes as they hurry back and forth between transports and the Tinian beachhead. This photograph was taken as Marine reinforcements were rushed ashore to capture a Jap airstrip, which lies just out of sight at the top of the picture. (*Marine Corps Photo.*)

(*right*) These Marines had an unexpectedly easy time when no Japs opposed a landing on one of the Tinian beachheads. Fortunately they held their rifles high, for there was action aplenty for them farther inland. (*Marine Corps Photo.*)

(*left*) Battle etchings. Officers and enlisted men aboard the cruiser BIRMINGHAM watch in fascination as Navy Grumman Hellcats etch vapor trails against the blue tropical sky, repelling Jap raiders during the Marianas campaign.

PLATE XLI—(*right*) Target: Guam! A salvo of 14-inch guns lets go at Jap entrenchments spotted on Guam. Much of this preliminary bombardment was done by battleships "destroyed to pieces" by the Japs at Pearl Harbor! This heavy gunfire not only was destructive to actual installations, but served also to demoralize Jap defenders.

(*left*) Some of the leaders of the Guam operation, *left to right:* Maj. Gen. Roy S. Geiger, commanding Third Amphibious Corps; his chief of staff, Col. M. H. Silverthorn; Rear Adm. R. L. Conolly, Amphibious Task Group Commander; Capt. W. E. Moore, chief of staff of the Command Task Force; and Brig. Gen. Pedro del Valle, commanding Third Amphibious Corps Artillery. (*Marine Corps Photo.*)

(*right*) Early on the morning of July 21, 1944, amphibious tanks, in orderly rows, moved unflinchingly toward the Guam shore under a rain of Jap mortar fire. This painting is the basis for a mural dedicated in the messhall of the U. S. Naval Academy, Annapolis, Md., in 1945. (*Painting by Official Navy Combat Artist, Lt. William F. Draper.*)

PLATE XLII (*upper left*) Sniper hunting, deep in the Guam jungle, a Marine pauses for a snack of K rations. The Marine is Paul Smith, former Navy public relations officer and Editor of the San Francisco Chronicle. (*Marine Corps Photo.*)

(*center*) First toll at Guam. Within two hours of the landings, American wounded are being moved from a dressing station to an LVT, which carried them back to transports to receive full medical care. The remains of a Japanese "Val" lies in the background. (*Painting by Official Navy Combat Artist, Lt. William F. Draper.*)

(*lower*) Under fire, every man hits the dirt except one! When Japanese snipers opened up on an advance Guam patrol, Marines on the ground, on amphibious tanks and elsewhere duck for any shelter available—all but one Leatherneck (center background) who sees a better spot, and takes off on the double for it. (*Marine Corps Photo.*)

PLATE XLIII—(*upper right*) Plasma on Guam. At an advanced first-aid station a Marine private lies relaxed, the empty plasma container at his head, as the precious fluid courses through his veins. Later he was removed to a base hospital in Pearl Harbor, where he recovered—thanks to the plasma derived from the blood of some generous person back home.

(*center*) When they wouldn't come out, the Marines blew them out—in pieces! Advancing along Agat Road toward Orote Peninsula, Guam, Marines found many caves and dugouts filled with snipers. If the Japs didn't accept an invitation to surrender, a dynamite charge was set, thereby removing one more enemy obstacle. (*Marine Corps Photo.*)

(*lower*) The price of victory—Marine Corps cemetery No. 1, Guam. The cross in the right foreground marks the grave of Lt. Col. Hector de Zayas, USMC, who, with Col. Carvel Hall, USMC, raised the first United States flag over recaptured Guam. (*Marine Corps Photo.*)

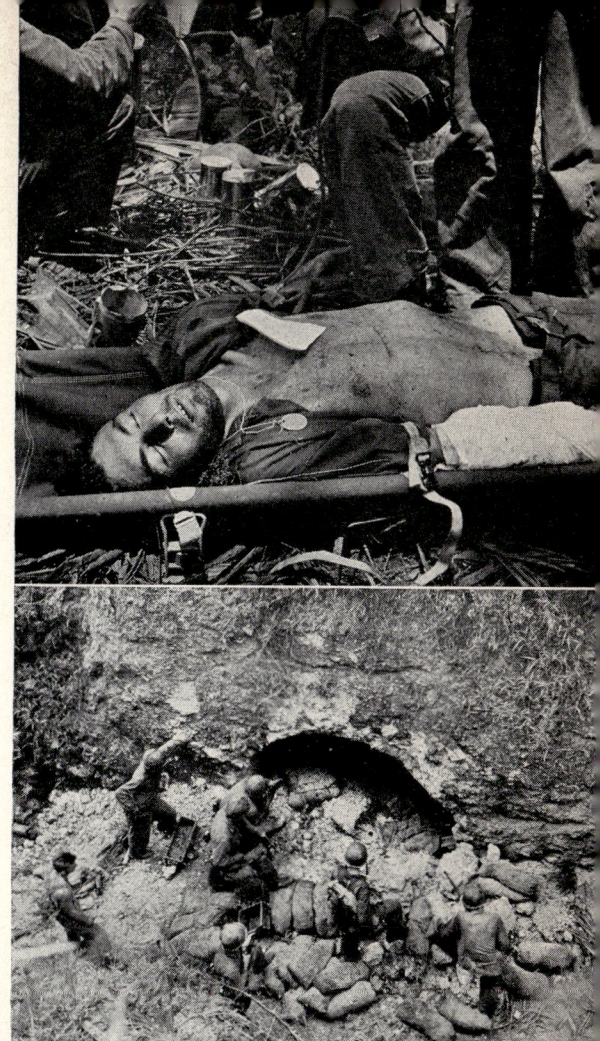

PLATE XLIV—A strange study in contrasts. The upper picture shows Japanese occupation forces on Guam, in 1941, about to execute three prisoners, who kneel before their open graves. In the lower picture, taken September 5, 1945, Japanese prisoners-of-war receive standard American Navy rations, served in Army-type mess kits. American personnel even had to show them how to hold their mess gear.

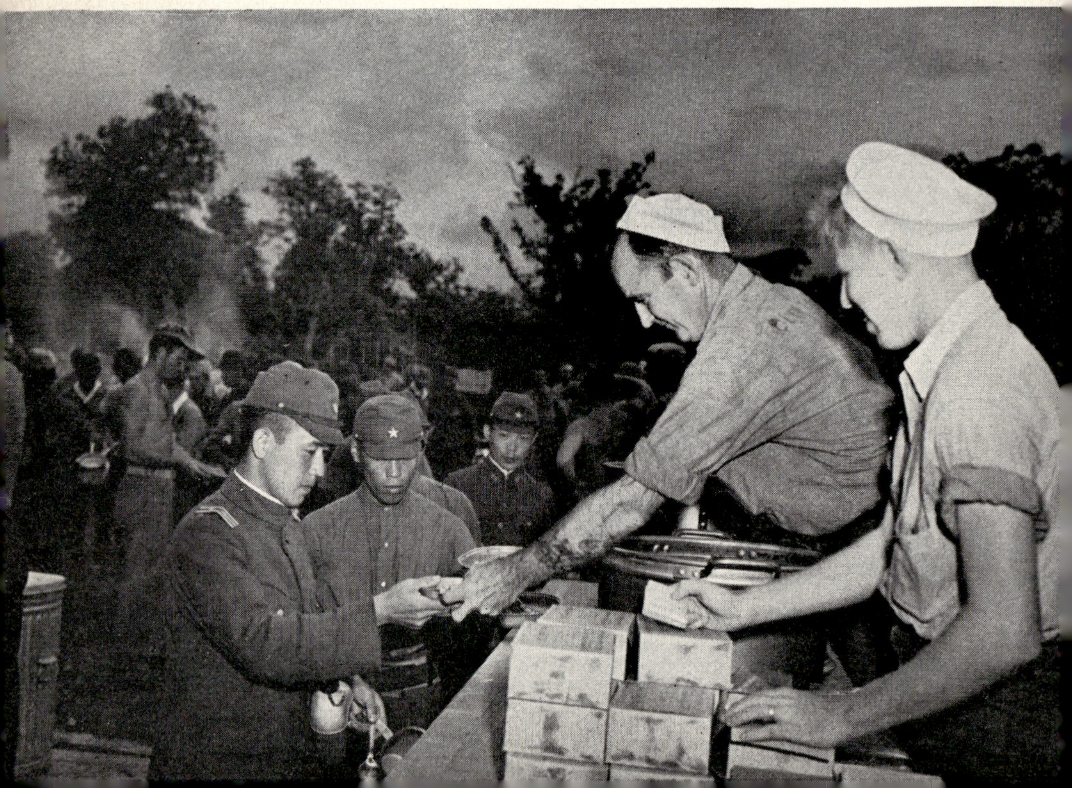

PLATE XLV—(*upper right*) A salute to the teamwork that won many a Japanese stronghold in the Pacific. Holding the sign are Marine Pfc. William A. McCoy (left) of Bisbee, Arizona, and Pfc. Ralph L. Plunkett, of Hammond, Indiana. (*Coast Guard Photo.*)

(*center*) During a respite from war duties, Naval officers and nurses relax at a Marianas beach party. *Left to right, front row:* Lt. (jg) H. Emerick, Baltimore, Md.; Ens. Ann Wareniski, Nanticoke, Pa.; Lt. (jg) G. W. Robinson, Houston, Texas; Ens. Katherine Wilson, Detroit, Mich. *Back row:* Ens. Frances Del Paine, Greensburg, Pa.; and Lt. (jg) L. J. Broussard, Los Angeles, Calif.

(*lower*) Cincpac (Commander in Chief, Pacific Fleet) moved his headquarters only twice during the war—from the sub base at Pearl Harbor, to Makalapa (above Pearl Harbor), and then to Guam. This aerial view shows the nerve center of our Pacific naval forces on Guam, with actual headquarters in the echelon of dark structures at lower left center.

PLATE XLVI—Combined Operations. Almost unnoticed in the excitement of larger mid-Pacific and European campaigns in the spring of 1944 were the operations of a task force of American, French, Dutch, British, Australian and New Zealand warships in the Indian Ocean, under the command of Admiral Lord Louis Mountbatten, Supreme Allied Commander, South East Asia Forces. (*above*) In the harbor of Trincomalee, Ceylon, the USS SARATOGA (left center) joins an Allied fleet poised to attack Japanese installations in the Dutch East Indies. The ship in the foreground is HMS CUMBERLAND, a British cruiser. (*Painting by Official Navy Combat Artist, Lt. Comdr. G. B. Coale.*)

(*left*) More "Combined Operations!" English officers play host to their American comrades-in-arms at a beer party in the wardroom of the British carrier ILLUSTRIOUS at "Trinco." While the serving of drinks is permitted aboard British ships, American vessels of war have been "dry" since World War I.

(*right*) Rendezvous at sea. To deceive any lurking Jap submarines, the task force that struck at Sabang, the Dutch East Indies oil shipping center, split into two parts, rendezvousing near Sumatra just before the raid, April 19, 1944. From the bridge of the "SARA," the British group can be seen coming up over the horizon.

PLATE XLVII—(*upper right*) Lord Louis Mountbatten inspects the USS SARATOGA at Trincomalee. Accompanying him (left) is Captain Page Smith. The Supreme Commander showed keen interest in every department of the famous, battle-scarred American flat-top temporarily under his command.

(*center*) Only American flyer shot down during the Sabang raid was Lt. (jg) D. C. Klahn (right) who was immediately rescued by the submarine HMS TACTICIAN, despite heavy gunfire from the shore. The submarine skipper points to his battle flag, which bears a life-raft symbol, denoting the rescue. Sabang was rendered oilless for a long time.

(*lower*) Seven smokes over Soerabaja. A month after the Sabang raid, the combined task force struck the important Java port of Soerabaja, destroying one of the world's largest oil refineries, an airplane parts factory, a drydock, ten ships in the harbor and twenty-two planes. En route home, a 5,000-ton Jap cargo ship was sunk for good measure.

PLATE XLVIII—(left) Closin[g] one of the last laps to th[e] Philippines, General Ma[c]Arthur, with Admiral Ba[r]bey's 7th Amphibiou[s] Force, struck at Morota[i] near Halmahera, Septem[ber] 15, 1944. From th[e] bridge of his flagship, USS NASHVILLE, General Ma[c]Arthur observes the bom[bardment of the Galela Ba[y] area, Halmahera Islan[d]. Facing him is Capta[in] C. E. Coney, commandi[ng] officer of the cruiser.

(right) Their bag during the "Marianas Turkey Shoot" —a 28,000-ton Japanese carrier! Pilots and crewmen of Air Group 24's torpedo squadron, which put three "fish" into a HAYATAKA class carrier, June 19, 1944. *Left to right, top row:* W. R. Omark, B. C. Tate, W. D. Luton; *middle row:* R. E. Ranes, J. R. Dobbs, P. E. Whiting, E. C. Babcock; *bottom row:* J. E. Prince, G. H. Platz, and J. A. Brookbank. *Inset:* G. P. Brown, missing in action.

(left) Rain and mud prov[ed] the chief obstacles to lan[d]ing forces at Morotai, J[ap] opposition being insigni[fi]cant. U. S. planes op[er]ating from the Seab[ee] built airfield on Moro[tai] soon cut the supply lin[es] to the remaining Japane[se] garrisons in the Molucc[as] thus isolating them.

task force and target, the two enemy destroyers were sunk (one at sea after a dash through the reef); four escort vessels and 20 auxiliaries and merchantmen, totaling 104,000 tons, were destroyed; 150 enemy aircraft were forever eliminated, and shore establishments, fuel stores, barracks, and supply facilities were bombed and burned.

The American losses were 25 airplanes. Of the 44 men downed in the carrier planes, 26 were saved by air-submarine rescue teams.

Palau was left in just exactly the condition MacArthur's plans required it to be, and for that the pioneering aerial minelayers deserve the greater credit.

Aerial minelaying differs radically from ordinary bombing or torpedo dropping, and merits special description. A bomb or torpedo falls free, but a mine has a parachute attached and even a not very strong wind can cancel the drop as effectively as a shell burst. A pilot can put his sights on the target with bombs and torpedoes, but not so with mines, in whose accurate placement timing is all-important. The target is located at the intersection of lines computed from two geographic reference points, or, if only one reference point is known, the planes fly a compass heading from that point. Each plane has to fly an exact course at an exact rate of speed, and drop its burden at the exactly calculated spot with immediate corrections for wind and weather. The whole business is something akin to counting the stitches in a baseball in flight.

The tactical solution at Palau demanded that the channels be mined immediately after the attack commenced, since all the ships that had sufficient steam up would try to escape. Consequently, all the mines were dropped in daylight despite enemy fighters and antiaircraft defenses.

The mining of Palau constituted the largest tactical use of mines ever made by U.S. forces. Torpedo planes from LEXINGTON, BUNKER HILL, and HORNET, escorted by fighters from these carriers, carried out the mission. At this time several outbound Jap ships were in or approaching the channel trying to seek safety in the open sea. Severe strafing turned all but two ships back into the lagoon and those escaping were later sunk. Sixteen mines were laid in the main channel alone, and the Japs were cornered. In all 78 mines were laid although only about 10 per cent of the effort of the carrier raid was used on these missions.

The effective result of the mining was summed up in a report by Commander Nakajima: "For a period of 20 days all channels were closed to navigation; the whole harbor was closed. Since the New Guinea campaign was looking more and more unfavorable, it was decided that Palau was no longer an effective naval base, so it was no longer used as a base. We thought that the southwest channel was not mined. The hospital ship TAKASAGO MARU was directed to come through, and after negotiating almost all that channel it hit a mine; the ship was beached to save from sinking."

Submarines did a lion's share of the rescue work. The TUNNY, mistaken by one of our own pilots for an enemy ship, received a 2,000-pounder close aboard. The explosion of the bomb buckled several plates and caused considerable damage. Submarines when furnished fighter cover proved much more successful. They could surface and locate downed pilots through reports from the planes.

As approaching dusk on the evening of March 30 heralded the close of the Palau mission, Admiral Reeves's Task Group 58.1 pulled away from the main force and by dawn was 100 miles southwest of Yap. Throughout the next day the group flew strikes against Ulithi and Yap, strategically important islands facing the Philippines. The fliers found little to shoot at; a few buildings and small craft were destroyed. On April 1 the group rejoined the task force for a passing strike on Woleai, after which Task Force 58 "headed for the barn." Whatever disappointment its leaders may have felt in the escape of the Japanese warships was well soothed by the knowledge, photographically confirmed, that Palau's usefulness to the Japanese as a major fleet anchorage had been canceled forever.

.5

And what of Koga, sitting in the wreckage of his headquarters, his plans worse ruined than the harbor?

"The line of defense must be held, even to the death."

Even to the death—a phrase that has many meanings to many peoples, but only one to a Samurai. The upstart Occident had a phrase coined only a few centuries back: "Dulce et decorum est pro patria mori." Barbarians! The ecstasy of dying for the Living Sun God, to cement with one's blood the ever-rising structure of the Japanese world-empire, that was something only a son of Nippon could realize.

But it was an ecstasy to be deferred. There remained Operational Plan Zed. Every good naval commander-in-chief has an alternate plan, and Koga had returned from Tokyo with one in his pocket.

"Operational Plan If," it should have been called.

If, by unpredictable chance, the Allies should attack before the Japanese Fleet had been rehabilitated, several courses were open:

If the attack was against the Marianas, Koga would direct the defense from Saipan.

If the attack was in the south, Koga would make his last stand on Davao, the southernmost of the Philippines, land of the Moros.

If Admiral Ozawa's carriers were not ready for the showdown, the Army would concentrate its land-based air at either site.

If—if—if—if. There was no fifth "if." Koga would die before it could confront him—the "if the American attack is successful—."

Admiral Koga put that thought from him. Palau was in ruins, its harbor blocked, its installations shattered. Part of the American task force had steamed westward. There were credible reports that an American transport group had moved in the same direction from the recently lost Admiralties.

It all added up to one thing in Koga's mind. The Allied blow would be launched at the south, with Davao the prime target via western New Guinea. So, he would meet them at Davao.

(Koga's reasoning was excellent, if inadequate. That was exactly the Allied plan, as conceived by MacArthur and accepted by the Joint Chiefs and the Combined Chiefs of Staff. But it was only half the plan.)

The Japanese who was Admiral Nimitz's opposite number put his reasoning into practice. He ordered Ozawa to get to Davao as quickly as he could. He stripped the Marianas of fighter planes, ordering them to Palau in preparation for the defense of the Philippines. He ordered a trio of four-engine Kawanishi flying boats to come down from Saipan and carry him and his staff to Davao.

He got two. Even Koga did not know how hard up his Navy had become under the terrible scourge of American marksmanship.

Well, then, the staff would fly in two Kawanishis instead of three! Koga conferred with his chief of staff, Vice Admiral Fukudome, as they walked down to the lagoon.

Koga would ride in one plane, Fukudome in the other. Koga had all the details of the Davao defense operation in his head; Fukudome had them in his briefcase.

Suddenly the air-raid signal shrieked its too-familiar warning. Men leaped to their guns, or fled to shelter.

"We'll take off," Koga said crisply.

It was not a rash decision, nor one of bravado. The big Kawanishis were certain to be destroyed if they sat there on the lagoon. If they were to fly off, they might as well carry the departing staff—and the chances of successful departure were better than even.

The Commander-in-Chief took off first. His aircraft, like a winged whale, circled the island once, and then, flying low, pointed its blunt nose westward into the night.

It was never seen again. How Meinichi Koga died for the Emperor no one will ever know, for there were no survivors when the sea engulfed his plane.

Before Vice Admiral Fukudome's craft left the water, the copilot ducked into view. He saluted, bowed, sucked in his breath, and reported that the air-raid alert had been a false alarm.

The Admiral uttered the Japanese equivalent of "Let's go." It was nine o'clock and at midnight he had to meet Admiral Koga in Davao.

Aloft, the pilot himself came in to report to the Vice Admiral. Humbly, and with more elaborate wind-sucking, for he had bad news. There was a storm ahead, a bad storm. They could turn back—or try to circle the lightning-slashed turbulence.

"Fly around it!"

The Kawanishi tipped to starboard as the pilot headed north.

With the storm evaded, the aviators apologetically but uncompromisingly declared it best to head for Manila instead of Davao. Davao was out of reach. The hungry motors ate much fuel, especially at high speed. At two in the morning the plane passed over a long, thin island—Cebu.

Cebu? Fukudome doubted it. If it was Cebu, they were nearer Davao than Manila. The pilot was sure it was Cebu. He rubbed his tired eyes and looked again. The Staff Navigation Officer was consulted. He was so groggy from lack of oxygen he could not offer a sound opinion. The moon had just gone down and the surface of the sea was dark. The pilot circled the lights of a small town at the southern part of the island. He would put the plane down near there. He had to do it. The airplane had to be refueled. Then, on to Davao . . .

Perhaps it was the darkness; perhaps it was because the pilot was exhausted after five hours of storm-battling flight. But the plane crashed from 150 feet while coming in for the landing.

6

Fukudome was thrown into the water by the impact. When he came up from where he had sunk, the surface of the sea was a burning mass of gasoline, but he was outside the ring of fire. Ten others escaped the flames—a Captain Yamamoto of the staff, a warrant officer, and eight sailors. All the others, of Koga's staff or the plane's complement, died in the fire.

The shore appeared to be about two and a half miles away—a fairly stiff swim. Fukudome grabbed a floating cushion and started kicking toward land, his briefcase of precious war plans on the improvised raft. The going was difficult. At dawn, after four hours of swimming, Fukudome was still not ashore. He could recognize the chimney of the Asano Cement Plant, so he knew he was in fairly safe territory. But he was alone in it. The younger men had swum on ahead in the darkness.

Then three canoes put out toward him. Fukudome had heard that the Filipinos had largely failed to co-operate with the missionaries of the Greater East Asia Co-Prosperity Sphere, and he was reluctant to accept rescue. He was so close to shore—and also somewhat closer to the end of his strength. He decided to take a chance.

Fukudome was tenderly lifted into a canoe, and taken ashore. The Filipinos seemed delighted to have him in their midst. With gestures and in halting English they made Fukudome understand he was to accompany them. When the road they took led into the mountains, and not to the Asano Cement Plant, Fukudome made objections, but they were swiftly overcome.

"The atmosphere was such," he later said, "that I feared I would be killed either by sword or by gun."

Cebu is one of the most populated islands of the Visayan group. Its fine network of roads and its well-developed interior made guerrilla operations on the island about as easy as they would be in Connecticut, but guerrillas there were, and Fukudome had been captured by them.

(The guerrilla leader was an American mining engineer, Jim Cushing. Another guerrilla leader, Iliff D. Richardson—Ensign, U.S. Naval Reserve; Major, Philippine Guerrilla Army—describes how Cushing got the job: "From the very beginning, after the surrender, Jim became famous. He didn't want the command of Cebu but Southwest Pacific said,

'You've got it!' 'I don't want it,' he said. They said, 'Do you know how to obey orders?' And he said, 'Sure.' ")

At the end of the first day's hike, Fukudome explained to a Filipino, who spoke English better than the others, the circumstances of the plane trip. The guerrilla suddenly became very interested. He had caught a bigger fish in the Visayan Sea than he had known.

"Shortly after that," related Fukudome in an interview after the war, "I was placed on a simple, primitive stretcher, and carried through the mountains for seven days. On the eighth day, which was April 8, I was carried into a fairly good native home where there were two Filipino doctors and nurses to attend to me. I was in a very weakened condition, my wounds having festered, and running a fever of around 104 degrees.

"Then there came to this home a Lieutenant Colonel 'Kooshing,' who said that he had control of Cebu, and that as long as I was in his hands I was safe. This lieutenant colonel, who was a mining engineer, had been to Japan several times, where he said he had many Japanese friends.

"At midnight of the 9th Kooshing came to me suddenly saying that there had arrived some Japanese Army men to recover the party and they were causing trouble to the natives. He promised to release me and my party if I would send word to the Army that they should not kill or injure the natives. Captain Yamamoto, who had been taken prisoner too, sent a message by Kooshing to which the Army apparently agreed, so that I was again placed on a stretcher and taken to Cebu."

The story behind Fukudome's release is not so simple as it appeared to him from his stretcher.

When he heard the report of his natives, Cushing knew immediately he had a big shot—at first he thought it was Koga. He already knew of the flight from Palau—American naval intelligence, having broken the Japanese codes, kept the guerrilla leader well informed of Japanese movements in his area.

Not only did the guerrillas pick up Fukudome, they also picked up his briefcase containing the detailed Davao war plans. Cushing radioed news of his haul to the powerful guerrilla relay station in Mindanao. From there it was beamed down to the Southwest Pacific. MacArthur's headquarters clicked their heels with joy. A submarine on patrol was diverted in to Cebu to pick up the prize prisoner of the war and his papers.

But the Japanese also heard of the capture and threatened to kill every Filipino on the island of Cebu unless Fukudome was given up. It was more than a threat—they started in on the job: "Causing trouble to the natives," as Fukudome euphemistically put it.

So there was only one thing to do—turn Fukudome loose. The Japanese got back their admiral, but not their war plans.

A few nights later a black-hulled submarine rendezvoused off Cebu with a small native canoe, picked up the briefcase and took it sub-haste to another rendezvous—this time with a SOWESPAC seaplane. The briefcase was then quickly flown to the waiting translators at Brisbane.

Chapter Thirteen

Hollandia

I

IN NEW GUINEA the Japanese had been pushed off Huon Peninsula except for an isolated force of about 16,000 in Madang, completely cut off by sea, its airfields destroyed by the constant attacks of the American Fifth Air Force and its Australian colleagues. About 100 miles to the west, at Hansa Bay, the Allied bombers and naval forces had boxed in 35,000 more enemy ground troops. To the northeast the Admiralties' "cork" had been wedged the tighter by occupation of Green and Emirau islands.

But stringing westward from Wewak along the north coast of New Guinea a series of Japanese airfields and garrisons blocked the road to the Philippines. They would have to be captured or neutralized. At Aitape there were 2,000 troops; at Hollandia 9,000 to 12,000; at Wakde, 3,000. An additional 15,000 were scattered over a number of airfields on the Vogelkop Peninsula at the western tip of the giant island.

With the Allied flanks protected by the isolation of Rabaul and capture of the Admiralties, MacArthur and his planners decided that a jump 400 miles up the New Guinea coast to Hollandia would be feasible.

Skipping like giant grasshoppers over a wall, American forces would thus by-pass strongly held Wewak and Madang, leaving the garrisons isolated by the sea on one side, swamp and jungle on another, and Allied forces on the remaining two.

Admiral Nimitz agreed with MacArthur that the operation merited maximum naval surface and air effort. Admiral Kinkaid's Seventh Fleet would be reinforced by units from the Central Pacific and Marc Mitscher's fast carriers would be loaned to furnish direct air support for the landings and to oppose the unlikely interference of enemy naval forces.

Lieutenant General Walter Krueger, boss of the Sixth Army and MacArthur's top planner, was assigned the job of co-ordinating naval, air, and ground operations.

Lieutenant General George C. Kenney promised that the Fifth Air Force would knock out the Hollandia airdromes, even though they were 150 miles beyond fighter protection range.

Kinkaid, MacArthur's naval chief, promised that he and "Uncle Dan" Barbey would haul the men and supplies, if given the ships. They got the ships, all right; 200 of them. It was to be the biggest landing to date for the seasoned Seventh Amphibs.

The show opened with strikes by the Fifth Air Force at Hansa Bay and Wewak. So far the pattern for an invasion had always been set by the big bombers hemstitching the target, and the Japanese thought Wewak certain to be our next objective.

It was April Fool for them—April 1, 1944. Feverishly the enemy started strengthening the defenses of Wewak and Hansa Bay. An armada of Japanese Army planes was flown into Hollandia from the Philippines. Hollandia's airstrips were known to be beyond the effective range of the Fifth Air Force fighters.

But at dawn on April 3 the startled Japanese found hundreds of Liberators droning over the jammed revetments of Hollandia's airfields and, sweeping high and sweeping low, P-38 Lightnings were clearing a path for the bombers and ground-strafing parked planes. Nearly 200 Japanese fighters and bombers were caught sitting on their roost. With one quick stroke, the enemy's 6th Air Division was crippled.

The Japanese, however, interpreted the attack as a raid. Wewak would be the next invasion point, they were sure, and they doggedly concentrated on building up its defenses.

Anxious to help the enemy in his self-deception, Admiral Barbey had meanwhile chosen a deceptive route for the invasion forces. First he steered a northerly course from Vitiaz Strait directly toward the Admiralties, then due west, and finally south to the landing beaches. The route was nearly 200 miles longer than a direct approach, but it provided less chance of early detection. Even if detected, the enemy would have a hard time guessing the convoy's real destination.

D-day was April 22.

Barbey's odd-shaped LCIs, LSTs, LSDs, and transports were toting 79,800 Army personnel, 50,000 tons of bulk stores, and more than 3,000 vehicles. They weren't just moving people. They were moving gas stations, bulldozers and construction equipment, lumberyards and sawmills, bridges, telephone companies, hospitals, tool shops, grocery and dry goods stores, and explosives. They were even bringing along a post office for good measure. It was like picking up a city the size of Galveston, Texas, and planting it in three different locations along the west coast of Florida.

The three invasion points were spotted along the north shore just below the humped shoulder of the dinosaur that New Guinea resembles on the map—at Aitape, Humboldt Bay, and Tanah Merah Bay—bracketing about 120 miles of coast. The big prizes were the three airfields near Lake Sentani, about 12 miles from Humboldt Bay in the direction of Tanah Merah Bay rather than Hollandia itself. These airfields lay behind a spine of coastal hills and to get behind this barrier was the job of the two flanking groups at Tanah Merah and Humboldt. The town of Hollandia, which gave its name to the operation, lies west and inland from Humboldt Bay, in the healthier hill country. It was, and is again, the capital of Dutch New Guinea.

Admiral Barbey himself was to direct the assault on Tanah Merah Bay, the "farthest north" of the march up the mucky coast. The Fifth Air Corps photo reconnaissance showed what appeared to be a broad road angling inland and westward, an important objective in itself and leading to Lord knew what more important enemy installation in the jungled valleys.

The landing was effected in fine style, but against no opposition. Into the jungle plunged the troops, moving cautiously, suspecting a trap, heading tree by tree for the military highway. Sweating, bemired, tree leeches clustered on their necks like bunches of grapes, the invaders reached the highway.

It was a silted river bed, a meandering road of stinking ooze, too thick for fishes to travel, too soft for a grasshopper to leap upon.

Disgustedly the Admiral called off the whole show and took his unit down to Humboldt Bay, where Rear Admiral W. M. Fechteler's attack force was on the job. That night the one serious interference was achieved by the enemy. A lone Japanese plane swooped over the hills to the beach and launched one of the luckiest bombs that ever made a solo flight, for it fell on the overburdened supply dump and wiped out the equivalent of eleven LST loads of food, ammunition, and medical stores.

Again, almost as at Tanah Merah, the Japanese at Humboldt and Aitape offered no organized resistance to the invaders. It was not because they could not; they chose not to. For a solid day the entire area had been plastered from the air by Admiral Mitscher's carrier forces, but the Japanese weren't being fooled! They "had the word"—the Americans were after Wewak.

Fast Carrier Task Force (TF 58) had sortied from Majuro on April 13 and arrived off Humboldt Bay on D-minus-1-day, April 21. Two days before, the task force had been sighted by enemy planes but there had been no attack. According to Admiral Mitscher, "all enemy planes seemed bent on reconnaissance work or escape, whichever was possible." The Japanese scouts were still taking most literally the orders issued at Palau weeks before by Admiral Koga.

Throughout D-minus-1-day the three groups of fast carriers launched bombers, torpedo planes, and fighters for the preinvasion air bombardment of the Hollandia fields and the minor airdromes at Wakde and Sawar, 100 miles west of Hollandia and a possible base for Jap air attack. The preliminary work of the Fifth Air Force had been so thorough that it was difficult for the Navy fliers to find really worth-while targets. They destroyed 67 planes on the ground at Hollandia and 21 at Wakde, and sank a 1,500-ton freighter, three coastal vessels, and numerous small craft. Ground installations, fuel and ammunition dumps, and quantities of stores were set afire.

That night—April 21–22—after the carrier planes withdrew, Rear Admiral L. T. DuBose, Commander Cruiser Division 13, in his flagship SANTA FE (Captain Jerauld Wright) conducted a night bombardment of the airfields at Wakde and Sawar. The accompanying cruisers were BILOXI (Captain Daniel M. McGurl) and MOBILE (Captain C. Julian Wheeler). Destroyer Division 91, commanded by Captain Carl F. Espe, including IZARD, CHARRETTE, CONNER, BELL, and BURNS, rounded out the bombardment group.

Next morning the Japanese were taken completely by surprise at the landing beaches. The nerve-shattering roar of naval gunfire at dawn was the first intimation the Japanese had that the American warships had not gone down to Wewak, as advertised, but were coming ashore at Hollandia and Aitape. There was no time to organize defenses, so the Japanese fled to the hills leaving behind unfired guns, stores of ammunition, all types of clothing, and—final proof of panic—half-eaten meals. Rice was scorching on the stoves where Jap cooks had been interrupted in preparing breakfast.

That the enemy should flee without a fight demonstrated that his morale was broken. These were not the same fighting men who had so bitterly resisted the Marines on Tarawa: their spirit was broken by weeks on short rations, no air support to contest a sky filled with Mitscher's 800 planes, and then the murderous naval bombardment when they were only half awake and confident the worst was over.

Not an American life was lost during the landings. As Admiral Barbey put it, "The amphibious ships ran up on the beaches and simply opened their front doors." General Krueger's Sixth Army went ashore unopposed.

The Hollandia operation was the first time carrier planes had ever been used as close air support in landings by Southwest Pacific forces. To augment the carriers there had been plans to fly land-based support from the Admiralties, Finschhafen and Gusap, but unfavorable weather intercepted all but one squadron. The Navy's fast-moving airfields, which could dodge bad weather or even use it to advantage to mask an approach, had the honors.

At that, the Air Force squadrons would have been supernumeraries at Hollandia. During the entire operation the Navy fighters shot down 13 of the enemy near the carrier force and 20 over the target area, at a cost of 10 planes of their own.

By noon of April 22 all beachheads were firmly secured. At Aitape the airstrips near Tadji were captured by nightfall and the town itself was occupied without opposition on the 24th, the day after Hollandia was captured without pitched battle. The important airdromes of Cyclops, Hollandia, and Sentani were seized on April 26, and by the 30th one strip was in use for MacArthur's fighters. PT bases were quickly built and an air and sea blockade was thrown out to stop any Jap movements along the coast. To the eastward 50,000 Japanese troops were isolated in the jungles and swamps.

CHAPTER FOURTEEN

Truk Revisited

I

HOLLANDIA HAD TURNED out to be easier than was expected. The area was secured at less cost of time and material than had been calculated. Admiral Mitscher's program called for his return to Majuro for relaxation and replenishment before undertaking an important job in the north.

But what to do with the bombs that had not been used at Hollandia? Majuro was a long distance to deadhead them. Besides, Truk was lying almost on the direct route, and Admiral Mitscher just couldn't pass that near without paying his respects. In fact, he decided that it would be just as well to remain overnight and render appropriate honors for two days.

The Admiral summoned his new chief of staff, "31-Knot" Burke, and briefly outlined his plan. Captain Burke called the other members of the small staff together to draw up the details of attack. Within an hour the targets for each task group had been designated; the strike plans had been laid out.

The plans were simple. Carrier planes would level "all shore installations," destroy "all aircraft" based at Truk, and in general finish up the job done on the first visit ten weeks earlier. This time the destroyers and cruisers were not going to play watchdog only; they were to train their guns on Satawan, south of Truk in the Carolines, on the 30th. The battlewagons and screening ships were assigned Ponape, midway between Truk and the Marshalls, for their exercise on the following day.

No one regarded the return to Truk as a push-over. As it turned out, the Japs had anticipated another visit and had sharpened their shooting eye considerably. The Navy pilots ran into the heaviest antiaircraft fire they had ever encountered and it was the exceptional plane that did not need patching after depositing its bombs.

Early in the morning of April 29 five Japanese planes took off for their normal routine search and patrol mission, unaware that the American task force was in the immediate vicinity. At about 4:20 A.M. the Truk radar picked up unidentified planes approaching the island. Shortly after that one of the search planes attempted to make radio contact with its home base, but before the report was received intelligibly communication was lost. None of the five patrol planes returned, but Truk's defenders could guess why.

So, when the first American fighters swept the island thirty minutes later, the forewarned Japanese had a reception committee of 57 intercepting aircraft aloft. Most of them landed unwillingly in the sea. The Commander of the 22nd Air Flotilla, based on Truk, when interviewed after the war, reported that he had 104 planes available for combat when the battle opened. When the American visitors went home he had eleven.

In one meeting, eight LANGLEY fighters, orbiting above the heavy clouds that were again co-operating in the defense of Truk, spotted an estimated 30 Jap Zeros approaching a few hundred feet below. The double quartet attacked at once, and destroyed 21 of the Zeroes in less than half as many minutes, without loss to themselves. In another fight, a LEXINGTON group of 11 Hellcats encountered 18 Japanese planes; final score, Navy 9, Opponents 1.

The Navy fliers lightened the task force's freight load by delivering 748 tons of bombs on Truk in 2,200 sorties, leaving the carriers' magazines empty. They destroyed 423 buildings, varying from barracks and offices to fish canneries and sugar refineries, besides six aircraft hangars and the several ammunition dumps and oil tanks set afire. Forty-four other buildings were badly damaged, and the lagoon cleared of the small cargo vessels that alone occupied it. An enemy submarine was also sunk outside the lagoon by the destroyer MACDONOUGH (Commander John W. Ramey) and to complete the tabulation, there were the 93 aircraft lost by the enemy.

This feat cost 27 planes—20 to AA fire—but 28 of the 46 airmen making water landings were rescued. Each Navy pilot knew before he took off his carrier that Admiral Mitscher would exert every possible effort to get him back safely. Rescue operations were poised as soon as the first fighter squadrons left the decks. The sumbarine TANG was alerted, and all surface ships with float-type planes had their aircraft on the catapults ready to take off for rescue.

2

The TANG's crew welcomed the orders to surface for lifeguard duty. It was a welcome relief from prowling underseas, and a box seat at the war besides.

"As we surfaced," related TANG's skipper, Lieutenant Commander Richard H. O'Kane, "we saw flights of up to fifty planes shuttling between Truk and the southwest. With the possible exception of a sinking Maru, this was the most encouraging sight we had witnessed in the Pacific war."

One of the most exciting fights the submariners witnessed came when Lieutenant (jg) Robert F. Kanze from Fighting 10 (ENTERPRISE) drew as his opponent a Japanese pilot who quickly demonstrated he was a master of his trade. Streaming long arabesques of vapor in the sky, the two aviators pushed their machines through every evolution in the books in as mortal single combat as ever crusader and Turk fought on the lists of the Holy Land. Finally, each pilot swerved out and pointed his bullet-spitting nose at the other in a head-on charge like two stags closing head on for a final thrust. Finally, indeed!

Both planes burst simultaneously into flames, and like well-rehearsed acrobats the two pilots bailed out and floated peacefully toward the lagoon.

Kanze's position after hitting the sea was not nearly as satisfactory as his opponent's. The currents would safely carry both ashore, where enthusiastic welcomes, differing in kind, if not in degree, would be accorded them. Kanze wanted no part of it.

The TANG, fishtailing in every direction, had already picked up three fliers, Lieutenant (jg) Scott Scammell, J. D. Gendron, AMM2/c, and H. B. Gemmell, ARM2/c, when she set out to save Kanze, guided by an airplane.

After navigating to a spot just one mile off the reef of Ollan Island, Commander O'Kane saw that he couldn't get any closer, because Kanze was on the other side of the reef and a Japanese shore battery was overjoyed at having a target at last in the submarine. He had to shoot his way to safety, without time to submerge, leaving Kanze bobbing about all alone.

Alone, but not forgotten.

Early next morning, Lieutenant John J. Dowdle, with his crewman,

R. E. Hill, ARM2/c, was catapulted off the NORTH CAROLINA to search for the downed pilot. They spotted Kanze on the first try, landed in the choppy sea of the lagoon and taxied over to the exhausted flier. Just as Kanze was hauling himself up on the wing, the plane got caught in a cross chop and capsized. So now there were three in the water, Dowdle, Hill, and Kanze, and a lot of water was in them.

The calamity had been witnessed, however, by a Kingfisher seaplane from the NORTH CAROLINA, piloted by Lieutenant (jg) John A. Burns. Burns, fully realizing that with three to rescue the odds were shorter that his plane, too, might suffer the same fate, throttled back his engine for a successful landing on the lagoon. The three men climbed aboard, and Burns, unable to lift the overburdened plane from the choppy sea, taxied on the surface to a rendezvous with the TANG.

The submarine slid up, and the rescued trio was transferred from the seaborne aircraft to its underwater partner. Then Burns soared off in his little Bug, to investigate three life rafts woefully drifting toward the eastern reef of the lagoon. Meanwhile, O'Kane's submarine added five more house guests to his growing list, Commander Alfred R. Matter, Lieutenant Harry Hill, Lieutenant (jg) James G. Cole, J. J. Lenaham, ARM2/c, and H. A. Thompson, AOM2/c. There was standing room only in the submarine, when once again Burns came skittering over the chop, but really loaded this time. Seven men were hanging on her wings and fuselage. Quickly the men jumped to the submarine—Lieutenant Robert S. Nelson, Lieutenant (jg) R. Barber, Ensign C. C. Farrell, and crewmen J. Livingston, R. W. Gruebel, J. Haranek, O. F. Tabrum.

"Got room for a couple more?" Burns hailed O'Kane.

"Keep 'em coming," the submarine skipper shouted back.

So Burns and his rear-seat man, Aubrey J. Gill, accepted the invitation themselves. Their airplane had been so battered by the seas she was unable to fly.

By the end of the day, the TANG had picked up 22 fliers. The submariners were more jubilant than if they had destroyed a whole convoy of Marus.

3

After the February raid on Truk, when 80 per cent of the repair facilities ashore were destroyed and 60 per cent of the fuel tanks damaged, the Japs had moved underground. Caves were blasted out of solid stone and made into barracks and repair shops. All the important installations that had not gone underground were either destroyed or heavily damaged by Mitscher's second raid and the air strength of the islands was completely wiped out.

Truk, as a major base, was finished.

(As a means of keeping fit, Vice Admiral Hara, in charge of the atoll, spent much of his time after the second raid tilling sweet potatoes for his staff. After the war, when he surrendered on Truk, he said: "I have what I call a South Seas Doctor of Potatoes degree. For morale purposes I should strut around giving orders, but one cannot act like a glorious Vice Admiral when he is naked with a potato hook in his hand.")

But if Truk was finished for good, there were other atolls near where the Japanese were believed to be building alternate airbases: Ponape and Satawan.

Rear Admiral Jesse B. Oldendorf, on April 30, and Vice Admiral Willis A. Lee, Jr., on May 1, were detached from the main task force to smother Satawan and Ponape, respectively. Admiral Oldendorf had eight destroyers and nine cruisers in his force [1] to take to Satawan and Admiral Lee had seven battleships [2] supported by destroyers and carrier aircraft for the reduction of Ponape. The bombardments were simply target practice, so far as any element of warfare entered the operations, but any

---

[1] Satawan Bombardment Group was divided into three bombardment sections under Rear Admiral Oldendorf for the firing mission on April 30, 1944:
  Bombardment Section 1, Rear Admiral Oldendorf
    Cruisers: LOUISVILLE, PORTLAND, WICHITA
    Destroyers: BRADFORD, CONNER, IZARD
  Bombardment Section 2, Rear Admiral Leo H. Thebaud
    Cruisers: BALTIMORE, BOSTON, CANBERRA
    Destroyers: BOYD, BROWN, COWELL
  Bombardment Section 3, Captain Samuel R. Shumaker
    Cruisers: NEW ORLEANS, MINNEAPOLIS, SAN FRANCISCO
    Destroyers: CHARRETTE, BURNS

[2] The Ponape Bombardment Group for May 1, 1944 under Vice Admiral Lee was also made up of three separate units:
  Bombardment Unit 1, Rear Admiral Olaf M. Hustvedt
    Battleships: IOWA, NEW JERSEY
    Destroyers: MILLER, OWEN, THE SULLIVANS, STEPHEN POTTER, TINGEY
  Bombardment Unit 2, Rear Admiral Glenn B. Davis
    Battleships: NORTH CAROLINA, INDIANA, MASSACHUSETTS
    Destroyers: CONVERSE, THATCHER, PRICHETT, CASSIN YOUNG
  Bombardment Unit 3, Rear Admiral Edward W. Hanson
    Battleships: SOUTH DAKOTA, ALABAMA
    Destroyers: CHARRETTE, CONNER, BELL, BURNS, IZARD

hope that the Japanese might have held for developing a strong airbase on those islands was obliterated.

Late in May a final carrier raid was made against Marcus and Wake to destroy aircraft, installations, and surface craft which might threaten the northern flank of U.S. supply lines to the Marianas area.

A secondary purpose of the raid was to indoctrinate new air groups which had just reported to the carriers. The Central Pacific was becoming a training school for new naval units presently to be gainfully occupied westward.

The ESSEX, WASP, and SAN JACINTO formed the carrier element of the striking force under tactical command of Rear Admiral A. E. Montgomery.

Montgomery's force sortied from Majuro on May 15, opened the attack with a night fighter sweep on Marcus during the predawn of May 19, and followed up with two days of heavy bombing and strafing. Although 150 tons of bombs were unloaded on Marcus, the strikes did not achieve complete destruction. A moderate amount of damage was done to buildings and installations, two small boats were sunk and one Betty, the only enemy plane seen, was shot down.

Heavy seas interfered with most of the Marcus attacks, but the comparatively meager results were more due to the inexperience of the fledgling air groups and the extremely heavy and accurate antiaircraft fire. Although only four Navy planes were shot down, nearly a quarter of all the carrier aircraft was hit by flak.

On May 23 the Montgomery raiders moved eastward to attack Wake Island, following the same pattern, and achieving about the same results, as the strike on Marcus. One U.S. plane was lost in combat.

But the small strikes on Marcus and Wake caused a bigger commotion in the Empire than Admiral Nimitz had hoped for, or even knew till the war's end. On May 20 the Japanese had commenced "To" Operation, a plan to intercept and annihilate any enemy fleet approaching the homeland. On May 24, when Montgomery's force moved eastward, and it was apparent that there was no further threat to the homeland, "To" Operation was canceled and the hastily assembled ships and aircraft dispersed. The nerves of Nippon's military leaders were on edge. All the evidence pointed to an Allied invasion of the southern Philippines. Here was a bold penetration of north-central waters. What was to be done? Where would the blow fall? With what could it be met?

4

To this period belongs the story of the greatest antisubmarine patrol in naval history. It is the story of the destroyer escort ENGLAND.

On May 18, the ENGLAND (Lieutenant Commander Walton B. Pendleton), together with two other destroyer escorts, RABY (Lieutenant Commander James Scott, II) and GEORGE (Lieutenant Commander Fred W. Just), received orders to sortie from Purvis Bay, form a hunter-killer group, and intercept a Japanese submarine that was reported to be running supplies into beleaguered Buin, the small island off the southeast tip of Bougainville. Commander Hamilton Hains, riding in GEORGE, was in command of the group.

The next afternoon, at a spot some 200 miles east of southern Bougainville, ENGLAND got sound contact with an "underwater object." Cautiously a trial run was made over the spot pointed to by the sensitive sound gear. Hunched over his instruments the sound officer made his evaluation: definitely a submarine.

The ENGLAND turned and came back for an attack on the unseen foe. As the range closed all hands, from skipper to seaman, waited tense and expectant. Then with a great hiss a mass of rocket-shaped projectiles sprang into the air, arced gracefully and plunged into the water in a clustered pattern. These were "hedgehogs," America's secret anti-submarine weapon. Seconds later there was a small underwater explosion but nothing spectacular.

The ENGLAND made four more runs on the fishtailing submarine, and on the fifth run hit the jackpot.

"This explosion was so violent," said Lieutenant Commander John A. Williamson, executive officer, "that it knocked men off their feet throughout the ship. At first we thought we had been torpedoed."

A huge oil slick began to spread out over a two-mile area. Boats were lowered from GEORGE and ENGLAND to pick up evidence of the kill. Papers, boards from decking, pieces of furniture, a mattress, life jackets, and a 75-pound bag of rice were recovered from the debris. There were no bodies but "that is perhaps explained by the fact that numerous large sharks were seen in the explosion area and the crew of the whaleboat had to actually fight them off while recovering wreckage."

The next day further orders were received from Admiral Halsey in the South Pacific: A scouting line of Japanese submarines is being formed between Manus and Truk. Go after 'em!

And the ENGLAND did, with a vengeance.

By May 31 the entire scouting line had been sunk and the ENGLAND, ably aided by her sister ships, had got them all.

The ENGLAND had chalked up the phenomenal score of six submarine killings in less than two weeks!

Commander Charles A. Thornwall, who saw the action from the bridge of the ENGLAND, presented his congratulations: ". . . as a result of your efforts Nip recording angel working overtime checking in Nip submariners in joining Honorable Ancestors."

It was an understatement.

5

The pressure was on Japan from sources other than the fast carriers and the dead-eyed hunter-killers.

As the number of ships in the Japanese Fleet decreased, the number of submarines in the U.S. Pacific Fleet increased. That was not a coincidence. By early 1944 there were sufficient submarines to keep the productive hunting areas continually occupied, with some left over to prowl less crowded lanes. Vice Admiral Lockwood, commanding Submarines Pacific, instituted a system of rotating patrols to give every submarine a fair chance on the shooting range.

Rotating patrols were in effect in six areas. The naming of these hunting grounds, and the method of locating the submarines in them, was not only ingenious but contained something rare in operational orders, a touch of whimsey.

The six areas were designated Hit Parade, Maru Morgue, Speedway, Dunker's Derby, Pentathlon, and Polar Circuit. Each was subdivided into beats appropriately named. Hit Parade, for example, had ten subdivisions, each with a musical-instrument name, five woodwinds and five strings. A submarine ordered to "play the trombone in Hit Parade" knew exactly where and when to patrol. He would not be duplicating the effort of submarines "strumming the banjo" or "tooting the flute."

Hit Parade covered the area east of the Empire itself. Maru Morgue embraced the Ryukyu Islands, where submarines played "coroner," "sleuth," "sheriff," "villain," and "bailiff." Speedway, in the Palau area, was subdivided into sectors named for automobiles, and Dunker's Derby, surrounding the Bonins, had its patrol lanes named for famous race horses. The PLUNGER on her eleventh patrol was riding Whirlaway. On the way to the area, someone discovered that among some of the new phonograph records was one song entitled "Whirlaway." Forthwith it was played and replayed as the sub's theme song, until the less—or maybe the more—musically appreciative among the crew threatened murder.

The Kurile run was the Polar Circuit. Here the submariners rode trains, the Challenger, the Chief, the Flamingo, the Streamliner. Around the Marianas it was Pentathlon, where five sectors were named after famous track stars, such as Nurmi and Eastman.

The Pentathlon was a whole Olympic games in itself. Submarine activity there took three forms: rotating patrol, reconnaissance patrol, and open-sea patrol. While the sea churned to the submarines' screws, the air overhead hummed with Navy PB4Ys and Army B-24s based on Eniwetok. It was the busiest over-and-under-the-ocean area in the Pacific.

On April 23, following the successful landings at Hollandia, New Guinea, Admiral Nimitz had ordered the assault on the Marianas.

That is getting ahead of the story. On April 23 that order was a top secret known to a very few. Meanwhile, down in New Guinea, on which the Japanese had their eyes fastened in a hypnotic stare, there was plenty going on.

Chapter Fifteen

Wakde and Biak

I

PERHAPS it was a burning desire to get to the western tip of New Guinea and get the hell off the malaria-ridden island; perhaps it was because the Japs were now definitely on the run; or perhaps it was just plain momentum. At any rate, three weeks after the mass movement into Hollandia the Seventh Amphibs were on the hop again.

First attraction was the 4,700-foot runway on Wakde Island, 115 miles westward from Hollandia. The Fifth Air Force could make use of that strip.

Captain Albert G. Noble, Admiral Barbey's new chief of staff, was in charge of the assault phase of the operation. His tools for the job were 14 destroyers, 6 destroyer escorts, 2 attack transports, 7 LSTs, 15 LCIs (three fitted with rockets) and 5 SCs (two fitted with rockets).

Big-gun cover was to be furnished by twin cruiser forces well used to working together: Rear Admiral V. A. C. Crutchley's Royal Australian Task Force 74 and Rear Admiral R. S. Berkey, USN, with his Task Force 75. Crutchley's was built around two Australian heavy cruisers, AUSTRALIA and SHROPSHIRE. Accompanying the big fellows were two veteran Australian destroyers, ARUNTA and WARRAMUNGA, plus two American destroyers, AMMEN (Commander Henry Williams, Jr.) and MULLANY (Commander Baron J. Mullaney). Berkey's force consisted of three light cruisers—PHOENIX (Captain Jack H. Duncan), Captain Noble's old ship, NASHVILLE (Captain Charles E. Coney), and BOISE (Captain John S. Roberts)—and six destroyers.[1]

From the big fleet anchorage at Manus—Seeadler Harbor—the twin task forces sortied together and headed west for a sea rendezvous with Captain Noble's attack group.

[1] HUTCHINS (Comdr. Caleb B. Laning), BEALE (Comdr. Joe B. Cochran), BACHE (Lt. Comdr. Robert C. Morton), DALY (Comdr. Richard G. Viser), ABNER READ (Comdr. Thomas B. Hutchins, III), and TRATHEN (Comdr. Fondville L. Tedder).

The Japanese, according to our intelligence reports, had a light cruiser, four destroyers, and eight submarines in the Palau area, and one heavy cruiser, two light cruisers, and four destroyers in the Davao area. They were not expected to send them out against us—yet. But there was no use taking chances.

The worst the naval forces had to contend against—and that was bad enough—came from an unexpected source: floating trees and heavy debris that littered the water as much as 50 miles from the coast, flotsam from some local jungle-twisting hurricane. Several of the destroyers bent their propellers. At night, speed had to be reduced and the officers of the deck had to be particularly alert to keep from colliding with the backwash from the primeval world of New Guinea.

Selected for the initial assault was a black sand beach just west of the small village of Arara on the New Guinea coast about 2½ miles from Wakde Island.

Wakde was the only spot where strong opposition was expected, so it was decided first to get a foothold on the mainland, opposite.

On D-day—May 17, 1944—7,000 men of the 163rd Regimental Combat Team (Brigadier General J. A. Doe) swarmed ashore unopposed at Arara and on Insoemanai Island, adjacent to Wakde. Naval gunfire covered the landing until Army artillery was firmly established ashore, but by noon there was no more need for the cruiser forces. Berkey gathered his ships together and headed for Humboldt Bay. Crutchley with his ships went out on patrol north and east of Wakde.

Next day attention was turned to Wakde—an island small enough to throw a short-tailed bull across. It started at daylight, with planes flying from the newly won airfields at Tanah Merah, Humboldt, and Aitape bombing specified targets. The destroyers WILKES (Commander Frederick Wolsieffer) and ROE (Commander Francis S. Stich) plugged either end of the channel between Wakde and Insoemanai and put down a heavy bombardment. Both vessels eased in close enough to use their 20mm guns. LCIs moved in and covered the beaches with a shattering sheet of rockets.

As the landing boats snubbed into the beach, they were greeted with stiff flanking fire from snipers and light machine guns. The LCIs coming under this fire managed to silence a number of pillboxes. Jap snipers infiltrated our lines to the beachhead and fired on our boats. The enemy opposition was stiffer than expected. This was no Hollandia. For about half an hour it was touch and go whether we could keep our foothold or not. But two days and 110 casualties later the Army had a new airstrip. Meantime Liki and Niroemoar islands were occupied on D-plus-2-day by rifle companies landed from the destroyer transports KILTY (Lieutenant Lloyd G. Benson) and SCHLEY (Lieutenant Commander Edward T. Farley).

Before landing on Wakde it was thought that 500 Japanese garrisoned the island. After the fighting was over, 759 bodies were counted. Only one prisoner was taken.

Hard by, a jungle-hidden Japanese shore battery on the mainland kept popping away at anything afloat that came within range, although its only success was with a gasoline barge that broke its mooring and grounded on a reef 500 yards from the emplacement.

2

The Japs were allowed to stay at Sarmi, even when the Toem-Wakde area was in use as a staging area. They had a particular use, as Navy Captain Richard M. Scruggs related: "Any time that the Army wanted to give new troops just in from the States some actual contact with the enemy, they would just march them to the westward until they met the Japs, and in that way they got some very good jungle training. . . . The Japanese did not bother the Americans unless the Army came close for some tactical exercises, in which case they would co-operate."

3

Wakde was only a way station. The real prize of the offensive westward from Hollandia was the island of Biak.

On May 9, 1944, a conference was held at faraway and almost forgotten Finschhafen. Present was most of the big brass of the Southwest Pacific: MacArthur's chief of staff; Lieutenant General Krueger, boss of the Sixth Army; Vice Admiral Kinkaid, Seventh Fleet commander; Lieutenant General Kenney, Fifth Air Force head; and Rear Admiral Fechteler, acting commander of the Seventh Amphibious Force, while Barbey was Stateside on a flying visit.

Although several airfields had been acquired with the Hollandia occupation, none could be used by the Army's heavy bombers, which had to use the strips near Lae or those in the Admiralties, 440 miles to the eastward. It was of strategic urgency to obtain heavy bomber fields closer to the operating area.

There was nothing suitable short of Biak, a large island in the Schouten group almost at New Guinea's western tip, where the Japanese had three excellent strips along the south coast.

The Japanese were not surprised, but there was not much they could do about it, when on May 26 their search planes spotted a large invasion convoy heading westward from Humboldt Bay.

After the landing at Hollandia the Japanese gambled that the Americans would not invade Palau as had been expected after the occupation of the Admiralties, so the Imperial 23rd Naval Air Flotilla headquarters were moved from Davao in the Philippines to Sorong on the northwestern tip of New Guinea. The 180 planes of this flotilla formed the main Japanese air strength in western New Guinea. It would be more accurate to say "on paper," because bad maintenance and the lack of spare parts left many of them useless.

Consequently, Admiral Fechteler sailed on unmolested.

The sea on the morning of May 27 was flat calm. The partially overcast sky, gray in the early light, promised to break fine and clear. Biak's cliff-humped profile was lost in a haze of smoke and dust, through which fires occasionally flickered brightly, marking the results of the dawn bombardment by destroyers and 52 B-24s.

Now it was time for Major General Horace Fuller's 41st Division to hit the beach.

Eighty-eight Buffaloes and DUKWs, disgorged from six mother LSTs, formed up in waves and headed for the smoke.

The point selected for the invasion of Biak was a place called Bosnik, on the south shore of the island about eight miles east of the nearest landing strip. The usual reefs had to be crossed, and a westerly current was expected at the landing beaches—but not two knots' worth. Some of the Buffaloes drifted considerably to the westward of the designated "Green" Beaches which could have had serious consequences if the enemy counterattacked. Quickly the LCI rocket boats moved in and nailed the defenders to the cliffsides, while the destroyers KALK and REID, on either flank of the landings, turned to with close fire support, the REID sinking six enemy barges.

4

Resistance at the beaches was quickly overcome. The defending Japanese of Colonel Kuzume's 222nd Infantry Regiment, scurried up the cliffs and retired to the northward. Now troop-filled LCIs and cargo-bulging LSTs could push their ramps against the two Jap-built stone jetties that stretched from the coral reef all the way to the beach. By 5:15 that afternoon, when all unloading ceased, 12,000 men had been landed with their heavy equipment of tanks, artillery, bulldozers, and 500 vehicles, and food and fuel for men and machines.

Throughout the day a dozen B-25s (Mitchells) and A-20s (Bostons) roamed the skies over the beaches ready to perform tactical missions assigned them by the Air Support Controller aboard the destroyer SAMPSON, headquartership for the operation. But fighter cover did not arrive until nearly noon because of a weather front between Biak and the fighter strips at Wakde and Hollandia. Remembering the like circumstances at Hollandia's capture, when fighter protection for troops and bombers would not have been available except for Admiral Mitscher's carrier forces, the decision was reached at Biak never to undertake a major amphibious operation again without the Navy's portable airstrips in support.

For all their fine airfield, the Japanese had few planes to contest the invasion. The first showing in any force came at five o'clock in the afternoon when two twin-engined bombers escorted by five fighters shot out over the cliffs. They had waited too long to do Dai Nippon any good. By that time the Army had set up some multiple 50s on the beach, which shot down the first bomber so close to the beach that it almost fell on top of the LSTs of Flotilla 7.

Captain R. M. Scruggs, flotilla commander, saw a fighter coming.

"I got down on the floor of the conn because he was strafing us and the bullets were rattling all around. Something went over my head that sounded like a couple of bumblebees. Those bumblebees were two bombs that fell on the second LST over, but they had been released from such a low altitude that they had not had time to arm. They cracked open when they hit a deck and spilled out their yellow contents." Which mess the ship's sweepers were for once glad to clean up, no doubt.

The second bomber was hit by AA fire over the water. Its pilot must have been an evangel of the Kamikazes to come, for with difficulty he maneuvered his burning airplane to crash into the largest ship present, the destroyer SAMPSON (Commander Thomas M. Fleck), with Admiral Fechteler on board.

"It was a very interesting thing to sit there and see how that deal was coming off," Captain Scruggs now recalls. "The bomber was out of gun range from us, so we were just spectators. The plane came so close to SAMPSON that at first I thought he hit her, but he hit just astern, where a sub-chaser, that had just been alongside the SAMPSON talking to the Admiral, was moving off. When the plane hit, as usual there was a big burst of flame. I thought certain the sub-chaser was gone but in about a minute, it seemed like 15 minutes, she came piling out of the smoke . . ."

The sub-chaser was the SC 699 (Lieutenant (jg) James W. Foristel) one of the breed of hard-riding little (110-ft.) wooden-hull ships that had done such good work as landing control boats in the Southwest Pacific while their brothers bounced in convoy off the Atlantic seaboard.

The plane, after the left wingtip struck the water, catapulted into the port side of the little vessel, burying its engine into the craft's hull near the waterline. A terrific explosion followed; mast-high flames enveloped the SC from bridge to stern. Many of the crew found themselves in the water not knowing whether they had been blasted overboard or whether they had jumped.

Within a matter of minutes the rescue and salvage tug SONOMA (Lieutenant George I. Nelson) was alongside. Lieutenant Commander Philip C. Holt, aboard the SC as control officer, helped man the fire hose as the sub-chaser's crew threw drums of exploding ammunition over the side. The fire was out in fifteen minutes.

Miraculously enough only two men were killed and nine injured. One of the men who died was William Henry Harrison, Radioman 2/c, who remained at his 20mm firing at the bomber until the plane actually crashed into his gun. His body was removed from the harness rigid, still crouched in firing position.

5

"With the progress of the Allied advance along the north coast of New Guinea, it became extremely important for the defense of the Halmaheras and Philippines that we hold Biak Island," said Captain Momochio Shimanouchi, formerly on the staff of the 16th Cruiser Division (KINU and AOBA), in an interview at Tokyo after the war. "When the Allies began the invasion of Biak, although our defense forces put up a very brave and skillful fight, we realized that unless fresh forces were thrown in regularly, it would be impossible in the long run to hold the island. Herein arose the necessity of the KON operation. This operation had as its main objective the transportation to Biak by Navy combat ships and small craft of the No. 2 Amphibious Brigade [about 2,500 troops] which was at that time in Zamboanga [Philippines]. The secondary objective was a naval bombardment of enemy land positions if the situation permitted."

The first attempt at a western New Guinea version of the Toyko Express run was made on the second and third of June. From Davao a force consisting of two cruisers and three destroyers screened by two other cruisers and six destroyers put to sea on the night of June 2 and headed for Biak. The next morning a periscope was sighted. Later two B-24s shadowed the force.

Admiral Soemu Toyoda, who had been made Commander-in-Chief Combined Fleet after the death of Koga, closely followed the movements of the KON force. The submarine and aircraft contacts were reported to him. He heard also that a strong Allied surface force was east of Biak. With the element of surprise gone, Toyoda decided to call off the operation, at least temporarily. Before midnight of June 3 the transport division was ordered to Sorong, the last Japanese stronghold on New Guinea. It has nothing to do with the sarong a certain movie star has popularized.

The force east of Biak, of course, was Admiral Crutchley's task force, combined from TF 74 and TF 75, on the prowl, alert for exactly the type of operation the Japanese had in mind. On June 4 the force was attacked by dive bombers. The NASHVILLE received a near miss that blew a sizable hole in her hull, and had to withdraw for repairs.

On June 7 the Japanese were ready to try again. This time the run was to be attempted with destroyers only: SHIKINAMI, URANAMI, and SHIGURE in the transport division each carrying 200 troops; and HARUSAME, SHIRATSUYU, and SAMIDARE as screening units. The cruisers AOBA and KINU were to stand by in the vicinity of Salawati Island, across from Sorong. For the operation Rear Admiral Shimounouchi shifted his flag from KINU to SHIKINAMI. Air cover was to be given by the 23rd Air Flotilla flying from Sorong.

At midnight the ships left Sorong and headed east toward Biak.

During lunch hour the next day, when sailors usually want a little rest, things were unusually active for the rice-filled Japanese. Twenty B-24s and thirty P-38s crisscrossed the six ships with low-level bombing and strafing runs. The HARUSAME, five minutes after a near miss, sank, hissing, to the bottom. A bomb fragment holed SHIRATSUYU but did not slow her down. The SHIKINAMI and SAMIDARE were messed up a bit topside by strafing. But this time the ships did not turn back. After picking up the survivors of the HARUSAME, they proceeded again toward Biak.

Orders were flashed from Admiral Kinkaid's headquarters to Admiral Crutchley and his impatient commanders that American aircraft had attacked a Japanese force, reported as two cruisers and four destroyers, about 130 miles west of Biak and heading east. Crutchley was given the "go ahead" signal. Soon after, fourteen destroyers—Desron 24 (Captain Kenmore M. McManes): HUTCHINS, DALY, BEALE, BACHE, TRATHEN, ABNER READ, MULLANY, and AMMEN; Desdiv 42 (Commander Albert E. Jarrell): FLETCHER, RADFORD, JENKINS, and LA VALLETTE, the two Australian destroyers ARUNTA and WARRAMUNGA, and three cruisers; the Australian heavy AUSTRALIA, the PHOENIX, wearing Admiral Berkey's flag, and the BOISE—filed out of Humboldt Bay and turned toward the approaching enemy.

First contact with the enemy was made at ten o'clock that night near Korim Bay, on the north coast of Biak, when a reconnaissance plane spotted five Japanese ships 60 miles to west-northwest. The destroyer MULLANY, appropriately captained by Commander Baron J. Mullaney, was sent to the entrance of Korim Bay for a quick look-see, but found nothing. At 10:30 P.M. a Japanese plane illuminated MULLANY with a bright, well-placed flare—but missed by a hundred yards with its bomb.

Radar contact with the enemy at 23,400 yards was made simultaneously 40 minutes before midnight by BOISE and FLETCHER.

Since the Japs were in a good torpedo firing position, Crutchley ordered the task force to turn north to let pass any torpedoes that might have been fired. The Japanese, by their maneuvering, had the task force spotted, and were running west at 32 knots.

After a few minutes' run to the north, Desdiv 42—FLETCHER (Commander Jarrell's ship), RADFORD (Commander Gale E. Griggs), JENKINS (Commander Philip D. Gallery), and LA VALLETTE (Commander Wells Thompson)—headed straight for the fleeing enemy. Desdiv 47—HUTCHINS, DALY, BEALE, BACHE, and TRATHEN—also gave chase. The Japanese fled in two columns, three ships on the left and two on the right.

Thus began a two and a half hours' chase. At twelve minutes after midnight FLETCHER opened up with her bow guns. Since the range was 17,000 yards—8½ miles—the shots were not so much expected to hit as to force the Japanese either to zigzag or to turn to starboard toward Desdiv 47. But they had confidence in the speed of their ships and kept on a bee line, firing their stern guns as they ran.

Admiral Crutchley had given the two destroyer divisions permission to keep after the Japs until 0230, at which time they must break off the chase, and head for rendezvous. It would not be good to have our destroyers beyond fighter coverage with the coming of daylight.

The range had closed to 13,600 yards when the four ships of Desdiv 42 swung out of column and opened up with broadsides for a good seven minutes. The bright flash of the Jap's return fire could be seen through the heavy columns of smoke.

At 0211 the lookouts and bridge personnel aboard FLETCHER saw an explosion on one of the Jap ships in the left column. The destroyer, hoping to catch a cripple, headed over in that direction, but the stricken ship, the SHIRATSUYU, continued to hold her lead. (She had only two weeks more to live, at that.)

With fifteen minutes to go before the 0230 deadline, Captain McManes's Desdiv 47 got within range of the enemy's right column. Tracers from their 5-inch shells disappeared into a thick smoke laid down by the fishtailing enemy destroyers. The Japs returned the fire. All even— no hits on either side.

Captain McManes's Desdiv 47 had whittled the range down to 11,000 yards but the clock had whittled the remaining minutes of chase down to zero.

The show was over. For over two hours both sides, never in view except as radar pips, threw hot shells at each other. Of the thousands of rounds exchanged, only one shell had landed, and that was on an enemy ship.

For the high command the bout was a tactical victory—the enemy reinforcements had not landed. For the engine-room gangs of the American destroyers victory was as good as complete for the first time, American destroyers had gained in a chase with their gazelle-footed Jap counterparts—gained 12,000 yards out of 24,000 in less than three hours. Now, if the Old Man had just allowed them another hour—half an hour even . . . !

6

The Japanese gathered their forces for one more attempt to crash the gate at Biak. Destroyers alone were not adequate for the job. That was obvious. So from the fleet anchorage at Tawi Tawi the Japanese brought out the largest battleships in the world—the monstrous sisters YAMATO and MUSASHI.

On June 11 the units for the new express run were gathered at Batjan in the Halmaheras Islands—YAMATO, MUSASHI, four cruisers, eight destroyers, and smaller supporting units. This force could easily have crushed the Allied naval strength in western New Guinea waters.

But Admiral Crutchley was saved from opposing the 18-inch guns of the Jap battleships with the 8-inch guns of the AUSTRALIA. On June 13 the Japanese canceled the expedition.

The double-crossing Americans were attacking the Marianas, when all the while they had made out to be coming up from the south.

The Japanese ships headed north for a rendezvous with the main fleet. All naval aircraft in New Guinea were ordered to Palau. What happened in New Guinea now was the Japanese Army's problem.

Chapter Sixteen

New Guinea Adieu

1

THE Japanese fought hard at Biak. After the original landings the Army found it tough going. The cliffs that frowned along the coast line made ideal defensive position for the Japanese, especially westward at the point where the cliffs closed nearly to the sea forming an almost impenetrable bottleneck.

Colonel Kuzume had about 10,000 men, a third of whom could be classed as combat troops, to defend the island. The Americans, unable to reach the airstrips by advancing along the coast, cut over the cliffs and drove westward across the flat terrain in an effort to take the airdromes from the rear.

Dominating the airdromes was a 100-yard-long cavern, the West Cave, which the Japanese had made the cornerstone of their defenses. It was a natural fort, and the Nipponese had improved on nature. As long as West Cave was occupied the airstrips were neutralized.

On June 20 the Japanese fell back before a co-ordinated drive of the American forces. Many of them took refuge in the West Cave. Next day the American troops dumped barrels of gasoline into the cave openings and added a squirt of flame-thrower. Then they lowered quantities of TNT into the caverns, and detonated it. That night Colonel Kuzume had had enough. After burning the regimental colors with impressive ceremony, he performed the traditional disembowelment ritual.

2

With the withdrawal of naval air support from New Guinea the Japanese Army could not hope to oppose the sure-footed hops of the Seventh Amphibious Force. Allied submarine and air blockade of the massive island was complete. The last supply ship that the cut-off Japanese saw sailing under their own colors left Manokwari on the Vogelkop Peninsula in May—outward bound. They saw plenty of American supply ships as they skulked along the swampy beaches, hunting snails and dead fish. New Guinea lay like a huge, dumb saurian awaiting the final death blow.

Even so it was amazing that Admiral Fechteler could make two more quick landings and lose only two men. But that's what happened.

The first landing [1] was on Noemfoor Island, 60 miles west of Biak and halfway to the Vogelkop (Dutch for "bird's head") Peninsula—the gasping head of the "dinosaur." Army scouts landed eleven days before D-day from PT boats to reconnoiter the reefs near Kamiri airdrome. They played a desperate game of hide-and-go-seek until they were tagged by the enemy—but they got "home free" with a valuable store of information.

The main obstacle to be overcome on the day of the landing, July 2, was the reef, not the Japs. After the usual covering fire from Admiral Berkey's cruisers and destroyers and air bombardment by Liberators, Mitchells, and Bostons of the Fifth Air Force, no opposition was encountered on the beaches until an hour after the landing. Then a burst of enemy mortar fire scored hits on one truck and one DUKW. One man was killed, the only D-day fatality. (By D-plus-6-day, eight had been killed.) The 2,000 Japs on the island did not have their heart in the fight.

Everything and everybody that went ashore went over the reefs at a spot where the Japs least expected a landing, for it was negotiable only at high tide. The LVTs cleared the rough edge of the reef in good order but the DUKWs had some difficulty getting up on the coral shelf. Several lodged on the coral heads. By fifteen minutes past the leisurely H-hour of eight o'clock the boat control officers, in four PCs, were working like traffic cops during the rush hour. LSTs, DUKWs, LCIs, and some LCMs choked the approach lanes. All except the LSTs, which were unloaded by smaller craft, beached at the reef. From there the 7,000 men of the 158th Infantry Regimental Combat Team (Brigadier General Edwin D. Patrick) walked ashore across the slippery, razor-edged coral through a foot of water, some of them dragging their heavy equipment in rubber boats.

[1] Force was divided into three parts: (1) Main Body (Adm. Fechteler): 15 DDs, 8 LSTs, 14 LCIs (3 rocket and 2 demolition), 8 LCTs, 4 PCs, and the rescue and salvage tug SONOMA; (2) Covering Force (Adm. Berkey): 1 CA, 2 CLs, 10 DDs; (3) LCT–LCM Unit (Lt. Comdr. J. S. Munroe): 3 PCs, 5 LCTs, and 40 LCMs manned by 3rd Engineer Special Brigade.

The same combination of Fechteler[1] and Berkey made the last landing in the New Guinea campaign. This time, on July 30, a reinforced regimental combat team (about 7,500 men under Major General Franklin C. Seibert) of the 6th Infantry Division was put ashore in the Cape Sansapor area of the Vogelkop Peninsula. The whole operation differed little from the practice landings in the Milne Bay area where the division had trained.

There were about 18,000 hungry Japanese troops trapped on Vogelkop, most of them concentrated at Manokwari, Babo, and Sorong. In the Cape Sansapor area the Japs had no defenses. The air and sea bombardment was called off and the Army went ashore unscratched on a perfect beach. Late in the day one man was killed in a minor skirmish.

Secondary landings were made on Middleburg Island and two days later Amsterdam Island was occupied with the object of setting up a PT operating base. That same night PTs went on patrol from there.

At last New Guinea was ours. Memories of the first amateurish landings on Woodlark and Kiriwina, with all its kinks and foul-ups, were hazy in the minds of the seasoned men of the Seventh Amphibs, who now turned out perfect landings with the precision of a cookie cutter.

3

Since those first beginnings, when Admiral Barbey's flag flew from the old repair ship RIGEL, the Seventh Amphibs had advanced more than 1,500 air-miles (many more than that if measured by LST) and had put MacArthur's men ashore in a dozen enemy-held places.

Sometimes these landings had been unopposed by-passes; often they had been contested from land and air. During the campaign most of the supplies for both sides were water-borne, except what little the Japanese sweated pickaback over the narrow, boggy, bug-infested, and sniper-haunted trails. Presently they had no supplies, because no ships brought any in.

In a little over twelve months more than 135,000 enemy troops had been cut off beyond all hope of rescue, and small hope for survival.

In that accomplishment the little PTs had played a part disproportionate to their size and numbers, although by the end of the campaign

[1] Attack Force: 11 DDs, 5 APDs, 8 LSTs, 19 LCIs (3 rocket), 4 PCs, and 1 rescue tug.

they had increased from one tender and six boats to eight tenders and fourteen squadrons of fifteen boats each.

The tiny water-wasps sank ships and blasted barges carrying the food and munitions for lack of which the Japanese lost their will to fight. The PTs prevented reinforcements from landing, and when the helpless, hapless Japanese wanted to pull out, the PTs firmly tied them down to the miry hell that had been Japan's farthest south on the march to conquest.

Now that was over and done with—so far as New Guinea was concerned.

From our new bases on the western extremity of the subcontinent, aircraft could now range over territory that heretofore had been penetrated only by submarines—the Molucca Passage and Macassar Strait.

Close by to the northwest the Halmaheras could be bombed at will.

Beyond them, a mighty ocean leap away, lay the waiting Philippines.

PART FOUR
The Marianas

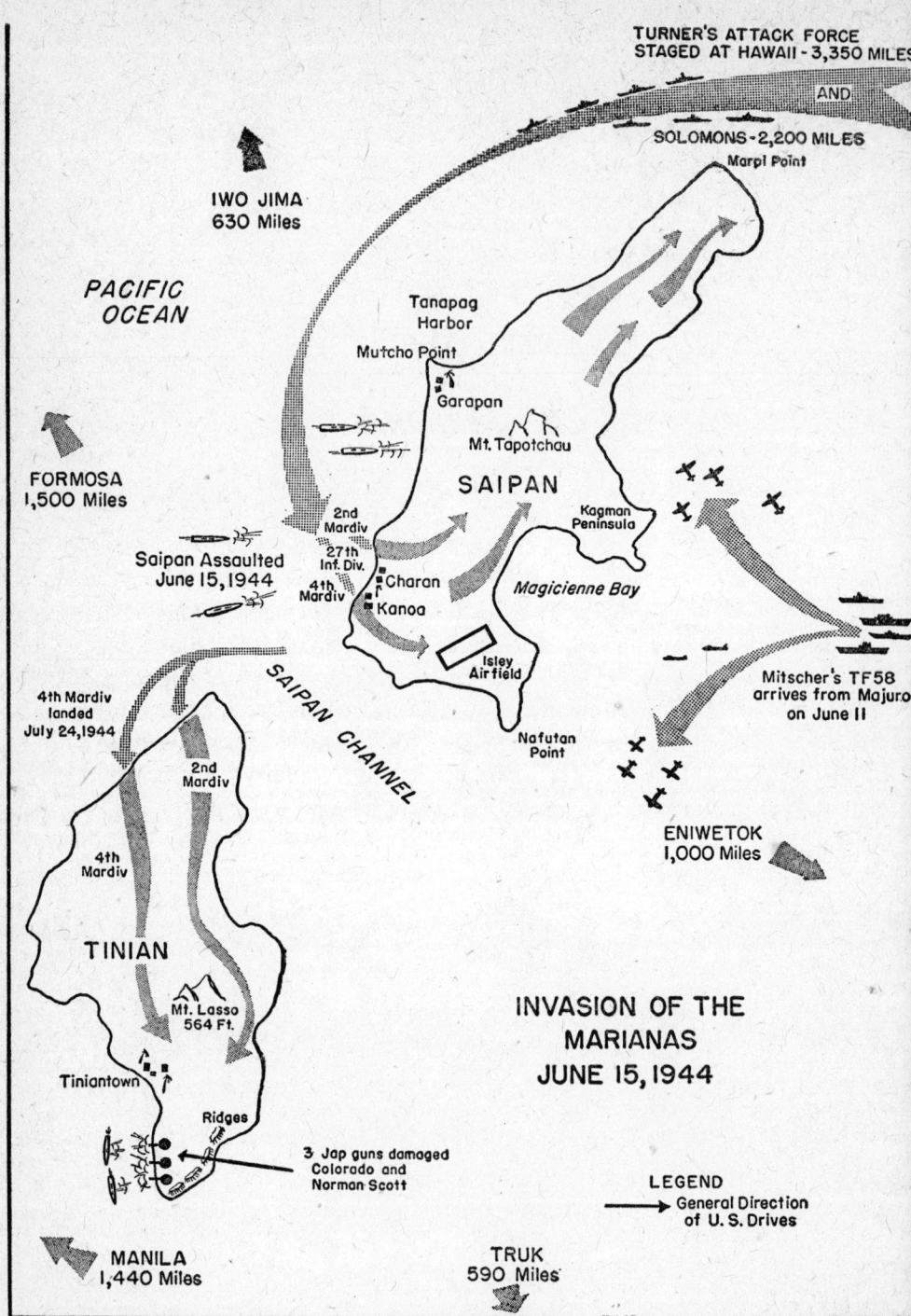
FIGURE II

Chapter Seventeen

"If Big Bombers From Japan..."

I

IN 1521, EN ROUTE to his rendezvous with death in the Philippines, Captain Fernando de Magelhaes—whom we remember as Ferdinand Magellan—brought his battered little squadron of high-pooped ships into the first decent anchorage he had found since rounding Cape Horn.

He had "discovered" Guam. The fact that somebody got there ahead of him, by the evidence of some thousands of sturdy, fine-featured inhabitants, was of no matter. The Guamanians, and their brethren on the smaller islands northward in the chain, were remarkable sailors. They could sail rings around Magellan's clumsy ships in their long, light, outriggered boats with triangular lateen sails. Magellan named the islands "Las Latinas." Although the great navigator christened more geography than any human being before or since, he was singularly unimaginative in his choice of names. Because he had been favored with good weather, he called the world's biggest ocean, which he was the first white man to cross, "the Pacific." Because the unshod natives in the rocky islands at South America's tip had grown splay-footed on the harsh terrain, he called their land "Patagonia," meaning the Big Foot Country.

And so Las Latinas—the lateen-sail islands. But the name did not stick very long. The Spaniards (Magellan was a Portuguese refugee in Spain's employment) went ashore and helped themselves to what they needed. The proud but somewhat awed Guamanians retaliated by stealing their property back, together with what loose gear they could pick up, and so the islands were renamed "Los Ladrones," the Islands of Thieves.

Some years later, when the Spanish throne tried to colonize the islands, the name was again changed to "Las Marianas," in honor of Philip IV's consort, Queen Mariana. The process is still employed by real estate promoters; thus Frog Hollows becomes Colonial Terraces in

America Suburbia. But the name "Ladrones" stayed on the charts till modern times.

Spain held the Marianas for 378 years. When Commodore Dewey sent the tottering Hispanic empire into ruins at Manila Bay, the Marianas were put up for sale. The United States took Guam at a bargain price, but refused—with understandable lack of foresight—to buy Saipan, Tinian, Rota, and the rest of the 400-mile chain. So the Germans, newcomers and greedy ones in the trade of international land-grabbing, bought the rest of the Marianas and lost them to Japan sixteen years later.

In 1941 the Japanese took over Guam. For details, see the first volume of the BATTLE REPORT series. For the strategic importance of the islands, which two Congresses could not recognize, see the map.

In the United States Strategic Bombing Survey (Pacific) the immediate military importance of the Marianas as of June, 1944, is described thus:

> Being directly across our path north to the Japanese Empire and west to the Philippines, Formosa and the coast of China [the Marianas] formed a natural barrier of islands whose location permitted the Japanese to stage land-based aircraft from the Empire and the Philippines to any island of the western Pacific. It was therefore possible for the enemy to concentrate an offensive or defensive air force on selected islands in the chain and to provide shore-based air cover and support for a surface fleet operating within combat range. Conversely the loss of the islands would mean a major break in the inner ring of defense, with advantages to the invading force. . . .

"Conversely" is to say, whatever use the Japanese had for the Marianas, the United States forces could employ as well. If big bombers could fly from Japan to Saipan, for example, they could also fly from Saipan to Japan.

2

The Japanese knew the importance of the Marianas as well as did Admirals King and Nimitz—knew it better because they knew how little they had to interpose against American surface and sky fleets based on the islands. Trouble was, there were so many areas of vital importance to guard!

Admiral Koga died—vanished in thin air, rather—on March 31, convinced that the big Allied push would be against the southern Philippines, via the New Guinea-Solomons-Admiralties route. His reasoning, as has been observed, was good as far as it went. That thrust was not only in the cards, it was in the plans of the Joint Chiefs of Staff. But it was only one of two. Admiral Nimitz was first going to blast a clear path from Hawaii straight across the Pacific, which meant the occupation of the Marianas. He issued his operation plan late in April. Within a fortnight the battle-hardened 2nd, 3rd and 4th Marine Divisions and the 1st Provisional Brigade and the Army's 27th Infantry Division were rehearsing the invasion in the Hawaiian and Solomon Islands.

The Japanese in the Marianas heard rumors and started yelling for help.

On May 3 Admiral Soemu Toyoda was named Commander-in-Chief Imperial Combined Fleet, Koga's old job. He also inherited Koga's old strategy. On the date of his accession he was given a program by the warlords in Tokyo "to concentrate majority of our forces for decisive battle . . . thwart the enemy's plans by smashing his fleet with one blow"—somewhere south of Truk! The date for the annihilation of the United States Navy and Allied forces was "within the last 10 days of May"; Army and Navy were ordered to "expedite operational preparations from the Central Pacific extending to the Southern Philippines and North of Australia Areas."

The Japanese Central Pacific Command in the Marianas called louder for reinforcements, for airplanes, ships, guns, men, barbed wire, cement. Early in May they started their own rehearsals for the anticipated invasion. Every day the 20-odd thousand men in the islands took turns being the barbaric Americans swarming ashore.[1]

The Marianas command received only a quarter of the material it asked for; not that Imperial Headquarters was unwilling to send more, but because the steadily declining industrial output of Japan's blockade-starved factories had to be spread thin from the Bonins to the Halmaheras.

---

[1] With the conquest of the Marshalls and the reduction of Truk, Saipan became the chief Japanese headquarters for the Central Pacific. Four large area headquarters were established there: (1) Headquarters, Central Pacific Fleet, commanded by Vice Adm. Nagumo; (2) Headquarters, Thirty-first Army, commanded by Lt. Gen. Obata; (3) Headquarters, Fifth Base Force, commanded by Rear Adm. Tsutjimura; and (4) Headquarters, Northern Marianas Defense Force, commanded by Lt. Gen. Saito. The main defense forces of Saipan were: 43rd Infantry Division, 47th Independent Mixed Brigade, 3rd Independent Mountain Artillery Regiment, 9th Tank Regiment, 7th Independent Engineer Regiment, 25th Independent AA Regiment, Independent Mortar Battalions, 55th Kiebita (Naval Guard Force), 1st Yokosuka Special Naval Landing Force. The estimated total was 22,700 troops and 7,000 naval personnel.

On June 7 the 118th Regiment arrived—at less than half strength and without weapons. Five of the seven transporting ships had been sunk en route by American submarines. Scarcely a day passed now without the Marianas garrisons being increased by half-clad, unarmed survivors of torpedoed vessels.

The Japanese had one advantage: they knew that the United States forces would inevitably hit Saipan first, and that Saipan could be invaded in force only from the west. Although only slightly more than a third of the heavy coastal and dual-purpose guns were in condition for a first-class shooting war, and fortifications had not progressed much beyond a single line of defense positions due to lack of materials, the Imperial forces had ample ammunition, plenty of food, and morale was high.

3

Morale was as high or higher among the men of the Japanese First Mobile Fleet, lurking cat-like in southern Philippine waters watching the mousehole gap between New Guinea and the western Carolines for the United States naval forces to come sniffing at the Palau cheese. In accordance with the plans for *Operation AGO,* the end of American sea power, the Army's land-based big bombing planes were poised to aid the Imperial Navy rewin the Pacific War in one strike.

The Marianas Command was waiting defensively. The First Fleet was waiting aggressively. On May 16, 1944, it assembled in all its might in the open anchorage of Tawi Tawi, between the Philippines and Borneo. Admiral Ozawa was there with his refurbished carriers, nine of them. There were five battleships, including HARUNA of the charmed life, twelve heavy cruisers, and four divisions of destroyers.

Eleven days later the American occupation of Biak was reported. Commander-in-Chief Toyoda smiled a little grimly. The Anglo-Austral-American opponent was doing the unexpected—Biak instead of Palau. He executed *Operation KON,* with the results recorded a few pages back. And while that plan was miscarrying, Toyoda sent out a search for Task Force 58.

On June 6, the reconnaissance reported. Admiral Mitscher's ships were in Majuro, on the yonder side of the Marshall Islands.

"Keep an eye on them," Toyoda ordered.

THE MARIANAS

The scouts leapfrogged back over the Carolines, the Marshalls, a third of the way across the Pacific at its widest.

Majuro was empty.

Toyoda, Kurita, and Ozawa sipped their thimble-cups of sake and pondered. An attack was imminent—but where?

June 11, and Task Force 58 was found—pounding the Marianas.

"It is the Yankees' new deceptive tactics—maybe. Remember Hollandia? They pounded Wewak to delude the Army into thinking that was the target . . ."

June 13, and all doubts were settled for Toyoda. The Americans were openly preparing to land on Saipan. If that was not enough, American submarines were prowling so thickly around Tawi Tawi that withdrawal into the shelter of the Philippines was urgent.

The Japanese Fleet moved fast, and rendezvoused again in the heart of the Philippine archipelago, off Guimaras Island near Panay. A hurry call was sent out for all elements to belay mouse-baiting and Biak-relieving, and join up quickly.

June 15, and the Marines were piling ashore on Saipan. Iwo Jima and Chichi Jima were under fire.

It was time to fight back, a now-or-never time. At a quarter past five on the afternoon of June 15, Toyoda returned Ozawa's bow—inclining just a hand's breadth less than his subordinate had, as befitted his superior station. The aviator-Admiral chugged to the flagship TAIHO, and the fleet headed into the Visayan Sea "with the burning desire to destroy the powerful enemy and place our Imperial country on safe ground." Admiral Toyoda flew back to Tokyo to await the outcome.

Nearly 20,000 Americans were on Saipan when the Japanese Fleet weighed anchor.[1]

---

[1] The enemy task force, First Mobile Fleet, was under tactical command of Jisaburo Ozawa, Vice Admiral, IJN. Organization of the force was as follows:

Third Fleet, Vice Adm. Ozawa
- First Carrier Division: TAIHO (same size as our Essex type carrier), SHOKAKU, ZUIKAKU
- Second Carrier Division: HIYO, JUNYO, RYUHO
- Third Carrier Division: ZUIHO, CHITOSE, CHIYODA
- Tenth Squadron: Light Cruiser YAHAGI, 4th, 10th, 17th, and 61st Destroyer Divisions

Second Fleet, Vice Adm. Keno Kurita
- First Squadron: Battleships YAMATO, MUSASHI, NAGATO
- Third Squadron: Battleships HARUNA, KONGO

4

Marc Mitscher led his Task Force 58 out of Majuro on Tuesday, June 6, 1944.

Before the week was out, the Central Pacific was streaked with converging columns of ships a hundred miles long, the greatest aggregation of sea power on earth headed for the best-rehearsed battle in history. The boss man afloat of the armada of 644 ships was Admiral Spruance, commander of the Fifth Fleet, in the INDIANAPOLIS, but at the head of the procession was Vice Admiral Mitscher with his fast carrier task force, and the Advance Minesweeping Group under Commander Wayne R. Loud close behind.

Mitscher's job was to clear the air for the invasion, Loud's was to clear the harbors. They had to get to Saipan days ahead of the main body, days ahead of D-day set by Admiral Spruance for June 18.

Aboard the hundreds of ships all hands were briefed in detail on the job to come, down to such details as had the Marines talking to themselves in elementary Japanese.

"Tay-oh-ah-geh-tay-deh-tay-koi. Tay-oh-ah . . ."

It was supposed to be a useful phrase. It was certainly going to be used a lot, but with small results. The translation: "Put up your hands."

Between lessons, there were bridge, poker, cribbage, acey-deucey, and crap games. And, of course, "calking off" catnaps in the shifting shade. One night early in the voyage the bull-horns blared:

"Now hear this. The invasion of France has started. That is all."

The men rolled out of their bunks, to talk it over.

"Thank God."

"Any Marines in that show?"

"I wisht I wuz—"

"Just like those dogfaces to shove off first and grab all the headlines."

They crowded around the mimeographed news bulletins and criticized the operation on the far side of the other ocean, as fighting men

Fourth Squadron:	Heavy Cruisers ATAGO, TAKAO, MAYA, CHOKAI
Fifth Squadron:	Heavy Cruisers MYOKO, HAGURO
Seventh Squadron:	Heavy Cruisers TONE, CHIKUMA, KUMANO, SUZUYA, MOGAMI
Sixth Destroyer Squadron:	Light Cruiser NOSHIRO, 27th, 31st and 32nd Destroyer Divisions
Supply Force:	12 ships

will with the professional wisdom of two years' intimacy with combat, until the ships caught up with their own war.

Admiral Mitscher's orders were to clear the area of air opposition on D-minus-3-day. As he approached the target he came to the conclusion that D-minus-3 might possibly be one day too late. Better to be forehanded than to expose the transports to air and submarine—and possibly surface—attack if they had to wait an extra hour or ten. The Japanese must have a powerful land-based air force on Saipan; if not there, they could assemble one from the tangle of islands.

He sent Admiral Spruance a dispatch requesting permission to launch a 200-plane fighter sweep over Guam, Rota, Tinian, and Saipan on D-minus-4. Admiral Spruance readily acquiesced.

The startled Japanese defenders lost 147 planes to that surprise attack, and thereby lost all aerial initiative. They were all naval planes, and most of them manned by novices, according to a Japanese official document later found in Tokyo, which was rather wistfully entitled "Lessons of the Battle."

On D-minus-3-day the bombers hit Saipan. They had virtually no aerial opposition, but the enemy had ample antiaircraft artillery, and it was not manned by amateurs. Of the eleven TF 58's planes shot down, that of Commander William I. Martin (who had trained that first night radar bomber squadron) was among the first. But Martin lived to tell the story:

"Our specific target was AA installations near a radio station at the Charan-Kanoa airstrip. We could see our target blinking at us when we pushed over in a 55 degree glide attack from about 8,000 feet. Two black bursts appeared almost in the line of our dive when Williams, the radio gunner, called out 'four thousand.' At 3,500 feet, I pushed the electric bomb release and was pulling the emergency manual release when there was a teeth-shattering jolt. The plane seemed to tumble around its lateral axis and I was on my back being forced out against the safety belt. I knew we were crashing. I felt a heat wave go past me and thought the plane was in flames. I groped for the microphone to tell Williams and Hargrove to jump, but couldn't find it.

"At this point involuntary reactions and instinct went to work; on the count of one I released the safety belt; on the count of two I pulled the rip cord; on the count of three I felt the parachute take up the slack in my harness and on the count of three and a half I hit the water. Our speed had been in excess of 300 knots, at which 3,000 feet are covered in less than six seconds. I do not believe that the parachute opened until I was within a few feet of the water. As there had been no abrupt jerk in the parachute, I was not sure it had opened at all and expected it to splatter."

Martin's parachute had been ripped, and it did little to slow his more than half-mile fall. It turned out to be a lucky accident. The enemy sharpshooters thought he was plummeting to certain death and conserved their bullets, but the Commander, glimpsing water under him, remembered the story of the Marine pilot who had straightened his body, pointed his toes, and split the sea with immunity from 2,000 feet.

But Martin fell through 3,000 feet of air and only four feet of water. When he revived from the stunning impact he found himself reciting the 23rd Psalm aloud.

". . . Yea, though I walk through the Valley of the Shadow of Death I will fear no evil, for Thou art with me . . ."

He wiped the water from his eyes.

"I was about 300 yards off the beach in a reef-encircled lagoon near the airstrip, and the Japs could be seen yelling 'Yippee' like our gun crews when they knock down an enemy plane. Our crashed plane was 30 feet upwind from me and burning with intense heat. No other parachutes were in sight. Williams and Hargrove had not got out. Parts of the tail structure were still falling lazily to the water.

"With the rifle fire peppering away, I started a bit of submarine navigation to the seaward edge of the reef, coming up only when my lungs ached for air. Once when I came up, I saw two boats moving toward me. At this point, with invasion obviously imminent, the Japs would have stopped at nothing to extract information from a prisoner. My output of energy was extended to the limit.

"Upon arrival at the reef, the firing had ceased and feeling quite secure I sat on a slope with my nose and eyes above water and peeked over the raft back at the shore. Having studied the charts meticulously in preparation for carrying out the duties of Air Co-ordinator, I recognized the shore line in front of me as the landing beaches. So I took cross bearings for an accurate fix of my position and began taking mental notes. It was hard to keep from thinking of Williams and Hargrove. They had been flying with me since the summer of 1942. They were just like brothers to me."

Mitscher's air-sea rescue team picked Martin up and flew him to Admiral Spruance's flagship, INDIANAPOLIS, where the Commander was given rest and restoratives and then called in to report his unscheduled observations to the boss. The priceless information was dispatched to all ships and Martin was transferred by breeches buoy to the destroyer MACDONOUGH, to be taken back to the ENTERPRISE.

"While en route the MACDONOUGH received a dispatch to bombard the western beach of Saipan, picking targets at discretion," Martin concludes. "I asked the skipper, Commander John W. Ramey, if he would mind shooting at that AA installation that knocked us down. If our bombs didn't knock out those Jap guns, the MACDONOUGH's main battery did, and I wished that Williams and Hargroves might have known of it."

Saipan bristled with antiaircraft weapons. Commander Robert H. Isley, skipper of the veteran Torpedo Squadron 16, lost his life while making a rocket run on a Jap airfield.

The pilots had been critical of the decision to convert the torpedo plane to rockets. They were slow, more designed for stability than for speed and maneuverability, and being rigged for rockets did not improve any of their characteristics. However, "the proof of the pudding . . ."

On D-minus-2-day, after completion of the bombing strikes, "Captain Bob" swallowed his doubts as to the merits of rockets on torpedo planes during the initial assault, climbed his torpedo plane to around 7,000 feet and winged over for the first rocket run on Saipan. His plane was hit while still about 4,000 feet in the air, burst into flames, and exploded at the south edge of the big airfield later named Isely field in honor of a pioneer of rocket-launching torpedo planes.

CHAPTER EIGHTEEN

Saipan: The Marianas' Turkey Shoot

I

SAIPAN WAS THE FIRST objective. Its all-but-Siamese-twin Tinian would be the third. Guam was the second target on the calendar; June 18 the tentative date for its re-entry to the catalogue of United States sovereignty.

Now the atoll war was over. For the first time in the Pacific War, all the forces engaged were battle-tested veterans, and, except for New Guinea, the battleground was for the first time considerably broader than Coney Island.

The incessant thunderblast of Rear Admiral Jesse B. Oldendorf and Rear Admiral Walden L. Ainsworth's two bombardment groups of battleships, cruisers, and destroyers was music to the ears of the incoming transports. To the Japanese it was more horrifying at night, when the close-lying destroyers lobbed over star shells whose parachuted magnesium flares either made the shore gunners see spots before their aching eyes or caused them to pinch their lids tightly shut. Either way, it didn't improve their shooting, which was too accurate for the Americans anyhow. The INDIANAPOLIS (Captain Einar R. Johnson), TENNESSEE (Captain Andrew D. Mayer), BIRMINGHAM (Captain Thomas B. Inglis), and REMEY (Commander Reid P. Fiala), two battleships, a cruiser and a destroyer, had all suffered some damage from near misses, and the destroyer BRAINE was hit by one hidden and hitherto silent shore battery while Commander William W. Fitts's gunners were silencing another. Three men were killed, and fifteen wounded.

Four days of almost incessant man-made thunder and lightning and hail beat upon the Japanese on or behind every possible landing beach, every airstrip, everything and anything that looked like a military installation on Saipan. Guam was repeatedly struck from the air. Tinian and Rota rocked under the impact.

THE MARIANAS

From deep in Philippine waters the submarine REDFIN (Lieutenant Commander Marshall H. Austin) reported the Japanese naval forces concentrated in Tawi Tawi roadstead to be heading north. Were they coming out to fight? Admiral Spruance figured there was a closer menace, some more of Japan's "unsinkable carriers" to the north. From Task Force 58 he split two groups, about half Mitscher's strength, and Rear Admirals Joseph J. ("Jocko") Clark and William K. Harrill steamed northward to smother the Bonin Islands, those "Jimas" soon to become household words in the United States. Forty determined Japanese aircraft sped out to meet the threat. Forty-four fighters from HORNET (Captain William D. Sample) and YORKTOWN (Captain Ralph E. Jennings) rose from the carriers to intercept the unwelcoming committee, and 37 of the enemy found theirs a one-way flight. Lieutenant (jg) "Barney" Barnard, somewhat to his own surprise, shot down two of the enemy in the first half minute of battle, and three more in the remaining 24.5 minutes. Of course, there were fewer to shoot at as the fighting progressed.

The bombers found ample targets in barracks, runways, and parked aircraft in the string of islands that formed the first ladder of descent from Japan itself to the Marianas and thence to the Carolines and what the Nipponese still optimistically called the "North of Australia Area." The temporary ruination of the Bonins, which severed the Marianas' aerial life line to Japan, was accomplished under extremely bad weather conditions. Thirty-foot waves tossed the carriers about like chips in a flood, making take-offs and landings most hazardous, but only one airplane was lost operationally, and six in combat.

In fact, more injuries were suffered to personnel from American gunfire than the enemy's. A twilight attack on Admiral Reeves's ships to the south by Japanese torpedo planes penetrated the task group's screen and made a determined attack on LEXINGTON (Captain Ernest W. Litch) and ENTERPRISE (Captain Cato D. Glover, Jr.), without achieving even a close miss. However, in fighting off the low-flying aircraft from the carrier's heaving decks the gunners, willy-nilly, sprayed other ships in the group, killing two and wounding 58. Seven enemy aircraft were destroyed.

Not only the Marianas and the Bonins shook under the tonnage of explosives poured upon them those mid-June days. In an arc from southwest to southeast, Army and Navy land-based air smashed at every enemy-occupied island in the Caroline-Marshall-Gilbert area. The entire Central Pacific was in an uproar, in a vast triangle of destruction more than

2,000 miles broad at its base and reaching to within 700 miles of Japan itself.

(Give credit where it is due. The Japanese First Mobile Fleet headed straightway for the heart of the trouble.)

2

Very early on the morning of the fourth day the signal was given that the landings would be made on schedule.

On the transports, the shoving, sweating, battle-geared Marines and doughboys paused as the chaplains spoke the prayers for men about to face death—and embrace it.

At 0540 the battleships TENNESSEE and COLORADO (Captain William Granat) gave the Japanese the first intimations where the landings would be made by laying down a shattering barrage. Twelve minutes later Admiral Richmond Kelly Turner passed the word "Land the landing force."

The LVTs and other amphibious craft came up to the line of departure like runners taking their places for a handicap race. Overhead was the unholy racket of shells speeding to the target; there was a pause as the battleships' big guns shifted, and the momentary silence was wiped out as 165 planes sped shoreward from the carriers to make the Marines' landing easier by sweeping the beaches with rockets and bombs.

At 13 minutes past 8:00 A.M., June 15, 1944, Landing Control Officer Commodore P. S. Theiss sent the first wave of troop-laden amphibs toward the beaches.

Another flight of carrier planes darted in as the bombers withdrew. No noise from the newcomers' burden when it was loosed on the Japanese. Instead of using bombs or rockets, these planes smothered the area with man-made fog, blinding the Japanese to the onchugging landing craft and swimming tanks. Destroyers and rocket-hurling LCI(G)s moved in close and poured their destruction through the smoke and fog.

The main landings were directed toward the southwestern slopes. Saipan, a mountainous rugged island of about 72 square miles, was designed by nature to resist invasion. Cliffs face the sea to north, east, and south; a barrier of saw-toothed coral reefs guards the western side. Admiral Hill, commanding the Western Attack Force, had ordered a feint to the northwestern side to divert attention from the main attraction. The

Japanese, who had guessed the landing area correctly (who should know the island's possibilities better than they?), took the bait. An entire enemy regiment was rushed to the spot, arriving too late too fire a shot at the faked assault, and weakening the defenses of the actual target area by 3,000 men.

The plan of attack for the Northern Troops and Landing Force called for the 2nd and 4th Marine Divisions to land abreast, with the 27th Army Division in reserve. The town of Charan-Kanoa on the lower western side of the island was to constitute the center of the landing zone. The initial objective assigned to the 2nd Division was the capture of Mt. Tapotchau, whose 1,554-foot summit dominated the entire island. The 4th was given the primary mission of seizing Aslito airfield.

When the leading wave was about 1,000 yards off the reefs, the enemy showered it by-guess-and-by-gosh with mortar shells and light artillery. Several of the landing craft were hit, but, unless rendered helpless, even the battered ones plunged for the beach. There were not many Japanese on the beaches as the first wave landed at 0843. The reason was soon apparent as the mortar and artillery fire shifted to the shore in an indiscriminate bombardment that groped for the scurrying, dripping troops.

Despite that opposition, in less than thirty minutes a force of 8,000 men was landed; by dusk, 20,000 men had been put ashore.

3

Around the landing force ships and planes strove to build a sheltering screen of explosives. Responsibility for the southern flank's security centered on the TENNESSEE.

The battleship's starboard lookout swallowed his five-stick wad of chewing gum as three plumes of foaming water rose out of the sea a few score yards from the ship. The ship was under fire from next-door Tinian, but before the lookout could yell his warning into the mouthpiece on his chest, the next salvo crashed aboard, killing eight men. One of the 5-inch guns of TENNESSEE's secondary battery was wrecked. Debris and shrapnel struck down twenty-six men with wounds of varying severity.

In the battleship's wardroom a mess attendant, not detailed to duty with guns or stretchers, was sitting out the battle in an attitude assumed to convince himself, more than anybody else, of his complete nonchalance.

The attitude was a posture unpardonable even under the circumstances, for he had taken off his shoes and propped his feet on a table.

Into the wardroom, checking on casualties, came Commander Lawrence E. Ruff, Batdiv 2's communications officer. He found the mess attendant, feet still table-propped, contemplating with slack-jawed horror the appalling fact he now had only nine toes. A stray shell fragment had performed the operation.

"Ah will never again no more prop mah feet on no wardroom table," he swore to the startled Commander.

4

At sunset most of the fleet stood out to sea, dispersing in avoidance of night submarine or aerial torpedo attack. Shortly after dusk a group of enemy planes slanted down over the smaller vessels left behind. Observers say that at no time during the Pacific War were more shots exchanged with less damage—in fact, no damage at all.

Aboard the main force, Admiral Turner recommended to Admiral Spruance that his tentatively scheduled June 18 invasion of Guam be confirmed. So far the schedule for Saipan had been exactly maintained at less than estimated cost.

The men who are called "brass hats" between wars hunched sleepless over the plans for the next day, and the Guam invasion day after that, while the men off watch hit the sack.

Commander Ruff blinked his red-rimmed eyes at the slip of paper that was to alter all these plans aborning. On the INDIANAPOLIS Admiral Spruance leaned back in his chair as the identical message was laid before him by his communicators.

It was a dispatch from the submarine FLYING FISH (Lieutenant Commander Robert D. Risser) prowling the Philippine coast.

"Sighted large enemy task force heading east from San Bernardino Strait. Speed 20 knots."

Admiral Spruance scratched his head and smiled quizzically, while his staff waited for the word.

"Well, it looks like they're coming," he said. "But I don't think they'll get here before the 17th."

So now all plans were shoved aside and work begun on a new set. To the Bonin-battering Clark and Harrill went instructions to do a one-day job on the Jimas. They were to rejoin the task force not where they had left it, but at a new rendezvous—on a collision course with the Japanese Fleet.

"When it became definite that the Japs were going to fight I went over to talk to Admiral Turner," Admiral Spruance recalls. "I always liked to do business by word of mouth.

"'Can you retire all of your ships to the eastward?' I asked Turner.

"'No,' he said. 'I've got to stay close to the troops and keep unloading their cargo. I must also keep fire support ships in the area.'

"I knew before I asked what Turner would say, but I just wanted to hear him say it. I knew that we barely had a toe hold on Saipan and that much of our amphibious force would be needed for support."

Spruance told Turner to stay on the job, then. But he would have to turn over to Mitscher all cruisers and destroyers he could spare, and the cargo ships and transports not discharging supplies to the troops were to put the Marianas between themselves and the brewing battle.

"We will load INDIANAPOLIS with ammunition, join Mitscher, and keep the Japs off these islands."

That was Spruance's promise to Turner. He kept it.

All approaches to the Marianas had been carefully studied to determine whether or not Toyoda could outflank our forces from north or south. All possibilities of approach and diversion were discussed, plotted, and counterbalanced. The amphibious forces and troops ashore were protected against a Japanese sideswipe by the force of old battleships, "jeep" carriers, and some cruisers and destroyers, while the rest of the Fifth tried to intercept the main enemy fleet.

The warships of the invasion forces regrouped to face the new situation. There was still no active proof that it would develop into a collision between fleets.

On June 16, from his flagship LEXINGTON, Admiral Mitscher communicated to his ships this estimate of the situation:

"Believe Japanese will approach from a southerly direction under their shore-based air cover close to Yap and Ulithi to attempt to operate in the vicinity of Guam. However, they may come from the west. Our searchers must cover both possibilities." The Admiral was taking no chances.

Early the next day Admiral Spruance, commander of the Fifth Fleet, issued his major battle plan dispatch. "Our air will first knock out enemy carriers as operating carriers, then will attack enemy battleships and cruisers to slow or disable them. Task Group 58.7 will destroy enemy fleet either by fleet action if enemy elects to fight or by sinking slowed or crippled ships if enemy retreats. Action against the retreating enemy must be pushed vigorously by all hands to ensure complete destruction of his fleet. Destroyers running short of fuel may be returned to Saipan if necessary for refueling."

He answered Mitscher's inquiry as to night movements by saying, "Desire you proceed at your discretion, selecting dispositions and movements best calculated to meet the enemy under most advantageous condition. I shall issue general directives when necessary and leave details to you and Admiral Lee."

Spruance still wasn't positive that the Japs were coming out to fight. However, Lee's battleships were taken out of the carrier task groups and moved ahead toward the enemy to maximum communication distance. The maneuver lessened close defense of the carriers against aircraft, but Spruance was hopeful of an opportunity to engage the enemy surface force with his superior battle line.

Back in Pearl Harbor, Admiral Nimitz, studying the approaching conflict as it was plotted on the CINCPAC charts, sent Spruance this postscript:

"You and the officers and men under your command have the confidence of the naval service and the country. We count on you to make the victory decisive."

As CINCPAC's message was distributed to the forces on the fighting line, more than one received it with comment to the effect of "sure, sure, but we've got to catch them first."

Admiral Spruance had calculated that the Japanese could not arrive in the Marianas zone until the 17th. The Americans had gone out to meet them, and here June 17 was nearly over, and still no clue to the enemy fleet's position.

Close to midnight, the answer was supplied by another submarine, CAVALLA (Commander Herman J. Kossler). The Japanese were on their way, all right.

Commander Kossler, an expert naval tactician, estimated that he had sighted, Marianas-bound, at least seven big ships on his night-seeing radar. One very large pip looked like a carrier and the others looked big enough to be battleships and cruisers.

"The biggest ship passed about seven miles from us," relates the skipper. "Although the night was black, the ship looked mighty big and I was in position to attack. I was afraid that I wouldn't get a second chance."

But where there had been seven ships there now appeared to be ten, then fifteen, then twenty, and Commander Kossler knew he had more important duties to perform than sinking one of them—first half of a ship-for-ship swap anyhow, because CAVALLA could never expect to survive. Of greatest importance was warning the fleet in the Marianas and giving Spruance the enemy's numbers, course, and speed.

The last entry in the log for the day was made close to midnight: "Got enemy contact report off. Chasing task force at four-engine speed. Hoping for a second chance."

He was to get it, indeed.

5

Admiral Mitscher headed for battle with just half his strength. Clark and Harrill, with the other half, were speeding from the Bonins to join up. Task Group 58.2 (Rear Admiral A. E. Montgomery) was designated as battle-line carriers. Twelve miles to the north was Task Group 58.3 (Rear Admiral J. W. Reeves, Jr.). Both groups were reinforced by cruisers and destroyers from Turner's amphibious forces.

At half past seven on the morning of June 18 the CAVALLA's second bulletin was welcomely received. The submarine was still hanging on to the Japanese enemy fleet and it was most certainly and determinedly steaming directly toward Saipan. A night surface engagement seemed to be in the making.

Admiral Mitscher sent the following message to Task Force 58: "Do you desire night engagement. It may be we can make air contact late this afternoon and attack tonight. Otherwise we should retire to the eastward tonight. Task Groups 58.1 and 58.4 [Clark and Harrill] are joining us at noon today."

The reply came from Admiral Lee: "Do not believe we should seek night engagement. Would press pursuit of damaged or fleeing enemy, however, at any time."

Spruance agreed with Lee. The latter's reasoning was that the Americans had the superior force and should avoid a night action, which would offset some of that advantage to the lighter, more compact enemy fleet. Spruance, concerned with—and responsible for—the entire operation, of which fighting off a Japanese fleet was only a part, was not so much indisposed to engage the enemy at night as he was disinclined to go westward to meet Ozawa. That would put too much open sea between TF 58 and the business in hand around Saipan, leaving the amphibious operation vulnerable to a Japanese sneak attack behind Spruance's back.

Mitscher was all for pushing westward and meeting the enemy head on, especially when Ozawa's approach was located by the Fleet's radio direction finders between 350 and 400 miles west-southwest, at 10:45 P.M. (2245).

"I studied Mitscher's message for some time," Admiral Spruance relates. "I thought of why we had been sent out to this area. We were sent to take Saipan. Our duty was to protect that amphibious force. If we couldn't do that, then we had no business being there.

"My feeling was that, if we were doing something so important that we were attracting the enemy to us, we could afford to let him come— and take care of him when he arrived."

So Spruance vetoed Mitscher's plan, and Task Force 58 remained on its sentry beat, only 40 miles west of the Marianas and 400 miles from the oncoming enemy, the direction of whose approach could only be estimated. At 1:15 A.M. (0115) on the morning of the 19th a Marine search plane out of Saipan spotted a fleet of about forty ships 470 miles west, precious news for Spruance could he have received it; some quirk in radio obliterated the message between the plane and the ships.

Reinforced 58, dispersed for greatest possible range of interception, rode out the night.

But if Spruance was playing his cards close to the vest, Ozawa had been slipped an ace from the bottom of the deck by Old Dame Nature. The wind was from the east, at 14 knots.

That meant the Japanese carriers could launch their planes while heading in toward the Marianas. As at Midway, the American flat-tops would have to turn their backs to the enemy to steam into the wind and provide their aircraft with the head-on lift of air currents.

Nor was Ozawa anybody's fool. His plan, and his appraisal of the Americans', contained many elements of victory. He reasoned from the evidence that Spruance would stick close to the lee of the islands, so the Japanese Admiral decided to launch his planes from 350 miles distant, shuttling them between his carriers and Guam, refueling and rearming at both ends and plastering the Americans coming and going. The plan was not original with Ozawa. He was copying the tactics employed by the ENTERPRISE flyers at Guadalcanal,[1] in destroying a Japanese reinforcement convoy.

Ozawa's trouble was, he did not have the likes of the Big E's aviators.

6

The story of the "Marianas' Turkey Shoot" has been often related, and in infinite detail.

First blood was drawn before sunrise on June 19 when fighter pilots from the MONTEREY (Captain Stuart H. Ingersoll) intercepted two Japanese "Judys" (dive bombers) and shot one down. The skirmish was significant only to the extent that it alerted all the American forces present to the imminence of climax.

Sunrise came to Guam at 0542—not quite a quarter before 6:00 A.M.—on June 19, 1944. Only about a third of the sky was cloud-masked: "ceiling and visibility unlimited."

Carrier planes flying CAP over Guam reported tremendous activity on the island's airstrips, and suggested the advisability of deterrents being applied. The Japanese were hauling gassed-up, armed planes out of the tree-covered revetments and pushing them off into the air with all the determination of bees swarming.

Reinforcements were rushed to the Combat Air Patrol, and, between 8:00 and 9:30 A.M., shot down 35 of the enemy without greatly interrupting the Japanese' dogged labors to get every plane into the air at no matter what cost.

At 9:50 enemy aircraft were detected around the full circle of the radar screen, with a large group orbiting about 130 miles to the westward of Mitscher's flagship at 24,000 feet. The Admiral himself bellowed the call to battle over the TBS, the old circus war cry "Hey, Rube!" the signal to the fighters over Guam to rally around for a more important fight.

Aboard every carrier the squawk-box gobbled its "Pilots—man-your-planes" and from the American ships rose their own swarms, stingers poised. Bombers and torpedo planes, however, flew east. Their job was

[1] See BATTLE REPORT, Vol. III, Chap. 9.

to make the airstrips on Guam worthless to the shuttling Japanese, while the fighters headed for the enemy concentrations.

Commander Ernest M. Snowden, who commanded the planes on the LEXINGTON, gives a vivid picture of what the approaching Japs looked like:

"We could see vapor trails of planes coming in with tiny black specks at the head. It was just like the sky writing we all used to see before the war. The sky was a white overcast and for some reason the planes were making vapor trails at much lower altitude than usual. That made it easier for our boys to find the incoming Japs. The air was so clear that you could see planes tangling in the sky. Then a flamer would go down. We would hope it was a Jap and from the radio chatter we could hear from the pilots, it seemed that the Japs were getting the worst end of it.

"One of our newest members of the fighter squadron, Ensign Bradford Hagie, shot down three Japs while ferrying from one carrier to another. Hagie had joined up with us as a replacement. On the day before he had motor trouble and couldn't land aboard LEXINGTON because we were launching planes. A carrier cannot land and launch planes at the same time. Hagie put down an another carrier about 3,000 yards away. He slept on her the night of the 18th. Next morning he took off about 9:30 to fly back to his carrier. While he was in the air, he heard the report about the Japs coming in and decided to go for a little hunt. He shot down three, which isn't bad for a 3,000-yard ferry flight."

There were seventy enemy planes in the group taken under attack. They were met 60 miles from the guardian battleships, and by the time the distance had been cut by 10 miles, half the attacking force was under water. It was three of the survivors that Hagie eliminated.

Another pilot who gloomily found his airplane apparently out of the fight was Lieutenant Alexander Vraciu, who had gained considerable combat experience flying wing for Butch O'Hare. His engine refused to make adequate speed, and the fighter control ordered him and five similarly indisposed aircraft to drop out and keep clear of trouble. But trouble headed for Vraciu and his five "orphan" brothers—a formation of Japanese planes, which, the cripples were told, were coming in fast in their direction.

Vraciu, his windscreen smeared with oil, shot off at a tangent from the monotonous circle he had been flying, followed by the five other fighters. One of the sextet could not keep up, falling behind and below.

THE MARIANAS

In his mind Vraciu was going over every little detail of his lessons in how to win an air battle. Butch O'Hare had told him never to shoot at a Jap until he was close enough to do some good. Always go after the bombers first. Always aim at the spot where the wing joins the fuselage because that is where he burns most easily. Ignore enemy fire—they probably couldn't hit you anyway. Mix it up as long as you have the advantage, but the moment you lose the advantage, break away. Never dive on an enemy plane until you have looked over your shoulder. Good, practical teaching this—if one had a good, practicable airplane.

"Tallyho, three enemy planes," radioed Vraciu to base. "Keep looking," came the reply, "those aren't the dangerous ones."

Vraciu took another look, including down, and there they were, 2,000 feet below and on the port side. He grabbed his radio: "Tallyho—at least thirty rats [Jap fighters]."

He dove in for the kill, and then saw the enemy formation was composed of bombers. That meant fighters in the vicinity, and, remembering O'Hare's Rule No. 6 he craned his neck for a look over his shoulder and saw seven planes speeding toward him! Before he could gulp back the lump in his throat he recognized them as Hellcats. Now they were twelve against the thirty and five seconds later Vraciu's exultant voice crackled through the radio phones "Scratch one Judy." He banked and came back at the other bombers all guns blazing. Two more tumbled wing-over-wing into the ocean.

"After we had been on them a few minutes they began to separate like a bunch of disorderly cattle," Vraciu relates. "Every time one of the Japs would try to lead a string of others out of formation the Hellcat pilots turned into 'cowboys' and herded them back into the group. If they had been able to separate we wouldn't have been able to shoot down as many as we did."

Another pass and two more "meat balls" were dunked. A third run, and Vraciu's bullets tore into the Judy's bomb. The Japanese plane blew up in the air, sending Vraciu's whirling like a feather, but still his voice came clear:

"Splash number six. There's one more ahead. He's diving on a BB. I don't think he will make it."

"He" didn't. The battleship's AA took care of that one.

Eight minutes later, with only 360 rounds of ammunition expended but most of his gasoline gone, Lieutenant Vraciu climbed out of his cockpit the Navy's ace, the six bombers bringing up his score to 18 planes shot out of the air and 21 destroyed on ground. For the day's high score, however, he was tied by Ensign Wilbur B. ("Spider") Well, of Fighting 2, who also had brought down six.

The 70-plane attack was completely broken up by the time it reached Admiral Lee's surface force. A few penetrated the aerial and AA interception, one planting a direct bomb hit on the SOUTH DAKOTA (Captain Ralph S. Riggs) which killed 27 men and injured 23. A second plane scored a near miss on the MINNEAPOLIS (Captain Harry B. Slocum) and a third, in a suicide dive, hit the INDIANA (Captain Thomas J. Keliher, Jr.) on the waterline. In another morning attack four dive bombers broke through to score near misses on BUNKER HILL (Captain Thomas P. Jeter) and WASP (Captain Clifton A. F. Sprague). Three were killed and 85 were wounded aboard the two carriers.

7

There was small compensation for Admiral Ozawa in those comparatively trifling dents in his adversary's armor. It is doubtful if he ever heard of them until days later, for the Japanese commandant's heart and mind had room for little but woe that morning.

As Ozawa stood exultingly on the bridge of his flagship TAIHO, watching his planes take off for the first strike at the American Fleet, his attention was diverted by the radical movements of three destroyers. He guessed immediately that they had spotted an enemy submarine. The guess was doubly confirmed. First, an orderly stumbled up with the transmitted warning of a torpedo attack.

Next, the TAIHO blew up under his feet.

The United States submarine ALBACORE, leader of the pack of five patrolling the Marianas area, had stuck her periscope into the sunlight at 0750 to reveal a submariner's vision of perfection. An aircraft carrier and a cruiser filled Commander James W. Blanchard's lens. They were now 6½ miles away and coming closer, other and unidentifiable ships following along. And as he watched, another and larger carrier came into view, until he could see nothing but ship overlapping ship, carriers and cruisers and destroyers.

The carriers were launching their planes. Blanchard knew what that meant. He closed the range between himself and the larger carrier to 2½ miles and let fly six torpedoes, whose wake spelled out on the water "Sayonara, TAIHO!"

The ALBACORE [1] dove, deep and very fast. Presently the familiar but never monotonous business started of sitting out the depth charges.

Three and a half minutes after the dive, the submarine was lifted, twisted and tossed by an explosion that made everybody aboard wonder what new kind of depth charge the Japanese had invented.

It was, however, TAIHO's boisterous departure from the naval registries. Blanchard's torpedoes had ripped into the carrier's tanks, flooding her decks with oil and gasoline. In a minute the pride of Japan's naval air forces had become a giant bomb with a lighted fuse. In ninety minutes, nothing remained but an oil slick and bits of garbage.

Ozawa was able to abandon the hulk, transferring to the carrier ZUIKAKU on a destroyer. He had barely been escorted to his new quarters by officers alternately congratulating him on his escape and bemoaning the tragedy that had necessitated it, when he was given the message that ZUIKAKU's sister ship, SHOKAKU, had been torpedoed!

(Ozawa's biggest concern for his airplanes then was not how they might be faring against the American Fleet, but how he could service them all on their shuttling operation with two of his best filling stations eliminated. He need not have worried. Not many of the Imperial First Fleet's planes completed a round trip that day.)

The SHOKAKU's destruction was the pay-off for Commander Kossler's patient stalking of the Japanese all the way from the Philippine straits. His submarine CAVALLA was on her first war patrol, and already she had paid back the cost of construction by warning Admiral Spruance that Ozawa had come out of hiding and was out to dispute the control of the Pacific.

All the early hours of June 19 Kossler had peered through his periscope at an empty disk of sea. At 10:39 he spotted some airplanes circling just above the eastern horizon, and he charged in their direction. As he tells it: "A few moments later we sighted masts of ships directly under the planes. They were on our starboard bow. I ordered an approach course and went to battle stations. At 10:52 I raised periscope and the

---

[1] Four months later ALBACORE failed to return from her fifth patrol. Under command of Lieutenant Commander Richard C. Lake she had accounted on two patrols for the Japanese cruiser TENRYU and destroyer OSHIO. Under Commander Blanchard her torpedoes cost the Japanese the destroyer SAZANAMI and carrier TAIHO.

picture was too good to be true. I could see four ships, a large juicy carrier, with two cruisers ahead on the port bow and a destroyer about 1,000 yards on their starboard beam. I could see that the destroyer on the cruisers' starboard beam might give me trouble, but the problem was developing so fast that I had to concentrate on the carrier and take my chances with the destroyer. I let the executive officer, Lieutenant Thomas B. Denegre, Jr. and the gunnery officer, Lieutenant (jg) Arthur G. Rand, Jr., take a quick look at the target for identification purposes. The target mounted a large bedspring type radar mast and was flying a large Japanese ensign that reflected in the morning sunlight. When sighted and during the attack she was in the act of taking on small single engine low winged planes. At the time of attack only one plane was seen left in the air and the forward part of the flight deck was jammed with planes. My guess is at least thirty or more.

"We fired a spread of six torpedoes. By the time the fifth torpedo was leaving the tubes, we already had nosed down for a deep dive. We had already heard three torpedoes hit the side of the carrier. For three hours the Jap destroyers worked us over. We were badly shaken by 56 of the 106 charges they dropped on us. About 2:00 P.M. and for three minutes thereafter, four terrific explosions were heard in the direction of the carrier. These were not depth charges or bombs, as their rumbling continued for many seconds."

They were SHOKAKU's death agonies.

8

Commander James H. Hean, tactical officer on Admiral Mitscher's staff, sums it up with "The Hellcats won the battle." [1]

Of 545 Japanese planes launched against Mitscher's task force, 19 were shot down by ships' antiaircraft and 366 were destroyed in the air by the American fighter pilots. Seventeen more were destroyed on Guam's rapidly deteriorating airstrips by the carriers' bombers and strafing fighters, for a total of 402. The American losses were 26 aircraft and 24 flying personnel, and 30 men killed on the bombed ships.

[1] The men in them, of course, had a lot to do with the success. So did superior American radar, the submarines both strategically and tactically, and the co-ordination between ships and air provided by fighter director teams. The Japanese carrier pilots, schooled in Singapore waters, were largely inexperienced, some with less than a hundred hours of combat flight training.

No, Ozawa did not have to worry where to refuel TAIHO and SHOKAKU's orphan aircraft. By nightfall his only worry was to withdraw what he had left of the Emperor's naval forces.

He knew that, sure as fate, the American Fleet would be down on his trail like hounds after a wounded stag.

Chapter Nineteen

"When the Lights Go On Again..."

1

ADMIRAL OZAWA did not know when he was licked. That was a characteristic of the Japanese in almost any area of conflict, but it was especially true of their naval forces, who did not suffer the corrosion of morale that starvation and isolation inflicted on the jungle-trapped troops.

So his withdrawal from the extravagantly fruitless attack on the American invasion forces was not a retreat. His plan was to move northwestward about 250 miles, rendezvous with his supply train, and ask Admiral Toyoda to fly out to his depleted carrier force every plane and pilot that could be sent.

Only 102 aircraft had survived the "turkey shoot"—44 fighters, 17 fighter bombers, 11 torpedo bombers, and 30 others.

But Ozawa, knowing the Americans' strength, knowing they would pursue him, was planning to reopen the engagement on June 22, if he could hide for 48 hours to replenish his strength.

Hide he could not. The air was full of American chatter, and no cryptographer was needed to translate the radio conversations into evidence that Spruance's hounds were on his trail. Ozawa ordered his supply ships to run northwest to Okinawa, while he led his fighting ships to the protective Philippine seas. In midafternoon a Japanese aerial scout discovered two United States carriers with escorts, and at 5:00 P.M. Ozawa risked his remaining torpedo planes in an attack which failed to come off because the ships had changed course and could not be found.

An hour later, though, the Americans found Ozawa.

2

Less Task Group 58.4 (ESSEX, COWPENS, and LANGLEY), which was sent back to cover the Marianas, Task Force 58 started in pursuit of the Japanese Fleet as soon as evidence of its retirement was confirmed.

PLATE XLIX—The same day that MacArthur invaded Morotai, September 15, 1944, a huge amphibious force hit Peleliu and Angaur, in the southern Palaus. Whereas Morotai was easy, Peleliu was hot, despite plenty of air and ship softening-up bombardment. (*above*) At dawn an F6F takes off from its carrier for the Palaus. (*Painting by Official Navy Combat Artist, Lt. William F. Draper.*)

(*below*) The rockets' red glare pierces the Stygian overcast of Peleliu beaches on the morning of D-day, preceding the landing of the 1st Marine Division. Waters around the Palau Islands were heavily mined and pillboxes fronted all the beaches.

PLATE L—The operation against the Western Carolines involved every major command in the Central and Western Pacific and employed 800 ships, 1,600 airplanes, and 19,600 Army, 28,400 Marine and 202,000 Navy personnel.

(*upper left*) Close by a landing party of Coast Guard and Marine invaders, a Japanese shell sends up a cloud of ugly black smoke over the beachhead of Angaur Island, the Palaus. (*Coast Guard Photo.*)

(*center*) At the moment the photographer clicked his shutter at the Marine (left) advancing upon the enemy lines at Angaur, an American shell scored a direct hit on a nearby Japanese ammunition dump. The island rocked, debris filled the air, but the cameraman got a remarkable picture. (*Coast Guard Photo.*)

(*lower*) Preceding the landing at Peleliu, Navy underwater demolition teams, braving enemy fire and sharks, planted more than 8,000 pounds of explosives among the mine fields surrounding the island. The massive wall of water marks the successful conclusion of another hazardous mission by the Navy's "warriors in trunks." (See also PLATE LVI.)

PLATE LI—Possibly the fiercest fighting on Peleliu centered around a rocky height, 1,000 yards north of the airfield, called "Bloody Nose Ridge" (the favorite Marine nickname for any costly objective). For six days it held out against pulverizing attacks by Marine and Army troops, ship gunfire and aerial bombing.

(*upper right*) Behind the thin shelter of a riddled tree, a Marine with a bazooka blasts a Japanese sniper nest in a cave, Peleliu. (*Marine Corps Photo.*)

(*center*) This photograph reveals clearly the rugged character of "Bloody Nose Ridge," which had to be captured in order to free the airport from sniper fire. The 1st Marine Division suffered 60 per cent casualties on Peleliu, before being relieved by the 7th Marines and the 321st Infantry Regiment of the Army. (*Marine Corps Photo.*)

(*lower*) The Amtrac, or amphibious tank, which brought them ashore, serves as a Marine shelter in repelling an enemy counterattack on the Peleliu beachhead. (*Marine Corps Photo.*)

PLATE LII—The next six pictures were taken from truly remarkable film "Fury in the Pacific," made under fire by combat cameramen of the Army, Navy, Marines, Coast Guard and Air Force during the Palau landings. Perhaps nowhere before or since, has the lens portrayed so vividly the stark grimness of modern warfare, the nightmare fatigue and the haphazard finger of Death, choosing whom it will.

(*left*) Two Army soldiers, approaching the beach at Angaur, listen to Japanese missiles and ponder the deadly gantlet they soon must run.

(*right*) "Never stop at the water's edge, that's what the Japs want you to do." Marines, recalling this warning from basic training, await the word to go forward at Peleliu, where fierce interdicting fire has pinned the first wave to the beachhead.

(*left*) Marines, en route to the Peleliu beachhead, maintain communications with the control ship. The officer (right) is Major Hunter Hurst, commander 3rd Battalion, 7th Marines, who, five minutes after landing, had advanced so enthusiastically that he found himself alone on the turning circle of the Japanese airfield. He quickly rejoined his troops!

PLATE LIII—(*right*) This is one of the most macabre pictures of the war. It shows a Japanese hurling a Bangalore torpedo (the piece of horizontal tubing just above his head) at the very moment he was struck dead by a Marine bullet. Fortunately the cameraman escaped the blast that followed, but the Jap's body seemed to dissolve in a cloud of smoke.

(*left*) Head tilted back, a Negro Marine watches for a sign of the foe. At Peleliu the first Negro unit of Marines—the 16th Field Depot—distinguished itself so often that it won the title, "the volunteer-in'est outfit of 'em all!"

(*right*) Half-crouched, and looking warily about, Marines advance up the slope of embattled "Bloody Nose Ridge" at Peleliu. Japanese camouflage, always good, seemed near perfection in the Palaus. Gun muzzles and enemy troops would suddenly come out of what appeared to be barren soil.

PLATE LIV — (*left*) Seconds before, these two Marines were firing at the Japanese from behind an embankment on Peleliu. The order came to advance. One Marine started over the top—looked down, lifted the head of his buddy beside him—then went on. The second Marine was dead.

(*right*) Although the Angaur landing met less resistance than that on Peleliu, mopping-up of enemy remnants by the 81st Infantry Division continued until October 22. Here two fellow soldiers bear a wounded Army man back from the front lines on Angaur, the Palaus.

(*left*) Major General William H. Rupertus (right) who commanded the 1st Marine Division, and Colonel Lewis Fuller, who commanded the 1st Marine Brigade, pay their respects to the honored dead at burial services on Peleliu. Capturing the southern Palaus cost the United States 7,794 casualties, including 1,209 dead or missing, while Japanese dead numbered close to 12,000.

PLATE LV—Led by Commander Norman H. ("Bus") Miller, of Winston-Salem, N. C., a squadron of Navy Liberators (PB4Y) sank or damaged nearly 150 Jap ships and destroyed or damaged 94 planes. This is an incredible record for a small unit, organized as a "search" group, but the giant LIBs always carried bombs and plenty of bullets—and usually found good use for them.

(*upper right*) Commander Miller, wounded by shrapnel in the right temple and the hand during a raid on Pulawat, remains at the controls of his plane during the long flight back to base.

(*center*) Flagship of the squadron was the "Thundermug," here shown in difficulty as she overran the strip upon return to base. Japanese anti-aircraft had damaged the landing gear during a low-level attack.

(*lower*) One of the groups that flew with Commander Miller in the "Thundermug." *Left to right:* L. B. Johnson, W. F. Fitzgerald, B. R. Jaskiewicz, J. A. Simmen, A. G. Whitson, P. K. Ramsey, Ira Smith, E. H. Kasperson, E. L. Dorris, and R. Gariel. *Standing:* Commander Miller.

PLATE LVI—Like a page out of Jules Verne reads the account of one of the unique UDTs, or Underwater Demolition Teams. From the chill waters off Normandy to shark-infested lagoons in the Pacific, these "warriors in trunks" preceded the first waves of landing craft to clear out, with explosives, both natural and man-made obstacles.

(*upper left*) A special underwater camera, developed by the Bureau of Ordnance, records a mine-disposal diver at work in Hawaiian waters. The small charge he is placing will cut the electrical leads to the firing mechanism inside the mine, rendering it inoperative.

(*center*) There being no gangway on a rubber raft, this UDT diver makes "the customary approach" after completing a mission. Rubber fins add to underwater swimming speed.

(*lower*) Like debris floating on the water, men and equipment of the UDT offer small targets for Jap marksmen, as they are dropped from a motor boat. Explosive charges (right) will be picked up by the men as they swim toward their assigned areas. Despite the extreme hazards of UDT operations, casualties were comparatively few. With characteristic humor, however, they referred to their work as "The Ensign Disposal Service!"

PLATE LVII—Pattern of assault. The great invasion of the Philippines is on, and, like figures in a gigantic ballet, hundreds of landing craft swing into orderly rows with the rhythm acquired from scores of previous Pacific amphibious operations. The scene is Leyte, the date October 20, 1944—two months ahead of schedule, thanks to the series of bold Navy carrier raids which proved that Japanese forces in the Philippines were not as strong as reported. (*above*) Leaving the transports, the first wave heads for shore. (*below*) Wave after wave they come, rocket boats (lower right corner) blasting the last enemy resistance.

PLATE LVIII—(*left*) The USS HONOLULU, or "Blue Goose," one of the spearheads of the hard-hitting Seventh Fleet, bombards shore installations prior to the first Philippines landing at Leyte. The choice of Leyte came as a surprise to "armchair experts," who reasoned that Mindanao was a logical point of entry. Later in the day the cruiser was hit by a Jap aerial torpedo, and by a salvo from one of our own ships.

(*right*) Prayer before battle. Officers and crew aboard a Navy warship attend church services preceding the Leyte landings, October 20, 1944. Chapel is where you find it aboard a man-of-war. In this case the signal flag rack makes a particularly apt background, resembling a miniature organ.

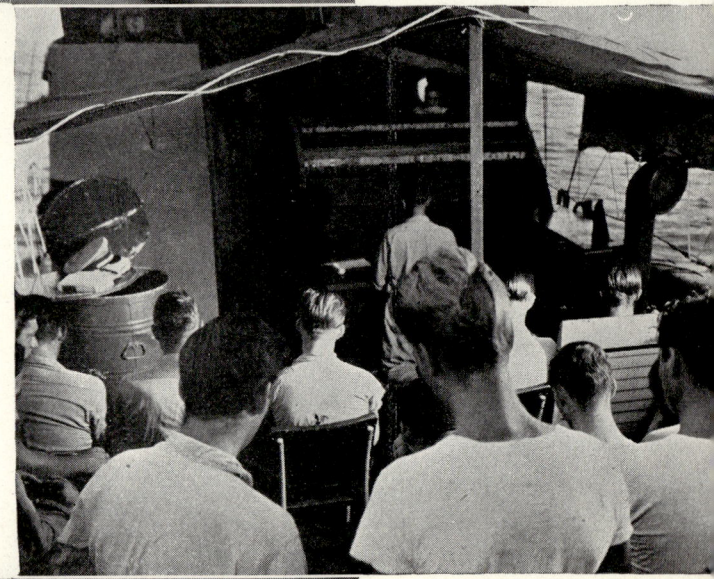

(*left*) Bound for the beach, all eyes turn upward as American planes battle Japanese planes attempting to raid transports and other "sitting ducks" of the 738-ship invasion fleet, lying off Leyte. The enemy planes were beaten off, and little resistance was encountered at the beachhead. It was at Leyte that the Japanese introduced a new aerial weapon, that instrument of desperation the "Kamikaze," or human-guided missile. Hitting the superstructure of the HMAS AUSTRALIA, the first one caused only slight damage. (*Coast Guard Photo.*)

PLATE LIX—(*upper right*) "I have returned!" General MacArthur fulfills a pledge to the Filipinos, made at Corregidor in 1942, when he steps ashore near Tacloban, Leyte's capital. There, 41 years earlier, he reported as a Second Lieutenant, fresh from West Point on his first assignment. With him (left) walks Rear Admiral Daniel E. Barbey, Commander Northern Attack Force, Leyte.

(*center*) Sergio Osmena, President of the Philippines, rides ashore with General MacArthur in a Navy landing craft on "A-day," to receive a tumultuous welcome from his people. MacArthur brought with him a liberating army of nearly 200,000 troops, which soon joined forces with Filipino insurgents, who had been operating as guerillas against the Japs for 2½ years.

(*lower*) The Leyte beachhead still smoulders from the devastating fire of battleships, cruisers, LCI rocket ships and destroyers, as landing craft nose up its marshy sands. The vessel in the foreground is an **LSM** (Landing Ship, Medium), making its combat debut.

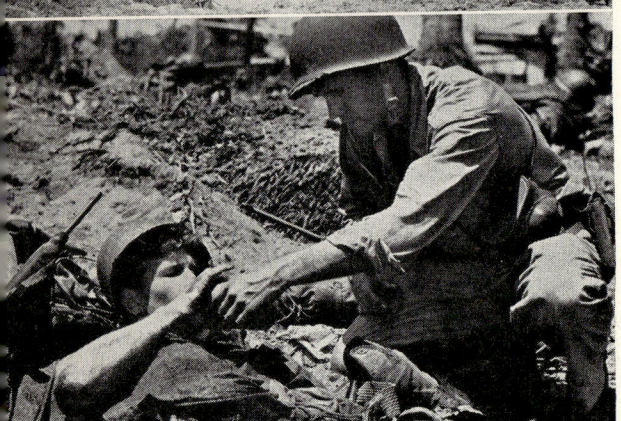

PLATE LX—Although the assault phases of the Leyte landings, as Admiral Halsey predicted, were completed quickly and cheaply, the real battle was yet to come, both ashore and afloat. Mortar fire did harass troops at Red Beach, however, until a cruiser lobbed a salvo over the Tolosa Hills—silencing the Japanese battery.

(*upper left*) Army troops move inland to meet the threat of Japanese Army resistance to the Leyte landing, soon to come.

(*center*) A Coast Guardsman, Carol Smith, gives a drink to an Army buddy, Pfc. Junior F. Happel, wounded during the landing at Red Beach, Leyte, by a Jap mortar shell. (*Coast Guard Photo.*)

(*lower*) When the Allied barrage lifted, throngs of Filipinos, half starved, war-torn but jubilant, swarmed in from the hills to welcome the liberation forces to Leyte. Many of their homes were smouldering ruins, but from the ashes rose the joy of freedom again. Tacloban's 30,000 people crowded the streets in carnival, as the U. S. First Cavalry marched in. Men and women thrust flowers into the troopers' gear, pressed food and wine upon them, and clung to their arms.

PLATE LXI — Logistics, which means food, fuel, and other supplies, became an increasingly vaster problem as our forces moved westward. Almost everything needed in the Philippines campaign had to be carried by ships 6,000 miles from West Coast ports. In October 1944, the fleet alone used enough oil to fill a train of tank cars over 260 miles long!

(*upper right*) Seabee "Seven League Boots." To unload ships, whose draft will not permit them to come close to shore at Leyte, the Navy's Construction Battalions spun out an attenuated pontoon causeway. Such a floating pier could be quickly taken apart and moved to the scene of the next operation.

(*center*) When LSTs (Landing Ships, Tanks) approached as close to the shore as they could, earth ramps were built to the bow doors in order that tanks, trucks and other equipment might be unloaded without damage. The men in the crow's nests over the bows are not sightseers—they are anti-aircraft crews on the alert.

(*lower*)—A few days previously this was a quiet beach, bordering the Japanese airstrip (whose outline can be seen center and left) at Tacloban. Now a score of big LSTs pours tons of Army supplies hourly into the area, as bulldozers scrape sand and earth from the beach to build and widen unloading ramps.

PLATE LXII—The saga of the USS PRINCETON is one of the war's most heroic stories of men fighting against overwhelming odds to save a ship. The carrier went down after more than 350 men had given their lives to keep her afloat.

(*upper left*) A single Japanese plane from Admiral Fukudome's Second Air Fleet scored a direct hit on the light carrier, starting flames which soon spread to the magazines. The PRINCETON was then (October 24, 1944) with Sherman's Task Group 38.3, east of Polillo Island, the Philippines.

(*center*) Damage-control parties attempted to enter the hangar deck, where planes, loaded with bombs and gasoline for the day's attack, were afire. Flames and dense smoke drove them back.

(*lower*) For eight hours the PRINCETON's crew fought to save the doomed ship. Then a terrific explosion ripped the PRINCETON from stem to stern and riddled rescue ships alongside. In life-rafts the crew of the carrier abandon ship, while the destroyer MORRISON stands by to take off the seriously wounded.

PLATE LXIII—(*upper right*) The riddled superstructure of the light cruiser USS BIRMINGHAM, which was directly alongside of the PRINCETON when the carrier's magazines exploded. Two hundred and twenty-nine of the BIRMINGHAM's crew were instantly killed and more than four hundred wounded.

(*center*) Accompanying carriers took aboard the planes of the ill-fated PRINCETON, seen smoking in the distance. When the Japanese air squadron struck the task force, eight planes from the PRINCETON's Fighting 27 were flying Combat Air Patrol. It was eight against eighty. Despite the odds, the Japanese were held in check for fifteen minutes, and lost 28 planes.

(*lower*) Just before the final disaster struck. The BIRMINGHAM (right) had several hoses playing on the flaming PRINCETON. Then one of the destroyers reported a submarine sound contact, and the BIRMINGHAM withdrew. When the attack failed to materialize, the cruiser came alongside again—unfortunately at the moment the PRINCETON's magazines let go.

PLATE LXIV—Death agony of a gallant, stout-hearted ship. (*above*) This remarkable photograph was taken at the moment the after magazines exploded, the force of the blast blowing the after elevator and part of the flight deck high into the air. (*below*) By late afternoon nothing remained of the PRINCETON but a smouldering hulk, but she just wouldn't sink! Finally the cruiser RENO moved in and administered the *coup de grâce* with two torpedoes. Within forty-five seconds all that could be seen was a patch of fire on the water.

The three groups steamed westward all night and at crack of dawn on the 20th sent the long arm of aviation to grope beyond the horizon for Ozawa.

All morning they searched, with radar, radio, and airplanes; no contact. The afternoon grew middle-aged; no Japanese fleet.

At 1542—nearly a quarter to four—a gabble of static-broken, distance-distorted language gave the task force some intimation that the enemy had been sighted by one of the searchers.

The communicators tuned their instruments to frog's-hair fineness, and after fifteen minutes brought in the report clearly. Ozawa's force, split into two—possibly three—groups, was 250 miles westward, and going fast.

Four o'clock in the afternoon, and a 500-mile round trip for the carrier planes to make, with a battle to fight in the middle of it. Could they make it?

Admiral Mitscher put the question to his tight little staff. For a moment no one answered. Each man was doing mental arithmetic, encumbered by all the human factors which the most hard-boiled would have had to contemplate. The young pilots would have to fly an extreme range at an extreme hour; they would be tired when they arrived over the enemy, infinitely more tired on the homeward flight over a darkening ocean with night coming out of the east to meet them and conceal the waiting carriers.

"We can make it," came the decision, "but it will be a tight squeeze."

"Then launch 'em," said Mitscher, biting off the words.

The decision first went to Mitscher's superior, Admiral Spruance, for approval. It was relayed to task group commanders, from them to the skippers, to the air officers, to the yeomen who beat out the summonses to the carriers' ready rooms. Precious moments of daylight were unavoidably lost in the process of translating decision to action.

"Start engines," roared the bull-horns.

The pilots were already burdened with their flight gear. They had not removed it all day, expecting the summons to go forth and do battle at any minute since dawn. Now they heard the call, and their throats were dry and their palms wet as they manned their planes to fly into the setting sun. All the odds—all the odds—were against them.

Into the wind the carriers turned their shovel-faced bows, and at 1624 —nearly 4:30 in the afternoon—Commander Bernard M. ("Smoke")

Strean led the parade of 216 planes into the air in his fighter. A second strike of as many more planes was to be launched as soon as the carriers' decks were cleared.

Then came a correction in the enemy's location. It wasn't good news. Ozawa was 60 miles farther west than had been reported. The second flight was canceled as the first formed up for the 300-mile-plus pursuit, fighters high and in the lead.

"There was no time to work out navigation," Lieutenant (jg) John Denley Walker recalls. "After we got into the air and orbiting, waiting for the other groups to assemble, we began to arrive at the answers—course, speed, estimated time of arrival at target, wind force and direction.

"One voice said, 'Did you get what I got?'

"Another answered, 'It won't get on my board!' [Meaning the figures were astronomical.]

"Then a third voice chimed in with 'No sense working this out both ways!' A lot were thinking the same thing, that there would be no return trip."

As the planes jockeyed for position, Walker recalls, there was the usual exchange of banter and joking criticism of each other's flying. But it was a strangely quiet trip to the target, he recalls, with the twilight gathering at their backs and the target over the horizon, aware of the pursuit and up to Lord knew what tricks to evade it.

The silence was broken by voice from one of the lead fighters shouting, "Look at that oil slick!" and then, on the echo, "Ships sighted." Commander Strean glanced automatically at his watch. It was 6:40 P.M.

A few Japanese fighters rose to intercept, but the Navy bomber and torpedo crews had come too far to worry about them. Leave 'em to the escort. Eyes burning, bones aching, the pilots of the lethal little carrier torpedo-bombers bored through the dogfights to the ships that erupted into what Lieutenant H. H. ("Hank") Moyers described as resembling "Fourth of July fireworks around the Washington Monument. The puffs contained more colors than a rainbow—white, pink, red, yellow, orange and black puffs. Thermite shells were all around, throwing white hot metal." (When that stuff hit it burned through anything, metal, flesh, or bone like a cigarette through tissue paper.)

The Japanese even brought their big guns into play. They were angry clear through. The SBDs and TBFs had to penetrate a wall of explosives 300 feet thick to get behind the range of shells. Then they had only machine-gun fire to worry about.

First through the wall was YORKTOWN's torpedo group, and Lieutenant Charles W. Nelson picked an aircraft carrier against which to lead Lieutenants (jg) John D. Slightom, James R. Crenshaw, Jr., and Carl F. Luedemann. The group leader's airplane was shattered by a direct hit as he dropped his torpedo.

3

Lieutenant (jg) George P. Brown, temporarily commanding a squadron of BELLEAU WOOD (Captain John Perry) torpedo planes, picked another carrier, one of the big HAYATAKA class of fast converted Pacific luxury liners. Following him in came Lieutenants (jg) Benjamin C. Tate and Warren R. Omark. Let Lieutenant J. D. Walker, Brown's friend and shipmate, recount one of the stories of great heroism that the battle produced.

"Brown found his section had been left alone. The other planes were headed for a glide bombing attack. He hoped to get enough protection from a huge black cloud to get to the level of attack unnoticed, but when the boys came out of the cloud they saw with consternation that they had 5,000 yards to go in the clear, with a gantlet of battleships, cruisers and destroyers to run—three TBFs against a big chunk of the Japanese Fleet.

"The tracers were so thick they wondered if they had room for their wings. At night you see them all. Black streaks of oil and bonfires on the water showed them the graves of their comrades and their enemies.

"Brownie broke up his group for the attack. Each was to come in on a different angle. The carrier, now fully alerted, began to circle tightly as the massed fire of her guns was brought to bear. Explosions rocked the three planes and tore into the sturdy TBFs. Tate ducked as the tracers cut through his cockpit, but one of them burned through his hand. A larger shell smashed his fuselage. Still they headed on.

"Brown's plane took the brunt of the Japanese fire; shell after shell struck home and suddenly it began to burn. He pulled up slightly and his crewmen, unable to live in the white-hot flame, bailed out.[1]

---

[1] The turret gunner, George H. Platz, finding himself enveloped in flames and unable to reach Brown over the intercom, scrambled into the bombardier compartment, which was an equally hot spot, to find Radioman Ellis C. Babcock stuck in the jammed

"Brownie pushed on, and pretty soon the flames went out, leaving his plane black and his recognition marks burned away. He reached the dropping point and released the torpedo straight and true.

"Not on the target, Tate and Omark still had to penetrate the murderous head-on fire through which Brown had persevered, and Brown knew it. He didn't hesitate. Comparative safety for his plane lay straight ahead. With his attack completed he could get away while the gunners concentrated on the incoming planes. But he had brought the boys in there and he would get them out if he could, so he turned his plane straight in to the carrier and then flew straight down the length of the ship. The surprised Japanese instinctively concentrated their fire on him, and in that moment of immunity the others sped their two torpedoes straight to the mark."

He did not go down under that mortal beating. Brown's blackened, smoking, tattered plane cleared the danger area but still headed westward. Omark overtook him, and flew so close the wingtips of the aircraft were only inches apart. He signaled to Brown to turn and follow him in the direction of the task force.

"Brownie waved a shattered arm to his friend. His khaki shirt was splattered with blood. Then his plane wavered and plunged nose first into the blackness below."

Behind them, the carrier HIYO was a tower of flames that turned to steam as the big ship rolled slowly over, and sank. Platz and Babcock, floating in the water half a mile away, saw her go.

4

The battle lasted only forty minutes. By twenty minutes after 7:00 P.M. the last American plane still able to fly was on its way back to the carriers.

Ozawa's surviving ships fled into the darkness. He was minus one more carrier, HIYO, and two fleet oilers (probably mistaken for carriers in the dusk by the attacking force). His flagship ZUIKAKU, three other carriers, the battleship HARUNA, a cruiser, and an oiler had all been

---

escape hatch. Platz lunged at the door and both men tumbled out over the Japanese Fleet, clothing ablaze. They "sat out" the battle in mid-stage, floating on their life jackets, and were picked up next day by the sea-air rescue team.

damaged in degrees ranging from fighting uselessness to minor leaks and bomb holes. Twenty-two Japanese planes were shot down.

The American losses in that battle will never be accurately listed. Twenty have been identified as lost in combat. There may have been more; there may even have been less.

Because an even 100 of them did not get home, and 38 men were lost with them.

All the survivors, let us say 196 of the 216, had small hope of ever putting landing gear to deck as they bored into the night in the general direction of the carriers. The dusk was deepening to cloudy darkness; they had more than 300 miles to fly, with gasoline tanks depleted by the long journey to the battle and 40 minutes of fuel-consuming combat.

They knew the fleet was required to be blacked-out and silent. How to get aboard the carriers—if they ever found them—if they even could fly that far—was a problem; well, it was a problem to be solved when they got there. The pilots nursed their fuel, using every trick they had ever been taught or heard rumored, to coax the ultimate BTU from each drop.

Then they began to fall. Over the radio would come a hoarse voice to a wing mate. "I've only got a couple of minutes' gas left, Tom. I'm going in while I still have power. So long, Tom."

Somewhere ahead a tropical thunderstorm lit up the clouds in intermittent flashes. Some of the exhausted pilots thought it was the task force firing.

"Don't shoot," they pleaded over the radio, repeating the recognition signals over and over. "For God's sake, don't shoot."

Others matter-of-factly discussed the situation from plane to plane, from cockpit to turret. One section decided to land in the sea in tight formation, so all could help each other. A pilot argued with his gunner whether the odds favored a parachute jump or putting the plane down on the sea.

A couple of hundred youngsters were in the air there. Most of them in their early twenties. Not many of them old enough to vote. College sophomores, high school kids, boys from the farms and apprentice benches. Thousands of miles from home, hundreds of miles from land, and none could guess how far from a friendly ship.

On board the task force flagship Admiral Mitscher pinched his weather-beaten face into a tighter mask. Down below-decks amidst the machinery a bluejacket blinked his eyes and wrote on a scrap of paper:

> "The friendly chickens are staggering back,
> Make, O Lord, thy night less black,
> For the friendly chickens are having hard flying
> And some of our boys are dying."

In the LEXINGTON's radio room Commander Robert A. Winston, author of aviation books, who had persuaded the authorities to release him from desk duty to fly a Hellcat against the enemy at thirty-seven, listened to the incoming pilots.

"Where's home, somebody? I'm plumb lost."

"Hello, any station. Any station! Where am I, please? Can someone tell me where I am?"

Winston recalls that "we knew there were Jap submarines about, and we were pretty sure some Jap planes were following our planes back in; but we weren't worrying about that. We wanted our boys back. That's all we thought about.

"But to keep radio silence and the protection of darkness was the logical thing to do. There were a couple of hundred men out there, but there were thousands in the task force, a couple of thousand on one carrier alone. If we turned on the radio or the lights, a Jap submarine or dive bomber could destroy one or more ships. We agreed that the logic of the situation compelled us to stay blacked-out and silent.

"Then we heard a commotion topside. We piled up to the deck—and the lights were on. Not the dim lights that reveal the paddles of the man signaling the pilots in, but the floodlights. Not only running lights but searchlights hitting the sky. Men were dancing around and hugging each other like crazy. The ships were even sending up starshells."

Admiral Mitscher had made up his mind to gamble his fleet against the lives of the youngsters he had sent on so desperate an errand, so brilliantly accomplished.

5

The homing planes started to come in. By the dozen they dropped into the water, unable to make the last mile.

Ensign E. G. Wendorf was thankfully preparing to land on the nearest carrier in that Times Square of the Pacific when a faltering plane above him nearly collided. Wendorf put his shaky craft into a quick dive from which it did not recover, dragging him underwater and then turning on its back as it sank. He managed to fight his way out of the trap, leaving one shoe stuck in the canopy through which he kicked his way. When he was picked up seven hours later in his self-inflatable one-man rubber raft he was barefooted. He lost the other shoe beating off sharks that kept nudging his bubble-craft all night.

The dark sea, as far as one could see, was dotted with scores of winking lights, like lightning bugs, Walker [1] relates. The destroyers, trying to maintain their function as antisubmarine patrol, eased into the maze of flashing lights, each one marking a man or a plane crew frantically blinking with the Navy issue waterproof flashlights.

The entire task force bent itself to the work of rescue. There was some discussion among the Admirals about sending the battleships after the battered Japanese, but Admiral Spruance ruled against it as uneconomical and of dubious success.

When the last man was fished out of the water, the roll call of all those who had set out the night before showed but 38 missing. Although four times as many planes fell exhausted into the sea as were shot down in combat, the comparatively slim casualty list would argue that virtually every man not lost in actual battle was rescued.

6

The Battle of the Philippine Sea was won, but the victory brought some criticism as well as congratulations. The enemy fleet, for the first time since the Solomons, had come out to fight but the bulk of it had escaped to fight again. One thing was certain:

Japanese carrier aviation was substantially finished as a naval force in the war. It was not the loss of its planes so much as the destruction of Japan's last cadres of experienced or even partially combat-tested naval pilots that wrote that finis. (The lack was to force the Japanese to resort

---

[1] Lieutenant Walker, when interviewed for this volume, insisted on telling the story of his shipmate George Brown "the bravest man I knew," instead of describing how he himself won the Navy Cross, Silver Star, three Distinguished Flying Crosses, five Air Medals, the Purple Heart, the Presidential and Secretary's unit commendations, and a letter of commendation from Admiral Mitscher, while acquiring twelve combat clasps on his Pacific Campaign medal.

to the desperate expedient of the Kamikazes, and the American Fleet still had much to pay in the future for the victory that drove the enemy to the fanatical lengths of human-guided flying missiles.)

"It would have been much more satisfactory if, instead of waiting in a covering position, I could have steamed to the westward in search of the Japanese Fleet," said Admiral Spruance after the battle. "To have done so would, however, have involved the possibility of our being drawn off by one Japanese detachment, while another made a run around our flank and hit our amphibious shipping at Saipan. The Japanese often operated with well separated forces, as at Midway and in the South Pacific previously, and as they did later at Leyte Gulf. The importance to us of capturing the Marianas and the critical stage of the landing on Saipan at the time made me unwilling to take the risks involved."

7.

The Japanese naval authorities, determined to salvage something from the twin disasters, prepared a document, entitled something like "Battle Lessons from the Battle of the Eastern Philippine Sea," from which the following paragraphs are quoted. Evidently the intent was to make hindsight on the defeat foresight for the next engagement.

"We felt that the main principle, to attack first, was correct but that military operations should not be based on dogmatic and hopeful judgment.

"It was planned by the authorities in Operation AGO that, if an attack developed in the Marianas, shore-based aviation would be the chief defensive weapon; if the attack developed in the western Carolines, our task force would be used.

"This was based on the assumption that the U.S. forces would attack the western Carolines. . . .

"The two-day period from the 13th to the 15th had a great effect on the outcome of the operations. During that two-day period the enemy could have been successfully attacked while he was defending himself from our remaining shore-based planes. There is a feeling we were a little slow in commencing operations.

"In the basic structure of the operation it was imperative that very close co-operation exist between the task force and shore-based air strength. It is felt that the decisive battle should have been staged, as planned, in an area where maximum shore-based air could have been employed.

"It reads in Chapter 49 in the Combat Sutra [Japanese Tactical Document—Ed.] that 'Tactics is like sandals. Those who are strong should wear them. A cripple should not dare wear them.' Although AGO Operation was minutely worked out, and the strategy of each operational unit had been checked in great detail, the training for each detachment of fliers was not complete. Therefore, it looks, as said in the Combat Sutra, as if well-made sandals were allowed to be worn by a cripple.

"Although we could not control the fortune of battle, the combat strength of each air force was inadequate because of lack of trained pilots. The First Flying Squadron went into action after 6 months' training; the Second Flying Squadron after 2 months; and the Third Flying Squadron after 3 months. The reconnaissance squadron received its first instrument check just prior to getting underway for battle and none of the pilots had more than 100 nautical miles of flying experience. The pilots knew nothing of communications, having never sent any transmissions, and the radars were totally unusable.

"In this crisis of battles, on which the fate of Japan depended, the Army Air Corps did not participate in this operation in the least and the Navy Air Corps was so scattered in the Co-Prosperity Area of Greater East Asia that there was presumably 'no place left undefended, and no place defended sufficiently.'

"Our antisubmarine defenses should be re-examined. Since the battle of a fleet is now mainly carried out by the aerial battle of its planes, the fleet frequently is required to stay in the same combat area to launch and receive planes. Our antisubmarine defense did nothing more than post lookouts for submarines in a circular fleet formation. The lookouts [destroyers] cruised unconcerned at a high speed with the blind trust that the submarine danger was not much to worry about. Three of our carriers were sunk in the same operation by submarines.[1]

"Enemy submarines participated in the battle while our submarines were restricted to water east of the line joining the archipelago. It would

---

[1] Actually two. The HIYO was sunk by torpedoes from the BELLEAU WOOD's three planes led by Lieutenant (jg) George P. Brown. The Japanese evaluation was that one aerial torpedo and one submarine torpedo hit the carrier. Actually the second came from Brown's teammates while he heroically distracted the enemy's attention by "buzzing" the HIYO.

have been much better if our submarines could also have participated in the battle. [Most of Japan's remaining submarines, at the Army's insistence, were being conserved to carry supplies to the troops cut off in the Solomons and New Guinea.—Ed.]

"However, the most important cause for the miscarriage of the operation was the failure of the base air force to afford close co-operation. The disposition of U.S. task forces steaming within 200 nautical miles of Saipan and Guam could not be clearly learned from land-based air reports, thus the Japanese Fleet had to rely entirely upon reports from its own scouting planes."

CHAPTER TWENTY

Marianas Completed

I

ASHORE ON SAIPAN—and offshore and over it, too—that part of the United States forces engaged in the primary objective of the Marianas operation was having less easy going than Mitscher's twice-triumphant fleet.

Although tactical surprise had been achieved on June 15, the Japanese had rallied quickly and used their massed mortars and light field artillery with vicious effect. By the end of the third day, the Marines and infantrymen lost very close to 5,000 men in killed and disablingly wounded.

Saipan was no coral atoll such as the Marshalls and Carolines. It was no trackless jungle, like Guadalcanal. It was a heavily populated, intensively cultivated island of 81 square miles, containing three well-developed communities of which Garapan on the west coast was not only the largest but the capital of the whole Marianas group. From almost the mathematical center of the island volcanic action had thrust Mt. Tapotchau's peak 1,554 feet high, with lesser mountains, hills, and ridges radiating from it, merging into a high plateau on the north and melting away into the broad, richly arable lowlands in the south. Thus, in a space 12 miles by 5 or 7, every kind of fighting terrain was concentrated.

The Japs knew the island from more than twenty-five years of ownership and development. The American forces knew it only from aerial reconnaissance, and the information was very inadequate. It especially fouled up the landing and penetration of elements of the 4th Marine Division, with the result that a strong enemy force remained established—although surrounded—in the center of the American lines and four bloody days were spent in eliminating it.

The plan of invasion called for the 2nd Marine Division under Major General T. E. Watson to land on the left and to drive north against Garapan along the west coast. On its right, Major General Harry Schmidt's 4th Division was to cut east across the island to Magicienne

Bay and then parallel the 2nd's advance on the east coast. The Army's 27th Infantry Division, under Major General Ralph C. Smith, had the job of cleaning up the southern fringe of Saipan and capturing Aslito airfield.

2

It took three days of bitter fighting for the Marine divisions to win the positions for their parallel march northward along the opposite coasts. By the end of the third day the 165th Infantry of the Army division had captured Aslito airfield, and with the 105th Regiment began the slow yard-by-yard task of herding the retreating Japanese into Nafutan Point, the small southernmost peninsula of Saipan.

Four times were the United States ground forces subjected to mass Japanese counterattacks, and thrice in spectacularly unorthodox fashion. The first came on the night of D-day. Puzzled Marine scouts reported something like an old-fashioned political rally taking place near Garapan that evening. There was much flag-waving, endless stump speeches from tank-tops, with the enemy troops cheering and milling about in a sort of emotional debauch.

What was happening, as events soon proved, was that the Japanese in reserve were whipping themselves up to fighting pitch. At eight o'clock that night the enemy troops started down the shore road in columns of platoons behind their tanks, still waving flags and whooping it up for the Empire.

The Marines' 6th Regiment braced itself. Tanks and half-tracks began to converge to break up the parade, and word was flashed to the bombardment ships.

Closer and closer came the Japanese, stealthy as the Third Ward Chowder Club marching to its annual picnic. And then some officer either detected signs of diminishing ardor, which is doubtful, or was overwhelmed by the urge to deliver himself of some patriotic epigrams conceived after the march began.

Anyhow, a halt was called and the 2,000 troops clustered for a final harangue. It was almost too good to be true, thought the Navy's spotters ashore. The range was flashed to sea, and a few broadsides from the fire support wound up the jamboree as effectively as a thunderstorm at a strawberry festival.

The 25th Marine Regiment lost 400 yards of hard-won territory to a determined Japanese counterassault carried out in strictly military fashion, ground that was rewon with interest the next day. But the two other grand assaults, while not accompanied by the grotesqueries of the first, ended just as disastrously. In one the Japanese massed their tanks for what appeared to be the makings of a German-style Panzer attack, but sent their armored vehicles against the waiting Marines two or three at a time, without infantry support. One Marine company, "B" of the 6th Regiment, took care of the slow-motion piecemeal drive without trouble. The enemy lost 31 tanks to the unscathed boys of Company B.

Third of the extraordinary Japanese counterattacks was directed against the Army elements which had penned the Japanese into narrow Nafutan Point. Some 600 of the enemy burst out the woods on the night of June 26 yelling "seven lives to repay our country" and fell upon a battalion of the 105th Infantry. They did not stop to fight the surprised soldiers, but raced through their lines toward Aslito airfield, now in full operation thanks to the quick repair job done by the Seabees.

The infantrymen shot the berserk Japanese like shooting rabbits from a blind. Many of the enemy reached the airfield and began smashing up three airplanes before the startled Seabees piled out of their beds and put an end to that—and an end to several score Japanese. The survivors then went whooping off to the northward, where they ran into a small reserve group of the 25th Marines, who were thoroughly irritated at having their rest disturbed.

No doubt some percentage of the Japanese escaped into the hills and woods to join up with the main enemy forces, but more than five hundred dead ones were found scattered along the route of the lunatic lunge. As for their slogan, instead of each Banzai-charger taking seven American lives, the five hundred who were killed were accompanied in death by a bare half dozen infantrymen.

In the first three or four days of fighting, a dead Japanese was a rare sight for the advancing invaders. A dead enemy is almost as valuable as a living prisoner to the intelligence officers, and sometimes more valuable, for he cannot tell lies or destroy important papers on his person.

Yet for all the desperate fighting and vigorous shelling with everything from mortars to the ships' big guns, apparently few Japanese were wounded and almost none killed. It was not for days that the enemy's secret was discovered. They carried all their dead with them in retreating, and buried them secretly.

3

On June 24 Lieutenant General Holland M. Smith, USMC, who was in over-all command of the landing forces, ordered Major General Ralph C. Smith, AUS, to be relieved of his command of the infantry division. He was succeeded temporarily by Army Major General Sanford Jarman, who had been brought along to command the Saipan garrison forces after the island's capture. Eventually Jarman turned the command over to Major General George W. Griner, Jr.

The incident unfortunately provoked a tempestuous newspaper debate, made all the sharper by the fact that officers of different services were involved, and that a general in the senior and larger service had been removed by a general in a junior branch.

The facts leading up to the event are not easy to delineate. On June 22 the two Marine divisions reached the widest part, and the most rugged, of the island. To maintain contact would stretch their cordon across Saipan too thin, so General Holland Smith ordered the 27th Division to fill the gap in the center.

Now, the Marines and the infantry, for all the fact that they are foot troops employing identical weapons, do not belong to the same school of warfare. Their functions are not identical, and their methods even further apart. Marine tactics are to drive ahead. They travel light, they move fast, and their method is to push the enemy off balance and to run him ragged, giving him no time to regain equilibrium or to reorganize defense or counterattack.

The infantry is trained to conserve its strength and to make no radical advances without first softening up the opposition with bombardment by air or artillery, and making sure there are no enemy pockets left in its rear. The Marines went ahead, leaving by-passed enemy forces to mopping-up parties. At night the Marines scooped out shallow individual foxholes in a double arc, the bulge toward the enemy. The soldiers were trained—and commanded—to dig in for the night well before dark and to establish a rather more elaborate system of defense.

What seems to have happened on Saipan was that the 27th Division (already shy some of its artillery which had not been landed when the APAs were ordered out of range of the Japanese carrier air strike) was too slow to keep up with the Marines on its flanks. That was not wholly the fault of the infantry system, for the terrain assigned to the troops was a little more difficult, being hilly and honeycombed with caves where Japanese snipers and mortar companies were holed up. Also, several units, according to War Department records made available for this narrative, became lost. The 165th Regiment took a wrong road and became snarled up in a traffic jam with the 106th, and on the next day the 106th took a wrong turning and left the 165th unsupported.

At any rate, for two days the infantry was as much as 55 minutes late in scheduled attacks, causing considerable confusion to the up-and-at-'em Marines. Lieutenant General H. M. Smith, finding his center sagging and full of holes, ordered the change in command of his Army component. Such changes had happened before in the war, and they were to happen again and again. As Major Frank O. Hough, USMCR, says in *The Island War*, "plenty of Marine officers recognized the value of certain Army tactics under the right circumstances. And many high Army officers leaned toward Marine Corps methods, as was to be demonstrated in subsequent operations (not involving Marine units) where commanding generals of adjoining Army divisions became involved in controversies similar in all essential respects to that of Smith *vs.* Smith."

Almost all of the uproar was created by persons thousands of miles from the scene and happy to relieve the tedium of war by ornamenting it with intimations of fratricidal quarrel. Under its new command, but employing the plans devised by the departed general, the 27th went on to finish the campaign with conspicuous success.

4

The battle for Saipan lasted twenty-four days. On July 9, at 4:15 o'clock in the afternoon, the northernmost tip of the island was in possession of the 4th Marine Division, whose battle-hardened men watched with horror the mass suicides of scores of Japanese civilians leaping from the cliffs or wading across the reef to drown themselves.

During the combat, the civilians had presented an endless series of problems to the United States forces, who had landed lamentably unequipped to care for refugees and noncombatant prisoners. The native Chamorros, their loyalty to the United States emotionally intensified by years of slavery, rushed to meet the Marines heedless of the scything machine guns. Blood brothers of the Guamanians, they had never been under American administration, but had always envied it, whether their rulers were German or Japanese. Now they were so drunk with promise of freedom that they forgot all danger, and many were killed—purposely by the Japanese, accidentally by the invasion troops.

The Koreans, imported as indentured labor by the Japanese, were a problem of another sort. Sullen and bitter against the Japanese, they were indifferent toward the Americans, except so far as the Marines and infantrymen promised a source of food and shelter. The Japanese civilians retreated with their troops when they could, and most often killed themselves when they could not—or meekly allowed the Japanese soldiers to kill them, with land mines or machine guns. Many a Marine, whose bayonet had often run red, felt his stomach twist with nausea as he saw, on the opposite cliff, kimono-clad women with babies on their backs submit to such murder.

Death, it seems, was welcomed by the Japanese to the incredibility of surrender to a nation they had been told was whipped and bargaining for peace.

At first the defending forces, under aged Lieutenant General Yoshige Saito, sent messages of great optimism to Tokyo. They were repaid in kind. Imperial Headquarters cheered the hopeless cause with gaudy dispatches of tremendous victories at sea, which left the United States with scarcely a ship afloat or a carrier plane to fly. Maybe Saito wondered why, in such desperate straits, the Americans maintained so large a fleet around the Marianas—and why the triumphant Japanese Navy did not clean up its work by sinking them.

Some aspect of realism overwhelmed him and he sent this report to Tokyo: "Please apologize deeply to the Emperor that we cannot do better than we are doing. However, the right-hand men of the Emperor are probably rejoicing because they are not in places of death during the fight. The Governor General of the South Seas will retreat to the north end of Saipan and the Army will defend its position to the very end, though that be death, to guard the island treasure.

"Praying for the good health of the Emperor, we all cry 'Banzai.'"

Carefully worded dispatches from Chief of Staff, Saipan, to Chief of Staff, Tokyo, copies of which were found by the 2nd Marine Division, told of the battle to defend Saipan. "The enemy, while assaulting various strong points with incessant night and day naval gunfire, further menaces us by brazenly low flying planes that bomb and strafe. Moreover, it is regrettable that we cannot match the enemy at sea.

"The enemy is under cover of warships near by the coast; as soon as our night attack units go forward, the enemy points out targets by using the larger star shells which practically turn night into day.

"The enemy naval gunfire, using mainly a shell with attached instantaneous fuse, has great destructive power. They also send over a shrapnel shell. The call fire on land from the ships is extremely quick and accurate."

A diary of a staff officer with General Saito, scribbled during the last days on Saipan, was found:

"I don't remember the exact date too well, as I am groggy from the intense bombardment and naval shelling. The 135th Infantry, robbed of the summit of Mt. Tapotchau, was chased to the northern end of the island.

"At new field headquarters, the fourth new headquarters, a conference was quickly held to decide how to extricate ourselves quickly from this predicament. Some officers proposed that 'we should die gloriously in battle with a final charge now, in this place.' However, General Saito ordered 'because there are many military units which were left scattered on the field of battle, they should all be brought together at a defensive line to the north and chew the American forces to pieces.'

"However, before this defensive line was completed, the enemy Marines were upon us. We did not stay long in our 4th headquarters. Caught in the concentration of naval gunfire the wounded and dead continued to increase. We stayed at 5th headquarters only two days. On about July 3 we moved to 6th and final headquarters. This area is generally called the 'Valley of Hell' and I felt this was an unpleasant hint concerning the future.

"On July 4 a unit appeared on the opposite side of the valley and started firing automatic weapons. At that time I felt we were entirely surrounded and lost all hope.

"General Saito was feeling very poorly because for several days he had neither eaten nor slept well and was overstrained. He was wearing a long beard and was a pitiful sight. I felt the final hour was drawing near.

"General Saito held a secret conference. Either we die in the caves or we make a last attack and fight to the finish. The opinion of Vice Admiral Chuichi Nagumo was probably received. [Nagumo was commander of the Central Pacific area and of the Fourteenth Japanese Air

Force. He had commanded the task force that struck Pearl Harbor and commanded the Japanese carriers at Midway.]

"Officer messengers took a period of four days to disseminate the orders. After issuing the orders it seemed that the work of headquarters was finished. Everybody put his personal belongings together. By the kindness of the cook, a farewell feast was prepared for General Saito. It consisted of sake and canned crab meat.

"Why did they have this last farewell feast? Since General Saito because of his age and the exhausted condition of his body would not be able to participate in the attack of the 7th and had decided to commit suicide in the cave. It was feted. Ten A.M., July 6! This time was set by the General himself as the final hour."

Just two hours before the General killed himself he stood before an assembly gathered in his cave to observe the final ceremony and delivered the following message:

"I am addressing the officers and men of the Imperial Army of Saipan.

"For more than twenty days since the American devils attacked, the officers, men, and civilian employees of the Imperial Army and Navy on this island have fought well and bravely. Everywhere they have demonstrated the honor and glory of the Imperial forces. I expected that every man would do his duty.

"Heaven has not given us an opportunity. We have not been able to utilize fully the terrain. We have fought in unison up to the present time but now we have not materials with which to fight and our artillery for attack has been completely destroyed. Despite the bitterness of defeat, we pledge seven lives to repay our country.

"The barbarous attack of the enemy is being continued. Even though the enemy has occupied only a corner of Saipan, we are dying without avail under the violent shelling and bombing. Whether we attack or whether we stay where we are, there is only death. However, in death there is life. We must utilize this opportunity to exalt true Japanese manhood. I will advance with those who remain to deliver still another blow to the American devils and leave my bones on Saipan as a bulwark of the Pacific.

"As it says in Senjinkum [Battle Ethics], I will never suffer the disgrace of being taken alive, and I will offer up the courage of my soul and calmly rejoice in living by the eternal principle.

"Here I pray with you for the eternal life of the Emperor and the welfare of the country and I advance to seek out the enemy.

"Follow me."

5

Aged and infirm General Saito did not physically lead his troops in that last banzai charge. Having made his speech, eaten his own funeral banquet, he parted his white kimono and thrust a dagger into his bowels. Sorrowfully an aide shot him through the temple and went forth from the cave to join the massing soldiers, sailors, and grounded aviators.

At dawn, Marine outposts felt their hair rise under their helmets as they saw the enemy massing for assault in columns that contained the bandaged wounded, the blind, one-legged men on crutches even. Some carried hand grenades, others had no more potent a weapon than the improvised spear of a bayonet lashed to a bamboo pole.

The Marine artillery went to work on the scarecrow regiments. Great gaps were blown into their ranks by the 105s, but with discipline and coolness the Japanese closed up and came doggedly on. The Marines lowered their field pieces, shortened their fuses, and then wrecked their own guns as the flood of wild-eyed, screaming Japanese engulfed the positions.

Now, backing up the Marines, came men from other batteries and regiments. The Seabees roared in by truckloads; clerks, cooks, mess attendants, sick men and wounded, snatched up any weapon to hand and dammed the breach in the lines.

The charge ended when there were no Japanese left to fight. More than 3,000 enemy dead lay on the field. There was one space fully an acre in extent where the corpses so overlapped it was impossible to walk without stepping on a dead man.

Thus Saipan was won, at a cost of 3,478 American lives and 23,811 Japanese. The United States wounded numbered 13,208; the Japanese military prisoners taken were 1,810 and in the stockades were 14,735 interned civilians, friend and foe, living in indescribable squalor, eating what the Marines and the ships offshore could supply out of overextended ration allowances.

Saipan was won but the fighting did not stop for over a year. Snipers lurked in the caves and kept shooting until starvation or an American patrol ended their solo war against the United States. And in that desultory warfare half a dozen Marines drew death upon themselves from the rifles of their own sharpshooters by indulging in the reckless horseplay of donning a Japanese general's uniform, complete with Samurai sword and strutting down a forest path just for the hell of it.

6

There were Americans who refused to surrender, too. The record for sustained refusal to call quits belongs to a Navy petty officer who saw the American flag lowered on Guam on December 10, 1941, and turned his back on the whole sorry business.

On July 10, eleven days before the invasion of Guam, the destroyers MCCALL and GRIDLEY were sent to that once-American island to provide rescue services for downed pilots, to direct the fighter planes to targets of opportunity, and to bombard pillboxes. The ships had been firing all day and were about to rejoin Task Group 58.1, when one of the signalmen observed a heliograph from a cliff on the island. "Investigation of the object revealed a man trying to send us a message by semaphore," related the MCCALL's skipper, Lieutenant Commander John B. Carroll. After establishing his friendly character, a heavily armed volunteer landing party was sent to the beach in a motor whaleboat. The MCCALL and the GRIDLEY, commanded by Commander Philip D. Quirk, covered the landing at a distance of about 2,500 yards from the beach. Although within range of a Japanese 6-inch battery, the landing party was not taken under fire by the enemy and succeeded in rescuing Navy Radioman 1/c George R. Tweed, who had been living on Guam since 1939 and had refused to surrender to the enemy when the island fell. Tweed had been living in the bush since that time. He had valuable information as to Japanese strength, morale, pre-landing casualties, and disposition of enemy guns on Guam.

7

There was no element of surprise to the landings on Guam. Surface bombardments had begun the day after the first landing on Saipan, when it was anticipated that W-day would be June 18.

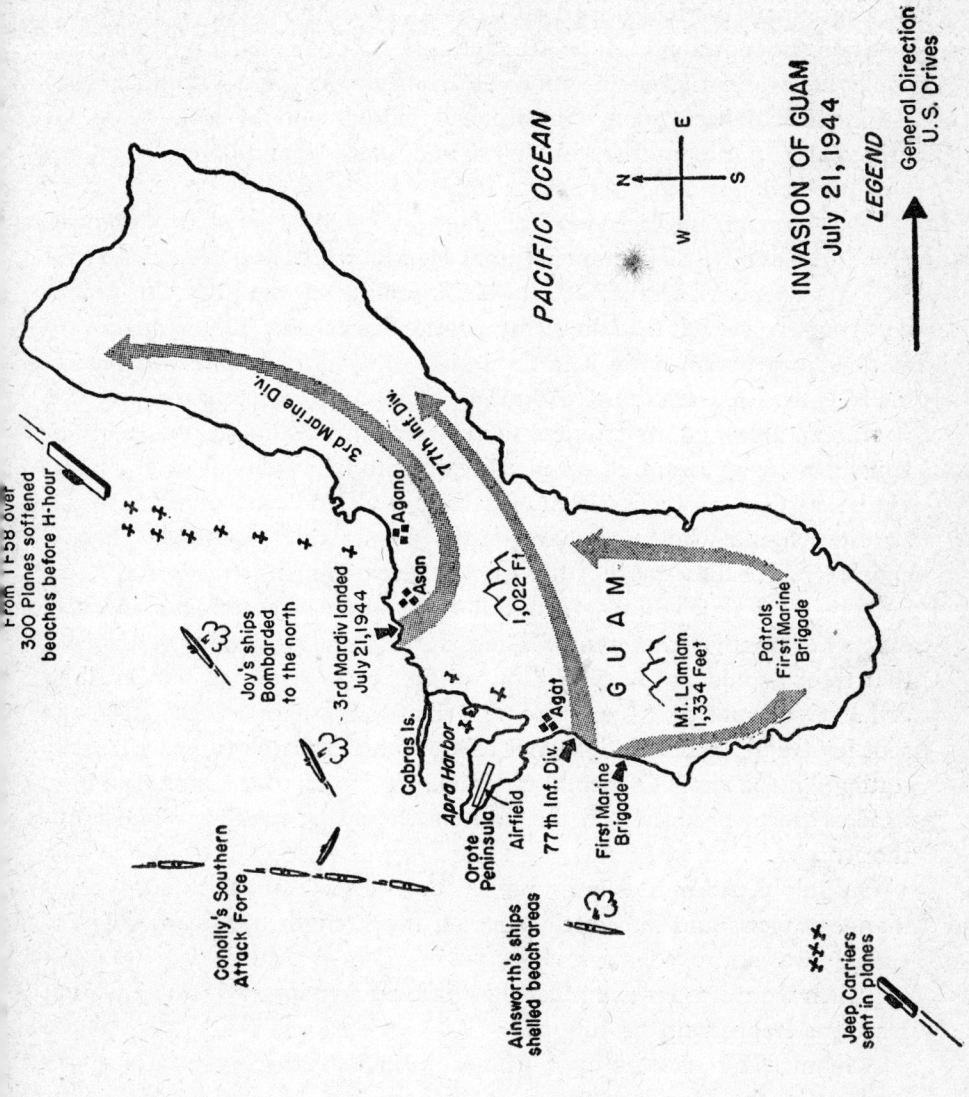

FIGURE 12

"The value of the early bombardment was questionable," later related Rear Admiral W. L. Ainsworth, who commanded one of the bombardment groups. "We had tipped off our hand with the two-hour bombardment on the morning of June 16. Nothing short of an engraved diagram could have told the enemy more clearly that our photographic reconnaissance had been good, that we had pin-pointed the location of his principal batteries and installations, and that our probable intentions were to land just about where we did."

A conference by Vice Admirals Turner and Mitscher, Rear Admirals Hill and Conolly, Lieutenant General H. M. Smith, and Major General Roy M. Geiger was called to consider carefully the time for the assault on Guam. It was felt that the Army's 77th Division should be immediately available for action upon its arrival on July 25, which date was recommended to Admiral Nimitz. Admiral Nimitz answered that July 25 was not acceptable and that unless there were compelling reasons why, of which he was unaware, it appeared feasible to fix W-day at or about the 15th. Any delay in the invasion of Guam, in CINCPAC's opinion, would slow down the whole schedule for the Central and Southwest Pacific campaign. He directed that the case be re-examined.

The next day, July 5, Admiral Spruance called only the Marine officers to another conference. They affirmed their previous judgment: that troops could not be pulled out of Saipan to reinforce the invading 3rd Division and that the entire 77th Division would be needed on the spot for Guam. Admiral Spruance sent another dispatch to Pearl Harbor stating, "if the views of the military commanders as to the military forces needed are to be overruled the decision should be made by higher authority . . ."

On July 6, Admiral Nimitz replied that in view of the military commanders' views and late intelligence on the strength of Guam, delay of the day was approved.

Then word was received that the 77th was arriving early and Invasion Day was stepped up to July 21.

Guam Island, resembling a peanut in shape, is the largest and southernmost of the Marianas group. The shore line varies from high cliffs to coral beaches. It is of practically no economic importance, but of great military and naval value, due to its strategic location.

Beginning on July 8, Guam was under constant surface bombardment until the landing on the 21st, by ships of Conolly's Southern Attack Force.

Nineteen bombardment ships—cruisers, destroyers, battleships—were standing off the western coast of Guam, to support the Marines' "homecoming." Rear Admiral Charles T. Joy's ships were off Agaña and "Pug" Ainsworth's off Agat. For the first time in Pacific amphibious operations, the plans called for naval gunfire and aircraft bombing in the same coastal area simultaneously. The pilots were instructed to fly at least 1,500 feet above the ground and gunnery officers were instructed to keep the gunfire trajectory below 1,200 feet. Living conditions, even in caves, under this volume of explosives were made extremely hazardous for the Japanese.

Otherwise the pattern of invasion was very much like all the rest. Bombardment, landing, attack, and resisting counterattack. Offshore, the ships pouring in the heavy punches from their big guns on the spots designated from the hills and forests.

Captain Ellis M. Zacharias's NEW MEXICO alone sent 2,464,000 pounds—1,100 long tons—of destruction into the Japanese positions.

"Two nights after the landing the enemy made heavy counterattacks," he relates. "The Japanese were also trying a flanking movement with barge-loads of troops sent to land behind our lines during the night. The Marines called for light to see what was going on, so we gave them constant illumination with a star shell every forty seconds."

Between battleship and Marines the Japanese maneuver was smashed. Major General Geiger, commanding the landing force, signaled Captain Zacharias: "Many thanks for your splendid work throughout the night. From all indications you saved the day." And later, to all the bombardment ships, he said: ". . . The enemy was never able to rally from the initial bombardment and the continued gunfire support kept him in a state of confusion to the end of the campaign. . . ."

Five days after the landing, Guam was back under the American flag again. "Organized resistance" ended on August 10. The United States forces[1] lost 1,919 killed, 7,122 wounded, 70 missing, of which the Army had 405 killed, 1,744 wounded, and 51 missing. Only 86 Japanese military personnel were taken prisoner; 10,971 were killed. That was far from the final score.

---

[1] On Saipan, the two Marine divisions lost 886 killed, 2,145 wounded, and 1,178 missing, almost all the latter being later identified as dead. The Army division had 81 killed, 362 wounded, 22 missing.

The Marines hitched up their belts and went about the tough, thankless task of digging out the holed-up Japs. Often at night the Emperor's stubborn soldiers made sneak raids into Marine-held territory.

One night, twenty-six days after Guam had been reported secure, Second Lieutenant Paul C. Smith and sixteen riflemen were ordered to set up a road block where a Nip raiding patrol was expected. Sure enough, the Japs attacked and were driven back. Later a Jap prisoner of war in describing the raid said: "Our troops encountered a heavy concentration of American forces which used machine guns, rifles, flames and gas. We were forced to disperse with heavy casualties . . ."

But Smith, who is now back at his desk as editor and general manager of the San Francisco *Chronicle*, tells what really happened:

"We set up our ambush on the edge of a grassy plain across which we felt sure the Japs would pass. All was quiet the first night. Next morning on a patrol we found several abandoned U.S. Army trip flares—used for illumination in night perimeter defense. All around our little outpost we strung hair wire which we attached to the flare pins.

"That night one of the trip flares suddenly fired. Twenty yards ahead we saw seven or eight Japs, apparently the part of a larger force.

" 'Let 'em have it!' I yelled.

"When our M-1s, BARs, and two light machine guns opened up about forty trip flares went off at once. There was a mad scramble as Japs scattered like ants from a disturbed anthill.

"Next morning we counted nine bodies right in front of our row of foxholes and twenty more near-by."

Smith's small group had suffered no casualties and had repulsed a Jap outfit of 220 strong, indicated by the 18 Hotchkiss heavy machine guns, tripods, 50 boxes of ammunition, Nambus (light machine guns), and Arisakas (antitank rifles) left behind.

Two months later the toll of enemy dead stood at 17,238, the prisoners —mostly wounded—at 463.

By ones and twos, the survivors of "organized resistance" took to the woods and caves, determined never to surrender and to take as many American lives as possible before death inevitably overtook them. Radioman Tweed had had the assistance of hundreds of loyal Guamanians while he hid throughout the Japanese occupation. The fierce little sons of the Sun Goddess had every man's hand against them, and no hope of rescue at all.

Nobody wasted any time in admiring the fanatical courage and patriotism of the Nipponese, however. It would have been just as philosophical, and far more fatal, as pausing to admire an angry hive of bees whose members give up their lives to sting an intruder.

Long after Admiral Nimitz had moved CINCPAC Headquarters to the first reconquered American territory, from which to direct the final dissolution of the Empire, gaunt Japanese snipers were still steadying their hunger-palsied hands on tree branches to draw a rifle bead on an American patrol. Their aim was, most fortunately, execrably bad.

But the Marines had come home to Guam, and the American flag flew there again, defiantly now, in promise of the forthcoming eclipse of the Rising Sun.

8

How does it feel to go into battle?

It is a feeling a considerable percentage of American manhood wants to forget; it is a feeling impossible to convey to those who have not experienced it. Perhaps no two men experience the same emotions—or the kind of lack of emotion that makes one almost an automaton, obeying messages from the brain that were photographed upon it in training.

One Marine voluntarily went ashore with the first wave on Guam with a small microphone strapped to his chest and with instructions to translate his every thought into spoken words, which were recorded. Here is his stream-of-consciousness description of how it feels to ride toward a bullet-spitting beach in an LCVP and to stumble ashore through surf in which the bodies of one's comrades are tossed:

"We are getting along toward the beach now. It is pretty rough. It's getting smoky. The acrid smell of gunpowder is all around. There is a destroyer standing in by the reef. If she can get in so close, without being hit, so can we.

"The Japs have started firing at us. We can see orange puffs from their machine guns. One fellow joked. 'Well, we can go back now, we have a combat star already.' Jap machine guns right ahead of us. They are firing right at us. Things are hotter than Scollay Square on Saturday night. We are a little out of their range. Boy, it would be nice to get back to the transport.

"I think we are well in range of their machine guns. I would like to get out of here. We have got to get to that beach. I can't see any of our boys on the beach. I don't blame them for getting off that beach. They are either across the sand or they are dug into it. An amtrac just hit. It's burning.

"Jap machine guns burst all over again. We are finally to the reef. It's gonna be rough. Everybody hold on, we are switching to an amtrac to get to the beach. Our machine guns have just opened up from our amtrac.

"I am thinking of my wife and my little daughter. Hope they are all right and that I can see them again. Hey, Dave! Keep your eyes on this stuff in case I get hit. I am walking behind the amtrac. The water is about $2\frac{1}{2}$ feet deep. I am stumbling. Getting tired. Just losing my breath. Say, you fellows, don't leave me all alone.

"Bullets are kicking up the water all around. One landed right next to me. What's the matter? Hey, everybody spread out! Spread out, you guys. Sure a lot of machine-gun fire in this water. Nobody has been hit. Just fell on some coral. How the hell are we going to get to that beach? Soaking wet now. We can see the Japs are shooting from the hills—walking on our knees now—smaller target. One of our men has been hit. He is lying on his side. I can't tell who it is. Another one has just been hit. Bullets. Bullets.

"We are about 100 feet from the beach. Everybody's mouth seems drawn. Another one just got hit. Another one just next to me on my right. Hey, Dave! Are you all right? One has been hit and is on his back. Blood is pouring out of his mouth.

"Marines are all over the beach but unable to move forward. I know we will move, but I don't know when. We have just got to keep our heads down. Can't tell where all the fire is coming from. Navy corpsmen are looking for casualties. They don't seem to take cover. We don't have the beach yet. It may take all day just to get that hill. Boy, something hit very close! One fellow just got his helmet shot off. He is crawling in behind a coconut tree for cover.

"I am still running, out of breath. Marines are pouring in from behind. Here comes a tommy gunner. His teeth are gritting. A Marine behind him stumbled. He looked up, his rifle still dry, smiled and said, 'What do we do now?' Marines now are everywhere. It is a strange thing."

At that point, the monologue ends.

9

J-day on Tinian—three days after the landing on Guam—opened the final phase of the Marianas campaign.

There were only three possible places to land troops on the island, and the Japanese guessed wrong. They expected the invasion at Tinian Town's beaches, as the Marines discovered when Captain James L. Jones (of Apemama and Majuro fame) sent picked scouts of his 5th Amphib Reconnaissance Battalion across the strait to study the lay of the land.

Creeping within sight of Japanese working parties, the reconnoiterers observed that a very hot welcome was being prepared for the invaders at the broad beaches of Tinian Town on the island's southwest. Two smaller beaches on the north-northwestern end, less than half the size of any ever before employed even in atoll warfare, were neglected by the defenders except for a few land mines obviously laid to booby-trap snoopers.

Saipan's conquerors were assigned to take Tinian—2½ miles across the strait. It was to be something new in warfare—the troops departing from dry land in their amphibious craft and landing boats.

Just to keep the Japanese happy in their delusion that the invasion was to be at Tinian Town, a brisk bombardment of that area was maintained from Saipan. Meanwhile the officers who were to lead the attack were flown over the terrain to study its geography at close hand. The 4th Marine Division was again to make the first assault, followed by the 2nd, with the 27th Infantry Division in reserve. An amphibious, ship-supported feint against Tinian Town was devised to preserve until the last minute the Japanese' naïve guess that the Marines would choose the obvious and easiest beach to land upon.

From the start, the Japanese garrison of 7,000 men had no chance at all.

The island was gently hilly, intensively cultivated, and served by a comprehensive network of roads. It was within easy artillery range of Saipan; the invasion was shore-to-shore instead of ship-to-shore, and unlimited supplies could be ferried across the strait in DUKWs and amtracs for delivery to the troops inland, instead of being dumped on the beach.

When the Marines landed on July 24, the Japanese, who had been expecting them for a month, had indeed watched the preparations with the naked eye, were taken completely by surprise. The Marines swarmed ashore through the bottleneck beaches, needing to reduce only two blockhouses manned by fifty Japanese, and by dusk were well inland with tanks and artillery. They set up a defense line on ground chosen without haste, and got set for the inevitable banzai counteroffensive. Except for the bitter fact that men were being killed or maimed, it was like an exercise.

The anticipated enemy charge came at three in the morning, and was repeated diminuendo until dawn, when the well-entrenched Marines put down their guns for the nasty chore of burying 1,241 Japanese dead.

Without their usual haste and dash, the Marines herded the diminishing Japanese troops into the southern tip of the island. Each night the Japanese turned against their grim shepherds in fanatical charges, one of which actually broke the Marine line only to be blasted to shreds by the point-blank fire of the howitzers.

The last organized enemy attack was made on the night of July 31-August 1. A bare company's strength of Japanese soldiers, sailors, and Marines, equipped with three battered tanks and led by a fanatical officer, made the final suicide dash against the leatherneck line and then that campaign was finished except for the tedious mopping up of guerrillas—which kept the troops on the other islands dangerously occupied, too.

The Marines lost 290 men killed in action, 24 missing and adjudged dead, and 1,515 wounded. The Japanese casualties were 6,050 killed and 255 prisoners. The enemy dead is not an exact figure.

Tinian's defenders were the 50th Infantry Regiment plus three batteries of artillery and one of the 135th Infantry, with some scattered naval and aviation minor units—without ships or planes. Most of the Japanese troops were veterans of the Manchurian campaign.

Ranking officer on the island was Vice Admiral Kakuta, commandant of the First Air Fleet: Kakuta was an extraordinary Japanese. He was six feet tall and a coward.

After the Marines had overrun the island, a prisoner who had suffered from the Admiral's drunken bullying offered to lead the Americans to the cave near Tinian Town where, he said, Kakuta was holed up. Two men were wounded by a hand grenade tossed from the cave as they explored its entrance. A few minutes later the cave had no entrance—or exit. A few demolition charges closed and concealed it forever.

Tinian, as the other landings, was covered by warship bombardment. Off Tinian Town, where the mock assault was being staged on D-day, occurred the only fatalities afloat—one of the ironies of war.

A trio of hitherto undetected, excellently camouflaged 6-inch guns at the base of low cliffs flanking the beach opened fire on the warships. The Japanese gunners were fast, their marksmanship excellent, and the battleship COLORADO had twenty-two holes in her hull before she could be maneuvered out of range. The battleship's commanding officer, Captain William Granat, and the division commander, Rear Admiral Theodore D. Ruddock, Jr., were among the wounded. Forty-seven men were killed.

While the COLORADO was being pounded, the destroyer NORMAN SCOTT was hit six times. Her skipper, Commander Seymour Owens, and the officer of the deck, Lieutenant Noyes D. Farmer, Jr., were killed.

10

The flying Navy was conspicuously among those present in the capture of the Marianas.

All four task groups of Marc Mitscher's TF 58, plus two divisions of escort carriers (CVEs), combined their best talents to give Guam the heaviest aerial bombardment that had ever fallen on a Pacific target. At Guam, Tinian, and Saipan they provided close tactical support for the ground forces, strafing enemy positions, bombing enemy concentrations and artillery posts, and parachuting supplies to the United States forces.

Such close co-operation with the air arm was a new experience for the Army boys. After the fighting was over, enthusiastic expressions of admiration and thanks were delivered to the naval aviators by the infantrymen.

Naval pilots also helped make the capture of Tinian as economical and efficient an operation as it was by carrying Marine and Army officers of all ranks over the island at almost treetop height to provide the ground forces with firsthand scrutiny of the terrain over which they would have to fight on foot.

Combat losses were very few among the fliers, and Mitscher's air-sea rescue teams kept the fatalities well under the number of planes lost. One rather melodramatic rescue was made by the submarine STINGRAY (Commander Sam C. Loomis, Jr.) under the shadow of the Japanese guns on Guam.

The submarine did not dare to surface at such close range. It had come close to being hit in rescuing Lieutenant Richard E. James and ARM 2/c David H. Smith from a rubber raft inside Apra Harbor, and it had been touch-and-go while Lieutenant John M. Searcy was hauled aboard earlier. Lieutenant Edwin G. Weed of STINGRAY had jumped overboard and brought that wounded pilot aboard.

With three aviator guests aboard, STINGRAY received the signal to pick up another, a scant mile off Orote Point, which at the time was well manned with Japanese gunners. Here is Commander Loomis's log of that mission:

1233—Sighted pilot dead ahead. Had to approach from lee or across wind. Velocity 10 to 12 knots.
1235—Two shell splashes ahead.
1238—Two more splashes and burst of AA fire near pilot. Can see him ducking in rubber boat.
1240—Pilot has sighted us and is waving. Holding up left hand which shows a deep cut across the palm.
1303—Approached with about ten feet of number one periscope and about three feet of number two periscope out of water. Pilot very close and no sign of life. Headed directly for him. Missed.
1319—Three shell splashes on port quarter.
1347—Heard shell land close aboard.
1349—Heard another close one.
1352—Almost on top of pilot. Now, he's paddling *away* from scope. Missed.
1423—Shell splash, about 500 yards.
1424—Heard shell splash. Heard another close one. Heard another close shell. Heard two more. Heard one shell.
1440—Heard and saw two splashes close aboard.
1453—Pilot missed the boat again. On this try, he showed the first signs of attempting to reach periscope. Maybe shell fire has made him think that a ride on a periscope might be all right after all. I am getting damned disgusted, plus a stiff neck and a blind eye.
1500—Heard another shell.
1516—Fourth try. Ran into pilot with periscope and he hung on! Towed him for one hour during which time he frantically signaled for us to let him up. His hand was cut badly and it must have been tough going hanging onto the bitter end of the line with one hand while bumping along in the whitecaps.
1611—Lowered towing scope, watching pilot's amazed expression with other periscope.
1613—Surfaced.
1618—Picked up Ensign Donald C. Brandt, USNR, suffering from deep wound in left hand. Glad to finally get him aboard. He said that during first and third approaches he was afraid periscopes were going to hit him and he tried to get out of the way and come in astern of me. He had been briefed on a rescue like this, but guess the shock of getting hit at 14,000 feet and

falling upside down in his parachute from 12,000 feet was too much. And then the shell fire shouldn't have done him much good either. He's taken quite a running, and taken it well. We're on speaking terms now, but after the third approach I was ready to make him captain of the head.

11

During the assaults on the Marianas, Mitscher kept his fast carriers from boredom by two significant raids.

The first took Carrier Groups 58.2 and 58.4 on a three-day tour of the western Carolines in late July. The Joint Chiefs of Staff in Washington had sent word that the seizure of Yap, Palau, and Ulithi might soon be considered necessary, and the carriers' visit was to reconnoiter the area and to destroy any installations which might constitute a threat to the Central Pacific program.

The second sweep in early August was against the Bonins, that string of islands in line with the Marianas on the air route to Japan. Carrier Groups 58.1 and 58.3 were sent to give those islands a second dose of neutralizing explosives.

Mitscher's orders to the two groups brought great cheer to all of mighty 58:

> "Get the planes
> Get the ships,
> Finish the Bonins,
> Head for the barn."

The "barn" meant Eniwetok, with beaches uncontested by Japs and no harsher sound of metal piercing metal than that produced by an opener on a can of cold beer.

So the two carrier groups sped off on the ultimate mission of the Marianas campaign like boys told to cut an armload of wood before playing football. When fliers from 58.1 discovered "a large enemy convoy" ahead of the fleet, the group commander, Admiral J. J. ("Jocko") Clark dispatched his cruiser division (Crudiv 13; Rear Admiral L. T. DuBose) SANTA FE, BILOXI, MOBILE, and OAKLAND, to intercept it. With the cruisers went Desdiv 91 (Captain Carl F. Espe) made up of BROWN, IZARD, CHARRETTE, and BURNS, with Desdiv 100 (Commander Harold T. Deutermann), INGERSOLL, KNAPP, and COGSWELL, coming up behind.

The wind was strong, the seas were rough, and the enemy was agile. At close to six o'clock in the evening the first Japanese ship was overhauled and obliterated by BROWN and IZARD. It wasn't much of a catch—a dumpy little steamer no bigger than an LCI. An hour later the four destroyers of 91 sank a small tanker.

With darkness, SANTA FE's radar picked up a pip of fair proportions, a "might be a cruiser" blob on the screen. She started the argument at 19,000 yards range, using radar control, and the target retorted with three shells—identifying itself thereby as a destroyer with two mounts forward and one aft.

All the other ships in the United States group, destroyers and cruisers, quickly joined in. Eleven ships, 70-odd 5-inch guns against one ship, three guns. It wasn't a good fight. It wasn't good shooting, either.

"There is too much shooting and not enough hits," Admiral DuBose warned the eight over the short-wave voice radio. "Watch your bullets!"

A few minutes later he ordered his cruisers to cease firing, and sent Desdiv 100 in to engage the Japanese at closer quarters. Two of the enemy's guns were still in shooting order, but not after the second firing run of INGERSOLL, KNAPP, and COGSWELL. The Japanese destroyer MATSU went down fast.

One other ship, a fair-sized cargo vessel, was sunk by BILOXI and MOBILE under brilliant illumination of the target by OAKLAND starshells. That ended the nameless battle, mentioned here only because it wrote finis to the Marianas campaign and to demonstrate fairly that American gunnery was not always of squirrel-rifle accuracy. But, be that as it may, the affray had more significance than sinkings. It occurred a scant 500 miles from Japan itself, and the repercussions in Tokyo were somewhat more shaking than the shell fire itself.

The cruisers and destroyers rejoined the task groups to give the Bonins the plowing-up by bomb and shell that would ensure the forces in the Marianas relative peace and quiet. Then Task Force 58 "headed for the barn" and rest, recreation, and repair.

12

Eighteen days after Saipan fell, so did Tojo's cabinet in Japan.

(When Rear Admiral R. A. Ofstie later asked Fleet Admiral Osami Nagano, supreme naval adviser to the Emperor, at what point Japan realized the war was lost, Nagano simply said: "When we lost Saipan, hell was upon us.")

It was, in literal fact.

Possession of the Marianas gave the United States forces a base from which the big far-flying Army bombers could operate against Japan's homeland industrial cities. The B-29s had not proved effective in China, because sea lanes were not open to feed them with fuel and explosives. From Saipan, where Navy tankers could fill the Army's bombers with high octane gas and the Navy's cargo ships would bring them all the bombs they could carry faster than they could drop them, the B-29s were to make history such as they had not written even in Germany.

The Japanese knew it. They knew it very well, and started dispersing their factories, moving some of them underground. Trouble was, the factories were not much good no matter how well protected, because they had few materials with which to work. The naval blockade had already reduced all of Japan's commerce with her shrinking "Southeast Asia Co-Prosperity Sphere" to little coastwise convoys that raced from haven to haven in shallow water. The factories were starving, and so were the people.

As the Japanese saw their own fleets dwindle, they saw the Pacific right up to their doorstep fill up with American warships, and they marveled.

There seemed to be two identical American fleets on the ocean, and the Americans were so infernally clever in deception that one bunch of ships was made to look exactly like the other, right down to rust stains and patches.

What the Japanese did not know was that the Third and Fifth fleets were only one. It remained almost continuously at sea because it had two commanders complete with staff—while one set of officers was ashore studying the next operation, the other set was ranging the seas on a mission of destruction.

Even had they known that much, the baffled Japanese would have disbelieved it, because ships have to be replenished, overhauled, repaired.

The answer to that was Admiral Nimitz's endless chain of supply, a bucket brigade of cargo ships that plied between Seattle, San Francisco, and other West Coast ports to the Central Pacific carrying oil, spare parts, fresh drafts of manpower, shot and shell, food and drink. In the captured islands great floating drydocks and fleets of repair ships mended and refurbished the battle-grimed and damaged American warships in days, instead of the months it would have required to send them back to Pearl Harbor and the United States for such attentions. Every type of ship had a "mother ship" to nurse it back to fighting trim. Damaged submarines, battleships, cruisers, destroyers, even the big carriers, had what British War Correspondent William Courtney called their "ladies in waiting."

The Pacific was a melon the United States had eaten down to the rind—the rind of the Philippines and Japan itself.

13

War is not all a business of killing and trying not to be killed. There is an endless list of accompanying tasks to be performed, tedious, unglamorous, but very, very important. The fruits of such labors are compressed into reports which find their way by devious routes to bureaus, where they are numbered, classified, studied, and filed.

One can feel sorry for Commander Hayashi of the Imperial Navy's Medical Corps. The capture of Saipan by the Americans set at naught a whole year's scientific labor, as set forth by him in this captured document:

CONCERNING THE SOILING OF NAVY MEN'S CLOTHING

1. Throughout the four seasons the shirts of cooks, firemen, and general duty personnel show a remarkably high degree of soiling. This is also true of their socks, which in the case of barbers, radiomen, and nurses show a low degree of soiling.

2. The progress of soiling is generally proportionate to the passage of time and is cumulative in effect. However, in the case of cooks, firemen, and general duty personnel the degree of soiling exhibited on the first day is equivalent to that noted on the 5th to 7th days for barbers and nurses. Taking an average for all branches, the soiling of shirts and drawers tends to show a cumulative increase, and this process accelerates sharply in the summer. This is also true of socks in all branches.

3. Considering the seasonal effect, it appears that shirts and drawers get dirtiest in the summer and autumn, in that order. Socks, however, get dirtiest in the summer and spring.

4. The order of greater soiling for various articles of clothing is as follows: socks; drawers; shirts. The differential in the degree of soiling is especially great as between spring and summer, somewhat less as between autumn and winter.

5. Throughout the four seasons the soiling of socks is particularly great in the case of the soles, which get approximately 1.5 to 1.8 times as dirty as the uppers. This difference is more pronounced in the spring and summer than in the fall and winter.

6. Shirts get dirtiest in the back, the chest and stomach following, and the sides showing the least soiling.

7. In the case of drawers, the seat gets dirtiest, followed by the knees and thighs in that order.

CONCLUSIONS

I have spent a year with the fleet studying sailors' soiled linen and have tentatively established the following laundry standards.

1. Shirts
    Firemen—every day in all seasons.
    Cooks and general duty personnel—2 days in winter and autumn, otherwise every day.
    Mechanics—3 days in all seasons.
    Other branches—3–4 days in summer, 5–7 days in other seasons.
2. Drawers
    General duty personnel and firemen—every day in all seasons.
    Cooks—2 days in winter, otherwise every day.
    Radiomen—every day in summer and autumn, 2 days in spring, 5 days in winter.
    Other branches—3–5 days throughout the year.
3. Socks
    As a standard in view of the dirtiness of the soles:
        Cooks and firemen—every day in all seasons.
        Other branches—every day in summer, 2–3 days in other seasons.

14

Meanwhile, behind the barrier of the East Indies, there was fighting too.

The war on the Asiatic continent was the stepchild of Mars. China, Indo-China, and most of Burma were occupied by the Japanese in the manner of goldfish occupying a pool. There was no "front." While men toiled with wheelbarrows, baskets, and shovels to build a thousand miles of truck highway over the trackless interior, Chennault's planes flew "over the hump" to carry men, munitions, and gasoline for other aircraft —probably the most costly per-man operation of the whole war. The campaign, if thus it can be called, was complicated by China's incomprehensible internal politics besides.

Hopes to bomb Japan's southern industrial cities from China had proved impracticable and almost utterly impossible. Control of the seas was needed to supply the Air Forces, and from Burma to Siberia the Japanese still dominated them. Not many big bombers can fly if they depend for fuel on the gasoline other bombers have to carry to the limit of their range—plus their own round-trip fuel.

The British, Dutch, and United States merchant marines lugged the implements of war through the submarine zones to ports in India and Ceylon, for piecemeal delivery from there to the fighting zones. In the summer of 1944 a United States War Shipping Administration Liberty ship, *Jean Nicolet*, crossing the Indian Ocean, was twice torpedoed. The even 100 persons on board—41 crew, 28 Navy Armed Guard, 31 passengers—took to lifeboats and rafts as the vessel listed 30 degrees to starboard.

Forty-five minutes later one of Japan's biggest submarines surfaced and bombarded the listing ship with two 5-inch guns. Leaving the ship ablaze, the submarine approached one lifeboat after another, and ordered the survivors to board the warship.

As each man climbed aboard he was stripped of all possessions, even identification disks, and bound. Then the Japanese sank the lifeboats and rafts with the four 20mm machine guns on deck. One crew member who did not come aboard smartly enough to suit a Japanese officer was killed with a pistol shot and his body kicked into the sea. The rest were made to kneel on the metal deck, wrists lashed behind them.

Four members of the naval armed guard group decided to take no chances on that kind of rescue. Sharks were more merciful. They swam off into the darkness.

That made the toll of prisoners 95. When they stirred or sagged from their cramped positions they were rapped to attention with a length of iron pipe.

No doubt the Japanese submarines were bored and craving amusement after long and precarious days at sea. They decided to play an exhilarating game. A dozen lined up in a double row, and one by one the bound prisoners were prodded to their feet and forced to run the gantlet. One Jap had a bayonet, another a length of pipe, some had guns, some used fists and feet. As the victims staggered bleeding to the end of the line, they were knocked overboard.

Twenty-five of the 95 had been thus disposed of when the ship's siren sounded its grating call to quarters. The Japanese sailors dashed for the conning tower hatch. It was slammed shut, and the submarine slid under the waves, with 70 helpless men on deck.

Miraculously, 23 survived. Seaman 1/c Kolczynski of the armed guard had a tiny pen knife in his pocket which the pirating Japanese had overlooked. Ship's Carpenter Van Ness managed to wriggle out of his bonds, found the knife while Kolczynski floated on his back, and cut the thongs of the bluejacket and of six others. The men then started to swim toward the still-floating *Jean Nicolet* and encountered a few others who were still gamely fighting for life, knowing that before she had been abandoned a radio message went forth from the Liberty ship giving her position and predicament.

With daylight—July 4—air-sea rescue planes came over the area and fished the 23 survivors, some still bound, from the water.

The Indian Ocean and adjacent waters were not exactly a Japanese monopoly. The British Far Eastern Fleet, with elements of the Royal Australian and New Zealand navies and the Royal Dutch Navy, kept the Nipponese close to shore or in port most of the time. First American warship to join the RNs was that venerable lady champion of the whole Pacific war, the "Sara"—USS SARATOGA, Captain John H. Cassady commanding. In the spring of 1944 Sara departed her Central Pacific stamping grounds via Australia for Ceylon. Vice Admiral Sir Arthur J. Powers, RN, commanding the Far Eastern Fleet, assigned SARATOGA to the frontline Group 2, as companion of HMS ILLUSTRIOUS, and the Commander of Carriers, Rear Admiral Clement Moody, RN, flew aboard to discuss the first operation—or co-operation.

United Nations seapower was more fully represented when the French battleship RICHELIEU joined the fleet, and on April 16, 1944, the international fleet sallied to give the Japanese in Southeast Asia a demonstration of what their confreres elsewhere had been forced to take.

Sabang, the Netherlands East Indies oil shipping center, was the first target. The SARATOGA furnished 39 of the planes that rendered Sabang oilless for a long time to come. One man only was shot down—Lieutenant (jg) Dale Klahn, who was handily rescued by the submarine HMS TACTICIAN under heavy fire from the shore.

At Soerabaja, Java, a month later, SARATOGA's fliers—opposed by only two enemy fighters, quickly eliminated—destroyed one of the world's larger oil refineries, a drydock, ten ships in the harbor, and twenty planes on the ground. The ILLUSTRIOUS's smaller air group meanwhile wiped out the extensive Bratt's Machinery Works and bombed the airfield, sinking a 5,000-ton cargo ship on the way home for good measure.

With Admiral Lord Louis Mountbatten's congratulations, SARATOGA's far-faring company worked the ship back to the center of activities, having contributed a token of thanks to the Royal Navy for its great services in the Pacific.

PART FIVE
The End's Beginning

Chapter Twenty-One

Closing the Gap to the Philippines

I

WITHIN A SCANT ten months after the terrible days on Tarawa, the complex sea-air-land machine of the United States and Allied forces had rolled 2,000 miles across the Pacific toward the ultimate goal.

The gigantic jaws of the MacArthur-Nimitz pincers pointed to the southern Philippines. Two impediments to the closing of those tongs existed in the Halmaheras group of the Moluccas archipelago off the northwestern tip of New Guinea and the Palau Islands 450 miles due east of Mindanao, southernmost and second largest of the Philippine islands.

Capture of these two groups was indicated not so much to destroy their value as outposts to the Japanese as to provide springboards for the Allied forces. Possession of each island group would cut the distance between the American perimeter and Mindanao in half on the two radii of attack, and provide bases for the heavyweight AAF strategic bombers which need long, substantial runways to take off with their heavy burdens for long-distance delivery.

For ten months Admiral Nimitz had been building a bridge across the Central Pacific. Palau was to be the last pier in that long span. Admiral Spruance's Fifth Fleet was now the Third Fleet under Admiral William F. Halsey. Mitscher's famous Task Force 58 was now TF 38. Vice Admiral Theodore S. Wilkinson's Task Force 31 could supply the heavy, grinding, relentless amphibious power to supplement the quick battering blows of the big guns and the carrier planes.

Admiral Nimitz's orders from the Joint Chiefs of Staff in Washington were terse: "You are directed to gain and maintain control of the eastern approaches to the Philippines—Formosa-China coast area."

CINCPAC translated that into an all-over policy, guiding the formation of detailed plans for specific tasks, which told his subordinate commands to "maintain and extend unremitting pressure against Japan; apply maximum attrition to enemy air, ground and naval forces by all possible means in all areas."

For those tasks, the United States industrial machine was now running in highest gear to pour into the combat areas anything and everything needed, and sometimes things that were not needed. By sheer weight of hurled metal alone, the doom of Japan was pronounced; in the mines, farms, mills and factories, the railroads and merchant marine, and in the will of 140,000,000 people, the United States had a preponderance of weight, reach, and power-punch that no nation had ever achieved. The Australians, the British, the Dutch, contributed to make the power accelerate faster than Japan's declined.

Brains were an important ingredient, too.

In midsummer of 1944 the Commander-in-Chief of the Army and Navy himself called a conference of his Pacific commanders at Pearl Harbor. President Roosevelt arrived aboard the new cruiser BALTIMORE (Captain Walter C. Calhoun). General MacArthur flew to the Hawaiian Islands from New Guinea, and Admiral Nimitz was host to both as the plans were discussed for the war's final stages.

The end was not in sight, but the means to achieve the end were in hand.

Japan knew she was whipped. But the Japanese would not admit it to themselves. They hoped that Ameterasu, the ancestral sun-goddess, would perform one final, sweeping miracle. Short of that, they were determined to make the Allied advance so costly in lives that Japan could bargain with blood for a peace which would leave the Empire some shreds of geographical profit.

That is why no chances were taken in closing the last gap to the Philippines—Peleliu, Angaur, Ulithi, and Morotai. There was no need any more to take chances, either.

2

America's fleet, sweeping across the Pacific, was doing a task that made the Labors of Hercules book like tiddlywinks. With exact precision, with perfect co-ordination, its ships of war were pushing the Japanese Empire in upon itself. Invasions ticked off with the methodical regularity that could be achieved only by having every plane, every ship, every gun of the fleet at the proper place at the proper time.

It was not mere coincidence that this was so. Behind each move of the fleet, so effortless when viewed from afar, were the sweat and ingenuity of tens of thousands of men—men of the long-armed Service Forces; men who riveted and painted and cut and welded and scraped and overhauled and supplied. In short, men who kept this fighting fleet fit to fight.

The Marianas had been tough, and to finish the job it had been necessary to keep the fleet at sea for two weeks longer than expected. This resulted in all ships running low on everything from beans to oil and in their being in urgent need of hull and machinery repair. But the schedule could not be delayed, regardless.

The general plan was for a great part of the fleet, after the Marianas, to go to the South Pacific, to the bases in the Solomons and New Caledonia area, for upkeep and replenishment in preparation for the next invasion. The servicing facilities in the area would be put under a great strain. In spite of the two weeks' delay, the target date for Palau had not been changed.

Rear Admiral Oscar C. Badger, Commander Service Forces South Pacific, decided that the lost fortnight could be made up by round-the-clock industry. Every dock, every tool, every loading crane, every shop, every fuel hose, every ammunition barge would have to be used day and night.

Ships began to arrive and things began to hum. Admiral Badger made a quick survey trip of his bases, especially the two principal ones, Tulagi (Captain George Lyttle), consisting mostly of floating repair and supply facilities, and Espiritu Santo. He reported to COMSOPAC that, in spite of the strain, the deadline would be met.

As he stepped from headquarters building, he was handed a dispatch from Captain Frank Mecleary, Officer-in-Charge of the Santo base. It was not good news. The battleships TENNESSEE and CALIFORNIA had been in collision and both ships were badly banged up—TENNESSEE with a crushed bow and CALIFORNIA with a ripped side. The base personnel at Santos were already sweating out a bulging repair schedule and yet TENNESSEE had to be ready for sea in six days and CALIFORNIA, more seriously injured, in twenty-two. What work, all vital for the coming invasion of Palau, should be deferred?

After a hurried conference with his staff, Admiral Badger sent his reply: "Defer no work projects. Six hundred welders, shipfitters and mechanics, including two underwater welding teams, will arrive your base by air within twenty-four hours. Complete work on TENNESSEE and CALIFORNIA in time to meet operational requirements."

From the Fijis, from Guadalcanal, from New Britain and New Caledonia men were pulled from jobs of lesser urgency and whisked by plane to Santos.

Within a week TENNESSEE was ready for sea and two weeks later CALIFORNIA followed.

That's the way the Navy's Service Forces operated.

3

Peleliu, in the Palaus, and Morotai, in the Halmaheras—or, to be more cartographically precise, the Moluccas—were invaded on the same day—September 15, 1944. The end of the war was just eleven months away. Almost everybody was sure it was five years distant.

Morotai was in General MacArthur's bailiwick, and once more Barbey's Seventh Amphibious Force was on the hop. ("Well, it's leap year, ain't it?" one philosophical bosun remarked as they shoved off.) The Seventh had the task of putting 16,852 Army troops ashore on the island—480 miles from Palau, which was 350 miles from Ulithi and Ulithi 350 miles from Guam.

To prepare for the landing a surface bombardment force of five cruisers and ten destroyers under Rear Admiral R. S. Berkey, and a carrier force of six CVEs and eight DEs under Rear Admiral T. L. Sprague, preceded the strike. Just in case of trouble from the Japanese Fleet, Vice Admiral McCain, Commander Task Group 38.1, stood by over the horizon with big, fast carriers. The bombardment and bombing groups worked over the island while Barbey's slower, troop-packed flotilla churned toward the beaches. The Admiral's flag flew from USS WASATCH, a communications ship.

On the second day out, a soldier fell overboard and speed was slacked to rescue him. It was a thrilling diversion for the sweating, sardine-packed troops.

On the third day another soldier splashed over the side. Admiral Barbey "hit the overhead." He reached for a dispatch blank, and scribbled a terse message to the force.

"No more men will fall overboard."

And none did!

The landings were accomplished on D-day with insignificant opposition. There were no beaches on Morotai, only tidal flats of green, steaming, thigh-deep mud. A couple of CVEs—escort carriers—and a dozen PTs were left to patrol the waters and Barbey went back for another load of soldiers. In another fortnight there were 45,000 troops on the island and Army planes flying from the new Seabee-built field. The large Japanese garrisons in the rest of the Moluccas were cut off from the Japan-Philippines supply line, out of the war.

4

The operation against the western Carolines was a different story. It was planned to follow in the same amphibious pattern as that employed in the Marianas, and it promised to be equally as difficult. Every major command in the Pacific area was involved; 800 ships and 1,600 airplanes would operate over the entire Central and Western Pacific. Of the personnel, 19,600 would be Army, 28,400 would be Marines, and 202,000 would be wearing the Navy's dungarees and khakis.

Except for a minor collision between two oilers, MILLICOMA and SCHUYLKILL, the cruise to the objective area was undetected and generally uneventful until September 12 when the fire-support ships approached the beachhead to commence their bombardment. Rear Admiral Oldendorf's force was divided into two groups—one to shell Angaur, the other Peleliu. Admiral Oldendorf himself had tactical command of the group attacking Peleliu; Rear Admiral R. W. Hayler, Commander Cruiser Division 12, riding in USS DENVER, the other, which was to hit near-by Angaur. The two groups were approximately four miles apart when, about four hours before sunrise, Admiral Oldendorf ordered his escort vessels to reorient the screen making it more sub-tight.

Just as the APD NOA (Lieutenant Commander Henry B. Boud) prepared to execute the order to move counterclockwise to the other side of the formation, the destroyer FULLAM (Commander William D. Kelly) swung into view on a collision course as it sought its new position. The destroyer sounded the four shrieking blasts for collision quarters. The NOA's quartermaster was so excited that he yanked the handle of the ship's siren too hard and its cable snapped. The whistle would have served no good, for at that moment the destroyer's bow crashed into the attack transport's starboard quarter.

All hands were safely evacuated from the APD in the ship's landing craft. Despite desperate salvage work, the vessel sank almost under Boud's feet a few hours later. The FULLAM, with her bow pushed back like an old pugilist's nose, was able to carry on.

The Japanese defending Peleliu had had plenty of time to get ready for the invasion, and they had used the terrain to best advantage in preparing the Americans' reception.

They realized that they had to hold the airfield at all costs, and planned their defenses accordingly, planting extensive minefields over land and sea. Single- and double-horned mines, even aerial bombs buried as land mines, formed a protective belt from the reefs to 100 yards inland. (Over 1,000 moored contact mines were swept in the Palau group and Ulithi, more than five times the number found in all previous Pacific operations combined.) Concrete and coral casemates and pillboxes fronted all the beaches. Road junctions were covered by strongly entrenched antitank guns and automatic weapons. Inland traps were constructed to channel tank movements into their line of fire. Artillery and heavy mortars studded the higher ground. The defense had been carefully rehearsed. The Japanese had been warned to be ready for the invasion by September 15. They had anticipated the time of invasion to the day.

Remembering the lessons learned at Tarawa, Admiral Oldendorf's big guns and gunners went to work. The bombardment ships, following in paths cut by the minesweepers, poured over twelve million pounds of explosives on Peleliu alone in three days. It messed up the Japanese defenses considerably, but did not destroy their esprit de corps. Speaking of esprit—

Living up to her reputation at Guam, the battleship PENNSYLVANIA (Captain Charles F. Martin) again had her nose up against the Peleliu beach searching for camouflaged Japanese installations.

There had been a large number of duds and ricochets in the area, and Rear Admiral T. D. Ruddock, commanding the battleship division, decided that PENNSYLVANIA was responsible because she was steaming so close to the beach. He signaled: "Suggest you open range somewhat. A large number of duds and ricochets were noted in your main battery firing."

The PENNSYLVANIA's gunnery department had great pride in its ability to move in and destroy. At its earnest request Captain Martin replied to the Admiral: "Our plane spotter reported 5 ricochets and 1 dud from this ship. Large number of ricochets from other ships. Our fire most effective in demolishing definitely located structures. Would like to continue our close-range firing at such targets." To paraphrase: "Please, Admiral, don't make us leave."

Admiral Ruddock hastily replied: "My last despatch not intended critically of your fine destructive fire which was noted but to suggest improvement by reducing duds. The MARYLAND had many duds also. Choose your own range to get best results."

5

The invasion of Peleliu was hot.

"Plenty hot," were the words of Pfc John F. Balla, USMC (Company L, 3rd Battalion, 5th Marines of the 1st Division). "The Japs had their mortars set so they could drop the explosives right on us as we went over the reef on Orange Beach. For about fifteen minutes after we made it to the beach, we couldn't move forward or backward. We cuddled up in the sand pulling our feet up and our head down to avoid the bullets. Remembering the final instructions of our battalion commander, 'Men, never stop at the water's edge, for that's what the Japs want you to do,' we plunged across the sand. We never worried about bullets we could hear. A bullet with a passing sound is usually a safe distance off, but the bullet that cracks like a whip is close. The one that you can't hear is usually too close."

In a reflective mood, the Marine private continued, "Peleliu wouldn't have been so bad if you could have avoided seeing your buddy—dead. Maybe someone you had worked and played with shoulder to shoulder through boot camp to Frisco, Pearl, and finally fought beside in combat. Suddenly pop, and your buddy is dead right beside you. In a few hours the guy you were just talking to is swollen and black beyond recognition. That is what hurts.

"One night on Peleliu they told our outfit to dig in. Dig in they say—why, I was in muck up to my thighs. Instead of digging, I had to climb into some vines above me and sleep there during the night."

Balla's experiences and reactions were much the same as those of the thousands of other 1st Division leathernecks who went ashore at Peleliu. They were told that in case they didn't know which direction to go from Orange Beach at dawn, to walk toward the sun. The big airport with the blinding white coral runways, their first and main objective, was in that direction.

Probably the first Marine to set foot on the airfield was a young major, Hunter Hurst, commander 3rd Battalion, 7th Marines. He was so eager to get inland that five minutes after landing he found himself alone on the turning circle of the airfield. Realizing his conspicuous predicament, he got off as quickly as he could. In his second appearance with an organized battalion the next day he went after the airfield for keeps.

Although they had to cross one of the worst coral reefs since Tarawa and face strong opposition from veteran Japanese troops, the Marines of the 1st Division as usual made a successful landing. At 0832 on September 15, following a lengthy ship and aerial bombardment, the Marines under Major General William H. Rupertus planted their toes in the southwest sands of Peleliu immediately adjacent to the airfield. Colonel Lewis B. Fuller led the 1st Marines, Colonel Harold D. Harris, the 5th, and an old Haitian veteran, Colonel Herman H. Hannekin, the 7th Marines. (In 1919 Hannekin won the Congressional Medal of Honor. Masquerading as a native he personally killed the Haitian bandit leader, Charlemagne Peralte, while serving as a Marine Corps sergeant and a captain in the Gendarmes of Haiti.) While enemy mortar shells walked up and down the beach in bloody regularity and enemy artillery churned the water into a dirty, debris-laden froth, the assault troops kept plunging across the reefs.

The vigilant bombardment ships stood close offshore contributing their hefty main battery punch when called on by the sweating Marines. A good example of the close co-operation that day between ship and shore was when HONOLULU (Captain Harry R. Thurber), late in the afternoon, broke up a threatening counterattack of twenty Jap tanks.

Possibly the fiercest fighting was against a ridge, 1,000 yards north of the airfield, at whose southern extremity was a commanding height— "Bloody Nose Ridge." For six long days, this pillbox-studded height was the scene of bitter, bloody fighting. During the afternoon of September 22 advance elements of the 321st Infantry Regiment, 81st Division, with the 7th Marines, moved from Angaur, by this time secured, to relieve the 1st Marines, who had suffered 60 per cent casualties.

Bitter hand-to-hand fighting continued for days. Flame-throwers, hand grenades, bazookas, rifles, knives, tanks, artillery, mortars, and machine guns were all used to blow the enemy out of his caves. Pin-point gunfire from ships exploded in the Japanese positions. Marine Corsair pilots flew one of the shortest missions on record from the airstrip to Bloody Nose Ridge—1,000 yards.

Here, too, the first Negro unit of Marines—the 16th Field Depot—distinguished itself, and won the title of "the volunteerin'est outfit of 'em all." Major Frank O. Hough, author of *The Island War*, relates the confusion of one officer who told a detachment of the 16th FD, "I need some volunteers . . ." The entire unit stepped forward as one man without waiting to hear the nature of the task, which was only to bury a dead Japanese.

The camouflage of the Japanese, always good, seemed near perfection in the Palau Islands. Gun muzzles and Japs would come out of what appeared to be barren soil.

The Japs tried desperately to hold out. The night of September 23 they even tried to send in reinforcements by sea. They loaded oil, gasoline, ammunition, and troops aboard fourteen big Army barges at Koror, a little island north of Peleliu, and cautiously felt their way down the shadowy coast line.

Rear Admiral George H. Fort, commander of the Peleliu Attack Force, had anticipated something of the sort. He kept the destroyer HEYWOOD L. EDWARDS and four LCIs patrolling the north side of Peleliu, with orders to shoot first and identify later.

Aboard the HEYWOOD L. EDWARDS it had been a dull night for the radar operators, until 2:00 A.M. when the scope showed activities around Ngesebus Island.

The destroyer's skipper, Commander Joe W. Boulware, notified the LCIs 347, 454, 455, and 726 that he would illuminate the objects with star shells. The LCIs moved in closely and spotted the enemy craft scuttling inshore under the white glare. All the ships opened fire, carefully sidestepping a minefield on the 20-fathom curve just beyond their position. The low profile of the barges and the extreme range made the 40mm fire from the LCIs not nearly so destructive as it was harassing to the Japs, so the destroyer, using one gun to fire star shells while the remaining four fired shrapnel, started picking the barges off like stripping grapes from a bunch.

Some exploded with a terrific roar, others in a sudden brilliant noiseless flash. After twelve barges had been thus wiped out, the destroyer ROBINSON arrived to lend a hand, but the battle was almost over.

A little more than three hours after the radar's first warning, the last barge exploded violently when hit by a full salvo. From the sight and sound of the explosions, six barges had been loaded with gasoline and oil, two with ammunition, and the remainder with troops. For HEYWOOD L. EDWARDS, it had been nothing short of a field day at night!

Officially confirming that the situation on Peleliu was well in hand, the American flag was raised in front of the 1st Marine Division Command Post at 0800, September 27.

The landing at Angaur met with much less enemy resistance. The 81st Infantry Division (Major General Paul J. Mueller) quelled all organized resistance on September 20 although mopping up of enemy remnants continued until October 22.

Capturing the southern Palaus cost the Uuited States 7,794 casualties —1,209 of these killed and missing. Japanese dead numbered close to 12,000. Bullets and loud-speakers persuaded only 301 to surrender.

6

Minesweeping has always been a sweaty, unglamorous—but necessary —business. Before the sleek, powerful ships—those which accumulate the praise and the glory—can move into a newly won harbor, or even before they can nose close to enemy-held shore for bombardment, a safe path of approach must be cleared by the dogged little sweepers.

It is always the minesweeps that spearhead an invasion; it is always the minesweeps that open up the vital gap through which the amphibious forces pour their massed weight. And it is almost always a minesweep that gets sunk first.

Back and forth they go, in slow orderly formation, dragging their long tails of magnetic cable behind them, streaming their paravanes to port and starboard, and rattling out sounds like a riveting machine from the trip-hammer mechanism beneath their bows. Thus all kinds of mines—magnetic, contact, and acoustic—are cut from their moorings or detonated.

It is hard work, always nerve-shatteringly noisy, and frequently hull-shatteringly dangerous.

The first ship to be sunk at Palau by enemy mines was the minesweeper PERRY.

It was about midafternoon on September 13. The PERRY was sweeping about 750 yards off the southeast coast of Angaur. Her skipper, Lieutenant Commander William N. Lindsay, Jr., only knows that "a sudden explosion on the starboard side caused an immediate list to port of about 30 degrees. The hole was beneath the water line. No. 2 boiler exploded, and forced live steam and hot oil through ventilation fittings and ruptured hatches. Both firerooms flooded at once." Lieutenant Commander Elward F. Baldridge brought the minesweeper PREBLE in close to save the PERRY but his efforts were fruitless as well as dangerous. Nine men of the PERRY's crew, who had been working near the explosion, were killed, and four members wounded.

The destroyer WADLEIGH (Commander Walter C. Winn) also suffered extensive damage three days later, while demolishing mines at the eastern entrance to Kossol Passage, so that it could be used as a fleet anchorage. Four of the crew were killed and 15 injured.

The last ship to strike a mine was YMS 19. Lieutenant John K. Mahaffey, Jr., was in command of the little ship's maiden cruise. According to Mahaffey, "We were sweeping at low tide. We could see moored mines all around about 10 feet under the surface. My only recollection of the explosion is that it resembled a bomb striking a lumber yard. Timbers went everywhere. About a third of the ship was blown into the air, and it heeled 90 degrees to port. The survivors, 26 in all, crawled to the starboard side of the hull and cut loose our two life rafts shortly before she righted herself and went down by what was left of the stern. Nine of our men were missing."

The mines that our fast carriers dropped in their March raid against Palau must have made an impression on the Japs. If our mines could close the port for one month, they reasoned, their mines would accomplish the same result against us. But the United States Navy was well supplied with men who knew how to sweep mines, and all the minesweepers needed to do the job.

But minesweepers cannot get at mines, booby traps, and obstacles planted in shallow water close to enemy shore batteries. Before the troops wade ashore, these have to be cleared, too. So the Navy developed its Underwater Demolition Teams combing the service for professional and amateur long-distance swimmers who incidentally didn't mind being shot at, at close range. As much psychology as physiology went into their selection.

Tough, fearless, and highly skillful, these men were always the very first to set foot on the beaches. While the minesweepers went about their methodical work in deeper water, these men piled into wooden Higgins boats—two officers and fifteen men to each—and started in toward God-knows-what. From the Higgins boats they transferred to rubber rafts, and from these, when close to shore, the swimmers slipped into the water.

In the Pacific (Navy Demolition Teams blasted a path through the thousands of man-made obstacles at Normandy, too) the beaches were often entirely uncharted and before a landing could be safely made it was necessary for the teams to reconnoiter an entire area a day or so before the first LST could spill its men ashore.

Coral heads and reefs were plotted, the slope of the beach was measured, mines were exploded—all this while looking down the barrels of disputatious guns! But the swimmers, brown and brawny, behaving with the nonchalance of professional poachers, systematically went about their oft-rehearsed tasks. The Japs never knew what they were about, or when.

Each man carried a watch and at a pre-set time all headed seaward, picked up and returned to their APDs. There intelligence officers, after piecing together the information brought back, made sketches of the beaches.

When the Marines charged ashore at Guam, they were greeted by the signs on the beaches—"Welcome Marines" and "Agat USO." Marines, traditionally the first to land, had to defer to the UDTs!

For three days prior to the Peleliu landings demolition teams probed the beaches and the shallow waters offshore. Each man risked his naked, undefended body to save the lives of hundreds who would go ashore armed under an umbrella of heavy gunfire.

7

The original plans for the western Carolines operation called for the occupation of both Yap and Ulithi, but then things started to speed up. On September 16, one day after the landing on Peleliu, a dispatch from Admiral Halsey directed Admiral Wilkinson, if the tactical situation permitted, to "retain afloat one Regimental Combat Team of the 81st Division for possible early employment in seizure of Ulithi." Later on the same day a second dispatch directed Wilkinson to "seize Ulithi as early as practicable—with the resources at hand." At noon on September 17,

Halsey, from the deck of his flagship, NEW JERSEY, personally set that expedition in motion and canceled another. Abandoned was the plan to capture Yap. The war's tempo had sped to a pace which made such lesser enemy strongholds negligible side issues, it was explained. That was a fairy tale, which concealed one of the most dramatic decisions of the entire war—as will be seen.

Rear Admiral W. H. P. Blandy was given the errand to pop Ulithi into the Navy's locker. Captured enemy charts and documents indicated that Ulithi Lagoon was heavily mined in certain areas. Leading the occupation force again, the minesweepers and demolition teams departed Kossol Passage on September 19.

On the morning of September 22 the fire-support group commanded by Admiral Hayler in DENVER (Captain Alfred M. Bledsoe), with the destroyers ROSS (Commander Benjamin Coe) and BRYANT (Commander Paul L. High), entered Ulithi Lagoon, and covered the reconnaissance work being done by the underwater demolition team on Sorlen and Mogmog beaches.

In the evening scouting parties were sent out from the destroyer-transport SANDS to reconnoiter enemy positions on the three nearer islands, and to estimate the effect of the bombardment.

The task was very quickly completed. Four native islanders had been fatally wounded. The handful of other Melanesians were very sorry about that, because they wanted to be happy about the American arrival. It seems that the Japanese had left a month before, and had taken all the young native women with them. The Ulithians wanted their wives and daughters back, and counted on the U.S. Navy to effect the rescue forthwith.

Ulithi, largest atoll in the western Carolines, consists of some thirty islands dotting a reef, which forms a lagoon 19 miles long from north to south, and from 5 to 10 miles wide east to west. The northern part of this lagoon is a good large-ship anchorage, in fact one of the best in the Central Pacific, and was large enough to anchor the entire combatant fleet.

One of the first improvements on the Pacific scene accomplished by Rear Admiral J. W. Reeves, Jr., when he took command of the atoll on September 25 was the establishment of a Fleet Post Office on board a big green LST in the lagoon. This LST soon became the object of every sailor's searching eye as his ship sailed into Ulithi.

The whole sprawling circle of islands was quickly converted to a fleet playground. Baseball diamonds were laid out on the beach. Native huts—the noun is a poor one for the graceful, sturdy thatched structures—were converted into cocktail lounges, beer halls, soda fountains, and "dairy lunches." There were bathing beaches for the sailors who did not insist upon sticking close to dry land after ten months at sea.

8

While all this was going on, the September cruise of TF 38 turned out to be more than a watchdog affair guarding the amphibious operations. The Halsey-Mitscher team was probably the most offensively minded duo in the Pacific, their theory being that the quickest way to eliminate Jap air power was to cut it off at its roots by shooting up the planes on their home grounds.

"There was another basic principle on which the Third Fleet operated," Rear Admiral Carney, Chief of Staff for Admiral Halsey, explains. 'This simple principle, of peculiar interest and vital importance in warfare, was of a fluid and changing nature.

"If it could be determined that the enemy had some plan afoot, the Third Fleet would strike, the purpose being to break up or interrupt whatever plan the enemy had before it could be consummated.

"To carry out this principle it was necessary for our 'dirty trick department' to maintain a continuous plot of enemy forces with the idea of trying to determine at the earliest moment any redisposition or movement of enemy forces which would indicate that something was afoot in their camp. The moment that such a movement or redisposition was spotted, we organized an attack either against those forces directly or made a diversionary attack which would freeze him in his tracks until he could figure out what skulduggery we were up to."

To start with, TG 38.4 under command of Rear Admiral Ralph Davison feinted a diversionary attack against the Volcano and Bonin Islands on August 31, hoping to open up the Japanese defense. Fighting 13 based on the carrier FRANKLIN opened and closed this phase with twenty-nine Hellcats, sixteen of which were armed with rockets, which roared over Iwo Jima and, finding no ships, blasted Iwo's No. 1 airfield, catching ten enemy planes taking off. Fighting 13 also sank one small cargo vessel, damaged and beached another, and left two small transports dead in the water.

The three remaining task groups went directly to the Philippine area to neutralize air activity on Mindanao Island during the Palau operations. Mindanao extends north and south approximately 250 miles and east and west an even greater distance, covering an area roughly equivalent to that of the British Isles. Intelligence information was limited, but it was believed that at least nine big operational airfields were located there, plus many times that number of small operational and emergency fields.

By early morning of September 9 our three task groups—38.1, 38.2 and 38.3—cruised undetected about 50 miles off the coast of Mindanao and sent off the early fighter sweep. Once more a much-vaunted Japanese stronghold proved to have been grossly exaggerated. Jap planes were scarce. However, there was considerable small shipping in the area, and shortly after nine o'clock on the morning of September 9 the planes reported a convoy of thirty-two small cargo vessels proceeding south along the eastern shore of Mindanao. Later it was learned that this convoy had been en route four months from Japan to Davao, and had only 150 miles to go with its desperately needed cargo when first spotted. Sherman's TG 38.3 was the nearest to the convoy so he immediately requested permission from Mitscher to send out a surface force to polish it off. The request approved, Admiral Sherman ordered Rear Admiral L. T. DuBose to take two cruisers and four destroyers and go to work.

It was old stuff for DuBose. The light cruisers SANTA FE and BIRMINGHAM with the destroyers LAWS (Commander Merle VanMetre), MORRISON (Commander Walter H. Price), LONGSHAW (Commander Robert H. Speck), and PRICHETT (Commander Cecil T. Caufield) required less than two hours to eradicate the entire convoy once they brought it into range. Destruction of the supply train was just as effective in pinning the Japanese Army air forces to the ground as the loss of airplanes themselves, for the chief burden of the convoy was oil and gasoline for the dry tanks of the enemy aircraft. Only two Japanese planes attacked the task force, which operated only 50 to 75 miles off the coast. This plus the lack of air opposition over the target area pointed to the fact that the Jap on Mindanao, far from being strong, was in fact extremely weak.

Original plans called for a four-day attack on Mindanao, but since all worth-while targets had been destroyed in two days, Admiral Mitscher used his spare time in attacks on the islands of Leyte, Samar, Cebu,

Negros, Panay, and Bohol. Not much was known of enemy strength in these islands in the central Philippines. There was strength, but not from the neck up.

The Japanese had ample aircraft in the interior islands, and ample warning that the United States carriers were in the neighborhood. Somehow the enemy could not combine these two facts into a plan for action. While they were wringing their hands on Cebu, sixteen carrier-fighters, eight ESSEX and eight LEXINGTON, flew over the island's big airfield, bulging with planes. The Americans knocked down the few that took to the air, picked off the 30-odd more as they took off, and then destroyed forty on the runways for an hour's bag of 78.

Two days later, when the task force was retiring, Mitscher and his staff began to add up the destruction: at least 373 airplanes, ten cargo ships, a transport, two precious oilers, three escort vessels, and more than 35 sampans, barges, and square-sailed luggers. And, of course, there were just as many ships damaged.

Planes from TF 38 had swept across all the islands south of Luzon. Inspiration! Why not go after Luzon? Luzon was one of the juiciest targets in the Empire—perhaps the most juicy outside of the Home Islands themselves. Docks, warehouses, repair yards, merchant ships made fat, tempting targets in the Manila Bay and Subic Bay areas. Furthermore, the highly developed network of airfields was being used as training bases for fledgling pilots and any disruption of this program would aggravate Japan's already acute shortage of trained aviators. There remained, however, the problem of dealing with the five hundred defending planes.

It was too good an opportunity for Mitscher to pass up.

Captain Arleigh Burke, in commenting on the approach, said, "The task force was not detected on its run in towards the eastern shores of Luzon. The initial launch was delayed until about 0800 the morning of the attack by extremely bad weather. It was foul. We didn't know whether to attack or not. Admiral Mitscher, by using a very simple method, decided to attack. Radar showed enemy aircraft aloft about 100 miles to the west. The Admiral reasoned rightly that if the enemy planes could take off, our planes could get in."

Commander Jackson D. Arnold, commanding HORNET's Air Group 2, was among those to go in. Here is his story:

"By midnight of September 20, the three task groups had reached a position 300 miles northeast of Manila. From that point a high-speed run-in was made to the plane-launching position, some 70 miles east of central Luzon.

"The attack was a complete surprise to the Japanese. Filipino stewards, who had lived in Manila, had worked on the details of the strike. The Filipinos knew where ships usually anchored in Manila Bay; knew the depth of the water, and that was our basis for determining the direction the torpedo bombers would attack. The Filipino boys said that the wind usually blew from the north, and that the ships at anchor would be swinging with their sterns away from the wind. That is just the way we found them—about fifty ships.

"There wasn't anything left floating in Manila Bay when we got through. The attack was co-ordinated in such a manner that as the dive bombers led by Commander Jack Blitch from WASP and Commander Grafton B. Campbell nosed over in steep dives, the torpedo bombers who had been circling low around the edge of the bay banked over for a bow approach on the shipping. Old Dewey Drydock that the U.S. Navy had towed from the East Coast through the Panama Canal to the Philippines was sunk, with a ship inside it. The drydock was hit seven times by bombers from the WASP. The entire bay was littered with burning wreckage and oil slicks. We flew very close to Bilibid Prison and could see it plainly. We wanted to drop cigarettes and rations but didn't get a chance. We hoped that sight of our planes would give our people strength to await our return."

While the air groups from "Slew" McCain's carriers, Air Group 2 from HORNET and Air Group 14 from WASP, went after the shipping, Bogan's fliers (Air Group 18, INTREPID; Air Group 8, BUNKER HILL) attacked Clark Field. Sherman's pilots (Air Group 15, ESSEX; Air Group 19, LEXINGTON) struck Nichols Field. Both Clark and Nichols field were within 30 miles of Manila.

Fighter sweeps were furnished by air groups from the light carriers PRINCETON, LANGLEY, CABOT, INDEPENDENCE, and COWPENS, each sending sixteen Hellcats.

The score in planes shot down was again lopsided, the Japs losing 66 in the air and many additional ones on the ground while TF 38 lost six.

Fighting 27 from the PRINCETON bagged the biggest score for the day and one of the best records for the war.

The sixteen Hellcats had swept over their area without locating even one enemy plane when the earphones cackled with a welcomed suggestion.

"Let's strafe the airfield," spoke up Lieutenant Commander Frederick A. Bardshar, who had recently taken over Air Group 27 after the loss of Lieutenant Commander Ernest W. Wood, Jr.

One of Bardshar's fighting aces, freckled-faced, sandy-haired Lieutenant Carl Brown, had just lit a fresh cigarette when he heard this message. As he pushed over for a dive he took a methodical glance toward the sky to see if all was clear and, to his astonishment, directly overhead was a complete armada of Japanese planes at about 16,000 feet.

"Fred, I see our welcoming committee topside," Brown called.

"Rendezvous!" shouted Bardshar immediately.

"Everybody knew Fred's voice," said Brown later, "and I have never seen such a rapid rendezvous in all my life. I didn't have time to take a puff on my cigarette before the fight started.

" 'Tony' pilots hit us the hardest. The painted noses of their planes resembled our Flying Tigers and the noses of our planes bore a face that made a shark look timid. It was weird to watch the funny-faced planes streak toward each other.

"Since we were outnumbered about five to one, we developed new fighter tactics by forming up into a tight ball like swarming bees as we moved toward the Jap formation. I saw five Japs flaming at once and I didn't think that ever happened outside of a Howard Hughes movie.

"When the fight ended, I had big blisters burned on my upper and lower lips from that cigarette. That was how long the fight lasted—one cigarette. My throat was so dry that I couldn't talk over the radio. That is how scared I was."

Although Fighting 27 had faced the toughest opposition, they had met with the greatest success. They had shot down thirty-eight planes without losing a single one of their own.

At the end of the day Admiral Halsey sent a dispatch to Admiral Nimitz:

"Approach to Luzon apparently undetected and surprise complete— thanks to convenient weather front. Weather over the target was good but in launching area weather was foul and operations were only possible because of superb judgment, skill, and determination of TF 38 and its commander Vice Admiral Mitscher.

"Our strikes hit Clark Field, Nichols Field, Cavite, Manila Bay Shipping, Subic Bay Shipping, convoys and swept north and south. Our pilots staged a field day. In addition to above, submarine HADDO while waiting to save some lives knocked off one destroyer. Some air opposition in morning but virtually none reported in afternoon.

"At time of writing this dispatch no damage to our surface forces and nothing on the screen but Hedy Lamar."

9

The path that had been charted on paper more than a year before was now built. It led directly to the Philippines, and the Joint and Combined Chiefs of Staff left it to MacArthur and Nimitz to work out the reconquest of the captured commonwealth their own way.

December 20 was the day selected for the invasion of Mindanao. It was General MacArthur's determination not to move until he had ample airfields, well supplied, for his land-based big bombers to cover his troops. The Army still had some doubts whether carriers and carrier aircraft could operate successfully against the striking power and fighting power of the swifter, heavier-armed land-based aircraft.

Admiral Halsey, Admiral Mitscher—a lot of admirals and a unanimous horde of lesser naval rank—did not share the Army's doubts and triumphantly produced the end-to-end raids on the Philippines to prove it. The argument had great weight, as is about to be demonstrated.

The sweep from Mindanao to Luzon had demonstrated another fallacy in the "estimate of the situation." As Admiral Carney states it, "with startling results we found that the enemy's efforts had been made on a shoestring. His forces in the Philippines were not in great strength, and his installations were not such as to preclude the possibility of early capture."

The fast carrier strikes between August 31 and September 24 had bagged over 1,000 Japanese airplanes and over 150 ships. No American carrier was damaged, and the total Navy planes lost were 54 in combat, 18 by accidents.

But MacArthur's plan called for another hop from Morotai to the Talaud Islands, closing the distance to Sarangani Bay in southern Mindanao by another 50 per cent. It was the companion piece to the Navy's planned capture of Yap.

It was the testimony of a reserve ensign that upset all these calculations. Thomas Cato Tillar, an F6F pilot from the HORNET, was shot down off the southwestern coast of Leyte Island. He was rescued by Filipinos who sheltered him, fed him, and told him in great detail all they knew about the Japanese strength in the area.

They knew a lot, a convincing lot, and when Tillar was returned to his ship he carried a mental chart of the Japanese positions on Leyte, and a round-number census of the enemy troops and equipment.

With that final piece of evidence, Admiral Halsey sped a message to MacArthur.

The General was aboard the NASHVILLE, returning to Hollandia on September 13 after viewing the easy occupation of Morotai. After reading Halsey's urgent top-secret dispatch, MacArthur paced his stateroom for four hours. Then he summoned the cruiser's commanding officer.

"Captain, I must ask you to break radio silence," he said.

"Break radio silence, sir?" Captain Coney was as startled as if General MacArthur had asked to be put ashore in Tokyo. "Why, General, that will not only let the Japs know where we are, but it will give them the location of all the ships with us."

The General waved Coney's protests aside, although the Captain explained further that breaking radio silence was almost the worst violation of Navy security rules.

"Send a message to my staff in Hollandia," MacArthur said, "telling them to have our alternate plan such-and-such for the Philippine invasion drawn up by the time I arrive tomorrow.

"And, Captain! Enter in the ship's log that radio silence was broken by my express order."

In all the trips the General made on the NASHVILLE, that was the only order he ever issued to Captain Coney.

The alternate plan was for the invasion of the Philippines at Leyte Gulf. And at once, not at Christmas.

Halsey laid his conclusions before Admiral Nimitz. General MacArthur presented his acceptance of them, and his plans for hitting the Philippines a blow in the belly instead of a kick in the pants.

But you can't turn a war off its ponderous course the way a traffic cop can divert a parade down another street.

The Navy was getting all set for Yap. Vice Admiral "Ted" Wilkinson's Third Amphibious Force had already shoved off from Hawaii and was nearly a week at sea, headed west.

There was also a chain of command to follow to its source, back in the United States. A radical change in the plans for the Pacific might complicate the plans in operation against Germany, where the Allied forces were crowding Hitler's forces back into the Reich. The Joint Chiefs of Staff were not even in Washington. They were in Quebec, at a United Nations conference.

In less than twenty-four hours after General MacArthur made his decision, the whole machinery of war from Quebec to Guam and Hollandia was in motion to execute it.

Chapter Twenty-Two

"I Have Returned"

1

THE day that General MacArthur ordered Captain Coney, NASH-VILLE's commanding officer, to break radio silence for the purpose of advising his staff back at Hollandia to have the alternate plan drawn up by the following morning, there were exactly thirty-seven days remaining before he would fullfil his promise to the Filipinos, "I shall return."

The Joint Chiefs of Staff were attending the Octagon Conference in Quebec when they were interrupted by the urgent request from the other side of the earth. Halsey's message came first. He recommended that the three projected intermediate landings on Yap, Mindanao, Talaud, and Sangihe islands be canceled and Leyte invaded as soon as possible. While the Joint Chiefs were still passing the message from hand to hand another arrived from Admiral Nimitz. He supported the change and committed the entire Pacific Fleet to accomplish the job.

Admiral Leahy, Admiral King, General Arnold, and General Marshall were about to move into a formal dinner party as guests of high Canadian officers when the messages arrived. Dinner had to wait while they met in unscheduled conference. The third dispatch arrived, from MacArthur.

"I am already prepared to shift plans to land on Leyte 20 October instead of 20 December."

It was not a difficult decision for the Joint Chiefs. They had utmost confidence in MacArthur, Nimitz, and Halsey. Within ninety minutes after the last dispatch had been received in Quebec, MacArthur and Nimitz had the answer in hand. It was instructions to execute the Leyte operation on October 20. The three previously approved intermediate landings were canceled.

2

Sad news from General Joseph Stilwell in China did not dampen the spirits of MacArthur. Stilwell radioed that the Japanese offensive in

Central China would soon result in the capture of Eastern China airfields. These were the airfields from which Major General Claire L. Chennault's B-29s had planned to support recapture of the Philippines. MacArthur told the War Department that Admiral Halsey's fast carriers had so reduced Japan's air capabilities in the Philippines, Formosa, and the Ryukyus that it would be possible to move from Leyte to Luzon without the Fourteenth Air Force.

The most pressing problem facing the United States was one of logistics. The transporting of supplies for an Army and Navy operating 6,000 miles from the West Coast ports would never be simple, regardless of the number of bottoms available to form a pipeline. The staggering amount of material necessary for fleet operations alone was revealed during October in the use of fuel oil. The fleet received $4\frac{1}{2}$ million barrels of fuel oil, enough to fill a train of tank cars over 260 miles long!

United States problems, seemingly great, did not compare with the endless difficulties facing the Japanese.

Their fleet was still strong, but unbalanced. They had cruisers and battleships, but no destroyers to provide protection. They had the remnants of a merchant marine, but no escort vessels to tussle with U.S. submarines. They had aircraft carriers, but only a few skilled pilots available to make them an effective weapon. Making the situation even worse was the shortage of fuel oil. Far-ranging American submarines through numerous tanker sinkings had reduced the flow of oil to a trickle. Pilot training and fleet operations and training in general were increasingly curtailed because of the fuel shortages.

But the strong Japanese Army, still undefeated and virtually untested in mass combat, was still full of confidence. Tough, battle-hardened reinforcements were brought from Manchuria to strengthen the Philippine defenses. The Army chose to man Luzon most strongly, and there organized a mobile counterlanding force which could be rushed through protected waters after the Americans committed themselves to an invasion point.

The goal of the Japanese was simple—to hold the Philippine defense line at all costs; to fight to the bitter end with the Navy, Army, and Air Forces. If the Army and Air Forces were lost they might possibly be replaced, but if the Navy was lost it would be gone forever. The chance had to be taken.

3

On September 15, the day the Joint Chiefs of Staff ordered invasion of Leyte, the ships that would be required for this operation were spread out all over the vast Pacific Ocean areas.

September 15 was D-day on Morotai and Palau. On that day, while at Morotai, Admiral Barbey was informed of the cancellation of the southern Philippine operation and advancement of the date and target to October 20 at Leyte. All of Barbey's ships were unloading at Morotai. His new job was to finish that task, return to the staging area, reload and shove off in time to arrive at Leyte, 1,900 miles away, on invasion day. He had exactly thirty-five days to do it all.

Admiral Wilkinson's Third Amphibious Force was rocking along in the middle of the Pacific en route to Yap when he learned of the stepped-up offensive. He had to scrap all instructions and plans, and prepare for a new target. He put in at Eniwetok as scheduled for replenishment, and there got his orders to proceed to the big anchorage in Seeadler Harbor, Manus. The big bay had started to pay dividends. His transport convoy arrived in Manus on October 3 and the slow-moving LST convoy a day later.

4

The planning for the invasion of Leyte was done at Hollandia, where MacArthur's headquarters had been moved from the temporary base at Port Moresby, Brisbane being the permanent base until the move. With a number of Quonset huts Admiral Kinkaid, head of "MacArthur's Navy," had built himself "quite a respectable headquarters."

"It was the only time during the Pacific War," recalled Kinkaid later, "that I had adequate time to plan. It was the only time I saw plans properly made. We had the ideal physical setup. Everyone was there.

"Wilkinson, who was second in command of the Seventh Fleet and a man in whom I had great confidence, lived in the same room with me at Hollandia for seventeen days while we made plans for the invasion. I just put up another bunk for him and we lived right there together. His staff was quartered right next to mine and they could shout to each other from their huts. Barbey was in his flagship at Humboldt Bay. Kenney, the Fifth Air Force Commander, Krueger, commander of the

Sixth Army, MacArthur—all were close by, within a half-hour calling distance. We were able to get together and work out an excellent plan while looking over each other's shoulder. Each man had a chance to get in his oar."

Lack of time precluded extensive reorganization of the amphibious task forces for the new and bigger operation. For example, the Third Amphibious Force, in preparing to land on the coral atoll of Yap, had on board numerous LVTs and DUKWs to carry troops from parent vessels over the dangerous fringing reefs. At Leyte, the smooth, marshy landing beaches, unobstructed by coral, made unnecessary the use of these versatile amphibious craft, but there wasn't time to remove them from the ships.

Late in September, Admiral Halsey and selected members of his staff spent three days with General MacArthur and Admiral Kinkaid at Hollandia perfecting details for full co-ordination of Third and Seventh fleets. The new organization of the Seventh consisted of three task forces, TF 77, 78, and 79. Admiral Kinkaid was in over-all command of this fleet and also served as Commander of Task Force 77, which was divided into:

> Fire Support Group, CTG 77.2, Rear Admiral Oldendorf
> Close Covering Group, CTG 77.3, Rear Admiral Berkey
> Escort Carrier Group, CTG 77.4, Rear Admiral T. L. Sprague
> Minesweeping and Hydrographic Group, CTG 77.5, Commander Loud
> Beach Demolition Group, CTG 77.6, Commander C. C. Morgan
> Service Group, CTG 77.7, Rear Admiral R. O. Glover
> Commander Support Aircraft, Captain Whitehead.

In command of TF 78 was Rear Admiral Barbey and Vice Admiral Wilkinson's title was changed from CTF 33 to CTF 79.

5

The invasion was to be on the eighth largest of the Philippine islands, northwest of Mindanao's farthest reach. Slightly larger than the state of Delaware, Leyte is very fertile and supports a normal population of more than a million. It is about 90 miles long from north to south and from 35 miles to 25 miles wide. Its northeastern corner is separated from the island of Samar by narrow, shallow San Juanico Strait, navigable only by small craft. The broad beaches of the east-central coast face Leyte

INVASION OF LEYTE
OCT. 20, 1944

Gulf, whose 40-mile square expanse is free of offshore reefs. Tacloban is the capital city.

The gulf generally faces the Pacific through the 10-mile gap between bigger Samar Island and very much smaller Homonhon. South of Homonhon Island is Dinagat Island, and between Leyte and Dinagat, Panaon Island splits Surigao Strait, which is one of the two deep-water exits from the Philippines' inland seas to the Pacific.

Panaon, Dinagat, Homonhon. These islands, commanding the gulf's exit and entrances, would have to be secured first, and they were the first objectives of MacArthur's invasion.

Leyte would provide space for a relatively big battlefield, compared with MacArthur's other excursions. True, his 193,841 attacking troops were a tiny force compared with the huge armies crowding the European fronts. The Pacific was the bigger campaign area. There, distances were measured in miles where it was measured in feet in the ETO, but most of the miles were water.

6

The basic concept of the operation visualized the seizure by major amphibious assault of the eastern coast of Leyte and strategic points on adjacent islands. The operation also called for complete control of contiguous waters.

As set forth in General MacArthur's operating instructions, Admiral Kinkaid's Seventh Fleet was given a heavy responsibility:

"The Navy will transport and land the Army inside Leyte Gulf; will sweep the mines and clear underwater beach obstacles; will sink opposing surface forces and clear the skies of enemy planes; will hover air power over our long attack and support convoys; will prevent the Japanese from reinforcing Leyte from the west; will clear all adjacent waters for future operations; will press a submarine offensive and at the same time provide lifeguard services and will establish in Leyte Gulf a naval force sufficient to support current and future operations."

In addition to this, Admiral Halsey had agreed to support the operation in the following manner:

During the period of A-minus-10 to A-minus-7 (A was used instead of D to designate invasion day), he would take his carriers into the shadows of the Empire of Japan. His swift and deadly planes would swoop down on Okinawa, Formosa, and the northern Philippine airfields to destroy planes that might be used for enemy reinforcements.

During the period from A-minus-4 to A-day itself he would steam up and down the eastern coastal areas of Leyte, Samar, and Luzon, and cruise off Leyte on A-day to support the invasion.

Following the invasion, his Third Fleet would remain in the area for strategic support and launch strikes as the situation required.

Most of the ships for the invasion assembled at Seeadler Harbor in the Admiralties, but some assembled at Hollandia. When Kinkaid flew over Seeadler on an inspection, there were 565 ships in the harbor and "room for plenty more."

7

Always in the van of the invasion forces, the slow minesweepers were first to sortie. They weighed anchor on October 11. Next came the Dinagat Attack Group, TG 78.4, which left Hollandia the following day, rendezvoused near Palau to be refueled, and was joined October 15 by the bombardment and fire-support ships. This latter group was built around six old battleships—MISSISSIPPI, MARYLAND, WEST VIRGINIA, PENNSYLVANIA, TENNESSEE, and CALIFORNIA—and included ten cruisers and twelve CVEs plus the beach demolition group. This advance force was commanded by Rear Admiral J. B. Oldendorf.

"We had a strong force," said Admiral Kinkaid. "There was no grave concern over whether we could land and stay there. But there was great concern over storms. We talked it over and decided that if a storm did come, each group would circle to the left and come back. We would delay an even twenty-four hours, in such a case, so that the schedule would still be the same.

"In order to have available the best weather information I had Wilkinson and his aerologists come in my group. So together with my weather men on the WASATCH we had the best of information. I gave MacArthur a cruiser [NASHVILLE] and he too came in my group.

"The bombardment group headed for the entrance of Leyte Gulf where they were to shell the islands of Suluan and Dinagat in preparation for landings on them. It was a strange thing but the only circular storm in the whole area built up right there where Oldendorf was."

The center of the typhoon was detected about 100 miles ahead of

Oldendorf's advance force on October 16. Waves 40 to 50 feet from crest to trough broke over the ships. Occasional gusts of wind swept across the sea at 125 knots.

Many of the ships lost their radio and radar antennas, sustained heavy damage to gyros and engines, as the angry sea swished gray water over the flying bridge. The strain on the smaller ships soon began to tell as one by one they dropped out of formation. Toward sunset on the first day of the storm, five minesweepers were straggling far behind and an Australian frigate, HMAS GASCOYNE, dropped out of formation to round them up.

When the sweepers reached their sweeping stations the sea was still rough. For YMS 70 the storm had been too much. She tried to sweep, but the heavy seas continued to pour through her ripped seams. Finally the little ship could be maneuvered no longer and at 1730, A-minus-3-day, YMS 70 became our first casualty in the Battle of Leyte Gulf—but to J. Pluvius, not S. Toyoda.

Before sunset of October 17 the minesweepers reported the gulf free of mines, and the remainder of fire-support and beach demolition groups entered the gulf. The sweepers' report was overoptimistic. Next day, as Admiral Sprague commenced air operations with his jeep-carriers, the destroyer ROSS, while screening sweepers that had retired for the night, was damaged by two floating mines. This was only the beginning of a series of misfortunes which were to plague ROSS. Up to October 19 she had successfully participated in several shore bombardments and fought off many an air raid. She rode out the preinvasion typhoon handily. Then two mines hit her, and she had to be dragged to the shelter of Homonhon Island by the fleet tug CHICKASAW (Lieutenant Louis C. Olson). Shelter? She was hit by a Japanese airplane shot flaming out of the sky by carrier fighters, and hit six times by erratic gunfire from her sister ships, before her turn came to enter one of the floating drydocks for repair. But, cripple though the ROSS was, her guns knocked two Japanese bombers out of the sky while she "sat waiting in the doctor's office."

8

A representative from the NASHVILLE, Commander Robert H. Taylor, went over to General MacArthur's headquarters, high on Cyclops Mountain near Hollandia, to complete arrangements for bringing the General aboard. What impressed Taylor most was that he had to "sleep under two blankets to keep warm on the mountain. Living in that climate should have put the General in fighting trim."

According to the NASHVILLE's log, "The Commander-in-Chief, Southwest Pacific Area, General Douglas MacArthur, and members of his staff embarked at Hollandia, Dutch New Guinea, at 1057, October 16, 1944 and Task Unit 77.1.2 consisting of NASHVILLE, ABNER READ and BUSH, got underway and proceeded to the specified rendezvous," where it joined the main attack force. All ships fueled from the tanker group, and then NASHVILLE fell in astern of Admiral Wilkinson's TF 79 to steam with WASATCH, Kinkaid's flagship, to Leyte.

When NASHVILLE joined up, Kinkaid sent a blinker message to MacArthur:

"Welcome to our city."

MacArthur's reply, also sent by flashing light, read: "Thanks for your message. Glad indeed to be in your domicile and under your flag. It gives me not only confidence but a sense of inspiration. As Ripley says, believe it or not we are almost there. MacArthur."

Probably the happiest man in the convoy was the General himself. To NASHVILLE's personnel he was a strange mixture of precise formality and completely informal affability. Although commander-in-chief of the operation, he never stepped on the cruiser's bridge without first requesting the Captain's permission, but he also willingly spent hours in writing his autograph for the bluejackets and Marines aboard. He sat in his cabin doorway, signing his name over and over again on anything the lined-up men presented—gum wrappers, dollar bills, old envelopes, and even tissue paper.

Captain Coney had known General MacArthur for a number of years. As they stood together on the bridge of the NASHVILLE, Coney took a quick glance through his binoculars at the horizon, McArthur gazed out toward the Philippines across the stretches of blue water, calmed now after the storm, and volunteered the promise that "when we get back to Manila, you and I will ride side by side in an open car up the middle of Dewey Boulevard!"

"He never complained about food and would ask for nothing special— except ice cream," Coney recalls. "General MacArthur is very fond of ice cream and when he would get the word that ice cream was being mixed, he would immediately dispatch his Filipino sergeant to the galley. He liked it plain or he liked it fancy, as long as the bowl was full.

"The only thing that irritated me about General MacArthur," concluded Captain Coney, "was that when he came topside to witness an aerial action or a bombardment, he refused a steel helmet or a life preserver. If he was on the bridge, he would push his familiar gold-covered cap back and coolly watch the show. If he was in his cabin, he would read a book while the guns were firing."

9

As the convoy neared Leyte Gulf, General McArthur's impatience to return to Tacloban, Leyte's capital, became more pronounced. That was the place where, forty-one years earlier, he had reported as a second lieutenant fresh from West Point on his first mission.

The General didn't have long to wait.

By nightfall October 19 the main attack force stood in for the entrance to Leyte Gulf, streaming their mine-severing paravanes. Two of the deadly steel bubbles were found and destroyed, one by the Australian cruiser SHROPSHIRE whose adroit handling of the mine won warm commendation from Admiral Berkey.

Only the sweep-arm on the face of the radar penetrated the night and revealed the vast convoy of 738 ships, all feeling their way through the swept channel into Leyte Gulf. On the radar screen each ship formed a small pip while the land made large blots of light on the edges. Like so many insects crowded near a porch light on a hot summer evening, the clusters of ships moved in a definite pattern on the orange and green lighted radar scopes.

Complex because large groups of ships of various speeds had to arrive practically simultaneously on both the northern and southern beaches, the approach plan provided an exact place in the pattern for each ship to be at the 10:00 A.M. assault. The fleet had to be deployed with chronometerlike precision, every ship exactly where it should be at every moment—and this in utter darkness save for radar's night-piercing eye. It was a ballet of the blind.

A light blinked from Homonhon Island. U.S. Rangers, who had been landed two days before, were reporting all well.

Still guided by radar, more than 700 ships fanned out over Leyte Gulf to get in positions assigned for the big assault.

LSTs from both attack groups arrived at their launching areas at 0800, two hours before H-hour. With the transports' arrival a few minutes later, all ships were present.

To the north the veteran Seventh Amphib was clustered in San Pedro Bay, in the Tacloban area. Its job was to put ashore the Tenth Corps, composed of the 1st Cavalry Division and the 24th Infantry Division, whose job in turn was to capture Leyte Valley. Rear Admiral Barbey himself would direct the assault on Red Beach, Rear Admiral W. M. Fechteler at White Beach, Rear Admiral A. D. Struble, with one Regimental Combat Team of the 24th Infantry Division, was sent south to Panaon Strait to gain a key position commanding the lower entrance to Surigao Strait, permitting passage of PT boats into Mindanao Sea west of Leyte.

Admiral Barbey's Northern Attack Force was supported by fire-support ships which had been bombarding Japanese defense positions for two days. These ships—battleships WEST VIRGINIA, MARYLAND, MISSISSIPPI, the destroyers AULICK, CONY, and SIGOURNEY—were augmented by Admiral Berkey's Close Covering forces, the cruisers PHOENIX, BOISE, HMAS AUSTRALIA, and HMAS SHROPSHIRE, and destroyers BACHE, BEALE, HUTCHINS, DALY, KILLEN, HMAS ARUNTA, and HMAS WARRAMUNGA.

"There were so many ships in the small area," Admiral Berkey relates, "that we had to take turns firing. When the battleships completed their firing mission, my cruisers, which had been milling around near-by, moved and blasted what remained of known Japanese defenses."

Admiral Wilkinson's Southern Attack Force, Task Force 79, meanwhile stood off the beach 11 miles south. Its beachhead was situated between Dulag, the town destroyed A-minus-2-day by bombarding ships supporting the underwater demolition teams, and San Jose. Assisting Wilkinson were Rear Admirals Conolly and Royal. Together they were to land the 24th Corps, composed of the 7th and 96th Divisions. Bombardment ships supporting Wilkinson included the battleships TENNESSEE, CALIFORNIA, and PENNSYLVANIA; the cruisers LOUISVILLE, PORTLAND, MINNEAPOLIS, HONOLULU, DENVER, COLUMBIA; the destroyers LEUTZE, NEWCOMB, BENNION, HEYWOOD L. EDWARDS, RICHARD P. LEARY, ROBINSON, ROSS, ALBERT W. GRANT, BRYANT, HALFORD, THORN, CLAXTON, and WELLES. Since more sea room was available around the southern beaches than up north all the ships were able to loose their salvos simultaneously.

From dawn until H-hour, all the bombardment ships laid down a methodically destructive fire against the hidden Japanese positions. Simultaneously, scheduled air strikes were made by planes from Admiral Sprague's eighteen CVEs which had been assigned to make bombing and strafing runs on the invasion points. LCI(G)s delivered a devastating rocket and mortar barrage during the last fifteen minutes.

Then the first wave darted landward, some riding in tanklike LVTs which had loaded for the invasion of Yap, some in fast wooden LCPRs, some in high-ramped LCTs, and some directly from the big LSTs, hit the marshy sands of Leyte on schedule, ten o'clock on the morning of October 20, 1944.

Troops encountered very little enemy resistance with the exception of those harassed by mortar fire off Red Beach. The mortars hit LSTs 452, 171, and 181 of Flotilla 7 injuring 75 men and causing some structural damage to the ships.

"The shooting came from the Tolosa Hills," recalls Captain Richard M. Scruggs, skipper of the flotilla, who had taken it through thirteen Pacific landings, from Woodlark Island to Leyte. "Our battleships and cruisers had done an excellent job, but of course they couldn't find everything."

The entire area was covered with dust, fire, and smoke. "Where the Jap shells were coming from was the question that had to be solved—and in a hurry," related Admiral Berkey.

"I ordered the cruisers to load with fragmentation projectiles and open up on the Tolosa Hills. It was my guess that the Japs might be located near the peak of the hill. Two of the cruisers' salvos passed over the summit before they exploded—and the Jap mortars were silenced! That was where they were hidden—behind the hills."

The assault waves and reserve battalions were all put ashore in the forenoon. After chow, the unloading of cargo was begun. The assault phase, as Admiral Halsey had predicted, was completed quickly and cheaply.

Threading their way out from shore, through the harbor-choking fleet, bobbing against the wakes of the landing craft and destroyers, came medieval-looking little craft filled with grinning, brown-skinned little men.

They were in an ecstasy that made them oblivious to everything but the necessity of welcoming the Allied Fleet; they were the real veterans of the war with Japan—Filipinos who had fought by night and bowed by day, and whose information had helped give Halsey the inspiration for the Leyte Gulf operation. Now they brought the news that all enemy planes on Leyte had been destroyed, that the Japanese had no torpedo craft on the far side of the island, and much other information of invaluable detail.

10

Aboard the NASHVILLE, Army Signal Corps specialists worked feverishly to install additional radio equipment, equipment which would cover the same frequency bands being used by the Filipino guerrilla leaders on Mindanao, Leyte, Visayas, and Luzon.

From the steel-plated decks of a Navy cruiser, plowing triumphantly along the newly won beachhead, General MacArthur made his historic speech to the Philippine patriots:

"This is the Voice of Freedom, General MacArthur speaking. People of the Philippines! I have returned. By the grace of Almighty God our force stands again on Philippine soil, consecrated in the blood of two peoples. As the line of battle rolls forward to bring you within the zone of operation, rise and strike. . . . Rally to me. Let the indomitable spirit of Bataan and Corregidor lead on . . . Let no heart be faint. Let every arm be steeled. The guidance of Divine God points the way. Follow in His name to the Holy Grail of righteous victory."

The time was two o'clock in the afternoon of October 20, four hours after the first soldier stepped on Leyte Beach.

Later that day, the General waded ashore to a point where he had stood forty-one years earlier as a second lieutenant on his first Philippine mission. From there he again broadcast his inspirational message to the guerrilla warriors. He had fulfilled his promise. He had returned.

11

Initial Japanese resistance was light. Before the day ended, the 1st Cavalry Division captured Tacloban airstrip and next day took Tacloban itself. The town's 30,000 people crowded onto the streets in carnival, cheering the triumphal re-entry with an enthusiasm that threatened to slow down the war as girls thrust flowers into the troopers' gear, pressed candy and wine upon them, and clung to their arms.

The General of the Sixth Army, Lieutenant General Krueger, took command of all Army forces in Leyte area on the 24th. To oppose him in the field, Japan was sending her greatest military leader, General Yamashita, known as the "Tiger of Malaya" to the Japanese and as the "Bloody Butcher of Bataan" to the Americans. Against the naval forces, Japan hurled what remained of her Philippine air force.

The first indication that the Japs were going to make it rough on ships came in the early morning of the first day, when a large force of planes attacked our fire-support ships, but without achieving even a reasonably near miss.

A little while later, so close as to seem almost a part of that raid, the Japanese struck with a new aerial weapon.

It was not recognized for what it was, the forerunner of a horrifying and inhumanly cold-blooded, and costly, instrument of desperation. The Japanese, in a self-immolating frenzy of destruction which was to reach specialized heights at which civilization still looks aghast, hurled their first Kamikaze at the invading fleet.

Kamikaze means "divine wind," and by tenuous threads of Nipponese association, related the suicide pilots to the "divine" wind which, centuries before, had converted defeat to victory by swamping a Korean fleet.

Other pilots had deliberately crashed their crippled planes on ships' decks before, but this was the first time that an explosive-laden aircraft had been piloted to its target for no other mission than to be a guided missile—a humanly guided missile.

It was not too successful, getting itself fouled up in the superstructure of HMAS AUSTRALIA and causing only a small fraction of the damage of which it was capable.

"The bloke must 'a' been sonky as 'ell," complained the bluejackets cleaning up the mess. "Got 'is brits up and froze to the blurry stick, I says."

But the bloke didn't have his brits up at all. He was as cool and determined as a bombardier dropping a 500-pounder on a barge from 20,-000 feet. And there were thousands like him, and factories turning out specially designed winged bombs for a devoted son of Nippon to ride straight to its mark.

At 4:02 in the afternoon, the cruiser HONOLULU was hit by an aerial torpedo. The enemy plane made its approach through a rain squall overhanging the northernmost ridge of hills off the southern landing beaches. The Japanese pilot knew the harbor was full of ships. All he had to do was drop his "fish" and he was bound to hit something.

The HONOLULU had participated in the early-morning shore bombardment and was standing by for another fire-support mission when the "Kate" appeared. Captain Harry R. Thurber tells the remainder of the story as viewed from the fighting bridge:

"Our lookouts were on the job, and spotted the brownish-green plane as it emerged from the mists overhanging Catmon Hill. It started its low run over many of our ships in that vicinity. They could not fire effectively, due to the ever-present danger of hitting our own people. The Jap apparently chose us as his intended victim, and made an approach from slightly abaft our port beam. We opened fire on him, but he kept coming on. From his approach angle, he was gunning for our engine room and I automatically ordered all engines crashed back full—a ship isn't worth much if she can't 'mote.' Shortly after this, the Jap torpedo made a slight splash as it entered the water. It was dropped in the shoals just off the beaches, and I sent up a prayer that it would stick on the bottom. But that wake began to show, pointing directly at our midriff. We felt powerless.

Although the "Blue Goose," as she was affectionately known to her men, had gained quite a bit of sternway, the torpedo could not be avoided. It was one of the enemy's biggest aircraft torpedoes with approximately 900 pounds of explosives. When it struck, it tore a jagged hole 25 feet wide and 29 feet high in the ship's hull.

Japanese torpedoes, it should be added, were better made than the American. There were fewer duds; fewer "went crazy," to run in circles.

The attack came at a critical time aboard ship because the 1600 to 2000 watch was in process of relieving. The blast killed sixty men. The ship took a 14-degree list and went down by the bow. Skillful work by the ship's damage-control parties localized the flooding. The destroyer RICHARD P. LEARY (Commander Frederic S. Habecker) came alongside to render first aid and supply emergency power. Two tugs, POTAWATOMI (Lieutenant Charles H. Stedman) and MENOMINEE (Lieutenant John A. Young, Jr.), arrived to pump out flooded compartments.

More bad luck was due the Blue Goose that night. Shortly after she had anchored in the transport area, with damage under control, another air raid commenced. A heavy smoke screen was laid, and the ships put up an umbrella of fire. A very badly misdirected AA burst from one of the fleet detonated the 40mm ammunition stowage on HONOLULU's flying bridge, killing five and wounding thirteen.

Admiral Halsey's message to the departing Blue Goose, a favorite ship that had participated in many of the grueling battles up the Slot, in the South Pacific, was very appropriate:

"Tough luck for a tough ship."

Although most of the early damage was minor, three ships were sunk during the amphibious phase of the operation. The SONOMA, the tough oceangoing rescue and salvage tug which had participated in all the invasions along the coast of New Guinea, was sunk on the 22nd. LCI(L) 1065 (Lieutenant Rudolph F. Liste) was struck by Jap shell fire and went down on the 24th. The EVERSOLE (Lieutenant Commander George E. Marix), a destroyer escort, was the victim of a submarine-launched torpedo and sank on the 29th. Other ships suffering more or less combat damage during the ten-day period included CALIFORNIA, DENVER, LOUISVILLE, and ROBERT WHEELER from what were now recognized as suicide planes; FREMONT, AUGUSTUS THOMAS, ASHTABULA, and PCE 848 from bombs and near misses.

Admiral Kinkaid, commenting on the Leyte invasion, says: "The amphibious part of this operation lost the headlines in the papers because of the big battle that followed, but it was the best planned and best executed amphibious operation I saw during the whole war. No naval commander could ask for a better plan."

CHAPTER TWENTY-THREE

Halsey Cuts the Pipeline

I

THE RESISTANCE to MacArthur's landing would probably have been stiffer, and the Japanese potential against the Allied fleet much higher, except for a brisk diversion created by Admiral Halsey in advance of the Philippine invasion.

MacArthur would have to have air supremacy at Leyte. Leyte was too far for his Army Air Forces to reach from the bases that had been captured in anticipation of the now-canceled Mindanao offensive. It was up to the carriers to supply the Army with bombers and fighters,[1] the latter especially dear to the soldiers for the close ground support in which the Navy and Marine fliers were so particularly well schooled—flying low to spy out enemy movements, strong points and traps, and dropping the written, sketched-out information; strafing and bombing the enemy ahead of the foot soldiers and tanks, and ferrying supplies in emergencies.

To provide all that, air superiority has to be obtained. One way of obtaining it is to hinder the enemy from getting his aircraft to the operation from other areas.

Halsey's plan, approved by Nimitz, was to cut the Japanese pipeline from the homeland to the Philippines, with an all-out punch against the way stations between.

Old Dame Nature, again quixotically taking sides with the Japanese, loosed the typhoon of October 3. There were two that month; the second

---

[1] In mid-December, at the Army's request, four Marine Aircraft Groups (MAGs 12, 14, 24, 32; Colonel Clayton C. Jerome, CO) were sent to Leyte to render the ground troops necessary close support. When Major General Verne D. Mudge led his troops into Manila on February 4 he said in an interview, "I depended solely on the Marines to protect my left flank from the air against possible Japanese counterattack. The job they turned in speaks for itself. We are here . . . The Marine dive bomber outfits are one of the most flexible I have ever seen . . . They will try anything, and from my experience . . . anything they try usually pans out. [They] have kept the enemy on the run. They have kept him underground, and enabled troops to move with fewer casualties and with greater speed . . ." (Hough, *The Island War*)

one, as described in the previous chapter, seemed intent on delaying the Leyte Gulf operation. More than half of Task Force 38 was anchored in Ulithi lagoon, and Halsey ordered it out in the face of the storm warnings. When it returned after ducking the typhoon, its task of making ready for the strike against Japan's lifeline was complicated by the loss to the storm's fury of 65 LCVPs and 14 LCMs, needed to ferry supplies from the stores ashore to the ships in deep water. But on October 7 the task groups made rendezvous north of Palau with their sister groups.

Group 38.1 was commanded by Vice Admiral John S. McCain; Rear Admiral Gerald F. Bogan had 38.2, with which Vice Admiral Willis A. ("Ching") Lee's TF 34—five battleships, three light cruisers, one light carrier, and fourteen destroyers—now merged. Task Group 38.3 was commanded by Rear Admiral Frederick C. Sherman and 38.4 by Rear Admiral Ralph E. Davison.

It was Halsey's scheme to use the typhoon to his own ends. He even gave it an official Navy designation—Task Force Zero.

As the revolving storm moved north and westward in counterclockwise violence, Halsey in the NEW JERSEY led his forces in the cyclone's wake. The armada stretched from horizon to horizon, lunging in the disturbed sea as it plowed toward Japan's home waters protected by a screen of continuous cloudbursts driven by a 100-knot wind. Meteorologists plotted the storm's course, and kept it enslaved as the task force's titanic camouflage.

Decks of the accompanying tankers were often under four feet of boiling sea as the crews transfused the vital oil into the warships' vitals. Hardened veterans of a generation at sea pushed back from the tables and left the mess hastily, sweat beaded and tight lipped.

Okinawa was the first target. Few persons in the fleet had ever heard of it before. In the United States it is doubtful if anybody except missionaries, geographers, and historians knew then of the island's existence at the elbow of the arm of Japanese islands that ends in the Big Fist of Formosa. But once it had been United States territory, informally and for a few months, when Commodore Matthew C. Perry annexed it in 1852, before Japan laid claim to it.

Lest rumors of his excursion be received and correctly interpreted by the enemy, Halsey detached a group of three cruisers and six destroyers [1]

---

[1] TG 30.2: Crudiv 5: Rear Admiral Allan E. Smith, with CHESTER (Captain Henry Hartley), PENSACOLA (Captain Allen P. Mullinnix), SALT LAKE CITY (Captain

to attack Marcus Island with instructions to "make a noise like a whole fleet." They did, with smoke screens, floating lights, pyrotechnics, and other razzle-dazzle.

The ruses all worked. Okinawa was "caught with its kimono up" at dawn on October 10. Planes from INTREPID, BUNKER HILL, HANCOCK, CABOT, INDEPENDENCE, ESSEX, LEXINGTON, PRINCETON, and LANGLEY hit the northern installations and those on the neighboring island of Ie. In the south, Okinawa's principal city of Naha and the airfields around it were smashed by the planes from WASP, HORNET, COWPENS, MONTEREY, FRANKLIN, ENTERPRISE, SAN JACINTO, and BELLEAU WOOD.

Juicy shipping targets were found in the harbors and anchorages off the west coast of Okinawa and these received their share of attention. Japanese air opposition was negligible. Only twenty planes were shot down over the target and three over the task force. An additional eight were destroyed on the ground or water. Our total loss was eight planes and eight men.

When the last carrier plane landed at five minutes after six in the evening four strikes of about 340 planes each had dropped 541 tons of bombs and expended 652 rockets and 21 torpedoes against Okinawa. Seventy-five ships from sampans to cargo types had been sunk. Two midget submarines were blown up by a single bomb dropped between them. Barracks, docks, hangars, warehouses, storage dumps, and airfields had been demolished, and, according to Japanese broadcasts, "the whole city of Naha was destroyed . . ."

When a fleet is at sea rigid radio silence must be maintained so as not to give away the position to the enemy. Halsey, however, had developed a procedure for breaking radio silence and thus getting eagerly awaited information through to headquarters. Dispatches were prepared and encoded during periods of strategic radio silence. When it was obvious that the enemy knew the fleet location, radio silence was broken and the dispatches were rapidly transmitted to Nimitz's Pacific headquarters at Pearl.

The strike was completely successful, even to the extent of obtaining good photographic reconnaissance of the area for Admiral Nimitz, who

---

LeRoy W. Busbey, jr.) ; Desron 4: DUNLAP (Lieutenant Commander Cecil R. Welte), FANNING (Commander James C. Bentley), CASE (Lieutenant Commander Robert S. Willey), CUMMINGS (Commander Paul D. Williams), CASSIN (Commander Vincent J. Meola), DOWNES (Commander Robert S. Fahle).

was looking past the Philippines to the time when the Home Islands themselves would be invaded.

Okinawa had been eliminated as a staging base—at least temporarily.

2

Formosa, an island 190 miles long and 50 miles wide, was the strongest and best-developed Japanese base south of Japan proper. It is flanked on the south by Luzon, 150 miles across Luzon Strait, and on the west by the China coast, 100 miles away. The Pescadores Islands lie 40 miles off Formosa's west coast. Reinforcements from Japan, only 700 miles away, could readily be flown into the twenty-eight operational airfields spread through Formosa and the Pescadores.

Commanding the Second Air Fleet with headquarters on Formosa was Vice Admiral Fukudome, now recovered from the injuries received in the crash off Cebu.

After that disastrous flight from Palau, it was decided by the Japanese Imperial Headquarters to keep Admiral Koga's death a secret. To ensure that secrecy Fukudome was given the rest cure in an isolated house near Togo Shrine. Meanwhile intelligent, well-informed Admiral Toyoda (who had once made strong efforts to keep Japan from going to war with the United States) was named Koga's successor as Commander-in-Chief Combined Fleet. Gradually, however, the fact of Koga's death became known and Fukudome was called back to duty in June.

Fukudome's Air Fleet was charged with the defense of the Kyushu-Okinawa-Formosa district. In September it became evident to the Japanese that the American offensive was directed at the Philippines, so on the 10th of October Fukudome shifted his headquarters from Kanoya, Kyushu, to Formosa.

On the island under his command were one hundred naval planes and two hundred Army aircraft. In Kyushu, 700 miles away, more were available.

3

Like Okinawa, Formosa had never before been attacked. To deceive the Japanese as to our intentions after the attack on Okinawa, a high-speed retirement was begun in the direction of Luzon. Japan proclaimed to the world that Halsey had been badly defeated. It was front-page news in the United States, not that anybody believed Halsey was whipped, but because nobody had known where Halsey was or what he had been doing except a necessarily close-lipped few in the Navy Department and on Guam.

To further the deception a fighter sweep was launched against Aparri on northern Luzon, 300 miles away, by Admiral McCain and Admiral Davison's task groups. It was a long 5-hour flight and, although the raid was not heavy (for the targets were not lush), enough damage was done to protect the left flank of the fleet against possible attack during the high-speed run into Formosa.

Fukudome, however, had not been fooled. Although the enemy's reactions were unpredictable and sometimes inexplicable, they were never stupid and often brilliant. When the fighter planes from the seventeen carriers swept over the island during the first light of morning on October 12, Japanese planes from the Second Air Fleet already were in the air to receive them.

The fight was fast and rough and the tenacious Jap continued strong during the first strike after the initial fighter sweep. But Fukudome's fliers could not keep it up for long against such opposition. By dusk the Japanese had knocked down forty-three of our planes but had lost over two hundred of their own. It was the beginning of the most violent air activity of the war, the consequences of which were to be decisive in the great Battle for Leyte Gulf.

After dark a number of sporadic air attacks were launched against Task Force 38. The night was lit up by the ghost-white light of Japanese flares but no planes got through to the ships. Our night fighters shot down three planes and antiaircraft fire got eight more. The only damage to the task force was reported by the destroyer PRICHETT—slight wounds from our own ships' antiaircraft fire directed at low-flying planes.

The next day the Third Fleet fliers returned to their task of making Formosa impotent as a base from which aircraft could fly south to attack the forthcoming landings at Leyte. During the old days of attacks on isolated islands, the method used to neutralize the airbases was to drop large quantities of bombs on airfield runways. But this was of only temporary benefit since the bomb craters could be quickly filled in. So at Formosa efforts were directed toward destroying aircraft and servicing facilities—hangars, fuel dumps, and shops. To accomplish this, however, required over one-half of the 772 tons of bombs dropped. The balance was used in attacks on already overburdened merchant shipping, industrial targets, and harbor installations.

The sky was heavily overcast and visibility was on the dark side of twilight as the men topside on the cruiser CANBERRA (Captain Alexander R. Early) watched the carriers recover their planes after the Friday-the-Thirteenth strike on Formosa.

Suddenly seven Japanese torpedo bombers were sighted coming in low, practically riding the ground swell. The WICHITA commenced firing as Admiral McCain ordered an emergency turn to the left. The antiaircraft fire was intense but the planes bore in. The WASP and MONTEREY downed three in flames.

At this point the four remaining planes veered sharply and headed for CANBERRA. In a simultaneous eruption of fire from all the machine guns on the starboard side of the cruiser—first American ship to be named for a foreign city—three of the attackers were sent crashing. The fourth had received its death wound but continued on.

A powerful jolt whipped CANBERRA fore and aft, and a large ball of flame shot up out of the after stack, burning men on their gun stations. In a matter of minutes the ship was dead in the water. The torpedo explosion had flooded both engine rooms and two fire rooms. All power was lost. Damage-control parties quickly went to work shoring the bulkheads near the flooded compartments.

The cruiser would have to be towed. The last dim light had faded from the west; Formosa was in that direction a scant 85 miles away. And Ulithi, nearest hospital for wounded ships, was 1,300 miles southeast.

The WICHITA (Captain Douglas A. Spencer), in a fine show of seamanship, came alongside and passed over a helping line. At three knots and leaving a trail of oil, under constant threat of air attack, the men aboard the cruisers thought Ulithi an almost impossible goal. One man aboard the CANBERRA remembers how, during the long hours of general quarters, he recalled a verse learned in school: "For I have promises to keep, and miles to go before I sleep."

The next morning, as planes from three of the carrier groups swept Formosa for the third time and one group struck at Aparri on Luzon, HOUSTON was ordered to take CANBERRA's place in Admiral McCain's task group. Rear Admiral Laurence T. DuBose's Cruiser Division 13 (SANTA FE, MOBILE, and BIRMINGHAM) plus six destroyers were detached to cover the towing group.

By noon the Third Fleet began retirement to the southeast leaving further chastisement of Formosa to the China-based B-29s. (Three B-29 attacks were carried out on October 14, 16, and 17 which further reduced Formosa as a staging point.)

By afternoon the enemy who had got his second wind, started an all-out air attack on the Third Fleet.

Rear Admiral Robert B. Carney, Chief of Staff to Admiral Halsey, tells of developments: "For a period of about 48 hours the Japanese were paralyzed. The damage that had been done at Okinawa successfully prevented staging of large quantities of aircraft through that area, and it was about 48 hours before any sort of reaction began to develop. At that time, about October 14, the Nips decided to throw everything they had in the way of air attack against our forces.

"The attacks took the form of formations of from 60 to 80 planes, but those of us who had seen the air operations earlier in the war in the South Pacific were immediately impressed by the fact that these aerial formations were nondescript in character, included all types of planes, and that the technical performance was not nearly of the same order as had been previously encountered. They attacked in daylight and they attempted their old tactic of the dusk attack.

"There was incessant activity. The fighter patrols over our forces shot down tremendous numbers of Japanese planes and those that broke through were, for the most part, destroyed by the automatic weapons of the ships.

"When this happened at dusk on the 14th, a very peculiar situation developed. Japanese planes were being sprayed around the ocean and, as they burst into flames on crashing, huge fires flared up on the surface. These were interpreted by other Japanese pilots to be American ships destroyed by the suicide attacks. These interpretations, and the reports of the Japanese pilots based upon them, were undoubtedly made in good faith. It is a well known fact that pilot observation of types and of damage is not always to be trusted either by our own forces or by the enemy's.

"Those enemy pilots that returned gave glowing reports of the success of their attacks: they saw ships burst into flame; a few minutes later there were no ships there. They reported ships had disappeared.[1] The

---

[1] Our side, too, found it difficult to estimate damage to distant ships. One of our task group commanders who had seen a Japanese plane fall and make an apparent cloud cover of smoke on one of his distant ships inquired as to the extent of the ship's damage and possible speed. The reply came back that this was a near miss, the ship had no damage, and could make full power.

people in the Empire, like all people in this world, hoping for miracles, received this information with the utmost enthusiasm, and Radio Tokyo, which we monitored continually, was putting out flashes every ten minutes or so reporting the complete destruction of the American force which had at last jumped into the Japanese trap. . . ."

The planes did succeed in seriously torpedoing HOUSTON in a dusk attack on the 19th, but, besides the crippling of CANBERRA, this was the only serious damage done to the fleet. One torpedo plane had ricocheted out of a crash and landed on the stern of the RENO, but little damage was done.

The HOUSTON, however, was hurt—bad. The seas rolled lazily over the main deck on the starboard side (the ship had a 16-degree list) and the men, who came up from below-decks, were greeted by buckets of water pouring down the escape trunks. She lay helpless, her keel broken, unable to move. At one time her skipper, Captain William Behrens, ordered the ship abandoned, but then it became evident that she would stay afloat. The BOSTON (Captain Ernest E. Herrmann) took her in tow and got in formation on the port beam of CANBERRA, the ship whose place HOUSTON had taken in the task group. Oddly enough, both of these damaged ships were named after cruisers lost earlier in the war.[1]

The Japanese gloried in the luxury of a fictitious victory. Tokyo newspapers devoted all their front-page space to the alleged exploits of Japan's "Wild Eagles" against American aircraft carriers and battleships. The excited Jap reports were studded with such phrases as "Turning the tide" and "Second Pearl Harbor." Joy swept the Empire like a divine wind.

One Japanese plane dropped leaflets over Peleliu containing the following message:

FOR RECKLESS YANKEE DOODLE:

Do you know about the naval battle done by the American 58th Fleet at the sea near Taiwan [Formosa] and Philippine? Japanese powerful Air Force has sunk their 19 aeroplane carriers, 4 battleships, 10 several cruisers and destroyers, along with sending 1,261 ship aeroplanes into the sea. From this result we think you can imagine what shall happen next around Palau upon you.

The fraud Rousevelt, hanging the President Election under his nose and from his policy ambition worked not only poor Nimitt [Nimitz]

---

[1] The original CANBERRA was an Australian heavy cruiser lost August 8, 1942, in the Battle of Savo Island. See BATTLE REPORT, Vol. III.
The original HOUSTON was lost off Java March 1, 1942, during the vain fight to keep the Japanese out of the Dutch East Indies. See BATTLE REPORT, Vol. I.

but also Macassir [MacArthur] like a robot, like this. What is pity you must sacrifice you pay! Thank you for your advice of surrender. But we haven't any reason to surrender those who are fated to be totally destroyed in a few days later.

The enemy was filled with pity over our perilous state. It is sad to think that one of our night fighters, insensitive and ungrateful, shot down this Jap plane.

Judging by the claims of Radio Tokyo, the American fleet had suffered a catastrophic disaster. Tokyo Rose stated flatly: "All of Admiral Mitscher's carriers have been sunk tonight—instantly." But Admiral Halsey, with characteristic resourcefulness and energy, set about saving the situation and soon was able to report:

> All Third Fleet ships reported by Tokyo radio as sunk have now been salvaged and are retiring in the direction of the enemy!

"About this time," related Admiral Carney, "it was decided that the misguided enthusiasm of the Japanese people as officially proven and demonstrated by the communiques that were being put out by Imperial Headquarters could be turned into something useful, so it was immediately decided to capitalize on the pitiful condition of the CANBERRA, and the HOUSTON and, to be perfectly frank with you, to troll a little bait for the Nips to work on.

"Salvage ships, which were kept up always with the service group, had been brought forward. The HOUSTON and the CANBERRA were under tow.[1] One carrier group was left in the vicinity to protect them and the other two groups were withdrawn to the eastward beyond what we believed to be enemy search radii.

"Throughout the 15th these two powerful groups remained unobserved and the Japanese high command decided to dispatch a surface force[2] to polish off the remnants of the Third Fleet. Admiral DuBose was in charge of the 'Bait Division'[3] and received some rather cold-blooded

---

[1] The fleet tug MUNSEE (Lt. Comdr. John F. Pingley), which was standing by at sea, relieved WICHITA of her tow. The PAWNEE (Lieutenant H. C. Gramer) latched on to HOUSTON.

[2] This was the Second Diversion Attack Force under Vice Admiral Shima. On the morning of October 15 this force left the protection of the Inland Sea and headed south. It consisted of two heavy cruisers, one light, and four destroyers.

[3] This group also known as "the crippled remnants of the Third Fleet," consisted of: (Task Unit 30.3.1, DuBose) the light cruisers SANTA FE (F), BIRMINGHAM, HOUS-

dispatches from Commander Third Fleet, outlining the glories of his task, which in effect was to be the sucker who would draw the Japanese fire and place them in a position where they could be intercepted and trapped."

Captain Thomas B. Inglis, commanding officer of the BIRMINGHAM, expressed the prevailing sentiments of the division in a message to Admiral DuBose. He said: "Now I know what a worm feels like on a fish hook."

"Throughout the 16th," continued Admiral Carney, "the Japanese threw everything they had at the HOUSTON and the CANBERRA, and those that got by Admiral McCain's covering force were badly mauled by the two CVLs, the CABOT (Captain Stanley J. Michael) and the COWPENS (Captain Herbert W. Taylor, Jr.), which were actually in company with the damaged ships under tow. Their performance was magnificent. The entire show was one of the outstandingly gallant jobs done in the course of the campaign.

"Throughout the 16th, until late afternoon, the two ambush groups still remained undetected and had high hopes that we were going to spring the trap. Late in the afternoon a lone Nip plane made contact and got away before it could be shot down by the CAP. He wasted no time in making his report and the enemy surface force, which we had had under observation some 400 miles to the north of us, also wasted no time in getting the hell out of there and returning to Empire waters—so the trap failed."

It was a U.S. Navy failure that cost Japan 41 more airplanes, however, at the price of another torpedo in the hull of the half-sunk HOUSTON. The 10,000-ton cruiser still stayed afloat, with 6,300 tons of water in the hull. The price for that costly torpedo hit was exacted by fliers from COWPENS and CABOT.

The greatest battle of the war to date between ship- and shore-based air was over. The Japanese had succeeded in damaging only HOUSTON and CANBERRA,[1] at a cost of over 650 planes and pilots destroyed in the air and on the ground. The Third Fleet lost 89 planes—76 in combat and 13 operationally.

TON; two heavies—including the cripple CANBERRA and the BOSTON; two fleet tugs, MUNSEE, PAWNEE; eight destroyers, CAPERTON, INGERSOLL, COGSWELL, THE SULLIVANS, STEPHEN POTTER, BOYD, COWELL, GRAYSON. (Task Unit 30.3.2; Rear Admiral C. T. Joy) one heavy cruiser, WICHITA (F); one light cruiser, MOBILE; two light carriers, CABOT, COWPENS; five destroyers, BURNS, CHARRETTE, KNAPP, BELL, MILLER.

[1] On October 27 these two cruisers were towed safely into Ulithi Harbor.

"The importance of Japan's losses in land-based planes to our carrier forces in September and early October is difficult to over-estimate and their cumulative impact on enemy air striking power was decisive. *Far smaller losses broke the Luftwaffe in the decisive battle of the war: then the greatest single day's loss was only 178 planes, and German losses over the two months of the Battle of Britain roughly equalled those suffered by the Japanese in October 1944 alone.* In retrospect the responsible Japanese commanders with one voice blamed the loss of the Battle of Leyte Gulf and the consequent loss of the Philippines on their weakness in land-based air, which was initiated by the United States carrier strikes. October saw the end of the Japanese air forces in the conventional sense; what had once been a formidable weapon was transformed perforce into a sacrificial army of guided missiles." [1]

With Japan's land-based and naval air power virtually eradicated as a factor in the Battle of the Philippines, and her pipeline of seaborne supplies ruptured, Admiral Halsey took his Third Fleet to its station off Leyte Gulf just as the events described in the preceding chapter began. This has been the story of why the Leyte Gulf landings could be accomplished with such speed and economy.

[1] *The Campaigns of the Pacific War* (Naval Analysis Division, United States Strategic Bombing Survey), page 283.

CHAPTER TWENTY-FOUR

Toyoda's All-or-Nothing Gamble

I

AT 8:00 A. M. on October 17 the first American Rangers went ashore on the small islands in the mouth of Leyte Gulf to wedge open the door for "The Return."

In his headquarters at the Naval War College on the outskirts of Tokyo, Admiral Toyoda, Commander-in-Chief Combined Fleet, the Japanese counterpart of Admiral Nimitz, read a dispatch telling of the American activity in the area. He was not surprised, although with the recent attacks on Formosa he had thought the Americans might decide to land there and by-pass the Philippines. But now it seemed certain that Leyte was the objective.

Toyoda turned to the attentive officer who stood beside him and gave a quiet command: "Alert the fleet for Sho Operation No. 1, the defense of the Philippines."

The time was 8:09 A.M.

2

After the loss of the Marianas the Japanese developed the "Sho" plans for the defense of the inner islands of their shriveled Empire. In Japanese the character "sho" means "to conquer."

American landings were expected in one of four possible areas, each area being covered by a Sho plan: the Philippines, Sho No. 1; Formosa-Nansei Shoto-Southern Kyushu, Sho No. 2; Kyushu-Shikoku-Honshu, Sho No. 3; and Hokkaido, Sho No. 4.

The Japanese plan was simple. In one last finish fight they were to throw all the Navy and as much Army and air strength as was available against the American forces. The plan was born of desperation, a device to delay the debacle that to the realistic minds seemed inevitable. Even if the Americans were defeated and pried loose from their beachheads,

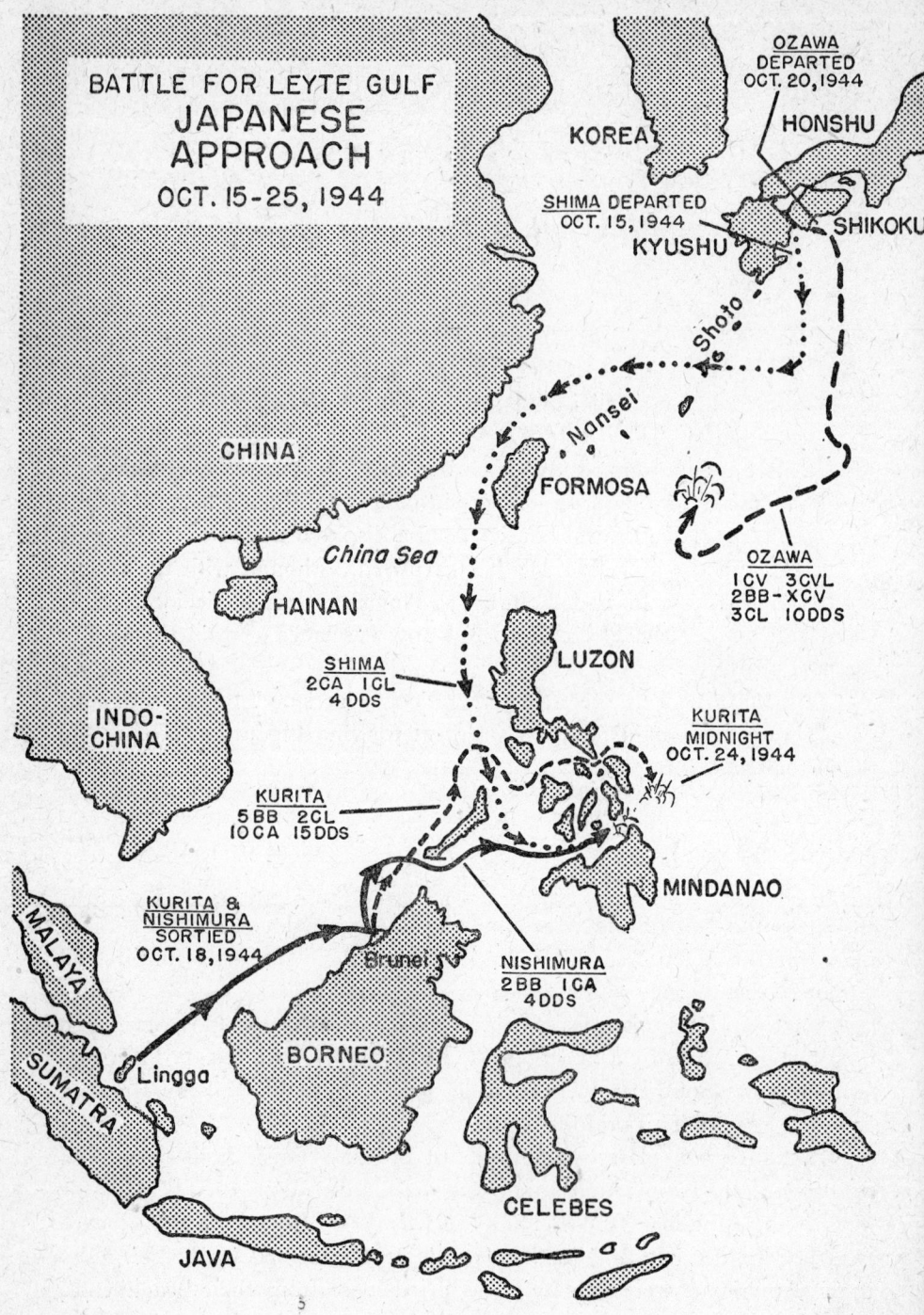

FIGURE 14

THE END'S BEGINNING

they would inevitably come back, and the Japanese had no plan for a second try. They would have nothing to try with.

After the war, Admiral Toyoda frankly told American naval officers of his dilemma: "Should we lose in the Philippines, even though the fleet were left, the shipping lane to the south would be completely severed. If the fleet came back to Japanese waters it would be without fuel. If it went south, it could not receive arms and munitions. There was no sense in saving the fleet at the expense of the loss of the Philippines."

As a result of the relentless attacks of U.S. submarines, the Home Islands were choked off from the oil of the Southern Resource Area. Without oil modern warfare is impossible, and the Japanese were already draining their last few barrels. Because of the lack of fuel, aviation training was grossly inadequate; sometimes pilots were sent into battle with only eighty hours of flying time. Because of the lack of oil movements of fleet units were increasingly restricted. Because of the lack of oil the fleet itself was divided and as a result unbalanced. For nearly three years U.S. submarines had bit deep at the arteries of the Empire, giving tankers preferential attention. The effect of this on the total defeat of Japan has never been fully appreciated. More dramatic acts of annihilation, which could not have been performed as well—if at all—had not the "silent service" of the submarines functioned to perfection, got the headlines.

Vice Admiral Jisaburo Ozawa was in a familiar predicament. In the Inland Sea he had the four remaining carriers of the Imperial Navy still suitable for fleet action. As ships they were good. As carriers they were a mockery, for he lacked trained pilots to fly from them. Ozawa's difficulties were reminiscent of those after the Allied landings on Bougainville, when his trained carrier groups were sacrificed in the Rabaul area, leaving him with a ghost fleet of empty-decked carriers. It had taken Ozawa six months of hard training in the Singapore area to rebuild his pilot strength. Then came the "Marianas Turkey Shoot" in June, and he was "behind of where he started." He was still there in October.

Ozawa kept his carriers in home waters, not only closer to the source of pilots and aircraft but closest to the kind of repair his ships had to have after the Marianas expedition. The heavy ships of the Japanese Fleet, under Vice Admiral Takeo Kurita, based at Lingga, near Singapore, where fuel was amply available.

Toyoda, realist though he was, had only his official reports to go on:

"a dozen or more enemy carriers and many other ships" sunk by the Japanese air forces between October 10 and 17.

To make the score a shutout he stripped Ozawa of 150 planes of his almost-trained carrier groups to reinforce Fukudome on Formosa. This left Ozawa with only 116 aircraft spread thin over four carriers.

The 150 never returned to their carriers.

3

As soon as orders were received for the Sho-1 alert, Admiral Kurita prepared to put to sea.

One hour after midnight on the morning of October 18, a long line of blacked-out ships steamed silently out into the dark waters of the South China Sea.

Kurita had a good fleet: battleships, including the mammoth YAMATO and MUSASHI, whose secret 18-inch guns dwarfed anything the Americans had; heavy and light cruisers, and destroyers. Not enough destroyers, though. The South Pacific campaign and U.S. submarines had taken quite a toll. Also he had no aircraft. Even most of the float planes from the battleships and cruisers had been sent to Mindanao. He depended on the land-based air from Luzon. But it was a good fleet with a lot of beefy punch.

When Kurita's ships put into Brunei on the northwest coast of Borneo to top off with fuel, the Americans had already started landing at Leyte and the Sho-1 plan had been definitely activated.

Although the basic planning had been done previously at Lingga, in the shadow of Singapore, there were a number of last-minute conferences during those two active days in Brunei Bay.

The fleet was divided into two forces: one commanded by haughty Vice Admiral Shoji Nishimura, "C" Force, and one commanded by Kurita himself, the First Diversion Attack Force. The plan called for a salt-water pincer movement on the American transports in Leyte Gulf. Nishimura's smaller force of two battleships, a heavy cruiser, and four destroyers would fight its way into the gulf from the south via Surigao Strait, while Kurita's attack force would pass through San Bernardino Strait to the north, and sweep down the coast of Samar and into Leyte Gulf from the east. Once inside the gulf the two forces would join together for a slaughter of the helpless transports and the Allies' Philippine adventure would come to an awful end. If the plan worked, it would be a long time before the Americans could replace their shipping. The war-weary Allies might even be willing to talk compromise peace.

There was one fly in the cup of sake—Admiral Halsey's Third Fleet. Kurita's force, strong as it was—five battleships, ten heavy cruisers, two light cruisers, and fifteen destroyers—could not hope to fight against the massed power of five carriers (100-plane capacity), six light carriers (33-plane capacity), six new battleships, seven light cruisers, two heavy cruisers, and forty-six destroyers.

The Third Fleet would have to be lured out of Kurita's path before he passed through San Bernardino Strait. That sacrificial function, under the revised Sho plan, fell to dignified Admiral Ozawa and his depleted carriers, the so-called Main Body.

Kurita, a veteran of thirty-eight years in the naval service, commanded the key force. The success or failure of the plan depended on whether the First Diversion Attack Force got through or not. It was a desperate plan and it was dangerous. But it was the only one the Japanese could have adopted.

When Kurita's attack force departed from Brunei Bay at eight o'clock in the morning of October 22, the timetable was set. He would advance along the west side of narrow Palawan Island at a speed of 16 knots; he would then turn eastward and circle to the south of Mindoro on the 24th, increasing speed at this time to 24 knots; then at sundown of the same day he would arrive at the east entrance of San Bernardino Strait, turn south, sweep down the coast of Samar, and at dawn of X-day, October 25, break into Leyte Gulf.

Admiral Nishimura's "C" Force departed from Brunei at three o'clock in the afternoon of the same day, the 22nd. After crossing the Sulu Sea, this southern prong of the pincer was to arrive at the Mindanao Sea entrance of Surigao Strait about sundown of the 24th. At dawn the next morning "C" Force was to push through to Leyte Gulf in co-ordination with Kurita's main force.

But between the inception of a plan and its execution there is many a slip—

Shortly after the gray beginnings of early light on the morning of the 23rd, the day after the departure from Brunei, Kurita sat in his sea cabin sipping a steaming cup of green-hued tea. His flagship was the heavy cruiser ATAGO. Beside him stood his chief of staff, Rear Admiral Koyanagi, explaining that all had gone well during the night. The submarines reported sighted the day before had all been false alarms, although it was known that the Americans kept submarines deployed along the route they were taking. The fleet was now zigzagging at 18 knots.

Kurita glanced at a sketch of the formation of his ships. They were divided into two groups: The first contained the heavy cruisers ATAGO, TAKAO, CHOKAI, MYOKO, HAGURO, and MAYA; the light cruiser NOSHIRO; and the battleships NAGATO, YAMATO, and MUSASHI. The second group contained the heavy cruisers TONE, CHIKUMA, KUMANO, and SUZUYA; the light cruiser YAHAGI; and the battleships HARUNA and KONGO, Admiral Koyanagi's old command. Each group was composed of two columns of heavy ships with the cruisers leading the battleships. Forming a rather thin protecting line around the whole formation were the fifteen destroyers.

Kurita put down his empty cup and rose from his chair to go to the bridge. Abruptly he found himself violently back in a sitting position, his ears ringing with the noise of explosion. The ship shuddered and seemed to start sliding downhill.

Four torpedoes from the American submarine DARTER had dug their way into the thick skin of the flagship.

Nineteen minutes after she was hit, she slid bow first under the gray choppy water. As Kurita sped in his barge to the destroyer KISHINAMI he saw another cruiser, the TAKAO, dead in the water, spurting smoke and steam.

Since the attack had come from the left, the force changed course to the right. But sitting on that flank was the submarine DACE. The water where ATAGO went down was still eddying when the MAYA was hit with four torpedoes. She disappeared within four minutes.

In twenty-three minutes three much-needed cruisers had been knocked out. The TAKAO did not sink, but neither could she fight. Two destroyers, NAGANAMI and ASASHIMO, escorted her back to Brunei.

4

The DARTER and DACE were proceeding side by side at 5 knots on the surface of reef-studded, swift-flowing Palawan Passage. The skippers were conversing by megaphone; two convoys were supposed to be in the area, and the submariners had agreed to divide the prey between them.

Commander Bladen D. Claggett of the DACE said "Roger! Well, so long, Dave."

The DARTER's Commander David H. McClintock waved back. Then —but let him tell the story himself:

"We were preparing to part company when, 16 minutes past midnight, from our conning tower came the report, 'Radar Contact, one three one true, 30,000 yards—contact is doubtful—probably rain cloud.'

" 'Rain cloud hell! That's the Jap Fleet,' flashed through my mind. Almost immediately the radar operator shouted back the contact was ships. I put my megaphone once more to my mouth and gave Claggett the range and bearing of ships too numerous to mention.

"He answered, 'Let's go get them.' By 20 minutes after midnight both DARTER and DACE were chasing the radar contact at full power. The enemy ships were strung out in Palawan Passage, headed north.

"It soon became apparent that we had not a convoy, but a large task force, which we assumed was headed for Leyte to interfere with our landing which we had heard about over the radio. We sent three contact reports, the final one estimating that the force included at least 11 heavy ships, the main body of the Jap fleet, we hoped! [Actually 31 ships.]

"The DARTER was attempting to gain position ahead of the port column and DACE a similar position on the starboard column. We waited for a periscope attack at dawn.

"At 0425 DARTER was 10 miles ahead of the left flank. At 0430 all hands were called for coffee before the attack. Ten minutes to 0500, battle stations! Ten minutes after 0500 we reversed course to head down the throat of the western column. It was getting faintly light in the east. There wasn't a cloud in the sky. In 20 minutes we would shoot. We submerged to 300 feet to get a trim, then returned to periscope depth.

"The first look in the periscope showed a huge gray shape; it was the whole Japanese column, seen bows on. Were they cruisers or battleships? A look to the southeast, where the light was better, showed battleships, cruisers, and destroyers. That column would pass about 3 miles to the east of us. Two destroyers could be seen part way between the columns. Our sound gear was silent. Weren't they echo-ranging at all?

"As I swung the periscope around to the east, some of my phrases are not recordable. At every point at which the periscope stopped, the Exec would say, 'What's there?' I said battleships. 'What's there?' Cruisers.

'What's there?' Cruisers. 'What's there?' Destroyers. I swung the periscope back to our own column.

"The gray ships kept getting larger. We were a little to the east of the column and would pass on parallel courses. At 0525 the first target could be identified as a heavy cruiser with huge bow waves. Sighs of disappointment went up from the conning tower when we discovered they weren't all battleships. A beautiful sight, anyway. They were in close column. We imagined we could see the Japs at general quarters, water-tight doors dogged down, the officers in white service pacing the bridge. We hoped the lead ship would be the flagship. It was!

"At 0527 all tubes were ready . . . range under 3,000 yards. The column zigged west to give a perfect torpedo range of just under 1,000 yards. Their profiles could be seen clearly . . . ATAGO cruisers! The barkward slant of the big leading cruiser's bridge seemed to accentuate her speed. Estimating angle of her bow was easy because we had done it before on models. The periscope was up while we watched and confidently waited. (Yes, it looked easy up there in the conning tower; but only because I knew that down below 80 officers and men were doing a perfect job; Ensign Bill Paseler, the diving officer, Chief Electrician's Mate Strother and his crew, all performing faultlessly.)

"Now the angle on the bow was getting bigger, 55, 60, 65 . . . range under a thousand . . . shooting bearing . . . mark . . . fire one! As the next five forward fish left us, the Jap flagship turned on a searchlight to signal to the east. Did she see our torpedoes? She was going by now. No, she wasn't zigging!

"Shift targets to second cruiser . . . bearing mark. 'Give me a range, give me a range,' sang out Lieutenant Eugene P. Wilkinson, the TDC [1] operator. 'You can't shoot without a range,' he complained. He finally got it. Fifteen hundred yards to the next cruiser. They were in line of bearing now. TDC ready . . . bearing, mark . . . fire seven! The first stern torpedo was on its way.

"As the torpedo left, heavy explosions started.

" 'Depth charges!' said Lieutenant Commander Ernest L. Schwab, Jr., the Executive Officer.

" 'Depth charges hell . . . torpedoes!' said I.

" 'Cripes, we're hitting 'em, we're hitting 'em,' shouted Walter Price,

[1] Torpedo Data Computer.

PLATE LXV—The Battle for Leyte Gulf. (*above*) Surprised by carrier-based Navy planes in the Sulu Sea, the Japanese battleship YAMASHIRO (foreground) and the heavy cruiser MOGAMI twist to evade winged attack. (*below*) Farther north, in the Sibuyan Sea, the giant Japanese battleship MUSASHI, escorted by the destroyer KIYOSHIMO, takes simultaneous hits from a Navy Helldiver and an Avenger torpedo plane.

PLATE LXVI—(*above*) Putting the transports to bed for the night. Word has been received of the approach of a Japanese fleet toward Surigao Strait. On the eve of the battle destroyers lay a dense smoke screen to hide the huge Allied squadron of transports, supply ships and auxiliaries. (*below*) Transport traveling, with built-in bunks crowding every inch, was no fun. It almost made one eager to reach one's destination—even though that meant battle.

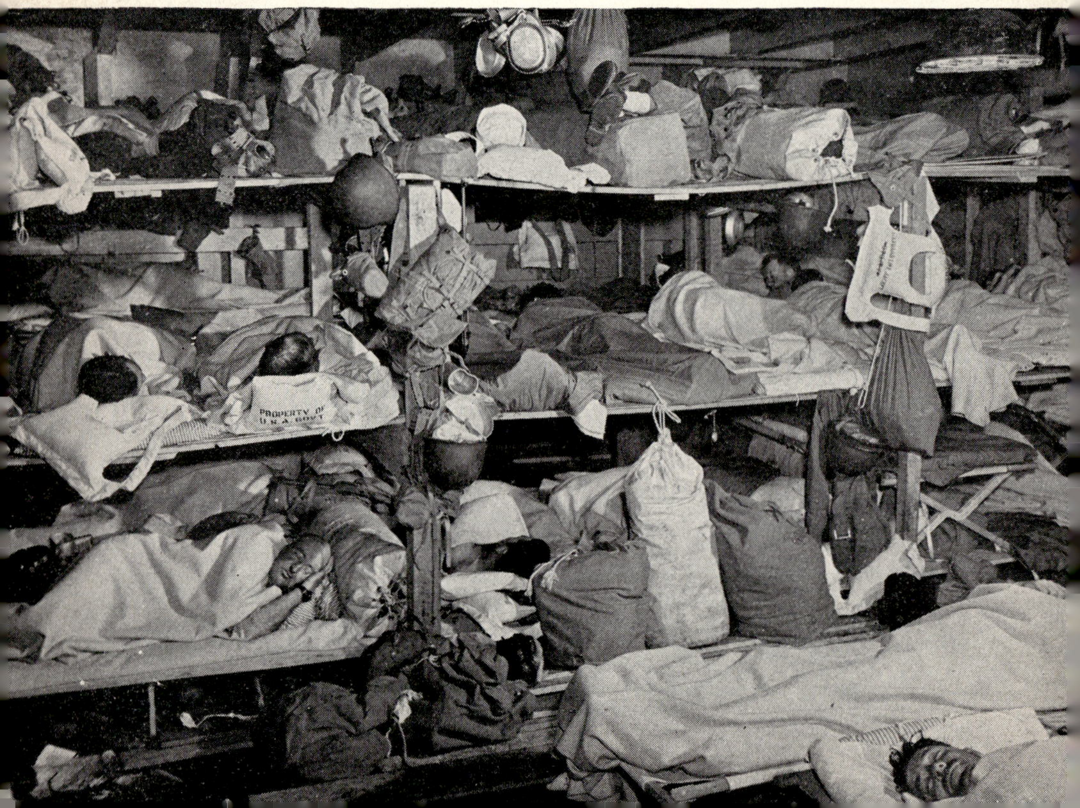

PLATE LXVII—A classic naval maneuver, and the dream of every fleet commander, came true for Oldendorf and his old battleships when the enemy's southern thrust at MacArthur's invasion forces was raked by American warships steaming at right angles to the Japanese course. (*above*) Flashes of gunfire at close quarters reveal cruisers of the American force to a cameraman in the USS PENNSYLVANIA. (*below*) Another view of the famous night action of October 25, 1944, when a heavy enemy force was turned back and most of its ships sunk.

PLATE LXVIII—(*upper left*) Like an etching on silver the sun sets on this Japanese cruiser, cornered by U. S. Navy carrier planes in the Sibuyan Sea, the Philippines. The vessel is bracketed by near misses, one of them so close aft that it caused severe damage. The central Japanese force took a heavy pounding in the Sibuyan Sea.

(*center*) Cautiously a PT boat crew picks up survivors of the Japanese fleet ambushed and sunk in Surigao Strait early on October 25, 1944. PT boats were first to contact the enemy in this night action.

(*lower*) Part of the central Japanese fleet which broke through San Bernardino Strait as it appeared to a U. S. Navy plane swooping down to attack it off Samar, the Philippines.

PLATE LXIX—When the small escort carrier group, commanded by Rear Admiral C. A. F. Sprague, was suddenly confronted by a formidable Japanese force east of Samar, October 25, 1944, there was nothing to do but run for it, and hope that reinforcements would arrive before the big guns of the enemy fleet could blast the jeep flat-tops clear out of the water. The carriers had plenty of planes, but most of them were loaded with anti-personnel bombs, for support of ground operations. There was no time to reload.

(*above*) Destroyers and destroyer-escorts promptly laid down a smoke screen between the carriers and the onrushing enemy. The Japanese force: 4 battleships, 7 heavy and light cruisers, and 11 destroyers. Sprague's force: 6 escort carriers, 3 destroyers, and 4 destroyer escorts.

(*center*)—The escort carrier GAMBIER BAY joins two DEs in laying smoke. The destroyers and DEs also loosed several dozen torpedoes at the approaching enemy capital ships.

(*lower*) From the carrier KALININ BAY, near misses from the big guns of the Japanese can be seen dropping among the ships of Sprague's little squadron. The battle is already two hours old.

PLATE LXX—(*upper left*) Shells from a Japanese cruiser fall around the doomed escort carrier GAMBIER BAY during the height of the engagement. Note the enemy cruiser (circled) on the horizon. This is one of the few instances during the "long-range war" in the Pacific when a major enemy ship could be seen in the same photograph with one of ours.

(*center*) Another salvo from the Japanese fleet brackets the GAMBIER BAY. She later was sunk after being hit by half a hundred salvoes. Among the Japanese vessels bearing down on the little American carrier force was the giant battleship YAMATO, whose 18-inch guns, largest afloat, had never before been fired in battle.

(*lower*) Aboard the KITKUN BAY damage-control parties hit the deck as a salvo from the Japanese fleet falls around the ship. The enemy, using armor-piercing ammunition, sometimes sent shells clear through the fragile escort carriers without exploding. The FANSHAW BAY, the WHITE PLAINS, and the KITKUN BAY were all severely damaged by Japanese shellfire.

PLATE LXXI—(*upper right*) Shells fired by Japanese battleships "walk" across the water toward a U. S. escort carrier, which this time walked away unharmed. Because the largest gun in Sprague's squadron was only 5-inch, most of the surface engagement developed into a contest between Japanese major-caliber gunnery and American seamanship. By making sudden and frequent changes in course, the captains of our jeep carriers were generally able to throw enemy gunnery off.

(*center*) In another phase of the action off Samar, the USS SUWANEE was hit by a Japanese suicide plane. Although smoke poured through a hole in the flight deck and out one of the side apertures, within ninety minutes the SUWANEE's damage-control parties had extinguished fires, repaired the flight deck and the ship was again underway.

(*lower*) Flight deck crews aboard the escort carrier KITKUN BAY feverishly launch planes as another CVE (the WHITE PLAINS, in the background) is bracketed by salvoes fired by the big guns of the Japanese fleet, which steamed out of San Bernardino Strait. Before retreating through the same strait, the Japanese lost three heavy cruisers and a destroyer.

PLATE LXXII — (left) Navy carrier planes from Task Force 38 have the Japanese fleet on the run off Cape Engaño, northern Luzon. This must have been early in the engagement, because the enemy ships are still proceeding in orderly columns, whereas later, breaking formation, it was every man-of-war for itself.

(right) A U. S. Navy pilot proves you can "fly on one wing" — almost! During the engagement off Cape Engaño, a TBM from the carrier USS SAN JACINTO took an anti-aircraft hit which damaged part of its right wing. Below, Japanese battleship ISE and a TERUTSUKI class destroyer come hard left, as they take evasive action against our air attack.

(left) Japanese ack-ack was thicker and more accurate during action off Cape Engaño, October 25, 1944, than at any time previously in the Philippines. Planes from Task Force 38 had to penetrate barrages of both high-level and low-level anti-aircraft fire to come within striking distance of the enemy fleet.

PLATE LXXIII — (*right*) Already burning furiously, the Japanese carrier ZUIKAKU is bracketed by bombs from U. S. Navy carrier planes of Task Force 38, during the action off the coast of northern Luzon, near Cape Engaño, October 25, 1944.

(*left*) Going around in the best circles, no doubt, but this Japanese warship still could not avoid being hit by bombers of the U. S. Third Fleet off Cape Engaño, the Philippines. The light streak, at right, is the track of one of our torpedoes, which missed the Japanese destroyer speeding away in the right background.

(*right*) Planes of the USS ESSEX, a part of Task Force 38, harass the disorganized Japanese fleet in the engagement off Cape Engaño, October 25, 1944.

PLATE LXXIV—(*above*) Her flight deck buckled by the force of an explosion, following a direct hit by a Navy torpedo bomber, the Japanese carrier ZUIHO vainly tries to escape near Cape Engaño. She was sunk a short time after this photograph was taken. (*below*) One of the strangest of the enemy's big ships also flees for its life during the Battle for Leyte Gulf. An ISE class battleship carrier clearly reveals its flight deck aft and huge pagoda foremast as it attempts to fight off the onslaught of Navy Hellcats, Helldivers, and Avengers.

PLATE LXXV—(*above*) Another remarkable aerial view of a Japanese ISE class battleship carrier under attack by U. S. Navy planes of Task Force 38, off Cape Engaño. A puff of smoke at the bow indicates that the big ship has just taken a direct bomb hit. (*below*) Last voyage for the ZUIKAKU. Here, the powerful Japanese carrier tries vainly to escape the bombs of Navy carrier planes in the action off Cape Engaño. An hour and a half after this photograph was taken came an aviator's terse message: "Heeled over on side, sank at 1430."

PLATE LXXVI—This series of photographs reveals how Kamikaze fliers were able to do their deadly work. The ship is the escort carrier USS SUWANEE, operating with a covering force off Leyte, October 26, 1944.

(*right*) While recovering her returning fighter planes, the SUWANEE is suddenly attacked by the unsuspected suicider (above and to left of mast) that came out of the clouds.

(*left*) At the moment of impact, gasoline flames spread a huge ball of fire across the midget carrier's deck. An F6F, which was about to land, clears the explosion and pulls away.

(*right*) Smoke billows high into the air from the USS SUWANEE, following the Japanese suicide hit. The ship appeared to be doomed, but its stout-hearted crew soon had the fire under control, and the SUWANEE later returned to the Pacific fighting, adding to an already impressive record.

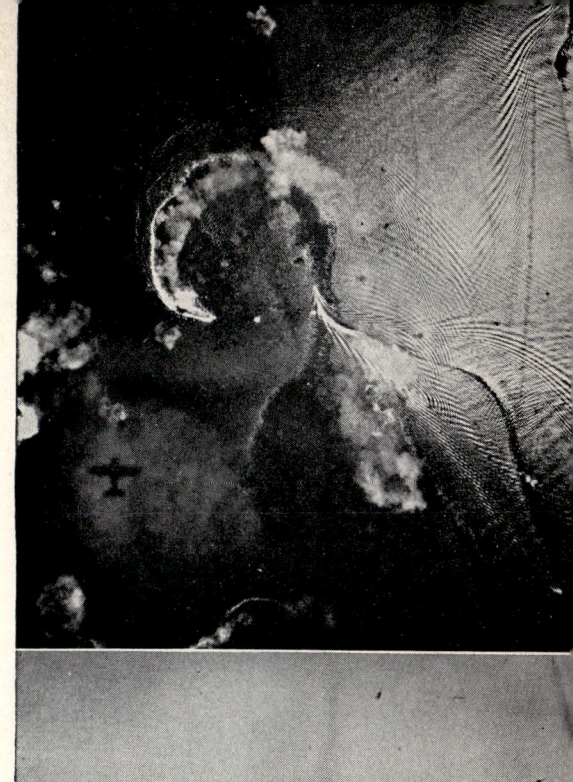

PLATE LXXVII—(*upper right*) Unconsciously the wake of a fleeing Japanese ship etched a gigantic question mark in the waters of Tablas Strait. But there was no question about its fate to U. S. Navy carrier planes of the Third and the Seventh Fleets, during the Battle for Leyte Gulf. The shadow of one of the planes can be seen on the cloud at lower left.

(*center*) Funeral pyre of one of the Japanese cruisers, repeatedly hit by U. S. carrier planes.

(*lower*) A Japanese dive bomber has just swept by the USS SANGAMON, and the flight-deck crew is still tense. Anti-aircraft gunners in the gallery follow the attacker with a barrage of bullets. The action took place off Leyte, during the Battle for Leyte Gulf.

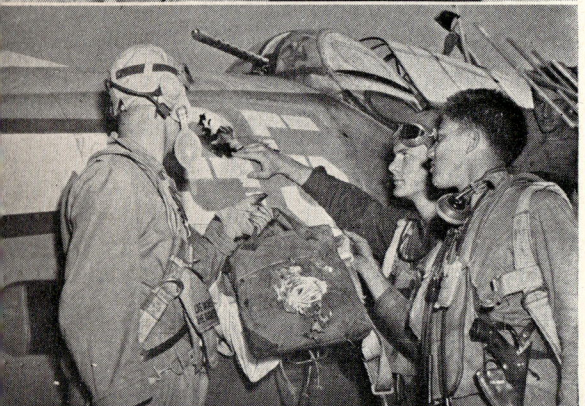

PLATE LXXVIII—(*upper left*) Through an intense halo of anti-aircraft fire these two daring Navy fliers bombed and then photographed (see below) Japan's newest and fastest battleship, the YAMATO, during the action in Tablas Strait in the western Visayans, October 25, 1944. *Left to right:* Aviation Radioman 2/c John L. Carver, of Hamilton, Montana, who took the pictures, and Lieutenant Commander Arthur L. Downing, of South Haven, Michigan, pilot.

(*center*) Navy planes, and parachutes, can take it! Examining the damage to their plane and a parachute pack are, *left to right:* turret gunner Donald L. Seig, pilot Lieutenant (jg) Jimmie Smyth, and radio gunner Gilbert C. Johnson. The plane, a General Motors Avenger from the USS ESSEX, took part in the Battle for Leyte Gulf.

(*lower*) This is one of the fine action shots made by Carver, with a hand-held camera, as Commander Downing pulled their Curtiss Helldiver out of an exceptionally steep dive. One bomb can be seen bursting just forward of the YAMATO's No. 1 gun turret.

PLATE LXXIX—(*upper right*) Again Old Glory flies over a free Philippines. A battle-shattered palm serves as a flagpole for the first American flag to fly in the Commonwealth for three years. It is secured by Robert Driscoll, Boatswain's Mate 2/c, of East Providence, R. I.

(*center*) When a Japanese plane attempted a night attack on the Tacloban airfield, Leyte, this fantastic tapestry of fire suddenly criss-crossed the heavens. The enemy plane expired in a ball of fire, lower left.

(*lower*) The waters of the Philippines cleared of enemy warcraft, transports again steam in impressive array along the coast of Leyte, carrying thousands of troops to enlarge the beachhead, which was to become a springboard for the reconquest of the entire Commonwealth. (*Coast Guard Photo.*)

PLATE LXXX—The Battle for Leyte Gulf has been won, and the Japanese Navy, as a navy, has ceased to exist. Enemy combat ship losses: 3 battleships, 4 carriers, 10 cruisers and 11 destroyers. U. S. losses: 1 light and 2 escort carriers; 2 destroyers, and 1 escort destroyer.

(*left*) The price of victory from the human point of view, however, again was high. One of the casualties of the Battle for Leyte Gulf, wounded by Japanese aerial attack, receives first aid on the flight deck of an escort carrier.

(*right*) The wardroom, normally the center of social life aboard a warship, takes on a grim aspect as it is converted into an emergency sickbay. These men were wounded aboard their carrier during the Battle for Leyte Gulf.

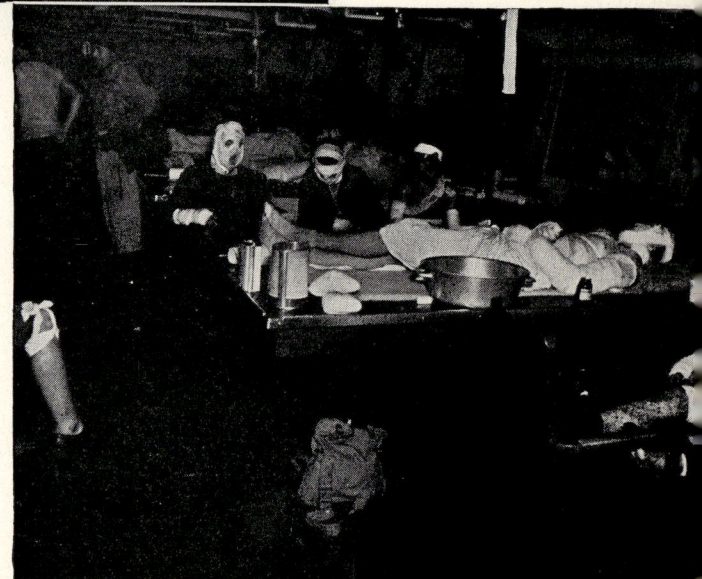

(*left*) Shipmates, some in battle helmets, stand with heads bowed as five members of a carrier's air group are committed to the sea.

Gunnery Officer who was punching the torpedo firing keys and jumping up and down on each torpedo hit.

"I swung the periscope back to the first cruiser and will never forget that sight. She was belching flame from the base of the forward turret to the stern. Five torpedoes had hit. Dense black smoke of burning oil covered her and she was going down by the bow. She was still going ahead but her number one turret was cutting the water. She was finished."

Meanwhile activity aboard DACE had been equally if not more exciting than aboard DARTER. That is, if you call depth charges excitement.

Commander Claggett and his executive officer, Lieutenant Commander Rafael C. Benitez, were standing on the bridge of DACE when DARTER slowly began to fade off their radar screen.

"The DARTER is diving," said Benitez.

"Order the crew to battle stations submerged," said Claggett.

The first streaks of morning light were breaking over the horizon when Benitez started down the hatch.

"Looks like a beautiful morning, Captain. Do you suppose we'll ever see another one like it?" remarked Benitez as he climbed down the ladder.

The Captain did not answer.

With all men at battle stations, the diving officer, Lieutenant Earl Jones, was soon able to get a perfect trim on DACE. The boat was ready; the crew was ready.

"Up periscope," calmly ordered Claggett.

At about this time loud explosions were heard in the direction of DARTER's column of ships.

"Good lord! It looks like the 4th of July out there. One is sinking and another is burning. The Japs are firing all over the place. What a show! Stand by for a setup—here they come," Claggett described the scene his periscope revealed.

The fire-control officers, Lieutenant William Dodsworth and Lieutenant (jg) Harry Caldwell, sounded ranges, bearings, and angles on the bow; the plotting officers, Lieutenants Sam Reid and Matt Godek, checked the fire-control officers; Benitez checked all four. Below, the diving officer with his assistants, Lieutenants (jg) Phil Banta and Ed Jones, kept the boat within inches of the depth ordered by Claggett. Throughout the ship, no less attentive, no less preoccupied than any one of the officers, was the crew; each man an expert at his particular task; each one of them a strong and necessary gear in the machine. All the information funneled to the skipper, who had his eye pressed to the periscope.

It was 0545. The skipper had two huge targets bearing down on him. Astern of the two cruisers he saw what looked like a battleship.

"Let them pass . . . they are only heavy cruisers," said the skipper.

"Bearing, mark, range, mark; angle on starboard bow about 10 degrees. She looks like a KONGO-class battlewagon."

"Fire one, fire two, fire three, fire four, fire five, fire six."

"Almost immediately our torpedoes began striking home and it was music to our ears," said Benitez. "Hardly had the sixth torpedo left the tube when the Old Man said, 'Take her deep, Earl. Let's get to hell out of here!'

"On our way down to deep submergence," continued Benitez, "we heard a crackling noise that sounded like cellophane being crumpled close to our ears."

It was the big heavy cruiser MAYA breaking up, and there was cause to worry that multi-tonned fragments might strike the submarine. Then another worry intruded:

"Hardly had we settled down to running depth when a string of depth charges exploding close aboard told us that Jap destroyers were on the scene," Benitez relates.

"Depth charges exploded all around us. The uncanny soundman, Junior Younger, gave the Captain a complete picture of what was going on above. Only the words of Younger and the Captain broke the deathly silence within the boat, while depth charges punctuated every remark. They had us cold.

" 'Four of them are making a run now, Captain,' Younger would say. We didn't really need to be told because as the Jap cans approached they sounded like an electric razor at work on a two-day beard. Some of the destroyers made dry runs. We would hear a fast 'chuchuchuchuchu,' and then wait. The waiting was worse than when the charges actually exploded.

"After what seemed years (it was 'only' one hour and 30 minutes) the Japs left. We stayed deep for a while and later came to periscope depth to·survey the cruiser which had been damaged by DARTER. She was being jealously guarded by two destroyers and two airplanes. We couldn't get her during the day, but we knew she would be a lame duck that night," concludes Benitez.

During the day the crews of both submarines were given some much-needed rest while McClintock and Claggett plotted the doom of the stricken Jap cruiser. Commander McClintock tells the remainder of the story.

"That night, October 24, 1944, DARTER and DACE were again steaming side by side to finish off the cruiser. We thought she would be towed inside the Palawan Barrier Reef. Instead, she got underway, making about 5 to 8 knots headed southwest. The DACE started 'ending around' to east and DARTER to west.

"At about midnight we had about an hour to go to gain position for attack ahead of the cruiser. The OOD, Lieutenant Ed Skorupski, and I were on the bridge on the pitch-black night. At five minutes past midnight we were making 17 knots, trying to attack before the cruiser could pick up more speed. The navigator was plotting in the conning tower; all officers and most of the crew were at battle stations.

"Something happened! We hit something and were riding over it as a whale noses out of the water. We took a large up-angle and the stern went under water as far as the engine-room hatch. Then all of a sudden the stern rode up, and we came to rest high and dry.

" 'What was that?' the navigator yelled, running to the bridge. I told him we were aground. He jumped into the conning tower to check the chart, was back on the bridge in a minute. 'Captain, it can't be that we are aground! The nearest land is 19 miles away.'

"But we were aground, just the same, on an uncharted reef.

"A Japanese destroyer with the cruisers started closing in, coming closer and closer until the range was 12,000 yards. That may not sound so close on shore, but it sounded close then to us sitting there on the reef with nothing but one 4-incher and a couple of pop-guns. When the Jap destroyer faded on our radar we breathed a little easier, and went to work in hopes of floating off at high tide. It was then or never as far as getting off that reef was concerned."

The crew threw everything movable overboard, except the deck-gun ammunition; food, furniture, anything to lighten ship. The torpedoes were dispatched through the stern tubes.

It was no use. The crew congregated in the submarine's stern to raise the bow. It was wedged. They tried to rock the bow free by dashing from port to starboard and back again.

"It was get off by dawn or fight the Jap destroyers and airplanes,"

McClintock continues. "We had radioed DACE shortly after running aground, and she abandoned her chase of the cruiser to try to pull us off.

"We gave up at about 0230. We were high and dry.

"Down below all equipment was destroyed. Sledge hammers were used on the radar and radios. Confidential gear was burned, choking everybody with smoke.

"At 0300 we commenced to abandon ship.

"Captain Claggett brought the DACE right up to the edge of the shoal. After setting the demolition time clock in the control room I went topside and was the last to leave the DARTER."

The DARTER did not explode and DACE tried to finish her off with torpedoes. They detonated on the reef without damaging the abandoned submarine. The two sub skippers decided to try gunfire.

Just as the deck gun went into action, the radarman reported a Jap plane at 6 miles.

"Clear the deck," ordered Claggett, and somehow all twenty-six men who were topside got below. There were bruised shins and trampled fingers but all noses were present when a count was made later.

Technically McClintock was still group commander, even with the group now wholly contained in the DACE.

"Do you think there is enough water for diving here, Claggett?" he said.

"I don't know and neither do you," came the quick reply, "but there is a Jap plane overhead."

The DACE dived—and started on the long voyage to her base in Australia.

5

Later in the day Admiral Kurita, having shifted ships again, this time to YAMATO, received an interesting dispatch from his boss, Fleet Admiral Toyoda, in Tokyo. He read the first sentence, and his fingers plucked at his bristly hair.

"Estimate of Enemy Plans: It is very probable that the enemy is aware of the fact we have concentrated our forces . . ."

Kurita murmured the Japanese equivalent of "You're telling me!" and read on:

"He will probably act in the following manner: (a) Concentrate submarines in great strength in the San Bernardino and Surigao Straits area. (b) Plan attacks on our surface forces, using large type planes and task forces, after tomorrow morning. (c) Plan decisive action by concentrating his surface strength in the area east of San Bernardino Strait and Tacloban where he has his transport group. He should be able to dispose himself in this manner by afternoon of 24th."

Kurita nodded. No crystal ball was needed to make those prophecies. He read on: "As to our plans: (a) Carry through our original plans. (b) In effecting the operations, the following points are specially emphasized: (1) Make up for our inferior surface strength by making every effort to direct the enemy to the north towards the Main Body of the Mobile Force. (2) Maintain an even stricter alert against submarines and aircraft. Utilize every possible trick to keep enemy submarines under control, particularly while breaking through the narrow straits. (3) Destroy enemy task force carriers with our shore-based planes, while his carrier-based planes are engaging our surface forces."

The Japanese plan was not bad. It was good enough to meet with dangerously partial success.

6

To the north, in the Inland Sea, Admiral Ozawa prepared his ships for death. The Americans had come too soon to Leyte, before he had time to complete the training of his airmen, before he could go south to command a large, balanced fleet in one big strike against the landings. More than half his pilots had been taken away from him for the defense of Formosa, and the ones left could hardly take off and land on carriers. He did not blame Toyoda for deciding to use his fleet as a decoy. That was all it was good for.

"I thought," Admiral Ozawa told interviewers after the war, "that at sacrifice of my fleet, which was very much weakened, Kurita's fleet could carry out its mission. I expected complete destruction of my fleet. If Kurita's mission was successful, that was all I wished."

On the afternoon of October 20, Ozawa with his force of decoy ships departed from the Inland Sea via Bungo Channel. Ozawa chose as his flagship the only large carrier of the group, a carrier that had participated in the attack on Pearl Harbor—the ZUIKAKU. Also in the force were three light carriers—CHITOSE, CHIYODA, and ZUIHO; two hermaphrodite vessels—half battleship, half carrier with a flight deck aft—HYUGA and ISE; three light cruisers, OYODO, TAMA, and ISUZU, and eight destroyers. The converted battleships carried no aircraft, their air groups having been part of the Formosa reinforcement. Divided sparsely among the carriers were only 80 fighters, 31 torpedo planes, and 7 dive bombers—118 planes in all. That was the Japanese carrier air force, complete, after a little less than two years of war with the United States Navy! Only the Americans didn't know it.

CHAPTER TWENTY-FIVE

Surigao Strait

I

THE BATTLE OF LEYTE GULF—much more accurately the Battle of Japan's Life—was complicated by factors of geography, psychology, logistics, and luck.

In its outcome, naval experts were given something besides the World War I Battle of Jutland to debate, diagram, and deliberate. If it is going to be something for the experts to argue, it presents a bewildering picture for the less learned to try to understand.

Look at the map again. There is Leyte, on the center-east of the Philippine Archipelago, between and a little back of the larger islands of Mindanao and Samar. On the northwest Leyte backs into the Visayan Sea, on the south into the Mindanao Sea.

Between Samar and Luzon to the north is one of the deep channels from the inland seas to the Pacific (or Philippine Sea, as the area west of the Marianas is called). That is San Bernardino Strait.

Between Leyte and Mindanao to the south is the other exit, Surigao Strait, which debouches into Leyte Gulf.

That mental image of Leyte explains many things, including why it was so important for the Allied forces to capture it. With Leyte in hand, all the 7,000 other islands in the Philippines were in radius. It also explains how and why the battle's three major phases shaped up as they did.

Admiral Kinkaid's forces were disposed to protect the landings inside Leyte Gulf. He had Admiral Oldendorf's battleship-cruiser combination plugging the southern approach by way of Surigao Strait. The mouth of the gulf was guarded by Rear Admiral T. L. Sprague's eighteen escort carriers, whose planes had been assigned the 360-degree job of fighting off submarines to seaward, supporting the ground troops to landward, and shooting down enemy aircraft in all directions.

Over the horizon, looking for trouble wherever it might appear, cruised Halsey's Third Fleet.

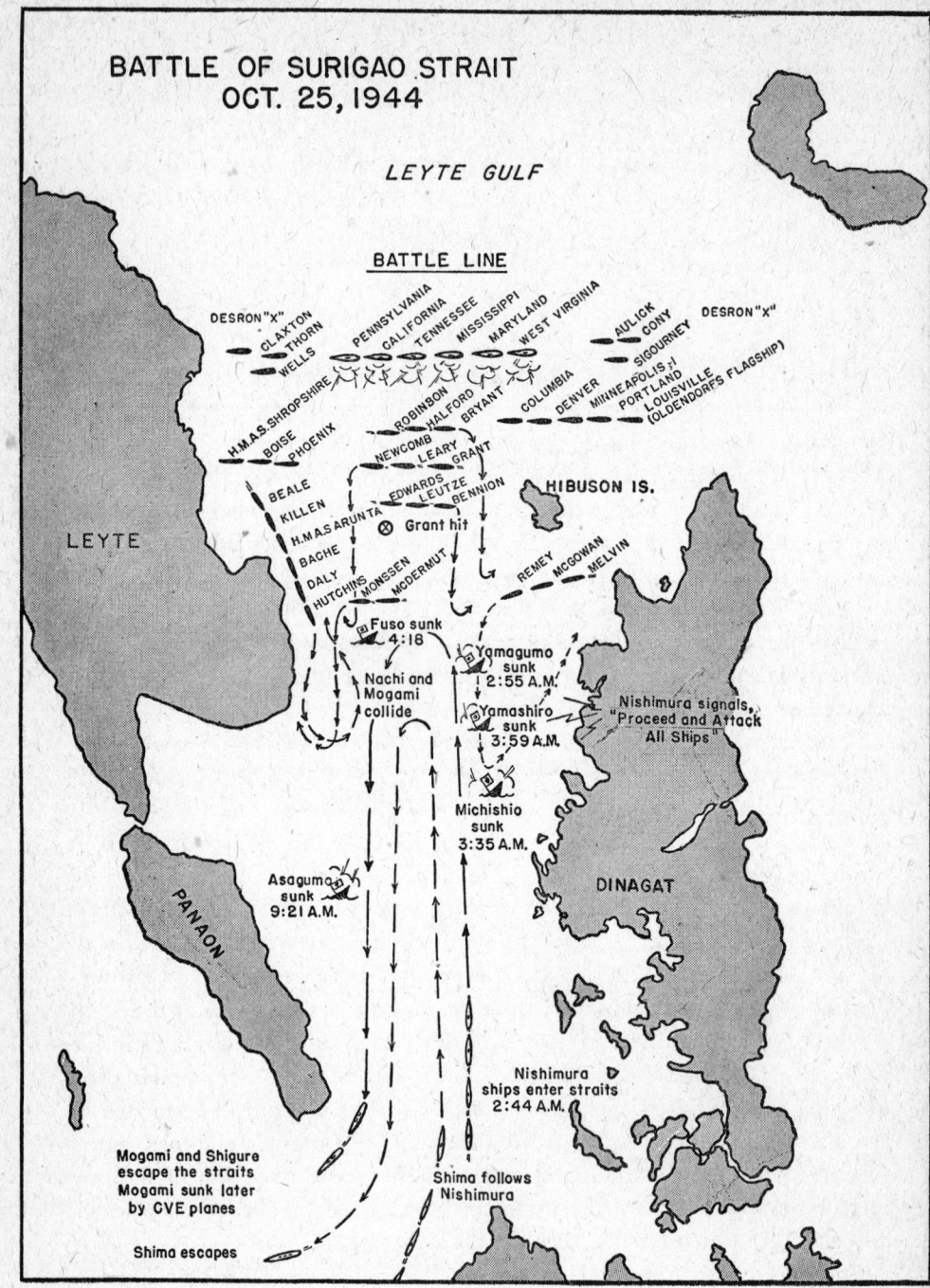

FIGURE 15

That, was, in simplest terms, the U.S.-Allied naval disposition.

The Japanese, it will be recalled, had their naval forces divided into three parts, too. One was to drive in upon Leyte through Surigao, the largest was to come out through San Bernardino and hit Leyte from the north, while Ozawa's pitiable carriers were to decoy the accurately surmised American forces at sea away from the hoped-for carnage.

Now, then, this is what happened. The preview will help the reader—and the authors as well—to keep in mind the pattern of that most decisive naval engagement. It all took place virtually at once, and each of the three battles had great influence on the others, far away.

The Japanese southern attack force bulled its way into Surigao Strait and was pounded to shreds by Oldendorf.

The enemy's central attackers were caught west of San Bernardino Strait and took such a pounding from Admiral Halsey's fliers that they turned back, but with no intention of retreat. That word was not in the Japanese lexicon for the operation, by orders of the High Command.

The northern force, Ozawa's "bait" carriers, managed to put on such a show of strength and daring that Halsey took his ships up to eliminate what seemed to him and his staff to be the greatest danger.

That gave the Central Force the chance to slip out through San Bernardino Strait and chew up the escort carriers guarding Leyte Gulf—a tour of sentry duty that had not been visualized as including a fight with some of the world's toughest warships. The carriers were on the verge of annihilation when the enemy broke off the action, reinserted the deleted word "retreat" into the orders for the day, and fled—shedding ships as it went. Not until after the war was that mystery cleared up. Admiral Kurita's big ships had taken such terrible punishment from the jeep force that he thought it to be more powerful than it was, and he also suspected he was about to be trapped by elements of Halsey's fleet.

What it all added up to was the end of Japan's sea power. It was a victory for the United States as complete and tidy as that of the Greeks over the Persians at Salamis—but it is a fair bet that after Salamis the Greek tacticians and columnists for years started arguments with "Now, if I had been Themistocles . . ."

There, then, are the broad outlines. Now for the details: For the sake of clarity, they will be related separately, Surigao first.

2

"Prepare for night engagement," radioed Vice Admiral Kinkaid to Rear Admiral Oldendorf, who was commanding the Leyte bombardment and fire-support ships. This dispatch was logged aboard "Lady Lou" (Admiral Oldendorf's flagship LOUISVILLE) at 1443, October 24, 1944.

All ships overheard Admiral Oldendorf's TBS message to his task force commanders. "Consider enemy night surface attack tonight Leyte Gulf via Surigao Strait imminent. Make all preparations. My dispatch orders are now being sent."

The electrifying words "night battle" raced throughout the fleet like lightning. It was definite. The Japs were coming through Surigao Strait. Blinker messages relaying battle instructions made the Lady Lou look like a Times Square advertising sign.

Scuttlebutt caused mixed emotions among the fighting sailors, but there wasn't much time for introspection. As they toiled to ready the ships for action, the old-timers—bearded old veterans of twenty-five years or even more—told new hands tall tales in the breathing spells. They would see billowing explosions, followed by steel bows pointing skyward and slipping beneath the surface. They would hear grating noises of twisted and torn steel and hear the screams from twisted and torn flesh.

"It won't take long," boasted one old sailor.

"And it will be easier than chippin' paintwork," spoke up another.

Aboard battleships and cruisers the stern cranes were lowered and secured on deck; airplanes were catapulted and sent to the beach to sit it out; fire hoses were faked down and unnecessary topside gear was secured; lifelines and stanchions were taken down and stowed; items that would splinter or burn were carried below or heaved over the side; fire-control instruments were checked and double-checked; radio and radar technicians made certain that secondary stations could be rigged immediately if primary stations were knocked out; torpedomen aboard the destroyers went over each tin fish as carefully as a trainer checks a boxer before his title fight. The ships were ready.

That is, all ships were ready but one—the cruiser NASHVILLE, up near the landing forces. General MacArthur was still aboard her.

Captain Charles Coney, the skipper, was doing everything within his power to get the NASHVILLE into action.

"With the Battle of Surigao Strait coming up, I naturally wanted to get in there and mix it up," Coney recalled wistfully. "I had fought in two wars and this was the opportunity of my naval career—to fight in that surface action.

"I went to General MacArthur and told him that I would like very much to take my ship into action and would it be asking too much of him if he would transfer his staff in order that we might participate."

General MacArthur had not planned to move ashore until the next day and he didn't seem anxious to change his mind.

"No, I do not desire to leave your ship, Captain," he replied. "I have never been able to witness a naval engagement and this is the opportunity of a lifetime. Proceed to the battle area when you wish."

Captain Coney thought the matter over and decided that he couldn't take the responsibility of sailing into battle with the Supreme Commander aboard. He radioed Admiral Kinkaid for advice on the matter. The Admiral, who was in the communications ship WASATCH, sympathetically replied that the General would be welcome aboard his flagship.

MacArthur's decision was firm.

"Transfer from a combatant ship to a noncombatant ship? Never! I have never been in the middle of a naval engagement and I would like nothing better than being in one tonight."

So, the risks being what they were, Admiral Kinkaid did not authorize NASHVILLE to enter the battle. Captain Coney did not take part in the action, and General MacArthur did not see it.

Also aboard NASHVILLE that night was Ensign (and/or Major) Iliff D. Richardson, the Philippine guerrilla leader, who, after crossing Leyte Gulf in a native canoe, had been picked up by the destroyer DAILEY. Three years earlier Richardson had been the executive officer on the PT 34 (Lieutenant Robert B. Kelly) when that boat, together with the other "expendable" PTs, took MacArthur and his party out of Bataan. After the loss of the PT 34 in Philippine waters during a strafing attack, Richardson became a guerrilla leader and set up a network of radio stations throughout the central Philippines. MacArthur had read every one of those guerrilla dispatches and now had invited Richardson to come aboard to tell all he knew of the guerrilla and enemy strength and disposition.

3

Admiral Oldendorf had anticipated the order to prepare for battle. Since first notice of enemy reactions was radioed from our vigilant submarines, he had made precautionary battle dispositions after sunset in Leyte Gulf.

"Upon receipt of the order to prepare for night action," Admiral Oldendorf says, "I issued a battle plan and then sent for the commander of the battleline [the six old battleships], Rear Admiral G. L. Weyler, and Rear Admiral R. S. Berkey, who was to command the right flank forces [cruisers and destroyers] and explained my plan to them.

"In essence, my plan was to plug up Surigao Strait. It was obvious that the purpose of the attack was to destroy our shipping in Leyte Gulf on which the success of General MacArthur's enterprise still depended. Since the south side of Leyte Gulf funnels into Surigao Strait, which in turn forms a canal-like passage into the Mindanao Sea, 50 miles farther south, I placed the battleline cruising squarely across the Leyte exit of the Strait. Weyler's battleline speed was to be 5 knots in order that the ships would not have to countermarch (reverse course) too frequently.

"I flanked both sides of the battleline to the south with cruisers and destroyers and sent five picket destroyers under command of Captain Jesse Coward deep into Surigao Strait.

"Our plan of battle was to use torpedoes and heavy gunfire, the former to slow down the enemy, the latter to destroy him completely."

All that day Japanese aircraft had been attacking over the entire area in numbers and fury exceeding anything the invasion fleet had so far experienced. By these all-out air attacks on the day before the planned smash into Leyte Gulf, the Japanese hoped to give their surface forces "indirect protection." Their pilots were too ill-trained and too ill-equipped to co-ordinate more closely.

Some of the Japanese aircraft were Army, flying from fields south of Luzon and directing their efforts against the Leyte beachheads. Some of the attackers were from Admiral Onishi's Manila-based First Air Fleet, now whittled down to 100 planes by Halsey's persistent attacks. It was this outfit that made the first Kamikaze attacks.

But most of the attackers who plagued Admiral Halsey's Third Fleet that day were from Admiral Fukudome's Second Air Fleet swelled to 350 by units from China and the homeland, which had been ordered down to Luzon from recuperating Formosa. Early in the morning they cost Admiral Sherman's Task Group 38.3 the carrier PRINCETON, who died so violently she nearly sank two ships trying to save her.

But air supremacy was being vigorously defended by United States naval fliers: fighters swarming against the Japanese torpedo bombers, and the American torpedo bombers searching for Japanese ships. It was from the air that the Japanese surface forces were detected standing in for Surigao Strait, and it was a short, sharp attack led by Commander Fred E. Bakutis, skipper of ENTERPRISE's Fighting 20, that drew first blood in the historic battle.[1] Bakutis had fourteen rocket-equipped F6F fighters escorting twelve SB2C dive bombers led by Commander R. Emmet Riera and Lieutenant Commander Ray Moore. They had only 500-pound bombs, but they attacked Admiral Nishimura's seven warships, causing damaging fires on the battleship FUSO and knocking out one turret on the destroyer SHIGURE.

Only one American plane was lost—Bakutis's. The pilot, after floating around the Mindanao Sea seven days in his rubber life raft, was picked up by Commander Francis A. Greenup's famed submarine HARDHEAD.

4

The Japanese warships assigned to the forcing of Surigao Strait approached in two groups, one 40 miles behind the other. They might as well have been strangers, for all they knew of each other's plans.

Vice Admiral S. Nishimura led with the "C" Force of two battleships, FUSO and YAMASHIRO, one heavy cruiser, MOGAMI, and four destroyers, MICHISHIO, ASAGUMO, YAMAGUMO, and SHIGURE.

The Second Diversion Attack Force (known also by the rather grandiloquent name of the Fifth Fleet) followed, under command of Vice Admiral K. Shima. It was composed of the two heavy cruisers, NACHI and SHIGARA, the light cruiser ABUKUMA, and four destroyers— SHIRANUHI, KASUMI, USHIO, and AKEBONO.

[1] More blood was spilled that morning, October 24, when a search team from FRANKLIN, part of Admiral Davison's TG 38.4, discovered three enemy destroyers heading south off the west coast of Panay. In the ensuing attack one destroyer, the WAKABA, was sunk.

Shima was not exactly clear in his mind what Nishimura was up to. He had come hurrying south from the wholly fruitless sortie against "the remnants" of Halsey's fleet which the Japanese aviators had reported to be limping away from the Formosa raid. He had orders to co-operate with Admiral Kurita by forcing Surigao Strait. Not until he intercepted a radio message not addressed to him did he know that Nishimura's group had been detached from Kurita's fleet and had a head start on him.

The radio message was a broadcast from Nishimura announcing he was under attack at the strait's mouth. The battle was joined before Shima had word to confirm what his radar had caused him to suspect more and more, that the force ahead of him was on an identical mission.

Their co-operation, consequently, was more with Oldendorf than each other.

5

Oldendorf's reception committee for the Japanese consisted of 39 sideboys in the shape of PT boats, thirteen sections, three boats to each. Three sections were stationed in the Mindanao Sea, patrolling as far as 60 miles from the mouth of the strait. Five sections were cruising around the entrance to the strait, and five were inside the channel itself.

Theirs was a Wagnerian setting. Sheet lightning dimmed the hazy blur of the setting moon and thunder echoed from the islands' hills, as fictional a prelude to battle as any writer of thrillers could conceive.

Radar contact was first established at 11:00 P.M. Lieutenant Weston C. Pullen, Jr., in command of the five sections at the strait's entrance, ordered motors muffled down and the boats steered on a collision course with the enemy.

Pullen was riding in PT 152, or LAKACOOKIE, as she was called by her crew. The LAKACOOKIE's radio failed, and PT 130, speeding behind her, made the radio contact with the PTs stationed up the strait. From one force to another the word was passed to the Admiral that the Japs were coming.

"We were 6,000 yards from the battlewagons and 4,000 yards from their destroyers when they turned on their searchlights and blanketed us with gunfire," Pullen relates. "Since our boats were at extreme torpedo range, we turned and scampered toward shallow waters as our radiomen clicked out identification and contact reports."

THE END'S BEGINNING

The LAKACOOKIE was hit forward and set on fire. Things looked desperate for a few seconds, until the Japanese obligingly extinguished the flames with a near miss that deluged the little boat with a half ton of foam.

PT 130, skippered by Lieutenant (jg) Ian D. Malcolm, was protecting LAKACOOKIE's withdrawal when one of her torpedo warheads was struck by an 8-inch armor-piercing projectile which tore out approximately a quarter of the TNT without causing the torpedo to detonate. PT 131 also was riddled by Jap gunfire, but the damage to the Japanese had greater significance.

Their identification, location, course, and speed were known to all our waiting warships.

It was then that Admiral Nishimura opened up on his radio to let Japanese forces know he was under attack by torpedo boats, and thus gave Admiral Shima the word that Nishimura's force was ahead of him—and in trouble.

6

The first round went to the Japanese on points. Two battleships, a cruiser, and a destroyer had messed up three little PT boats, but in so doing they had revealed everything they had to fight with.

Round two was with the American Destroyer Squadron 54—REMEY (Commander Reid P. Fiala), MCGOWAN (Commander William R. Cox), and MELVIN (Commander Barry T. Atkins)—on the east side of the strait; on the west, the MONSSEN (Commander Charles T. Bergin) and MCDERMUT (Commander Carter B. Jennings).

Lieutenant Leonard H. Hudson, officer of the deck of the flagship REMEY which carried Squadron Commander, Captain Jesse Coward, now relates:

"When I came to the bridge my skipper, Commander R. P. Fiala, had just turned on the ship's speaker to address all hands. 'This is the Captain speaking. Tonight our ship has been designated to make the first torpedo run on the Jap task force that is on its way to stop our landings in Leyte Gulf. It is our job to stop the Japs. May God be with us tonight.'

"The statement 'May God be with us tonight,' was found in practically every letter that left the REMEY after the battle.

"All hands were aware that the REMEY would be first to steam into the big Jap battleships. The men who were survivors from destroyers that had fought in the Solomons well knew what torpedo attack meant.

"The PTs were on the job. They kept sending in reports and we knew exactly where the Japs were. The Japs tried to jam their radio transmitters but they tried too late. The next patrol had already picked up the message and the news was relayed up the strait from one group of boats to another until it reached us. [The Japanese at this time were formed up in their approach disposition: the destroyers MICHISHIO and ASAGUMO leading, followed in column by the battleships YAMASHIRO, Nishimura's flagship, and FUSO, with the heavy cruiser MOGAMI bringing up the rear. Broad on the port and starboard bows of the flagship were the destroyers SHIGURE and YAMAGUMO.] We decided the Japs would be on us shortly and we prepared to attack. Captain Coward radioed to Admiral Oldendorf that the five ships of Desron 54 were divided into two groups and were going in to attack. Admiral Oldendorf replied, 'Affirmative, but keep close to the shore prior to the attack and during the withdrawal afterwards.'

"Our group, the eastern, formed its attack disposition at 0227. We circled north of Hibuson Island and stood down the strait on a due south course. Soon we were making over 30 knots and closed the target at the rate of over a mile a minute.

"Our radar picked them up at 16 miles. When the target was less than 5 miles, the Captain radioed to ships astern: 'Follow me.'

"Then came the rapid orders: 'Stand by to fire torpedoes. Fire torpedoes! Torpedoes away!' About the time we fired our torpedoes the Jap radar picked us up. This was 0301. They quickly turned on their searchlights and they were right on target. I felt like my picture was being taken with a flash bulb camera.

"We were in so close that they shot over us with their AA guns. They shot in front of us; behind us and straddled us, but we got out without a scratch and so did all the other ships of Desron 54."

As the Japs concentrated on the retiring Eastern Group, the Western Group, MCDERMUT and MONSSEN, commanded by Comdesdiv 108, Commander Richard H. Phillips, streaked down the shore line on the other side, and swung at the Japanese with a right cross.

(Some of the Jap ships took these destroyers under fire but visibility was bad and radar action poor. Commander Nishino of SHIGURE attempted to aim by radar but "could not differentiate between the ships and the land," getting just one merged reaction on the screen.)

The Japanese, apparently still unhurt, plowed on up the strait, determined to reach Leyte Gulf. Nishimura gave the signal to form battle disposition and SHIGURE and YAMAGUMO started pulling into column ahead of the flagship.

Then came the second big destroyer torpedo attack. This time it was Destroyer Squadron 24 (Captain Kenmore M. McManes), also in two groups, HUTCHINS (Commander Caleb B. Laning), DALY (Commander Richard R. Bradley, Jr.), and BACHE (Commander Robert C. Morton) on the west, and, opposite, HMAS ARUNTA (Commander Alfred E. Buchanan, RAN), KILLEN (Commander Howard G. Corey) and BEALE (Commander Doyle M. Coffee), laying a smoke screen.

The results of this well-aimed torpedo attack were decisive. The three leading enemy destroyers and the lumbering flagship, YAMASHIRO, were all hit. One of the destroyers, the YAMAGUMO, sank and the other two were left unnavigable.

From his stricken flagship Admiral Nishimura informed his group of the damage and gave his last orders: "You are to proceed and attack all ships."

Only FUSO, MOGAMI, and SHIGURE could comply.

From his bridge on the KILLEN, Commander H. G. Corey eyed one enemy ship that seemed to be in pain. He recognized it as the YAMASHIRO and at once ordered all torpedoes set to a depth of 22 feet. The evidence is that Commander Corey's quick thinking brought YAMASHIRO to sudden death. Commander Nishino testified after the war that it was the deep-running torpedoes striking amidships that caused YAMASHIRO'S ammunition to explode, breaking the battleship's back.

But still the Japanese kept coming up the strait.

There was still time for one more destroyer torpedo attack before our cruisers and battleships, silently cruising back and forth on station, had their turn at the enemy.

Desron 56 (Captain Roland N. Smoot), divided into three sections, turned to attack. Section I—NEWCOMB (Commander Lawrence B. Cook), the flagship, RICHARD P. LEARY (Commander Frederic S. Habecker), A. W. GRANT (Commander Terrell A. Nisewaner)—went down the center; Section II—HALFORD (Commander Robert J. Hardy), BRYANT (Commander Paul L. High), ROBINSON (Commander Elonzo

B. Grantham, Jr)—charged down the westward side; Section III—
HEYWOOD L. EDWARDS (Commander Joe W. Boulware), LEUTZE (Commander Berton A. Robbins, Jr.), BENNION (Commander Joshua W. Cooper)—to the eastward.

Both Sections II and III were at once taken under extremely heavy gunfire by the enemy. They fired their torpedoes and retired along the coast as ordered without suffering damage. "The Jap bullets were so close I could smell them," said Captain Smoot.

Section I, in the center, and in a position 4 miles directly west of Hibuson Island, was likewise under enemy fire. At 0405 the three ships splashed their fish into the water and tried to make their getaway toward the shore lines as Admiral Oldendorf had instructed, but enemy fire was so intense that they were forced to retire due northward up the center of the strait toward our own battleline. It was, of course, the same route the Japanese ships were taking, and when our cruisers went into action our center destroyers were in the line of fire. Only the A. W. GRANT was hit, the only one out of twenty that made torpedo attacks to get hurt, but the hurts were grievous.

"At this stage of the battle the Captain of FUSO, Captain Ban, took charge," said Nishino. "The FUSO, MOGAMI, and my destroyer SHIGURE proceeded north to continue battle."

Instead of retiring south while in condition to do so, the remnants of Admiral Nishimura's force sailed majestically northward in column; straight into Admiral Oldendorf's death trap of floating steel; straight into the textbook position that all admirals dream of, the position of a crossed T.[1]

7

Now it was the cruisers' turn.

Admiral Oldendorf, aboard the LOUISVILLE, was thinking about his

---

[1] Oldendorf was like a man holding a hand full of aces; it was a gunnery tactician's dream, to T (or cap) the enemy's column, throwing at him the full broadsides of one's own ships. This maneuver had been executed at the Battle of Tsushima Strait in 1905, when the slowness and weakness of the Russian Imperial Fleet permitted Admiral Togo to do it. It had occurred again without being taken advantage of in 1916 at the Battle of Jutland when, in low visibility, Admiral von Scheer unknowingly ran his column headlong into the broadside of Lord Jellicoe, who did not know until long after the battle that he had his enemy perfectly capped.

ammunition and fuel. He was low on both after five days of shore bombardment and night cruising in Leyte Gulf. Because the primary mission of the battleships and cruisers had been fire support, their normal allowance of armor-piercing shells had been cut 25 per cent and the difference made up in lighter ammunition designed for destroying shore installations—and people. And even these shells were down to 12 per cent of magazine capacity.

So Admiral Oldendorf had told his heavy ship commanders that he did not intend to fire "until I see the whites of their eyes." He thought he could detect the gleam in the darkness.

"What range do you get, Sam?" he asked Captain Hurt of the flagship, who was leaning over the rail of his bridge looking at the Admiral on his flag bridge below.

"Seventeen thousand yards, sir."

"Got a good setup?"

"Yes, we have."

Admiral Oldendorf waited a minute pecking his fingernails against the steel rail of LADY LOU's bridge—8½ miles, a moderate range, he thought.

"Well, all right, give the order to open fire."

At 0350 Hurt spoke into his phone—from the crowded "flag plot" order repeater—it blared forth from every squawk-box on every ship—and on the instant (every finger must have been tensed at the guns)— BLAM!

This was modern war at sea; they fired at something they couldn't see, and it fired back.

There was a terrific rolling roar as the main battery cut loose. Then a moment of silence and the hiss as the air blast cleared the gun barrels. Next the whirring of reloading, rammers and elevating gears grinding away. Stand-by buzzer sounds and flash—roar!

"Upon giving the order to 'open fire,' " said Admiral Oldendorf, "it seemed as if every ship in the flank forces and the battleline opened at once, and there was a semicircle of fire which landed squarely on one point, which was the leading battleship [FUSO]. The semicircle of fire evidently so confused the Japanese that they did not know what target to shoot at. I remember seeing one or two salvos start toward my flagship but in the excitement of the occasion, I forgot to look where they landed."

With the nod from Rear Admiral Theodore D. Ruddock, Jr., WEST

VIRGINIA (Captain Herbert V. Wiley) opened fire for the battleships, which all night long had been performing the difficult maneuver of marching and countermarching at slow speed across the Leyte Gulf end of the strait by stop-watch and radar: steam west for such-and-such a time, reverse and steam east.

The TENNESSEE (Captain John B. Heffernan) spoke a second later, with CALIFORNIA (Captain Henry P. Burnett), MARYLAND (Captain Herbert J. Ray), and MISSISSIPPI (Captain Herman J. Redfield) following in that order. The PENNSYLVANIA (Captain Charles F. Martin) chose that time to have radar trouble, and missed joining in the chorus.

The destroyers had ringside seats. They saw FUSO's pagoda mast crumble like a sand castle in the tide. But there were three destroyers who found themselves not ringside, but in the ring. The NEWCOMB, RICHARD P. LEARY, and A. W. GRANT, retiring up the center of the channel, shouted for succor. Admiral Oldendorf ordered firing to cease. There wasn't much left to shoot at, anyhow.

8

The A. W. GRANT was caught between the fire of the two battlelines, catching shells from both sides. The first shell landed aft at 0407 and exploded among empty powder cases stacked across the fantail. Thirty seconds later several shells hit amidships and steam began to pour out of the forward stack. The forward fire rooms and engine rooms were out of commission.

An entry in the ship's log gives details:

"0408½ Additional shell hits began to riddle ship. Hit forward at waterline flooded forward storeroom and forward crews berthing compartment. Hit in 40mm gun #1 exploded 40mm ammunition and started fire. Hit through starboard boat davit exploded killing ship's Doctor, Lieutenant Charles Akin Mathier, 5 radiomen, and almost entire amidships repair party. Other hits in forward stack, one hit on port motor whale boat, one hit and low order explosion in galley. One hit in scullery room, one hit in after crews berthing compartment, and one additional hit in forward engine room. All lights, telephone communications, radars, and radios out of commission. Steering control shifted aft."

All the above happened in one minute. It gives some idea of what the Japs took in fourteen minutes.

Using blinker gun, Commander T. A. Nisewaner sent the following message toward his battleline: "From DD649 we are dead in water. Tow needed." The message was sent over and over. No acknowledgment was received from our ships. None was really expected.

Commander Nisewaner, a big, powerful man, entered the engine room amidst escaping steam, and groping through the darkness and the rapidly rising water personally carried several of the men out on his back. In his action report he said, "following the battle damage our medical setup became pretty grim. Prior to the operation we transferred our Chief Pharmacist's Mate without replacement. Within a minute after the first shell hit, the medical officer was killed outside battle dressing station forward, and the PhM2/c was instantly killed outside sick bay amidship. This left one PhM1/c working in the aft head [toilet] under emergency lighting to treat approximately 45 dying men and 50 with serious injuries."

In his executive officer's report Lieutenant Hunt Hamill mentions some of the activity that went on during the ghastly few minutes of absorbing both enemy and friendly shell fire.

"The reaction of the crew in a dire emergency requiring medical help was remarkable," Hamill wrote. "The remaining PhM 1/c, W. H. Swaim, Jr., took charge of a staggering crisis to carry aid to the wounded about the ship. In addition to maintaining his own battle dressing station in the crew's head aft, Swaim issued instruction for those setting up operations in other parts of the ship.

"Swaim had some able assistance. J. C. O'Neill, Jr., a soundman, whose association with his father, a physician, enabled him to turn to on some of the ugly wounds, improvised makeshift tourniquets and administered morphine to relieve pain. He bound up numerous open wounds and stumps, and rigged an emergency oxygen tent for a man at the point of death from burns. The Chief Commissary Steward, L. M. Holmes, organized a first-aid station in the wardroom, where the doctor would have worked, and showed a great amount of talent in a field far removed from his own.

"The wounded cared for the wounded. W. G. Hertel, WT 3/c, badly wounded and unable to move his legs, asked to be propped up against the base of a boat davit and from there administered morphine syrettes to all within his reach. J. M. Flaherty, RT 1/c, severely wounded by shrapnel and bleeding profusely, rigged a makeshift dressing on his badly torn thigh, and then proceeded to give aid to the other wounded. One boy, W. M. Selleck, RM 1/c, with both legs torn off and near death, looked up to the Chief Commissary Steward and said before he died, 'There's nothing you can do for me, fellows. Go ahead and do something for those others.'

"At his battle station with Repair 3, on the fantail, R. H. Parker, MM 1/c, heard the safety valves of the forward engine plant blow. Showing complete disregard for his own safety, he ran through the intense shell fire and shut off the escaping steam below, saving at least a half dozen lives of men trapped by live steam in the forward fire and engine rooms.

"Hit by shrapnel from one of the first shells to explode, severely wounded and weak from loss of blood, Ensign F. D. Case refused medical aid for himself, carried stretcher cases to the battle dressing station until he collapsed and fell to the deck. Unable to regain his feet, he lay against the deckhouse and directed efforts to treat the wounded about him. Unable to walk himself, he gave his shoes to a shipmate whose shoes had been burned off his feet.

"The Engineering Officer, Lieutenant Bethuel B. V. Lyon, Jr., rushed below to check the boilers. Discovering that one boiler could still be operated, he organized a crew and entered the steam-filled compartment. There were no lights and most of the work had to be done by sense of touch. He worked steadily until he was able to get the GRANT underway."

The report seems to cite every living—and dying—man on the ship— King, Brown, Bennett, DeMarco, Kelly, Jone, Ogden, Bradfield, and more. A book could be written for the A. W. GRANT's minutes of agony.

The ship's damage-control officer Lieutenant William J. E. Crissy, organized parties to seal the twenty big holes in the hull, half of them from American shells. The men plugged them with mattresses, tables, anything handy.

At 5.00 A.M. the NEWCOMB sent a motor whaleboat alongside with her medical officer, Lieutenant (jg) John J. McNeil, and two corpsmen. About an hour later, Commander Lawrence B. Cook, skipper of NEWCOMB, took the crippled GRANT in tow.

9

Sailing into all this mess, Vice Admiral Shima entered Surigao Strait, and barely got inside when a torpedo from one of the shore-hugging PTs struck the light cruiser ABUKUMA. Her bow drooped and her speed dropped.

A ship passed the force headed south. From the Admiral's flagship a challenge blinked.

"I am the SHIGURE," came the reply. It was Commander Nishino, taking the sole survivor of Admiral Nishimura's task force the hell out of there.

"I am the NACHI," acknowledged Shima's flagship, and swept on. No questions about what lay ahead or why the SHIGURE was wrong-way bound. It seems that Shima did not care much for Nishimura, and vice versa.

Shima just sailed on, and on, and on.

His radar picked up a group of ships in motion. Obviously they were not Japanese, because the group was now passing MOGAMI, burning rather briskly and apparently motionless. So the advancing Japanese fired a broad fan of torpedoes.

The target was the crippled GRANT, in tow and guarded by two other destroyers. All the torpedoes missed.

By now Admiral Shima was sure the upper end of Surigao Strait was no place to go. He ordered a turn, and his flagship collided with the crippled MOGAMI. That settled it. He called off the whole business and headed south, his cruiser limping badly.

10

Admiral Oldendorf detected SHIGURE proceeding south at high speed on his radar and ordered Destroyer Squadron X,[1] which had been acting as battleline screen, to pursue the enemy. He told Admiral Weyler to

---

[1] Destroyer Squadron X, which was unable to overtake either SHIGURE or Admiral Shima's force, was composed of CLAXTON (Commander Miles H. Hubbard), THORN (Lieutenant Commander Frederick H. Schneider, Jr.), WELLES (Lieutenant Commander John S. Slaughter), CONY (Commander Allen W. Moore), SIGOURNEY (Lieutenant Commander Fletcher Hale), AULICK (Commander John D. Andrew).

maintain the battleline in its assigned location while he gave chase to the crippled remnants of the Japanese force. Admiral Oldendorf took all the cruisers of the left flank force (LOUISVILLE, Captain Sam Hurt; PORTLAND, Captain Thomas G. W. Settle; MINNEAPOLIS, Captain Harry B. Slocum; DENVER, Captain Alfred M. Bledsoe; COLUMBIA, Captain Maurice E. Curts) to make sure that nothing would escape.

Trailing Admiral Oldendorf came Rear Admiral Berkey with his flagship PHOENIX (Captain Jack H. Duncan), BOISE (Captain John S. Roberts), and HMAS SHROPSHIRE (Captain Charles A. Godfrey Nichols, RAN).

Our cruisers were making fast work of the once-proud Jap fleet until 0540, when they were forced to retire because of the possibility of enemy torpedo attacks.

At 0643 Admiral Oldendorf ordered Admiral Hayler to take DENVER and COLUMBIA ("The Gem"), screened by the destroyers ROBINSON, BRYANT, and HALFORD, down the strait and sink any ships found in a floating condition.

A few minutes later the Jap destroyer ASAGUMO, with its bow blown off just forward of the bridge, gamely opened fire on DENVER and COLUMBIA. After one flurry of 6-inch shells, the water was dotted with survivors from ASAGUMO. That ended the surface action in Surigao Strait.

Morning found all hands very tired but supremely happy. One of the greatest victories in naval history was theirs and they knew it.

Describing what happened to the Japs more graphically than any action report from our fleet, the dispatch sent to Toyoda that morning by the lone ship of Nishimura's force to survive, the destroyer SHIGURE, tells the story:

"C Force has been annihilated, location of enemy unknown, please send me instruction. I have trouble with my rudder, my wireless, my radar, and my gyro, and I received one hit."

The Japanese said that the damaged MOGAMI[1] temporarily escaped Surigao Strait, but she was caught along with one cruiser from Admiral Shima's force, ABUKUMA, and both were sunk that morning by planes from our escort carriers. The remainder of Admiral Shima's force turned away before engaging our main forces and saved themselves the fate of Admiral Nishimura's force.

[1] Admiral Oldendorf believes that the ship his cruisers engaged just prior to daylight was MOGAMI. If so, she was sunk by his surface forces.

Our destroyers had just begun to pick up Jap survivors when an urgent radio message was beamed down the strait from Admiral Kinkaid:

"The Main Jap Force which cleared San Bernardino Strait at midnight is attacking our CVEs."

The Battle off Samar was underway. Oldendorf collected his ships and headed for the trouble. His lockers were practically bare, but he was ready and willing to fight with cutlasses, if nothing better could be supplied.

Chapter Twenty-Six

And Still They Come

I

TO STRAIGHTEN OUT the thread of narrative so that the account of this involved three-way battle will not become hopelessly knotted, it is necessary to shift the scene back in time and space, to Halsey and his fleet.

After the smashing strikes on Formosa, the Third Fleet turned its attention to the Philippines, especially Luzon, where the main enemy airfields were located. Then, when the Third and the Seventh Amphibious Forces spilled their human cargoes ashore at Leyte on October 20, carrier planes from Admiral McCain's and Admiral Davison's groups flew overhead in direct support of the troops.

Things had been quiet—too quiet—at the beachheads. The troops had gone ashore almost unscratched, and there had been practically no air reaction on the part of the Japs. So Halsey and his nimble-witted staff —the famous Dirty Trick Department—were intensely interested in what the Japs were up to.

Since momentous decisions were soon to be made by this staff, a brief description of how it worked might be in order.

The title "Dirty Trick Department" had its origin in the dim first days of the war when someone on Halsey's staff remarked at one of the meetings: "I wonder what dirty tricks we can play on the little sons of bitches today." The idea stuck and from then on the staff wore its new name as jauntily as a cocked hat.

The streamlined staff worked together, ate together, lived together, and were in "sight contact" with each other practically all the time, except when they "hit their bunks."

"This was the key to the success of the staff," said Chief of Staff Carney, "and in spite of this closeness there was no snapping at each other."

Halsey's flag quarters aboard NEW JERSEY were the working space for the staff. Extending the width of the second superstructure deck, Halsey's quarters consisted of a large messroom to starboard and a smaller office to port where Halsey and Carney each had a desk. Off the office was Halsey's cabin; Carney slept in a cabin adjacent to the messroom.

When the oblong table in the messroom was not being used for victualing purposes, it served as a workbench for the staff heads and their immediate assistants. Instead of laboriously sending memos to each other from separate offices scattered throughout the ship, they were able to settle questions quickly by talking directly across the green felt cover of the table. The policy committee of the Dirty Trick Department consisted of "Mick" Carney, Captain Ralph ("Rollo") Wilson, the operations officer, Captain Horace ("Doug") Moulton, the air operations officer, Captain Leonard ("Ham") Dow, communications officer and in charge of radio deception and countermeasures, Captain Marion ("Mike") Cheek, intelligence officer, Captain Herbert ("Jack") Hoerner, assistant operations officer, and Commander Harold Stassen, assistant Chief of Staff (Administration), aide, and flag secretary. Also included on the staff were Marine and Army liaison officers.

Directly above the Admiral's quarters, and only a hop up the ladder away, was the heart of the staff organization—the flag plot. There on visual display was the whole strategic picture, and instead of having to read through lengthy reports and operation orders, the staff, at one glance, could see what was happening. Plots, charts, radar displays showed everything—the enemy disposition in the contact areas; the estimated damage done to the enemy—and what he in turn had inflicted; the position of all ships of the Third Fleet; the position of all aircraft—both enemy and friendly—within a radius of 100 miles; and even positions of all downed aviators, all essential voice radio channels were piped in and the more important ones recorded. The business manager of this elaborate information room was Harold Stassen.

It was from here, with the flag bridge just on the other side of the door, that Halsey fought the Third Fleet.

Twice a day the staff met; in the morning and in the evening. At each meeting the entire strategic and tactical situation was reviewed. Enemy movements and dispositions were closely studied. All hands were encouraged to make suggestions. "What do the Nips have we can get at?" "What will they do if we do strike?" were questions always asked.

Intelligence made its estimate of the current situation to operations.

Operations in turn made its estimate of capabilities. The estimates were then funneled to Mick Carney.

After reading through the dispatches of the previous few hours, Admiral Halsey would come into the cabin where the staff was at work, sit down, and say, "Well, what do we do now?"

Then the possible plans and alternatives were laid before him. He made the decision "yes" or "no" and if "yes" the operation order was shot out quickly to the fleet.

It was not Halsey's policy to sit back and wait to see what the enemy plan was before doing something about it. "Break it up before it gets started" was his aggressive axiom. As early at the 21st of October, while messages of congratulations on the Okinawa-Formosa sweep poured in, staff studies were being made as to the best way of breaking up any action the Japs might take in reaction to the Leyte landing.

"By the 23rd," said Admiral Carney, "it became apparent from air sightings and from submarine sightings notably in the South China Sea, that the Japs were milling around and that something on a grand scale was under foot. The decision was made to move in close to the east coast of the Philippines and project reinforced searches across the Philippines into the South China Sea to find out just what was going on.

"If you will remember, beginning with the 10th of October at Okinawa these carriers and their air groups had been fighting almost continuously for fourteen days. They needed replenishment and they needed rest in the worst way. Nevertheless, this was no time to give too great consideration to that sort of thing."

One group, McCain's Task Group 38.1, had been ordered back to the fleet anchorage at Ulithi to rearm. On the way it was to make an air slap at Yap. The BUNKER HILL escorted by two destroyers, STEPHEN POTTER and BENHAM, had been detached and sent to Manus in the Admiralties to pick up a replacement air group.

During the night of October 23 the three remaining groups made a high-speed run in toward the Philippine coast. Davison's group moved in east of Leyte to cover Surigao Strait. Bogan's group, including NEW JERSEY, took the middle position off the entrance of San Bernardino Strait, while "Ted" Sherman's carriers, with Marc Mitscher aboard the LEXINGTON, went north off the little bight in Luzon near the Island of Polillo.

The Jap navy was on the move and Halsey knew it. During the night word was received that the submarine GUITARRO (Commander Enrique D. Haskins) had sighted a force of fifteen to twenty warships west of Mindoro heading east, obviously the force that had been attacked earlier by DARTER and DACE.

At dawn the three carrier groups launched a fan of searches that completely covered the western approaches to the Philippines spreading out over a huge area 300 miles deep and 1,000 miles long.

The distinction of being the first aircraft to spot Kurita's attack force fell to a search plane from CABOT.

In flag plot aboard NEW JERSEY the amplifier crackled as a voice came in, thin and indistinct:

"Four battleships, eight cruisers, thirteen destroyers off the southern tip of Mindoro Island, course 050, speed 10 to 12 knots . . ."

This was it—definitely! Within a matter of minutes the Commander of the Third Fleet passed the word to all of the waiting admirals spread over half the globe: to King in Washington, to Nimitz at Guam, to Kinkaid in Leyte Gulf, to Mitscher near-by to the north, to Sherman and Davison.

Things began to happen as Halsey went into high gear. Davison's group to the south and Sherman's group off Luzon were told to concentrate toward Bogan's center group at best speed and to launch strikes against the strong Jap force sighted by the CABOT plane. McCain on his way to Ulithi and at the time 635 miles from the coast of Samar was ordered to come about and join the fray. An urgent top-secret dispatch was sent to Mitscher aboard the LEXINGTON stating that the enemy carrier strength had not been located and directing that the area to the north be kept under observation by planes from Sherman's Task Group 38.3.

At a quarter to nine INTREPID (Captain Joseph F. Bolger), CABOT (Captain Stanley J. Michael), and INDEPENDENCE (Captain Edward C. Ewen) launched their first strike against the spotted Japanese. Roaring to the west went 31 fighters, 16 torpedo planes, and 12 dive bombers.

It was the beginning of a hot day for Admiral Kurita.

2

On the morning of October 24, Sherman's Task Group 38.3 was east of Polillo Island and within 150 miles of Manila. Its job that day was to cover its search sector and to send a fighter sweep over Manila. On the after deck of each carrier sat torpedo planes, loaded and gassed, with wings folded, waiting to fly against the Japanese fleet, once it was spotted.

"At dawn," related Captain William H. Buracker of the PRINCETON "as was usually the case when we were close to Japanese strong points, we had fire hoses led out in the hanger and on the flight deck and, since we anticipated a long stretch at general quarters, we prepared to feed the crew at battle stations.

"About ten minutes of eight radar picked up a group of from 40 to 50 unidentified aircraft approaching from the westward, from Manila, and almost immediately thereafter a second group of about the same size was detected 15 miles behind the first group. Our two small fighter divisions in the air were immediately sent to intercept.

"Admiral Sherman ordered all carriers in our task group to launch all available fighters and then he maneuvered us into the rain squalls for cover."

The PRINCETON's Fighting 27, the same outfit that had staged a field day over Manila during the September raids, was flying Combat Air Patrol when the Jap raids were detected.

"We estimated that there were 65 fighters and 15 bombers in the attack," related Lieutenant Carl Brown. "Ordinarily we would not have tackled 80 planes with 8 Hellcats, but it was get them before they reached our ships. It had been drilled into us from the time we were in preflight school that the primary task of a Navy fighter pilot is to protect his ship.

"With this thought in mind we went after them with all guns and throttles wide open.

"We held off the 80 planes for 15 minutes, shooting down 28 of them. During that time they only made 10 miles good toward our task force. When Dave McCampbell's scrambled fighters arrived, we headed for home . . ."

But they were never again to land on the deck of the PRINCETON.

"At 0938," continued Captain Buracker, "one of our PRINCETON lookouts detected a single unidentified plane in a shallow dive making an attack on our ship from sharp on the port bow. Because of the low clouds we had very little warning.

"When the bomb hit, I felt no immediate major concern. I saw the hole, which was small, and I visualized slapping on a patch in a hurry and resuming operations. But, unfortunately, we had six of our torpedo planes loaded with gas and torpedoes, in the hangar. The bomb passed directly through one of these torpedo planes and exploded between the hangar and the second deck. Flames shot down through engineering spaces aft and back into the hangar. Immediately the fire started to spread. Smoke was intense from the start and very soon it started billowing out from the sides of the ship."

For the next eight hours her crew fought to save the burning ship. Fire room and engine rooms were filled with smoke; but men put on oxygen masks, and continued to operate pumps and machinery until ordered out about 10:00 A.M. when a number of major explosions began to shake the ship. Pressure in the fire mains failed immediately.

By this time Admiral Sherman was departing with the remainder of the task group to close with Admiral Halsey off San Bernardino. Four destroyers, CASSIN YOUNG (Commander Earl T. Schreiber), IRWIN (Commander Daniel B. Miller), GATLING (Commander Alvin F. Richardson), and MORRISON (Commander Walter H. Price), a light cruiser, BIRMINGHAM, and an antiaircraft cruiser, RENO, were detached to assist the stricken ship.

A little before one o'clock, when the MORRISON was on the starboard side amidships and the BIRMINGHAM on the port quarter, both streaming water into the flaming PRINCETON, it began to look as if the ship could be saved.

"At the time when conditions looked most favorable," said Captain Buracker, "Jap aircraft had to appear. I observed from the after part of the flight deck of the PRINCETON that the Commanding Officer of the BIRMINGHAM was directing that his fire hoses and personnel be returned. When I inquired into the matter, I was told that there were Jap planes snooping around within a radius of about five miles. Also I later learned that at that particular time one of the destroyers had reported a submarine sound contact. With the close danger of both Japanese aircraft and submarines, Captain Thomas B. Inglis felt that he should not permit BIRMINGHAM to remain dead in the water alongside PRINCETON, so he decided to pull clear. The MORRISON followed shortly after."

When the attack failed to materialize, BIRMINGHAM came back alongside once again to help fight the fire and if possible to give PRINCETON a tow. By this time the wind had risen to 20 knots. Deck hands were having a hard time getting approach lines over when without warning tragedy struck.

"The explosion was as surprising as it was terrifying," related a survivor. "I think it can well be compared to a small volcano. A considerable portion of the after part of the PRINCETON was blown into the air and fell in the water astern. Flying fragments, some huge, some small, burst outwards and upwards, showering the deck of PRINCETON from stem to stern."

The BIRMINGHAM, directly in the path of the explosion, had a large number of her officers and crew exposed topside—men who were working on tow lines; others who were manning antiaircraft guns; turret crews, repair parties and engineers, who were handling hoses. The carnage was unbelievable and the decks literally ran red with blood. Two hundred and twenty-nine men lay dead—killed instantly. Four hundred and twenty more were injured, among them Captain Inglis.

Still the PRINCETON floated on an even keel, without list or change of trim, but with huge fires raging. All the personnel that had remained aboard were now wounded or dead (7 known dead, 99 missing, and 190 wounded).

"Captain John M. Hoskins," continued Buracker, "who was to take command of PRINCETON after this operation, had been standing with me amidships on the port side where we were to receive the lines from the bow of the BIRMINGHAM. When those of us in that immediate vicinity first hit the deck and then started to run forward to get behind some planes for protection, someone noticed that Captain Hoskins couldn't move. I turned around and saw he had his right foot hanging by a shred.

"I called for Commander Roland Sala, our senior medical officer, who had been with us just before this explosion, but by some means unknown to him he found himself on the forecastle. He was injured, but he proceeded to render first-aid treatment to Captain Hoskins. Captain Hoskins fortunately had fallen near a piece of line which he, with great presence of mind, used to apply a tourniquet to his leg. The doctor made his way to him with some sulfa powder and morphine, and using a sheath knife cut off the part of the leg that was dangling. Shortly afterwards Dr. Sala himself had to be given treatment for his wounds." [1]

Reluctantly Captain Buracker decided to abandon ship.

The RENO (Captain Ralph C. Alexander) moved in at 5:49 P.M. and fired two torpedoes. There was a terrific explosion in the vicinity of the

---

[1] On November 18, 1945, a new PRINCETON (CV37) was commissioned at the Philadelphia Navy Yard. The commanding officer was Captain John Hoskins, the only naval officer afloat with only one foot.

forward magazines and PRINCETON seemed to disintegrate. Within forty-five seconds all that could be seen was fire on the water. Thus passed a gallant ship.

Captain Inglis of BIRMINGHAM wrote in his action report: "Ever since James Lawrence's dying words, 'Don't give up the ship,' our Service has been indoctrinated to exert every effort to save damaged ships. This doctrine is sound and has paid dividends through the years, not only in a material, but also in a moral sense. It was most unfortunate that BIRMINGHAM's crew suffered so grievously. Nevertheless, this tragedy should be considered the exception which proves the rule. 'Don't give up the ship' is still as sound as it is inspiring."

3

Before the first American air strike of the day arrived, Kurita's attack force had rounded the southern tip of Mindoro and was heading north through Tablas Strait. His ships—five battleships, seven heavy cruisers, two light cruisers, and thirteen destroyers—were divided into two roughly equal groups, one 5 miles behind the other, with each group in a ring formation, heavy ships to the center, ready to repel air attacks. Kurita knew that Manila had been attacked earlier that morning and he felt sure that soon it would be his turn.

Then, at about 10:15 A.M., his radar picked up a large group of bogies 60 miles to the east.

The Americans had come.

The action was short but intense. Kurita, having no proctective aircraft over his head, tried to make up for it with the fierceness of his AA fire. But the pink and purple and black bursts (the Japanese used different colors to facilitate spotting for each ship) and the explosion that seemed to roll through the sky like a fiery hoop stopped neither the dive bombers screaming down with their 1,000-pound bombs nor the torpedo planes slipping in low and fast with their belly load of death.

When the first attack was over, the heavy cruiser MYOKO had received a torpedo hit and could make only 15 knots. The giant MUSASHI also had taken a torpedo but hardly seemed to notice it. The MYOKO was ordered to retire alone to Brunei.

In the meantime, while the first strike was in progress, the second strike of thirty-five planes was being launched from INTREPID, CABOT, and

INDEPENDENCE. When these planes struck at a quarter to one in the afternoon, MUSASHI, the proud ship that had once flown the flag of the late Admiral Koga, was the chosen victim. Three more torpedoes dug into her blister-protected sides. Many near misses threw a spray of water and steel across her decks. When the planes retired, she had slowed down and was circling, deeply wounded.

Kurita was taking an awful pounding, and he knew there was more to come. He was afraid that Ozawa's lure to the northward was not working, so after the second attack he sent out a message: "We are being subjected to repeated enemy carrier-based air attacks. Advise immediately of contacts and attacks made by you on the enemy."

Kurita also sent a call for fighter protection to Fukudome and Onishi in Manila. But there was no reply, no planes. They had more than they could handle in Ted Sherman's carrier group off Luzon.

While Kurita was sending his call for help, Davison's carriers ENTERPRISE (Captain Cato D. Glover, Jr.), FRANKLIN (Captain James M. Shoemaker), SAN JACINTO (Captain Harold M. Martin), BELLEAU WOOD (Captain John Perry), now out of range of Nishimura's Surigao force, which had been spotted and attacked earlier, sent sixty-five planes against Kurita's desperately squirming fleet.

Commander Dan Smith (Commander Air Group 20, ENTERPRISE) tells of coming in over Kurita's pounded force: "The sky had cleared up by the time we arrived. The force was making about 20 knots eastward and opened up on us before we got within range. We circled a long time to gain altitude because we were heavily loaded with armor piercing bombs and torpedoes.

"I kept my high-powered binoculars on their fire as we slowly made our climb. Their colored bursts were always trailing and soon we stopped worrying. The YAMATO and MUSASHI were now in separate groups. About this time Air Group 13 from FRANKLIN swooped down on the YAMATO force. We took the MUSASHI.

"When we winged over for our dive, we entered a cloud bank and the Jap guns went silent because they couldn't see us. When we emerged from the clouds, they opened up again like the hammers of hell. I personally saw all eight of our torpedo planes score direct hits on the bow of MUSASHI, and saw five direct hits and three near misses from our bombers. The last time I saw MUSASHI, she was stopped dead in the water and her entire forecastle was awash."

THE END'S BEGINNING

By four o'clock that afternoon Kurita was groggy from five waves of air attacks extending over a six-hour period. The MYOKO was out of action and on its way back to Borneo. The MUSASHI, down by the bow, could not continue to fight. Guarded by the destroyer KIYOSHIMO she was to proceed to Bako. But on the fifth attack KIYOSHIMO had been badly bombed as had the battleship NAGATO. The YAMATO received several bomb hits that exploded on deck, but her fighting power was unimpaired. The destroyer YAHAGI had been severely damaged from near misses. The battleships HARUNA and KONGO also suffered their share of bomb hits.

"Originally the main strength of the First Diversion Attack Force," wrote Admiral Kurita in an estimate of the situation, "had intended to force its way through the San Bernardino Strait about one hour after sundown, co-ordinating its moves with air action. However, the enemy made more than 250 sorties against my force between 0830 and 1530, the number of their planes involved and their fierceness mounting with every wave. Our air forces, on the other hand, were not able to obtain even expected results, causing our losses to mount steadily. Under these circumstances it was deemed that were we to force our way through, we would merely make of ourselves meat for the enemy, with very little chance of success to us. It was therefore concluded that the best course open to us was to temporarily retire beyond the range of enemy planes and reform our plans.

"Apparently the main body of our Mobile Force (Ozawa's carriers) was not succeeding in diverting or attacking the enemy. Our various forces were not successfully coordinating their actions and because of this my force was placed in a position of fighting the entire battle alone, was being whittled down with nothing to show for its sacrifices.

"If the First Diversion Attack Force were to continue eastward in the face of these circumstances, it seemed very likely that it would be subjected to terrific pounding from enemy aircraft in the narrows to the east of Sibuyan Sea."

At four o'clock Kurita came about in the Sibuyan Sea and headed westward.

Still he got no rest. Fliers from the carriers of TG 38.2—INTREPID, CAROT, and INDEPENDENCE—made one last attack a little before six, when the sun had dropped low behind a cloud bank to the west. To them it appeared as if the Jap fleet, heading toward the setting sun, had had enough.

The giant MUSASHI was in its death throes. During the long, seemingly endless day she had received 10 torpedo and 16 bomb hits. (Captain Kenkichi Kato, executive officer of MUSASHI, claims she was hit by 30 bombs and 26 torpedoes.) Two torpedo attacks had hit in exactly the same place on the port side. This was her death wound. After vain attempts to beach her on the north coast of Sibuyan Island, she capsized to port under a twilight sky and sank. Over half her crew of 2,200 were lost.

In Tokyo, Admiral Toyoda received Kurita's dispatch telling of his retreat to the westward. Toyoda did not like this. The assault on the Philippines had to be turned back, even if it meant the loss of the entire Japanese fleet. The machine was in motion now, and the operation could not be stopped.

Toyoda sat down and quickly penned a short dispatch in reply:

"With confidence in heavenly guidance the entire force will attack!"

But an hour before, small, wind-withered Kurita—tough sea warrior that he was—had once again reversed course and headed toward San Bernardino.

Later that evening, when estimates had been made and a schedule drawn, Kurita radioed a message to Toyoda and to Nishimura: "Main Force (4 battleships, 6 cruisers, 2 light cruisers, and 11 destroyers) plans to pass through San Bernardino Strait at 0100, 25 October; proceed southward down the east coast of Samar and arrive in Leyte Gulf at about 1100 same day . . ."

The night was clear and there was a moon. Kurita was thankful for this as he stood on the bridge of YAMATO looking at the dark humps of islands on either side. Behind him his ships threaded out in single column as the whole force weaved through the narrow waters at twenty knots leaving bubbly phosphorescent wakes.

Occasionally a white shiny streak would cut through the water toward the ship like a torpedo, but it would be only a large fish. The night had brought a respite from the torpedoes and the bombs.

But Kurita knew the respite was only temporary. On the other side of San Bernardino, in the Philippine Sea, he felt sure there would be submarines and planes and even surface ships waiting. He would have to be prepared to fight his way into the open sea. He wondered if Nishimura, to the south, would be able to fight his way through Surigao—

4

"Where in the hell are those Jap carriers?" asked Captain Doug Moulton, Halsey's air operations officer, as he pounded his fist on the chart-covered table.

The question was asked again and again during that very eventful day, the 24th.

"With the forces that were spotted, the surface forces coming from the South China Sea," said Admiral Carney, "it was felt that there must be a missing piece to this puzzle. No operation on such a scale would be undertaken without the use of what the Japs had in the way of a carrier force. If that carrier force was to be used we felt it would be north and east of the Philippines."

Soon after the sighting of the Center Japanese Force on the morning of the 24th, Admiral Halsey had told "Pete" Mitscher to keep a weather eye open to the north and northeast, where he was sure the Jap carriers would be.

Mitscher, riding the "Blue Ghost" (LEXINGTON) in Ted Sherman's Task Group 38.3 had a rough time of it that morning, for this group took the entire weight of the Japanese air attack—Fukudome's "indirect protection" to Kurita. Throughout the morning Sherman, ducking in and out of rain squalls, played an elusive game of tag with the Japanese and at the same time managed to shoot down half of the three hundred attackers, among whom were a large number of carrier-type planes, thus strengthening suspicions of enemy carriers near-by.

When PRINCETON was disabled, Sherman, short of fighters, fought on a shoestring. In spite of this, LEXINGTON (Captain Ernest W. Litch), ESSEX (Captain Carlos W. Wieber), and LANGLEY (Captain John F. Wegforth) were able to launch two strikes against Kurita.

When Commander Hugh Winters (Commander Air Group 19) got back to the LEX after his strike against the plodding ships in the Sibuyan Sea, Admiral Mitscher called him to the bridge.

"Well, son, what did it look like?" asked Mitscher, looking over the tops of his glasses, which he had pulled down on his nose.

"We hit them hard, Admiral, but they aren't severely crippled," replied Winters. "They're still heading for San Bernardino Strait."

The Admiral grunted and looked northward.

Just as the second strike was launched, a little before two in the afternoon, a large group of enemy planes was reported coming in from the *northeast*. That meant carriers—without a doubt.

"We sent a few planes to the northeast in hopes that they would be able to pick up something," related Arleigh Burke, now a commodore and Mitscher's chief of staff. "Sure enough, at about 4:40 P.M. they did contact an enemy force, about 200 miles from Cape Engano off northern Luzon, which was reported as being three battleships, half a dozen cruisers, and six destroyers. Later there was another contact in a different position, of three carriers, three cruisers and three destroyers heading west. The distance to the enemy and the fact that our planes were out on a strike against other enemy ships in the Sibuyan Sea prevented us from launching an attack that day against those to the north."

At last all of the Jap fleet was present and accounted for. Doug Moulton stopped pounding on the chart table. The time had come for decisive action.

"We knew," explained Admiral Carney, "that the Japanese carriers had a very beautiful technique, a theory of employment of their carrier planes against our forces called shuttling. They could make a one-way trip from a carrier to an airfield via the target, which was our forces, and by doing that their carriers could be effectively employed from a distance such that our carriers could not make a round trip from carrier to objective and back to carrier. If they could employ this very clever tactic they had us on the hip. We had recognized that from their efforts in the First Battle of the Philippine Sea and had decided that should this occasion arise we would make a high-speed run in on them, preferably at night, and prevent them from getting away with any such scheme. The problem that faced the Commander Third Fleet on the night of the 24th was as momentous as any fleet commander ever had laid in his lap."

Indeed, "Bull" Halsey had a tough decision to make. His own action report is probably the best explanation of the final decision and the reasoning behind it:

"A curious point was apparent from the contact reports of the three [Japanese] forces—northern [carrier] central [San Bernardino] and southern [Surigao]: they were all proceeding at deliberate speed and it was inferred that there was a predetermined focus of geographical location and time. The movements indicated that a carefully worked-out co-ordinated Japanese plan was in motion with October 25 as the earliest date of planned concerted action.

THE END'S BEGINNING 379

"Throughout the day [24th] carrier strikes had been launched against the Center Force and all reports indicated that the Center Force was being effectively and heavily damaged. In the face of these continued strikes the Center Force kept coming with a determination that commanded respect. By dusk the following damage had been reported: At least 4 and probably 5 BB torpedoed and bombed, one probably sunk; a minimum of 3 heavy cruisers torpedoed and others bombed; 1 CL sunk; 1 DD sunk; 1 DD probably sunk and 4 damaged—flash reports indicated beyond doubt that the Center Force had been badly mauled with all of its BB and most of its CA tremendously reduced in fighting power and life.

"Although the Center Force continued to move forward, the Commander Third Fleet decided that this enemy force must be blindly obeying an Imperial command to do or die, but with battle efficiency greatly impaired by torpedo hits, bomb hits, topside damage, fires, and casualties. From long experience with the Japs, their blind adherence to plan and their inability to readjust disturbed plans, the Commander Third Fleet had long ago adopted a policy of attacking first. The Southern and Center Forces had been under heavy and persistent air attack while proceeding through inland waters in daylight. Jap doggedness was admitted, and Commander Third Fleet recognized the possibility that the Center Force might plod through San Bernardino Strait and on to attack Leyte forces, à la Guadalcanal, but Commander Third Fleet was convinced that the Center Force was so heavily damaged that it could not win a decision, while the possible maximum strength of the Northern Force as reported by CTF 38, Admiral Mitscher, constituted a fresh and powerful threat. It was decided that earliest possible attack on the powerful Northern [carrier] Force was essential for breaking up the enemy plan and retaining the initiative.

"The choices were to:

"First, divide the forces leaving TF 34 (Vice Admiral W. A. Lee, Jr.'s, heavy surface striking force, built around six new battleships, that had been integrated with Task Force 38 at Ulithi) to block San Bernardino Strait while the carriers with light screens attacked the Northern Force.

> ("Ching" Lee was itching to get at the Japanese with his big battleships, not just "ride herd on the carriers" as he had been doing across the Pacific.

"We thought we could clean them up," said Lieutenant Gil Aertsen, Lee's flag lieutenant and aide.

That afternoon Lee sent a message to Halsey giving his views on the situation. Lee knew from his Solomons experience—Lee had been in the Pacific continuously since October, 1942—that the Japanese often tried to divert attention with decoy ships while sneaking in a solid punch from another direction.

"Lee thought we shouldn't trust the sons of bitches," commented Aertsen after the war. "He wanted to take his battleships and stand up and down in front of the straits. Lee's sole purpose was to take on the Jap fleet. It was the chance of a lifetime for the battleships.")

"Second, maintain integrity of our own entire striking strength, concentrated off San Bernardino Strait.

"Third, strike the Northern Force with all of our own striking strength, concentrated, and leave San Bernardino Strait unguarded.

"The first was rejected; the potential strength of the undamaged Northern Force was too great to leave unmolested. Requiring TF 34 to engage the Center Force while at the same time exposed to attack by land-based and possibly carrier-based air attack was not sound. This choice would spread our strength and risked unprofitable damage in detail.

"The second was rejected because it permitted the Northern Force to function as planned, unmolested, and because destruction of Japan's carrier force would mean much to future operations.

"The third was adopted; it maintained the integrity of the Blue striking fleet; it offered the best possibility of surprise and destruction of enemy carrier force. It was particularly sound and necessary if the strength of the Northern Force proved to be the maximum reported. It was recognized that the Center Force might sortie and inflict some damage, but its fighting power was considered too seriously impaired to win a decision. Finally it was calculated that the Third Fleet forces could return in time to reverse any advantage that the Center Force might gain and Commander Third Fleet was firmly convinced that this would contribute most to the over-all Philippines campaign even if a temporarily tight situation existed at Leyte."

Halsey had no way of knowing that aboard the four Japanese carriers to the north there were only twenty-nine planes.

The lure was working.

5

The decision made, Halsey acted quickly. It was a little after eight in the evening when he directed the two task groups then off San Bernardino—Davison's 38.4 had by then joined Bogan's 38.2—to head north. An urgent dispatch was sent to Admiral Kinkaid in Leyte Gulf informing him that at 7:25 P.M. the enemy Center Force was off Sibuyan Island, that strike reports indicated heavy enemy damage and that Halsey was heading north with three groups to attack enemy carrier force at dawn.

Night fighters from INDEPENDENCE shadowed Kurita's force as it threaded its way to the east. The reports were relayed to Kinkaid, whose old battleships by that time were preparing to cross the T at Surigao. The last report from the snoopers, before they had to return to their carrier which was rapidly drawing away to the north, was that at 9:45 P.M. the Center Force had reached the southern tip of Burias, trailing a large oil slick the length of the island, and had turned northeast between Burias and Ticao. Obviously it intended to break through San Bernardino Strait.

At 11:30 that night the third task group, Ted Sherman's TG 38.3, joined up with Admiral Halsey and the other two groups in their run north. Mitscher then took tactical command.

6

During the day Admiral Kinkaid, aboard his headquarters ship, WASATCH, anxiously watched the progress of the Central Japanese Force in the Sibuyan Sea. Through intercepted dispatches he was able to reconstruct the whole show, blow by blow, except for one important item. He assumed in the absence of information to the contrary that Third Fleet forces would plug up San Bernardino the same way his Seventh Fleet units were plugging Surigao. During the afternoon he was busy getting his ships ready for a night torpedo and gunnery action in Surigao. But he also kept his eye cocked on the larger enemy force to the north. He was sure the Japanese Navy was after his soft-shelled transports in the gulf.

In the middle of the afternoon Kinkaid intercepted a dispatch from Halsey to all Third Fleet subordinate commands announcing preliminary orders to form Task Force 34, consisting of battleships, cruisers, and destroyers. Kinkaid assumed that this force was being separated from the rest of the Third Fleet in order to engage the Japanese Central Force when it tried to come through San Bernardino. Later that evening, at 8:24 P.M., when Halsey informed Kinkaid that he was "proceeding north with three groups to attack the enemy carrier force at dawn," Kinkaid assumed that Task Force 34 was still guarding San Bernardino Strait.

The assumption was incorrect. Halsey had sent a dispatch at 3:12 P.M. stating that Task Force 34 would be formed but he had not *executed* the signal. In other words, he had told his ships to stand by and be ready to form into a separate force, but he had not given the order actually to do it.

"I remember reading the dispatch about Halsey's forming Task Force 34," recalled Kinkaid after the war, "and at the time I was not aware that it was not addressed to me. We later got the dispatch telling of Halsey's taking the three carrier groups northward. In my mind, and in the minds of my staff, there was no doubt; we thought there were four groups. At the time I remember wondering why Halsey had not left one carrier group to cover the battleships that we thought were opposite San Bernardino Strait. It never occurred to me that San Bernardino would be left open.

"That night, or actually it was morning by this time, I was checking with my operations officer, Captain Richard H. Cruzen, my planning officer, Captain David S. Crawford, my intelligence officer, Captain Arthur H. McCollum, and several others making sure all our plans were in order, making sure nothing was left out or undone. By that time the Surigao picture was pretty clear. Oldendorf was chasing the remaining Jap ships down the strait. In Sprague's carrier outfit we had an attack group set up—about a dozen planes. At dawn they were to go after the cripples of Surigao. I also ordered the carriers to send a dawn search to the northward.[1]

---

[1] This search was never instituted. Also a night sweep off the coast of Samar northward to San Bernardino Strait by Black Cat search planes failed to contact the enemy.

"Everything seemed clear. At the end of the conference, just as a check, just as a safeguard, I decided to send a message to Halsey inquiring as to the whereabouts of Task Force 34. However, the assumption was so basic that the battleships were up there plugging the strait that neither I, nor any of my staff, really doubted it for a minute.

"There were a number of secret dispatches to be sent out, so I am not sure when this dispatch left the ship. [It was originated at 0412 and also contained a report of the Battle of Surigao Strait.—Ed.] L didn't receive a reply from Halsey until five minutes before Sprague reported sighting the Jap Force off Samar."

Chapter Twenty-Seven

Jeeps vs. Giants

I

"ENEMY SURFACE FORCE of 4 battleships, 7 cruisers, and 11 destroyers sighted 20 miles northwest of your task group and closing at 30 knots!" The pilot's voice sounded thin and frantic over the radio.

Combat Information Center on the escort carrier FANSHAW BAY (Captain Douglas P. Johnson) quickly relayed the message to the bridge where Rear Admiral C. A. F. Sprague watched the planes from his carriers take off for another day of long, hard work—antisubmarine patrols, photographic missions, searches, combat air patrol, support to the troops on Leyte: enough to keep everyone on the jump till sundown.

"Air Plot, tell that pilot to check his identification," shouted Cliff Sprague into the squawk-box. He felt annoyed. He had enough to worry about without having some screwy aviator report some of Halsey's fast battleships as enemy.

"Identification confirmed," the pilot, Ensign William C. Brooks, snapped back. "Ships have pagoda masts."

Pagoda masts! Sprague looked to the northwest. The sky beyond the squall was speckled by antiaircraft bursts. That was enough for him.

"Come to course 090. Flank speed. Launch all aircraft!"

Brooks looked around him and saw the sky begin to blossom with thick puffs of antiaircraft bursts. He had expected to find submarines when he took off shortly before sunrise. Instead he had found the whole damned Jap fleet.

Nosing his plane over he headed down for the nearest cruiser to paste her with what he had been saving for a Nip sub—two depth charges.

A minute after the launching of planes had started, at two minutes before seven, the foretops of a large force of ships were sighted from the carrier bridge.

Kurita had arrived.

2

Cliff Sprague's escort carrier group that so unexpectedly found itself blocking the path of Kurita's charge for Leyte Gulf consisted of six escort carriers, three destroyers, and four destroyer escorts.

These escort carriers (CVEs) were known by a number of unflattering names: "baby flat-top," "jeep carrier," "Kaiser coffin," "tomato can," "bucket of bolts," "wind wagon." Green sailors coming aboard for the first time were told by the old hands that CVE stood for "Combustible, Vulnerable, Expendable."

The "jeeps" were a type ship the Navy turned out en masse by slapping a runway on a hull designed for a tanker or a merchantman. The resulting ship was short (about half the length of a big carrier), slow ("What makes that thing run—squirrels?"), and thin skinned (a "grease monkey" in the engine room could touch the hull and be only a half-inch from salt water). In a calm sea and with a following breeze these little ships might make 18 knots provided the engineering officer had been leading a good life.

The destroyer escorts, too, were thin skinned, and were designed for antisubmarine work. Never in their wildest dreams had the designers thought that either of these types would have to fight a battle with the heaviest units of the Japanese Navy.

Cliff Sprague's group was one of three similar groups. At the time of first contact his group was 50 miles off the southern half of Samar; Rear Admiral Felix Stump's group was about 30 miles southeast, off Homonhon Island; and Rear Admiral Thomas L. Sprague (no kin), who was in over-all command of the eighteen carriers, had his group 120 miles away and roughly east of Dinagat Island. The operation plans for the Leyte landing directed the escort carriers to furnish combat and antisubmarine patrols, as well as air support and spotting services for the troops ashore. The three groups had arrived on October 18 and had been busy ever since.

The first indication that the Japanese had broken through San Bernardino came at 6:37 A.M. when the Combat Information Center on FANSHAW BAY heard excited Japanese jabbering on the interfighter director net, but this was regarded as no more than an attempt at jamming.

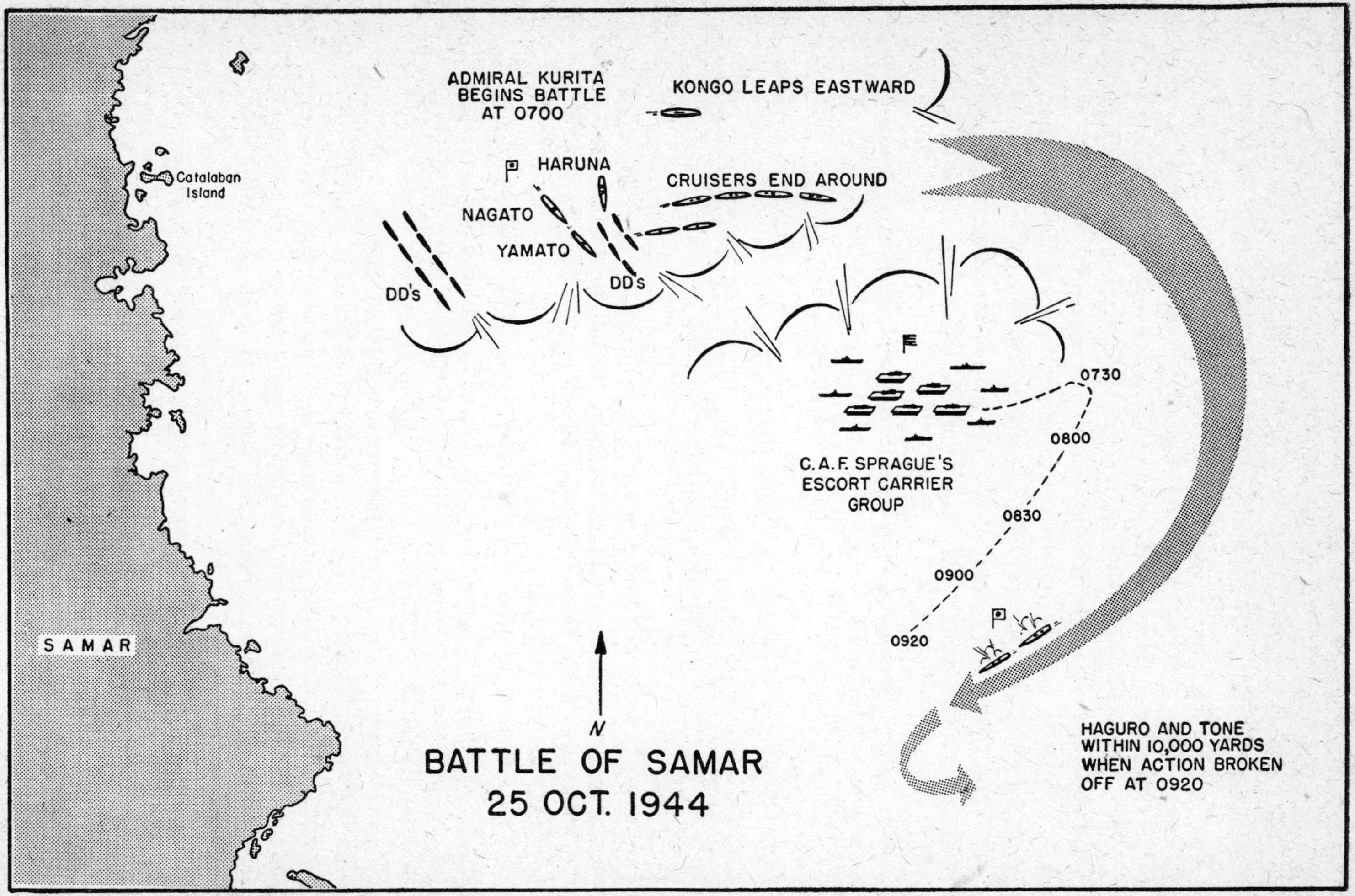

BATTLE OF SAMAR
25 OCT. 1944

FIGURE 16

ADMIRAL KURITA BEGINS BATTLE AT 0700
KONGO LEAPS EASTWARD
HARUNA
NAGATO
YAMATO
DD's
DD's
CRUISERS END AROUND
C.A.F. SPRAGUE'S ESCORT CARRIER GROUP
0730
0800
0830
0900
0920

HAGURO AND TONE WITHIN 10,000 YARDS WHEN ACTION BROKEN OFF AT 0920

Catalaban Island

SAMAR

At 6:45—18 minutes after sunrise—antiaircraft fire was observed to the northwest and three minutes later Ensign Brooks made his startling announcement to unbelieving ears.

"Five minutes after the sighting of the Jap force," said Captain John P. Whitney, captain of the KITKUN BAY, "we were taken under heavy major caliber gunfire. We started scrambling our deck loads. There wasn't time to give them any instructions as to how they were to make their attacks or how they were to coordinate their attacks. We simply had to rely on their training to insure that they would be able to carry on and carry through.

"The wind was out of the northeast that morning, what little there was of it, which meant that as we launched our deck loads we continued to close this big task force very rapidly since they were on a southerly course, headed for the entrance to the gulf."

From the bridge of YAMATO Kurita sighted the Americans at almost the same time he was spotted—first he saw two carrier planes and then the masts of Sprague's ships, hull down over the horizon. Groping blindly without search planes, it was the first he knew of the presence of American carriers.

At the time his ships were shifting from night- to day-cruising disposition, which resulted in his formation being somewhat straggly. The battleships YAMATO and NAGATO were in column on a southeasterly course with the other two battleships, KONGO and HARUNA, on the port quarter maneuvering independently. Also to port of the flagship were the six heavy cruisers attempting to form up. Screening on the starboard beam were the light cruiser NOSHIRO and her seven destroyers. Ahead and a bit to port of YAMATO was the light cruiser YAHAGI with her four destroyers. Leyte Gulf was 60 miles away, to the south-southwest.

When the American carriers were sighted, the range was about 38,000 yards, 19 miles. Kurita immediately changed the course of his formation more to the east with the intention of getting upwind from the carriers and at the same time closing the range. When the range had closed to 18 miles, Kurita gave the order for YAMATO to open fire. For the first time her 18-inch guns, whose size had been one of the most closely guarded secrets of the Japanese Navy, were fired in anger. The time was 6:59 A.M.

Almost immediately the Japanese salvos started falling less than 2,000 yards away from the little carriers, who were rapidly launching all available planes. One by one, as the salvos crept closer, the fighters and torpedo planes ran the length of the deck and took to the air. Most of them, in anticipation of a day of routine support work, were loaded with small general-purpose bombs or depth charges—not enough to make a battleship flinch. But there was no time to reload.

The first destroyer to leap at the Japanese was the JOHNSTON. Without orders, like a mother lion who instinctively protects her young, JOHNSTON started making smoke ten minutes before the other escorts. Then when the shells began to drop so close that it seemed as though JOHNSTON would soon be hit, Commander Ernest E. Evans, the commanding officer, decided to launch a torpedo attack alone, before his ship was incapacitated.

Unaided, JOHNSTON dashed in toward a heavy cruiser and at 7:20 A.M. launched a spread of ten torpedoes from a range of 8,000 yards. Her 5-inch guns fired continuously. The JOHNSTON was not hit until she started to retire. Then three 14-inch shells and three 6-inch shells smashed into her fragile hull, slowing her speed to 16 knots.

As the Japanese rapidly drew closer, their fire became more intense and more accurate. Cliff Sprague ordered his destroyers and destroyer escorts to spread a curtain of smoke between the carriers and the onrushing enemy.

After launching planes on an easterly course, the carriers eased, in small increments, toward the south, giving their sterns to the Japanese. Smoke pouring from the sterns of the galloping destroyers and DEs spread thick and woolly over the sea and at 7:20, when the carriers jumped into a seagoing foxhole, a heavy rain squall, Japanese fire slackened and became less accurate.

Meanwhile Cliff Sprague ordered his escorts to form up for two torpedo attacks—the first by destroyers HOEL, HEERMANN, and JOHNSTON; the second by the slower, lighter destroyer escorts, JOHN C. BUTLER, DENNIS, RAYMOND, and SAMUEL B. ROBERTS.

The JOHNSTON was badly hurt, by this time, and had expended all her torpedoes, but Commander Evans turned and followed HOEL and HEERMANN in as best he could to provide fire support while they launched their attacks.

The Japanese were pouring on steam. Kurita ordered all ships to make their best speed. The heavy cruisers, faster than the battleships, started a flanking movement to the left at 30 knots. The KONGO bolted formation and headed eastward with the enthusiasm of an unleashed puppy. The YAMATO and NAGATO closed from astern while HARUNA cut corners across their wakes. The YAHAGI and her destroyer squadron remained to port of the flagship while NISHIRO and her destoyers remained to the rear on the starboard flank. The attack was on.

"We were the southernmost destroyer of the three," related Commander Amos T. Hathaway, captain of the HEERMANN, "and had to thread our way through the formation to join on the HOEL. I didn't know exactly where the enemy was. We had no radar contact due to jamming, and as the visibility was very bad, I had not seen the enemy, nor had anyone in my ship . . .

"I took the middle of the radar jamming section and headed in that general direction. It was rather difficult threading through the carriers as the shell splashes were rather heavy in some spots . . .

"About this time, I realized that we were on our way to make a daylight torpedo attack. The progress of the war and the natural instinct of the Japs to seem to want to fight at night had made me believe that I would never have such an opportunity. But I was on my way. I turned to the officer of the deck, Lieutenant Robert F. Newsome, and said, 'Buck, what we need is a bugler to sound the charge.' He looked at me like I was a little crazy and said, 'What do you mean, Captain?' I said, 'We are going to make a torpedo attack.' Buck gulped and went about his job.

"After that we had little more opportunity for such conversations, as things started to happen rather rapidly. First, we had to maneuver violently to avoid the SAMUEL B. ROBERTS, one of the destroyer escorts that was laying a smoke screen.

"About this time I think I had better say a little bit about the weather. The visibility was anything from 100 yards up to about 13 miles. There were many squalls. The rain was dense and heavy at any time you were in a squall. You came out and you might see a short distance to another squall, or maybe several miles. Most of the time the visibility was very bad.

"All the destroyers and destroyer escorts were continuing to lay smoke. The whole area was beginning to be covered with a dense black and white smoke screen.

"We avoided the DENNIS and proceeded at full power to join the HOEL. A few minutes later I had to back emergency to miss the HOEL.

I did not realize it at the time, but she had already been damaged. I thought she had slowed down to wait for me.

"We followed the HOEL in on a co-ordinated torpedo attack led by Commander William Thomas [Screen Commander using HOEL as flagship]. There were no orders issued as none were necessary. It was made according to doctrine, in the manner in which we had planned such an attack during the many conversations and conferences we had held in port.

"The JOHNSTON, who had already made a torpedo attack, joined and followed some place astern of HOEL and HEERMANN to aid with her battery in supporting the attack. After HOEL cut loose with her fish, an enemy heavy cruiser took us under fire. We fired seven torpedoes at him.

"By this time, we were under heavy fire and could hear the express train roar of the 14-inchers going over.

"The gunnery officer, Lieutenant William W. Meadors, said that he watched with fatal fascination as they fired. First they fired two turrets. Then they fired two more turrets. Then all four. All the shells went on over. Lieutenant Meadors took our five-inch director and moved our fire up and down their superstructure. Much to our surprise this must have done something to their fire-control system, or at least to their morale, because they quit shooting at us and for about four minutes we were able to shoot at them without any interference.

"We fired our last three torpedoes at the battleship at about 4,400 yards closing. It was a good beam shot.

"After firing, I went inside the pilothouse, called the Admiral on the TBS, and told him my exercise was completed. I don't know quite why I used these words. I remember having an idea in my head that the Japs might be listening on the circuit and I didn't want them to know that I didn't have any more torpedoes."

The HOEL did not return after her torpedo attacks. Two minutes before launching her first half salvo (five) of torpedoes at the leading Jap battleship (KONGO) she was hit for the first time—on the director platform. Nevertheless, torpedoes were launched at a range of 9,000 yards. Immediately afterwards a 14-inch shell dug its way into the after turbine causing the loss of the port engine. Another hit from a battleship shell knocked out the after guns and the electrical steering gear.

In the melee it was hard to see if the torpedoes hit or not. The smoke screen, the rain squalls, and all the ships dashing in and out made it difficult to get a smooth idea of which ships were which.

Commander Leon Kintberger, skipper of the HOEL, felt that it was necessary to stop both columns of enemy ships—the battleships and the cruisers—if the escort carriers were to be saved. So he selected the leading heavy cruiser as a target for his second half salvo of torpedoes. Using one engine, hand steering, and training the torpedo mount manually (all electric power was disrupted) HOEL loosed her second load of torpedoes at 7:35. Geysers of water were seen to shoot up from the cruiser [probably KUMANO] at about the time the torpedoes should have hit.

"With our ten fish fired," said Lieutenant Maurice F. Green of the HOEL, "we decided that it was time to get the hell out of there. We attempted a retirement to the southwest but this was impossible for we were boxed in on all sides by enemy capital ships—battleships 8,000 yards on the port beam and heavy cruisers 7,000 yards on the starboard quarter. By fishtailing and chasing salvoes and making all posible speed we were able to remain afloat for more than an hour in this precarious position. We had only two guns left to fire. They were forward, which made it difficult to continue firing while attempting a retirement. The gun crews did almost a miraculous job. Each gun expended between 250 and 300 rounds. Before the ship sank we had to send people up to those two guns and chase the men out of there and make them cease firing and get off the ship. They did not leave the gun mounts until there was a good list on the ship and she was settling by the stern."

At 0855, after having received over 40 hits from 5-inch, 8-inch, and 14-inch shells, the HOEL sank.

Under cover of the rain squall the carriers had gradually changed course to the southward, feeling their way toward Leyte Gulf and the protection of Admiral Oldendorf's heavy ships. By this time carriers, too, were laying a thick carpet of black smoke.

(In the northern transport area in Leyte Gulf Admiral Wilkinson, aboard his flagship MOUNT OLYMPUS, lying to alongside Admiral Kinkaid's WASATCH, anxiously followed reports of the battle. Admiral Barbey had gone south with his group but most of Wilkinson's group was still in Leyte Gulf unloading cargoes sorely needed by the troops ashore.

"I felt," remarked Wilkinson, "much like the heroine watching the hero and the villain struggle for her favors.")

When the baby flat-tops came out of the squall at 0730, they were still in good formation—a large circle with ST. LO to the north and in clockwise rotation KALININ BAY, GAMBIER BAY, KITKUN BAY, WHITE PLAINS, and FANSHAW BAY (Admiral Cliff Sprague's flagship).

"The enemy's main body, that is, the battleships," related Captain Walter V. Vieweg, commanding officer of the GAMBIER BAY, "were about ten miles to the north of us. A division of four cruisers [HAGURO, CHOKAI, TONE, CHIKUMA] had gained station about 15,000 or 16,000 yards to the northeast of the formation. The wind was generally from the northeast. As a result GAMBIER BAY and KALININ BAY were on the exposed windward flank of the formation where our own smoke provided very little coverage between us and these cruisers to the northeast. It did offer more protection to the other ships of the formation. And the destroyer smoke and their attacks momentarily, at least, suppressed the fire from the main enemy battleship body to the north.

"These cruisers, to the northeast and closing our port flank, were unopposed and in an excellent position to pour in a rather heavy fire upon GAMBIER BAY and KALININ BAY which they proceeded to do without delay. However, their fire was somewhat inaccurate, not very fast, salvos were about a minute or a minute and a half apart and not particularly large. Their spotting was rather methodical and enabled us to dodge.

"I maneuvered the ship alternately from one side of the base course to another as I saw that a salvo was about due to hit. One could observe that the salvos would hit some distance away and gradually creep up closer and from the spacing on the water could tell that the next one would be on if we did nothing. We would invariably turn into the direction from which the salvos were creeping and sure enough the next salvo would land right in the water where we would have been if we hadn't turned. The next few salvos would creep across to the other side and gradually creep back and would repeat the operation. The process lasted for, believe it or not, a half hour during which the enemy was closing constantly.

"When the range was finally reduced to about 10,000 yards, we weren't quite so lucky and we took a hit through the flight deck, followed almost immediately by a most unfortunate piece of damage which I believe was caused by a salvo which fell just short of the port side of the ship. The shell exploded very near the plates outside of the forward engine room, flooding it rapidly. With the loss of this one engine my speed dropped from full to about 11 knots. Of course I dropped astern of the formation quite rapidly and the range closed at an alarming speed.

"The Japs really poured it on then, hitting us with practically every salvo. During the period from this first hit, which was around 8:10 until we sank, which was about 9:10, we were being hit probably every minute."

The three destroyers had made their torpedo attacks. Now it was time for the slower, thin-skinned destroyer escorts to get rid of their "fish" in a follow-up attack.

"Small boys form for our second attack," came the orders from Cliff Sprague over the voice radio.

The DEs had become scattered in the rain and smoke, so each attack was an individual affair. The SAMUEL B. ROBERTS, under smoke cover, approached to within 4,000 yards of a heavy cruiser before launching her three torpedoes about 0800. The DENNIS (Lieutenant Commander Samuel Hansen) and RAYMOND (Lieutenant Commander Aaron F. Beyer) also launched theirs about the same time but from greater range.

Their torpedoes expended, except for JOHN C. BUTLER (Lieutenant Commander John E. Pace), who had not been in a firing position, the scrappy DEs began to slug it out with the Japanese cruisers. It was as if a bantamweight had been put in the ring with a ham-fisted heavy. For destroyers with their five 5-inch guns to take on the Japanese heavies was plucky enough, but for DEs with only two 5-inchers—well, it was unbelievable.

"Gunner's Mate 3/c Paul Henry Carr, was the gun captain of No. 2 gun," related Lieutenant William S. Burton of the SAMUEL B. ROBERTS. "That gun in less than an hour expended something in excess of three hundred rounds of 5-inch ammunition including star shells when all common and AA projectiles were gone. In fact they expended every round except one which was available to them in their part of the ship.

"The rapid and continuous fire from Gun 2 was an inspiration to every man on the ship. We had to maneuver radically in order to avoid the oncoming salvos, and although we operated with very little fire-control equipment, Carr was able to obtain a great many hits on a Jap heavy cruiser. We positively knocked out their number three 8-inch gun turret, demolished their bridge and started fires aft under their secondary control tower.

"After we had been in action perhaps fifty minutes, during which time Lieutenant Commander Robert W. Copeland, captain of the ship, did a marvelous job chasing salvos, we received our first hits. At that time Carr's ammunition hoist went out of commission. That did not delay his rate of fire in the least. The Japanese had our range by this time and we were being hit continuously by salvos of 8-inch and 14-inch shells, which finally disrupted all power and communication to the gun mount. Our action report tells the story: 'After all power, air, and communications had been lost and before the word to abandon ship was passed, the crew of No. 2 gun, who as a crew distinguished themselves throughout the entire action, loaded, rammed and fired six charges entirely by hand and with a certain knowledge of the hazards involved due to the failure of the gas-ejection system caused by the air supply having been entirely lost.

" 'While attempting to fire the seventh round, the powder charge cooked off before the breech closed, wrecking the gun and killing or wounding all but three crew members, who were critically injured and two of whom were blown clear of the mount and the ship as a result of the explosion.

" 'The first man to enter the mount after the explosion found the gun captain, Carr, on the deck of the mount holding in his hands the last projectile [weight 54 pounds] available to his gun, even though he was severely wounded from his neck down to the middle of his thighs. He was completely torn open and his intestines were splattered throughout the inside of the mount. Nevertheless, he held in his hand the 54-pound projectile, held it up above his head and begged the petty officer who had entered the mount to help him get that last round out. You must appreciate that the breech of the gun had been blown into an unrecognizable mass of steel. The mount, itself, was torn to pieces. He was the only man capable of physical movement within the mount and yet his only idea was to get out that last round.

" 'The petty officer, who entered the mount, took the projectile from Carr and removed one of the other men, who was wounded and unconscious, to the main deck in order to render him first aid. When he returned to the mount, there was Gunner's Mate Carr again with the projectile in his hand, still attempting, although horribly wounded, to place the projectile on the loading tray and thereby utilize his last chance to do damage to the Japanese.' "

THE END'S BEGINNING

Carr was immediately removed from the mount but died within five minutes.

Although the jeep carriers were making smoke and taking violent evasive turns at full speed, the dye-colored shells from Kurita's battleships and cruisers continued to fall near. As the four fast cruisers continued to close in on the port quarter of the fleeing ships, the four destroyers and one light cruiser of Kurita's Desron 10 pressed in on the right flank in a flying pincer movement. When the men aboard KALININ BAY—"Tail-End Charlie" of the carrier formation—first saw these destroyers approaching head on, they thought them to be friendly, but when the destroyers opened fire, they changed their minds and immediately began firing back with the only thing at their disposal—a single 5-inch gun on the stern.

As they ran, all the carriers fired steadily with their stern "peashooters."

"Being able to fire that one 5-inch gun," commented Captain John Perry Whitney, commanding officer of the KITKUN BAY, "contributed greatly to the morale of the crew because they felt that at least we were throwing something at the enemy. It was pretty tough for the men because all the 40mm and 20mm gun crews, all the flight deck personnel and other topside personnel had nothing to do except watch the progress of the battle."

A 40mm battery officer tried to lift the spirits of his gun crew. "It won't be long now, boys," he said "we're sucking them into 40mm range."

The great danger to the carriers came from the heavy cruisers on their port quarter. In spite of air and torpedo attacks and heavy shelling, they continued to draw nearer and nearer the eggshelled carriers and their salvos were connecting: FANSHAW BAY, KALININ BAY, and GAMBIER BAY had all been hit before 0830. Many of the Jap shells were armor piercing and passed entirely through the ships without exploding.

Over the noise of battle the voice radio barked out an urgent order from Sprague: "Small boys [DDs and DEs] on my starboard quarter intercept enemy cruiser coming in on my port quarter!"

Forty seconds later the order was repeated in short, quick tones: "Intercept enemy heavy cruiser coming in on port quarter. EXPEDITE!"

The 8-inch guns of HAGURO were finding their range.

"Intercept" the order had been, but there was not much to intercept with. The HOEL was sinking under heavy fire. The JOHNSTON, mortally wounded, could make only 15 knots. Only two of her guns were in full operation. Killed and wounded littered her decks, but the captain, Commander Evans, holed by numerous shrapnel wounds and with two fingers blown off continued to fight his ship. The HEERMANN was still in good shape.

But in the entire force there was not a single torpedo left.

"Smoke hung heavy on the sea," said HEERMANN's skipper, Commander Hathaway, "as we started to cross the formation to the port quarter. Immediately it was obvious that the JOHNSTON was badly damaged and couldn't make the speed we could. The radar was hanging down on her yardarm and Evans sent me a signal: 'Only one engine, no radar, and no gyros.' We left him and started to the port quarter of the carrier formation by ourselves.

"Actually I guess he made a better trip across than we did, because our haste only slowed us up. I had the ship trying to make 35 knots when suddenly the FANSHAW BAY was very close ahead of me. I gave an emergency crash back. We avoided the FANSHAW BAY and went crash ahead again. No more had we started forward than here was the JOHNSTON coming out of the smoke on the port bow. I crash backed again. This time it was too close for comfort. We missed the JOHNSTON by a mere matter of inches. People could have touched as our bows missed each other. Everyone thought we would hit. As we cleared a spontaneous cheer arose from each ship.

"As we passed under the JOHNSTON's stern, we came out of the smoke and saw the GAMBIER BAY lying to in the water. She had about a 20-degree list to starboard, and an enemy cruiser of the TONE class had her under fire. There were other enemy cruisers firing at her too.

"When we started to fire at the TONE-class cruiser, she shifted fire from the GAMBIER BAY and engaged us. Actually this didn't do the GAMBIER BAY very much good, because there were so many Jap ships there firing at her that I don't believe one made much difference. We paralleled the TONE at about 12,000 yards and started to slug it out. As she shifted her fire to us, we noticed three more heavy cruisers astern of her.

"Four minutes later, at 8:45, we received a shrapnel hit on the bridge which killed three men and mortally wounded the steersman. John P. Milley, Chief Quartermaster, was thrown to the deck. He rose to his knees, reached over the mortally wounded steersman, took the wheel and carried out an unexecuted order I had given.

"I conned the ship from the top of the pilothouse, where I could see better, and we continued to chase salvos while engaging the enemy cruisers—we were under fire from four of them now. I realized that it was four ships by the fact that there were several colors of splashes. There were red, yellow, green and no-color splashes all around us. It looked like a rainbow. There was more red than anything else. In fact it looked kind of rosy, looking through it, although I guess it was probably rosier for the Japs than it was for us at that particular moment.

"One shell hit tore a jagged hole in the hull and flooded the forward magazines. One hit a stowage locker full of dried navy beans and reduced the beans to paste. Another hit the uptake from the forward boiler. The bean paste was sucked up by the hot blast of the uptake and thrown in the air. Lieutenant Bob Rutter was nearly buried in the stuff.

"The HEERMANN plunged down by the bow until her anchors were dragging in the bow wave. It seemed as if the ship would dive headfirst beneath the surface. Racing at flank speed torrents of water were coming up over the deck. But only one gun had been knocked out and we continued firing."

The four cruisers CHOKAI, HAGURO, TONE, and CHIKUMA—SUZUYA having dropped out to aid the injured KUMANO—continued to close, forcing Cliff Sprague's carriers more and more toward Samar only 15 miles away. The battleships pressed the attack from astern, gaining ground each minute.

The smoke screen was getting thinner and the salvos were creeping closer.

"Small boys on my starboard quarter interpose with smoke between men [CVEs] and enemy cruisers," cracked Sprague's order over the TBS at 8:30.

For the next forty minutes the "small boys" did the work of giants—zigzagging back and forth at their best speeds, laying great rolling clouds of smoke, shooting at any Jap within range: the four heavy cruisers to port or the destroyers to starboard. It was during this phase of the battle that the limping JOHNSTON was fatally hit.

In spite of these heroic efforts the cruisers continued to close. By this time the torpedo planes of the task group had expended all their bombs and torpedoes and were forced to make dummy torpedo runs on the enemy ships. The fighters strafed, but it was like rain falling on a tin roof. The carrier's 5-inch guns were low on ammunition, having been firing since 0740.

By 9:10 A.M. the carrier formation had been forced around to a southwesterly course and was heading straight for Leyte Gulf.

Ten minutes later the four Japanese destroyers on the starboard flank, led by the light cruiser YAHAGI, made a last torpedo attack from 10,000 yards. The first indication that KALININ BAY (Captain Charles R. Brown) had of the attack was when a torpedo plane from ST. LO, which had been circling the formation, went into a steep glide and strafed the wake of KALININ BAY, about 100 yards astern. Two torpedoes exploded. Immediately after this another torpedo was sighted broaching directly astern in the wake. The 5-inch gun on the fantail opened fire. An exploding shell near the approaching torpedo caused it to veer to port.

All the torpedoes fired in this attack paralleled the course of the fleeing carriers and no damage was done.

Then the Japanese did a strange and puzzling thing. By 9:20 two flanking cruisers to port had closed to 10,000 yards—point-blank range for their 8-inch guns—forcing the jeep carriers more and more to the right, and threatening to cut off the escape route to Leyte Gulf. The GAMBIER BAY had been sunk; HOEL, JOHNSTON, and SAMUEL B. ROBERTS were either sunk or sinking; FANSHAW BAY, KALININ BAY, DENNIS, and HEERMANN were badly hit. But just when the situation seemed most desperate, the Japanese quit.

The Jap's last gesture was two salvos, which fell short, and a minor torpedo attack from the cruisers. With that they broke off the engagement, turned about, and headed north.

The battle was over. A strange quietness settled over carriers. There was no more gunfire and no more shells fell near the ships. On the bridge of one carrier the silence was broken by a signalman:

"Damn it. They got away."

3

After the first early-morning contact, Kurita's attack force was harassed continuously by fighters and torpedo planes from the jeep carriers. Time after time they made runs on the cruisers and battleships. One pilot, after dropping his torpedo, made six dummy runs on the Jap ships, causing them to maneuver violently and break formation. Strafers continued to zoom low over the ships even though their ammunition was exhausted.

"The impression I got when I dived in," said one pilot, "was that YAMATO and NAGATO were the two biggest things I had ever seen afloat. They started letting us have it with everything, including shells from their main batteries. Different colored AA bursts boxed us in all around—yellow, orange, green, pink; just like a Christmas tree."

Help came quickly to Cliff Sprague from the other two carrier groups to the south. "While Clifton was having this little morning exercise," said Rear Admiral T. L. Sprague, "the carrier groups to the south were doing what they could about it. It so happened that since the enemy approached from the north, we had an excellent disposition to counter his attack; we were what is called 'disposed in depth.' In other words, while Cliff Sprague was attacked, the other two carrier groups were in the rear, as it were, so we were in position to launch attacks continuously at the enemy fleet.

"Admiral Stump, who was in the center, launched six full-scale strikes at the enemy with torpedoes and semi-armor-piercing bombs, machine guns, rockets, and as a matter of fact they threw everything they had in the locker at the Japs. As luck would have it, Stump's ships were not injured by any of the attacks, either by suicide planes or by shell fire, although they were under fire for a few minutes.[1] Completely untouched, they carried a heavy part of the load of turning back the enemy.

"There may have been a torpedo or two left over, but in general all of the ships used all of their torpedoes and all of their armor-piercing bombs in attacking the Japs. My group, which was to the south, had a torpedo and bomb strike airborne [to attack the Jap remnants of the Surigao battle] when we got the report. We immediately diverted the strike up to the new Jap fleet."

At 7:40, just as the destroyers far to the north were making their torpedo runs, four single-engined planes approached T. L. Sprague's southern group at high altitude. His carriers had just launched their second strike.

Without warning a bomb-loaded Zeke dived at SANTEE (Captain Robert E. Blick), crashed on her deck forward of the elevator, and ex-

[1] During the last half hour of battle, when TONE and HAGURO were flanking the carriers, they closed to within 12 miles of the screen destroyers (HAGGARD, FRANKS, HAILEY) of the center carrier force. A total of 23 rounds, fired in salvos from one of the cruisers, fell near the destroyers.

ploded. Simultaneously two other planes dived at SANGAMON (Captain Maurice E. Browder) and PETROF BAY, "The Mad Russian" (Captain Joseph L. Kane), but, hit by AA fire, they narrowly missed and fell into the water close abeam.

A few minutes later the injured SANTEE was hit by a torpedo fired from an undetected enemy submarine.

At 7:59 the fourth plane dived at her victim—the SUWANNEE (Captain William D. Johnson, Jr.). The explosion on the hangar, where it hit, caused heavy casualties and serious damage.

Two of the attacking planes had hit their targets; two had come desperately close. "Divine Wind" tactics seemed to be paying off.

But the wounds of the little carriers were quickly doctored. Within an hour SANTEE reported that she could make maximum speed and was ready to launch and land aircraft. The SUWANNEE, with a huge hole in her deck, took two hours to get back into action condition.

Tacloban airfield, on Leyte, had been captured by American troops the day after the landings, on October 21. Four days later, by the time Kurita showed up off Samar, the Army had a strip in good enough condition for emergency use. It was to this strip that many of the planes from the escort carriers went for rearming and refueling when they could not land on their own mother ships during the battle.

Cliff Sprague's ships deserved a rest after their exhausting fight but they didn't get it.

At ten minutes to eleven, as planes were returning from Tacloban in driblets, a formation of about six Zekes appeared over the five tired carriers. They started their dives simultaneously. Two headed for WHITE PLAINS (Captain Dennis J. Sullivan) and were taken under heavy AA fire. At last the 40mm and 20mm crews had their chance to shoot. One plane was hit and started to smoke. Suddenly this plane turned and dived into the deck of ST. LO (Captain Francis J. McKenna). The plane itself bounced overboard but its bomb penetrated the flight deck. A series of violent explosions followed.

The second plane continued its dive on WHITE PLAINS from astern, taking continuous hits as it came. When only a few yards astern, it suddenly rolled over on its port side and dived into the water.

Another plane crossed ahead of KITKUN BAY, climbed rapidly, rolled and made a dive directly at the bridge, strafing as it came. It passed over the island and crashed into the port catwalk.

The KALININ BAY, already holed from 15 shell hits, was attacked by three suicide-minded Zekes. Two hit the flight deck and the third dived into the sea on the port beam.

By 11:30 the attack was over. But there was one less carrier. The ST. LO had broken in two and sunk, stern first, seven minutes before.

What the 18-inch guns of YAMATO had failed to do, a single Kamikaze had done.

Chapter Twenty-Eight

The Great Sacrifice

I

AND WHAT OF Admiral Ozawa, who had sortied from the Inland Sea on his mission of lure and sacrifice?

For the first day and a half, after sidestepping a reported submarine, he took his ships south. His fleet, the so-called Main Body, looked formidable from afar—or from the air—with its four carriers, two battleship-carriers, three light cruisers, and eight destroyers. But, lacking adequate aircraft, it was a hollow fleet and Ozawa knew it.

On October 22 radio monitors aboard HYUGA heard what they thought were voice transmissions from a U.S. task force. That meant it was time to begin the decoying in earnest, so a long radio message was put on the air with the hope that the Americans would pick it up and be drawn north, like a cat to spilled milk.

On the 23rd the Main Body headed directly for Luzon. Ozawa was not confident that the lure would work, but he carefully laid his plans. The next day—X-minus-1-day, October 24—would mark the beginning of the great battle. At dawn he would send out his first patrols, and if the Americans were sighted, he would attack immediately with what little air strength he had. The Main Body would proceed on a southwesterly course until discovered, then it would maneuver in such a way as to suck the Americans northward out of Kurita's path. It was the old trick of feinting with the left, hoping the opponent would not see the haymaker coming from the right.

Soon after dawn on the morning of October 24 nine search planes took off from the white-lined decks of Ozawa's carriers. After orbiting the mother ships, they headed south.

The first report of contact with the American carrier force came from Manila. Fukudome's land-based planes had found Ted Sherman's task group in the Luzon bight. Shortly after this, Ozawa's planes also found the American carriers, who by this time were running in and out of rain squalls, playing a game of hide-and-seek with their winged attackers.

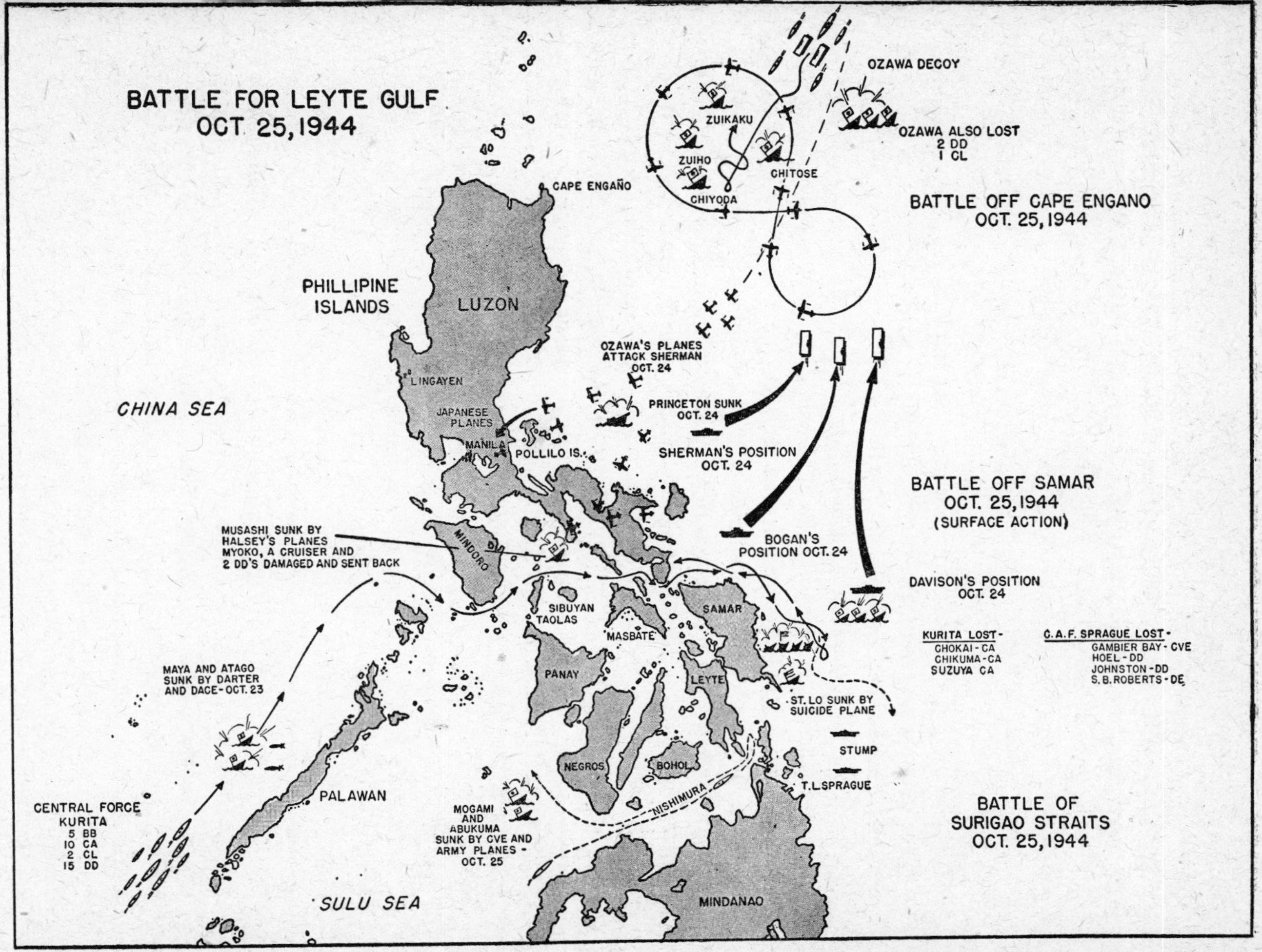
BATTLE FOR LEYTE GULF
OCT. 25, 1944
PHILLIPINE ISLANDS
CHINA SEA
SULU SEA
LUZON
LINGAYEN
JAPANESE PLANES
MANILA
POLLILO IS.
CAPE ENGAÑO
MINDORO
SIBUYAN
TAOLAS
MASBATE
PANAY
NEGROS
BOHOL
LEYTE
SAMAR
PALAWAN
MINDANAO
ZUIKAKU
ZUIHO
CHIYODA
CHITOSE
OZAWA DECOY
OZAWA ALSO LOST
2 DD
1 CL
BATTLE OFF CAPE ENGANO
OCT. 25, 1944
OZAWA'S PLANES ATTACK SHERMAN OCT. 24
PRINCETON SUNK OCT. 24
SHERMAN'S POSITION OCT. 24
BOGAN'S POSITION OCT. 24
BATTLE OFF SAMAR
OCT. 25, 1944
(SURFACE ACTION)
DAVISON'S POSITION OCT. 24
KURITA LOST-
CHOKAI-CA
CHIKUMA-CA
SUZUYA CA
C.A.F. SPRAGUE LOST-
GAMBIER BAY-CVE
HOEL-DD
JOHNSTON-DD
S.B.ROBERTS-DE,
ST. LO SUNK BY SUICIDE PLANE
STUMP
T.L.SPRAGUE
NISHIMURA
BATTLE OF
SURIGAO STRAITS
OCT. 25, 1944
MUSASHI SUNK BY HALSEY'S PLANES
MYOKO, A CRUISER AND 2 DD'S DAMAGED AND SENT BACK
MAYA AND ATAGO SUNK BY DARTER AND DACE-OCT. 23
CENTRAL FORCE
KURITA
5 BB
10 CA
2 CL
15 DD
MOGAMI AND ABUKUMA SUNK BY CVE AND ARMY PLANES - OCT. 25

FIGURE 17

The distance from Ozawa was too great for an immediate attack, 250 miles, so he continued on in toward the brawl.

By 11:45 A.M. the distance had been closed to 150 miles, near enough to strike. An attack unit of 76 planes—40 fighters, 28 bombers, 6 torpedo, and 2 reconnaissance—was launched with orders to attack the American carriers and then continue on in to the Luzon airfields.

"We planned," said Captain Toshikazu Ohmae, Ozawa's sharp-minded chief of staff, "that the planes go to the American fleet, bomb and torpedo, and then go to land because our ships would be sunk because we went too near on purpose to lure your ships to the north. Surely we would be sunk, that was our duty."

With the one attack Ozawa had shot his wad. He never knew how it came out, for communications with the shore bases were very poor. He also lost contact with his search planes.

Ozawa did receive reports, however, of the many attacks on Kurita's ships in the Sibuyan Sea. Ozawa felt he was not succeeding in his mission of drawing the American fleet northward. Drastic action had to be taken.

About four in the afternoon an advanced guard unit, consisting of the hermaphrodite ships ISE and HYUGA and four large destroyers, was detached from the carrier force and sent ahead in the hope of forcing a night engagement with the Americans.

When the search plane from LEXINGTON sighted the Japanese fleet later that afternoon, the Japanese also sighted him and listened as he reported his discovery back to Task Force 38.

Ozawa's hopes began to rise as he headed his ships southeast. The trick might work after all.

2

During the dark early-morning hours of October 25, while Kurita's attack force was heading south along the coast of Samar after having slipped through San Bernardino Strait, Mitscher's Task Force 38 was sniffing out Ozawa's carrier force known to be about 250 miles east of Cape Engaño, the northern tip of Luzon.

Night search planes from INDEPENDENCE probed the darkness with their owl-eyed radar. At 2:05 A.M. one of them made contact with a force of five ships only 80 miles to the north of Task Force 38. Soon after, a second group of six large ships was found 40 miles astern of the first group.

THE END'S BEGINNING

This was close, too close for good carrier work. If the Japs maintained even a moderate speed, a surface engagement might develop by 4:30 A.M., while it was still dark.

In preparation for this possibility Mitscher, in tactical command, shuffled the fleet. Admiral Lee's Task Force 34, consisting of six battleships, two heavy cruisers, five light cruisers, and eighteen destroyers, was formed up and sent 10 miles out in front of the rest of the fleet. This massive concentration of gunpower was fully capable of chewing up anything the Japs might put in the way. Proudly the ships swept on through the night.

Unfortunately the night snooping plane which had been tracking Ozawa had to return to INDEPENDENCE about 3:00 A.M. because of engine trouble. Contact was not regained during darkness.

Pete Mitscher got no sleep that night. When his night search planes lost contact, he was frantically worried, for he figured that the Japs had spotted him also and were steadily tracking his ships. Not knowing that the Jap carriers did not have their air groups aboard, he was afraid they would get their punch in first.

At dawn Mitscher sent out searchers east, west, and north. Attack groups, containing approximately 60 fighters, 65 dive bombers, and 55 torpedo planes, took to the air immediately following. They orbited about 50 miles in advance of the fleet waiting to pounce on the enemy carriers as soon as they were sighted by search planes. Commander David McCampbell of Air Group 15 flying from ESSEX was in charge of planes from Task Group 38.3 (Sherman); Commander William Ellis (Air Group 18 from INTREPID) had the planes from TG 38.2 (Bogan); and Commander Daniel Smith of ENTERPRISE's Air Group 20 commanded the fliers from TG 38.4 (Davison).

Weather was excellent, clear with a 16-knot wind from the northeast. There were no clouds for enemy ships to hide under. A perfect day for an attack.

At 6:48 A.M., while tensely waiting for battle, Halsey received Kinkaid's dispatch asking if Task Force 34 was still guarding San Bernardino Strait. It was Kinkaid's dispatch sent at 4:12 A.M. Halsey quickly answered that Task Force 34 was with the carrier groups heading north to attack an enemy carrier force. But by the time this reply arrived Kurita's battleships were shelling the escort carriers off Samar.

Some members of Mitscher's staff thought that the enemy carrier force might be to the east of the assigned search sectors, so Mitscher ordered four planes from the ESSEX Combat Air Patrol vectored out to conduct a high-speed search to the northeast. This decision paid off. At 0730 Ozawa's carrier force was sighted by the ESSEX fliers 130 miles from Task Force 38 on a northeasterly course. The Japs had obviously been running at high speed to the northward during the night after the radar search plane was forced to break contact.

For fifty minutes the ESSEX fliers circled over the Japanese ships reporting their position, composition, and maneuvers.

Radio silence on the carriers was broken with a message from Mitscher's flag plot:

"Ninety-nine Rebel [Dave McCampbell's call] take charge of this strike and get the carriers."

"McCampbell opened up on his radio," related Dan Smith, "to give Ellis and me instructions. I don't remember exactly what he said, but I do know that he said 'Follow me in.' But Ellis and I were not virgins at this business and we knew what to do.

"We turned our noses toward the Jap task force and gave the planes full throttle. 'Pick one out, boys, and let him have it' was the only instruction I gave my air group."

The first strike arrived about eight o'clock. Eighteen intercepting fighters were quickly disposed of and for the rest of the day American fliers had the sky to themselves, but, of course, had to dodge the colored AA bursts that the Japanese threw up thickly and accurately, even from battleship main batteries.

"I was over the target about three hours," related ace McCampbell. "We gave each task group a carrier to strike during which all four carriers were hit. Since I was leading the entire strike, our group was in the lead. As we approached, one carrier turned out of formation as if to launch planes. So I sent our group in on him. The bombers that went in first did such a bang-up job that I called the torpedo planes off and put them on a battleship. The carrier sank in about fifteen minutes."

"The Japs were steaming in a beautiful screen when we went in," continued Smith. "When we left them they looked like a disorderly mob and every ship was trailing oil."

As the planes came in, the Japanese formation broke up into violent individual maneuvers. But they could not get out from under the hawk-eyed fliers. The ZUIKAKU, the large carrier, was hit aft with a torpedo which disrupted its steering gear. The CHITOSE was smothered under a rain of bombs and sank—it was the carrier McCampbell saw go down. The destroyer AKITSUKI blew up and sank instantaneously. The TAMA, a light cruiser, received a torpedo hit and was slowed to 13 knots. The two other light carriers, ZUIHO and CHOYODA, received bomb hits, and CHOYODA was forced to drop out of formation. The light cruiser ISUZU and the destroyer MAKI were assigned to guard her.

While the planes of the first strike were still in the air, Halsey received an urgent message from Kinkaid: Jap battleships and cruisers were 15 miles astern of his baby carriers off Samar and firing at them.

Eight minutes later, at 0830, Halsey received a second urgent dispatch: fast battleships urgently needed immediately at Leyte Gulf.

Halsey was in a tough spot. His own ships were about to engage a force which he considered to be a much greater threat, in the long run, than the Center Force, and he thought that Oldendorf's old battleships and cruisers should be able to take care of the Japanese he had bruised so badly the day before.

McCain's carrier group, Task Group 38.1, had come about the day before on orders from Halsey and now it was fueling 400 miles to the northeast of Leyte Gulf. Halsey directed McCain to strike the Japanese force off Samar and to proceed at best speed toward Leyte Gulf. Kinkaid was told of this.

At 9:00 another urgent dispatch came in requesting that Task Force 34 proceed at top speed to cover Leyte Gulf and requesting immediate strikes by fast carriers. (Kinkaid had sent the message at 0730 when the escort carriers were emerging from the rain squall.)

Still a fourth leather-lunged call for help was received at 9:22. This time Kinkaid informed Halsey that his old battleships, after five days of bombardment and the battle in Surigao Strait, were low on ammunition.

It was a hard decision to make. The battleline of the Third Fleet, which included Halsey's flagship, NEW JERSEY, was within 40 miles of the enemy carrier force which, according to flash reports, was already badly damaged. Halsey was all set to take part in the first surface engagement of his naval career—an engagement that he hoped would break Japanese seapower forever.

Taut with anticipation of battle Halsey had been irritated by Kinkaid's frantic cries for help, for he thought Kinkaid could handle the Japs with what he had already. But then came the message from Kinkaid stating that his ships were low on ammunition. It was the first time Halsey knew of that.

On Guam, Admiral Nimitz, who was following the battle closely from the dispatches, also was confused as to the whereabouts of "Ching" Lee and his battleships. "Where is Task Force 34?" was the message Halsey received from CINCPAC at 10:00 A.M.

After receiving a fifth urgent request for assistance from Kinkaid, Halsey made his decision. He ordered Bogan's Task Group 38.2 and Task Force 34 [1] south. Mitscher, with the two remaining carrier groups, was to carry on the attack against Ozawa. At 11:15 A.M. Halsey turned south.

About eleven o'clock, after the second wave of American planes had struck, Ozawa decided to change flagships. The ZUIKAKU could still do 20 knots but could be steered only with difficulty and her communications facilities were badly damaged. So during a lull in the air attack he and his staff transferred by small boat to the light cruiser OYODO.

Ozawa's expectations of complete destruction were rapidly coming true. Before the third attack, which came about one in the afternoon, Ozawa made a terse estimate of the situation:

"Considerations which influenced the decision of whether to continue with our diverting operations or to counterattack with our considerably damaged force:

    (a) No aircraft available for our use.

         Reconnaissance strength, attacking strength: nil.

    (b) Enemy position unknown.

"Decided to draw the enemy farther north."

The third wave, which included about 150 aircraft that had returned from the first strike to rearm and refuel, was directed by Commander Richard L. Kibbe (FRANKLIN, Air Group 13) and Commander Hugh Winters (LEXINGTON, Air Group 19).

"I got over the target about 9:15 and Admiral Mitscher told me to stay as long as my gas held out," related Winters. "By the time I relieved McCampbell as strike leader and air co-ordinator, there were three car-

---

[1] The ships in this formation of TF 34 were: the battleships WASHINGTON (Captain Thomas R. Cooley) Admiral Lee's flagship, ALABAMA (Captain Vincent R. Murphy), MASSACHUSETTS (Captain William W. Warlick), SOUTH DAKOTA (Captain Ralph S. Riggs), IOWA (Captain Allan R. McCann), NEW JERSEY (Captain Carl F. Holden); the light cruisers VINCENNES (Captain Allen D. Brown), MIAMI (Captain John G. Crawford), BILOXI (Captain Daniel M. McGurl); and eight destroyers of Desron 52.

riers, two battleships, and three or four cruisers left. They were more or less spreading out, trying to get away. Some of them were cripples which we flew over on the way in. It was a great temptation to stop and knock them off. But two carriers, ZUIKAKU and ZUIHO, had full speed left in them and were getting away to the north. So we took our groups on up farther north and hit them.

"I put my group on the ZUIKAKU and they really smothered her. When the torpedoes hit, a narrow plume of water went high into the air like a fire plug that had been run over by a car.

"The ZUIKAKU slowly burned for about two hours and then sank. But it took several strikes to sink the ZUIHO, which was smaller, faster and more maneuverable. Finally she rolled over and sank after about three hours of attack. There was no exploding or going up in a mass of flames or anything spectacular like you see in movies. The carriers just smoked slightly all over and gradually listed more and more. Pretty soon they just rolled over, without any explosion, and went down.

"The advantage of having one person stay over the scene of action and co-ordinate things is that damaged ships are prevented from escaping. Kid O'Mara, my wing man, and I circled around the Japs like a shepherd tending his flocks. One cruiser and destroyer tried to escape to the northwest. I marked them down on my knee pad and when the next strike came in I said to the air group commander: 'Follow that oil slick to the northwest and you will find a big Jap cruiser.' It was just like a treasure hunt.

"I had quite a time restraining some of the new fliers when they came in for the first time. Most of them wanted to go after the carriers, not knowing that they had already been hit and were sinking. I knew it was no good wasting more bombs and torpedoes on them, so sometimes I had to get tough. 'Goddammit, these are orders from Admiral Mitscher,' I would say. 'Lay off the carrier and go after that cruiser.'

"Later over my radio I confessed to Jimmy (Commander James Flatley) back in flag plot on the LEX what I had been doing. 'Jimmy,' I said, 'I'm using Admiral Mitscher's name in vain.' 'Use anything you want to, but sink those ships,' Jimmy came back."

During the course of the air attacks, it became evident that there would be a number of enemy cripples that could be finished off if overtaken by surface forces. So a little after 2:00 P.M., while ZUIKAKU was sinking, Mitscher ordered Rear Admiral L. T. DuBose, of "Bait Division" fame, to take two heavy cruisers, WICHITA (Captain Douglas A. Spencer) and NEW ORLEANS (Captain Jack E. Hurff), two light cruisers, SANTA FE (Captain Jerauld Wright) and MOBILE (Captain Charles C. Miller), and twelve destroyers [1] and start out after the Jap stragglers.

"On the way back about 4 o'clock in the evening," continued Hugh Winters, "I came across the one carrier [CHOYODA] that was still afloat. She had no way on and was still smoking a little bit from fires started by the first morning strike. I thought possibly she had been deserted or abandoned but when I flew down close to her she started shooting.

"We had no air strikes in the vicinity at that time so I swung south a little bit and found a fast force of four of our cruisers. I called them on the radio and the reception was perfect. They had evidently been manning our circuit. I had them change course to the right about 45 degrees and in about twenty minutes they came up at high speed to within range of this stricken carrier. After I had searched around and told them there were no battleships near, they came on in and were very happy to polish her off."

By 4:40 P.M., CHOYODA was a mass of flames. DuBose ordered a division of destroyers to close the carrier and sink her—with torpedoes, if necessary. The destroyers headed in under cover of the heavy smoke pouring from the hull of the carrier but, at 4:47 P.M., CHOYODA rolled over to port, lay momentarily on her side, and then sank.

"All day long, back on the LEX," continued Winters, "they kept saying 'Get the carriers. Get the carriers.' This time when they repeated the familiar directions, I replied in a disgusted tone: 'They're all going under the water.' I heard them laugh over the radio and then say, 'That's all we wanted to know.'

"I turned for home and landed with ten minutes' gas in my tanks. I had been in the air about nine hours. I was so tired that my knees would not hold me and I practically collapsed in the ready room as I told the story. All of us got some sleep that night, for the story was simple—all carriers sunk."

Two more air strikes, a small one and a large one, went in that day between three and five in the afternoon. They were more or less over-

---

[1] The PORTERFIELD (Captain Carleton P. Todd), CALLAGHAN (Commander Francis J. Johnson), KNAPP (Lieutenant Commander William B. Brown), COGSWELL (Commander Wallace J. Deutermann), INGERSOLL (Commander Alexander C. Veasey), CAPERTON (Commander George K. Carmichael), C. K. BRONSON (Commander Gifford Scull), COTTEN (Lieutenant Commander Philip W. Winston), PATTERSON (Lieutenant Commander Walter H. Hering), HEALY (Commander John C. Atkeson), DORTCH (Commander Robert C. Young), and BAGLEY (Commander William H. Shea, Jr.).

lapping and were co-ordinated by the same man—Commander Malcolm T. Wordell (Air Group 44 of LANGLEY). Several 1,000-pound semiarmor-piercing bombs dropped by planes from this strike sank ZUIHO.

"It was my third strike of the day," said Dan Smith. "I was flying with the help of two benzedrine pills and a desire to see all the Jap ships go down."

The rest of the efforts of these last strikes were directed against the two battleship-carriers, ISE and HYUGA, and the light cruiser OYODO, fleeing northward at 20 knots. The OYODO was hit with one bomb, which caused only slight damage. The waterline blisters of ISE were damaged from near misses, but neither she nor HYUGA received a direct hit from bomb or torpedo.

DuBose did not linger over the grave of CHOYODA. Within fifteen minutes his group was sweeping north looking for more killings, while there was still light.

A LANGLEY search plane reported at 6:40 P.M. that one Jap cruiser was dead in the water to the northward and was being circled by two destroyers.

Actually the Jap ships were three destroyers—HATSUTSUKI, WAKATSUKI, and KUWA. The HATSUTSUKI, a large 2,400-ton destroyer, was probably mistaken for a cruiser.[1] These destroyers were picking up survivors from two of the sunken carriers.

Soon DuBose's ships made radar contact with the Japs. Two of the targets seemed to be pulling away to the north, so DuBose ordered his heavy cruisers to take these ships under fire (range 14 miles) and ordered his light cruisers to concentrate on the closer target. At 6:53 P.M., MOBILE opened up and was followed three minutes later by WICHITA.

When the shooting started the two smaller destroyers beat a hasty retreat, while HATSUTSUKI laid a smoke screen. Building her speed up to 26 knots, HATSUTSUKI twisted violently dodging salvos from MOBILE and SANTA FE. When the range had closed to six miles, HATSUTSUKI started firing back.

After dusk Ozawa received word of the attack on HATSUTSUKI. He decided to go to her aid with ISE, HYUGA, OYODO, and the destroyer SHIMOTSUKI. Coming about, he headed south. A little later he asked HATSUTSUKI by radio for her position. There was no reply.

[1] Throughout the day airmen had confused these large destroyers with light cruisers, which in turn led them to believe that the light cruisers were heavy cruisers.

One of the fleeing destroyers joined up with Ozawa's ships en route and told her story: the three destroyers had been attacked by an American surface force estimated as two large cruisers, two apparent battleships, and a destroyer squadron. The HATSUTSUKI, at last sighting, was making smoke. What happened after that was not known.

What had happened was that, after an hour's running fight, DuBose's cruisers had closed the range to 6,000 yards. The SANTA FE illuminated HATSUTSUKI with star shells, and by 8:45 P.M. she had been brought to a stop with many heavy hits. Fifteen minutes later she sank rapidly, going down by the bow.

DuBose decided after that to call it a day. His destroyers were low on fuel and the nearest Jap was 46 miles to the north. Also he had to rendezvous the next day with the carrier groups. So he broke off the chase and headed back toward the task force.

Ozawa searched until about midnight but made no contact with friend or foe. So he turned north and headed for Japan with the remains of his fleet.

Chapter Twenty-Nine

The End of a Navy

I

KURITA'S Attack Force, after breaking off the attack on Cliff Sprague's eggshelled carrier group, behaved in a most peculiar manner. For some three and a half hours it circled about, now heading in one direction, now in another, like a groggy boxer trying to decide how to hit his opponent.

At 10:45 A.M. the Japanese ships were reported as retiring to the northeast, but ten minutes later they had changed course to the south. About noon they came about to a southwesterly course and for about forty-five minutes headed directly for Leyte Gulf, seemingly intent on forcing an entrance. Meanwhile the baby flat-tops, scraping the bottom of the ammunition lockers, kept the Japanese ships under attack much of the time.

By 1:10 in the afternoon the Japanese were 13 miles west of where they had been at 7:22 that morning. Once again they circled about and headed north, this time for good.

While the Japs were milling around deciding what to do, Kinkaid kept Halsey informed about the tight situation off Samar. Help, Kinkaid kept repeating, was urgently needed. In all nine requests were sent to the Third Fleet.

By this time Halsey with his fast battleships and cruisers and Jerry Bogan's carrier group, TG 38.2, was racing down from the north but would not be in the Leyte area until eight o'clock the next morning. "Slew" McCain's carrier group, the largest in the Third Fleet (three large carriers, and two light carriers), was making full speed toward Leyte and at ten-thirty launched its first air strike from HANCOCK (Captain Fred C. Dickey), HORNET (Captain Austin K. Doyle), and WASP (Captain Oscar A. Weller) while still 335 miles from the Japanese. This was beyond the striking range of the aircraft, but with the carriers closing at 30 knots, the distance home after the strike would be much less

The combat ships available to Kinkaid were deep in Surigao Strait and after the early-morning engagement with Nishimura's Southern Force and after five days of almost continuous shore bombardment were very short of ammunition and fuel. Furthermore, the destroyers had expended most of their torpedoes. However, a striking force under Oldendorf, consisting of three battleships, four cruisers, and two destroyer squadrons, was organized and at 9:53 A.M. was ordered to proceed to the aid of the escort carriers. But when the enemy turned north the first time, these orders were canceled. Again at 11:27 A.M., when it seemed that the Japanese were returning toward Leyte, the force was ordered out, but when the Japanese again reversed course, the order was again canceled. Oldendorf did not leave Leyte Gulf.

McCain's fliers found Kurita heading north along the coast of Samar at 1:10 P.M. Ninety-nine planes swooped down in a co-ordinated attack—fighters strafing ahead of bombers, with bomb-loaded torpedo planes coming in last.

Later in the afternoon, about three o'clock, a second strike of 53 planes hit at the fleeing ships with bomb and rocket. The rainbow-colored antiaircraft fire from Kurita's ships was intense, and by the end of the day had accounted for eleven American planes. Most of the attackers returned to their carriers, but eight made landings on the half-completed strip at mud-bound Tacloban.

By the middle of the afternoon Halsey knew that the Japanese Central Force had given up the attempt to plow through to Leyte Gulf and that it was backtracking toward San Bernardino. Halsey wanted to block that exit, so at four o'clock he took his two fastest battleships, IOWA and NEW JERSEY, three cruisers, VINCENNES, MIAMI, and BILOXI, and eight destroyers of Squadron 52 out of formation and headed at high speed toward San Bernardino. Rear Admiral Oscar C. Badger was in tactical command of the group.

But Kurita won the race and slipped through San Bernardino Strait at 9:30 that evening, three hours before Halsey arrived. That is, all his remaining ships slipped through—except one.

At twenty-six minutes past midnight the destroyer LEWIS HANCOCK reported a surface radar contact 15 miles to the south. Bushy-browed Oscar Badger ordered his light forces, cruisers and destroyers, to engage the straggling Jap. Range was closed for half an hour. Then VINCENNES, BILOXI, and MIAMI opened up with main and secondary batteries. Within five minutes the enemy ship was erupting flame from stem to stern. The destroyers OWEN (Commander Carlton B. Jones) and MILLER (Lieutenant Commander Dwight L. Johnson) were then sent in for the kill. A half salvo of torpedoes from OWEN did the trick and the unlucky Jap went down hissing. The OWEN illuminated the area with star shells but nothing could be seen. At 0147 the sea shook with a final underwater explosion. Then all was quiet.

For the first time in his long naval career Admiral Halsey had witnessed a gunnery fight between surface ships.

"It was a heavy cruiser of the ATAGO class."

"No, it was a large destroyer."

"Definitely a light cruiser."

No one could agree on what it was they had sunk. Actually it was the NOWAKE, a large 2,400-ton destroyer, the kind that throughout the day had been mistaken for light cruisers by American airmen. When sunk, she was loaded with survivors from the cruiser CHIKUMA.

Throughout the remainder of the night the force swept south along the coast of Samar hoping to find more cripples. But there were none. At early light the ships passed through waters dotted black with survivors of the engagements of the previous day. The majority of the survivors were Japanese, so Halsey ordered some "samples" picked up. Eleven American aviators and crewmen also were recovered.

At dawn the same morning the carriers of Jerry Bogan's TG 38.2 rendezvoused with McCain's TG 38.1 coming up from the south at full speed. A combined strike was launched about 0600 against the fleeing Japanese. This time Kurita was caught heading south in Tablas Strait, along the east coast of Mindoro.

On the first attack a torpedo was put into the light cruiser NOSHIRO, stopping her dead in the water. She was a sitting duck for the dive bombers of the second strike—McCain's carriers sent over three strikes that day—and she finally sank under a hail of bombs.

The limping KUMANO [1] was also hit again with torpedo and bomb, and was left dead in the water.

Twenty-four B-24s of the Fifth Air Force also attacked Kurita that

---

[1] In the words of Admiral Carney, KUMANO "was discovered a month or so later hiding and camouflaged on the west coast of Luzon minus one bow complete and received special attention in the form of about 14 torpedoes which completed the action begun on October 24."

day, October 26, but the closest they got to a hit was a near straddle on the YAMATO.

By that afternoon what remained of Kurita's First Diversion Attack Force had fled into the Sulu Sea, beyond range of the Third Fleet carriers.

At midnight Halsey considered the action with the Japanese fleet terminated and sent the following message to the Third Fleet:

"For brilliance, courage, and tireless fighting heart the all hands performance since early October will never be surpassed. It has been an honor to be your commander. Well done. Halsey."

2

Under cover of the great sea battles the Japanese had managed to sneak 2,000 men ashore at Ormoc from a convoy of four transports protected by the destroyer URANAMI and the light cruiser KINU. The next morning, while Kurita was being pounded in retreat, Admiral Stump's rugged CVE air groups found these ships heading northward between Cebu and Leyte. After a full day of persistent attacks with bullet, rocket, and contact bomb—all heavy bombs and torpedoes had been used the day before—they managed to sink URANAMI, KINU, and two transports.

The next day one of Admiral Shima's destroyers, the SHIRANUHI, who had escaped death at Surigao Strait, was sent out to rescue survivors from the sunken cruiser but succeeded only in getting herself sunk off Panay by carrier planes.

She was the last ship sunk in the Battle for Leyte Gulf.

3

The Japanese fleet had been decisively defeated. The Sho Operation had not worked. The entire Imperial Navy had been gambled on a long chance—and the Japs had lost.

"After this battle," said Vice Admiral Ozawa, "the surface force became strictly auxiliary, so that we relied on land forces, special attack [Kamikaze] and air power."

The whole Sho plan was exceedingly complex and difficult to carry out, requiring very precise timing and a good deal of luck. "I think that it was the best possible plan," related Ozawa after the war, "considering the location of the three forces and also the condition of training of the three forces—I know it was very difficult and complicated, so I was not surprised by events; under the circumstances there was no other method of procedure—I do not think it was foregone conclusion that this operation was doomed from the very beginning, although lack of air power was a decisive factor leading to the defeat. I think that if we had not sent reinforcement of Formosa from the carriers, the outcome of the operation would have been more successful."

Indeed, the Sho Operation had come dangerously close to succeeding. The Third Fleet had been lured to the north according to plan. Kurita had sortied unmolested through San Bernardino during the night, dashed down the coast of Samar and had surprised a weak escort carrier group only 60 miles from Leyte Gulf. He had engaged these brittle-bottomed ships and by sheer weight had forced them clear. The way was open to Leyte Gulf and he was in a position to accomplish his primary mission —the destruction of the soft transports near the landing beaches. But then Kurita had done a puzzling thing. On the verge of victory he had turned back.

Why?

On the morning of October 25 Kurita sighted Cliff Sprague's force at about the same time he was sighted—just before seven o'clock. Having no reconnaissance aircraft himself, Kurita had no accurate information about the composition of the American force. He estimated that it was one group of a task force and was probably composed of five or six carriers, two or three battleships, a few cruisers and destroyers.

The attack on the American forces that followed was a wild chase, each Japanese ship going at its individual top speed, each ship fighting on its own. Soon the formation became widely scattered and the YAMATO, down by the bow from bomb hits of the previous day, was left far behind the faster cruisers. Since so much depended on visual sighting, the American smoke screen was very troublesome to Kurita.

The American torpedo attack further disrupted and slowed the Japanese formation. Kurita estimated that the Americans were retiring at 30 knots—a rare tribute to the engineering officers on the 18-knot jeep carriers! From the bridge of the lagging YAMATO Kurita, because of squalls and smoke, lost sight of the fleeing Americans and his pursuing cruisers. Thinking the Americans too swift, he decided to call off the chase. He did not know that at the time his two leading cruisers—TONE and HAGURO—were only 10,000 yards from the American ships.

Kurita, when he broke off the chase at 9:30 A.M., still intended to push through into Leyte Gulf. But first he had to collect his ships, piece together his information, and in general, weigh the situation.

His cruisers had taken some heavy hits. The CHOKAI and CHIKUMA, two of the four cruisers that had flanked Sprague from the east, had both been bombed and shelled heavily and were unmaneuverable. The KUMANO, a heavy cruiser, had been disabled by a destroyer torpedo. The SUZUYA, who had been standing by to aid KUMANO, was hit with a torpedo and a bomb.

The KUMANO could still navigate at a reduced speed of 15 knots, so she was ordered to proceed independently to Manila in company with the destroyer HAYASHIMO. Nothing could save the other three cruisers. After the crews had been removed, they were sunk by torpedoes from the destroyers FUJINAMI, NOWAKE, and OKINAMI. These destroyers with the survivors aboard then headed back toward San Bernardino Strait hugging the coast of Samar.[1]

That left Kurita with four battleships, two heavy cruisers, two light cruisers, and seven destroyers. Still a formidable group, but strong enough to fight the Americans in the confined waters of Leyte Gulf? Kurita began to doubt it, so he called a conference of his staff.

The Japanese had intercepted American voice radio transmissions which led Kurita to believe that the Tacloban and Dulag airstrips were operational and that carrier planes were being concentrated there for an attack on his force. A plain-language cry for help also had been picked up by Japanese monitors and the plain-language reply promised aid in two hours. Kurita interpreted this as meaning air aid and thought a strong carrier force was closing in on him, and would strike at just the time he was entering the gulf. (Actually this plain-language cry for help was meant for Kurita's ears as much as Halsey's. It was the idea of Captain Richard H. Cruzen, Kinkaid's operations officer, that if Kurita thought Halsey was closing in on him he would either slow down to discuss the situation or possibly even turn back. So the message was put on the air with the deliberate intention of having it picked up by Kurita's monitors. It was a long shot that paid off—one of the best bits of deceptive intelligence of the war.)

---

[1] The HAYASHIMO was sunk south of Mindoro on the 26th by a carrier torpedo plane; FUJINAMI, with survivors of CHOKAI aboard, was sunk also south of Mindoro on the 27th by carrier planes.

Kurita, operating blindly, his reconnaissance information confined to his field of vision, felt that American surface forces were prepared to engage him in Leyte Gulf. He imagined a huge trap ready to spring as he entered narrow waters—land-based planes, carrier-based planes, surface ships; all would attack him.

"The American preparations to intercept our force apparently were complete whereas we could not even determine the actual situation in Leyte Gulf," he logged.

Also he was behind schedule. He should have entered the gulf at 6:00 A.M. He thought that by the time he arrived his principal target, the soft invasion shipping, would probably be dispersed and safely out of the danger zone (actually unloading operations had not even been stopped). He had received word, in a brief message from the destroyer SHIGURE, that Nishimura's force had been wiped out. The original plan had been to exit by way of Surigao Strait after sweeping around Leyte Gulf, but that seemed impossible now.

An intercepted radio message from the Japanese Northern Force led Kurita to believe that Ozawa was preparing a night torpedo attack on the American forces in that area. It was just what Kurita needed. Backed unanimously by his staff he decided to give up the idea of penetrating Leyte Gulf, but come about and head north, hoping to join forces with Ozawa for the attack.

Thus ended the naval threat to the landings on Leyte.

By 5:30 after an afternoon of almost continuous air attack Kurita reached a position northeast of Samar without contacting any American force. His ships were now low on fuel, so he gave up the search, and headed for San Bernardino.

4

Often the outcome of a battle depends on some fortuitous twist of Fate that can be neither anticipated nor guarded against. Perhaps the Battle for Leyte Gulf would have had a much different ending if it had not been for a faulty radio transmitter on Ozawa's flagship, the ZUIKAKU.

Ozawa sent three important messages to Kurita, none of which was received. The first message that was not received outlined Ozawa's plans for attacking the Third Fleet on the morning of the 24th from east of Luzon. (The message giving the results of this operation also was not received.) The second message stating the plan for ISE and HYUGA to conduct a night attack on the American fleet was not received. And the last message, giving news of Task Force 38's attack on the Japanese carriers, was not received.

"The influence of these lost messages," testified Captain Toshikazu Ohmae, Ozawa's chief of staff, "was: first, since Admiral Kurita did not receive word of our attack on your carrier force east of Luzon, he turned back on the afternoon of the 24th for a time and thus lost time; second, had he known that your forces were attacking us on the morning of the 25th, he could have continued on into Leyte Gulf."

5

Submarines had drawn first blood in the Battle for Leyte Gulf when DARTER and DACE attacked Kurita's force in Palawan Passage. Before the battle was over, they made another killing.

By dawn of October 25 Admiral Lockwood had ordered sixteen of his Pacific submarines to form a patrol net that would cover all logical Japanese escape routes. In Luzon Strait, the stretch of water between Formosa and northern Luzon, he stationed seven submarines. To submariners this area was known as "Convoy College."

"Chance of a lifetime for convoy college," Lockwood had radioed. "Go get 'em!"

Farther north, off the northeast tip of Formosa guarding the approaches to the East China Sea, were three submarines. Six more were placed off Luzon covering the escape paths to the Home Islands.

When Lockwood got word that Halsey was engaging Japanese Northern Force, he ordered two "wolf packs" to intercept any of Ozawa's ships that might survive and try to flee. The two packs, alliteratively known as "Roach's Raiders" (Commander John P. Roach) and "Clarey's Crushers" (Commander Bernard A. Clarey), were composed of three submarines each: Raiders—HADDOCK (Commander Roach), TUNA (Lieutenant Commander E. F. Steffanides, Jr.), and HALIBUT (Commander Ignatius J. Galantin); Crushers—JALLAO (Commander Joseph B. Icenhower), ATULE (Commander John H. Maurer), and PINTADO (Commander Clarey).

About eight o'clock in the evening of the 25th, JALLAO picked up a fleeing Jap cruiser escorted by a destroyer and immediately began tracking. Within an hour PINTADO joined up.

By 11:00 P.M., JALLAO was in a position to attack. The target was the cruiser, 1,200 yards away. With a jolt three torpedoes leaped from the bow tubes, but the cruiser turned and all three missed.

The range had closed to 700 yards by the time Icenhower could swing his sub around for a stern shot. Four torpedoes were fired from the stern tubes and three of them found their mark.

The JALLAO then went deep.

Surfacing twenty minutes later, there was nothing in sight. From Clarey on the PINTADO came a message saying he had seen the cruiser explode, break in half, and sink.

It was the light cruiser TAMA, damaged by a torpedo dropped that morning by one of Mitscher's airmen. Unable to continue the fight, she had been ordered by Ozawa to proceed to Okinawa for repairs.

6

The historic Battle for Leyte Gulf will be studied and debated by strategists and tacticians for years to come. The complete story of what went on in the minds of the commanders probably never will be known. Decisions in battle are a product of many complex and tenuous factors: intelligence and reconnaissance reports, both accurate and inaccurate; subtle shades of emphasis given to bits of information; the basic plan of the commander; the press of the moment and the necessity of making a choice quickly; and not least of all the character of the commander himself. A very thin line marks the difference between a good decision and a bad one—or a good decision and a better one. In battle the supreme necessity of immediate action must receive as much emphasis as deliberate balance and evaluation. As one veteran fighting man said: "It is hard for anyone but a combat man to judge a combat man." Even then two combat men often differ.

"In analyzing naval actions," said Admiral Kinkaid, whose "soft" shipping in Leyte Gulf came perilously close to disaster, "one must keep in mind the *missions* of the forces. The key to the Battle for Leyte Gulf lies in the missions of the two fleets.

"The mission must be clearly understood. The mission of the Seventh Fleet was to land and support the invasion force. My title was Commander of the Central Philippines Attack Force. Our job was to land troops and keep them ashore. The ships were armed accordingly with a very low percentage of armor-piercing projectiles. The CVEs carried anti-personnel bombs instead of torpedoes and heavy bombs. We were not prepared to fight a naval action . . ."

"Kurita was an example of a fellow who failed to keep his mind on his mission. If he had come down Samar, pressed the fight against the CVEs and their escorts, I believe he would have got into Leyte Gulf.

"About thirty of our destroyers had expended all their torpedoes, and all the battleships were low on ammunition and low on fuel. There would would have been some of the advantages of Surigao Strait, since the Jap ships would have had to go through a passage between two islands. I can't say they would have definitely got in, but there was a good chance. Had Kurita carried out his mission the story would have been different, but instead of coming on in as he should have, he just took half-baked, half-hearted action.

"The only thing I can think of that I would have done differently if I had known Kurita was definitely coming through San Bernardino unopposed is that I would have moved the northern CVE group more to the south and I would have had a striking group from the escort carriers up looking for him at dawn.

"What mistakes were made during the battle were *not* due to lack of plans. Any errors made were errors of judgment, not errors of organization. The two areas coming together—the Central Pacific and the Southwest Pacific—posed a difficult problem of command, but one head would not have altered things."

In spite of differences of opinion as to what the best course of action would have been, the fact remained that action had been taken and the Battle for Leyte Gulf had been won. How decisively it had been won can only be realized by looking at the box score:

COMBATANT SHIPS SUNK

Japanese	*American*
3 battleships	
MUSASHI	
YAMASHIRO	
FUSO	
1 large carrier	
ZUIKAKU	

3 light carriers
   CHITOSE
   CHOYODA
   ZUIHO

6 heavy cruisers
   ATAGO
   MAYA
   CHOKAI
   SUZUYA
   CHIKUMA
   MOGAMI

4 light cruisers
   ABUKUMA
   TAMA
   NOSHIRO
   KINU

11 destroyers
   WAKABA
   YAMAGUMO
   MICHISHIO
   ASAGUMO
   HATSUTSUKI
   AKITSUKI
   NOWAKE
   HAYASHIMO
   FUJINAMI
   URANAMI
   SHIRANUHI

1 light carrier
   PRINCETON
2 escort carriers
   GAMBIER BAY
   ST. LO

2 destroyers
   JOHNSTON
   HOEL

1 destroyer escort
   SAMUEL B. ROBERTS

The Japanese Navy, as a fighting fleet and not merely as an unbalanced group of air and surface raiders, had ceased to exist. Long since, the merchant fleet had been put under by the U.S. Navy's submarines and aircraft, and now the combatant ships had followed.

Japan had lost everything except the will to fight. Her people, from Emperor to peasant housewife, knew that the end was only a matter of time—the time it would take the Americans to kill the last defender of the sacred homeland—and they prepared accordingly.

For the United States the problem was to cut the time short, to bring about the end at the least cost of life. And the United States, too, prepared accordingly.

Already accomplished but not acknowledged, the end of the war was to be attained only after both adversaries had struck at each other with new weapons of appalling character. Tens of thousands were yet to die, and to die as humanity had never before met death, in order to prove that which already had been clearly indicated.

The Japanese Empire was finished.

Appendix

TASK ORGANIZATIONS

Because of space limitations and in order to avoid repetitious listings of ships and men, the task organizations of the operations that took place during the period of the Pacific War covered in this volume have not all been listed. It is felt, however, that the lists are representative and that they include most of the ships involved in the assault landings and the fleet engagements in the Central and Southwest Pacific Areas. Also included in this appendix is the organization and composition of the Japanese Combined Fleet at the time of the Battle for Leyte Gulf.

Lae, 4 September 1943: REAR ADMIRAL DANIEL E. BARBEY

Headquarters Group 76.1
    CONYNGHAM   Commander J. H. Ward
    FLUSSER   Commander J. A. Robbins, 2 DDS *

APD Group 76.2   Commander J. S. Willis
    BROOKS (F)   Lt. Comdr. C. V. Allen
    GILMER   Lt. Comdr. J. S. Horner
    SANDS   Lt. Comdr. L. C. Brogger
    HUMPHREYS   Lt. Comdr. F. D. Schwartz, 4 APDS

LST Group 76.3   Captain J. B. Mallard
    13 LSTS

LCI Group 76.4   Commander H. F. McGee
    20 LCIS

LCT Group 76.5   Lt. Comdr. B. C. Allen, Jr.
    1 APC
    14 LCTS

Destroyer Group 76.6   Captain J. H. Carter
    PERKINS   Lt. Comdr. G. L. Ketchum
    SMITH   Commander R. A. Theobald, Jr.

* See KEY TO ABBREVIATIONS, pp. 463 to 464.

MAHAN	Lt. Comdr. J. T. Smith
LAMSON	Commander P. H. Fitzgerald
MUGFORD	Commander H. G. Corey
DRAYTON	Lt. Comdr. R. S. Craighill, 6 DDS

APC Task Group 76.7—Lt. Comdr. F. J. Leatherman
- 14 APCS
- 9 LCTS
- 2 SCS

Service Group 76.8—Captain R. Dudley

RIGEL (AD)	Captain R. Dudley
SONOMA (AT)	Lieutenant (jg) G. I. Nelson

- 3 LSTS
- 10 SCS
- 5 YMS
- 1 YO

Tarawa, 20 November 1943: CENTRAL PACIFIC FORCE—VICE ADMIRAL RAYMOND A. SPRUANCE

CARRIER FORCE (TF 50)—Rear Adm. C. A. Pownall

Task Force 50.1—Rear Adm. C. A. Pownall

YORKTOWN	Captain J. J. Clark
LEXINGTON	Captain F. B. Stump, 2 CVS
COWPENS	Captain R. P. McConnell, 1 CVL
WASHINGTON	Captain E. Mather
SOUTH DAKOTA	Captain A. E. Smith
ALABAMA	Captain K. F. Durrel, 3 BBS
IZARD	Commander E. K. Swearingen
CHARRETTE	Commander E. S. Carpe
CONNER	Commander W. E. Kaitner
NICHOLAS	Lt. Comdr. R. F. S. Keith
TAYLOR	Commander B. Katz
LA VALLETTE	Lt. Comdr. R. L. Taylor, 6 DDS

Task Force 50.2—Rear Adm. A. W. Radford

ENTERPRISE	Captain G. B. H. Hall, 1 CV
BELLEAU WOOD	Captain A. M. Pride
MONTEREY	Captain L. T. Hundt, 2CVLS
MASSACHUSETTS	Captain T. D. Ruddock
INDIANA	Captain W. F. Fechteler
NORTH CAROLINA	Captain F. P. Thomas, 3 BBS
BOYD	Commander U. S. G. Sharp, Jr.
BRADFORD	Commander R. L. Morris

APPENDIX

BROWN	Lt. Comdr. T. H. Copeman
FLETCHER	Commander R. D. McGinnis
RADFORD	Commander G. E. Griggs
JENKINS	Lt. Comdr. M. Hall, Jr., 6 DDS

Task Force 50.3—Rear Adm. A. E. Montgomery

ESSEX	Captain D. B. Duncan
BUNKER HILL	Captain J. J. Ballentine, 2 CVS
INDEPENDENCE	Captain R. L. Johnson, 1 CVL
CHESTER	Captain F. T. Spellman
PENSACOLA	Captain R. E. Dees
SALT LAKE CITY	Captain L. W. Busbey, Jr., 3 CAS
OAKLAND	Captain W. K. Phillips, 1 CL
BULLARD	Commander B. W. Freund
KIDD	Commander H. G. Moore
CHAUNCEY	Commander M. VanMeter
ERBEN	Commander J. H. Nevins, Jr.
HALE	Commander K. Poehlmann, 5 DDS

Task Force 50.4—Rear Adm. F. C. Sherman

SARATOGA	Captain J. H. Cassady, 1 CV
PRINCETON	Captain G. R. Henderson, 1 CVL
SAN DIEGO	Captain L. J. Hudson
SAN JUAN	Captain G. W. Clark, 2 CLS
WILSON	Lt. Comdr. C. K. Dunkin
STACK	Lt. Comdr. P. K. Sherman
STERETT	Lt. Comdr. F. G. Gould
EDWARDS	Lt. Comdr. P. G. Osler
LAND	Lt. Comdr. H. Payson, Jr., 5 DDS

TASK FORCE 51—Vice Adm. R. A. Spruance

Task Force 51.1—Vice Adm. R. A. Spruance

INDIANAPOLIS (FF)	Captain E. R. Johnson, 1 CA

TASK FORCE 52, NORTHERN ATTACK FORCE—Rear Adm. R. K. Turner

IDAHO	Captain H. D. Clarke
MISSISSIPPI	Captain L. L. Hunter
NEW MEXICO	Captain E. M. Zacharias, 3 OBBS
MINNEAPOLIS	Captain R. W. Bates
SAN FRANCISCO	Captain A. F. France, 2 CAS
LISCOME BAY	Captain I. B. Wiltsie
CORREGIDOR	Captain S. G. Mitchell
CORAL SEA	Captain H. W. Taylor, Jr., 3 CVES
PHELPS	Commander John E. Edwards
DEWEY	Commander J. P. Canty

MACDONOUGH	Lt. Comdr. J. W. Ramey
MAURY	Lt. Comdr. J. W. Koenig
GRIDLEY	Lt. Comdr. J. H. Motes, Jr.
MORRIS	Commander F. T. Williamson
HUGHES	Lt. Comdr. E. B. Rittenhouse
MUSTIN	Commander M. M. Riker
HOEL	Commander W. D. Thomas
FRANKS	Commander N. A. Lidstone
BURNS	Commander D. T. Eller
KIMBERLY	Commander H. Smith
REVENGE	Commander F. F. Sima, 13 DDS

TASK FORCE 53, SOUTHERN ATTACK FORCE—Rear Adm. H. W. Hill

MARYLAND	Captain C. H. Jones
TENNESSEE	Captain R. S. Haggart
COLORADO	Captain W. Granat, 3 OBBS
PORTLAND	Captain A. D. Burhans
BALTIMORE	Captain W. C. Calhoun
NEW ORLEANS	Captain S. R. Shumaker, 3 CAS
MOBILE	Captain C. J. Wheeler
SANTA FE	Captain R. S. Burkey, 2 CLS
SANGAMON	Captain E. P. Moore
SUWANEE	Captain F. W. McMahon
CHENANGO	Captain D. Ketcham
BARNES	Captain G. A. Dussault
NASSAU	Captain S. J. Nicholl, 5 CVES
HARRISON	Commander C. M. Dalton
JOHN RODGERS	Commander H. O. Parish
MCKEE	Commander J. J. Greytock
MURRAY	Commander P. R. Anderson
RINGGOLD	Commander H. Crommelin
SIGSBEE	Commander B. V. Russell
HAZELWOOD	Commander H. Wood, Jr.
BAILEY	Lt. Comdr. M. T. Munger
GANSEVOORT	Lt. Comdr. J. M. Steinbeck
MEADE	Commander J. Munholland
ANDERSON	Commander J. G. Tennent, III
RUSSELL	Commander W. H. McClain
AYLWIN	Commander R. O. Strange
FARRAGUT	Lt. Comdr. E. F. Ferguson
MONAGHAN	Commander P. H. Horn
COTTEN	Commander F. T. Sloat
COWELL	Commander C. W. Parker
HULL	Lt. Comdr. A. L. Young, Jr.
CALDWELL	Commander H. A. Lincoln

APPENDIX

WHITMAN	Lt. Comdr. C. E. Bull
WILEMAN	Lt. Comdr. Aaron F. Beyer, Jr., 21 DDS

Trans Div 4

ZEILIN	Commander T. B. Fitzpatrick
VIRGO	Commander C. H. McLaughlin
ORMSBY	Commander L. Frisco, 3 APAS

Trans Div 6

HARRIS	Commander A. M. VanEaton
HARRY LEE	Commander J. G. Pomeroy
MIDDLETON	Captain S. A. Olsen, USCG, 3 APAS
BELLATRIX	Commander C. A. Joans, 1 AKA

Trans Div 18

J. F. BELL	Captain O. H. Ritchie
FELEND	Captain C. A. Misson
MONROVIA	Commander G. A. Parsons
SHERIDAN	Commander J. J. Mockrish
DOYEN	Commander J. G. McClaughry
HEYWOOD	Commander J. P. Dugan
W. P. BIDDLE	Commander L. F. Brown, 7 APAS
THUBAN	Commander J. C. Campbell, 1 AKA
ASHLAND	Captain C. L. C. Atkeson, 1 LSD
REQUISITE	Lt. Comdr. H. R. Peirce, Jr.
PURSUIT	Lieutenant R. F. Good, 2 AMS
LASALLE	Commander F. C. Fluegel
FRAZIER	Lt. Comdr. E. M. Brown
SCHROEDER	Commander J. T. Bowers, Jr., 3 DDS

TASK FORCE 54, ASSAULT FORCE—Rear Adm. R. K. Turner

PENNSYLVANIA (F)	Captain W. A. Corn, 1 OBB
DALE	Lt. Comdr. C. W. Aldrich
BANCROFT	Lt. Comdr. R. M. Pitts
COGHLAN	Lt. Comdr. B. B. Cheatham, 3 DDS
LE HARDY	Lt. Comdr. J. H. Prause
W. C. MILLER	Lt. Comdr. F. G. Storey, Jr.
C. R. GREER	Lt. Comdr. W. T. Denton
H. C. THOMAS	Lt. Comdr. V. H. Craig, Jr., 4 DES
PRESIDENT POLK	Commander C. J. Ballreich
PRESIDENT MONROE	Captain G. D. Morrison, 2 APS
JUPITER	Commander D. S. Baker, 1 AK
SS YOUNG AMERICA	
SS ISLAND MAIL	
SS CAPE CONSTANTINE	
SS CAPE SAN MARTIN	

SS DASHING WAVE
SS CAPE FEAR
SS ROBIN WENTLY
SS CAPE STEVINS
SS CAPE ISABEL
B. R. HASTINGS
JANE ADDAMS   11 AKS (Civilian)
25 LSTS
11 LCTS

Trans Div 20

LEONARD WOOD	Captain M. O'Neill
NEVILLE	Commander O. R. Swigart
PIERCE	Commander A. R. Ponto
CALVERT	Commander E. J. Sweeney, 4 APAS
ALCYONE	Commander J. B. McVey, 1 AKA
BELLE GROVE	Commander M. Seavy, 1 LSD
HEERMANN	Commander D. M. Agnew
DASHIELL	Commander J. B. McLean, 2 DDS

Carrier Task Force 58, 30 January 1944: REAR ADMIRAL MARC MITSCHER

Task Group 58.1—Rear Adm. J. W. Reeves, Jr.

YORKTOWN (FF)	Captain J. J. Clark
ENTERPRISE (F)	Captain M. B. Gardner, 2 CVS
BELLEAU WOOD	Captain A. M. Pride, 1 CVL
WASHINGTON (F)	Captain E. J. Maher
MASSACHUSETTS	Captain T. D. Ruddock
INDIANA	Captain W. M. Fechteler, 3 BBS
OAKLAND	Captain W. K. Phillips, 1 CL(AA)
C. K. BRONSON (F)	Commander W. S. Veeder
COTTEN	Commander F. T. Sloat
DORTCH	Commander R. C. Young
GATLING	Commander A. F. Richardson
HEALY	Commander J. C. Atkeson
COGSWELL	Commander C. F. Chillingworth, Jr.
CAPERTON	Commander W. J. Miller
KNAPP	Commander F. Virden
INGERSOLL	Commander A. C. Veasey, 9 DDS

Task Group 58.2—Rear Adm. A. E. Montgomery

INTREPID (F)	Captain T. L. Sprague
ESSEX	Captain R. A. Ofstie, 2 CVS
CABOT	Captain M. F. Schoeffel, 1 CVL
SOUTH DAKOTA (F)	Captain A. E. Smith
ALABAMA	Captain F. D. Kirtland

APPENDIX

NORTH CAROLINA	Captain F. P. Thomas, 3 BBS
SAN DIEGO	Captain L. J. Hudson, 1 CL(AA)
OWEN (F)	Commander R. W. Wood
MILLER	Commander T. H. Kobey
THE SULLIVANS	Commander K. M. Gentry
STEPHEN POTTER	Commander C. H. Crichton
HICKOX	Commander W. M. Sweetser
HUNT	Commander H. A. Knoertzer
LEWIS HANCOCK	Commander C. H. Lyman
LANG	Commander H. Payson, Jr.
STERETT	Commander C. J. Stuart
STACK	Lt. Comdr. P. K. Sherman, 10 DDS

Task Group 58.3—Rear Adm. F. C. Sherman

BUNKER HILL (F)	Captain J. J. Ballentine, 1 CV
MONTEREY	Captain L. T. Hundt
COWPENS	Captain R. P. McConnell, 2 CVLS
IOWA (F)	Captain J. L. McCrea
NEW JERSEY	Captain C. F. Holden, 2 BBS
WICHITA	Captain J. J. Mahoney, 1 CA
IZARD (F)	Commander E. K. Van Swearingen
CHARRETTE	Commander E. S. Karpe
CONNER	Commander W. E. Kaitner
BELL	Commander L. C. Petross
BURNS	Commander D. T. Eller
BRADFORD	Commander H. F. Morris
BROWN	Commander T. H. Copeman
COWELL	Commander C. W. Parker
WILSON	Lt. Comdr. C. K. Duncan, 9 DDS

Task Group 58.4—Rear Adm. S. P. Ginder

SARATOGA (F)	Captain J. H. Cassady, 1 CV
PRINCETON	Captain W. H. Buracker
LANGLEY	Captain W. M. Dillon, 2 CVLS
BOSTON	Captain J. H. Carson
BALTIMORE	Captain W. C. Calhoun, 2 CAS
SAN JUAN	Captain G. H. Bahm, 1 CL (AA)
MAURY	Lt. Comdr. J. W. Koenig
CRAVEN	Lt. Comdr. R. L. Fulton
GRIDLEY	Lt. Comdr. J. H. Motes, Jr.
MCCALL	Commander E. L. Foster
DUNLAP	Commander C. Iverson
FANNING	Lt. Comdr. J. C. Bentley
CASE	Commander C. M. Howe, III
CUMMINGS	Commander P. D. Williams, 8 DDS

Kawajalein, Southern Attack Force (T.F. 52), 30 January 1944: REAR ADMIRAL R. K. TURNER

TASK ORGANIZATION

Force Flag
   ROCKY MOUNT   Captain S. F. Patten, 1 AGC

Support Aircraft, T.G. 52.1—Captain H. B. Sallada

Southern Landing Force, T.G. 52.2—Major General C. H. Corlett, USA
   Seventh Infantry Division, plus attached units.
   Southern Garrison Force, Brig. Gen. Gibson, USA
   Southern Base Support Aircraft, Colonel Collar, USA

Channel Island Transport Group, T.G. 52.3—Lt. Comdr. D. K. O'Connor
   MANLEY   Lieutenant R. T. Newell, Jr.
   OVERTON   Lt. Comdr. D. K. O'Connor, 2 APDs

Advance Transport Unit, T.U. 52.5.1—Captain J. B. McGovern
   Transdiv 4—Captain J. B. McGovern
      ZEILIN (F)   Commander J. B. Fitzpatrick
      ORMSBY   Commander L. Frisco
      WINDSOR   Commander D. C. Woodward, 3 APAS
      PRESIDENT POLK   Commander C. J. Ballreich, 1 AP
      VIRGO   Commander C. H. McLaughlin, 1 AKA
      ASHLAND   Captain C. L. C. Atkeson, 1 LSD

   Tractor Unit No. One—Commander R. C. Webb, Jr.
      LST UNIT   8 LSTS
      LCT UNIT (Deck Load) 3 LCTS

Southern Transport Group, T.G. 52.5—Captain H. B. Knowles
   Transdiv 6—Captain T. B. Brittain
      HARRIS (F)   Commander A. M. Van Eaton
      FAYETTE   Captain J. C. Lester
      HARRY LEE   Commander J. G. Pomeroy
      LEEDSTOWN   Commander H. Bye, 4 APAS
      CENTAURUS   Captain G. E. McCabe, 1 AKA
      LINDENWALD   Commander W. H. Weaver, Jr., 1 LSD

   Transdiv 18—Captain H. B. Knowles
      MONROVIA (F)   Commander J. D. Kelsey
      J. F. BELL   Captain O. H. Ritchie
      PIERCE   Captain A. R. Ponto
      FELAND   Commander G. M. Jones, 4 APAS
      THUBAN   Commander J. C. Campbell, 1 AKA
      BELLE GROVE   Commander M. Seavey, 1 LSD

APPENDIX

Tractor Unit No. Two—Commander A. M. Hurst
- LST UNIT — 8 LSTS
- LCT UNIT (Deck Load) — 3 LCTS

Control Group, T.G. 52.6—Commander Coleman
- SC UNIT — 3 SCS
- LCC UNIT — 2 LCCS

Transport Screen, T.G. 52.7—Captain E. M. Thompson
   Advance Transport Screen—Captain E. M. Thompson

JOHN RODGERS (F)	Commander H. O. Parish
HAZELWOOD	Commander Hunter Wood, Jr., 2 DDS

   Southern Transport Screen, T.U. 52.7.2—Captain Crommelin

HAGGARD (F)	Commander D. A. Harris
FRANKS	Commander N. A. Sidstone
SCHROEDER	Commander W. T. Bowers, Jr.
HAILEY	Commander P. H. Brady, 4 DDS
ZANE	Lt. Comdr. W. T. Powell, Jr.
PERRY	Lieutenant I. G. Stubbart, 2 DMSS
SC UNIT	2 SCS

Fire Support Group, T.G. 52.8—Rear Adm. R. C. Giffen
   Fire Support Unit No. One—Commander J. J. Greytak

MCKEE (F)	Commander J. J. Greytak
STEVENS	Lt. Comdr. W. M. Rakow, 2 DDS

   Fire Support Unit No. Two—Rear Adm. R. C. Giffen

MINNEAPOLIS (F)	Captain R. W. Bates
NEW ORLEANS	Captain S. R. Shumaker, 2 CAS
IDAHO	Captain H. D. Clarke
PENNSYLVANIA	Captain W. A. Corn, 2 OBBS
BAILEY	Lt. Comdr. M. T. Munger
FRAZIER	Commander E. M. Brown
MEADE	Commander J. Munholland, 3 DDS

   Fire Support Unit No. Three—Rear Adm. R. C. Giffen

NEW MEXICO (F)	Captain E. M. Zacharias
MISSISSIPPI	Captain L. L. Hunter, 2 OBBS
SAN FRANCISCO	Captain H. E. Overesch, 1 CA
COLAHAN	Commander D. T. Wilber
MURRAY	Commander P. R. Anderson
HARRISON	Commander C. M. Dalton, 3 DDS

   Fire Support Unit No. Four—Commander H. Crommelin

RINGGOLD (F)	Commander T. F. Conley, Jr.

434　　　　　　　　BATTLE REPORT

    SIGSBEE　　　　　　　　Commander B. V. Russell, 2 DDs
    LCI UNIT　　　　　　　　Lt. Comdr. T. Blanchard, 12 LCI(L)s

Carrier Support Group, T.G. 52.9—Rear Adm. R. E. Davison
    MANILA BAY (F)　　　　Captain B. L. Braun
    CORAL SEA　　　　　　　Captain H. W. Taylor, Jr.
    CORREGIDOR　　　　　　Captain R. L. Bowman, 3 CVEs
    BANCROFT　　　　　　　Lt. Comdr. R. M. Pitts
    COGHLAN　　　　　　　 Commander B. B. Cheatham
    CALDWELL　　　　　　　Lt. Comdr. D. R. Robinson
    HALLIGAN　　　　　　　Commander C. E. Cortner, 4 DDs

Mine Sweeping and Hydrographic Group, T.G. 52.10—Comdr. F. F. Sima
    Sweep Unit One—Commander F. F. Sima
    REVENGE　　　　　　　 Commander F. F. Sima
    PURSUIT　　　　　　　 Lieutenant R. F. Good
    REQUISITE　　　　　　 Lt. Comdr. H. R. Pierce, Jr., 3 AMs

    Sweep Unit Two—Lieutenant J. H. Pace
    YMS UNIT　　　　　　　4 YMSs
    LCC　　　　　　　　　 1 LCC

Southern Salvage Unit, T.G. 52.11
    TEKESTA (F)　　　　　　Lieutenant John O. Strickland
    TAWASA　　　　　　　　Lieutenant F. C. Clark
    ARAPAHO　　　　　　　 3 ATs

Kawajalein (Roi-Namur), Northern Attack Force (T.F. 53), 30 January 1944: REAR ADMIRAL R. L. CONOLLY

Force Flagship, 53.1—Captain J. M. Fernald
    APPALACHIAN　　　　　Captain J. M. Fernald, 1 AGC

Transport, 53.2—Captain P. Buchanan
  TransDiv 24—Captain P. Buchanan
    DUPAGE (F)　　　　　　Captain G. M. Wauchope
    WAYNE　　　　　　　　Commander T. V. Cooper
    ELMORE　　　　　　　　Commander D. Harrison
    DOYEN　　　　　　　　 Commander J. G. McClaughry, 4 APAs
    AQUARIUS　　　　　　　Captain R. V. Marion, 1 AKA

  TransDiv 26—Captain A. D. Blackledge
    CALLAWAY (F)　　　　　Captain D. C. McNeil, USCG
    SUMTER　　　　　　　　Captain T. G. Haff
    WARREN　　　　　　　　Commander W. A. McHale
    BIDDLE　　　　　　　　Lieutenant R. H. Hopkins, 4 APAs

APPENDIX

ALMAACK	Lt. Comdr. C. O. Hicks, 1 AKA
EPPING FOREST	Commander L. Martin, 1 LSD

TransDiv 28—Captain H. C. Flanagan

BOLIVAR (F)	Captain R. P. Wadell, 1 AP
SHERIDAN	Commander J. "J." Mockrish
CALVERT	Commander E. J. Sweeney
LASALLE	Commander F. C. Fluegel, 3 APAS
ALCYONE	Commander J. B. McVey, 1 AKA
GUSTON HALL	Commander D. E. Collins, 1 LSD

Raider Unit—Lt. Comdr. E. J. Farley

SCHLEY	Lieutenant C. H. Myers, 1 APD

Transport Screen—Captain J. G. Coward

REMEY	Commander R. P. Fiala
MACDONOUGH	Commander J. W. Ramey
HUGHES	Lt. Comdr. E. B. Rittenhouse
ELLET	Commander T. C. Phifer
FLETCHER	Commander R. D. McGinnis, 5 DDS
STANSBURY	Lt. Comdr. D. M. Granstrom
HAMILTON	Commander R. R. Sampson, 2 DMSS

Minesweepers, 53.3—Commander W. R. Loud
  DMS Unit—Lt. Comdr. R. H. Thomas

PALMER	Lt. Comdr. R. H. Thomas, 1 DMS

AM Unit—Commander R. S. Moore

CHIEF (F)	Lt. Comdr. J. M. Wyckoff
HEED	Lieutenant M. Dent, Jr.
MOTIVE	Lt. Comdr. G. W. Lundgren, 3 AMS

  YMS Unit—4 YMSS

Northern Landing Force, 53.4—Major Gen. H. Schmidt, USMC
  FOURTH Marine Division (Reinforced)

Northern Support Group, 53.5—Rear Adm. J. B. Oldendorf
  Battleships

TENNESSEE (F)	Captain R. S. Haggart
MARYLAND	Captain H. J. Ray
COLORADO	Captain Wm. Granat, 3 OBBS

  Cruisers—Rear Adm. L. T. DuBose

SANTA FE (F)	Captain J. Wright
LOUISVILLE	Captain S. H. Hurt, 2 CAS
INDIANAPOLIS	Captain E. R. Johnson
MOBILE	Captain C. J. Wheeler
BILOXI	Captain D. M. McGurl, 3 CLS

Screen—Captain E. A. Solomons

MORRIS (F)	Commander G. L. Caswell
ANDERSON	Commander J. G. Tennent, III
MUSTIN	Commander M. M. Riker
RUSSELL	Lt. Comdr. L. R. Miller
PORTERFIELD	Commander J. C. Woelfel
HARADEN	Commander H. C. Allan, Jr.
JOHNSTON	Commander E. E. Evans
HOPEWELL	Commander C. C. Shute
PHELPS	Captain E. R. McLean, Jr., 9 DDS

Carrier Group, 53.6.1—Rear Adm. V. H. Ragsdale
CarDiv 22—Rear Adm. V. H. Ragsdale

SANGAMON	Captain E. P. Moore
SUWANEE	Captain F. W. McMahon
CHENANGO	Captain D. (n) Ketcham, 3 CVES

Carrier Screen—Captain I. H. Nunn

FARRAGUT	Captain I. H. Nunn
MONAGHAN	Commander P. H. Horn
DALE	Commander C. W. Aldrich, 3 DDS

Initial Tractor Group, 53.7—Captain A. J. Robertson

LST Unit	Captain A. J. Robertson, 9 LSTS

Destroyer—Commander R. L. Taylor

LA VALLETTE	Commander R. L. Taylor, 1 DD
SC Unit	Lieutenant W. C. Coughenour, 3 SCS
LCI Unit	Commander M. J. Malanaphy, 12 LCIS

Reserve Tractor Group, 53.8—Captain J. S. Lillard

LST Unit	Captain J. S. Lillard, 8 LSTS

Destroyer—Commander R. O. Strange

AYLWIN	Commander P. O. Strange, 1 DD
SC Unit	2 SCS

Northern Salvage Group, 53.12—Lt. Comdr. H. O. Foss

MATACO	Lieutenant W. G. Baker
CHICKASAW	Lieutenant (jg) G. W. McClead
MOLALA	Lieutenant R. L. Ward, 3 ATS

Neutralization Group, 30 January 1944: REAR ADMIRAL ERNEST G. SMALL

TASK GROUP 50.15

Taroa Neutralization Unit

CHESTER (F)	Captain F. T. Spellman
PENSACOLA	Captain R. E. Dees, 2 CAS

APPENDIX

ERBEN   Captain J. T. Bottom, Jr.
HALE   Commander K. F. Poehlmann
BLACK   Commander J. Maginnis, 3 DDS

Wotje Neutralization Unit
SALT LAKE CITY (F)   Captain L. W. Busbey, Jr., 1 CA
ABBOTT   Commander M. E. Dornin
WALER   Captain J. E. Hurff
KIDD   Commander A. B. Roby, 3 DDS

Carrier Unit
NASSAU (F)   Captain S. J. Michael
NATOMA BAY   Captain H. L. Meadow, 2 CVES
BULLARD   Commander C. E. Carroll
CHAUNCEY   Lt. Comdr. L. C. Conwell, 2 DDS
PREBLE   Commander F. S. Steinke
RAMSAY   Lt. Comdr. R. H. Holmes, 2 DMS

MAJURO TASK GROUP 51.2—REAR ADMIRAL HARRY W. HILL
PORTLAND   Captain A. D. Burhans, 1 CA
NASSAU   Captain S. J. Michael
NATOMA BAY   Captain H. L. Meadow, 2 CVES
BULLARD   Commander C. E. Carroll
BLACK   Commander J. Maginnis
KIDD   Commander A. B. Roby
CHAUNCEY   Lt. Comdr. L. C. Conwell, 4 DDS
CHANDLER   Lt. Comdr. H. L. Thompson, Jr., 1 DMS
SAGE   Lieutenant F. K. Zinn
ORACLE   Lt. Comdr. J. R. Fels, 2 AMS
CAMBRIA   Captain C. W. Dean, USCG, 1 APA
KANE   Lieutenant F. M. Christiansen, 1 APD
LST 482   Lieutenant R. E. Eddy, 1 LST

Eniwetok Expeditionary Group, 17 February 1944: REAR ADMIRAL HARRY W. HILL

Flagship Group—Captain C. W. Dean, USCG
CAMBRIA, 1 APA

Transport Group—Captain C. A. Misson
  TransDiv 20
  LEONARD WOOD (F)   PRESIDENT MONROE, 1 AP
  ARTHUR MIDDLETON   ELECTRA, 1 AKA
  HEYWOOD, 3 APAS

  TransDiv 30
  CUSTER (F)   MERCURY, 1 AK

NEVILLE, 2 APAS   ASHLAND, 1 LSD
WHARTON, 1 AP

Scout Detachment
KANE   SCHLEY, 2 APDS

Control Unit
SC 539
SC 1066, 2 SCS   LST Unit, 9 LSTS
                         LCI Unit, 6 LCI(L)s

Transport Screen
HALL   MONAGHAN
HAZELWOOD   FARRAGUT
PHELPS   HULL
AYLWIN   DEWEY
DALE   MACDONOUGH, 10 DDS

Expeditionary Troops—Brig. Gen. T. E. Watson, USMC
  Landing Forces:
    22nd Marine Regiment (reinforced)
    106th Infantry Regiment (reinforced)
    5th Amphibious Corps, Reconnaissance Co.
    Co. "D," 4th Marine Tank Bn. (Scout)
    Provisional Amphibian Tractor Bn., 7th Infantry Division
    Co. "A," 780th Amphibian Tank Bn., 7th Infantry Division
    Provisional DUKW Battery, 7th Infantry Division

Fire Support Group—Rear Admiral J. B. Oldendorf
  Fire Support Section 1
  COLORADO, 1 OBB   HAILEY
  LOUISVILLE, 1 CA   JOHNSTON, 3 DDS
  HAGGARD

  Fire Support Section 2
  TENNESSEE   MCCORD
  PENNSYLVANIA, 2 BBS   HEERMAN, 2 DDS

  Fire Support Section 3
  PORTLAND   TRATHEN
  INDIANAPOLIS, 2 CAS   HOEL, 2 DDS

Escort Carrier Group—Rear Adm. V. H. Ragsdale
  SANGAMON (F)   HUGHES
  SUWANNEE   MUSTIN
  CHENANGO, 3 CVES   ELLET, 4 DDS
  MORRIS

APPENDIX

Carrier Task Group 4—Rear Adm. S. P. Ginder
    SARATOGA (F), 1 CV
    PRINCETON
    LANGLEY, 2 CVLS
    CANBERRA (F)
    BOSTON, 2 CAS
    SAN JUAN, 1 CL(AA)
    MAURY
    CRAVEN
    GRIDLEY
    MCCALL
    DUNLAP
    FANNING
    CASE
    CUMMINGS, 8 DDS

Minesweeping Group
    Northern Minesweeping Unit
        CHANDLER
        ZANE, 2 DMSS
        REQUISITE, 1 AM

    Southern Minesweeping Unit
        ORACLE
        SAGE, 2 AMS
        YMS 262
        YMS 383, 2 YMSS

Service Group
    CHICKASAW
    MOLALA, 2 ATS
    GAZELLE
    GEMSBOK, 2 XAOS

AT Group
    MILLER, 1 DD
    TAWASA
    TEKESTA, 2 ATS

Tanahmerah Bay—Humboldt Bay—Aitape, 22 April 1944

Task Force 77—Rear Adm. D. E. Barbey
    BLUE RIDGE   Commander L. R. McDowell, 1 AGC

Task Group 77.1, Western Attack Force—Rear Adm. D. E. Barbey
    SWANSON (F)   Lt. Comdr. J. C. Snider, 1 DD

Transports—Captain P. S. Stevens
    H. T. ALLEN   Captain J. Meyer
    MANOORA   Captain A. P. Cousin, RANR (S)
    KANIMBLA   Commander N. H. Shaw, 3 APAS
    CARTER HALL   Lt. Comdr. F. Harris, 1 LSD
    TRIANGULUM   Lt. Comdr. R. E. Loughborough, 1 AK

LCIs—Lt. Comdr. J. P. Hurndall
    15 LCIS

LSTs—Commander T. C. Green
    7 LSTS

Destroyers—Commander W. S. Veeder

HOBBY	Commander G. W. Pressey
NICHOLSON	Commander W. W. Vanous
WILKES	Commander F. Wolsieffer
GRAYSON	Lt. Comdr. W. V. Pratt
GILLESPIE	Commander J. S. Fahy
KALK	Lt. Comdr. H. W. Fuller, 6 DDS

Special Service Vessels—Captain N. D. Brantley

RESERVE	Lt. Comdr. G. A. Keith, RANVR, 1 AT
2 SCS	
1 LCI	
2 YMSS	

Beachmaster Unit No. 3—Lt. Comdr. E. R. Halloran

Task Group 77.2, Central Attack Group—Rear Adm. W. M. Fechteler

REID (F)	Commander S. A. McCornock, 1 DD

Transports—Commander A. V. Knight, RANR

WESTRALIA	Commander A. V. Knight, RANR, 1 APA
GUNSTON HALL	Commander D. E. Collins, 1 LSD
GANYMEDE	Lt. Comdr. G. H. Melichar, 1 AK
HUMPHREYS	Lt. Comdr. F. D. Schwartz
BROOKS	Lt. Comdr. C. V. Allen
SANDS	Lt. Comdr. L. C. Brogger
GILMER	Lt. Comdr. J. S. Horner
HERBERT	Lt. Comdr. J. N. Ferguson, Jr., 5 APDS

LCIs—Commander H. F. McGee

    16 LCIS

LSTs—Captain R. M. Scruggs

    7 LSTS

Destroyers—Captain R. F. Stout

STEVENSON	Commander F. E. Wilson
STOCKTON	Lt. Comdr. W. W. Stark, Jr.
THORN	Commander E. Brumby
ROE	Commander F. S. Stich
WELLES	Commander D. M. Coffee
RADFORD	Commander G. E. Griggs
TAYLOR	Commander N. J. Frank, Jr., 7 DDS

Special Service Vessels—Captain B. Anderson

HOVEY	Lieutenant A. A. Clark, III
LONG	Lt. Comdr. R. V. Wheeler, Jr., 2 DMSS

APPENDIX

SONOMA   Lieutenant (jg) G. I. Nelson, 1 AT
2 LCIS
2 YMSS
2 SCS

Beach Master Unit No. 4—Lieutenant (jg) E. J. Zinzer

Task Group 77.3, Eastern Attack Group—Captain A. G. Noble

LAVALLETTE (F)	Commander W. Thompson, 1 DD

Transports—Commander D. L. Mattie

KILTY	Lieutenant L. G. Benson
WARD	Lt. Comdr. F. H. Lemly, Jr.
CROSBY	Lt. Comdr. W. E. Sims
DICKENSON	Lt. Comdr. J. R. Cain, Jr.
TALBOT	Lt. Comdr. C. C. Morgan
SCHLEY	Lt. Comdr. E. T. Farley
KANE	Lieutenant F. M. Christiansen
DENT	Commander R. A. Wilhelm
NOA	Lt. Comdr. H. W. Bond, 9 APDS
EPPING FOREST	Lt. Comdr. L. Martin, 1 LSD
ETAMIN	Lt. Comdr. G. W. Stedman, 1 AK

LSTs—Lt. Comdr. D. M. Baker
7 LSTS

Destroyers—Captain W. D. Chandler

NICHOLAS (F)	Commander R. T. S. Keith
O'BANNON	Commander R. W. Smith
JENKINS	Commander P. D. Gallery
HOPEWELL	Commander C. C. Shute
HOWORTH	Commander E. S. Burns, 5 DDS

Special Service Vessels—Captain J. W. Jamison

HAMILTON	Commander R. R. Sampson
PERRY	Lieutenant I. G. Stubbart, 2 DMSS
CHETCO	Lieutenant (jg) R. E. Gill
4 SCS	
2 YMSS	

Beachmaster Unit No. 5—Lieutenant (jg) M. H. Williams

Task Force 78, Escort Carrier Force—Rear Adm. R. E. Davidson

Task Group 78.1—Rear Adm. V. H. Ragsdale

SANGAMON	Captain M. E. Browder
SUWANEE	Captain W. D. Johnson
CHENANGO	Captain D. Ketcham
SANTEE	Captain H. F. Fick, 4 CVES

Destroyers

MORRIS	Commander G. L. Caswell
ANDERSON	Lt. Comdr. J. F. Murdock
HUGHES	Lt. Comdr. E. B. Rittenhouse
MUSTIN	Commander T. H. Tonseth
RUSSELL	Lt. Comdr. L. R. Miller
ELLET	Lt. Comdr. E. C. Rider
LANSDOWNE	Lt. Comdr. W. S. Maddox
LARDNER	Lt. Comdr. O. C. Schatz, 8 DDs

Task Group 78.2—Rear Adm. R. E. Davison

NATOMA BAY	Captain H. L. Meadow
CORAL SEA	Captain H. W. Taylor
(later changed to ANZIO)	
CORREGIDOR	Captain R. L. Bowman
MANILA BAY	Captain B. L. Braun, 4 CVEs

Destroyers

ERBEN	Lt. Comdr. M. Slayton
WALKER	Commander H. E. Townsend
HALE	Commander D. W. Wilson
ABBOT	Commander M. E. Dornin
BULLARD	Commander B. W. Freund
KIDD	Commander A. B. Roby
BLACK	Lt. Comdr. E. R. King
CHAUNCEY	Lt. Comdr. L. C. Conwell
STEMBEL	Commander W. L. Tagg, 9 DDs

Task Force 74, Covering Force—Rear Adm. V. A. C. Crutchley, RN

AUSTRALIA	Captain H. B. Farncomb, RAN
SHROPSHIRE	Captain J. H. Collins, RAN, 2 CAs
WARRAMUNGA	Captain E. F. V. Dechaineaux, RAN
ARUNTA	Commander A. E. Buchanan, RAN
AMMEN	Commander H. Williams, Jr.
MULLANY	Commander B. J. Mullaney, 4 DDs

Task Force 75, Covering Force—Rear Adm. R. S. Berkey

PHOENIX	Captain J. H. Duncan
BOISE	Captain J. F. Roberts
NASHVILLE	Captain C. E. Coney, 3 CLs
HUTCHINS	Commander C. B. Laning
BEALE	Commander J. B. Cochran
BACHE	Lt. Commander R. C. Morton
DALY	Commander R. G. Visser
ABNER READ	Commander T. B. Hutchins, III
BUSH	Commander T. A. Smith, 6 DDs

APPENDIX

Carrier Task Force 58, June 1944

TASK FORCE 58—Vice Adm. Marc. A. Mitscher

Task Group 58.1—Rear Adm. J. J. Clark

HORNET (F)	Captain W. D. Sample
YORKTOWN	Captain R. E. Jennings, 2 CVS
BELLEAU WOOD	Captain J. Perry
BATAAN	Captain V. H. Schaeffer, 2 CVLS

CruDiv 10—Rear Adm. L. H. Thebaud

BOSTON (F)	Captain E. E. Herrmann
BALTIMORE	Captain W. C. Calhoun
CANBERRA	Captain A. R. Early, 3 CAS
OAKLAND	Captain W. K. Phillips, 1 CL(AA)

DesRon 46—Captain C. F. Espe

IZARD (F)	Commander M. T. Dayton
CHARRETTE	Lt. Comdr. G. P. Joyce
CONNER	Commander W. E. Kaitner
BELL	Lt. Comdr. J. S. C. Gabbert
BURNS	Commander D. T. Eller
BOYD (F)	Commander U. S. Sharp, Jr.
BRADFORD	Commander R. L. Morris
BROWN	Commander T. H. Copeman
COWELL	Commander C. W. Parker, 9 DDS

DesDiv 11—Captain E. G. Fullinwider

MAURY	Lt. Comdr. J. W. Koening
CRAVEN	Lt. Comdr. R. L. Fulton
GRIDLEY	Commander P. D. Quirk
HELM	Lt. Comdr. S. K. Santmyers
MCCALL	Lt. Comdr. J. B. Carroll, 5 DDS

Task Group 58.2—Rear Adm. A. E. Montgomery

BUNKER HILL (F)	Captain T. P. Jeter
WASP	Captain C. A. F. Sprague, 2 CVS
MONTEREY	Captain S. H. Ingersoll
CABOT	Captain S. J. Michael, 2 CVLS
SAN JUAN	Captain J. F. Donovan, 1 CL(AA)

CruDiv 13—Rear Adm. L. T. DuBose

SANTA FE	Captain J. Wright
MOBILE	Captain C. J. Wheeler
BILOXI	Captain D. M. McGurl, 3 CLS

DesRon 52—Captain G. R. Cooper

OWEN (SF)	Commander R. W. Wood

MILLER	Commander T. H. Kobey
THE SULLIVANS	Commander K. M. Gentry
STEPHEN POTTER	Commander L. W. Pancoast
TINGEY	Commander J. O. Miner
HICKOX	Lt. Comdr. J. H. Wesson
HUNT	Commander H. A. Knoertzer
LEWIS HANCOCK	Commander W. M. Searles
MARSHALL	Commander J. D. McKinney, 9 DDS

DesDiv 1

DEWEY (F)	Lt. Comdr. R. G. Copeland
HULL	Lt. Comdr. C. W. Cansolvo
MACDONOUGH	Commander J. W. Ramey, 3 DDS

Task Group 58.3—Rear Adm. J. W. Reeves, Jr.

ENTERPRISE (F)	Captain C. D. Glover
LEXINGTON (FF)	Captain E. W. Litch, 2 CVS
SAN JACINTO	Captain H. M. Martin
PRINCETON	Captain W. H. Buracker, 2 CVLS
INDIANAPOLIS (FFF)	Captain E. R. Johnson, 1 CA
RENO	Captain R. C. Alexander, 1 CL(AA)

CruDiv 12—Rear Adm. R. W. Hayler

MONTPELIER	Captain H. D. Hoffman
CLEVELAND	Captain A. G. Shepard
BIRMINGHAM	Captain T. B. Inglis, 3 CLS

DesRon 50—Commander C. F. Chillingworth, Jr.

C. K. BRONSON (SF)	Commander G. Scull
COTTEN	Commander F. T. Sloat
DORTCH	Commander R. C. Young
GATLING	Commander A. F. Richardson
HEALY	Commander J. C. Atkeson
COGSWELL (F)	Commander H. T. Devtermann
CAPERTON	Commander W. J. Miller
INGERSOLL	Commander A. C. Veasey
KNAPP	Commander F. Virden, 9 DDS

DesDiv 90

ANTHONY (F)	Lt. Comdr. C. J. Van Arsdall, Jr.
WADSWORTH	Commander J. F. Walsh
TERRY	Lt. Comdr. J. M. Lee
BRAINE	Commander W. W. Fitts, 4 DDS

Task Group 58.4—Rear Adm. W. K. Harrill

ESSEX (F)	Captain R. A. Ofstie, 1 CV

APPENDIX

LANGLEY	Captain W. M. Dillon
COWPENS	Captain H. W. Taylor, Jr., 2 CVLS
SAN DIEGO	Captain W. E. A. Mullan, 1 CL(AA)

CruDiv 14—Rear Adm. W. D. Baker

VINCENNES	Captain A. D. Brown
HOUSTON	Captain W. W. Behrens
MIAMI	Captain J. G. Crawford, 3 CLS

DesRon 12—Captain W. P. Burford

LANSDOWNE	Lt. Comdr. W. S. Maddox
LARDNER	Lt. Comdr. J. D. Parker
MCCALLA	Lt. Comdr. E. K. Jones, 3 DDS

ComdesDiv 4—Commander J. L. Melgaard

LANG	Commander H. Payson, Jr.
STERETT	Lt. Comdr. F. J. Blouin
WILSON	Lt. Comdr. C. J. MacKenzie
CASE	Lt. Comdr. R. S. Willey
ELLET	Lt. Comdr. E. C. Rider, 5 DDS

DesRon 23—Captain T. B. Dugan

CHARLES F. AUSBURNE (SF)	Lt. Comdr. H. W. Baker
STANLY	Lt. Comdr. J. B. Morland
DYSON	Lt. Comdr. J. D. Babb
CONVERSE (F)	Commander J. B. Colwell
SPENCE	Lt. Comdr. J. F. Andrea
THATCHER	Commander L. R. Lampman, 6 DDS

Battle Line Task Group 58.7—Vice Adm. W. A. Lee, Jr.

BatDiv 6—Vice Adm W. A. Lee, Jr.

WASHINGTON (F)	Captain T. R. Cooley
NORTH CAROLINA	Captain F. P. Thomas, 2 BBS

BatDiv 7—Rear Adm. O. M. Hustvedt

IOWA (F)	Captain J. L. McCrea
NEW JERSEY	Captain C. F. Holden, 2 BBS

BatDiv 8—Rear Adm. G. B. Davis

INDIANA (F)	Captain T. J. Keliher, Jr., 1 BB

BatDiv 9—Rear Adm. E. W. Hanson

SOUTH DAKOTA (F)	Captain R. S. Riggs
ALABAMA	Captain F. D. Kirtland, 2 BBS

CruDiv 6—Rear Adm. C. T. Joy

WICHITA	Captain D. A. Spencer

MINNEAPOLIS	Captain H. B. Slocum
NEW ORLEANS	Captain J. E. Hurff
SAN FRANCISCO	Captain H. E. Overesch, 4 CAS

DesDiv 12

MUGFORD (F)	Lt. Comdr. M. A. Shellabarger
CONYNGHAM	Lt. Comdr. B. Taylor
PATTERSON	Lt. Comdr. A. F. White
BAGLEY	Commander W. H. Shea, Jr.
SELFRIDGE	Lt. Comdr. L. L. Snider, 5 DDS

Desdiv 89—Commander E. B. Taylor

HALFORD (F)	Lt. Comdr. R. J. Hardy
GUEST	Lt. Comdr. M. G. Kennedy
BENNETT	Lt. Comdr. P. F. Hauck
FULLAM	Commander W. D. Kelly
HUDSON	Lt. Comdr. R. R. Pratt, 5 DDS

DesDiv 106—Commander T. Burrows

YARNALL (F)	Commander B. F. Tompkins
TWINING	Commander E. K. Wakefield
STOCKHAM	Commander E. P. Holmes
MONSSEN	Commander C. K. Bergin, 4 DDS

Saipan, 14 June 1944: BOMBARDMENT GROUPS

FIRE SUPPORT GROUP ONE—Rear Adm. J. B. Oldendorf

TENNESSEE	Captain A. D. Mayer
CALIFORNIA	Captain H. P. Burnett, 2 OBBS
INDIANAPOLIS	Captain E. R. Johnson, 1 CA
BIRMINGHAM	Captain T. B. Inglis, 1 CL
REMEY	Commander R. P. Fiala
WADLEIGH	Commander W. C. Winn
NORMAN SCOTT	Commander S. C. Owens
MERTZ	Commander W. S. Estabrook, Jr., 4 DDS

Fire Support Unit Two—Commander P. H. Fitzgerald

ROBINSON	Commander E. B. Grantham, Jr.
BAILEY	Commander M. T. Munger
ALBERT W. GRANT	Commander T. A. Nisewaner, 3 DDS

Fire Support Unit Three—Captain H. B. Jarrett

HALSEY POWELL	Commander W. T. McGarry
COGHLAN	Lt. Comdr. B. B. Cheatham
MONSSEN	Commander B. A. Fuetsch, 3 DDS

Fire Support Unit Four—Rear Adm. J. B. Oldendorf

LOUISVILLE (F)	Captain S. H. Hurt, 1 CA

APPENDIX

MARYLAND	Captain H. J. Ray
COLORADO	Captain W. Granat, 2 OBBS
MCDERMUT	Lt. Comdr. C. B. Jennings
MCGOWAN	Commander W. R. Cox
MELVIN	Commander W. R. Edsall
MCNAIR	Commander M. L. McCullough, Jr., 4 DDS

Fire Support Unit Five—Rear Adm. R. W. Hayler

MONTPELIER	Captain H. D. Hoffman
CLEVELAND	Captain A. G. Shepard, 2 CLS
YARNALL	Commander T. Burrowes
TWINING	Commander E. K. Wakefield
STOCKHAM	Commander E. P. Holmes, 3 DDS

FIRE SUPPORT GROUP TWO—Rear Adm. W. L. Ainsworth

Fire Support Unit Six—Rear Adm. Ainsworth

HONOLULU (F)	Captain H. R. Thurber, 1 CL
PENNSYLVANIA	Captain C. F. Martin
IDAHO	Captain H. D. Clarke, 2 OBBS
ANTHONY	Commander B. VanMater
WADSWORTH	Commander J. F. Walsh
HUDSON	Lt. Comdr. R. R. Pratt, 3 DDS
DICKERSON	Lt. Comdr. J. R. Cain, Jr., 1 APD
HOGAN	Lt. Comdr. J. P. Conway, 1 DMS
WILLIAMSON	Lt. Comdr. J. Pridmore, 1 AVD

Fire Support Unit Seven—Rear Adm. G. L. Weyler

NEW MEXICO (F)	Captain E. M. Zacharias, 1 OBB
MINNEAPOLIS	Captain H. B. Slocum
SAN FRANCISCO	Captain H. E. Overesch, 2 CAS
HALFORD	Commander E. B. Taylor
TERRY	Lt. Comdr. J. M. Lee
BRAINE	Commander W. W. Fitts, 3 DDS
TALBOT	Lt. Comdr. C. C. Morgan, 1 APD
STANSBURY	Lt. Comdr. D. M. Granstrom, 1 DMS

Fire Support Unit Eight—Rear Adm. C. T. Joy

WICHITA (F)	Captain D. A. Spencer
NEW ORLEANS	Captain J. E. Hurff, 2 CAS
ST. LOUIS	Captain R. H. Roberts, 1 CL
GUEST	Lt. Comdr. M. G. Kennedy
BENNETT	Lt. Comdr. P. F. Hauck
FULLAM	Commander W. D. Kelly, 3 DDS

CARRIER SUPPORT GROUP ONE—Rear Adm. G. F. Bogan
Carrier Unit One—Rear Adm. Bogan

FANSHAW BAY (GF)	Captain D. P. Johnson
MIDWAY	Captain F. J. McKenna, 2 CVEs
CASSIN YOUNG	Commander E. T. Schreiber
IRWIN	Commander D. B. Miller
ROSE	Commander B. Coe, 3 DDs

Carrier Unit Two—Captain O. A. Weller

WHITE PLAINS (F)	Commander D. J. Sullivan
KALININ BAY	Captain C. R. Brown, 2 CVEs
PORTERFIELD (SF)	Lt. Comdr. D. W. Wulzen
CALLAGHAN	Commander F. J. Johnson
LONGSHAW	Commander R. H. Speck, 3 DDs

CARRIER SUPPORT GROUP TWO—Rear Adm. H. B. Sallada

Carrier Unit Three—Rear Adm. Sallada

KITKUM BAY (F)	Captain J. P. Whitney
GAMBIER BAY	Captain H. H. Goodwin, 2 CVEs
LAWS (DF)	Commander L. O. Wood
MORRISON	Commander W. H. Price
BENHAM	Commander F. S. Keller, 3 DDs

Carrier Unit Four—Rear Adm. F. B. Stump

CORREGIDOR (F)	Captain R. L. Bowman
CORAL SEA	Commander R. W. Watson, 2 CVEs
BULLARD (F)	Commander Bernard W. Freund
KIDD	Commander A. B. Roby
CHAUNCEY	Lt. Comdr. L. C. Conwell, 3 DDs

Transport Screen—Captain R. E. Libby

NEWCOMB (SF)	Commander L. B. Cook
BENNION (FD)	Commander J. W. Cooper
HEYWOOD L. EDWARDS	Commander J. W. Boulware
BRYANT (FD)	Commander P. L. High
PRICHETT (FD)	Commander C. T. Caufield
PHILIP	Lt. Comdr. J. D. Rutter, Jr.
CONY	Lt. Comdr. A. W. Moore
MUGFORD	Lt. Comdr. M. A. Shellabarger
SELFRIDGE	Lt. Comdr. L. L. Snider
RALPH TALBOT	Lt. Comdr. W. S. Brown
PATTERSON	Lt. Comdr. A. F. White
BAGLEY	Commander W. H. Shea, Jr.
PHELPS	Lt. Comdr. D. L. Martineau
SHAW	Commander R. H. Phillips
RENSHAW	Commander J. A. Lark, 15 DDs
KANE	Lieutenant F. M. Christiansen, 1 APD
4 PCs	

APPENDIX

Marianas (Saipan), 15 June 1944, Western Landing Group (T.G. 52.2):
REAR ADM. H. W. HILL

TASK ORGANIZATION
Group Flagship
    CAMBRIA   Captain C. W. Dean, USCG, 1 APA

Northern Landing Force—Lt. Gen. H. M. Smith, USMC
    Corps Troops
    Second Marine Division, plus Attached Units—Major Gen. T. Watson
    Fourth Marine Division, plus Attached Units—Major Gen. H. Schmidt

Transport Group ABLE—Captain H. B. Knowles
    TransDiv 10—Captain G. D. Morrison

CLAY (F)	Captain W. E. Abdill
NEVILLE	Captain B. Bartlett
MIDDLETON	Captain S. A. Olsen, USCG
FELAND	Lt. Comdr. M. A. MacPhee, 4 APAS
ALHENA	Commander M. D. Sylvester, 1 AKA
JUPITER	Lt. Comdr. T. A. Whitaker
HERCULES	Commander W. H. Turnquist, 2 AKS

    TransDiv 18—Captain H. B. Knowles

MONROVIA (F)	Commander J. D. Kelsey
FUNSTON	Captain J. E. Murphy
CAMBRIA	Captain C. W. Dean, USCG, 3 APAS
WARHAWK	Commander S. H. Thompson, 1 AP
ALCYONE	Commander H. P. Knickerbocker, 1 AKA
LINDENWALD	Commander W. H. Weaver, Jr., 1 LSD

    TransDiv 28—Captain H. C. Flanagan

BOLIVAR (F)	Commander R. P. Waddell
DOYEN	Commander J. G. McClaughry
SHERIDAN	Commander H. E. Mockrish, 3 APAS
COMET	Lt. Comdr. T. C. Fonda, 1 AP
ELECTRA	Commander C. S. Beightler, 1 AKA
OAK HILL	Commander C. A. Peterson, 1 LSD

    SECOND *Marine Division Landing Force*—Major Gen. T. E. Watson, USMC

    SECOND Marine Division, plus Attached Units

Transport Group BAKER, 52.4—Captain D. W. Loomis
    TransDiv 20—Captain D. W. Loomis

LEONARD WOOD (F)	Captain H. C. Perkins
PIERCE	Captain F. M. Adams

O'HARA	Commander E. W. Irish, 3 APAS
LASALLE	Commander F. C. Fluegel, 1 AP
THUBAN	Commander J. C. Campbell, 1 AKA
ASHLAND	Lt. Comdr. W. A. Caughey, 1 LSD

TransDiv 26—Captain R. E. Hanson

CALLAWAY (F)	Captain D. C. McNeil
SUMTER	Captain T. G. Haff
LEON	Captain B. B. Adell, 3 APAS
STORM KING	Captain H. B. Krick, 1 AP
ALMAACK	Lt. Comdr. C. O. Hicks, 1 AKA
WHITE MARSH	Commander G. H. Eppelman
BELLE GROVE	Commander M. Seavy, 2 LSDS

TransDiv 30—Captain C. A. Misson

KNOX (F)	Commander J. H. Brady
CALVERT	Commander E. J. Sweeney
FULLER	Commander N. Pigman, 3 APAS
JOHN LAND	Commander F. A. Graf
GEORGE F. ELLIOTT	Commander A. J. Couble, 2 APS
BELLATRIX	Commander E. J. Anderson, 1 AKA

Marianas (Saipan), 15 June 1944: COMMANDER R. S. MOORE

Minesweeping Group

Unit One—Commander W. R. Loud

HOPKINS (SF)	Lieutenant D. P. Payne
PERRY	Lieutenant W. N. Lindsay, Jr.
LONG	Lieutenant S. Chaplan
HAMILTON	Lt. Comdr. J. Claque, 4 DMSS

Unit Two—Lt. Comdr. H. L. Thompson, Jr.

CHANDLER (F)	Lt. Comdr. H. L. Thompson, Jr.
ZANE	Lt. Comdr. W. T. Powell, Jr.
PALMER	Lieutenant W. E. McGuire
HOWARD	Lieutenant O. F. Salvia, 4 DMSS

Unit Three—Commander R. S. Moore

CHIEF (SF)	Lt. Comdr. J. M. Wyckoff
CHAMPION	Lt. Comdr. J. H. Howard, Jr.
HERALD	Lieutenant E. P. Dietrich, 3 AMS

Unit Four—Lt. Comdr. J. R. Fels

ORACLE (F)	Lt. Comdr. J. R. Fels
MOTIVE	Lt. Comdr. G. W. Lundgren
HEED	Lieutenant M. Dent, Jr.

APPENDIX

Unit Five—Lt. Comdr. M. T. Lambert, Jr.
YMS Unit—3 YMSs
Unit Six—Lieutenant C. A. Bowes
YMS Unit—6 YMSs
Mobile Hydrographic Unit—Commander A. D. Sanders
YMS Unit—2 YMSs
LCC Unit—2 LCCs

Saipan

List of submarines employed in the strategic area surrounding the Marianas from June 12 until June 22, 1944.

Bonin Island Area:

PLUNGER	Lt. Comdr. E. J. Fahy
GAR	Lt. Comdr. G. W. Lautrup, Jr.
ARCHERFISH	Lt. Comdr. W. H. Wright
SWORDFISH	Lt. Comdr. K. E. Montross
PLAICE	Lt. Comdr. C. B. Stevens, Jr.

Area southeast of Formosa and later athwart route from Marianas to Nansei Shoto:

PINTADO	Lt. Comdr. B. E. Clarey
PILOTFISH	Lt. Comdr. R. H. Close
TUNNY	Commander J. Scott

Area east and southeast of Marianas:

ALBACORE	Commander J. W. Blanchard
SEAWOLF	Lt. Comdr. R. B. Lynch
BANG	Lt. Comdr. A. R. Gallaher
FINBACK	Lt. Comdr. J. L. Jordan
STINGRAY	Lt. Comdr. S. C. Loomis, Jr.

Area between Ulithi and Philippines:

FLYING FISH	Lt. Comdr. R. B. Risser
MUSKALLUNGE	Commander M. P. Russilo
SEAHORSE	Lt. Comdr. S. D. Cutter
PIPEFISH	Lt. Comdr. W. N. Deragon
CAVALLA	Lt. Comdr. H. J. Kossler

Area southeast of Mindanao:

HAKE	Commander J. C. Broach
BASHAW	Lt. Comdr. R. E. Nichols
PADDLE	Lt. Comdr. B. H. Nowell

Tawi Tawi area:

HARDER	Commander S. D. Dealey

HADDO	Lt. Comdr. C. W. Nimitz, Jr.
REDFIN	Lt. Comdr. M. H. Austin
BLUEFISH	Lt. Comdr. C. M. Henderson

Area off Surigao Strait:

GROWLER	Lt. Comdr. T. B. Oakley, Jr.
PIPEFISH	Reported on June 21

San Bernardino Strait:

FLYING FISH	Until 17 June; 21 June, CAVALLA

Luzon Area:

JACK	Lt. Comdr. A. E. Krapf
FLIER	Commander J. B. Crowley

Third Fleet, October 25, 1944: ADMIRAL WILLIAM F. HALSEY
TASK FORCE 38—Vice Adm. M. A. Mitscher
Task Group 38.1—Vice Adm. J. S. McCain

WASP (GF)	Captain O. A. Weller
HORNET (F)	Captain A. K. Doyle
HANCOCK	Captain F. C. Dickey, 3 CVS
MONTEREY	Captain S. H. Ingersoll
COWPENS	Captain H. W. Taylor, Jr., 2 CVLS
CHESTER	Captain H. Hartley
PENSACOLA	Captain A. P. Mullinnix
SALT LAKE CITY	Captain L. W. Busbey, Jr.
BOSTON	Captain E. E. Herrmann, 4 CAS
SAN DIEGO	Captain W. E. A. Mullan
OAKLAND	Captain K. S. Reed, 2 CL(AA)
DUNLAP	Lt. Comdr. C. R. Welte
FANNING	Commander J. C. Bentley
CASE	Lt. Comdr. R. S. Willey
CUMMINGS	Commander P. D. Williams
CASSIN	Commander V. M. Meola
DOWNES	Commander R. S. Fahle
FARENHOLT	Commander K. S. Shook
WOODWORTH	Commander C. R. Stephan
MCCALLA	Lt. Comdr. E. Vinock
GRAYSON	Commander W. V. Pratt
IZARD	Commander M. F. Dayton
CONNER	Commander W. E. Kaitner
BROWN	Commander T. H. Copeman
COWELL	Commander C. W. Parker, 14 DDS

Task Group 38.2—Rear Adm. G. F. Bogan

INTREPID (GF)	Captain J. F. Bolger, 1 CV

APPENDIX

CABOT	Captain S. J. Michael
INDEPENDENCE	Captain E. C. Ewen, 2 CVLs
IOWA (F)	Captain A. R. McCann
NEW JERSEY (FFF)	Captain C. F. Holden, 2 BBS
BILOXI	Captain D. M. McGurl
VINCENNES	Captain A. D. Brown
MIAMI	Captain J. G. Crawford, 3 CLs
OWEN	Commander C. B. Jones
MILLER	Lt. Comdr. D. L. Johnson
THE SULLIVANS	Commander R. J. Baum
TINGEY	Commander J. O. Miner
HICKOX	Commander J. H. Wesson
HUNT	Commander H. A. Knoertzer
LEWIS HANCOCK	Commander W. M. Searles
MARSHALL	Commander J. D. McKinney
CUSHING	Commander L. F. Volk
COLAHAN	Commander D. T. Wilber
HALSEY POWELL	Commander S. D. B. Merrill
UHLMANN	Commander S. G. Hooper
YARNALL	Commander J. H. Hogg
TWINING	Commander E. K. Wakefield
STOCKHAM	Commander E. P. Holmes
WEDDERBURN	Commander C. H. Kendall, 16 DDS

Task Group 38.3—Rear Adm. F. C. Sherman

LEXINGTON (FF)	Captain E. W. Litch
ESSEX (GF)	Captain C. W. Wieber, 2 CVs
PRINCETON	Captain W. H. Buracker
LANGLEY	Captain J. F. Wegforth, 2 CVLs
MASSACHUSETTS	Captain W. W. Warlick
SOUTH DAKOTA	Captain R. S. Riggs, 2 BBS
SANTA FE	Captain J. Wright
BIRMINGHAM	Captain T. B. Inglis
MOBILE	Captain C. C. Miller
RENO	Captain R. C. Alexander, 4 CLs
C. K. BRONSON	Commander G. Scull
COTTEN	Lt. Comdr. P. W. Winston
DORTCH	Commander R. C. Young
GATLING	Commander A. F. Richardson
HEALY	Commander J. C. Atkeson
PORTERFIELD	Captain C. R. Todd
CALLAGHAN	Commander F. J. Johnson
CASSIN YOUNG	Commander E. T. Schreiber
IRWIN	Commander D. B. Miller
PRESTON	Commander G. S. Patrick

LAWS	Captain M. VanMetre
LONGSHAW	Commander R. H. Speck
MORRISON	Commander W. H. Price, 13 DDS

Task Group 38.4—Rear Adm. R. E. Davison

ENTERPRISE	Captain C. D. Glover
FRANKLIN (GF)	Captain J. M. Shoemaker, 2 CVS
SAN JACINTO	Captain H. M. Martin
BELLEAU WOOD	Captain J. Perry, 2 CVLS
WASHINGTON (F)	Captain T. R. Cooley
ALABAMA	Captain V. R. Murphy, 2 BBS
WICHITA (FF)	Captain D. A. Spencer
NEW ORLEANS	Captain J. E. Hurff, 2 CAS
MAURY	Commander J. W. Koenig
GRIDLEY	Commander P. D. Quirk
HELM	Commander S. K. Santmyers
MCCALL	Lt. Comdr. J. B. Carroll
MUGFORD	Commander M. A. Shellabarger
RALPH TALBOT	Lt. Comdr. W. S. Brown
INGERSOLL	Commander A. C. Veasey
KNAPP	Lt. Comdr. W. B. Brown
PATTERSON	Lt. Comdr. W. A. Hering
BAGLEY	Commander W. H. Shea, Jr.
WILKES	Lt. Comdr. F. E. McEntire, Jr.
NICHOLSON	Commander W. C. Bennett, Jr.
SWANSON	Lt. Comdr. W. K. Ratliff
COGSWELL	Commander W. J. Deutermann
CAPERTON	Commander G. K. Carmichael, 15 DDS

Central Philippine Attack Force, 20 October 1944: VICE ADM. THOMAS C. KINKAID

TASK FORCE 77—Vice Adm. Kinkaid
FLAGSHIP GROUP 77.1
Fleet Flagship Unit 77.1.1—Captain A. M. Granum

WASATCH	Captain A. M. Granum, 1 AGC
AMMEN	Commander J. H. Brown
MULLANY	Commander A. O. Momm, 2 DDS

Cruiser Unit 77.1.2—Captain C. E. Coney

NASHVILLE	Captain C. E. Coney, 1 CL
ABNER READ	Commander A. M. Purdy
BUSH	Lt. Comdr. R. E. Westholm, 2 DDS

Commander Support Aircraft—Captain R. F. Whitehead

BOMBARDMENT AND FIRE SUPPORT GROUP 77.2—Rear Adm. J. B. Oldendorf

APPENDIX

Fire Support Unit North 77.2.1—Rear Adm. G. L. Weyler
   BatDiv 3
    MISSISSIPPI   Captain H. J. Redfield
   BatDiv 4—Rear Adm. T. Ruddock
    MARYLAND   Captain H. J. Ray
    WEST VIRGINIA   Captain H. V. Wiley, 3 OBBS

   Div X-Ray
    AULICK   Commander J. D. Andrew
    CONY   Lt. Comdr. A. W. Moore
    SIGOURNEY   Lt. Comdr. F. Hale, 3 DDS

Fire Support Unit South 77.2.2—Rear Adm. J. B. Oldendorf
   BatDiv 2—Rear Adm. T. E. Chandler
    TENNESSEE   Captain J. B. Heffernan
    CALIFORNIA   Captain H. P. Burnett
    PENNSYLVANIA   Captain C. F. Martin, 3 OBBS

   CruDiv 4—Rear Adm. Oldendorf
    LOUISVILLE   Captain S. H. Hurt
    PORTLAND   Captain T. G. W. Settle
    MINNEAPOLIS   Captain H. B. Slocum, 3 CAS

   CruDiv 9—Rear Adm. W. L. Ainsworth
    HONOLULU   Captain H. R. Thurber

   CruDiv 12—Rear Adm. R. W. Hayler
    DENVER   Captain A. M. Bledsoe
    COLUMBIA   Captain M. E. Curts, 3 CLS

   DesRon 56—Captain R. N. Smoot
    LEUTZE   Commander B. A. Robbins, Jr.
    NEWCOMB   Commander L. B. Cook
    BENNION   Commander J. W. Cooper
    HEYWOOD L. EDWARDS Commander J. W. Boulware
    RICHARD P. LEARY   Commander F. S. Habecker
    ROBINSON   Commander E. B. Grantham, Jr.
    ROSS   Commander B. Coe
    A. W. GRANT   Commander T. A. Nisewaner
    BRYANT   Commander P. L. High
    HALFORD   Commander R. J. Hardy

   Div X-Ray
    CLAXTON   Commander M. H. Hubbard
    THORN   Lt. Comdr. F. H. Schneider, Jr.
    WELLES   Lt. Comdr. J. S. Slaughter, 13 DDS
    SAN CARLOS   Lt. Comdr. D. Mills, 1 AVP

CLOSE COVERING GROUP 77.3—Rear Adm. R. S. Berkey
 CruDiv 15
PHOENIX	Captain J. H. Duncan
BOISE	Captain J. S. Roberts, 2 CLS

 RAN CruSqdr—Commodore J. A. Collins, RAN
AUSTRALIA	Captain A. Wylie, RAN
SHROPSHIRE	Captain C. A. G. Nichols, RAN, 2 CAS

 DesDiv 47—Captain K. M. McManes
BACHE	Lt. Comdr. R. C. Morton
BEALE	Commander D. M. Coffee
HUTCHINS	Commander C. B. Laning
DALY	Commander R. G. Visser
KILLEN	Commander H. G. Corey
ARUNTA	Commander A. E. Buchanan RAN
WARRAMUNGA	Commander J. M. Alliston, RAN, 7 DDS

ESCORT CARRIER GROUP 77.4—Rear Adm. T. L. Sprague
Panaon Carrier Group 77.4.1—Rear Adm. T. L. Sprague
 CarDiv 22—Rear Adm. Sprague
SANGAMON	Captain M. E. Browder
SUWANEE	Captain W. D. Johnson
CHENANGO	Captain G. VanDeurs
SANTEE	Captain R. E. Blick

 CarDiv 28—Rear Adm. G. R. Henderson
PETROF BAY	Captain J. L. Kane
SAGINAW BAY	Captain F. C. Sutton, 6 CVES

 DesRon 47—Captain I. H. Nunn
MCCORD	Lt. Comdr. F. D. Michael
TRATHEN	Lt. Comdr. J. R. Millett
HAZELWOOD	Commander V. P. Douw, 3 DDS

 CortDiv 63—Commander J. V. Bewick
R. S. BULL	Lt. Comdr. A. W. Gardes
R. M. ROWELL	Commander H. A. Barnard, Jr.
EVERSOLE	Lt. Comdr. G. E. Marix
EDMONDS	Lt. Comdr. J. S. Burrows, Jr.
COOLBAUGH	Lt. Comdr. S. T. Hotchkiss, 5 DES

Southern Carrier Group 77.4.2—Rear Adm. F. G. Stump
 CarDiv 24—Rear Adm. Stump
NATOMA BAY	Captain A. K. Morehouse
MANILA BAY	Captain F. Lee

APPENDIX

CarDiv 27—Rear Adm. W. D. Sample
MARCUS ISLAND	Captain C. F. Greber
KADASHAN BAY	Captain R. N. Hunter
SAVO ISLAND	Captain C. E. Ekstrom
OMMANEY BAY	Captain H. L. Young, 6 CVEs

DesRon 47
HAGGARD	Commander D. A. Harris
FRANKS	Commander D. R. Stephan
HAILEY	Commander P. H. Brady, 3 DDs

CortDiv 69—Commander J. C. Phifer
R. W. SUESENS	Lt. Comdr. R. W. Graham
ABERCROMBIE	Lt. Comdr. B. H. Katchiniski
OBERRENDER	Lt. Comdr. S. Spencer
W. C. WANN	Lt. Comdr. J. W. Stedman
LERAY WILSON	Lt. Comdr. M. V. Carson, Jr., 5 DEs

Northern Carrier Group 77.4.3—Rear Adm. C. A. F. Sprague
  CarDiv 25—Rear Adm. Sprague
FANSHAW BAY	Captain D. P. Johnson
SAINT LO	Captain F. J. McKenna
WHITE PLAINS	Captain D. J. Sullivan
KALININ BAY	Captain C. R. Brown

CarDiv 26—Rear Adm. R. A. Ofstie
KITKUN BAY	Captain J. P. Whitney
GAMBIER BAY	Captain W. V. Vieweg, 6 CVEs

DesRon 47
HOEL	Commander W. D. Thomas
HEERMANN	Commander A. T. Hathaway
JOHNSTON	Commander E. E. Evans, 3 DDs
DENNIS	Lt. Comdr. S. Hansen
S. B. ROBERTS	Lt. Comdr. R. W. Copeland
J. C. BUTLER	Lt. Comdr. J. E. Pace
RAYMOND	Lieutenant A. F. Beyer, Jr., 4 DEs

MINESWEEPING AND HYDROGRAPHIC GROUP 77.5—Commander W. R. Loud
  Minesweepers 77.5.1—Commander W. R. Loud
    Sweep Unit One
PREBLE	Lt. Comdr. E. F. Baldridge
BREESE	Lt. Comdr. D. B. Cohen, 2 DMs
HOVEY	Lieutenant A. A. Clark, III
SOUTHARD	Lieutenant J. E. Brennan

CHANDLER	Lieutenant F. M. Murphy
LONG	Lieutenant S. Caplan
HAMILTON	Lt. Comdr. J. Clague
HOWARD	Lt. Comdr. O. F. Salvia
PALMER	Lieutenant W. E. McGuirk, 7 DMSS
CHICKASAW	Lieutenant L. C. Olson, 1 ATF
SANDS	Lieutenant M. M. Samuels, 1 APD

Sweep Unit Two

ZEAL	Lt. Comdr. E. W. Woodhouse
TOKEN	Lieutenant W. T. Hunt
TUMULT	Lieutenant W. K. McDuffie
VELOCITY	Lieutenant G. J. Buyse
SCOUT	Lieutenant E. G. Anderson, Jr., 5 AMS

Sweep Unit Three

REQUISITE	Lt. Comdr. H. R. Peirce, Jr.
PURSUIT	Lt. Comdr. R. F. Good
REVENGE	Lt. Comdr. J. L. Jackson
SAGE	Lt. Comdr. F. K. Zinn
SENTRY	Lt. Comdr. T. R. Fonick, 5 AMS

Sweep Unit Four

YMS 1	Lieutenant R. N. Compton
YMS 81	Lieutenant P. F. Beville
YMS 140	Lieutenant R. J. Staehli, Jr.
YMS 219	Lieutenant M. R. Winfield
YMS 319	Lieutenant R. F. Hellrung, 5 YMSS

Sweep Unit Five

YMS 238	Lieutenant (jg) W. C. Ling
YMS 243	Lieutenant (jg) W. C. Kayser
YMS 286	Lieutenant D. L. Middleton
YMS 293	Lieutenant J. W. Holmes
YMS 335	Lieutenant (jg) R. C. Wilkins
YMS 398	Lieutenant W. A. Latta, 6 YMSS

Sweep Unit Six

YMS 6	Lieutenant (jg) J. H. Skog
YMS 39	Lieutenant (jg) R. M. Sullivan
YMS 49	Lieutenant J. A. Lynch, Jr.
YMS 52	Lieutenant W. A. Semmes
YMS 340	Lieutenant P. Schminke
YMS 342	Lieutenant W. M. Reilly, 6 YMSS

Sweep Unit Seven

YMS 70	Lieutenant (jg) O. L. Blackett

APPENDIX

YMS 71	Lieutenant E. O. Saltmarsh
YMS 73	Lieutenant H. C. Dunson
YMS 314	Lieutenant F. X. Gallagher
YMS 341	Lieutenant H. O. Arend, 5 YMSS

Sweep Unit Eight
4 LCPRS

Hydrographic Unit
HMS GASCOYNE

YMS 316	Lieutenant R. J. Dalton
YMS 393	Lieutenant J. W. Montgomery, 2 YMSS
HMAL 1074	

Beach Demolition Group
  TransDiv 12

MANLEY	Lieutenant R. T. Newell, Jr.
TALBOT	Commander C. C. Morgan
GOLDSBOROUGH	Lieutenant W. J. Meehan
KANE	Lt. Comdr. F. M. Christianson

  TransDiv 14

BROOKS	Lieutenant S. C. Rasmussen, Jr.
BELKNAP	Lieutenant R. Childs, Jr.
OVERTON	Lt. Comdr. D. K. O'Connor
HUMPHREYS	Lt. Comdr. O. B. Murphy

  TransDiv 16

RATHBURNE	Lt. Comdr. R. L. Welch
BADGER	Lt. Comdr. A. T. Enos
CLEMSON	Lieutenant W. F. Moran, 11 APDS
UDT 3	Lieutenant T. C. Crist
UDT 4	Lt. Comdr. W. G. Carberry
UDT 5	Lieutenant J. K. DeBold
UDT 6	Lieutenant D. M. Logsdon
UDT 8	Lt. Comdr. D. E. Young
UDT 9	Lt. Comdr. J. B. Eaton
UDT 10	Lieutenant A. O. Choate, Jr., 7 UDTS

Service Group 77.6—Rear Adm. R. O. Glover
Leyte Gulf Unit

ASHTABULA	Lt. Comdr. W. Barnett, Jr.
SARANAC	Commander H. R. Parker
CHEPACHET	Lt. Comdr. H. K. Wallace
SUAMICO	Commander A. S. Johnson
KISHWAUKEE	Lieutenant F. M. Hillman
SALAMONTE	Captain L. J. Johns, 6 AOS

MAZAMA	Captain P. V. R. Harris, 1 AE
SS DURHAM VICTORY	1 Ammunition Ship
BOWERS	Commander F. W. Hawes
WITTER	Lieutenant G. Herrmann, III
WILLMARTH	Lt. Comdr. J. G. Thorburn, Jr.
LOVELACE	Lt. Comdr. E. L. deKieffer
MANNING	Lt. Comdr. J. I. Mingay
WHITEHURST	Lieutenant J. C. Horton, 6 DES

Kossol Roads (Palau) Unit

SS MERIDIAN VICTORY
SS BLUEFIELD VICTORY
SS IRAN VICTORY, 3 Ammunition Ships
SS PUEBLO
SS W. C. YEAGER, 2 Overseas Tankers

NEUENDORF	Lt. Comdr. R. C. Barlow
THOMASON	Lt. Comdr. C. B. Henriques, 2 DES

Others

ARETHUSA	Lieutenant R. L. Barrington
CARIBOU	Lieutenant H. G. Owens
MINK	Lieutenant W. J. Meagher
PANDA	Lt. Comdr. W. A. Porteous, Jr., 4 IXs
INDUS	Lt. Comdr. A. S. Einmo, 1 AKN
TEAK	Lieutenant B. P. Hollett
SATINLEAF	Lieutenant P. F. Taylor
SILVER BELL	Lieutenant H. N. Berg, 3 ANs
CABLE	Lt. Comdr. H. Pond, 1 ARS
ACHILLES	Lieutenant C. O. Smith, 1 ARL
MURZIM	Lt. Comdr. D. S. Walton, USCG, 1 AK

COMPOSITION OF JAPANESE COMBINED FLEET
Involved in Sho Plan—October 1944

Combined Fleet, ADMIRAL SOEMU TOYODA
First Mobile Fleet, VICE ADMIRAL JISABURO OZAWA
Second Fleet, First Diversion Attack Force—Vice Admiral Takeo Kurita
First Section, First Night Combat Unit—Vice Admiral Takeo Kurita
Battleship Division 1—Vice Admiral Matome Ugaki

    YAMATO (F)
    MUSASHI
    NAGATO, 3 BBS

Cruiser Div 4

    ATAGO (FF)
    TAKAO
    CHOKAI
    MAYA, 4 CAS

APPENDIX

Cruiser Div 5—less MOGAMI
    MYOKO (F)
    HAGURO, 2 CAS
DesRon 2—less DesDiv 27
    NOSHIRO (F), 1 CL
    SHIMAKAZE
DesDiv 2—less KIYOSHIMO
    HAYASHIMO
    AKISHIMO
DesDiv 31
    KISHINAMI
    OKINAMI
    ASASHIMO
    NAGANAMI
DesDiv 32
    FUJINAMI
    HAMANAMI, 9DDS

Second Section, Second Night Combat Unit—Vice Admiral Yoshio Suzuki
    BatDiv 3
        KONGO (F)
        HARUNA, 2 BBS
CruDiv 7
    KUMANO (F)
    SUZUYA
    TONE
    CHIKUMA, 4 CAS
DesRon 10—less DesDiv 4, 41, 61 plus NOWAKE, KIYOSHIMO
    YAHAGI (F), 1 CL

DesDiv 17
    URAKAZE
    ISOKAZE
    HAMAKAZE
    YUKIKAZE
    NOWAKE
    KIYOSHIMO, 6 DDS

Third Section, Third Night Combat Unit—Vice Adm. Shoji Nishimura
    BatDiv 2
        YAMASHIRO (F)
        FUSO, 2 BBS
        MOGAMI, 1 CA
DesDiv 4—less NOWAKE
    MICHISHIO
    ASAGUMO
    YAMAGUMO

DesDiv 27
      SHIGURE, 4 DDS
Third Fleet, Main Body—Vice Adm. Jisaburo Ozawa
   CarDiv 1—not as yet operational
      AMAGI (F)
      UNRYU, 2 CVS
   CarDiv 3—Rear Adm. Sueo Obayashi
      ZUIKAKU (FF), 1 CV
      ZUIHO
      CHITOSE
      CHOYODA, 3 CVLs
   CarDiv 4—Rear Adm. Chiaki Matsuda
      HYUGA (F)
      ISE, 2 BBs–CV
      JUNYO
      RYUHO, 2 CVLS
      OYODO
      TAMA, 2 CLS
   DesRon 11—less DesDiv 52 plus DesDivs 41, 61
      ISUZU (F), 1 CL
   DesDiv 43
      KIRI
      KUWA
      MAKI
      SUGI
   DesDiv 41
      SHIMOTSUKI
      FUYUTSUKI
   DesDiv 61
      SUZUTSUKI
      HATSUZUKI
      AKITSUKI
      WAKATSUKI, 10 DDS
Fifth Fleet, Second Diversion Attack Force—Vice Adm. Kiyohide Shima
   CruDiv 21—less TAMA, KISO
      NACHI (FF)
      ASHIGARA, 2 CAS
   DesRon 1—less DesDiv 1
      ABUKUMA (F), 1 CL
   DesDiv 7
      USHIO
      AKEBONO
   DesDiv 18
      SHIRANUHI
      KASUMI

APPENDIX

DesDiv 21
    WAKABA
    HATSUHARU
    HATSUSHIMO, 7 DDS

Sixth Fleet, Advance Expeditionary Force—Vice Adm. Shigeyoshi Miwa
    Approximately 50 operational submarines, of which some 10–15 engaged in transport of supplies to by-passed areas; most of the remainder at bases in the Inland Sea.

First Air Fleet, Fifth Base Air Force—Vice Adm. Takajiro Onishi
    Approximately 150 aircraft disposed throughout the Philippines with the principal concentration in Central Luzon.

Second Air Fleet, Sixth Base Air Force—Vice Adm. Shigeru Fukudome
    Approximately 450 aircraft disposed in Formosa, the Ryukyus, and Kyushu.

EXPLANATION OF SYMBOLS OF TYPES OF NAVAL VESSELS

AD	— Destroyer Tender
AE	— Ammunition Ship
AGC	— Amphibious Force Flagship
AK	— Cargo Ship
AKA	— Cargo Ship—Attack
AKN	— Net Cargo Ship
AM	— Minesweeper
AN	— Net Laying Ship
AO	— Oiler
AP	— Transport
APA	— Transport—Attack
APc	— Coastal Transport—Small
APD	— High-Speed Transport—Ex-Destroyer
ARL	— Repair Ship—Landing Craft
ARS	— Salvage Vessel
ATA	— Ocean Tug—Auxiliary
ATF	— Ocean Tug—Fleet
ATR	— Ocean Tug—Rescue
AV	— Seaplane Tender
AVD	— Seaplane Tender—Converted Destroyer
AVP	— Seaplane Tender—Small
BB	— Battleship
CA	— Heavy Cruiser
CL	— Light Cruiser
CL(AA)	— Light Cruiser (anti-aircraft)
CV	— Aircraft Carrier
CVE	— Aircraft Carrier—Escort
CVL	— Aircraft Carrier—Light

DD	— Destroyer
DE	— Destroyer—Escort
DM	— Light Minelayer
DMS	— High-Speed Minesweeper
IX	— Unclassified
LCI	— Landing Craft—Infantry
LCT	— Landing Craft—Tank
LSD	— Landing Ship—Dock
LST	— Landing Ship—Tank
OBB	— Old Battleship
PC	— Submarine Chaser (steel hulled)
SC	— Submarine Chaser (wooden hulled)
YMS	— Motor Minesweeper
YO	— Fuel Oil Barge
F	— Flag
GF	— Group Flag
FF	— Force Flag
FFF } FlF }	— Fleet Flag
DF	— Division Flag
UDT	— Underwater Demolition Team

OFFICER CASUALTIES—ACTIVE AND INACTIVE

List of Dead in Pacific and Asiatic Areas Between 1 December 1943 and 1 November 1944

As of 15 October 1947

ABERCROMBIE, Lt. Warren H.
ADAMS, Lt. (jg) Randal B.
ADAMS, CWO Roy C.
AGAR, Lt. (jg) Geo. J.
ALLEN, Lt. Cdr. Chas. J.
ALLEN, Ens. John C.
ALLEN, Lt. Robert W.
ANDERSON, Ens. Geo. G.
ANDERSON, Ens. Jack
ANDERSON, Lt. Romane C.
ARMBRUSTER, Ens. Geo. M., Jr.
ARMSTRONG, Lt. Leroy F.
ARNOLD, Lt. (jg) Raymond P.
ARNOT, Ens. Geo. E.
ARTHUR, Ens. Chas. L.
ARTHUR, Ens. Geo E.
ASTILL, Lt. (jg) Clarence J.
ATHEY, WO John F.
ATWELL, Lt. Melvin K.
AUTREY, WO Benj. F.
AVERILL, Cdr. Jas. K.

BAILEY, Ens. Paul E.
BALSLEY, Lt. Wm. A.
BANE, Ens. Wm. K.
BANEY, Ens. John F.
BANNISTER, Ens. Wm. P.
BARALDI, Lt. (j) Thos. R.
BARCLAY, Lt. Cdr. McClelland
BARDIN, Ens. Geo. G., Jr.
BARKER, Ens. Donald K.
BARNARD, Ens. Jas. F.
BARRETT, Lt. (jg) Guy J., Jr.
BARRY, Lt. John E., Jr.
BARRY, Ens. Leonard F.
BARTLETT, Ens. Phil F., Jr.
BARTON, Ens. Chas. W., Jr.
BARTON, Lt. Cdr. Wm. A.

BATES, Lt. (jg) John H.
BAYLESS, Lt. Cdr. Walter B.
BEAN, Ens. Russel C.
BEANE, WO Hubert C.
BECHTOL, Lt. (jg) Roy A.
BEEDON, Lt. John W.
BEGGS, Lt. Cdr. Lloyd S.
BEGHDEL, Lt. (jg) John K.
BEHREND, WO Carl W.
BELCAVITCH, CWO Chas.
BELL, Ens. Thos. O.
BELL, Lt. Vereen M.
BENEKE, Ens. Jas. R.
BENNETT, WO John W.
BENNETT, Lt. (jg) Wm. A.
BENNETT, Ens. Wilmurt A., Jr.
BENNION, Ens. Herald C.
BENTON, Lt (jg) John L.
BENTON, Lt (jg) John O.
BEREOLOS, Lt. (jg) Hercules
BERGERON, Lt (jg) Justin
BERGMAIER, Ens. Milton H.
BERSSENBRUGGE, Lt. (jg) Oscar W.
BERTON, Lt. (jg) Berdett B.
BIEDELMAN, Lt. Fredk. W., Jr.
BIGELOW, Lt. John O., Jr.
BIROS, Lt. Cdr. Edmund W.
BIXBY, Ens. Chas. H.
BJERTNESS, Ens. Sigurd J.
BLAIR, Lt. Clarence F.
BLAIR, CWO Roland F.
BLAUVELT, Lt. Robt. P.
BLIND, Lt. Howard J.
BLOEDOW, WO Rudolph F.
BLOSSOM, Ens. Louis F.
BLOWERS, CWO Ralph A.
BOLE, Lt. Cdr. John A., Jr.
BOSWORTH, Lt. (jg) Arthur S., Jr.

Bowen, Lt. Russell E.
Bowker, Lt. Gordon A.
Boyce, Ens. Neil R.
Boyd, Ens. Jas. B.
Boyd, Lt. John C.
Boyle, Lt. Gerald F.
Boyter, Ens. Jas. L.
Bradley, Lt. Robt. G.
Bradshaw, Lt. (jg) Eugene
Brady, Ens. Chas. E.
Brane, Lt. Richey S.
Brannon, Ens. Wm. P.
Branson, Lt. (jg) Guilford F., Jr
Brantley, Ens. H. R.
Bratcres, Ens. Chas. R.
Breed, Lt. Edgar R., Jr.
Bretland, Lt. Chas. W., Jr.
Brightman, WO Wm. C.
Brines, Lt. (jg) Earl E.
Brittain, Lt. Alex F., Jr.
Broedel, Ens. Ralph L.
Brokenshire, Lt. Cdr. Herbert C.
Bronson, Lt. Cdr. Ward
Brossy, Lt. Cdr. Henry E.
Brown, Ens. Douglas C.
Brown, Lt. Ivan L.
Brown, Lt. Rich. T.
Bruner, Lt. Harold T.
Buckelew, Lt. (jg) Wm. G.
Budd, Lt. Isaac W.
Buderus, Lt. Wm. H., Jr.
Buford, WO John D., Jr.
Bundy, Ens. Lloyd W.
Burckhalter, Lt. (jg) Wm. E.
Burgess, Ens. Warren C.
Burk, Lt. (jg) Jas. R.
Burkhardt, Lt. (jg) Carl
Burnham, Lt. Cdr. Bruce P.
Burns, CWO Jas. P.
Burns, Ens. Wm. H., Jr.
Burrows, Ens. Ward H.
Burton, Lt. Cdr. Paul W.
Bush, Ens. Paul B.
Bushey, Ens. Otto L.
Buswell, Lt. Karl P.
Butler, Ens. Geo. F.
Butler, Lt. Cdr. Geo. L.
Butler, Lt. Robinson P.

Cady, Cdr. Gordon D.
Caldwell, Capt. Kenneth C.
Cale, WO David L.
Calhoon, Ens. Gordon A.
Calhoun, Ens. Robt. W.
Callahan, Ens. Howard J., Jr.

Campbell, Ens. Archibald H.
Campbell, Lt. Clarence G., Jr.
Campbell, Lt. Cdr. Jack G.
Canter, Lt. (jg) Lloyd M.
Canty, Lt. (jg) W. H.
Captain, Ens. Eugene S.
Carawan, Ens. Henry F.
Carby, Lt. (jg) Henry C., Jr.
Carey, Lt. (jg) Philip W.
Carlin, Ens. Robt. W.
Carlson, Lt. (jg) Carroll L.
Carlson, Ens. Harold L.
Carocari, Lt. Alvin J.
Carruth, Ens. Wilson A.
Carson, Lt. (jg) Arthur Q.
Carson, Ens. Clyde L.
Carson, Lt. (jg) Harold H.
Cary, Lt. (jg) Cyrus G.
Case, Ens. Ernest W., Jr.
Cassleman, Ens. Robt. W.
Catching, Ens. Marvin R.
Cate, Lt. Jas. S.
Caudle, Ens. Wilburn R.
Cauthan, Lt. Weldon D.
Cavanaugh, Lt. (jg) John A., Jr.
Cecil, R. Adm. Chas. P.
Chaney, Ens. Rich. A.
Chapman, Lt. (jg) Kermit E.
Chase, Lt. (jg) Kenneth C.
Cheney, Lt. John F.
Chestney, Lt. (jg) Browne R., Jr.
Chester, Ens. John D.
Childs, Ens. Leroy W.
Christie, Ens. Alex A.
Clapp, Lt. (jg) John A.
Clark, Lt. Carl E.
Clark, Ens. Lennox B.
Clark, Lt. (jg) Norman
Clark, Lt. Robt. S.
Clark, Lt. Warner, Jr.
Clem, Ens. John R.
Cole, Lt. Harry L., Jr.
Coleman, Lt. (jg) Lee J.
Combs, WO Claude D.
Connell, WO Raymond E.
Conners, Ens. Jas. R., Jr.
Conway, Lt. Anthony J.
Cook, Ens. Emeral B.
Cook, Ens. Kenneth D.
Cook, Ens. Robt. S.
Cook, Lt. Stanley H.
Coons, Cdr. Paul K.
Cooper, Lt. Roland
Costello, Ens. Lourde G.
Cotton, Lt. Kenneth E.

CASUALTIES

Covington, Lt. Claude W., Jr.
Cox, Ens. Jos. E.
Craig, Lt. Cdr. Earl F.
Craig, Lt. Cdr. John R.
Cranny, Lt. Jos. R.
Craver, Ens. Bates B., Jr.
Crellin, Lt. (jg) Conrad W.
Criblet, Ens. Philip S.
Cronin, Ens. Malcolm K.
Crutcher, Lt. (jg) Wm. R.
Crutchfield, Lt. Jack R.
Culver, Ens. Wm. S.
Cummings, Lt. (jg) Jess C.
Cunningham, Lt. Russell P.
Curry, Lt. Robt. O.
Curtin, Lt. (jg) Edw. D.
Cyphers, Ens. Leon L.

Dahlen, Lt. (jg) Walter A.
Dahlgren, WO John A.
Dailey, Ens. Geo. F.
Dana, Lt. (jg) Paul
Davis, Ens. Bonner A.
Davis, Lt. Rich. W., Jr.
Davis, Lt. (jg) Robt. G.
Davis, CWO Robt. L.
Degenkolb, Ens. Edwin B., Jr.
Deger, Lt (jg) Chas. H.
Delesdernier, Lt. (jg) Warren W.
Deluca, Ens. Dan G., Jr.
Demers, Lt. Adam W.
Demler, Ens. Arthur M.
Dempsey, Ens. Jack W.
Devereaux, Lt. Wm. S.
Devries, Lt. Henry
Diana, Ens. Vincent F.
Dicrocco, Lt. (jg) Phil. P.
Dierking, Lt. Wm. E.
Diesch, Lt. (jg) Forrest J.
Diffenbaugh, Ens. Clarence M.
Ditter, Lt. (jg) Anthony J.
Dobbins, Ens. Chas. H.
Dolan, Lt. (jg) Clarence R.
Donnelly, Lt. (jg) Robt. E., Jr.
Downs, Ens. Jos.
Doyle, Lt. Jas. Q.
Dryer, Lt. (jg) Wm. H.
Duckworth, Ens. John C., Jr.
Dunn, Lt. Jas. A.
Dunson, Lt. (jg) Bernarr A.
Dye, Ens. Kenneth E.
Dyer, Ens. Lance C.

East, Ens. Jas. G.
Eaton, Lt. (jg) Paul M.

Edmondson, Lt. (jg) Jos. C.
Edwards, Ens. John M.
Egenthal, Midn. Meyer
Eichmann, Lt. John H.
Ekstrom, Lt. Stanley E.
Eley, Cdr. Francis L.
Ellingboe, Ens. Edw. R.
Ellis, Ens. Keith E.
Engel, Ens. Gwynn
Entrikin, Ens. John M.
Epply, Lt. Walter G.
Erickson, Ens. Lyle A.
Ernst, WO Chas. G.
Ervin, Lt. (jg) Henry N.
Eubank, Lt. (jg) Elwyn P.
Everett, Ens. Jas.
Everett, Lt. John L., Jr.
Evins, Lt. Cdr. Robt. C.

Farber, Lt. (jg) Benj. F., Jr.
Farmer, Lt. (jg) Noyes D., Jr.
Farrell, Lt. Daniel J.
Farrell, Ens. Wm. F., Jr.
Faulkenberry, Lt. (jg) Mack A.
Fearing, Ens. Thos. C.
Felsenthal, Ens. David S.
Felt, Lt. Robt. S.
Fend, Ens. Roland S., Jr.
Ferguson, Lt. Geo. T.
Ferguson, Lt. (jg) Wm. J.
Filipozak, Lt. (jg) Edwin S.
Finger, Lt. (jg) Walter E.
Finlay, Ens. Arthur W.
Fisher, Ens. Harlan R.
Flatau, Ens. Leroy H.
Fleming, Lt. Joe E.
Flynn, Lt. (jg) Van V.
Forell, Lt. Cyrus M.
Formanek, Lt. Geo., Jr.
Forsythe, Lt. Cdr. Rich. M.
Forys, Ens. Harry J.
Foster, Ens. Wm. B.
Fox, Ens. Gordon W.
Fox, Lt. Cdr. Jos.
Fox, Lt. Louis W.
Fox, CWO Robert H.
Francis, Ens. Meador D.
Frasier, WO Clarence A.
Freeland, Lt. Frank
French, Lt. Willard B.
Frese, Lt. (jg) Raymond L.
Fritts, Lt. (jg) John F.
Fullenlove, Ens. John J.
Fuller, Lt. (jg) Chas. E.
Fuqua, Lt. Forney O.

GALLAGHER, Lt. Robt. A.
GALLAHER, CWO Wm. L.
GAMMON, WO Eugene A.
GANNETT, Ens. Geo. B., Jr.
GARFINKLE, Lt. (jg) Max
GARRETT, Ens. Chas. H.
GARRETT, Lt. Cdr. Walter K.
GAVER, Ens. Henry C.
GEVELINGER, Ens. Paul A.
GIDEON, Lt. (jg) Delbert L.
GIFFORD, Lt. Walter S., Jr.
GILL, Lt. (jg) Athel L.
GILLAN, Ens. Dale G.
GILLIATT, Lt. (jg) Dean W.
GISH, Lt. Russell C.
GLADNEY, Ens. Jas. B.
GLASS, WO Wm. H.
GOETSCH, Lt. Chas. F.
GOFORTH, Lt. (jg) Robt. H. H.
GOHEEN, Lt. (jg) John R.
GOLDEN, Lt. Philip E.
GOODING, WO Geo. B.
GOODMAN, Ens. Howard E.
GOODMAN, Lt. (jg) Paul F.
GORDON, Lt. Cdr. Edw. M.
GORDON, Ens. Jacques
GORDON, Lt. Wm. M.
GOTHIE, Lt. Dan S.
GRAHAM, Ens. John E.
GRAHAM, WO Turner
GRAVES, Lt. Cdr. Sidney C.
GRAYSON, WO Elton
GREEN, Ens. Howard C., Jr.
GREEN, Ens. Worth S.
GREENAMYER, Lt. Cdr. Lloyd K.
GREENBERG, Lt. (jg) Marvin
GREENHAGEN, Ens. David F.
GRESHAM, Ens. Winfrey E., Jr.
GRIEBEL, Lt. (jg) Russell J.
GRIFFITH, Lt. Geo. A., Jr.
GROSSE, Lt. (jg) Francis G., Jr.
GROTHAUS, Lt. Arend
GROVE, Lt. Cdr. Alfred E.
GRUMBINE, Ens. Roy J.
GUILER, Lt. Robt. P., 3d
GUILMETTE, Lt. (jg) Dudley
GURVIS, Ens. Milton
GUTENKUNST, Lt. (jg) Douglas H. C.

HAHN, Lt. (jg) Roland D.
HAIGLER, Lt. Wm. C.
HALES, Lt, (jg) Henry B., Jr.
HALL, Lt. (jg) Robt. T.
HALL, Ens. Thos. A.
HALLOWELL, Ens. Alton W.

HALLOWELL, Ens. Thos. E.
HALVA, Ens. Virgil H.
HAMILTON, Ens. Jas. O.
HANISCH, Ens. Alton W.
HANNAH, Ens. John C.
HANSCHE, Lt. (jg) Richard H.
HARLAN, Lt. (jg) Sam R.
HARNEY, Lt. (jg) John J.
HARSMA, Ens. Raymond F.
HARWOOD, Cdr. Bruce L.
HASTINGS, Lt. Abbott Q.
HAUGE, Lt. Robt. J.
HAUPT, Lt. Edw. P.
HAYEK, Ens. Marvin A.
HAYES, Ens. John W.
HAYWOOD, Ens. Alfred W., Jr.
HEFFERNAN, Lt. (jg) John R.
HENDRICKS, Lt. (jg) Lucille
HENNING, Lt. (jg) Wm. V.
HERBER, Ens. Denton A.
HESSLER, Ens. Robt E.
HESTER, Ens. Harold L.
HEWITT, Lt. Chas. G.
HIGGINBOTHAM, Lt. (jg) Paul
HILL, Lt. (jg) Geo. E.
HILL, Ens. Norman C.
HINDENLANG, Ens. Warren A.
HOAGWOOD, WO Geo. H.
HOCH, Ens. Dwight R.
HOECKER, CWO Esper H.
HOGSHIRE, Lt. Cdr. Geo. H., Jr.
HOLIDAY, Ens. Robt. B.
HOLT, Lt. (jg) Wm. A.
HOOVER, Lt. (jg) Chas. C.
HOPFNER, Ens. Paul
HOPPER, Lt. Stephen F.
HOWARD, Ens. Rich. H.
HOWE, Lt. (jg) Geo. T., Jr.
HUDSON, Lt. (jg) Harmon R.
HUEY, Ens. Ralph L.
HUMSJO, Lt. (jg) John G. M.
HUNICKE, Lt. (jg) David C.
HUNTER, Lt. Adrian C.
HUNTLEY, Lt. Cdr. John D.
HUSK, Ens. Wm.
HUTCHESON, Lt. Cdr. Homer H.
HUTCHISON, WO Wm. A.
HYDE, Lt. Cdr. John L.
HYNES, Lt. Wildric F., Jr.

IRVINE, Lt. Hamden C.
IRWIN, Ens. Bruce J.
ISKE, Ens. Jas. L.

JACKSON, Ens. Ernest D.

CASUALTIES

JACKSON, Ens. Geo. B.
JAMES, Lt. Rich. F.
JANSON, Ens. Robt. E.
JENKINS, WO Alvin
JESTER, Ens. Clifford C.
JOHNSON, Lt. (jg) Carl A.
JOHNSON, Ens. Carl A.
JOHNSON, Ens. David E., Jr.
JOHNSON, Lt. (jg) Edwin O.
JOHNSON, Lt. (jg) Howard B.
JOHNSON, Lt. Howard L.
JOHNSON, Lt. Leonard A.
JOHNSON, Lt. Perry H.
JOHNSON, Cdr. Robt. A.
JOHNSON, Lt. (jg) Thos. C.
JOHNSON, Ens. Wm. J.
JOHNSTON, Lt. (jg) Lawrence C.
JOLLIFF, Lt. (jg) Julian K.
JONESON, Ens. Wilbur E.
JONES, Lt. (jg) Alfred A.
JONES, Lt. Chester C.
JONES, Ens. Rich. B.
JORDAN, Lt. Cdr. Francis D.
JOYCE, Ens. Stephen J.

KACZOR, Ens. Myrl M.
KAFER, Lt. (jg) August G.
KANE, Capt. John D. H.
KASER, Lt. (jg) John M.
KASPERSON, Lt. Elmer H.
KEELY, Lt. Warren L.
KEESEE, Lt. Eustace N.
KELLOGG, Lt. (jg) Geo. C.
KELLY, Ens. Dan B.
KELLY, Ens. Jas. J.
KELLY, Lt. Thos. A.
KELSCH, Lt. Cdr. Walter L., Jr.
KENAH, Lt. Wm. H., Jr.
KENDALL, Ens. Harrison E.
KENNEDY, Ens. Jesse O., Jr.
KENNEY, Lt. (jg) Leo T.
KENT, Ens. Wm. H.
KERR, Ens. Robt. C.
KEYSER, Lt. (jg) Jerome D.
KILPATRICK, Ens. Chas. H.
KILRAIN, Lt. Raymond F.
KIMMELMAN, Lt. Isadore E.
KING, Ens. Paige M.
KINNAN, Lt. Leonard E.
KLEMMER, Lt. Cdr. Roland N.
KNIGHT, Lt. Jas. P.
KNOSPE, Lt. Everell C.
KOCIS, Ens. Geo. H.
KOSOWICZ, Ens. Thadeus J.
KOST, Ens. Kemper J.

KRAMER, Lt. Henry H.
KREMER, Lt. Chas. F., Jr.
KROM, Ens. Max M.
KULMAN, Lt. (jg) Walder L.
KUSH, Lt. Stanley J.
KYSER, Lt. (jg) Robt. R.

LAMB, Ens. Chas. R.
LAMBERT, Ens. Mitchell F.
LANDES, Lt. (jg) Jos. P.
LANKFORD, Lt. (jg) John H.
LARSON, Lt. Wm. R.
LAWLER, Lt. Cdr. Chas. H.
LAWTY, Lt. (jg) Malcolm
LEAKE, Lt. (jg) Herbert T.
LEBOW, Lt. (jg) Douglas O.
LECLERCQ, Lt. (jg) John S., 3d
LEE, Ens. Leon E.
LEHMAN, Lt. (jg) Stephen M.
LETSON, Lt. (jg) Chas. F.
LEWELLYN, Ens. Jas. E.
LEWIS, Lt. John B.
LEWIS, Lt. (jg) Ross, Jr.
LIGHT, Ens. Calvin I.
LIGHTFOOT, Lt. (jg) Chas. J.
LILIENTHAL, Lt. (jg) Albert F.
LITTLE, Lt. Cdr. John R.
LLOYD, Lt. (jg) Demarest, Jr.
LLOYD, WO Harry M.
LONG, Ens. Keith V.
LORD, Lt. (jg) Henry S., Jr.
LOVE, Lt. Gordon A.
LOVEN, Lt. Otto E.
LUSK, Lt. (jg) Robt. J.
LYFORD, Lt. (jg) Benj. L., 2d
LYNN, Ens. Edw. W.
LYONS, Ens. Gordon W.

MAASS, WO Adolph R.
MACDOUGALD, Ens. Edw.
MACKENZIE, Lt. Cdr. Geo. K., Jr.
MACKERT, Lt. Cdr. Robt. W.
MACKEY, Ens. John C.
MACKIE, Lt. (jg) Norman W.
MACRAE, Lt. Jas.
MADSEN, Ens. Robt. B.
MAGAS, Lt. (jg) Alfred E.
MAGNUSSON, Lt. Eric
MALAKOWSKY, Lt. (jg) Irvin R.
MALLETTE, Lt. (jg) Earl C.
MALLORY, Lt. (jg) Chas. H.
MALONE, Lt. Thos. F.
MALONEY, Lt. (jg) Jas. R.
MANNOCCIR, Lt. Cdr. Ferdinand D., 2d
MANTELL, Ens. Chas.

Marquios, Ens. Chas. R.
Martin, Ens. Robt. H.
Massa, Lt. John A., Jr.
Mathews, Ens. Lewis A., Jr.
Mathews, Ens. Robt. E.
Mathieu, Lt. Chas. A.
Mattison, Ens. Donald A.
Mauser, Lt. (jg) Adolph
Maxey, Lt. John C., Jr.
Mayhew, Ens. Ralph A.
McAfee, Lt. Wm. M.
McCabe, Lt. (jg) Francis J. M.
McCausland, Lt. Orrin J.
McCluskey, Lt. Edw. S.
McCormick, Lt. Donald
McCutchan, Cdr. Geo. T.
McDanel, Ens. Donald M.
McDonald, Lt. (jg) Jas. W.
McElroy, Lt. Leroy
McElroy, WO Warren M.
McFall, Lt. Jas. W.
McGibony, Lt. (jg) Wm. N.
McGowan, Cdr. Richard
McGowan, Ens. Robt. J.
McGrath, Ens. Thos. E.
McGurk, Lt. (jg) Sidney W.
McHolland, Lt. Arthur V.
McIlwaine, Ens. Robt. D.
McIndoo, Lt. Wm. F.
McIntyre, Lt. (jg) Thos. R.
McKay, Ens. Percy E., Jr.
McKee, Lt. Carlos R., Jr.
McLain, Lt. Wm. W.
McLemore, Ens. Wm. M.
McLure, Ens. Otis J., Jr.
McMillan, Lt. (jg) Jesse I.
McNinch, Ens. Jesse E.
McNulty, Ens. Frank B., Jr.
McRae, Ens. Alexander D.
Means, Lt. (jg) Roger E.
Mendenhall, Ens. Geo. L., Jr.
Merritt, Lt. (jg) John A.
Mesick, Lt. (jg) Warren K.
Miller, Ens. Geo. H.
Miller, Ens. John A.
Milligan, Ens. Dale M.
Mills, Ens. Geo. R.
Mills, Lt. (jg) Wm. J.
Miltner, Lt. (jg) Blaine G.
Minier, Lt. Arthur F.
Mitchell, Ens. Geo. R.
Mize, Ens. Richard R., Jr.
Mooney, Lt. Pierce M.
Mooney, Ens. Robt. H.
Morgan, Lt. (jg) Donald E.

Morgan, Lt. (jg) Vernon R.
Moriarty, Ens. Anthony M.
Morrison, Lt. Edw. T.
Morrison, Lt. (jg) John H.
Morrison, Lt. (jg) Robt. N.
Morton, Lt. (jg) Harry S.
Mowry, Lt. Mark P.
Mroczkowski, Lt. (jg) Stephen G.
Mueller, Ens. Clifford M.
Mulkey, Ens. Harry F., Jr.
Mullen, Lt. (jg) Paul
Mullins, Lt. Grady L.
Murphy, Lt. (jg) Henry L.
Murphy, Ens. Jas. J.
Murphy, Lt. Cdr. John T.
Murphy, Lt. Ramund R.
Murphy, Lt. Wm. J.
Murray, Lt. (jg) Howard L.

Names, Lt. (jg) Richard P.
Namoski, Lt. Elmer C.
Nason, Lt. (jg) Earle A., Jr.
Neighbours, Lt. Jas. B.
Neill, Lt. John R. J.
Nelson, Lt. Chas. W.
Nelson, Lt. Clayton E.
Nelson, Ens. Gordon L.
Newcomb, Lt. (jg) Leland L.
Newhall, Lt. Eliot M.
Newman, Ens. Edgar T.
Nixon, Ens. Thos. D.
Noe, Lt. (jg) Merle J.
Nolte, Ens. Wm. F.
Norling, Lt. (jg) Milton W.

Oberlin, Lt. (jg) Jos. W.
O'Brien, Ens. Frank
Och, Lt. (jg) John T. S.
O'Connor, Lt. Edw. R.
Odem, Ens. Robt. H.
O'Donnell, Lt. Richard J.
Ogden, Lt. Sam'l I.
Ooghe, Ens. Thos. W.
Orr, Lt. Lester F., Jr.
Osborn, Lt. Isaac J.
Oster, CWO Jas. C.
O'Sullivan, Lt. (jg) Cornelius D.
Overmier, Lt. (jg) Robt. E.
Overton, Ens. John H.
Owens, Cdr. Seymour D.

Paine, Lt. Leonard F.
Palmer, Lt. John A.
Parish, Lt. Warren G.
Parker, Lt. Dale R.

CASUALTIES

PARKER, Lt. (jg) Glenn G.
PARKER, Lt. Lloyd E.
PARKMAN, Lt. (jg) Dan K.
PARKS, Lt. Edw. S., Jr.
PARSONS, CWO Frank D.
PASSI, Ens. Walter L.
PATELLA, Lt. Sam'l J.
PATTERSON, Ens. Edw. A.
PATTERSON, Lt. (jg) Johnny W.
PATTEN, Lt. (jg) Robt. A.
PAYNE, Lt. Harold G., Jr.
PAYNE, WO Jas. B.
PAYTON, Lt. (jg) Arthur M., Jr.
PAYTON, Ens. John J., Jr.
PEABODY, Ens. John E.
PEARSON, Lt. (jg) John K.
PEASE, Ens. Vinton L.
PEEL, Lt. Gordon L.
PERKINS, Lt. Bill M.
PERKINS, Cdr. Van O.
PETERSON, Lt. (jg) Albert L.
PETERSON, Lt. Leonard D.
PETERSON, Lt. Sam'l C.
PETTIT, Ens. Thos. M.
PEYTON, Ens. Geo. A. Jr.
PFAHNL, Lt. (jg) Jos. F.
PHIFER, Ens. Jim B.
PHIFER, Ens. Wm. L.
PIERCE, Lt. Cdr. John R.
PIERCY, Lt. (jg) Wilburne E.
PINEUR, Lt. Noel J.
PITT, Lt. Stephen B.
PILSKA, Lt. (jg) Jos. B.
POLK, WO Marley O.
POMEROY, Lt. Woodman B.
PORTER, Ens. John I., Jr.
POTTS, Cdr. Wm. H.
POWELL, Lt. Cdr. Harold V.
POWNING, Ens. John R.
PREMO, Lt. Clarence J.
PRICHARD, Lt. (jg) Bryant E.
PROPST, WO Othro B.
PULLEN, Lt. (jg) Curtis F.
PUTERBAUGH, Lt. (jg) John L., Jr.

RADOWIEC, WO Michael
RAITHEL, Lt. Stanley O.
RAMEY, Ens. Owen H.
RAMSEY, Lt. (jg) John R.
RANSON, Ens. Wm. H.
RAUEN, Ens. John F.
REAMS, Ens. Clyde F., Jr.
REED, Lt. Alan
REED, Ens. Thos. B., Jr.
REEDER, Lt. Paul P.

REESE, Ens. Phil. F.
REGAN, WO Richard A.
REGISTER, Lt. (jg) Francis R.
RIECHEL, Lt. Lenard O.
REICHERT, Ens. Jos., Jr.
RICHARDSON, Ens. Rich. R.
RICHARDSON, Ens. Robt. A.
RICHEY, Lt. John W.
REIBENBAUER, Ens. Leopold P.
RIFFE, Lt. (jg) Herbert W.
RIGLEY, Lt. Frank
RING, Ens. John M.
RISTAU, WO Herbert P.
RITCHIE, Lt. Cdr. Paul J.
RITTER, Lt. Edw. F., Jr.
ROACH, Midn. Floyd W.
ROACH, Lt. Melvin C.
ROACH, Lt. (jg) Thos. D.
ROBERTS, Lt. Jack D.
ROBERTS, Lt. Stuart W.
ROBERTS, Ens. Thos. H.
ROBERTS, Lt. Waring
ROBERTSON, Lt. (jg) Chas. A.
ROBERTSON, Lt. (jg) David H.
ROBERTSON, Lt. Robt. N.
ROBINSON, Lt. (jg) Cecil R.
ROBINSON, Lt. John L.
RODEBACK, Ens. Lorenzo C.
ROEHLER, Ens. Helen M.
ROGERS, Ens. Kent B.
ROHLEDER, Lt. (jg) Andrew H., 3d
ROLKA, Ens. Chester
ROQUEMORE, Ens. Joe H.
ROSE, Lt. Jack A.
ROTH, Lt. Cdr. Egbert A.
ROZUK, Ens. Raymond E.
RUFFCORN, Ens. Alfred N.
RYAN, Ens. Donald J.

SACKRIDER, Ens. Wm. T.
SADICK, Lt. (jg) Gordon P.
SAMUELSEN, Lt. Wm. W.
SANDERS, Lt. (jg) Wm. P.
SANDERSON, Lt. John P., Jr.
SANDELL, Lt. Ivan J.
SARGEANT, Lt. (jg) Warren
SATTERFIELD, Lt. Karl B.
SAUL, Lt. (jg) Robt. M.
SAVIKKO, Lt. (jg) Albert H.
SAVILLE, Ens. Kenneth W.
SAWYER, Ens. Stephen F.
SAYERS, Ens. Wm. J.
SBISA, Lt. Alvin F.
SCHMIDT, Ens. Edw. F.
SCHMITT, Lt. Max F.

SCHOENFELDER, Ens. Chas. H.
SCHRADER, Cdr. Fredk. R.
SCHREINER, WO Alex. J.
SCHROEDER, Lt. Jos. L., Jr.
SCHUG, Ens. Ivan C.
SCHULER, Lt. Edwin F.
SCHULTE, Ens. Robt.
SCHULTZ, Ens. Fredk. E.
SCHUNCKE, Lt. Geo. W.
SCOPELITIS, Ens. Andrew
SCOTT, Lt. (jg) Merle D.
SCULLEY, Lt. Geo. F.
SEAMAN, Lt. Cdr. Allen L.
SEGUNDA, Midn. John W.
SEIBEL, Lt. Cdr. Marshall G.
SEIDELL, Ens. Daniel R.
SETSER, Lt. (jg) Beverly L.
SEYMOUR, Ens. Hovey
SHANAHAN, Ens. Wm. M.
SHAW, Ens. Chas. A.
SHEPARD, Ens. Jos. W.
SHERMAN, Ens. Leonard R.
SHIPMAN, Ens. Wm. A., Jr.
SHORT, WO Wm. L.
SHRIBMAN, Lt. (jg) Philip A.
SHULTZ, Midn. Bernard
SHUMAKER, Capt. Sam'l R.
SICKEL, Capt. Horatio G.
SIEBERT, Lt. Niles R.
SILLS, Lt. (jg) Donald R.
SIMONEAU, Lt. Forrest W.
SIMONCIK, Ens. Steve E.
SIMPSON, Lt. (jg) John C.
SIMPSON, Lt. Wm. E.
SINCLAIR, Lt. (jg) Robt. L.
SINGLETARY, Ens. Douglas K.
SKINNER, Ens. Jas. B.
SLAHETKA, Lt. (jg) Peter
SLATER, Ens. Walter L.
SLAWSON, Cdr. Paul S.
SMITH, Ens. Andrew F.
SMITH, Lt. Cdr. Douglas E.
SMITH, Ens. Heidle J.
SMITH, Ens. Melvin C.
SMITH, WO Mirel R.
SMITH, Ens. Ralph E.
SMITH, Ens. Richard P.
SMITH, Cdr. Wayne O.
SNEAD, Ens. Wm. S., Jr.
SNELL, Ens. Earl L.
SNOW, Ens. Norman W.
SNYDER, Ens. Chas. W.
SNYDER, Cdr. Geo. W., 3d
SOBOTA, Ens. Jerome J.
SORENSEN, Lt. Vernon F.

SOUTH, Ens. Robt. M.
SPEARS, Ens. Horace E.
SPEER, Lt. Kenneth R.
SPENCER, Lt. (jg) Herbert A.
SPILLANE, Lt. Jas. D.
SPINDLER, Ens. Arthur W.
SPRIGGS, Lt. Cdr. Morris H.
SQUIRES, Ens. Wayne P.
STACK, Lt. (jg) Edw. D.
STEARNS, Lt. (jg) Howard J.
STEELE, CWO, Jas. C., Jr.
STERLING, Ens. Theo. W., Jr.
STERN, Lt. (jg) Rich. G., Jr.
STEWART, Lt. Cdr. Wayne H.
STICKELL, Lt. John H.
STOCKER, Ens. Merrill S.
STONE, Lt. Fred M.
STONER, Lt. Robt. F.
STRONG, Lt. Byron W.
STURGELL, WO Stephen R.
SUAREZ, WO Jesse L.
SULLIVAN, Lt. (jg) Wm. J., Jr.
SULTZER, Lt. (jg) Jos. C., Jr.
SWEET, Ens. Walter F.
SZALAY, Ens. Andrew

TAMBS, Lt. (jg) Clifford M.
TAYLOR, Ens. Chas. B.
TAYLOR, Lt. (jg) Cyrus R.
TAYLOR, Lt. (jg) Norman A.
TEARNEY, Lt. (jg) Jas. E.
TENNENT, Cdr. John G., 3d
THOMAS, Lt. Daniel U.
THOMPSON, Lt. (jg) Raymond B.
THORNBURG, Lt. Harold B.
THURMAN, Lt. (jg) Ralph E.
TILGHMAN, Cdr. Geo. H.
TIMONEY, Lt. (jg) Floyd B.
TITUS, Ens. Mark L.
TOLMAN, Cdr. Chas. E.
TOMME, Lt. (jg) M. M., Jr.
TOQUAM, Ens. Ruby A.
TOTEMEIER, Ens. Everett L.
TRAVIS, Lt. (jg) Roland F.
TRAYNOR, Lt. Raymond N.
TRIBLE, Ens. Geo. B., Jr.
TROWBRIDGE, Lt. Herbert W.
TUCKER, Lt. (jg) Chas. W.
TULLY, Ens. Orville B.
TUOHY, Lt. (jg) John E.
TURINO, Lt. Thos. R.
TURNER, Lt. Stanley K.

ULRICH, Lt. Robt. H.

VANDENBERG, Lt. Edw. J.
VANDERWALL, Ens. Clarence J.
VANFLEET, Ens. Donald E.
VANROOSEN, Lt. (jg) Hugh C.
VAUGHN, Lt. (jg) Thos. M.
VAUGHAN, Lt. (jg) Robt. W.
VAUGHN, Ens. Garrett E.
VERNER, Ens. Robt.
VITCUSKY, Ens. Frank T.
VLIET, Ens. Jackson
VONSPRECKEN, Lt. (jg) Frank, Jr.
WAGNER, Ens. Anthony C.
WAGSTAFF, Lt. (jg) Henry M., Jr.
WAINWRIGHT, Ens. Jas. A., Jr.
WALKER, Lt. John K.
WALLING, Lt. Victor G.
WARD, Lt. Cdr. Robt. M.
WARNKE, Ens. Harry
WARREN, Ens. Jas. A.
WARREN, Lt. (jg) Thos. J.
WATERS, Lt. (jg) Francis M.
WATSON, Lt. (jg) Henry H., Jr.
WATSON, Lt. Norman H.
WATSON, Lt. Wm. W.
WATTS, WO Jos. H.
WEBB, Ens. Wm. F., Jr.
WEBER, Lt. (jg) Henry C., Jr.
WEBER, Ens. Wm. H.
WEBSTER, Ens. Robt.
WEGNER, Ens. Vernon A.
WEIPPERT, Lt. (jg) Wm.
WERNTZ, Ens. Robt. C.
WHALEY, Ens. Jas. D.
WHITAKER, Lt. Cdr. Frank M.
WHITAKER, Ens. Rich. C.

WHITE, Lt. (jg) Kemble, Jr.
WICKER, Lt. (jg) Chas. R.
WIGGIN, Ens. Alex K.
WILBUR, Ens. Gustave A.
WILI, WO Albert T.
WILLIAMS, WO Ben. W.
WILLIAMS, Ens. Glendle D.
WILLIAMS, Ens. John M.
WILSON, Lt. (jg) Henry M.
WILSON, WO Jas. L.
WILSON, WO John D.
WILSON, Lt. (jg) Paul J.
WILSON, Lt. (jg) Sherwood L.
WINGFIELD, Ens. Henry W.
WINSTEAD, Lt. (jg) Hubert H.
WINSTON, Ens. Joe G.
WINTERS, Lt. (jg) Donald E.
WITTSCHEN, Ens. Theo. P., Jr.
WOOD, Lt. (jg) Ernest W., Jr.
WOOD, Lt. Leonard E.
WOOD, Ens. Rich. H.
WOOD, Ens. Walter A., Jr.
WOODY, Lt. Frank A.
WOOLMAN, Lt. (jg) Alan D.
WRIGHT, Ens. Hector S.
WRIGHT, Lt. Robt. P.
WYMAN, Lt. Newell P.

YARASHES, Ens. Vincent
YARBRAY, Lt. (jg) Paul K.
YORK, Lt. Cecil R.
YOUNG, Lt. (jg) Lawrence H.

ZALEWSKI, Ens. Henry J. V.
ZEHRUNG, Lt. (jg) John A., Jr.

ENLISTED CASUALTIES—ACTIVE AND INACTIVE

List of Dead in Pacific and Asiatic Areas Between 1 December 1943 and
1 November 1944

As of 15 October 1947

AAB, Howard D., S1/c
ABAIR, Russell, Jr., S1/c
ABOOD, Geo., S2/c
ABRAJANO, Pedro, S3/c
ABRAM, Avery W., ACOMA
ABRAMSON, Albert L., S2/c
ABRUZZINO, Thos. J., AM1/c
ACCARDI, Vito T., PhM2/c
ACFALLE, Vincente R., StM3/c
ACIERTO, Antonio, Ck1/c
ACKART, Stanley P., AMM3/c
ACTON, Francis T., S2/c
ADAMS, Calvin E., S2/c
ADAMS, Cecil L. PhM3/c
ADAMS, Gerald J., BM2/c
ADAMS, Harry E., S1/c
ADAMS, Jos., Jr., S2/c
ADAMS, Thos. W., ARM3/c
ADDINGTON, Norman E., Jr., FCO3/c
ADKINS, Lawrence H., F2/c
ADOLPH, Adrian L., F1/c
AGNER, Robt. G., S2/c
AGNEW, Chas. V., RDM3/c
AGNEW, Rich. J., CM3/c
AGRIMONTI, Louis, EM2/c
AGUIGUI, Felix T., StM3/c
AGUON, Pedro I., NSEA2/c
AHARONIAN, Harry, SOM2/c
AHLERS, Henry J., PhM3/c
AHLFINGER, Paul WT2/c
AISTON, Lester E., SC3/c
AKERMAN, Phillip A., S1/c
AKERS, Wm. C., CS2/c
AKEY, Saml. J., Cox.
AKIN, Noel D., F1/c
ALAMINSKI, Edwin V., CM2/c
ALBANESE, Rosario V., ARM3/c

ALBERICO, Jos. M., S2/c
ALBERT, Reny, Cox.
ALBITZ, John F., Jr., AMM3/c
ALBRIGHT, Fred W., S1/c
ALBRIGHT, Roger R., AMM3/c
ALDAY, Thos. L., CGMP
ALDERSON, Frank T., S2/c
ALDRICH, Donald R., S2/c
ALDRICH, Ralph E., Jr., F1/c
ALESI, Biaggio J., ARM3/c
ALEXANDER, Chas. H., Y1/c
ALEXANDER, Robt. D., QM2/c
ALEXANDER, Thedora L., MM1/c
ALLARD, John F., Cox.
ALLEN, Chas. C., S1/c
ALLEN, Glenn L., ARM2/c
ALLEN, Lonnie, S2/c
ALLEN, Robt. H., S2/c
ALLEN, Robt. K., Cox.
ALLEN, Robin E., PhM2/c
ALLEN, Roger R., PhM2/c
ALLEN, Solon L., Jr., F1/c
ALLEN, Willard, S1/c
ALLEVA, Jos. G., S1/c
ALLISON, Harry J., ARM3/c
ALLISON, John E., Jr., TM3/c
ALLMON, Mervin W., MoMM1/c
ALLYN, Hyrum L., S1/c
ALMANZA, Eulalio J., S2/c
ALSBROOKS, Barney V., PhM2/c
ALSPAUGH, John A., ACMA
ALTAMIRANO, Robt. D., SM2/c
ALVARADO, Edmund J., CCSA
AMBRO, Eugene A., PhM2/c
AMENDA, John C., EM2/c
AMES, Ralph H., AMM3/c
AMSPOKER, Walter H., SM3/c

CASUALTIES

ANCONA, Anthony, S1/c
ANDEEN, David W., Y3/c
ANDERSEN, Robt S., HA1/c
ANDERSON, Aron L., S2/c
ANDERSON, Arthur D., S2/c
ANDERSON, Carl V., S1/c
ANDERSON, Cecil Theodore, AOM3/c
ANDERSON, David E., AOM3/c
ANDERSON, Edw. F., F2/c
ANDERSON, Harold Reuben, Cox.
ANDERSON, Harris C., EM1/c
ANDERSON, Howard H., AMM1/c
ANDERSON, Irwin H., PhM2/c
ANDERSON, John M., HA1/c
ANDERSON, Jos. A., WT3/c
ANDERSON, Loran W., SK2/c
ANDERSON, Perry A., S2/c
ANDERSON, Raymond J., S1/c
ANDERSON, Robert Burns, PhM2/c
ANDERSON, Roy B., BM2/c
ANDERSON, Wade, WT2/c
ANDERSON, Wm. J., Cox.
ANDIFF, Francis P., EM2/c
ANDRADA, Jack, S2/c
ANDREWS, Edward J., StM2/c
ANDREWS, Harry E., GM3/c
ANDREWS, Laurin C., SM3/c
ANDREWS, Thos. D., S2/c
ANGLIN, Chas. L., CCSP
ANGLIN, Donald W., F1/c
ANGLIN, Lewis E., AOM3/c
ANTOLOSKY, John, S1/c
APPICIE, Chester, CBMP
APPLEFELD, Jos. A., ARM2/c
APPLING, Jas. I., EM2/c
AQUINO, Dominic R., AOM3/c
ARCHAMBEAU, Carl, F1/c
ARCHERD, Lynn Simmons, ARM2/c
ARCHIBALD, Edwin D., AMM1/c
ARMSTRONG, James Herbert, MM2/c
ARMSTRONG, Marvin M., F1/c
ARMSTRONG, Robt. L., PhM3/c
ARNAUD, John B., BM2/c
ARNOLD, David Joe, FCM3/c
ARNOLD, Geo. M., PhM3/c
ARNOLD, Warren H., F2/c
ARNOLDY, Theo. F., S2/c
ARPIN, Louis W., S1/c
ARSCIS, Michael G., EM1/c
ARTLEY, Arthur E., ARM3/c
ARTOWICZ, Theo. J., S2/c
ARTRIP, Ebert E., EM1/c
ASH, Alma S., Jr., QM2/c
ASHMORE, Floyd V., MM2/c
ASHTON, Thos. E., Jr., EM3/c

ASHWORTH, Geo. E., S2/c
ASPROMONTE, Dominick, S2/c
ATEN, Frank R., GM3/c
ATKINS, Lawrence A., Y2/c
ATKINSON, Othello, AMM3/c
ATUN, Hyman, ARM2/c
AUCOIN, Lee E., S1/c
AUDIBERT, Benoit B., GM1/c
AUERBACK, Edw. H., PhM3/c
AUGE, James J., S2/c
AUGUSTINO, Joe Paul, Cox.
AUSTIN, Carl S., S2/c
AUSTIN, Chas. G., S1/c
AUSTIN, Eddie, StM2/c
AUSTIN, Garland, S1/c
AUSTIN, Milton H., FCO1/c
AUSTIN, Thos. K., WT1/c
AUTHIER, Chas. H., Jr., F2/c
AVERILL, Donald E., S1/c
AVERY, Alfred F., MM1/c
AVERY, Benj. B., Jr., S1/c
AVERY, Roy E., HA1/c
AVILA, Geo. J., S1/c
AYERS, Herbert W., S2/c

BABAYAN, Vahanier G., RM3/c
BABBS, Marshall L., S2/c
BARBER, Geo. R., S1/c
BABYAK, John M., MM2/c
BACA, Jose, PhM3/c
BACILE, Marion A., SC3/c
BACKSTROM, Louie C., BM2/c
BACKUS, Jos. B., AMM2/c
BACON, Douglas M., GM3/c
BADYRKA, Peter, PhM3/c
BAER, Robt. W., HA1/c
BAGBY, Walter Franklin, SF2/c
BAGEN, John P., PhM2/c
BAILEY, Albert H., S1/c
BAILEY, Frank L., MM2/c
BAILEY, Harold Raymond, S2/c
BAILEY, James W., S1/c
BAILEY, Robt. E., TMV3/c
BAILEY, Vincent L., SK1/c
BAILEY, Walter E., S2/c
BAIZE, Reathel C., S2/c
BAK, Frank D., PhM3/c
BAKER, Chas. H., CMoMMA
BAKER, David H., S1/c
BAKER, Edward S., SOM3/c
BAKER, Feltner, S1/c
BAKER, Kenneth W., GM1/c
BAKER, Mark M., GM1/c
BAKER, Oliver F., PhM3/c
BAKER, Oren P., S1/c

BAKER, Trannie O., S1/c
BAKER, Wm. A., Jr., RM3/c
BALAS, Wm. G., MM3/c
BALCERAK, Harry F., AMM3/c
BALDRIDGE, Clyde T., S1/c
BALDWIN, Chas. M., Jr., MoMM2/c
BALDWIN, Edmund J., PhM1/c
BALDWIN, John B., MM3/c
BALES, Paul E., C2/c
BALFREY, Robt. E., AMM2/c
BALISTRERI, Tom D., S1/c
BALL, Charley E., WT3/c
BALL, Louis D., MoMM2/c
BALL, Robt. N., S1/c
BALL, Walter B., CCMA
BALLARD, Jas. D., MoMM2/c
BALLOU, Wm. E., CEMA
BALON, John, S2/c
BALTURSHOT, Wm., CS1/c
BALUT, Andrew J., F1/c
BANDY, Ira B., AOM3/c
BANISTER, Paul C., MoMM2/c
BANKS, Earl D., SC3/c
BANKS, Frank Andrew, St3/c
BANKS, Geo. W., S2/c
BANKS, Herman W., EM2/c
BANKS, Mitchell, MM3/c
BANOS, Raul F., PhM2/c
BANOVICH, Peter S2/c
BARACCO, Steve J., S1/c
BARBER, Milton M., F2/c
BARBER, Ursel W., MM2/c
BARCALA, Santiago, ARM3/c
BARCIO, Chas. W., AOM3/c
BARD, Francis P., WT3/c
BARFIELD, Jas., AMM2/c
BARGER, Thos. E., EM2/c
BARHAM, Elmer C., S2/c
BARHAM, Lewis W., RM2/c
BARKER, Dick Colver, Ptr2/c
BARKER, Paul L., S2/c
BARKLEY, Howard, EM3/c
BARKS, Chas. W., S1/c
BARKS, John W., S1/c
BARLOW, Russell J., AMM2/c
BARLOW, Wm. V., ARM3/c
BARNARD, Frank P., ARM3/c
BARNES, Frank K., S1/c
BARNES, Jas. E., BM1/c
BARNES, Paul James, WT2/c
BARNETT, Fred Lee, Cox.
BARNETT, Herman D., S1/c
BARNETT, Kenneth E., PhM2/c
BARNETTE, Chas. P., S2/c
BARNEY, Wallace A., ARM3/c

BARNHART, Chester A., CGMP
BARR, Luther V., MM3/c
BARRESE, Samuel J., MM3/c
BARRETT, Arthur P., Jr., F1/c
BARRETT, Marshall C., S1/c
BARRICKMAN, Carlisle, Jr., PhM2/c
BARRON, John F., ARM3/c
BARRON, Saml. J., S1/c
BARRY, Wm. J., RM2/c
BARTELL, Fredk. O., GM1/c
BARTELLO, Leo, Jr., PhM3/c
BARTLETT, Geo. W., Jr., S2/c
BARTLETT, Melvin D., CCMP
BARTLETT, Ray. E., F1/c
BARTLETT, Robt. D., S2/c
BARTLETT, Willie E., WT3/c
BARTLEY, John W., F1/c
BARTLEY, Robert Joseph, F3/c
BARTON, Edward J., CTMP
BARTON, Phil S., ARM2/c
BARTON, Robt. D., Y1/c
BARTON, Sherman L., S1/c
BARTONEK, Eugene J., S2/c
BARTOLI, Renato, S1/c
BARVINSKI, Henry, HA2/c
BASEL, John, EM2/c
BASEY, John S., F2/c
BASSETT, Albert J., Jr., S2/c
BASSO, Louis D., MM1/c
BASTANCHURY, Jean A., GM2/c
BATCHELDER, Wm. C., BM2/c
BATCHELOR, Clifford, GM2/c
BATES, Dennis, CBMA
BATES, Fred W., S2/c
BATES, Raymond L., S1/c
BATES, Robt. H., QM1/c
BATHGATE, Walter K. W., CTMA
BAUCOM, John B., S2/c
BAUER, Lewis L., M1/c
BAUER, Richard F., RM3/c
BAUGHMAN, Geo. W., Jr., GM3/c
BAULIS, Robt. G., F1/c
BAUM, Wm. P., Cox.
BAUMANN, Bernard N., PhM2/c
BAUSERMAN, Owen R., SC2/c
BAXTER, Arthur J., F1/c
BAYLESS, Merrill J., WT1/c
BAYLOR, Ralph C., AOM2/c
BAYNOR, John, CMMA
BEAL, John W., SSMB3/c
BEARCE, Wm. C., S1/c
BEARDSLEY, Wm. F., PhM2/c
BEASLEY, Willie F., StM2/c
BEATTY, Jas. W., PhM3/c
BEATTY, Robt. K., S2/c

CASUALTIES

BEAULIEU, Rich. J., S1/c
BEAUPRE, Emilien, S1/c
BECK, J. W. Coleman, S2/c
BECKELHEIMER, Geo. E., TM3/c
BECKER, Roy E., Jr., SC2/c
BECKMAN, Vernon N., S1/c
BEDNAR, Jas., S1/c
BEECHAM, Thos. W., CEMP
BEED, Bilton R., EM2/c
BEHRENDT, Donald P., Y3/c
BELDERES, Geo., SF2/c
BELEY, Michael, Jr., S2/c
BELHUMEUR, Normand P., F1/c
BELL, Jack D., AOM2/c
BELL, Jas. H., HA1/c
BELL, Morris A., S1/c
BELL, Ralph E., MM2/c
BELL, Richard E., Cox.
BELL, Robt. G., CM1/c
BELL, Thos. W., S2/c
BELL, Willis, StM2/c
BELTRAN, Eulogio, CStA
BELTZ, Wm. H., ARM2/c
BELVIN, Jas. J., CMMA
BEMIS, Richard V., MM2/c
BENBOW, William, M1/c
BENDER, Franklin E., S1/c
BENDER, John., Jr., SK2/c
BENKO, Frank, Jr., SC3/c
BENNETT, Dewey Douglas, RM3/c
BENNETT, Forest E., S2/c
BENNETT, Garnett I., MoMM2/c
BENNETT, Jas. K., Jr., GM3/c
BENOIT, Edw. M., AOM3/c
BENOIT, Theogene, AMM3/c
BENSMAN, Paul P., AOM2/c
BENTLEY, John S., MM1/c
BENTLEY, Richard W., HA1/c
BENTRUP, Lloyd T., S1/c
BENZIE, Paul, GM3/c
BERDAMI, Jos. B., AM2/c
BERENS, Edward J., SF1/c
BERG, Max D., MoMM3/c
BERGADO, Marcelino T., StM1/c
BERGERON, Freddie P., ARM3/c
BERGMAN, Reynold M., S1/c
BERNING, Leslie E., S2/c
BERRESFORD, Niel T., TM1/c
BERRY, Forrest D., FC2/c
BERRY, Harvey J., S1/c
BERRY, Max W., S1/c
BERRY, Wallace P., S2/c
BERTINETTI, Frank, M1/c
BESECKER, Dean O., Ptr2/c
BESOAIN, Wm. H., Jr., AOM3/c

BESSONETTE, Chas. T., S2/c
BETTINGER, Wm. A., F2/c
BETZ, Herbert H., QM2/c
BIANCO, Angelo L., S1/c
BIANCO, John A., F2/c
BICKNELL, Alex B., S2/c
BIEBER, Jess J., AMM3/c
BIEGEL, Chas. N., FCM3/c
BIENIEWICZ, Frank J., TM2/c
BIGALKE, Theo. J., BM2/c
BIGGS, Harold L., S2/c
BIGGS, Herbert C., Jr., ARM3/c
BIGGS, Perry J., MoMM2/c
BIGGY, Vernon J., MoMM1/c
BIGLOW, Robt., S2/c
BILLINGS, Harold, ARM3/c
BINDER, Paul B., CPHMP
BINGAMAN, Richard A., F1/c
BINNING, Geo. H., S2/c
BIRKINSHAW, Jerome, S1/c
BIRKMEYER, Eugene A., Jr., S1/c
BIRNSCHIEN, Lawrence J., AMM1/c
BIRON, Arthur, SC1/c
BIRTWISTLE, James J., MM3/c
BISCARDI, Leonard, ARM2/c
BISHOP, Chas. A., SC3/c
BISHOP, Gail Adair, S2/c
BISHOP, Jos. E., CEMA
BISTROWITZ, Abe, S2/c
BLACK, Curtheal, St3/c
BLACK, Luther L., S2/c
BLACKBURN, Wm. L., S1/c
BLACKWELL, Cletus E., S2/c
BLACKWELL, Ernest S., PhM2/c
BLACKWOOD, Cecil E., S1/c
BLACKWOOD, Lawrence, S1/c
BLADT, Jacob A., TM3/c
BLAIR, Ernie B., S2/c
BLAIR, Kenneth S., CSMA
BLAIR, Stanley, S2/c
BLAKE, Donald Jay, S2/c
BLANCETT, Jesse R., PhM2/c
BLANCO, Anthony P., S1/c
BLANKENSHIP, Cleo, S2/c
BLANKENSHIP, Oran W., PhM2/c
BLANSETT, Elija J., MoMM1/c
BLATTNER, John R., AOM2/c
BLAYDES, Wilbur K., Jr., PhM2/c
BLAZ, Vicente C., Cox.
BLEWETT, Kenneth L., HA1/c
BLISKEY, Jos. J., Jr., ART1/c
BLOECHER, Fred W., Bkr1/c
BLOMSTROM, Russell C., S1/c
BLODIN, Oscar E., EM2/c
BLOOD, Leon W., GM3/c

BLOOMINGDALE, Leslie F., PhM3/c
BLOSCHOK, John F., S1/c
BLYTHE, Clifford L., S1/c
BLYTHE, Robt. A., SC3/c
BOARDMAN, Earl W., MM2/c
BOATMAN, Saml. W., PhM3/c
BOBO, Allen W., Jr., SM3/c
BOCKUS, Frank L., Cox.
BODAK, John B., MoMM2/c
BODISH, Edw. M., SSMT2/c
BODNAR, John P., SC1/c
BOEHM, Fred W., Cox.
BOESKOOL, Donald, MoMM2/c
BOGDAN, Cyril M., MoMM2/c
BOGGS, Thos. H., EM2/c
BOHLER, Robt. J., TM3/c
BOLAND, Geo. W., EM3/c
BOLANDER, Kenneth R., S1/c
BOLEWSKI, John R., S2/c
BOLEY, Mitchell, CM3/c
BOLING, Frank E., S1/c
BOLTON, Harry A., MM1/c
BOLTON, James W., CAPA
BOLTZ, Darwin B., F1/c
BOLZE, John F., FCM1/c
BOND, Beecher O., PhM3/c
BOND, Raymond T., PhM3/c
BONDS, Hollis A., TM2/c
BONE, Freddie R., S2/c
BONETTI, Anthony J., F1/c
BONHAM, Glenn M., S1/c
BONNAFE, Richard L., MM2/c
BONNELL, Bert H., CM3/c
BONNER, John H., StM1/c
BONSHIRE, Wm. O., RDM2/c
BOOKS, Robt. L., F2/c
BOONE, Baldwin, GM1/c
BOONE, Jesse W., HA1/c
BOONSTRA, Dirk B., ARM1/c
BOOTH, Jerome M., S2/c
BOOTH, Raymond, F1/c
BOOTH, Wm. L., CFCA
BOREN, Edw., S2/c
BORK, Edward, CFCA
BOROUGH, John R., WT2/c
BOSSHART, Maurice L., S2/c
BOSTON, Gordon L., ARM2/c
BOTSFORD, Marvin R., MM3/c
BOTTOMS, Horace B., S2/c
BOTWRIGHT, Wm. C., S1/c
BOUCK, Ralph R., BM2/c
BOUDREAUX, Ernest J., BM1/c
BOUGERE, Louis C., MoMM2/c
BOUNDS, Claude W., S2/c
BOURKE, Frank F., F1/c

BOUTOS, Nicholas J., ARM2/c
BOVEE, Chas. F., AMMP2/c
BOWEN, Earl E., TM3/c
BOWEN, Thos. H., EM2/c
BOWERS, Frank H., F1/c
BOWERS, Harry L., CRTA
BOWLBY, Donald W., RM3/c
BOWLING, Chas. T., MM1/c
BOWMAN, Elmer A., ARM2/c
BOWMAN, Forest, EM1/c
BOWMAN, Glenie W., S1/c
BOWMAN, Jas. W., TM3/c
BOWMAN, Wilburn G., EM3/c
BOWMAN, Wm. F., EM3/c
BOYD, Bill F., S1/c
BOYD, Chas. E., Jr., F1/c
BOYD, Donnas H., Cox.
BOYD, Jas. D., EM3/c
BOYD, Stephen S., EM2/c
BOYD, Thos., Jr., S2/c
BOYDSTON, Arthur W., ARM1/c
BOYER, Hiram R., ARM3/c
BOYER, Hubert F., Cox.
BOYLE, Lawrence J., S2/c
BOYT, Robt. H., CMoMMP
BRACE, Leonard W., S1/c
BRACHA, Melvin G., RM2/c
BRACKETT, Albert G., CSFA
BRADFORD, Donald W., ARM2/c
BRADLEY, Donald J., F1/c
BRADLEY, Stephen M., Jr., S1/c
BRADLEY, Thos. C., AOM2/c
BRADSHAW, Chas. A., S1/c
BRADY, Chas. W., S2/c
BRADY, Norbert F., MM3/c
BRAGG, John H., AM1/c
BRAKE, Elmer C., S2/c
BRAND, Jos. J., WT1/c
BRAND, Kenneth P., F1/c
BRANNAN, Robt. J., EM1/c
BRANNEN, Wm. T., PhM3/c
BRANT, Fredk. J., S2/c
BRANT, Harold J., SC2/c
BRASEL, Thos. L., S2/c
BRASHEAR, Jas. G., AEM2/c
BRASHER, Jas. F., Jr., AMM3/c
BRAUN, Alois J., PhM3/c
BRAUN, Eric W., F1/c
BRAY, Wylie R., EM1/c
BRAYMAN, Burr, Jr., S2/c
BRAZEL, Willie G., CK2/c
BRAZZELL, Jas. R., S1/c
BREHM, Jerome C., BM1/c
BRENNAN, Jas. D., SF1/c
BRENNAN, Jos. L., S2/c

CASUALTIES

Bress, Dwight D., ARM3/c
Brett, Geo. H., BM1/c
Brett, Jesse R., Jr., PhM2/c
Brewer, Earl O., AMM2/c
Brewer, Leander, Jr., StM1/c
Brickerd, John M., Jr., S1/c
Brickman, Ernest L., MM3/c
Bridges, Alfred J., GM1/c
Briear, Geo. H., F1/c
Brien, Harris John, S1/c
Brien, Theodore Arthur, S2/c
Briggs, Lynus N., AMM3/c
Briggs, Robt. G., CYA
Briley, Gordon E., MM2/c
Brillon, Alcide E., MM3/c
Brimer, Merril C., S2/c
Brine, Wm. E., S1/c
Brinkley, Tony W., AM3/c
Brisco, Johnny H., StM2/c
Bristol, Harry D., WT2/c
Brittingham, Otis B., CRMP
Brittingham, Richard C., CYP
Britten, Wesley Malvin, S1/c
Brochu, Walter R., S2/c
Brodie, Geo. S., EM2/c
Brodsky, Chas., CBMP
Brody, H. Nathaniel, SOM3/c
Brohman, Henry G., PhM1/c
Brollair, Lemont G., F1/c
Brooks, Calvin B., PhM3/c
Brooks, Francis Doyle, S2/c
Brooks, Francis L., S2/c
Brooks, Malcolm M., MoMM2/c
Brooks, Raymond L., S2/c
Brooks, Russell H., EM1/c
Broome, Ernest K., F1/c
Broome, James T., ARM2/c
Broome, Lewis, RM2/c
Brose, Geo. E., SF2/c
Brouillet, Vern Clarence, S2/c
Brousseau, Herbert D., S2/c
Brousseau, Maurice J., S2/c
Brow, Earl H., S1/c
Brower, Edward R., S2/c
Brower, Wm. A., S1/c
Brown, Amos, S1/c
Brown, David, SC3/c
Brown, Ernest A., GH2/c
Brown, Ernest F., S2/c
Brown, Eugene R., AOM1/c
Brown, F. E., StM2/c
Brown, Floyd N., MM3/c
Brown, Fred P., S1/c
Brown, Geo. G., AOM2/c

Brown, Gordon N., S1/c
Brown, Hugh D., MoMM2/c
Brown, Jas. H., S1/c
Brown, Jos. E., Jr., AMM2/c
Brown, John F., S2/c
Brown, Kenneth, StM1/c
Brown, Kenneth V., S1/c
Brown, Laurence W., HA1/c
Brown, Leonard J., S1/c
Brown, McLain R., FC3/c
Brown, Milton V., MoMM2/c
Brown, Oral R., SK1/c
Brown, Raymond C., SoM3/c
Brown, Robt. M., SK3/c
Brown, Russell, SK3/c
Brown, Stanley I., MM1/c
Brown, Steven L., S2/c
Brown, Theo. H., S1/c
Brown, Thos. L., BM1/c
Brown, Warren W., F1/c
Brubaker, Harley, FCM2/c
Bruce, Joe S., S1/c
Bruce, Robt. W., MM2/c
Bruckshaw, Robt. E., MM1/c
Bruderer, Werner L., MoMM1/c
Bruggensmith, Robt. L., SC3/c
Bruggman, Alfred B., S1/c
Brun, Roland J., TM3/c
Brunelle, Jos. A., S1/c
Brunner, Friedrick L., GM2/c
Bruns, Walter A., Jr., CRMA
Brunson, Jos. A., Jr., ARM3/c
Bryan, Ted P., PhM2/c
Bryant, Arthur E., F2/c
Bryant, Clifford Irving, GM2/c
Bryant, Jas., Ck2/c
Bryant, James J., F2/c
Bryant, John E., F2/c
Bryant, Othar E., StM1/c
Bryant, Theo. W., SF1/c
Bryant, Thomas Crawford, S2/c
Bryce, Russel G., MM3/c
Brzozowski, Stanley A., Cox.
Bucar, Jos. S., MoMM2/c
Buccanero, Evert C., AMM1/c
Buchan, John W., MoMM1/c
Buchan, Wilson N., EM1/c
Buchel, Edw. F., ARM1/c
Buchman, John M., AMM2/c
Buckingham, Ernest A., MM2/c
Buckley, Harland G., GM3/c
Buckley, Walter E., WT3/c
Budd, Wallace G., ARM2/c
Bugajsky, Edw. J., S2/c

BUGANICH, Paul, CAPP
BULLARD, Howard M., TM2/c
BULLINGER, Roy G., MM3/c
BULLOCK, Richard, Bkr3/c
BULLOCK, Wm. J., SM2/c
BUNCH, Preston L., AOM2/c
BUNCH, Wm. H., S1/c
BUONOMO, Dan A., RM1/c
BURCH, John C., F1/c
BURCH, Marion Oliver, S1/c
BURCHELL, Chas. D., S1/c
BURCKHARD, Mike T., S1/c
BURDECKI, Bernard A., MM3/c
BURDEN, John W., CMMP
BURDETTE, Bobby N., S2/c
BURDETTE, Boyd A., CSFP
BURDETTE, Wm. E., MM3/c
BURGER, Earl R., S2/c
BURGESS, Franklin, Cox.
BURGESS, Wm. E., MM1/c
BURGHARDT, Frank, PhM1/c
BURKE, Edmund J., MM3/c
BURKE, Edw. G., ARM2/c
BURKE, John P., FC2/c
BURKOWSKI, Walter F., AMM2/c
BURMAN, Kenneth J., S2/c
BURMAN, Willard E., S1/c
BURNETT, Geo. M., S2/c
BURNETT, Wm. R., PhM3/c
BURNHAM, Robt. L., S1/c
BURNS, Edward J., S1/c
BURNS, Frank Robert, S2/c
BURNS, Robt. G., F1/c
BURNS, Rodger M., Cox.
BURNS, Wm., CBMA
BURRELL, Hershel S., S1/c
BURRIDGE, Geo. T., CRMA
BURRIS, John Elbert, S2/c
BURROUGHS, Eugene W., S2/c
BURROWS, Orbie B., S2/c
BURTON, Leland S., ARM2/c
BURTON, Robert Everett, Cox.
BURWELL, Clifford R., MM2/c
BUSBY, Rance Glenn, S2/c
BUSCHUR, Paul A., S2/c
BUSH, Arlyn, MM3/c
BUTKIEWICZ, Dan, S1/c
BUTLER, Collie H., S2/c
BUTLER, Geo. D., SF3/c
BUTT, Howard E., Jr., CCMA
BUTTI, Jos. P., S2/c
BUZEK, Rudolph F., EM3/c
BYLOW, Vernon E., S2/c
BYRD, Floyd B., HA1/c

BYRD, Frank L., StM1/c
BYRD, Hershel W., PhM3/c
BYRD, Virgil, CQMP
BYRNS, Dennis M., S2/c
BYRUM, Nolan R., SF3/c

CACCIATO, Diego, Jr., TM3/c
CADDARETTE, Jos. W., Jr., BM2/c
CAFIERO, Anthony F., CCMA
CAHIR, Wm. R., F1/c
CAHL, James F. P., TM3/c
CAIQUEP, Arsenio, St1/c
CALDERON, Manuel V., AOM3/c
CALDWELL, Billy W., WT3/c
CALDWELL, Leland J. D., S2/c
CALHOUN, Waid B., Cox.
CALLAHAN, Jos. T., SM3/c
CALLAHAN, Melvin C., S1/c
CALLAWAY, Enoch E., EM3/c
CALLIHAN, Clyde, Jr., HA1/c
CAMACHO, Jose. S., NS2/c
CAMBRA, Edw., S1/c
CAMERLINCK, Bernard V., Sr., S2/c
CAMERON, Bruce, S2/c
CAMERON, Glenn, GM2/c
CAMMARATA, Philip J., S2/c
CAMPBELL, Carl A., F1/c
CAMPBELL, Chas. W., GM2/c
CAMPBELL, Crawford K., MoMM2/c
CAMPBELL, David E., S1/c
CAMPBELL, John E., StM2/c
CAMPBELL, Jos. H., AMM2/c
CAMPBELL, Loyd L., S2/c
CAMPBELL, Mack E., Y3/c
CAMPBELL, Neil J., S2/c
CAMPBELL, William Felix, S2/c
CAMPFIELD, Barton F., CMMP
CANNON, Houston R., CAPA
CANNON, Jerald D., S2/c
CANTLIN, Wayne B., S2/c
CANTRELL, Herbert E., S1/c
CANTWELL, Wm. J., S2/c
CAOUETTE, Armand N., TM2/c
CAPENER, Merrill E., AMM3/c
CAPPS, Alvie E., F1/c
CAPUTO, Vincenzo J., RDM3/c
CARAWAN, Benago G., PhM2/c
CARDELL, Jos., SF1/c
CARDEN, Clarence, Cox.
CARDINALE, Carl L., PhM2/c
CARDOZA, David F., MM3/c
CARDWELL, Norman W., SoM2/c
CAREY, Jas. E., ARM1/c
CAREY, Wm. P., ARM1/c

CASUALTIES

Carey, Jerry D., PhM2/c
Cariello, Vincent J., S2/c
Carina, Wm. G., F1/c
Carkhuff, Wm. H., PhM2/c
Carl, Jeff C., GM3/c
Carl, Robt. P., S1/c
Carlin, Wm. J., Jr., Y1/c
Carline, Frank Joseph, CCMP
Carlisle, Stanley H., MoMM1/c
Carlsen, Wallace K., CRMP
Carlson, Chas. L., S1/c
Carlson, Chester E., FC3/c
Carlson, Edwin D., F1/c
Carlson, John Robert, MM2/c
Carlson, Kenneth V., ARM2/c
Carlson, Lyle A., S2/c
Carmichael, Elmer G., GM2/c
Carmody, Kenneth J., GM3/c
Carnahan, Lee P., RDM3/c
Carnahan, Ralph B., TM2/c
Carney, Wm. A., Jr., F1/c
Carpenter, John R., MMS2/c
Carpenter, Robt. A., RM2/c
Carpenter, Wm. T., BM1/c
Carr, Clifford H., F2/c
Carr, Donald D., S2/c
Carr, Jas. R., SF3/c
Carr, Lorraine Golden, S1/c
Carr, Paul H., GM3/c
Carraway, Kermit L., CWTA
Carrithers, Chas. C., S1/c
Carroll, Elbon L., S1/c
Carroll, Eugene D., AMM3/c
Carroll, John F., S1/c
Carson, Geo. R., CGMA
Carter, Arthur D., ARM2/c
Carter, Larned A., AMM1/c
Carter, Raymond L., S1/c
Carter, Ted A., AM2/c
Cartmell, Walter A., CMoMMP
Cartwright, Wm. E., S1/c
Carvalho, Antone, S2/c
Carvalho, Benedict M., F1/c
Carwile, Nathanial G., AMM1/c
Cary, Oran F., RM1/c
Case, Leonard P., RM2/c
Casey, John F., MM1/c
Casey, Richard F., HA1/c
Cash, Allen C., MM3/c
Casimiri, Nunzio N., S1/c
Caskins, James E., S1/c
Castille, John L., StM1/c
Castle, Jos. W., Jr., BM1/c
Catalano, Vincent Chris, F1/c

Cavender, Garnett L., S2/c
Cecconi, Nello, S2/c
Centola, Victor J. L., CSKA
Cepeda, Juan S., NS2/c
Cercone, Michael A., S1/c
Cerny, Jos. L., WT3/c
Cerra, Felix C., S1/c
Cerrinack, Chas. J., CGMP
Chaffin, Elmer E., F1/c
Chaffin, Kenneth L., S1/c
Chagnon, Oscar O., AM2/c
Chaison, Marshall F., RM1/c
Chalmers, John W., Jr., ARM1/c
Chalmers, Wm. J., S2/c
Chambers, Fredk. L., S1/c
Chambers, Herbert Y., WT2/c
Chambers, John B., St1/c
Chambers, Robt. W., WT1/c
Chamberlin, Rollo D., F1/c
Champaco, Vicente A., NMM3/c
Chandler, Martin L., S2/c
Chaney, John D., S1/c
Chapin, Virgil Freeland, WT2/c
Chapman, Arthur E., S2/c
Chapman, Arthur G., MoMM3/c
Chapman, Jos. R., S1/c
Chapman, Vernon Dow, S2/c
Chappell, Wm. R., S1/c
Charette, Paul R., F1/c
Charfauros, Arthur B. L., StM3/c
Charfauros, Francisco N., NS2/c
Charles, Thos. F., ARM2/c
Charles, Virgil W., F1/c
Chase, Howard Eugene, S2/c
Chase, Kenneth W., S1/c
Chase, Theo. J., CBMA
Chatman, Jos., MM3/c
Chavarrias, Alfonso, GM3/c
Cheek, Dan S., S2/c
Cheney, William Henry, StM1/c
Chenowith, Jos. G., TM2/c
Cherry, Alph T., S2/c
Cherry, Eugene T., St3/c
Cherry, Perry L., S2/c
Chestna, Jos., MM2/c
Childress, Aubury H., Jr., ARM2/c
Chiles, James R., BM2/c
Chism, Jas. D., Jr., CMMA
Chmura, John J., ARM2/c
Choate, Howard A., Cox.
Choate, J. C., EM2/c
Choin, Robt. E., RDM2/c
Chopchik, Geo. J., BM1/c
Chotos, Harry Z., S1/c

CHRISTEN, Herbert G., F1/c
CHRISTENSEN, Clarence F., CM1/c
CHRISTENSEN, David A., AMM2/c
CHRISTENSEN, Donald R., S1/c
CHRISTENSEN, Ernest L., PhM3/c
CHRISTENSEN, Maynard E., MM3/c
CHRISTENSEN, Robt. V., SF1/c
CHRISTIANSEN, Chas. W., MoMM2/c
CHRISTIANSEN, Peter Elmer, S1/c
CHRISTY, Frederic H., SC2/c
CHRISTY, Kenneth M., AOM2/c
CHUITES, Geo. R., EM3/c
CHUN, Louis F., CM2/c
CHURCH, Chas. D., MM2/c
CHURCH, Wm. V., BM1/c
CHURCHILL, Harold S., MoMM2/c
CIEPLY, Norbert J., ARM2/c
CILLEY, Lester E., GM2/c
CITARELLA, Henry, TM3/c
CIULLA, Michael A., SC2/c
CLABITE, Estiban B., St1/c
CLACK, Roy L., EM3/c
CLARK, Benj. L., TM1/c
CLARK, Carl D., S1/c
CLARK, Chas. C., PhM2/c
CLARK, David R., S2/c
CLARK, Elliott W., PhM1/c
CLARK, Frank E., EM1/c
CLARK, Jerry L., QM3/c
CLARK, John H., SF2/c
CLARK, Kenneth P., F1/c
CLARK, Marvin N., PhM3/c
CLARK, Merle J., S1/c
CLARK, Myles T., PhM2/c
CLARK, O. C., AMM3/c
CLARK, Robt. J., S2/c
CLARK, Rowe, MM1/c
CLARK, Terence H., M2/c
CLARKE, John O., CBMA
CLARKE, Robt. M., CEMA
CLARKE, Thos. C., S2/c
CLARY, Gilbert J., MM1/c
CLAYPOOL, Archie P., S1/c
CLAYTON, Marion J., S2/c
CLAYTON, Orville Frederick, GM3/c
CLEARY, Fredk., PhM2/c
CLEMENT, Virgil C., S1/c
CLEMENTS, Emory J., S1/c
CLEVENGER, Estell A., MM2/c
CLIFFORD, Geo. D., S1/c
CLINE, Gymal W., S2/c
CLINE, Roy C., GM1/c
CLINE, Thos. R., MM2/c
CLINTON, Edw. R., S1/c
CLONINGER, Ivan L., PhM2/c
CLOPP, Harry E., Jr., F1/c
CLOTFELTER, Clifton B., S1/c
CLOYD, Lyle T., S1/c
CLUGSTON, John W., S1/c
CLUTTER, Leroy A., S1/c
COBBE, Geo. B., ARM2/c
COBLE, Jas. W., AMM1/c
COCA, Johnny J., Cox.
COCHRAN, Charlie S., S1/c
COCHRAN, Henry H., S2/c
COCKRELL, Douglas, StM1/c
CODY, Claude L., EM2/c
CODY, Dalton L., MoMM2/c
CODY, Jos. W., St3/c
COGLIANESE, Frank J., S1/c
COHEN, Michael M., ARM2/c
COHEN, Rene, EM3/c
COLANGELO, Leonard V., BM2/c
COLATACCI, America A., S1/c
COLGUN, Steve, Jr., MM2/c
COLE, Geo. H., ACMMP
COLE, Norman L., S2/c
COLE, Sam D., S1/c
COLELLA, Domenic G., S2/c
COLEMAN, Chas. F., BM1/c
COLEMAN, Donald A., GM3/c
COLEMAN, James L., GM2/c
COLEMAN, Leland A., S2/c
COLEMAN, Leroy Ernest, SC1/c
COLEMAN, Royce Earl, S2/c
COLEY, Henry P., MoMM1/c
COLGAN, Wm. W., PhM2/c
COLLARD, Jos. H., HA2/c
COLLIER, Calvin C., S1/c
COLLINS, Alva B., Cox.
COLLINS, Arthur A., F1/c
COLLINS, Eugene M., S2/c
COLLINS, Fred E., CPhMP
COLLINS, Horace R., BM1/c
COLLINS, Nathan M., MM1/c
COLLINS, Paul E., ARM3/c
COLLINS, Thos. R., QM3/c
COLLINS, Thos. V., Jr., ARM2/c
COLLINS, Wm. G., AM3/c
COLLURA, Jos. P., S1/c
COLVIN, Jas. B., ARM3/c
COLWELL, Carl L., MoMM2/c
COLYER, Wesley A., Jr., S1/c
COMBAS, Nicholas W., S1/c
COMEAUX, Jos. D., S2/c
COMER, Henry M., HA2/c
COMPOMIZZO, Marvin L., S1/c
COMPTON, Robt. A., Jr., S2/c

CASUALTIES

COMSTOCK, Wm. L., MoMM3/c
CONKLIN, John L., S1/c
CONLEY, Thos. L., EM1/c
CONN, Chas. G., F1/c
CONN, Frank Jackson, F2/c
CONNELL, Jas. L., F1/c
CONNELLY, Joseph Michael, S2/c
CONNER, Wm. J. B., CGMP
CONNER, Wm. L., SF3/c
CONSTANTIN, Eugene A., S2/c
CONVIRS, Russell L., MM1/c
CONWAY, John P., S1/c
COOK, Claude J., CM2/c
COOK, Ellard F., AS
COOK, Ernest M., ACOMP
COOK, Hugh F., CWTP
COOK, Kenneth J., EM2/c
COOK, Norman G., GM2/c
COOKE, Harrison L., AOM2/c
COON, Benj. F., CM3/c
COOPER, Claude David, S2/c
COOPER, Jack H. W., ARM2/c
COOPER, Jack W., S1/c
COOPER, Jas. W., FC3/c
COOPER, Lige H., Jr., F1/c
COOPER, Marcus W., MoMM1/c
COOPER, Walter J., F1/c
COPAUS, Odis Lee, S2/c
COPE, Horace L., EM3/c
COPELAND, Walter V., AOM3/c
COPP, Leroy F., PhM1/c
CORBIN, Chas. O., S2/c
CORBIN, Emmett D., S1/c
CORBIN, Ivan B., RM1/c
CORDER, Eugene F., S1/c
CORINI, Carlo L., S1/c
CORNATZER, Joe C., S1/c
CORNELL, Harry A., S1/c
CORNETT, Carl E., HA1/c
CORNETTO, Vito D., MoMM2/c
CORNETTE, Wm. H., BM2/c
CORP, Thos. D., MM1/c
CORSON, Chas. A., CBMP
CORTEZ, Derle, S2/c
CORUM, Paul L., S1/c
CORUM, Richard E., MoMM2/c
COSTA, Chas., SF3/c
COSTANZA, Anthony B., Jr., F2/c
COSTELLO, Ernest R., ARM2/c
COSTIGAN, Jos. F., S2/c
COTE, Arthur F., ARM2/c
COTE, Real J., F1/c
COTTAM, Milan W., S1/c
COTTEN, Robt. A., S2/c
COTTON, Clarence, CCSA
COTTRELL, Claude C., Jr., F1/c
COTTRILL, Harold R., S2/c
COUGHLIN, Chas. J., S2/c
COUGHLIN, George Wm., ARM3/c
COULTAS, Wm. E., MoMM2/c
COURTNEY, Robt. E., ARM3/c
COVERLY, Kenneth Willis, EM2/c
COVINO, Jos. A., S2/c
COWGILL, Donald F., F2/c
COWLES, Marion D., MM3/c
Cox, Alfred, F1/c
Cox, Alvin J., GM1/c
Cox, Dale F., S1/c
Cox, Emmette G., CCSA
Cox, Gene A., EM3/c
Cox, Jas. L., RM1/c
Cox, Jas. R., F1/c
Cox, Jos. T., S1/c
Cox, Raymond N. SK1/c
Cox, Robt. R., ARM2/c
COY, Everett Verel, F2/c
COYLE, Matthew Lewis, S2/c
COYNE, Martin A., F1/c
COZAD, Ralph I., RDM3/c
CRABTREE, Jos. J., SM2/c
CRAFT, Willard R., RDM3/c
CRAGIN, Marleau J., PhoM1/c
CRAIG, Graham I., PhM1/c
CRAIG, Harold C., HA1/c
CRAIG, Judson S., S2/c
CRAIG, Robt. A., Jr., TM3/c
CRAIG, Willard H., BM1/c
CRAIG, Wm. L., Cox.
CRAMER, Rich. K., HA1/c
CRAMER, Robt. C., QM2/c
CRAMER, Winfred L., S1/c
CRANFORD, Theo., StM2/c
CRANSTON, Richard L., EM2/c
CRAWFORD, Geo. A., ACMMP
CRAWFORD, Griffin B., StM1/c
CRAWFORD, Hugh E., AS
CRAWFORD. Robt. M., WT1/c
CRAWFORD, Wm. E., S2/c
CREAL, John G., S1/c
CREAVEN, John A., Cox.
CREEKMUR, Herbert O., SM1/c
CRIMMINGS, Paul J., ARM3/c
CRIPPS, Glen A., BM2/c
CRITTENDEN, Arthur G., S2/c
CROCKETT, Forest, S2/c
CROCKETT, Thaddeus H., SC3/c
CROCKFORD, Ernest H., MM1/c
CRODDY, John J., FC3/c

CROFT, Rich. M., EM2/c
CROMPTON, Calvin C., F1/c
CRONIN, Jos. J., WT3/c
CRONIN, Michael J., S1/c
CRONIN, Paul B., SSML3/c
CROSS, Walter J., ARM2/c
CROSS, Wm. R., SoM3/c
CROTEAU, Thos. E., S2/c
CROWE, Willard A., QM1/c
CROWLEY, Wm. M., S2/c
CROWN, Richard H., S1/c
CRUMP, Carl P., PR2/c
CRUNELLE, Halden L., AMM3/c
CRUZ, Jose A., NS1/c
CUDDY, Francis D., WT2/c
CULBERTSON, Paul E., AM2/c
CULOTTA, Dominic P., S1/c
CUMMINGS, Jas. M., S1/c
CUMMINGS, John L., Jr., S2/c
CUNNINGHAM, Edwin J., MM3/c
CURRAN, John F., SK3/c
CURRAN, John R., ARM3/c
CURRIER, David H., S2/c
CURRY, Joe, EM2/c
CURTIS, Lamar, MM1/c
CURTIS, Wm. A., FC3/c
CUSHING, Daniel F., Jr., S2/c
CUSHMAN, Lawrence W., SM1/c
CUSHMAN, Ralph C., S1/c
CUSHING, Thom. M., S2/c
CUTSHALL, Harry E., AOM2/c
CUTTING, Robt. S1/c
CYR, Robt. L., Jr., ARM2/c
CZERWIEC, Anthony C., ARM3/c

DABAKIS, Jas. J., TM2/c
DABNEY, John D., CK3/c
DABROWSKI, Edward J., SK3/c
DAGG, Clark E., S2/c
DAHLMEIR, Raymond M., EM1/c
DAILY, Joe F., WT2/c
DALE, Fritz E., F2/c
DALEY, Stanley A., CYA
DALEY, Wm., Jr., MoMM1/c
DALTHROP, Geo. L., CWTP
DALTON, Nealous M., ARM2/c
DALTON, Stanley F., AOM2/c
DALTON, Virgle R., TM3/c
DALY, Jos. P., AOM2/c
DALY, Walter L., EM3/c
DAMARSKI, John, MoMM1/c
DANFORTH, Wm. M., AOM2/c
DANIEL, Geo., OS3/c
DANIEL, Matt A., F1/c

DANIEL, Rex U., PhM3/c
DANKS, Paul B., AMM3/c
DANKSHA, Louis D., CCMA
DANLEY, Noah E., MM2/c
DANMIER, Donovan Darald, S2/c
DANNA, Peter, Jr., CM1/c
DANNUNZIO, Nello, EM3/c
DARAH, Job, S2/c
DARCY, Edw. M., S2/c
DARDE, Harry R., WT2/c
DASCH, John C., F1/c
DAUGHERTY, Elwood A., BM2/c
DAUGHERTY, Howard E., S2/c
DAUGHERTY, Wm. L., ARM2/c
DAVENPORT, Elton E., F1/c
DAVENPORT, J. W., AMM2/c
DAVID, Robt. B., ARM1/c
DAVIDSON, Howard L., Jr., MM3/c
DAVIDSON, Leonard H., AMM1/c
DAVIDSON, Odis M., ARM2/c
DAVIDSON, Rodney C., GM3/c
DAVIE, John W., Cox.
DAVIS, Chas. B., Jr., F1/c
DAVIS, Clifford M., HA1/c
DAVIS, David W., PhM3/c
DAVIS, Dwight G., RM3/c
DAVIS, Edward S., S1/c
DAVIS, Elmer L., CRMA
DAVIS, Frank G., Jr., S2/c
DAVIS, Glenn E., GM2/c
DAVIS, Glenn F., SK2/c
DAVIS, Jas. T., S1/c
DAVIS, John Eldridge, S2/c
DAVIS, John K., S2/c
DAVIS, Kenneth W., Cox.
DAVIS, Larry L., StM1/c
DAVIS, Lee L., GM3/c
DAVIS, Leroy C., EM3/c
DAVIS, Richard L., AMM2/c
DAVIS, Robt. J., ACMMP
DAVIS, Warren W., S2/c
DAVIS, Wilson H., Jr., CEMP
DAVIS, Wm. E., SF1/c
DAVISON, Edw., StM1/c
DAVISON, Jas. H., S1/c
DAVISON, Max E., HA1/c
DAY, Chartley B., Jr., GM3/c
DEACHMAN, John W., SK1/c
DEAKIN, Billy W., MM2/c
DEAN, Alford B., RT1/c
DEAN, Myran Pearl, CSKP
DEAN, Russell L., S1/c
DEANE, Norwin G., CWTA
DEANGELIS, Earl A., S2/c

CASUALTIES

DEBAIN, Clifford L., S1/c
DEBELLIS, John H., F1/c
DEBERNARDO, Marco L., S2/c
DEBISSCHOP, Robt. E., AMM2/c
DEBOER, Dick, SF2/c
DECENZO, Frank J., F2/c
DECK, Vernon M., MM2/c
DECKER, Oscar E., S1/c
DECOUDREAUX, Alton H., S1/c
DECUBELLIS, Ralph, S1/c
DEEDS, Buferd A., BM2/c
DEEDS, Warren A., S1/c
DEERE, Troy O., TM2/c
DEES, Douglas C., PhM3/c
DEES, La Mark, AOM2/c
DEES, Merle D., S1/c
DEGLER, Lester Raymond, S2/c
DEGOEDE, John, SK3/c
DEGROOT, James, F1/c
DEGUZMAN, Victorino, StM1/c
DEISINGER, Geo. M., S1/c
DEJOURNETT, Homer, S1/c
DELANEY, Henry E., PhM3/c
DELEGARD, Chas. L., ARM3/c
DELEO, Edward Anthony, S2/c
DELISLE, Allen P., S2/c
DELLAMORE, Geo., Jr., PhM3/c
DELMENICO, Arnold J., AMM2/c
DELONG, Ralph W., SC1/c
DELUCA, John M., BM2/c
DELUCA, Peter W., S2/c
DELUCIA, Jas. M., Jr., F1/c
DEMANIO, Jos. J., RM3/c
DEMASTERS, Warren W., S1/c
DEMETRESCU, Aur, S1/c
DEMUTH, Paul V., PhM2/c
DENISON, Albert I., PhM1/c
DENNERY, John E., S1/c
DENNIS, Walter R., SPM1/c
DENNISON, Jos. J., Jr., PhM2/c
DENSON, Carl N., AMM1/c
DENSON, Starlie Edgar, S2/c
DEPANICIS, Vincent J., S2/c
DEPEW, Clifford R. L., S2/c
DEPEW, John M., TM3/c
DERINGER, Philip G., AMM1/c
DERMODY, Michael V., Jr., S1/c
DESCOTEAU, Rene L., PhM2/c
DESHAIES, Robt. J., S1/c
DESINGER, William Delbert, AS
DESMARAIS, Cyril A., RM3/c
DESTREE, Robert, Frank, S2/c
DETERESI, Philip S., TM3/c
DEVARNEY, Victor, S1/c

DEVENY, Roy Y., Jr., AOM3/c
DEVEREAUX, Fredk L., Cox.
DEVEY, Sterling M. V., S1/c
DEVORE, Thos. L., F1/c
DEWBERRY, Charlie L., S2/c
DEWILDT, Frank A., PhM3/c
DEXTER, Robt. L., NM3/c
DEXTER, Warren E., CEMA
DHUYVETTERS, John J., ARM2/c
DIAMOND, James, Jr., F2/c
DIANA, Daniel A., S1/c
DIAZ, Arthur I., CPhMP
DIBELLO, Vito J., WT1/c
DICK, Harold L., GM2/c
DICK, Robt. J., PhM3/c
DICK, Walter M., WT2/c
DICKENSON, Donald B., M1/c
DICKERSON, Alfonzo, J., S1/c
DICKERSON, Robt. H., StM1/c
DICKEY, Donald D., AMM3/c
DIELMAN, Galen R., SM3/c
DIETLIN, Francis W., TM3/c
DIETRICH, Howard R., GM1/c
DIETRICH, Robt., AMM2/c
DIETZ, Edward J., EM3/c
DIGHT, Paul N., S2/c
DIGIACOMO, Henry J., Cox.
DILKES, Robt. E., S2/c
DILKS, Thos., MoMM2/c
DILLARD, Jack J., St2/c
DILLARD, Robt. L., ARM2/c
DILLION, Jos. E., SF1/c
DILLS, Andrew C., Jr., ARM2/c
DILUCCA, John, MM1/c
DINDINGER, Robt. E., ACMMA
DIRKES, John B., GM3/c
DISCHNER, Donald H., MoMM2/c
DISCIANO, Frank J., MM1/c
DISTER, Geo. W., MoMM2/c
DITTY, Quinten Alvin, MM1/c
DIXON, Cletus H., MM3/c
DIXON, Elba L., S2/c
DIXON, James B., Jr., S2/c
DIXON, Joel H., SM3/c
DOAN, Clifford, S1/c
DOAN, Ellis J., F2/c
DOAN, Howard F., QM3/c
DOAN, Raymond, S2/c
DOBBINS, Robt. H., S2/c
DOBBS, Louis J., PhM3/c
DOBSON, Geo. W., Jr., AMM3/c
DOBSON, Harold L., MoMM1/c
DOCTOR, Steve E., S1/c
DODD, Thos. F., S1/c

Doenges, Gerald G., Y2/c
Doerr, Paul J., S2/c
Doheny, Thos. B., PhM3/c
Doherty, Jas. B., SF3/c
Dollard, Chas. M., S1/c
Dominguez, John, GM3/c
Donahue, Edw. C., ARM3/c
Donehue, Wm. E., PhM3/c
Donelan, Walter, F2/c
Donnelly, Darrell Russell, S2/c
Donor, Jos. J., CTMP
Dooner, Edw. J., ACOMA
Doran, Edward J., S2/c
Dorraugh, Thos F., PhM1/c
Doss, John M., PhM3/c
Doster, Edw. J., SF2/c
Dotson, Chas. R., S2/c
Dotson, Fred H., S2/c
Dotson, Leonard D., EM1/c
Doty, Rex L., S2/c
Doubrava, Herbert J., QM2/c
Dougherty, Wm., Jr., QM1/c
Doughman, Clarence L., S2/c
Douglas, Rich. E., SM3/c
Doulette, Raymond H., S1/c
Doupnik, Milo C., S2/c
Dour, Jacob N., MM3/c
Douthit, Harmon C., MM2/c
Downey, Jack C., AMM1/c
Downey, John D., ARM2/c
Downs, Elroy, S2/c
Doyle, Chas., MoMM1/c
Doyle, Jas. R., AOM2/c
Doyle, Reginald F., StM1/c
Doyle, Theo. J., RM3/c
Drager, Ervin O., GM3/c
Dragon, James Wm., Jr., S1/c
Drake, Douglas R., S1/c
Drake, Robt. F., ARM2/c
Draper, Clede Mayo, S2/c
Drennen, Clarence G., S1/c
Driesbach, Geo. C., Jr., ARM3/c
Driscoll, Geo. C., CTMP
Driscoll, Roy R., ACMA
Drobot, Frank J., WT3/c
Droles, Jas. G., CAPA
Drop, Louis B., AOM2/c
Dropkin, Jack, EM3/c
Droste, Albert H., SSML3/c
Drummond, Harry M., S1/c
Dryden, Walter J., RT3/c
Duben, Peter F., F1/c
Ducharme, Donald, QM3/c
Ducharme, Marvin J., CYA

Duchesne, Rodrick L., ARM2/c
Duchin, Paul E., WT3/c
Dudek, Bronislaus L., MM3/c
Dudek, John E., S2/c
Dudley, Clifford E., S2/c
Dudley, Harold R., AMM2/c
Dudley, Herman, S2/c
Dudy, Wm. K., RM1/c
Dufault, Lucien J., MM1/c
Duff, Thos. D., ARM3/c
Dugan, Robt. L., S1/c
Dugas, Sylvain Eugene, CEMA
Duggan, John E., S2/c
Duke, Clarence C., S2/c
Duke, Robt. C., S2/c
Duke, Wm. R., S2/c
Dumlao, Delfin, MM2/c
Dunbar, Harry J., Cox.
Duncan, Deward W., Jr., S2/c
Duncan, Geo. A., ARM2/c
Duncan, John G., QM3/c
Duncan, Ralph E., S1/c
Duncan, Wm. E., CPhMA
Dunlop, David W., HA1/c
Dunn, Jas. M., F2/c
Dunn, John P., S1/c
Dunn, Rich T., ARM2/c
Dunn, Robt. L., MoMM3/c
Dunnavant, Jesse H., MoMM1/c
Dunton, Willard E., AOM1/c
Dupree, Russell Joseph, AS
Duquette, Wm. G., S1/c
Durant, John F., F2/c
Duren, Jas. M., S1/c
Durham, Chas. M., S2/c
Durham, Irwin W., HA1/c
Durkee, Donald A., F1/c
Durney, Chas. E., SF2/c
Durrance, Wm., S2/c
Dutro, Wm. E., S1/c
Dutton, Leon M., S1/c
Dycus, Johnnie D., S2/c
Dye, Howard B., EM1/c
Dyer, Rufus, StM2/c
Dyke, A. R., MME3/c
Dykeman, Donald A., S2/c
Dykes, Dennis W., Jr., WT3/c
Dymond, Chas. D., S1/c
Dzinbak, Richard P., S1/c

Earl, Robt. S., PhM3/c
Earles, Marion N., PhM1/c
Early, Edward E., EM1/c
Eastman, Alton G. H., TM2/c

EASTWOOD, Harry M., TM1/c
EBERLINE, Jos., S1/c
ECKART, Francis J., Cox.
ECKERT, Harold A., AM3/c
EDDINGTON, Garland S., S2/c
EDELMAN, Louis, S1/c
EDGELL, Henry C., F1/c
EDGINGTON, Gale Benton, GM1/c
EDIGER, Norvin, S1/c
EDLIN, Wilber Earl, F2/c
EDMONDS, Aubrey D., S1/c
EDWARDS, Houston E., CEMP
EDWARDS, Jas. F., S1/c
EDWARDS, Rich. P., S1/c
EDWARDS, Walter, F1/c
EDWARDS, Walter, S2/c
EDWARDS, Wm. L., HA1/c
EEONOMIDES, Jim T., SoM2/c
EFIGENIO, Albert L., S2/c
EGAN, John M., S1/c
EGGER, Roland L., ARM1/c
EGGERSGLUSS, Harvey H., AMM2/c
EGNER, Jos. D., S1/c
EHINGER, Donald A., AOMB3/c
EHRHARDT, Melvin E., EM3/c
EICHELBERGER, Paul E., MM1/c
EICHLER, Wm. F., Jr., S1/c
EIDSON, Fredk. M., Jr., WT2/c
EIFERT, Raymond Gibson, S2/c
EISBERG, William Isadore, S2/c
EKLEBERRY, Bernard, S1/c
ELKEY, John R., AMM2/c
ELKIND, Benj., CPhMP
ELKINS, Samuel E., S2/c
ELLEDGE, Alonzo John, S2/c
ELLINGTON, John, S1/c
ELLIOT, Nelson W., WT3/c
ELLIOTT, Carl A., Jr., MoMM1/c
ELLIOTT, Willard C., SC1/c
ELLIOTT, Wm. L., PhM3/c
ELLIS, Frank D., CWTP
ELLIS, Milford, CWPT
ELLIS, Wm. A., Sr., SK2/c
ELLIS, Wm. M., Jr., AMM2/c
ELLISON, Everett O., ARM2/c
ELLISON, Harold P., Jr., S1/c
ELLISON, Jack D., EM3/c
ELMER, Richard V., F1/c
ELSASS, Fred W., FC1/c
ELSINGER, Francis J., S2/c
ELSON, Wm. J., F1/c
EMERSON, Chas. T., S2/c
EMERY, Maynard W., F1/c
EMILLIANOWICZ, Edward, ARM3/c

ENGEBRETSEN, Wilbert F., CM1/c
ENGLERT, Harry J., S1/c
ENGLISH, Geo., S1/c
ENLOW, Raymond W., AS
ENNEFER, Paul R., F1/c
ENNEN, Henry M., HA1/c
EPLEY, Everett E., S2/c
EPPING, Thos. R., S1/c
EPPLER, Chris G., S1/c
ERICHSON, Ralph, ARM2/c
ERICKSEN, Ralph J., WT1/c
ERICKSON, Ervin J., GM1/c
ERNO, Dan. S., S1/c
ERNST, Wm., CMMP
ERSKINE, Roger H., MoMM1/c
ERWIN, Walter Wendell, S2/c
ESCHUCK, Wm. T., ARM3/c
ESCOBAR, John W., S2/c
ESLINGER, Jos. W., MM1/c
ESTERHAZY, Stephen J., BM1/c
ESTES, Geo., S2/c
ESTES, Henry H., AP1/c
ESTES, Van Henderson, FCM3/c
ESTILL, Jas. E., S1/c
ESTLE, Robt. C., GM3/c
ETHIER, Edmond J., MoMM1/c
EURE, Everett J., EM3/c
EVANKOE, Steve, F1/c
EVANOWSKI, Thos. P., SoM2/c
EVANS, Chas. F., PhM2/c
EVANS, Ezra W., SK2/c
EVANS, Leo V., GM3/c
EVERETT, Ernest J., RT1/c
EWALL, Ralph, MM3/c
EWELL, Parker T., RM2/c
EXUM, Earl W., F2/c
EYL, Robt. A., S2/c
EYMAN, Harold L., AM3/c

FAATZ, Albert J., S2/c
FACCHINI, Dario F., MoMM2/c
FAGER, Elmo Edwin, S2/c
FAGER, Burl D., SM3/c
FALKNER, Ralph W., S1/c
FALLEN, Robert E., S1/c
FALUSZCZAK, Tadeusz Josep, S2/c
FANNING, Orville F., Jr., CS3/c
FARABEE, Albert E., TM3/c
FARISH, Jas. W., MM1/c
FARLEY, Jack Dempsey, S2/c
FARLEY, Rudolph J., QM2/c
FARMER, Loyd Edwin, S2/c
FARR, Wm. R., Jr., AMM1/c
FARRAUG, Herbert K., S2/c

FARRELL, Henry E., Jr., S1/c
FARRELL, Lee R., HA1/c
FARRELL, Thos. P., AMM1/c
FARRIS, Harold D., S1/c
FAUBION, Robt. G., MM3/c
FAUST, Anthony S., RM3/c
FAWL, Lloyd C., B2/c
FAZEKAS, Michael G., CMMA
FEDDERSON, Arthur O., PhM2/c
FEDORA, Clarence E., Bkr3/c
FEDORCHAK, Jos., S1/c
FEJARANG, Antonio S., NS2/c
FEJARANG, Francisco M., NS2/c
FELCZANK, Walter J., BM1/c
FELIX, Alfredo R., Ck1/c
FELTER, Frank C., MM1/c
FELTON, Lewis D., S1/c
FENDSACK, Wm. F., MM3/c
FENNER, Donald M., StM1/c
FENTON, Alfred H., EM3/c
FENTON, Lewis J., ARM2/c
FERANEC, John, F1/c
FERCHEN, Richard H., RM2/c
FERDINAND, Rich. W., S2/c
FERENTZ, John, S2/c
FERFOGLIA, Jos. E., MM1/c
FERGUSON, Chas. V., S1/c
FERGUSON, Harold G., S2/c
FERGUSON, Oral Ralph, F2/c
FERGUSON, Wyatt, Jr., S2/c
FERRELL, Robt. H., EM1/c
FERRIER, Lavane H., HA1/c
FERRIL, Robt. L., ART2/c
FESHOH, Wm. E., PhM3/c
FICKETT, Robt. W., S2/c
FICKLING, Bobby W., AOM3/c
FIELDER, John R., Cox.
FIELDS, Delmer E., BM1/c
FIELDS, Edw., WT1/c
FIELDS, Glen., S1/c
FIELDS, Hoyt S., EM3/c
FIELDS, John M., S2/c
FIELITZ, Ray D., TM2/c
FILIP, Jas. W., CSPAA
FINA, Jos., AMM1/c
FINCH, Eugene E., S1/c
FINCHER, John E., MM1/c
FINDLEY, Leland A., S1/c
FINK, Jos. J., F2/c
FINKENBINDER, Laverne W., ARM3/c
FINLEY, Alvin W., MM1/c
FINLEY, Geo. W., BM2/c
FINNEY, Alexander W., StM1/c
FIORITA, Frank E., SF3/c

FIREBAUGH, Harold E., F2/c
FISCHER, Lester H., RT2/c
FISCHER, Wm. H., TM3/c
FISHER, Geo. H., MM1/c
FISHER, Hale D., AMM1/c
FISHER, Jas. R., S2/c
FISHER, John C., MM3/c
FISHER, Lewis S., Jr., PhM3/c
FISHER, Orlando K., S2/c
FISHER, Oshel O., SF2/c
FISHER, Raymond E., S2/c
FITTIPALDI, Philip, S1/c
FITZGERALD, Donald F., S1/c
FITZGERALD, Jas. F., PhM1/c
FITZGERALD, Lorelza N., S1/c
FITZGERALD, Wm. H., MM3/c
FITZGERALD, Wm. W., GM1/c
FITZHARRIS, Robt. P., S1/c
FITZMIER, James Alfred, S1/c
FITZWATER, Hurley, WT2/c
FLANAGAN, Estle D., SK1/c
FLANNAGAN, Clarence, St3/c
FLATHMANN, John S., S1/c
FLATT, Paul E., ARM2/c
FLEMATTI, John A., S1/c
FLEMING, Grandville, StM1/c
FLEMING, Kenneth E., PhM1/c
FLESHER, Stanley R., S1/c
FLICKINGER, Clyde P., S1/c
FLOOD, Edwin W., MM1/c
FLOREA, Randall F., ARM3/c
FLORES, Tino M., AMM3/c
FLOWERS, LeRoy, StM1/c
FLOYD, Jewell M., SF1/c
FLUKER, Geo. A., Ck3/c
FLYNN, Gerard E., GM3/c
FLYNN, John F., EM2/c
FOGLEMAN, Rich. R., S2/c
FOLKEDAHL, Charles Bernar, Cox.
FOLKMAN, Leon J., SK3/c
FOLTZ, Cletis E., S1/c
FONTENOT, Jos. S., Jr., GM3/c
FORCUM, Leonard F., CMMP
FORD, Francis M., ARM2/c
FORD, Geo., TM3/c
FORD, Jos. E., S2/c
FORD, Melvin T., S1/c
FORD, Simon P., Cox.
FORD, Willie, Jr., GM3/c
FORMENTI, Mario J., SC2/c
FORNELLA, Dominic, CM3/c
FORSBERG, Robt. L., PhM3/c
FORTNEY, Saml. G., Jr., SC3/c
FOSNESS, Melvin M., MM3/c

CASUALTIES

Foss, Clarence S., F2/c
Foster, Chas. L., S2/c
Foster, Jesse, S1/c
Foster, Leonard C., ARM2/c
Foster, Linton B., CRMA
Foulke, Stanley L., S1/c
Foust, Arthur C., AOM1/c
Fowler, Arthur J., GM3/c
Fowler, Arthur J., F1/c
Fowler, Edward, ACMMP
Fowler, David H., EM3/c
Fox, Chas. J., AOM3/c
Fox, Dave F., EM1/c
Fox, Fredk. J., SF2/c
Fox, Wilton G., EM3/c
Foyle, Donald C., SC3/c
Frame, Charlie M., RM1/c
Francis, Lloyd J., PhM3/c
France, Kenneth C., MM1/c
Franco, Jas. A., WT3/c
Frandsen, Warren, MM3/c
Frank, Robt. D., F1/c
Franklin, Paul J., PhM3/c
Frantz, Warren Gamaliel, F1/c
Frappier, Benedict H., ARM3/c
Frazier, Lawrence O., CBMP
Frazier, Paul D., S1/c
Frazier, Paul, Jr., S1/c
Fread, Clyde D., CSFA
Fredette, John A., F1/c
Freeman, Earl W., Y2/c
Freese, Everrett D., EM2/c
Freitas, John AMM3/c
French, Lloyd E., SK2/c
Freund, Harry J., GM3/c
Friday, Otto Rudolph C., Jr., S2/c
Friedel, Geo. J., HA1/c
Frierson, Chas. M., Jr., F1/c
Friesen, Bernhardt, S2/c
Fritz, William Curtis, S2/c
Frost, Evan E., AMM1/c
Fry, Clifford E., S1/c
Fryback, Wm. C., ARM2/c
Frye, Richard D., ARM2/c
Fuglie, Carlyle J., AMM1/c
Fuller, Earl B., ARM1/c
Fuller, Eddy W., PhM3/c
Fullerton, James C., EM2/c
Fulton, Jas. M., SF3/c
Fulton, Judson P., PhM2/c
Fulton, Richard E., MM3/c
Funk, Wm. R., CPhMA
Fuqua, Bruce, S2/c
Furlong, Burl F., S1/c

Furnas, Robt. W., S2/c

Gable, Frank H., SK2/c
Gabryszewski, Ted S., MME3/c
Gaffney, Norman F., ARM2/c
Gaffney, Wm. E., Jr., PhM2/c
Gagnon, Walter J., S1/c
Gaither, Jas. R., CMMP
Gal, Michael, AMM2/c
Galbraith, Sidney S., MM1/c
Gallagher, Thos. W., MM3/c
Gallaher, Robt. N., PhM1/c
Gallerini, Leonard N., MM3/c
Galvin, Thos. J., F1/c
Gambino, Vincent, ARM2/c
Gamel, John J., AOM1/c
Gangloff, Edw., S2/c
Gant, Saml. W., StM1/c
Garay, John, AMM3/c
Garcia, Angelo, WT3/c
Garcia, Francisco M., NS2/c
Gardella, Francis A., PhM3/c
Gardiner, Carl T., Cox.
Gardner, Chas. L., HA2/c
Gardner, Earl W., QM3/c
Gardner, Everett K., BM2/c
Gardner, Jas. R., AMM1/c
Gardner, Rudolph S., ARM3/c
Gargano, Michael A., ARM2/c
Gargis, Dalton, CMMA
Garner, John M., CSFA
Garrison, Dorris O., RM3/c
Garry, Clifford M., S1/c
Garst, Eugene E., S2/c
Garton, Chas. P., GM1/c
Garwood, Clarence R., AMM3/c
Gary, Lester E., TM2/c
Garza, Jesus D., MoMM2/c
Gasko, John, BM2/c
Gaspa, Leonard J., PhM2/c
Gatlin, Jas. D., Jr., F2/c
Gavin, Michael L., CM2/c
Gaylord, Robt. F., S1/c
Gebauer, Chester W., S1/c
Gebhardt, Henry A., S1/c
Geho, Thos. E., ARM3/c
Geiger, Clair J., CGMA
Geil, Francis J., S2/c
Geist, Raymond H., FC2/c
Gellas, John G., MM2/c
Gentry, Landon M., Jr., Cox.
George, Donald R., TM3/c
George, Robt. T., Jr., S2/c
Geppelt, Robt. G., CRMP

GERBENSKY, Carl H., MoMM3/c
GERDON, Cecil S., CCSA
GERMAN, John L., QM3/c
GEROU, John F., S2/c
GERRITY, Wm. B., ARM2/c
GERSON, Paul W., WT3/c
GIACCANI, Floyd R., Bkr2/c
GIBBS, John J., Jr., BM2/c
GIBNEY, Wm. R., Jr., MM3/c
GIBSON, Bertrand E., S1/c
GIDDENS, John W., St3/c
GIDDENS, Roy Arthur, MM1/c
GIFFORD, Winford B., Cox.
GIGUERE, Wm. V., WT1/c
GILBERT, Chas. H., Jr., EM1/c
GILHULY, James F., F1/c
GILL, Geo. F., BM2/c
GILL, Russell C., S1/c
GILLARD, Geo. H., Jr., F2/c
GILLES, John L., S1/c
GILLESPIE, Jas. A., Sr., CM2/c
GILLETTE, Leigh, EM3/c
GILLIAM, Norman, StM2/c
GILLILAND, John A., Jr., S1/c
GILLILAND, Ralph J., PhM1/c
GILLIS, Alexander Hugh, MM2/c
GILLIS, Frank G., TM2/c
GILMAN, Clinton O., S1/c
GILMARTIN, Wm. H., S2/c
GILMORE, Wm. F., PhM1/c
GIRKIN, Farrel C., EM2/c
GITELSON, Seymour B., AOM2/c
GIVENS, Arthur, S2/c
GLADD, Jack N., CWTA
GLADSTONE, Geo., ACMMP
GLASCOCK, Robt. W., F2/c
GLASER, Edw. J., ARM3/c
GLASSNER, Lawrence F., ARM2/c
GLAZER, Albert, AMM2/c
GLEASON, Lawrence M., MoMM2/c
GLEN, Richard H., F2/c
GLENZ, Fredk. G., CGMA
GLETTIG, Henry J., Jr., Cox.
GLEW, Raymond, ARM3/c
GLICK, David A. M., PhM3/c
GLORY, Johnny, S2/c
GLOVER, Herbert P., PhM2/c
GLOVER, Jas. G., Jr., F2/c
GLOVER, Millidge E., S2/c
GLUSCIC, Jos. J., S1/c
GNAGNI, Armando D., F2/c
GOAD, Wm. R., Jr., PhM3/c
GOBLE, Robt. G., SC2/c
GOCKEL, Walter J., RM2/c

GODAY, Benj. M., Jr., CTMP
GODDARD, Leslie E., F1/c
GODFREY, Albert D., S2/c
GODIN, Vincent R., Y2/c
GODWIN, Luther H., PhM3/c
GODWIN, Norman B., S2/c
GOFORTH, Rich. L., S2/c
GOGGIN, John P., CBMP
GOGGINS, J. C., Cox.
GOLDBERG, Roy A., S2/c
GOLDEN, Audley M., GM2/c
GOLDEN, Marion E., S2/c
GOLDSTEIN, Leonard S., S2/c
GOLITKO, Edw. P., S2/c
GOMBOS, Jos., EM3/c
GOMEZ, John E., S2/c
GONZALES, Ermino, SC3/c
GONZALES, Robt. J., Jr., AMM3/c
GOODE, John H., S1/c
GOODE, Louis V., F1/c
GOODE, Saml. P., GM3/c
GOODEN, Leonard D., S2/c
GOODMAN, Robt. E., S1/c
GOODRUM, Herbert C., MoMM1/c
GOODSON, Ether E., ACMMP
GOODSPEED, Victor R., CM2/c
GOOTEE, Geo. H., F1/c
GORDON, Elgin Warren, Cox.
GORDON, Finley A., PhM3/c
GORDON, Harold D., S2/c
GORDON, Harvey, PhM1/c
GORMAN, John P., ARM1/c
GORMLEY, John F., AOM2/c
GOSCINIAK, Thaddeus, MoMM2/c
GOSHORN, Ray L., GM2/c
GOSLIN, Edgar H., MM3/c
GOSSMAN, Orval A., S2/c
GOTHELF, Louis, RM3/c
GOTOWT, John, S2/c
GOTTLIEB, Jacob M., PhM2/c
GOULD, Robt. R., Jr., MoMM2/c
GOURLEY, Lawrence W., S2/c
GOWEN, Culmer F., EM1/c
GRABER, Hector J., AMM2/c
GRABILL, Ernest D., PhM2/c
GRACEY, Howard Thomas, CMMP
GRAEF, Billy E., S2/c
GRAFTON, Ernest O., S2/c
GRAHAM, Edgar H., Jr., SK2/c
GRAHAM, Geo., Cox.
GRAHAM, Jas. P., S1/c
GRAHAM, Noah A., CM2/c
GRAHAM, Noel H., Cox.
GRAHAM, Robt. P., S2/c

CASUALTIES

GRAHAM, Sterling E., ARM1/c
GRAHEK, Edw. J., SK3/c
GRANT, Edw. C., S1/c
GRATER, Geo. W., S1/c
GRAVELL, Wm. M., AMM2/c
GRAVES, Elmer P., ACMP
GRAVES, Joe E., S1/c
GRAY, Arland L., SK2/c
GRAY, Jas. H., AOM3/c
GRAY, John R., EM2/c
GRAY, Paul E., S2/c
GRAY, Ralph J., SF3/c
GRAY, Virgil F., AM1/c
GRAYARD, Wm. P., AMM3/c
GREAVES, Wm. B., ACMP
GREEBON, Oliver H., SF1/c
GREEN, Clifford A., S2/c
GREEN, Dayton, F1/c
GREEN, Harold G., AMM3/c
GREEN, Hezzie, StM2/c
GREEN, John E., StM1/c
GREEN, Robt. E., MM2/c
GREEN, Robt. F., WT2/c
GREENE, Donald H., Cox.
GREENE, Everett A., Y3/c
GREENWALD, John, S2/c
GREENWALD, Sylvester T., PhM2/c
GREENWOOD, Chas. W., PhM3/c
GREER, Wm. A., Jr., PhM2/c
GREER, Wm. J., S1/c
GREGG, David F., S2/c
GREGORY, Jas. A., S1/c
GREGORY, Robt. A., RM3/c
GREIFZU, Fredk. C., F1/c
GREITZER, Michael J., MME1/c
GRELL, Geo. W., EM1/c
GREMILLION, Roy Charles, MM2/c
GRESHAM, Hugh P., Jr., PhM2/c
GRESSWELL, John, Jr., MoMM3/c
GRGURICH, Andy S., S1/c
GRIBBONS, Geo. T., CCMA
GRIBI, Jack D., AMM2/c
GRIEB, John H., S2/c
GRIFFIN, Earl E., MoMM3/c
GRIFFIN, Thos. S., PhM1/c
GRIFFITH, Arthur M., RM1/c
GRIFFITH, Edwin C., PhM1/c
GRIGER, Arthur, Y/3
GRIGGERS, Edw. L., S2/c
GRIGSBY, John E., HA1/c
GRIMMINCK, Bernard C., SC1/c
GRISSOM, O. C., SC2/c
GRISSOM, Walter E., AMM2/c
GRISWOLD, Carleton W., PhM3/c

GRIZ, Nick, SoM3/c
GRIZZELL, Leslie R., MM1/c
GROLLER, John J., GM3/c
GROOM, Eugene, PhM2/c
GROOMS, Bert J., PhM1/c
GROSS, Robt. C., S1/c
GROSSE, Wm. F., CMMP
GROTH, Gordon W., S2/c
GROUND, Orlo L., MM3/c
GROVE, Fredk A., CWTA
GRYGIEL, Thos. W., S1/c
GUESS, Teddy O., SF1/c
GUICO, Justiniano G., StM1/c
GUIDRY, Clifford, ARM2/c
GUIDRY, Jerry M., SM3/c
GUILL, John C., Cox.
GUNTER, Berchard K., RM2/c
GUNTER, Wm. L., SSML3/c
GURLEY, Thos. R., QM3/c
GUSTAFSON, Burton A., MM2/c
GUSTAFSON, Edw. W., SF2/c
GUSTISON, Richard J., F2/c
GUTE, Dewayne R., ARM1/c
GUTHKE, Thomas Albert, SF2/c
GUTHRIE, Geo. T., PhM3/c
GUTIERREZ, Anthony A., CEMA
GUTOWSKI, Thos. M., PhM3/c
GUY, Levi, Jr., S1/c
GUYNN, Wendell G., CM3/c
GUYON, Harold A., AMM3/c
GUZIK, Leon Francis, PhM1/c
GWINN, Chas. P., S1/c

HAAG, Justin C., MM2/c
HAAKE, Emmett B., PhM3/c
HAAPA, Leslie A., RM2/c
HAAS, Edw. J., S1/c
HAAS, Elmer V., S1/c
HAAS, Geo. H., Jr., S1/c
HACKER, Donald, S2/c
HADRA, Ernest, GM3/c
HAFLING, Bernard C., S1/c
HAGAN, Geo. T., BM2/c
HAGEDORN, Geo. E. L., F1/c
HAGUE, John C., CSKA
HAHN, John E., GM3/c
HAIGHT, Bruce S., ARM1/c
HAIGHT, James Harrison, Jr., S1/c
HAKENSON, Robert Clifford, ARM2/c
HALE, Donald E., S1/c
HALEY, Jack D., F2/c
HALEY, Robt. H., QM3/c
HALL, Arlis I., MM3/c
HALL, Bernard F., F1/c

HALL, Bud C., MM1/c
HALL, Donovan G., CMMP
HALL, Harry L., Jr., CBMP
HALL, John P., ARM3/c
HALL, Millard P., Sr., S2/c
HALL, Raymond E., S2/c
HALL, Thos. W., M1/c
HALL, Virgil E., S2/c
HALLAHAN, Rich. G., SK1/c
HALLQUIST, Wm. L., Cox.
HALVERSON, Lloyd H., Jr., PhM3/c
HALWEG, Stanley M., PhM3/c
HAMILTON, Carl B., PhM3/c
HAMILTON, Chas. W., AOM2/c
HAMILTON, Edw. A., AMM2/c
HAMILTON, Francis A., TM3/c
HAMILTON, John W., MoMM2/c
HAMILTON, Morris G., S1/c
HAMLETTE, Wallace W., SC2/c
HAMMERSMITH, Geo. A., SC2/c
HAMMOND, Robt. D., S2/c
HAMNER, Lawrence H., F1/c
HAMPTON, Clyde F., WT1/c
HAMPTON, Rupert L., MM2/c
HAMRICK, Gilbert T., MoMM3/c
HANCOCK, Jack, ARM2/c
HANCOCK, Stanley T., B3/c
HANDY, Wilbur, S1/c
HANEY, John R., MoMM1/c
HANKE, Kenneth E., F1/c
HANLEY, Gaylord G., S1/c
HANNA, John M., S1/c
HANNAMAN, Harry C., S1/c
HANSEN, Edward J., EM2/c
HANSEN, Tommy Fritz, S2/c
HANSON, John L., AMM3/c
HANSON, Paul V., CWTP
HANSTEAD, Leonard R., PhM2/c
HANTON, Edw., StM1/c
HARBAUGH, Rondall C., MM3/c
HARBER, Emmit D., SC3/c
HARBISON, Robt. N., TM3/c
HARBOLD, Robt. L., S1/c
HARDEE, Armestead S., ARM2/c
HARDEMAN, L. C., StM1/c
HARDGROVE, Chas. C., Y2/c
HARDING, Joe, F2/c
HARDING, Larry C., S2/c
HARDY, Eugene G., S1/c
HARGROVE, Wesley R., AOM2/c
HARLAN, Andrew E., AM1/c
HARLAN, Harold, GM3/c
HARMES, John C., PhM1/c

HARMON, Clayton H., SC3/c
HARMON, Dan, Jr., S2/c
HARMON, Floyd R., S1/c
HARMS, Frederic M., ACMMP
HARNUTOVSKY, Frank M., S1/c
HARPER, Oswald H., Jr., S2/c
HARRELL, Robt. R., WT3/c
HARRELL, Roland E., CEMP
HARRINGTON, Edw. D., PhM2/c
HARRINGTON, Edw. R., AM1/c
HARRIS, John M., S2/c
HARRIS, Jos. J., S2/c
HARRIS, Lorenzo S., CM2/c
HARRIS, Robt. D., Jr., S2/c
HARRIS, Saml., STM2/c
HARRIS, Thos. W., S2/c
HARRIS, Warren D., RDM3/c
HARRIS, Willis W., AMM3/c
HARRISON, Edw. N., EM3/c
HARRISON, Ernest H., SC3/c
HARRISON, John F., QM3/c
HARRISON, Roy F., S2/c
HARRISON, Vernon F., Y1/c
HARRISON, Wm. H., RM2/c
HART, Earl F., S1/c
HART, Earl P., Jr., S2/c
HART, Francis E., S1/c
HARTENSTINE, Roy, Jr., F1/c
HARTER, Henry H., CEMA
HARTGRAVES, Mayo M., S1/c
HARTIGAN, John P., ARM2/c
HARTLE, Raymond L., S2/c
HARTMAN, Dennis R., MoMM2/c
HARTMAN, Leon A., Bkr1/c
HARTMANN, Raymond K., EM1/c
HARTSOC, Jas. L., MM3/c
HARTZ, Wm. A., PhM3/c
HARVEY, Glenn H., PhM1/c
HARVEY, Luis W., CEMP
HARVEY, Malcolm L., SF1/c
HARVEY, Marion N., CMMA
HARVEY, Virgil C., CCSP
HARVEY, Wm. J., PhM2/c
HASBROOK, Howard S., AOM1/c
HASELDEN, Chas. L., CM1/c
HASELGARD, Edwin W., AMM2/c
HASKELL, Chas. O., F1/c
HATEM, Abraham E., PhM2/c
HATFIELD, Graham C., AMM3/c
HATLEN, Edwin A., S1/c
HATTENBACH, Robert Eugene, S2/c
HAUBRICH, Edw. U., S1/c
HAUPT, Robert Lawrence, S2/c

CASUALTIES 493

HAUSAM, Alfred W., TM1/c
HAUSER, Gary, Ptr3/c
HAUSER, John L., F1/c
HAWKINS, Benton F., MoMM2/c
HAWKINS, Hubert B., S2/c
HAWKS, Jas. E., S2/c
HAWKS, Wm. G., CM2/c
HAYDEN, Edw. C., S1/c
HAYES, Jas. C., ARM3/c
HAYES, John S., S1/c
HAYES, Loys V., CPhMA
HAYES, Postell, St3/c
HAYES, Robt. J., F1/c
HAYES, W. H., S2/c
HAYES, Willie, S2/c
HAYNES, Wm. F., StM1/c
HAYS, Geo. H., MM1/c
HAYSE, Harold T., WT1/c
HEAD, Paul W., CM3/c
HEAL, Thos. E., RDM2/c
HEARD, Lonnie, Ck3/c
HEARN, Robt. E., S1/c
HEATH, Jas. M., StM1/c
HEBERT, Edw. J., AMM2/c
HEBERT, Ellis J., S1/c
HEBERT, Ernest W., CM3/c
HEBERT, Francis X., Y3/c
HECKENDORN, Gordon F., ARM2/c
HEDGE, Robt. W., AMM2/c
HEDGES, Dan H., S2/c
HEDGES, Wilbert, GM3/c
HEEBNER, Lester C., S2/c
HEFFEL, Reuben B., S1/c
HEFFINGTON, Rich. C., EM3/c
HEIDE, Wm. H., AMM2/c
HEIDELER, John C., Jr., HA2/c
HEIDEMANN, Reuben F., MM3/c
HEIGHTON, Carl V., Jr., ARM3/c
HEINRICH, Wm., Jr., AOM3/c
HEINZE, Virgil R., Cox.
HEISCH, Chessher F., S1/c
HEISLER, Donald R., S1/c
HELDORFER, Jos. N., AOM1/c
HELFOND, Jacob, SK2/c
HELLMAN, Edw. J., SF2/c
HELM, Milton W., ARM2/c
HELMICK, Maynard E., MM2/c
HELMS, Wm. A., PhM2/c
HEMMERLING, Leonard R., Pr1/c
HEMPELMAN, Wayne V., HA1/c
HEMSTREET, Chas. R., F1/c
HENDERSON, Edw. F., QM2/c
HENDERSON, Felix, S2/c

HENDERSON, Jas. D., SC2/c
HENDERSON, Lawrence R., F1/c
HENDERSON, Leo J., Cox.
HENDERSON, Lloyd G., EM2/c
HENDERSON, Raymond W., AMM2/c
HENDERSON, Rich. D., F1/c
HENDERSON, Robt. W., AOM1/c
HENDERSON, Wm. I., Cox.
HENDRICKS, Marion L., S1/c
HENDRICKS, Robt. H., S1/c
HENDRICKS, Wm. F., PhM3/c
HENDRICKSON, Imanuel, SF3/c
HENDRIX, Thos. E., EM3/c
HENDRIX, Wm. T., BMKR2/c
HENDRY, Walter C., F2/c
HENKE, Wm. L., S1/c
HENNEBERRY, Geo., Cox.
HENNINGER, Howard C., S2/c
HENRY, Guy D., ARM3/c
HENRY, Wilfred, RM3/c
HENSLEY, Earl L., S1/c
HENSLEY, Gale E., AMM3/c
HENSON, Mat, StM1/c
HEPER, Arthur A., Jr., S1/c
HEPFLER, Geo., TM2/c
HEPP, Claude W., CM3/c
HEPPER, Arthur E., S2/c
HEPWORTH, Samuel D., AMM2/c
HERBIEN, Louis E., S2/c
HEREDIA, Manuel V., RM3/c
HERIFORD, Glenn E., S1/c
HERKERT, Willard W., AM1/c
HERLIHY, Wm. W., ARM1/c
HERMESDORF, John A., SF2/c
HERMLEY, Wm., S1/c
HERNANDEZ, Elias L., S2/c
HERNANDEZ, Rafael L., AMM3/c
HEROLD, Eugene E., S1/c
HERR, Eugene L., RM2/c
HERREN, Albert F., Jr., AMM3/c
HERRIN, Hollis E., S1/c
HERRING, John C., ARM2/c
HERRMANN, Chas. L., S1/c
HERRON, David. MM3/c
HERRON, Terence J., ARM3/c
HERSHEY, Wm. L., S2/c
HERSHMAN, Jos. A., S2/c
HERSTICH, Martin L., Jr., TM1/c
HERZOG, Robt., S2/c
HESS, Robt. W., BM1/c
HESSION, Chas., S1/c
HETZLER, Marvin L., PhM2/c
HEWITT, Wm. R., PhM3/c

HIATT, Don L., EM3/c
HIBLER, Raymond E., Jr., SC2/c
HICKMAN, Ronald, Bkr3/c
HICKS, Hollis W., S2/c
HICKS, W. L., ARM2/c
HIGDON, Harley R., MM1/c
HIGGINBOTHAN, Albert L., Bkr2/c
HIGH, Thos. P., S1/c
HIGHFILL, Leonard E., S2/c
HILER, Robt. L., S2/c
HILL, Adam, MM1/c
HILL, Burl A., S2/c
HILL, Donald N., AM3/c
HILL, Ernest J., S1/c
HILL, Garnett G., S2/c
HILL, John E., SK1/c
HILL, Lewis P., Cox.
HILL, Mark D., MM1/c
HILL, Samuel, Ck3/c
HILL, Willis W., F1/c
HILL, Wm. M. O., F1/c
HILLMAN, Robt. S., MM3/c
HIMEL, Ernest P., CBMP
HIMES, Arnold J., F2/c
HINDLE, Robt. E., S2/c
HINES, Rich. C., ARM3/c
HINEY, Henry M., PhM2/c
HIPPLER, Rose E., PM2/c
HIRLEMAN, Richard D., WT3/c
HIRSCH, Willard E., SC2/c
HIRST, Allen A., EM1/c
HITCHCOCK, Lawrence S., F1/c
HIZER, Norbert J. W., MoMM1/c
HOAGLAND, Namie C., MM3/c
HOBBS, Chas. S., MM1/c
HOBBS, Lee H., EM3/c
HOCH, Phlete A., PhM2/c
HODGES, Grant M., WT1/c
HODGES, Sam'l, Jr., PhM1/c
HODGES, Troy T., MM3/c
HODOS, Steve James, CEMA
HOEGERL, Anthony J., MM2/c
HOERMANN, Fred H., MoMM2/c
HOFELMANN, Russell H., S1/c
HOFER, Berthold Oscar, FCM3/c
HOFF, Leo A., AOM3/c
HOFF, Ralph W., SSML3/c
HOFFENPRADEL, John F., S1/c
HOFFMAN, Donald S., S1/c
HOFFMAN, Edw. T., ARM2/c
HOFFMAN, Jerry R., S2/c
HOFMANN, James L., AOM2/c
HOFMANN, Walter N., FC1/c
HOFSTEE, John D., S1/c

HOGAN, Harold Dan, PhoM2/c
HOGAN, Jas. E., Jr., S2/c
HOGG, Francis M., MoMM2/c
HOGG, Jesse T., Jr., GM3/c
HOGROGIAN, John, S2/c
HOGUE, Wm. A., EM1/c
HOLDEN, Paul L., EM3/c
HOLDER, Wm. B., S1/c
HOLLADAY, Darwin A., PhM2/c
HOLLAND, Clyde, Jr., MoMM2/c
HOLLAND, Elmer B., Cox.
HOLLAND, Michael, CTMA
HOLLAND, Velvin W., SKD2/c
HOLLAND, Walker K., Jr., PhM2/c
HOLLEY, Hubert H., S2/c
HOLLIMAN, Oliver L., S1/c
HOLLINGSWORTH, Talbert G., Cox.
HOLLOWAY, Arney L., MM1/c
HOLLOWAY, Earnest T., S1/c
HOLLOWELL, Chas. J., F2/c
HOLMBERG, John L., SoM3/c
HOLMES, Byron J., HA1/c
HOLMES, Wm. A., MM1/c
HOLQUIST, Donald E. W., CMoMA
HOLT, Clayton M., ACMMP
HOLT, Jas. D., PhM3/c
HOLT, John G., QM3/c
HOLTE, Victor R., SM3/c
HOLTHOUSE, Hugh J., CMoMMa
HONE, Earl E., F1/c
HONIGMAN, Carl G., F2/c
HONNOLD, Harry E., F1/c
HOOD, Enoch, S2/c
HOOK, Mike, S2/c
HOOKS, Carson L., Cox.
HOOVER, John H., PhM2/c
HOPKINS, Fred, S2/c
HOPKINS, Thaine L., S2/c
HOPKINS, Thos. L., S2/c
HOPPER, Arthur B., S1/c
HORAK, Robt. A., PhM3/c
HORAN, Edw. T., S2/c
HORCHLER, Edw. W., S1/c
HORN, Edw. T., HA1/c
HORN, Eugene K., AMM2/c
HORN, Robt. C., HA1/c
HORNBECK, Wm. H., Jr., F2/c
HORNE, Robt. P., CRMA
HORNER, Harold E., EM3/c
HORNER, Robt. L., S2/c
HORNYAK, Andrew J., F2/c
HORTON, Myron B., Jr., S2/c
HORTON, Ray E., StM2/c
HOSZOWSKI, John, EM3/c

CASUALTIES 495

HOTTEL, Maurice C., EM1/c
HOUDEK, Jos. V., WT1/c
HOUFF, Clayton J., HA2/c
HOUGH, Paul G., F1/c
HOUGH, Warren C., SM1/c
HOULDITCH, Jas. E., GM2/c
HOVLAND, Arnold J., PhM3/c
HOWARD, Ernest L., F1/c
HOWARD, Henry F., S2/c
HOWARD, Wm. S., Ptr1/c
HOWERTON, Claud F., Jr., S2/c
HOWIE, Gilbert J., Jr., RT2/c
HOWLEY, Jas. T., SK3/c
HOWZE, Jas. E., QM3/c
HOXWORTH, Theodore W., S1/c
HOYLE, Jack M., PhM3/c
HOYT, Jack W., PhM3/c
HRABE, Chas. J., PhM2/c
HRAPCHAK, Jos. A., PhM2/c
HUARD, Robt. B., MoMM2/c
HUBBARD, Bernard W., EM2/c
HUBBARD, Lewis Benton, MoMM1/c
HUBBARD, Paul R., S1/c
HUBBLE, Asa J., S1/c
HUBERT, Douglas L., SM2/c
HUBNER, Emil J., S1/c
HUCKABY, Broudis D., S2/c
HUDAK, John, Jr., F1/c
HUDSON, Billy J., RM1/c
HUDSON, Ellis, StM2/c
HUDSON, Francis G., RDM2/c
HUEBSCHER, Otto F., MM3/c
HUERTAS, Sotero, NSK3/c
HUEY, Hubbard P., S1/c
HUFF, Amos L., Cox.
HUFF, Delmar Lloyd, ARM1/c
HUFF, John K., CTMA
HUFFORD, Herbert V., CM1/c
HUGGARD, Thos. J., S1/c
HUGHES, Clarence H., CTMP
HUGHES, Lawrence T., MM2/c
HUGHES, Lewis W., S1/c
HUGHES, Lyall A., RM2/c
HUGHES, Wm. A., S2/c
HULL, Delmar D., BM1/c
HULL, Wm. A., Cox.
HULS, Jos. F., S2/c
HULSEBUS, Wm. L., S1/c
HUME, John F., S2/c
HUME, Lloyd E., AMM3/c
HUMMEL, John H., F2/c
HUMPAGE, Howard W., MM1/c
HUMPHREY, Derryl I., Cox.
HUMRICH, Clark L., MM3/c

HUNDLEY, Noble, S1/c
HUNT, Ambrose, CCMA
HUNT, Jack E., PhM3/c
HUNT, Thos. W., S1/c
HUNT, Wm. L., MM2/c
HUNTER, Alfonse, StM3/c
HUNTER, Billy G., ARM3/c
HUNTER, Chas. W., MM1/c
HUNTER, Norman E., S2/c
HUNTER, Ray, S2/c
HUNTER, Sam E., Jr., S1/c
HUNTINGTON, Louis Edward, CMMP
HUNTON, Arthur C., S1/c
HUNTZINGER, John R., EM2/c
HURON, William Harold, ARM3/c
HURTT, Maurice T., PhM2/c
HUSCHKA, Geo. L., ARM2/c
HUTCHINS, Robt. D., Cox.
HUTCHISON, Virgil E., S1/c
HUTCHMAN, John D., Ptr1/c
HYDE, Howard, S2/c
HYDE, Stanley L., BM2/c
HYLA, Frank G., EM3/c
HYMEL, Jos. M., MM2/c
HYMER, Roy E., Jr., S2/c
HYSS, Walter P., Y3/c

IANNAZZO, Frank B., S1/c
IBBOTSON, John L., S1/c
IGNACIO, Enrique M., NS2/c
ILGES, Harry J., Jr., S2/c
INDA, Frank R., Jr., S2/c
INMAN, Lorenzia D., Jr., S2/c
INMAN, Morton B., Jr., S1/c
INNINGS, Geo. T., TMV3/c
INOCENTI, Alfred, F1/c
IOVINO, Angelo R., S2/c
ISAAC, Lewis J., MM3/c
ISOM, Lyman L., MM3/c
IZZI, Jos. S., S1/c

JACKSON, David E., S1/c
JACKSON, Guy A., GM3/c
JACKSON, Jimmie L., StM1/c
JACKSON, John M., StM1/c
JACKSON, Maurice E., AOM3/c
JACKSON, Vernon T., MoMM2/c
JACKSON, Wilton A., FC3/c
JACOB, Jos. E., F1/c
JACOBS, Geo. O., S1/c
JACOBS, Jos. M., S1/c
JACOBSEN, Benj. F., PhM2/c
JACQUIN, Robt. G., CMoMMA
JAEGER, Harry A., F1/c

JAKLE, Richard H., AMM2/c
JALAD, Michel M., Jr., S1/c
JAMBOIS, Raymond A., F1/c
JAMES, Hershel D., F1/c
JAMES, Homer E., EM2/c
JAMES, Raymond, S1/c
JANACEK, Method C., S2/c
JANNEY, General A., Jr., PhM3/c
JANSEN, Lyle J., RM2/c
JANUSEZ, Stanley J., GM3/c
JARAMILLO, Wm., S2/c
JARRELL, Jas. C., S1/c
JAVARAS, Thos. G., S1/c
JAY, John P., PhM3/c
JEAN, Albert B., S2/c
JEFFRES, Willard T., F1/c
JELACIC, John, ARM2/c
JELAK, Andrew J., AMM2/c
JENKINS, Donald N., Y3/c
JENKINS, Geo. S., CQMP
JENKINS, Jack W., PhM2/c
JENKINS, Wm. H., S1/c
JENNINGS, Frank R., MM2/c
JENNINGS, Lawrence, S2/c
JENNINGS, Preston E., Cox.
JENNINGS, Robt. F., S2/c
JENSEN, Arthur R., MoMM2/c
JENSEN, John W., S1/c
JENSEN, Robt., AOM3/c
JEONG, Wing J., S1/c
JERDO, Fredk W., S2/c
JETER, Thos. E., CSPVA
JETER, Wm. L., SM3/c
JETT, Melvin S., SF3/c
JETTE, Augustin E., MM2/c
JEWELL, Thos. E., CSMP
JIMERSON, Bernice L., StM3/c
JOHNS, Harold Wesley, MM2/c
JOHNS, Otto J., Jr., S2/c
JOHNSON, Alan, CK2/c
JOHNSON, Bonnie H., F2/c
JOHNSON, Earnest, STM2/c
JOHNSON, Eddie J., STM3/c
JOHNSON, Elmo, S1/c
JOHNSON, Floyd W., ARM2/c
JOHNSON, Frank M., S2/c
JOHNSON, Harold D., MM2/c
JOHNSON, Harold H., ARM1/c
JOHNSON, Jack G., GM3/c
JOHNSON, Jas. A., MM2/c
JOHNSON, Jas. R., MM3/c
JOHNSON, Jas. W., S2/c
JOHNSON, Jesse L., S2/c
JOHNSON, Joe M., CSFA
JOHNSON, John D., BM2/c
JOHNSON, John T., S1/c
JOHNSON, John T., Jr., S1/c
JOHNSON, Leon, S2/c
JOHNSON, Leon, AMM1/c
JOHNSON, Louis M., S2/c
JOHNSON, Martin J., S2/c
JOHNSON, Meredith B., PhOM1/c
JOHNSON, Neal K., MoMM3/c
JOHNSON, Norman F., M1/c
JOHNSON, Ralph M., S1/c
JOHNSON, Robt. J., PhM1/c
JOHNSON, Russell H., HA1/c
JOHNSON, Sam, StM2/c
JOHNSON, Tarpley, CMMP
JOHNSTON, Carl E., S1/c
JOHNSTON, Harry L., AOM3/c
JOHNSTON, Hilton W., S2/c
JOHNSTON, Jas. A., MM2/c
JOHNSTON, Jas. W., HA1/c
JOHNSTON, Leonard A., SK1/c
JOHNSTON, Richard H., GM3/c
JOHNSTON, Virgil E., RDM2/c
JOHNSTON, Walter W., F1/c
JOLLEY, Cerell C., MoMM2/c
JONES, Alfred D., HA1/c
JONES, Benj. L., Jr., ARM3/c
JONES, Dave C., F1/c
JONES, Edwin E., S1/c
JONES, Geo. F., FCO3/c
JONES, Herman H., MM1/c
JONES, Jack E., ARM3/c
JONES, Jesse, S1/c
JONES, John N., WT3/c
JONES, Johnnie L., STM1/c
JONES, Karl K., EM3/c
JONES, Louis H., STM1/c
JONES, Louis H., STM1/c
JONES, Marsh, CQMA
JONES, Paul J., S1/c
JONES, Raymond H., CCMA
JONES, Rhett, S1/c
JONES, Robt. G., S1/c
JONES, Roy E., STM1/c
JONES, Shelbie A., F1/c
JONES, Thos. L., F2/c
JONES, Victor B., AOM2/c
JONES, Wayne E., SK3/c
JONES, Willard F., TM3/c
JOPLIN, Ottice C., F1/c
JORGENSEN, Donald P., EM1/c
JOY, Myron C., S1/c

JOYCE, Michael P., MM3/c
JUDD, Chas. W., AMM3/c
JULISON, Stanley J., CM3/c
JUNE, Harold A., S1/c
JUNEAU, Raymond T., S1/c
JUNKER, Dana S., PhM2/c
JURICK, Melvin F., ARM3/c

KABALA, Albert, MM2/c
KAHN, Edw. L., PhM2/c
KAISER, Geo. E. W., WT1/c
KALAMAJA, Leo B., QM3/c
KALBE, Walter H., CMMA
KALE, Ruben C., GM3/c
KAMENAR, Robt. J., F1/c
KANAE, John E., S1/c
KANAVEL, Walter J., S2/c
KANDYBOWICZ, Stanley J., F1/c
KANE, Sam, F1/c
KANNE, Robt. D., F2/c
KAPLAN, Gerald, S2/c
KARAIWU, Paul P., Jr., S1/c
KARAKO, Steven L., Cox.
KARAU, Dean R., S2/c
KARETSKI, Jos. P., PhM3/c
KARPAWICZ, Geo. W., HA1/c
KARSEMEYER, Henry, ACRMA
KARWACKI, Frank R., RM3/c
KARWOSKI, Henry E., S1/c
KASMAN, Brennan W., MM2/c
KASTER, Rich. A., S1/c
KASTER, Vernon W., MM1/c
KATALINICH, Daniel A., S2/c
KATH, Wm. H., BM2/c
KATHOL, Leonard J., Cox.
KATIC, Milo J., RT2/c
KATSAROS, Nicholas, ARM2/c
KAUFMAN, Leonard C., S1/c
KAUFFMAN, Harry, S1/c
KAWALEC, Frank, WT2/c
KAYLOR, Fredk G., PhM1/c
KAYLOR, John C., AERM3/c
KEAN, Hyman E., CBMA
KEAN, Kenneth, S1/c
KEATON, Thos. J. S., CMMP
KEEFE, Jos. F., TM3/c
KEEGAN, Frank Henry, Jr., BM2/c
KEENAN, Gerald J., EM3/c
KEENER, Jimmie C., AMM1/c
KEETCH, Jim M., PhM2/c
KEILMAN, John J., S1/c
KEIRN, Keith, MoMM3/c
KEITH, Otis J., S2/c
KELEKIAN, Harry, WT3/c

KELIMOFF, Victor P., ARM1/c
KELLER, Erven F., AOM1/c
KELLER, Goldwin C., AP1/c
KELLER, Jos. A., MoMM3/c
KELLEY, Dan L., S1/c
KELLEY, Floyd E., SC3/c
KELLEY, Geo. E., RM1/c
KELLEY, James A., MoMM1/c
KELLEY, James M., CAPA
KELLIHER, John P. J., AOM2/c
KELLY, Edward Thomas, S1/c
KELLY, Henry H., S2/c
KELLY, Jos. A., BH1/c
KELLY, Patrick F., Jr., S1/c
KELLY, Percy Howard, Bkr3/c
KELLY, Shirley H., PhM2/c
KELLY, Thos. C., S1/c
KELLY, Thos. J., MM3/c
KELLY, Wilbur L., Cox.
KELLY, Wm. E., SC2/c
KEMEOS, John J., S2/c
KEMKEM, Jas. B., S1/c
KEMMIE, Howard J., PhM1/c
KENAN, Dean F., EM2/c
KENDRICK, Ralph E., AMM3/c
KENLEY, Lee C., F1/c
KENNEDY, Marion J., BM2/c
KENNY, Dan R., Jr., CM2/c
KENSLER, Jacob D., F1/c
KENT, Philip L., PhM3/c
KENT, Texas T., S1/c
KENTNER, Robt. E., S2/c
KEOUGH, Robt. L., AMM2/c
KEPP, Guy W., S2/c
KERR, Jas. R., Jr., S2/c
KERR, John J., S1/c
KERTZMAN, Abraham, F1/c
KESLER, Gerald Leonard, BM2/c
KESLER, Merrel R., AMM2/c
KESSINGER, Harold, SC1/c
KESSLER, Walter W., PhM1/c
KEVILLE, John P., HA1/c
KIDD, Franklin B., RM3/c
KIDD, Kenneth T., AM3/c
KIDWELL, Laurence E., TM3/c
KIENE, Chas. B., F1/c
KIFFER, Lester J., Bkr1/c
KILGARD, Earl E., S1/c
KILGORE, Wm. W., SoM2/c
KILGO, Jas. A., F1/c
KILLIAN, Chas. H., BM2/c
KILPATRICK, Duane J., SM1/c
KIMBALL, Joe W., MM1/c
KIMBALL, Murry B., MM1/c
KIMREY, Hugh B., RT3/c

KING, Frank, S1/c
KING, Glennon E., S1/c
KING, Melvin L., MM3/c
KING, Orville W., PhM2/c
KINGERY, James C., S1/c
KINGSLEY, Lewis A., F1/c
KINGSBURY, Glen W., AMM2/c
KINGSTON, Francis P., MoMM1/c
KINLEY, Morris Richard, S1/c
KINTZ, Francis C., F1/c
KIPPER, Carl K., S1/c
KIRBY, Forrest H., SK1/c
KIRBY, Henry L., PhM2/c
KIRBY, Howard F., MM2/c
KIRCHNICK, John S., F2/c
KIRK, Bob, S2/c
KIRK, Jas. J., AOM1/c
KIRKHAM, John Lee, F2/c
KIRKLEY, B. K., HA1/c
KIRKSEY, Andrew J., TM2/c
KIRTLEY, Wilbert W., F1/c
KIRWIN, John F., S1/c
KISTLER, Ralph E., CMMP
KITSON, Neil V., F2/c
KIVISTO, Toivo S., F2/c
KLAJBOR, Peter P., AOM3/c
KLAUSE, Oscar, PhM3/c
KLAYSMAT, Raymond H., S2/c
KLEIN, Irving, S2/c
KLEIN, Jos. L., TM2/c
KLEKOTKA, Alexander J., MoMM1/c
KLEMCKE, Robert Lee, S2/c
KLIMOSEWSKI, Johnny P., MoMM1/c
KLINE, Albert P., S1/c
KLINGA, Tauno T. J., S1/c
KLOACK, Marlin H., MM3/c
KLOCK, Donald R., MoMM2/c
KLOTKOWSKI, Henry S., S2/c
KLUGE, Hugo L., ARM2/c
KLUGER, Seymour, F1/c
KLUMKER, Geo. G., PhM2/c
KLUPP, Adam J., EM2/c
KMIEC, Zegmond W., S2/c
KNAPP, Arthur L., QM3/c
KNAPP, Wm. E., S1/c
KNAUSS, Wm. A., Cox.
KNOCKE, Reuben H., ARM3/c
KNUTSON, Thos. S., AMM2/c
KOCHER, Alvin G., MoMM2/c
KOCHER, Harry A., SC1/c
KOCHON, Theo. P., S2/c
KOEHLER, Arthur J., CQMA
KOEHLER, Ralph C., PhM2/c
KOEPP, Geo. L., ARM2/c
KOHLER, Morris B., MM3/c

KOKTA, Chas. E., S2/c
KOLACHICK, Michael, M1/c
KOLCZYNSKI, Raymond R., S1/c
KOLLER, Frank M., TM3/c
KONOPKA, Frank P., S1/c
KOONS, John A., CAPA
KOPPANG Warren E., SF1/c
KOREYVA, Victor J., MoMM1/c
KORPETER, Michael, GM2/c
KOSA, Frank S., MM2/c
KOSCHUCH, Wm. P., S2/c
KOSESAN, Frank L., Bkr1/c
KOSMATKA, Ambrose L., S2/c
KOSTECHKO, Anthony, MM3/c
KOSTOLNIK, Sylvester S., EM3/c
KOT, Chester A., Bkr3/c
KOTLAS, Johnny, EM3/c
KOTLINSKI, Harry J., S1/c
KOZAK, John E., AOM1/c
KOZERA, Melvin, S1/c
KOZLOFF, Benj. B., PhM2/c
KRAMER, John Albert, GM3/c
KRANTZ, Francis R., AOM3/c
KRATOSKA, Richard T., F2/c
KRAUSE, Walter P., S1/c
KRAYER, Arthur D., RM1/c
KREISER, Chas. J., S1/c
KREY, David P., S1/c
KROHN, Arthur R., S2/c
KROPF, Richard Stanley, S1/c
KRUEGER, Albert F., MM3/c
KRUMHOLZ, Wm. A., PhM3/c
KRUPINSKI, Sylvester F., HA1/c
KRUPP, Jas. H., GM3/c
KRUSE, Donald D., RT1/c
KUDELLA, John, S1/c
KUEBKER, Kenton W., Bkr1/c
KUGEL, Ralph R., FC1/c
KUMINGA, Chester S., M3/c
KUMPUNEN, Otto E., Jr., SoM3/c
KUNES, Floyd E., Jr., MoMM3/c
KUNKEL, A. J., Jr., S1/c
KUPIDLOWSKI, Chester P., F1/c
KURLAND, Jos. B., ARM2/c
KUSHELOFF, Jos. M., RM2/c
KUSIELEWICZ, Albert S., MM3/c
KWAPICK, Frank S., QM2/c
KWITKOWSKI, Peter P., BM1/c
KWOLEK, John J., MM3/c
KYLE, Gilbert E., ARM2/c

LAACK, Wulfert J., MoMM3/c
LABO, Stanley B., AMM3/c
LACHANCE, Adelard R., Jr., BM1/c
LACK, John D., F1/c

CASUALTIES

LACY, Harold D., S2/c
LADUE, Fredk M., F1/c
LAFOSSE, Harvey A., S2/c
LAIRD, Richard F., GM2/c
LAKEMAN, Harry H., SK1/c
LALE, Elmer Paul, HA1/c
LAMAR, Gainer B., PhM3/c
LAMB, Jas. S., Jr., Y3/c
LAMB, Lonnie L., EM3/c
LAMBERT, Albert L., MM3/c
LAMBERT, Andrew J., S1/c
LAMBERT, David L., AOM3/c
LAMBERT, Wilfred T., Jr., AOM2/c
LANDERS, Chas. W., MM3/c
LANDIN, Johan A., F1/c
LANDRUM, Donald R., S1/c
LANDRETH, Robt., Mus1/c
LANDSPERGER, Jas. C., S1/c
LANG, Clyde Nelson, MM1/c
LANG, Robt. F., HA1/c
LANGENEGGER, Nolan M., S1/c
LANGFORD, Orbie, WT3/c
LANGSTON, Robt. L., STM1/c
LANGWORTHY, Archie L., CSPAA
LANKFORD, Alfred B., ARM2/c
LANKFORD, Thos., SKT3/c
LANTRON, Conrad A., ARM2/c
LANZELOTTI, Wm. A., S1/c
LAPOMA, Dan L., MM3/c
LAPRADE, Arthur, S1/c
LARACE, Wm. E., CCSA
LARAMEE, Romeo A., MoMM2/c
LARGE, Geo. H., SC3/c
LARGO, Phillip D., ARM3/c
LARKINS, Walter H., EM1/c
LARSON, Harris R., EM1/c
LARSON, Herbert V., ARM1/c
LARSON, Robt. R., PhM2/c
LARUSSA, Paul J., S2/c
LASKOWSKY, Stefan John, WT3/c
LASURE, Sam'l A., Jr., RT3/c
LATHAM, David L., S2/c
LATHROP, Harvey H., S1/c
LATORRE, Jos., S2/c
LATTANZI, Querino L., S1/c
LATTIMER, Robt. W., QM3/c
LAUBACH, Leo J., CMMP
LAUDER, Guy E., TM2/c
LAUDERDALE, Kenneth B., SF1/c
LAURN, Alvin E., WT1/c
LAURSEN, Kenneth A., PhM3/c
LAVALLE, John A., S2/c
LAVELLE, Peter F., S1/c
LAVIN, Martin T., ARM3/c
LAW, Vernon W., GM3/c

LAWLER, John W., F2/c
LAWLER, Orville E., CGMP
LAWLESS, Martin J., MoMM2/c
LAWRENCE, Austin L., Jr., Bkr3/c
LAWRENCE, Kenneth, S1/c
LAWRENCE, Thos. E., CBMA
LAWSON, Wm. D., M3/c
LAY, Geo. E., MoMM2/c
LAYTON, Albert E., RM3/c
LAYTON, John D., S1/c
LAZROVITCH, Geo., S2/c
LEACH, Clayton M., GM3/c
LEACH, Wm. E., S2/c
LEAMING, Joe, Jr., PhM3/c
LEAR, Wm. H., EM1/c
LEASE, Earl H., F1/c
LEASURE, Karl E., PhM3/c
LEAVERTON, Chas. C., EM1/c
LEBEAU, Ralph Joseph, AOM2/c
LEBEL, Alfred A., F2/c
LEBLANC, Louis A., S1/c
LEBLANC, Osias J., S1/c
LEBLANC, Peter A., SC1/c
LECAPTAIN, Bernhard, PhM2/c
LECCI, Jos., F1/c
LECHLER, Wm. R., S1/c
LECLAIRE, Ovila J., S2/c
LECLERC, Albert V., MM2/c
LEDBETTER, Edw. H., PhM3/c
LEDFORD, Chas. A., S1/c
LEE, Don, S2/c
LEE, Geo. W., S1/c
LEE, Jas. A., PhM3/c
LEE, James J., AOM3/c
LEE, James William, S1/c
LEE, Robt. E., SC3/c
LEE, Walter, S1/c
LEE, Wm. D., S1/c
LEFTWICH, Leo J., S1/c
LEGLER, Kenneth R., RM3/c
LEGROTTAGLIE, John J., MM2/c
LEHMBECKER, Leroy B., S1/c
LEHNER, Wm. W., S2/c
LEIBIK, Albert J., PhM2/c
LEINBACH, Barto J., Jr., PhM3/c
LEIST, Frank J., PhM2/c
LELAND, Lawrence D., CRMP
LEMACKS, Francis G., S2/c
LEMAIRE, John R., S2/c
LEMAY, Anthony H., SC3/c
LEMIEUX, Paulk M., ACOMA
LENON, Raymond E., EM1/c
LEONARD, Dan, Jr., SC3/c
LEONGUERRERO, Jesus C., St2/c
LEONHARDT, Eugene C., F1/c

Leopard, David P., Jr., GM2/c
Leopard, John L., S1/c
Lermusiaux, Jimmie Joe, SC2/c
Lerner, Lawrence, SF2/c
Leroux, Clarence S., EM3/c
Lesage, Dollard A., MM3/c
Lesiuk, Wm., MME3/c
Leslie, Chas. E., AOM1/c
Lester, Robt. L., S2/c
Leszczynski, Casimir A., SC2/c
Leta, Domenico M., S2/c
Letton, Jas. W., SC3/c
Leu, Robt. C., SM2/c
Levendowski, Lennie L., S2/c
Levesque, Raymond A., EM2/c
Levine, Bernard, PhM3/c
Levy, Jos., S1/c
Lewandowski, Edmund P., S1/c
Lewin, Jas. R., ARM1/c
Lewis, Donald R., PhM3/c
Lewis, Fredrick H., EM3/c
Lewis, John L., EM2/c
Lewis, John S., S1/c
Lewis, Lloyd S., S1/c
Lewis, Oaksie G., S1/c
Lewis, Richard James, S1/c
Lewis, Richard Warren, S1/c
Lewis, Wm. G., PhM2/c
Lewis, Wm. T., CBMA
Lexow, Wm. E., AMM3/c
Libby, Raymond N., TM1/c
Libengood, Jas. R., QM3/c
Liebman, Marion A., S1/c
Life, John R., EM3/c
Lifset, Leonard C., ARM2/c
Lightfoot, Earl A., AMM2/c
Light, Jas. D., CTMA
Ligrisse, Virgil N., EM3/c
Likevich, Steve, Jr., PhM1/c
Liles, James Joseph, S2/c
Lilly, Philip A., ARM3/c
Limen, Epifanio, CK2/c
Limpinsel, Anthony L., ARM2/c
Lind, Farris R., AMM3/c
Lind, Herbert J., SM2/c
Linder, Asby C., S2/c
Linder, Chas. F., MM2/c
Linder, Wallace R., S1/c
Lindgren, Geo. W., MM1/c
Lindstrom, Wm. R., F1/c
Lines, Walter E., MoMM2/c
Lingham, Geo. J., AOM3/c
Link, Leonard A., S1/c
Link, Raymond F., S2/c
Linville, Jess, Jr., PhM3/c

Linway, Clifford H., QM3/c
Lipinski, Francis J., F1/c
Lischeron, Anton G., MoMM1/c
Litka, Raymond W., PhM2/c
Little, Jas. D., AM3/c
Little, Vernon J., S2/c
Littledave, Anderson, S1/c
Litzsinger, Marion A., AMM2/c
Lively, Venal C., S2/c
Lizama, Simon F., St3/c
Lloyd, Garland L., BM2/c
Lloyd, Lucious W., PhM2/c
Loar, Geo. B., S2/c
Locke, John, Jr., S1/c
Locke, Willis J., BM2/c
Lockhart, Raymond B., WT1/c
Lockhart, Samuel Lincoln, StM1/c
Lockwood, Chas. W., Cox.
Loeber, Edw. C., RT3/c
Loeber, Robt. W., QM2/c
Loeffler, Ernest E., S2/c
Lofing, Raymond D., S2/c
Logan, Harold L., CMoMMP
Logan, Oscar F., CM3/c
Logsdon, Herbert H., ARM2/c
Lokey, Geo. A., EM2/c
Long, Earl N., S2/c
Long, Herman V., MM3/c
Long, Jas. E., RM3/c
Long, Lynn S., Jr., S2/c
Long, Percy E., TM2/c
Long, Wm. F., GM3/c
Long, W. S., Jr., PhM3/c
Longberry, Jas. T., HA1/c
Longkabel, Gordon, Jr., S2/c
Longo, Louis V., F1/c
Loomis, Richard R., PhM3/c
Lorenz, Bill E., SK2/c
Losbanes, Zody L., StM1/c
Losty, Wm. M., BM2/c
Loughlin, Jas. E., S1/c
Love, Dan M., S1/c
Love, David Wilson, AMM2/c
Love, Erclas G., Jr., AMM2/c
Lovelle, David A., PhM1/c
Lovelady, Obed L., S1/c
Lovering, Lauren L., CEMA
Low, Fredk. J., S1/c
Lowe, Burnis W., F1/c
Lowe, Wm. J., ARM2/c
Lowery, John T., WT1/c
Lowman, Ralph S., SC3/c
Lowman, Widner S., WT1/c
Lowrey, Gordon C., AOM2/c
Lowrey, John J., S1/c

CASUALTIES

Lowrimore, Orval D., AMM2/c
Lowy, Edwin A., RT1/c
Luby, Wm. E., ARM2/c
Lucas, Jos. B., Jr., MoMM2/c
Lucchesi, Louis L., S2/c
Luce, Roy E., Jr., ACOMP
Luchs, Tilden L., MM3/c
Luckett, Thos. E., MM1/c
Ludemann, Dan H., WT3/c
Luebke, Celestine C., BM1/c
Luke, Elmo StM1/c
Luketic, Anthony R., F1/c
Lukowski, Evgene T., TM2/c
Lum, Hoong C., CSTP
Lund, Loyd, AMM1/c
Lupisan, Arsenio, CK1/c
Lupshu, Chas. K., HA1/c
Lupton, Harold L., CEMA
Luster, Clarence, StM3/c
Luther, Ernest D., S1/c
Lutts, Earnest R., S2/c
Lutz, Arthur C., PhM3/c
Lyle, Richard P., AEM2/c
Lyle, Wagner D., AMM1/c
Lynch, Jas. T., Jr., PhM3/c
Lynch, Ralph M., HA1/c
Lynch, Robt. J., RM2/c
Lyon, Guy, PhM2/c
Lyon, Otto J., S1/c
Lyons, Wilmer V., S1/c
Lytton, Verle J., CM2/c

Maccarra, Robt. F., SoM3/c
Maccani, Jean E., PhM2/c
Macdonald, John B., S2/c
Macdonald, Robt. B., SC3/c
Macfarland, Howard, MM2/c
Macidyn, Frank J., BM2/c
Mack, Ralph D., MME1/c
Macleod, John M., S1/c
Macon, Shirley R., CGMA
Macri, Francis A., F1/c
Macy, Marvin R., RM2/c
Madden, Henry, SK2/c
Maddox, Jas. L., AMM1/c
Madej, Paul P., S2/c
Madely, Lawrence A., EM2/c
Madren, Phil S., S2/c
Magnan, Jas. A., PhM3/c
Magrath, Bernard L., GM3/c
Mahan, Chas. R., Jr., PhM2/c
Maher, Edw. M., RM3/c
Mahin, Chas. W., Sr., SK2/c
Majors, Jos. W., AMM3/c
Maker, Bion E., CPHMP

Malanuk, Walter, S2/c
Malcolm, Julian D., AMM2/c
Malley, Harry, HA1/c
Malone, Carl Edwin, MM2/c
Maloney, Richard M., Jr., TM1/c
Manchester, Berkeley, SC2/c
Manetz, Walter, F1/c
Manibusan, Juan C., NSK3/c
Manion, Geo. F., EM1/c
Mankowski, Edw., MoMM2/c
Mankus, Bruno C., AMM2/c
Mann, Maybern C., WT1/c
Mann, Robt. C., WT3/c
Manning, Jesse R., AMM2/c
Mannon, Paul M., AMM2/c
Mansfield, John P., SF2/c
Mantooth, Loyd Ray, F2/c
Mara, Geo. P., Jr., Cox.
Marchetti, Jos. A., ARM2/c
Marchi, Arthur J., F1/c
Mariette, Maxwell A., PhM2/c
Marineau, Rich K., S1/c
Marker, Franklin L., GM3/c
Marker, Paul E., S2/c
Markey, Leo E., ARM2/c
Markham, Daniel L., MM2/c
Markham, Walter, MM3/c
Marks, Geo. F., EM2/c
Marmar, Aaron C., PhM3/c
Marmon, Jas. A., MM1/c
Marousky, Leonard L., F2/c
Marquez, Robt. N., S2/c
Marquard, Rich F., PhM2/c
Marriott, Oscar F., CEMP
Marsh, Arnold, ARM2/c
Marsh, Chas. W., PhM3/c
Marsh, Dodson A., ARM1/c
Marsh, Geo. W., ARM2/c
Marshall, Arthur G., WT1/c
Marshall, Deward D., Cox.
Marshall, DeWitt, Jr., S2/c
Marshall, Ezra S., S2/c
Marshall, Leslie B., MM2/c
Marshall, Thos. H., EM3/c
Marshall, Walter F., SC3/c
Marshall, Wm. L., PhM3/c
Marsland, Alvah I., MM3/c
Martell, Louis W., MM2/c
Martin, Chas. H., PhM2/c
Martin, Chas. L., EM3/c
Martin, Edward, S1/c
Martin, Geo. S., S1/c
Martin, J. B., S2/c
Martin, Jack M., ARM2/c
Martin, James, StM2/c

MARTIN, John, Jr., S2/c
MARTIN, Jos. E., PhM2/c
MARTIN, Jos. R., SC3/c
MARTIN, Larry J., MoMM3/c
MARTIN, Leonard G., SC1/c
MARTIN, Milford C., WT2/c
MARTIN, Paulino P., StM2/c
MARTIN, Raymond L., BM2/c
MARTIN, Saml. D., S1/c
MARTIN, Theo. S., SF1/c
MARTIN, Thos. J., PhM3/c
MARTIN, Wendell L., S1/c
MARTIN, Wister A., Jr., WT1/c
MARTIN, Wm. B., Jr., S1/c
MARTIN, Wm. L., ARM2/c
MARTINEZ, Moyses A., S2/c
MARTS, Lyle C., CM1/c
MARZIE, Jesse J., GM3/c
MASCARELLA, Seymore Georg, Cox.
MASCHO, Geo. L., F1/c
MASKE, Fredk. P., ARM3/c
MASON, Booker T., Jr., StM2/c
MASON, Chas. P., BM1/c
MASON, Farrell D., S2/c
MASON, Frank C., SF1/c
MASSEY, Arthur R., StM2/c
MASTERSON, Herbert N., S2/c
MASTRANGELLI, Louis J., MoMM1/c
MATANANE, Jose, MM2/c
MATCHETT, Kenneth J., BM2/c
MATHESON, Roy L., PhM3/c
MATHEWS, Benj. F., S2/c
MATHEWS, Levon L., S1/c
MATHEWS, Virgil Vernon, F3/c
MATHIEU, Lester J., GM2/c
MATHISEN, Gilbert N., PhM2/c
MATHIAS, Eugene, RM3/c
MATHIS, Clarence B., PhM1/c
MATHIS, Clyde, AMM3/c
MATHIS, David B., CM1/c
MATSON, Fred M., PhM1/c
MATTHEWS, Arthur, Jr., StM2/c
MATTHEWS, Floyd H., GM3/c
MATTHEWS, Victor Y., MM1/c
MATTHEWS, Wanza E., Jr., S2/c
MATTHEWS, Wilbur F., F1/c
MATTHIES, Herbert A., F2/c
MAUCK, Geo. M., PhM3/c
MAUERMAN, Ben A., CFCA
MAULDIN, Glenn H., AMM3/c
MAUS, Philip O., BM2/c
MAUTER, Paul T., F1/c
MAXAM, Darwin I., EM3/c
MAXEY, Barney F., S2/c
MAXFIELD, Russell A., HA2/c

MAXSON, Henry D., MM2/c
MAY, Chas. V., S1/c
MAY, Vincent Ronald, S1/c
MAYE, Fred L., F2/c
MAYES, Dewey L., S2/c
MAYES, Morrison W., S1/c
MAYES, Paul D., SC3/c
MAZY, Manuel, S1/c
MAZZAROPPI, Arthur C., S1/c
MCALISTER, Farmer L., CMMA
MCATEE, Edmund H., PhM2/c
MCAULEY, Claude C., MM3/c
MCAVOY, John S., Mus3/c
MCBRATNEY, Harold E., FC3/c
MCBRIDE, Elmer A., Jr., S2/c
MCBRIDE, Tony N., CWTP
MCCAIN, Ralph C., ARM3/c
MCCALL, Eugene B., S1/c
MCCALOP, Hermon T., StM1/c
MCCALLUM, Jack E., PhM2/c
MCCANN, Francis J., HA1/c
MCCARTER, Merl E., B1/c
MCCARTY, Ollie J., S2/c
MCCASLIN, Loyd W., CM2/c
MCCLARY, Chas. A., AMM3/c
MCCLANAHAN, Paul R., Cox.
MCCLATCHEY, Virgil F., PhM3/c
MCCLAUGHRY, Wm. G., HA2/c
MCCLEASE, Geo. C., AMM2/c
MCCLELLAND, Elmo, EM3/c
MCCLOSKEY, Emmett W., S1/c
MCCLOSKEY, Jas. F., PhM3/c
MCCLUNG, Harvey J., PhM3/c
MCCLURE, Jack W., S1/c
MCCLURE, Kenneth G., S1/c
MCCLURE, Wm. J., S1/c
MCCONNELL, Wm. D., ARM2/c
MCCONVILLE, Jas. J., S2/c
MCCORKLE, James W., ARM1/c
MCCORMICK, Jos. A., S1/c
MCCORMICK, Russell E., AOM2/c
MCCRANIE, Wm. T., S1/c
MCCRAY, Thos. J., StM3/c
MCCUEN, Walter R., MM2/c
MCCUISTON, Gordon W., S1/c
MCCULLEY, Robt. A., RM3/c
MCCULLOUGH, Harvey Claude, S2/c
MCCUMMING, Sam L., S2/c
MCCURDY, Wm. A., S1/c
MCDANIEL, Clarence E., S2/c
MCDANIEL, Ray, S1/c
MCDERMOTT, John D., S1/c
MCDONALD, Chas., Jr., F1/c
MCDONALD, Joe B., F2/c
MCDONALD, Russell, ARM2/c

McDowell, Chas. A., F2/c
McDowell, Norvie L., S2/c
McElroy, Geo. H., S1/c
McEnaney, Thos. F., GM3/c
McEvoy, Jos. D., BM2/c
McFarland, Harry J., S2/c
McFarland, Hooper E., CBMP
McFarland, John Arthur, S1/c
McFarling, Wesley H., CTMA
McGann, Thos. J., ARM2/c
McGee, Donald E., S1/c
McGee, Jas. C., S1/c
McGee, John R., S1/c
McGee, Jos., Cox.
McGee, Thomas Owen, ARM3/c
McGillinn, Robt. P., SM3/c
McGinnis, Arthur J., S1/c
McGinnis, Orville L., S1/c
McGinnis, Richard C., GM2/c
McGivney, John P., Cox.
McGlone, Albert R., M1/c
McGowan, Paul, S2/c
McGrath, Theo. J., SPV3/c
McGrath, Wm. L., MM2/c
McGraw, Wm. F., CTCP
McGregor, Wm. P., AOM1/c
McGrew, Elton B. D., S2/c
McGrory, Thos. E., S2/c
McGuffin, Jas. E., AMM1/c
McGuffin, Wm. A., F2/c
McGuinness, Jas. F., PhM2/c
McGuire, Edw. F., SF3/c
McHugh, John F., Jr., CM2/c
McIlrath, J. B., SC3/c
McInturff, Thos. S., S2/c
McKay, John, PhM3/c
McKee, Harold R., MM2/c
McKee, Rich S., TM1/c
McKeller, Neil, CMMP
McKenna, Francis X., F1/c
McKenzie, Kenneth K., S1/c
McKenzie, Lloyd C., TM1/c
McKernan, Jos. E., S1/c
McKiernan, Chas. H., SC1/c
McKinlay, William F., S1/c
McKinney, Geo. H., PhM1/c
McKinnon, Richard L., PhM3/c
McKnight, Carl H., PhM2/c
McKnight, John J., MM2/c
McKoon, Charlie W., S2/c
McLain, Chas. E., F1/c
McLain, Wm. H., SC2/c
McLaughlin, Jos. O., Jr., S1/c
McLean, Robt. A., TM1/c
McLendon, Darwin A., PhM3/c

McLendon, Wallace H., WT2/c
McMahan, Jack T., S1/c
McMakin, Wm. C., WT1/c
McMillan, Marvin R., RM3/c
McMillan, Roy L., MM2/c
McMillon, Ben, S2/c
McMillon, Isaac B., BM2/c
McMillon, Thee J., S1/c
McNella, Robt. T., RT3/c
McNeely, Billy, S1/c
McNeill, Wayne D., AMM3/c
McNew, Thos. H., S1/c
McPhee, Francis J., S1/c
McQuiston, Wm. J., AMM2/c
McReynolds, Jas. F., S1/c
McWatty, Jas. F., Sr., S2/c
Mead, Harvey, S1/c
Mead, James Hilra, F2/c
Meade, Jack, RM2/c
Meadows, Robt. F., MM1/c
Mears, Wm. E., M1/c
Meaux, Robt. A., S1/c
Meckley, Geo. W., S1/c
Mecoli, Ernest J., S2/c
Medellin, Pedro M., S1/c
Medina, Norberto, RT3/c
Medlock, Franklin C., MM2/c
Meehan, Arthur J., SPP1/c
Meehan, Francis Cornelius, MM1/c
Meek, Saml., MM3/c
Meetze, Franklin W., CM1/c
Meeve, Edw. K., GM3/c
Meifert, Clifford A., Bkr2/c
Meili, Robt. R., GM3/c
Meinking, Peter W., S2/c
Melancon, Gauthier, MM2/c
Mellott, Thos. B., S2/c
Mendenhall, Gordon C., SF3/c
Menius, Billy O., MM3/c
Meno, Jose M., NSEA2/c
Mensenkamp, Walworth T., S1/c
Mentlick, Wm. E., ART1/c
Mercado, Salvador B., F2/c
Merico, Domineck J., S1/c
Merkel, Rueben E., AMM3/c
Merna, Wm. B., S1/c
Merritt, Geo. H., FC3/c
Messenger, Edward R., AMM2/c
Messer, Jas. H., MoMM1/c
Messer, John A., Jr., PhM1/c
Messer, R. B., EM2/c
Messer, Robt. W., F1/c
Messina, Wm. F., WT3/c
Metallo, Nunzio D., BM2/c
Metcalf, Junior W., S1/c

METCALF, Louie E., CM3/c
METROPOLIS, Chas., PhM3/c
MEUSCH, Robt. L., S1/c
MEYER, Eugene R., F1/c
MEYER, Herman E., F1/c
MEYER, Melvin F., S2/c
MEZA, Vicente O., SKD3/c
MICHAEL, Rayhugh G., SC1/c
MICHALIK, Geo. E., S1/c
MICHAUD, Roland Isidore, PhM1/c
MIDGETT, Chas. F., Jr., MoMM3/c
MIERZEJEWSKI, Paul R., WT2/c
MIESEN, Arthur, F2/c
MIGNAULT, John F., MM3/c
MIKITY, Edw. E., FC3/c
MIKULA, Julius S., S2/c
MIKULICH, Geo. T., AOM2/c
MILANO, Ralph F., S1/c
MILES, Robt. V., Prt3/c
MILEY, Harold J., Cox.
MILLER, Albert E., S1/c
MILLER, Chas. E., S1/c
MILLER, Clarence I., CWTA
MILLER, Claude H., Jr., WT1/c
MILLER, Earl L., S2/c
MILLER, Frank A., Jr., S1/c
MILLER, Herbert G., CWTA
MILLER, Jos. J., Cox.
MILLER, Max M., Cox.
MILLER, Mike, GM2/c
MILLER, Ralph A., ARM2/c
MILLER, Robt. H., EM2/c
MILLER, Robt. W., FC3/c
MILLER, Thos. W., ACMMP
MILLER, Walter D., S1/c
MILLER, Walter F., Jr., S1/c
MILLER, Wm., Jr., S1/c
MILLER, Wm. C., ARM2/c
MILLIGAN, Finas A., Jr., S2/c
MILLIGAN, Robt. S., Jr., SK2/c
MILLIKEN, Thos. W., MM3/c
MILLING, Willie, Jr., S2/c
MILLS, Robt. W., SC2/c
MINAHAN, John P., S1/c
MINIKUS, Wm. L., MM3/c
MINKS, Everett R., S2/c
MINOFSKY, Abraham, S1/c
MIRANDO, Mario G., AMM3/c
MISBACK, Carl E., CMoMMA
MITCHELL, Geo. W., MoMM1/c
MITCHELL, Harvey Marshall, F2/c
MITCHELL, Jos. R., BM2/c
MITCHELL, John H., ARM2/c
MITCHELL, Wade R., FCM3/c
MITCHELL, Wallace H., S2/c
MIZZI, Jos. R., PhM1/c
MODLIN, Robt. C., S1/c
MOELLER, Willard, CEMA
MOFFITT, Chester M., SM1/c
MOG, Victor O., AOM2/c
MOGENSEN, Carl J., S2/c
MOLANICK, Francis, S1/c
MOLINARI, Frank J., S2/c
MOLZAHN, Albert L., WT2/c
MONK, Saml. O., CCMA
MONROE, Calloway B., S1/c
MONROE, Robt. B., SM1/c
MONROE, Warren E., AOM3/c
MONTAGUE, Wallace, StM1/c
MONTESI, Marcello G., F1/c
MOODY, Roscoe J., F2/c
MOOERS, Howard S., ARM3/c
MOON, Bernard P., S1/c
MOORE, Albert S., ARM3/c
MOORE, Beachel, S1/c
MOORE, Carroll E., MM2/c
MOORE, Chas. G., BM2/c
MOORE, Donald E., Cox.
MOORE, Ebbie C., S2/c
MOORE, Franklin J., PhM3/c
MOORE, Hall E., S2/c
MOORE, James E., S1/c
MOORE, Jas. E., SM3/c
MOORE, John, Cox.
MOORE, Rufus E., Jr., CK3/c
MOORE, Wayne M., S1/c
MOOS, Robt. F., WT2/c
MORAN, Chas. R., RM2/c
MORAN, Jesse W., S1/c
MORAN, John J., MM1/c
MORAN, Lewis R., WT1/c
MORENO, Alfred J., HA2/c
MOREY, Earl J., S1/c
MORGAN, Carl L., AMM2/c
MORGAN, David Benjamin, GM3/c
MORGAN, Harrison P., QM1/c
MORGAN, Thos. M., FCM3/c
MORGAN, Thos. W., MM3/c
MORKEN, Clarence A., AM2/c
MORRIS, Alfred, CWTA
MORRIS, Carroll E., S1/c
MORRIS, Currie B., S2/c
MORRIS, John Owen, AMM1/c
MORRIS, Robt., Jr., SC3/c
MORRIS, Wesley J., ARM3/c
MORRISON, Edw. J., F1/c
MORRISON, Lewis H., AMM3/c
MORRISON, Oneal P., CM3/c
MORRISON, Robt. J., RM3/c
MORRISSEY, Fred J., AMM3/c

CASUALTIES

MORRISSEY, John E., ARM3/c
MORRISSEY, Thos. L., EM2/c
MORROW, Fred B., S1/c
MORT, Wm. C., WT3/c
MOSCARITOLO, Alphonse V., S1/c
MOSCHELLE, Wm. H., Jr., FCO3/c
MOSELEY, Chas. O., Jr., S2/c
MOSSMAN, Clifford W., SM1/c
MOTT, Joe Leland, S2/c
MOUDREE, Robt. C., SK1/c
MOULE, Benj. A., Jr., GM1/c
MOUNT, Jas. W., S2/c
MOUSER, Clarence A., Cox.
MOUSER, Louie E., S2/c
MOUSER, Willie, SF3/c
MOUSSEAU, Jos. F., EM3/c
MOWRY, Prescott M., TM2/c
MOYER, Lyle G., TM2/c
MROZEK, Albert C., MM2/c
MUDRE, Steve, S1/c
MUEHE, Wm. V. W. F., EM3/c
MUELLER, David Jonathan, ARM2/c
MUGRAUER, Herbert, ARM2/c
MUGRIDGE, Paul C., Cox.
MUIR, Chas. R., CTMP
MULCAHY, Wm. P., AOM2/c
MULKERRIN, Vincent C., HA1/c
MULLER, Newton B., MM1/c
MULLIGAN, Fredk. J., SC1/c
MULLINS, Albert, Jr., S1/c
MULLINS, Jas. T., S2/c
MULZER, Hilbert P., S1/c
MUNIZ, Eugene, WT2/c
MUNN, Rogers R., ARM2/c
MUNROE, Arthur R., PhM3/c
MUNSEY, James W., Jr., SM3/c
MURAWSKI, Richard T., GM3/c
MURPHY, Bernard F., ARM2/c
MURPHY, Clifford J., S2/c
MURPHY, David, Jr., EM2/c
MURPHY, John, MM2/c
MURPHY, John J., ARM2/c
MURPHY, John W., Jr., MM3/c
MURPHY, Patrick M., Jr., SC3/c
MURPHY, Thos. E., EM1/c
MURPHY, Walter A., ARM3/c
MURPHY, Wm. C., HA1/c
MURRAY, Eugene T., S1/c
MURRAY, Jas. D., CBMA
MURRAY, Leon G., ARM1/c
MURRY, Wm. F., AEM1/c
MUSE, Clyde J., GM3/c
MUSE, John W., PhM1/c
MUSGROVE, Vernie E., SF2/c
MUSHILL, Peter, Cox.

MUSICK, Arthur B., F1/c
MUSSELMAN, Blake D., S1/c
MUSSER, Calvin D., RM3/c
MUSTIN, Emmett R., MM1/c
MYER, Urban E., F1/c
MYERS, Harold K., S2/c
MYERS, Hollace H., CM1/c
MYERS, Homer A., Cox.
MYERS, Stanley M., S2/c
MYERS, Wm. H., Jr., S1/c
MYRICK, Harry M., Sr., CEMA
MYSLIWIEC, John L., GM2/c

NAGEL, Adolph Victor, F1/c
NAGEL, Harold S., S1/c
NAGY, Jos. A., S2/c
NAHANCHUK, John, WT3/c
NALL, Woodrow W., Cox.
NALLY, Richard A., S1/c
NANNEY, Robt. M., CQMA
NANOMANTUBE, Jas. J., MM3/c
NAPPEN, Arthur F., S1/c
NARDIELLO, Alexander, S2/c
NARROW, Thom A., Jr., S1/c
NASH, Alvin N., MoMM3/c
NASH, Clarence R., SK2/c
NASH, Jack K., CTMP
NASH, Jos. H., MoMM1/c
NATION, Edward H., MM3/c
NAUTA, Pedro Q., NS2/c
NAWROCKI, Edmund L., AOM2/c
NEAL, Earl A., AMM3/c
NEATHERY, Chas. W., S1/c
NEELD, Samuel, S2/c
NEELY, Albert A., Jr., ARM2/c
NEITSCH, Marvin Robert, S1/c
NELLIGAN, John J., PhM3/c
NELSON, Albert L., AOM1/c
NELSON, Douglas P., ACOMA
NELSON, Frederick Ray, MM1/c
NELSON, Laverne N., S2/c
NELSON, Leslie V., S2/c
NELSON, Lowell R., GM3/c
NELSON, Mauritz H., ARM2/c
NELSON, Max Richard, S2/c
NELSON, Milo G., MM1/c
NELSON, Norman R., AEM3/c
NELSON, Richard P., MM3/c
NEMETH, Edw. W., S1/c
NENDEL, Robt. H., S2/c
NETTLES, Edw. M., S1/c
NETTLES, Nicodemus, Cox.
NEVILLE, Lawrence H., S2/c
NEVITT, James L., MM1/c
NEWBERRY, Elroy R., S1/c

NEWBY, Leonard N., EM3/c
NEWCOMB, Hiram Adair, S2/c
NEWELL, Rich L., ARM3/c
NEWLAND, Chas. A., ACMMA
NEWMAN, Dellaware R., Jr., Y2/c
NEWMAN, Howard T., MM3/c
NEWMAN, Maurice R., CCSA
NEWMAN, Wm. H., Jr., BM1/c
NEWMILLER, John J., S2/c
NEWTON, Lester F., F1/c
NICHOLAS, Roland F., EM3/c
NICHTER, Geo. A., HA1/c
NICKSON, David Merlin, SF2/c
NICODEMO, Guido, Cox.
NIDERMAYER, Elmer G., Y2/c
NIELSEN, Kenneth R., WT3/c
NIELSEN, Milo W., S1/c
NIELSON, Sterling J., HA1/c
NIEMAN, Millard R., S1/c
NIEMEYER, Harold L., S2/c
NIEPOZESKI, Jos. L., AMM3/c
NIESS, Edmund R., MM1/c
NIEZGODA, Jos. A., MoMM3/c
NILSON, George Wm., S1/c
NILSON, Irving L., AOM1/c
NIMMO, Raymond H., S1/c
NITCHMAN, Louis O., ARM3/c
NITZEL, Billie J., AOM1/c
NIX, Norman P., S1/c
NIXSON, Russell B., S1/c
NIZZARDI, Wm. E., PhM3/c
NOBILE, Jos. S., S1/c
NODELL, Leonard M., MM3/c
NODES, Gilbert V., MM3/c
NOEL, Claudius, RM3/c
NOLEN, Wyley P., S2/c
NOLETTE, David D., GM1/c
NORGREN, Oscar W., CTMP
NORRIS, Victor, STM1/c
NORWOOD, Johnny A., SC2/c
NOTT, Lyle J., S2/c
NOTTAGE, Owen, GM3/c
NOVACICH, Paul L., S2/c
NOWAKOWSKI, Michael R., PhM3/c
NOYES, Elton L., PhM1/c
NULL, Edmund W., MM1/c
NYLANDER, Edw. D., RM3/c

OBARR, Byron Denman, F2/c
OBERG, Gordon F., RdM3/c
OBERHOLTZER, Herman R., EM3/c
OBLIGACION, Benj. R., NS1/c
O'BRIEN, Clifford W., S1/c
O'BRIEN, John E., Jr., F1/c
OCHS, Frank A., CBMA

O'CONNELL, James P., ACOMP
O'CONNOR, Dudley B., Jr., WT2/c
ODEGAARD, Wallace E., S1/c
ODOM, Shuler J., S1/c
O'DONNELL, Geo. M., MoMM3/c
OEHME, Paul R., CGMP
OFFER, John P., PhM2/c
OGILVIE, Donald George, MM2/c
OGILVIE, Harold B., TM2/c
O'HARA, Jas. M., EM3/c
O'HARA, Olin M., GM1/c
OKTAVEC, Jan L., ARM2/c
OLAH, Alex S., AOM3/c
OLATI, Louis J., PhM3/c
OLDHAM, Herschel T., CMMA
OLDHAM, Jas. M., HA1/c
OLDS, Percy J., St2/c
O'LEARY, Jas. J., AMM3/c
OLEN, Leo J., RM1/c
OLESEN, Chas. V., ARM3/c
OLESON, Harald R. A., CTCA
OLEXA, David E., MoMM2/c
OLIVER, Clarence E., MM3/c
OLIVER, John D., MM2/c
OLSEN, Clarence S., QM2/c
OLSEN, Wm. J., ARM2/c
OLSON, Chas. L. Jr., AOM2/c
OLSON, Hi F., Ptr2/c
OLSON, Richard R., S1/c
OLSON, Robt. H., F1/c
OLSON, Wesley F., MM2/c
OLVEY, Russell B., Y2/c
O'MALLEY, Francis K., Jr., AMM3/c
O'MALLEY, Robt. C., PhM3/c
ONAN, Wm. F., AMM3/c
ONEAL, Casper L., S1/c
ONEAL, James W., CPhMA
O'NEILL, John B., S1/c
O'ROURKE, Earl E., ARM2/c
ORR, John W., FC3/c
ORR, Robt. N., SF1/c
ORTEGO, Bernard J., S1/c
ORVALD, Robt. P., MM2/c
OSAKOWICZ, John Stanley, SK3/c
OSBORN, Clarence R., ARM2/c
OSBORN, Jerry G., WT1/c
OSBORNE, Jas. V., Jr., ARM1/c
OSBORNE, Raymond D. A., RM1/c
OSIECKI, Thos. A., MM1/c
OSOWICKI, Chette, MME2/c
OSOWITT, John T., S1/c
OSTMAN, Edwin E., S2/c
OTTENSMAN, Walter George, GM2/c
OTTERSON, Roy O., TM1/c
OUDERKIRK, Daryl M., MoMM3/c

CASUALTIES

Ouzts, Cleveland M., Jr., MoMM1/c
Overby, Leon E., EM3/c
Overby, Uzell C., StM2/c
Owen, Harris K., SC2/c
Owens, Luther B., S1/c
Owens, Wm. H., Jr., SC3/c
Oyervides, David M., F1/c

Pace, Gwyn S., S2/c
Pacel, Jos. P., MoMM2/c
Pacheco, Edw. E., S1/c
Pack, Arless A., F1/c
Packard, Fred C., MM1/c
Padgett, Wm. J., Bkr3/c
Padula, Jos. M., S1/c
Page, John Q., MoMM2/c
Page, Nelson K., F2/c
Page, Otis T., Sr., CCMA
Page, Robt. E., RM3/c
Paige, Eugene S., PhM3/c
Paine, Robt., Jr., CGMA
Palermo, Pasqual, AMM2/c
Palmer, Clifford E., FC2/c
Palmer, Jas. L., S1/c
Palmer, Paul W., ARM2/c
Palombo, Antonio, CMoMMA
Panno, Thos., ARM1/c
Panther, Melvin F., S2/c
Paone, John J., S2/c
Pappanghelis, Theo., GM3/c
Paquette, Dennis J., AMM3/c
Paradis, Clayton O., MM3/c
Parduhn, Elmer E., Cox.
Paris, Manley L., Y1
Parish, Rodrick D., Jr., CM2/c
Park, Percy D., Prt2/c
Parker, Andy L., CCKP
Parker, Aubrey M., S2/c
Parker, Billie B., S1/c
Parker, Doyle D., AMM2/c
Parker, Emory L., MM1/c
Parker, John J., S1/c
Parker, Theo., MoMM2/c
Parker, Walter E., AOM3/c
Parks, Archie P., RM1/c
Parks, Raymond J., S1/c
Parmelee, Erwin Clark, CCMP
Parrott, Robt. G., S2/c
Parsons, Edw. J., S1/c
Parsons, Ernest Dean, S1/c
Parsons, Rolla, Jr., RM2/c
Pasamonte, Norberto, CCKP
Pashkowsky, John, S1/c
Passmore, Duward N. B., S1/c
Pasternak, Frank J., SC2/c

Patch, James C., PhM3/c
Patrick, Chas. W., CMoMMA
Patrick, Wm. H., BM1/c
Patterson, Gerald, S1/c
Patterson, Jas. W., PhM2/c
Patterson, Jas. W., Y1/c
Patterson, Richard D., S2/c
Patterson, Woodrow D., EM1/c
Patton, Cleveland, S2/c
Patton, Jimmy D., S2/c
Patton, Willie L., StM3/c
Paul, Frank, S2/c
Paulk, Jack S., EM2/c
Paulson, Eugene J., MoMM2/c
Pavlin, Bruce F., EM2/c
Pavlos, John W., SF3/c
Payan, Sam'l, AERM3/c
Payne, Clyde Belmont, MM1/c
Payne, Harold K., AERM3/c
Payne, John D., EM3/c
Payton, Larus E., SF2/c
Pazinick, Jos. M., SC3/c
Peachey, Gerald R., PhM3/c
Peck, Marion P., MoMM2/c
Peden, Norman C., MM3/c
Peeler, Willie L., F2/c
Peery, Chas. W., MoMM1/c
Peet, Geo. V., MoMM2/c
Peevey, James W., EM3/c
Peightal, James A., CM3/c
Peine, Edwin W., EM2/c
Pekkala, Wilho A., AMM2/c
Pelc, John S., F1/c
Pelletier, Lucien E., AMM2/c
Penland, Robt. C., WT3/c
Penter, Loren B., S1/c
Peoples, John A., Jr., St3/c
Perciful, Victor F., PhM1/c
Peregud, Harry, S2/c
Perera, Louis, F1/c
Perez, Abelardo J., S1/c
Perez, Rafael M., S2/c
Perkins, Earl M., S2/c
Perkins, Jas. G., S2/c
Perkins, Thos. E., FC3/c
Perry, Gene L., S2/c
Perry, Jos. V., S2/c
Perry, Wm. J., Jr., AS
Person, Clifford E., AMM3/c
Person, Gilbert R., AMM2/c
Peters, John R., S1/c
Petersen, Dennis B., SF2/c
Peterson, Clarence H., AMM2/c
Peterson, Dean W., F1/c
Peterson, Robt. H., EM2/c

PETERSON, Wm. F., S1/c
PETITO, Frank J., S1/c
PETITTI, Angelo P., S2/c
PETRI, Earl V., S1/c
PETRIK, Clifford, S2/c
PETRIK, Theo., Jr., F1/c
PETRONE, Anthony F., RM2/c
PETRUN, John, MoMM2/c
PETTIT, Edw. G., ARM2/c
PETTY, Forrest, SC1/c
PETTYPIECE, Wm. J., CM3/c
PEVESTORF, Richard P., GM3/c
PFEIFFER, Raymond A., S1/c
PFERSICH, Gordon, S2/c
PHELPS, Frank, Jr., S1/c
PHELPS, Geo. F., EM3/c
PHELPS, Robt. J., CFCP
PHIFER, Everett C., AMM2/c
PHILLIPPI, Frank D., S1/c
PHILLIPS, Arnold L., S1/c
PHILLIPS, Floyd T., FCO2/c
PHILLIPS, Geo. W., Cox.
PHILLIPS, Joe F., SF3/c
PHILLIPS, John F., CM1/c
PHILLIPS, Sidney A., Jr., CM1/c
PHILLIPS, Wm. J., Jr., S1/c
PHILPOTT, Gordon C., PhM2/c
PHILSON, Clark A., HA1/c
PHIPPS, Donald A., PhM2/c
PHIPPS, Jack A., MM3/c
PIAS, Rich. J., HA1/c
PICKETT, Geo. R., F1/c
PICKRAIN, Leo G., MoMM2/c
PIERANTOZZI, Anthony, CPhMA
PIERCEFIELD, Ziegler F., Ptr3/c
PIERSON, Hilan R., CMMA
PIETSCH, Myron J., PhM2/c
PIGGOTT, Tom E., Bkr3/c
PIKE, Anthony W., MM2/c
PIKKARAINEN, Tauno O., ARM3/c
PILGRAM, Edw. F., CWTA
PILLARS, Benj. D., EM2/c
PILLSBURY, Howard C., Y1/c
PINCE, Francis Floyd, EM3/c
PINION, John O., Jr., EM3/c
PINKES, Chas. P., Jr., WT1/c
PINKHAM, Eben L., GM2/c
PINKHAM, Lucius S., MM1/c
PINKHAM, Paul W., MM3/c
PINO, Manuel L., WT3/c
PINTO, Albert A., S2/c
PINZINI, Jos. J., S2/c
PIOTROWSKI, Geo. F., SC1/c
PIPES, Billy T., S1/c
PIRES, John P., F1/c

PISARSKI, Henry, MM3/c
PISTOLE, Frank L. H., AMM3/c
PITT, Willis M., WT1/c
PITTINGTON, Ira F., PhM2/c
PITTMAN, Harry T., CM2/c
PITTS, Wilbur J., ARM2/c
PLANTE, Hubert, S2/c
PLASKETT, Fredk. C., S2/c
PLETCHER, Vernon D., ARM3/c
PLILER, Luther M., CPhMP
PLUCKBAUM, Alvin J., F2/c
PLUMMER, David G., MM3/c
PLUNKETT, Walter J., S2/c
PODGORSKI, John J., AMM1/c
POE, John W., Jr., S1/c
POEHLER, Lloyd E., Bkr1/c
POLK, Chas. E., ARM2/c
POLZELLA, Patsy G., AMM2/c
POMICHOWSKI, Benj. A., S1/c
POMPLUN, Lester A., S1/c
PONDS, Charlie, StM1/c
PONZAR, Alfred G., ARM2/c
POOL, Robt. W., S1/c
POOLE, Wm. A., F2/c
POOLER, Robt. W., EM3/c
POOVEY, Lloyd W., ART2/c
POPA, Emil, S1/c
POPE, John R., S1/c
POPE, Ralph M., ARM1/c
POPE, Waymon L., S2/c
POPOVICH, Robert George, S2/c
POPPEN, Wilroy E., BM1/c
PORRAS, Chas. V., Jr., PhM3/c
PORTAS, Francisco N., RM2/c
POSTLE, Lewis W., Jr., RM3/c
POTE, Robt. L., S2/c
POTISMAN, Paul J., PhM3/c
POTTER, Frank J., EM2/c
POTTER, Norman A., SK3/c
POTTS, Edwin L., MM3/c
POTTS, Loys E., SF3/c
POULSON, Samuel H., AOM2/c
POWELL, Carson F., Cox.
POWELL, Jas. D., S2/c
POWELL, John M., BM1/c
POWELL, Joho F., S2/c
POWELL, Ludlow J., S2/c
POWELL, Odeen D., PhM3/c
POWELL, Vester H., MM2/c
POWELL, Walter D., Jr., EM2/c
POWERS, Carroll R., F2/c
POWERS, Richard John, F3/c
POYNEER, Chas. F., RM1/c
POYNER, Thos. E., F1/c
PRANGE, Edw. H., PhM2/c

CASUALTIES

Prasser, Chas. E., PhM2/c
Premier, Michael, S2/c
Prentice, Robt. L., StM2/c
Presley, Lois E., CGMA
Pressendo, Phil, MM1/c
Preston, Leland R., S2/c
Preston, Victor M., CM2/c
Prestwood, Thos. G., S1/c
Price, Frank L., S2/c
Price, Lloyd R., S1/c
Prillaman, Leonard W., Jr., AMM2/c
Prince, Paul A., SF3/c
Prisco, Albert J., S2/c
Pritchard, Wayne L., F1/c
Pritchard, William L., AS
Probasco, Ellsworth L., Jr., WT2/c
Probst, Herbert L., PhM2/c
Procelo, Tadeus, ARM3/c
Proctor, Wm. A., ARM2/c
Profitt, Arnold Woodurth, AS
Proffit, Leonard M., PhM3/c
Prokop, Edw. J., AMM3/c
Pronovost, Wm. E., EM3/c
Protsman, Wm. O., F2/c
Pruchniewski, Jerome J., QM3/c
Pruitt, Forest W., BM1/c
Prusinski, Jos., MM1/c
Puder, Jas. A., GM2/c
Pudiack, Franklin A., HA1/c
Pugh, Coy D., GM2/c
Pugsley, Harry E., MM2/c
Pulice, Anthony J., S1/c
Pumphrey, Clyde C., F1/c
Purcell, John F., EM1/c
Purcell, Patrick R., S2/c
Purdom, Verl M., TM3/c
Purvis, John M., GM3/c
Pusateri, Jos. M., ARM2/c
Putnam, Avery C., S1/c
Puzerski, Albert R., S1/c
Pye, Thos. W., CEMA
Pyrch, Geo., S1/c
Pytynia, Ted S., GM2/c

Quesenberry, John T., PhM3/c
Quinn, Edw. J., Jr., S1/c
Quintero, L., F1/c

Rada, Edw. R., S1/c
Radke, Edw. E., AMM3/c
Raffles, Herbert J., S1/c
Rakyta, John G., S1/c
Ramey, Glenn A., MM3/c
Rampini, John, Jr., AOM2/c
Ramsey, Chas. H., Cox.

Ramsey, Kenneth H., ARM3/c
Ramsom, Larry B., AMMP2/c
Randall, Lewis D., MM3/c
Ranger, James A., RM2/c
Ranta, Arvo A., AMM2/c
Raschella, Patrick F., AS
Rash, Oscar S., CWTA
Rasimas, Algerd J., CEMA
Raslich, Geo., S2/c
Rassfeld, Kenneth W., EM2/c
Rathbun, Fredk. H., TM3/c
Rathbun, Jas. A., AMM3/c
Rathgeb, Robt. L., S2/c
Ratliff, Jas. W., StM1/c
Rauch, Benj. N., Jr., RM3/c
Rauscher, Fred, S1/c
Rawdon, Glenn D., F1/c
Rawlings, Cecil A., S1/c
Ray, Jack M., RM1/c
Ray, Orval Franklin, AS
Raymond, Ralph N., BM2/c
Razborsek, Frank M., MM3/c
Razes, Jos. A., MoMM2/c
Reach, Wm. A., SC3/c
Read, Harry E., AS
Read, John Francis, F2/c
Reames, Spencer W., S2/c
Reardon, Thos. E., GM2/c
Reavis, Edw. B., ARM3/c
Reay, Fred J., EM2/c
Rector, Roy J., BM2/c
Red, Harold G., MM3/c
Reddick, Wm. W., S1/c
Redfern, Floyd J., F2/c
Rediske, Manley A., FCM2/c
Redman, Winifred E., ARM2/c
Reed, Chas. W., Y3/c
Reed, Donald O., S1/c
Reed, Donald K., AOM2/c
Reed, Harold O., S1/c
Reed, Homer H., SF2/c
Reed, Jas., Jr., StM1/c
Reed, Mack H., Ptr3/c
Reed, Robt. E., S2/c
Reed, Wayne M., S1/c
Reek, Paul Henry, MM1/c
Rees, David V., F1/c
Rees, Lewis E., MoMM1/c
Rees, Robt. V., S2/c
Reese, Alphonzo, S1/c
Reeve, James W., AMM3/c
Reeve, Milton A., S1/c
Reeves, Solomon, CWTP
Refco, Emil, AOM3/c
Rehn, Ray P., MM3/c

REID, Algie Durham, AS
REID, Curtis C., SF2/c
REIHL, Jos. D., S2/c
REIMERS, Fred L., Y3/c
REINHEIMER, Harold R., PhM2/c
REINSCHMIDT, Theo. CMMP
REISER, Herbert, MM3/c
RELAMIDA, Anastacio, NF2/c
REMICK, Daniel Joseph, GM3/c
REMICK, Mayland V., MoMM1/c
REMILLARD, Paul B., SM2/c
REMINGTON, Ralston F., MM2/c
REMY, Earl T., Jr., AOMB2/c
REMY, Rock N., MM2/c
RENNARD, Lashley, S1/c
RENSBERGER, Loyal H., TC1/c
RESSINGER, Robert Russell, S2/c
RETERSTORF, Arnold G., Cox.
REYES, Paul E., F2/c
REYNOLDS, Arthur M., Jr., F2/c
REYNOLDS, David K., S1/c
REYNOLDS, Earl R., Ptr3/c
REYNOLDS, Eugene C., RM2/c
REYNOLDS, Harold L., S1/c
REYNOLDS, Ralph C., ARM3/c
REYNOLDS, Thos. J., SF2/c
RHODES, Donald, S1/c
RHUE, Harry M., S1/c
RHYNE, Eual T., S2/c
RICE, Jack, PhM3/c
RICE, Jas. W., MoMM2/c
RICE, Robt. C., CWTP
RICE, Victor L., MoMM1/c
RICE, Willis F., S1/c
RICHARD, Omar A., S2/c
RICHARDS, Gilbert Roland, S2/c
RICHARDS, Jack L., ARM3/c
RICHARDSON, Clifford C., AOM3/c
RICHARDSON, Howard H., CM1/c
RICHARDSON, Ivan L., CCMA
RICHARDSON, Willie, St1/c
RICHIE, Eugene A., S1/c
RICKETTS, Clinton A., AMM1/c
RICKETTS, Henry T., S1/c
RIDDLE, Arthur R., QM1/c
RIDEOUT, Edw. A., S1/c
RIDGWAY, Wm. H., TM1/c
RIECHMAN, Irvin J., S1/c
RIESTER, Walter A., PhM2/c
RIGBY, Sidney C., MM2/c
RIGDON, David M., Jr., S1/c
RIGGS, Clay H., AOM2/c
RIHN, Burnell Vincent, TM1/c
RIHN, Jas. J., PhM1/c
RIKER, Dorman N., PhM2/c
RILEY, Wm. F., WT3/c
RINGER, Rich. M., PhM3/c
RINGO, Oscar Lee, StM1/c
RINGWELSKI, Frank, S2/c
RINICK, Dan L., AOM2/c
RIORDAN, Robt. T., SC2/c
RIORDAN, Wm. J., HA1/c
RITCHEY, Edw. G., MM2/c
RITTER, John R., Jr., AMM2/c
RITTERBUSCH, Martin R., MoMM2/c
RIVERA, Fabian A., S1/c
RIVERS, Geo. P., MM3/c
RIZZO, Chas. V., SC3/c
RIZZO, Richard L., S2/c
ROACH, Dewey, CM3/c
ROACH, John Perry, S1/c
ROBBE, Robt. R., S1/c
ROBBIN, Agur, Jr., F1/c
ROBBINS, Ernest W., EM3/c
ROBBINS, Greeley H., MM3/c
ROBBINS, Harry E., Jr., PhM3/c
ROBBINS, Kermit, F1/c
ROBEDEAU, Jas. J., Jr., F1/c
ROBERGE, Jos. R., ARM3/c
ROBERG, Ernest C., S1/c
ROBERTS, Albert D., S2/c
ROBERTS, Darwin A., S1/c
ROBERTS, Earl F., MM3/c
ROBERTS, Jas. D., WT3/c
ROBERTS, Leland H., TM3/c
ROBERTS, Luther E., CYP
ROBERTS, Percy T., SK3/c
ROBERTS, Raymond M., S1/c
ROBERTS, Robt. C., GM3/c
ROBERTS, Robt. E., CCSP
ROBERTS, Seacil R., Jr., CM2/c
ROBERTS, Wm. M., S2/c
ROBERTSON, Harden W., Sr., S2/c
ROBERTSON, Roy R., GM2/c
ROBERTSON, Thos. S., EM1/c
ROBEY, Raymond K., HA1/c
ROBICHAUD, Arthur C., PhM1/c
ROBIE, Jas. L., S1/c
ROBINSON, Charlie K., MoMM2/c
ROBINSON, Coleman W., PhM2/c
ROBINSON, Donald P., GM3/c
ROBINSON, Jas. W., PhM2/c
ROBINSON, Pedro, F1/c
ROBINSON, Richard C., ARM2/c
ROBINSON, Thos. F., S1/c
ROBINSON, Thos. V., RM3/c
ROBINSON, Wm. A., StM1/c
ROBINSON, Wm. F., CMMA
ROBINSON, Wm. T., ARM3/c
ROBLES, Joe A., S1/c

ROBLES, Jos. R., MM1/c
ROCKWELL, Fred M., AMM2/c
ROD, Ernest D., S1/c
RODRIGUEZ, Jose G., Cox.
ROESCH, Earl J., S1/c
ROGER, Jos. E., Jr., MoMM1/c
ROGERS, Everett K., F1/c
ROGERS, Graydon G., ARM3/c
ROGERS, Harold F., S1/c
ROGERS, Harry T., Jr., ARM1/c
ROGERS, Jas. B., Jr., SM3/c
ROGERS, Louis R., S2/c
ROGERS, Saml. E., S2/c
ROGERS, Theawell John H., RdM3/c
ROGERS, Wm. E., Pr3/c
ROHDE, Bernard J., MoMM2/c
ROHLFS, Gordon F., MM3/c
ROHSFELD, Otto H., AMM1/c
ROLEDER, Howard S., MM2/c
ROLFE, Wendell, S2/c
ROLLAND, Harold L., CGMP
ROLLINS, Benj. C., AOM2/c
ROLLINS, Gerald M., S1/c
ROLLINS, Pernell O., HA1/c
ROMAN, Edwin, PhM3/c
ROMANO, Dominic, S2/c
ROMANS, John J., FC1/c
ROMEOS, Raymond A., BM2/c
ROMERO, Lupe, CCStP
ROMO, Jesuse A., S2/c
RONDY, Donald R., ARM2/c
ROOFENER, Joe F., MoMM2/c
ROOP, Edw., S2/c
ROSANDICH, Jos. F., MM1/c
ROSBURY, Chas. W., F2/c
ROSE, Melvin B., AMM3/c
ROSE, Warner William, Cox.
ROSENBAUM, Merrill K., CEMA
ROSENBERG, Jos., MoMM1/c
ROSERO, Federico, MM3/c
ROSS, Bernard M., F1/c
ROSS, Burnel C., S1/c
ROSS, George Alvin, S2/c
ROSS, Jack H., S1/c
ROSS, Norman M., PhM3/c
ROSS, Thos. M., GM1/c
ROSSETTO, Gino, CM2/c
ROSSUM, Althon L., MM2/c
ROTHE, Donald T., F1/c
ROTHWELL, Bernard J., MM3/c
ROTHWELL, John D., AOM2/c
ROTRUCK, Neoman E., S1/c
ROULEAU, Raymond A., MoMM2/c
ROUP, Marion F., MoMM1/c
ROURKE, Glenn G., MoMM3/c

ROUSE, Wm. J., S2/c
ROUSH, Howard J., S1/c
ROWAN, Paul F., S1/c
ROWDEN, Arthur, Jr., FCR2/c
ROWE, John L., QM2/c
ROY, Robt. J., SF1/c
ROYTER, Geo., S1/c
ROZMAN, Rudolph J., AMM3/c
ROZMARYNOWSKI, Arthur A., EM3/c
RUDD, Chester E., TM3/c
RUDRUD, Paul H., HA1/c
RUFFNER, Frank H., S1/c
RULE, James, MoMM2/c
RULE, Raymond H., S1/c
RUMENS, Wm., MM1/c
RUMSE, Henry E., PhM3/c
RUNDELL, Elton R., MoMM1/c
RUNKOWSKI, Chester L., TM3/c
RUNNELS, Geo. R., S1/c
RUNYON, Fredk. M., S1/c
RUSSELL, James M., ARM2/c
RUSSELL, John Kenneth, S1/c
RUSSELL, Othel L., AMM1/c
RUSSO, Anthony T., MM2/c
RUTLEDGE, Chas. W., Cox.
RUTLEDGE, Mack, Jr., S2/c
RUTT, Walter C., S1/c
RYALL, Lewis R., MoMM1/c
RYAN, Ernest Harold, MM1/c
RYAN, Patrick W., PhM1/c
RYAN, Thos., MoMM2/c
RYAN, Wayne A., S1/c
RYBINSKI, Anthony F., S1/c
RYDER, Wm. E., CCSA
RYTHER, Lavere M., AMM2/c

SAALFIELD, Herbert A., Jr., S2/c
SABELLO, Cyril A., S1/c
SABINO, Peter A., S1/c
SABLAN, Pedro T., NS2/c
SABLICK, Eugene J., S1/c
SABOL, Albert J., S1/c
SACUNDO, Flaviano, Ck2/c
SAFKO, Frank J., F1/c
SAGANIEC, Stanley A., SC2/c
SAGER, Robt. V., MoMM1/c
SAHM, Kampsey B., S1/c
SALADONIS, Geo. P., AOM2/c
SALADRIGAS, Manuel, F1/c
SALAS, Harold, S2/c
SALERNO, Jos. J., EM3/c
SALLBERG, Floyd W., S2/c
SALLEE, Coy K., SC1/c
SALLENSON, Seymour, S2/c
SALONEK, Theo. R., S1/c

SAMBO, John A., F1/c
SAMED, Ernest D., S1/c
SAMMARTINO, Vito A., F1/c
SAMPLES, Fenton W., S1/c
SAMS, Edgar H., MM3/c
SAMUELSEN, Laurenc A., S1/c
SAMUELSON, Herbert G., SK3/c
SANCHEZ, Frank, MM2/c
SANDERS, Bryant L., AMM1/c
SANDERS, Chas. E., S1/c
SANDERS, Floyd O., StM1/c
SANDERS, Jerry, HA1/c
SANDFORD, Darrell L., ARM1/c
SANDONE, Theo., S2/c
SANDS, Norman, BM2/c
SANFORD, Jas. L., MM1/c
SANFORD, Jas. R., S1/c
SANFORD, Tebe D., Jr., PhM3/c
SANTOS, Joaquin Q., NMM3/c
SAPPINGTON, Charlie W., S1/c
SARGENT, Melvin, S1/c
SARGENT, Wm. T., S2/c
SARVER, Milton D., S2/c
SASS, Herbert M., Jr., BM1/c
SASSENBERGER, Jas. A., S2/c
SATCHO, John F., MM3/c
SATTERFIELD, Clifford M., AMM1/c
SAUNDERS, Earl F., Cox.
SAUNDERS, Geo. B., Jr., AM3/c
SAUVOLA, Roy H., F1/c
SAVAGE, Jack M., CPhMA
SAVEY, John H., S511
SAXTON, Wm. A., Jr., AM3/c
SAYERS, Walter H., WT2/c
SAYLOR, Arthur E., Jr., F1/c
SAYLOR, Clyde E., CCSP
SAYLOR, Harry W., S2/c
SCAFOGLIO, Vincent S., WT3/c
SCANNELL, Donald H., PhM3/c
SCARBOROUGH, Burtis M., AEM2/c
SCARBROUGH, A. V., F1/c
SCARBROUGH, David Kent, SoM3/c
SCHAEFER, Wm. A., MM3/c
SCHAFER, Darl H., CM2/c
SCHAFER, Herman, MM3/c
SCHAFER, Robt. P., CSFA
SCHARMUCK, David A., GM3/c
SCHATZ, Emanuel, CM3/c
SCHAUER, Harold E., MM3/c
SCHEIB, Robt. H., RT1/c
SCHEIDLER, Robt., S2/c
SCHEIDT, Francis E., F1/c
SCHELL, Walter A., S1/c
SCHEMPP, Fred E., TM3/c
SCHEPIS, Louis F., CM1/c

SCHEPMANN, Amos C., MM1/c
SCHEUFELE, Carl, CCSTDP
SCHIELDGE, Erwin Fred, S1/c
SCHIEBER, Arthur W., F1/c
SCHIEBLE, Robt. F., S1/c
SCHIPPER, Wm. A., FC2/c
SCHLABECKER, Harry R., TM1/c
SCHLAUDT, Emil, Jr., MM1/c
SCHLECHTER, Anton S., RdM3/c
SCHLENZ, Ervin E., S1/c
SCHLESINGER, Alexander, S1/c
SCHMID, Jas. D., S1/c
SCHMIDT, Everett A., S1/c
SCHMIDT, John M., S1/c
SCHMIDT, Stanley L., Cox.
SCHMIDT, Wm. B., EM1/c
SCHMIEDEKE, Cleo E., MM1/c
SCHNEIDER, Conrad A., MM1/c
SCHNEIDER, Leonard M., F1/c
SCHNEIDER, Lester P., TMM2/c
SCHNEIDER, Wm. F., AQM2/c
SCHNELL, Richard J., S2/c
SCHOEN, Roy A., BM2/c
SCHOENER, Wm. F., EM3/c
SCHOMER, Donald O., S1/c
SCHOPF, Harry E., ACRMA
SCHRAMBECK, Edw. J., ARM3/c
SCHRECK, Jas. J., S1/c
SCHREIER, Earle C., MoMM2/c
SCHROEDER, Vincent S., MM2/c
SCHUELKE, John H., SC2/c
SCHUETZ, Wallace J., AMM2/c
SCHULTZ, Alvin L., Cox.
SCHUMACHER, Leonard J., F2/c
SCHWAIRY, Edw. L., ART2/c
SCHWENDEMAN, Peter, AMM1/c
SCIABA, Natale J., PhM3/c
SCIULLO, Jos. P., S2/c
SCOTT, Curry E., F1/c
SCOTT, Dale A., BUG2/c
SCOTT, Franklin A., StM1/c
SCOTT, Marvin W., WT2/c
SCOTT, Paul T., BM1/c
SCOTT, Raymond E., RM1/c
SCOTT, Wesley O., F1/c
SCRAFFORD, Bert, Jr., AMM2/c
SEABROOKS, Charlie, Ck3/c
SEALEY, Donald V., S2/c
SEAMSTER, Wiley E., S2/c
SEANNON, Wm. J., AMM3/c
SEAR, Wm. J., Jr., S1/c
SEARS, Billy D., S2/c
SEARS, Franklin M., EM2/c
SEARS, Hugh T., MM2/c
SEARS, Walter L., Jr., StM3/c

CASUALTIES 513

SEDICAVAGE, Stanley F., Bkr2/c
SEGO, Edgar L., CM2/c
SEHLER, Cecil T., CYP
SEIDEL, Herman C., CMMP
SEIDMAN, Walter F., RM3/c
SEIVWRIGHT, Geo., Jr., AOM1/c
SELDEN, Carrol B., MM3/c
SELLECK, Wm. M., RM1/c
SELTENREICH, Theo. S., AMM3/c
SENTER, Claude D., S1/c
SENTERFITT, Cecil S., CBMP
SERAFINI, Hugo J., MoMM2/c
SERAFINI, Tullio J., CRMA
SEREY, John N., AOM2/c
SEVERANCE, Edwin S., CMoMA
SHAFFER, Hyrum L., ARM2/c
SHAFRANSKI, Francis D., S1/c
SHANAHAN, John L., CBMP
SHANDLEY, John W., S2/c
SHANER, Chas. B., AMM3/c
SHANKLIN, Edgar G., AMM3/c
SHANNON, John F., F1/c
SHARP, Eugene R., S2/c
SHARP, Leonord J., S2/c
SHAVER, Frank, Jr., Bkr1/c
SHAW, J. T., MM2/c
SHAW, Kenneth, CYP
SHAW, Kenneth H., PhoM2/c
SHAW, Omer L., WT2/c
SHAW, Robt. M., CM2/c
SHEA, Robt. L., HA1/c
SHEEKS, David C., Y2/c
SHEELEY, John M., F1/c
SHEIL, Jos. P., S1/c
SHELL, Jos. W., AOM1/c
SHELTON, Billy M., ACMMA
SHEPARD, Marcus W., TM2/c
SHEPHERD, Laurence, MM3/c
SHEPPARD, Curtis E., ACMMA
SHEPPARD, Joe E., S1/c
SHERMAN, Edw. W., Y3/c
SHERWOOD, Jas. E., PhM3/c
SHETLER, Carl E., ARM3/c
SHIELDS, Ellis H., CPhMA
SHIFLET, Willie L., S1/c
SHIFLER, Wm., ARM1/c
SHILLINGTON, Thos. W., PhM3/c
SHINE, Jesse L., FCR3/c
SHINGLE, Robert Ward, SF1/c
SHIPMAN, Wesley E., HA1/c
SHIVERS, Dellie, St2/c
SHOCKEY, Harold C., AM3/c
SHOCKLEY, Carlos Edward, MM2/c
SHOEMAKER, John S., S2/c
SHOPE, Rodney D., WT3/c

SHORE, Earl, PhM2/c
SHORT, John H., S2/c
SHORT, Keith L., S1/c
SHORT, Robt. J., S2/c
SHOULDERS, Robert Maurice, RM2/c
SHREVE, Denver A., F1/c
SHROM, Amos R., PhM2/c
SHUMAN, John M., F2/c
SHUMATE, Robt. W., QM3/c
SHUMWAY, Kenneth W., PhM2/c
SHUPE, Willard L., PhM3/c
SIDOR, John, S1/c
SIDOTI, Carmelo R., SC3/c
SIEGEL, Clinton C., SF1/c
SIEGRIST, Geo. E., ARM2/c
SIEK, Geo. P., MoMM2/c
SIGLER, Elwin W., MoMM1/c
SIGMAN, Carter E., CCSP
SIGNS, Howard H., Cox.
SIKES, Homer L., ARM3/c
SIKI, Chester S., Jr., S2/c
SIKKING, Geo. S., M1/c
SILEO, Leonard, MoMM2/c
SILL, Chas. H., 3rd, AMM2/c
SILVA, Alvin, MM1/c
SILVERMAN, Arthur B., SoM3/c
SILVERSTEIN, Leon, S1/c
SIMAR, Albert S., SF3/c
SIMKINS, Clarence M., GM2/c
SIMMONS, Hubert, S1/c
SIMMONS, Mancel W., MM1/c
SIMMONS, Paul H., WT2/c
SIMMS, Warren C., F2/c
SIMON, Warren B., AMM2/c
SIMPSON, Emmett E., AMM1/c
SIMPSON, Ivan A., CRMA
SIMS, William Trabue, ACMP
SIRKIN, Leon, PhM2/c
SISSON, Harry C., SK3/c
SKANES, Dan K., S1/c
SKEFFINGTON, Francis X., AOM2/c
SKELTON, Emmett R., SK2/c
SKELTON, Herbert G., SK1/c
SKILLMAN, Ralph R., AOM2/c
SKIPPER, Sterling P., SC1/c
SKOSKIE, Stanley J., F2/c
SKOTZKE, Frank R., S1/c
SKUDERA, Dan G., B2/c
SLACK, Eugene, BM2/c
SLATER, Wm. F., CEMP
SLATON, Ira N., S2/c
SLATON, Pete, PhM3/c
SLATSKY, Mike, CQMA
SLIGER, John Z., F2/c
SLOAN, Geo. S., ARM3/c

SLOAN, Jas. J., S1/c
SLOAN, Winson, S2/c
SLUDER, Wm. H., SK1/c
SMALL, Carl B., AOM3/c
SMALLWOOD, Charlie, S2/c
SMAY, Thos. F., S1/c
SMELLAGE, Alva A., S1/c
SMITH, Anderson B., MM3/c
SMITH, Arthur R., MM3/c
SMITH, Chas. H., S2/c
SMITH, Chas. J., Jr., SC3/c
SMITH, Chas. N., CMMA
SMITH, Chas. W., AMMF3/c
SMITH, David W., S1/c
SMITH, David W., RM1/c
SMITH, Donald B., AMM1/c
SMITH, Earl Christian, F2/c
SMITH, Eddie H., M1/c
SMITH, Edward Herbert, ARM2/c
SMITH, Edw. R., PhM3/c
SMITH, Elwood W., ARM1/c
SMITH, Ernest J., GM/3c
SMITH, Frank S., SC2/c
SMITH, Fred L., StM1/c
SMITH, Friend Haroldbyrne, CM1/c
SMITH, Geo. T., S1/c
SMITH, Gewin F., ACOMA
SMITH, Harold E., SF3/c
SMITH, Harold T., F1/c
SMITH, Harry L., BM2/c
SMITH, Harry R., S1/c
SMITH, Hasting J., Jr., St2/c
SMITH, Herbert, OC3/c
SMITH, Hervey D., CCMA
SMITH, Howard B., CFCA
SMITH, Howard L., MoMM3/c
SMITH, Hoyt G., RdM3/c
SMITH, Jas. E., MM3/c
SMITH, Jas. L., S1/c
SMITH, Jerry A., StM3/c
SMITH, John R., S2/c
SMITH, Lawrence R., F2/c
SMITH, Leroy, StM2/c
SMITH, Maurice G., MoMM1/c
SMITH, Maurlin R., EM3/c
SMITH, Max W., S1/c
SMITH, Milford H., Bkr3/c
SMITH, Owen L., PhoM1/c
SMITH, Paul E., MM2/c
SMITH, Ralph L., MM1/c
SMITH, Rufus R., MM1/c
SMITH, Theo. A., ARM2/c
SMITH, Thos. L., CBMA
SMITH, Vernon L., BM2/c
SMITH, Victor N., S1/c
SMITH, Walter N., WT3/c
SMITH, Willis I., GM3/c
SMOTHERMAN, Harvey F., CM1/c
SMOLEN, Geo., RM3/c
SMOROL, Paul P., F1/c
SNAPP, Albert F., S1/c
SNEED, Chas. R., Jr., S2/c
SNIDER, Manning, MM2/c
SNOW, Ethan A., CMMP
SNOW, John R., Jr., ARM2/c
SNOW, Johnnie M., StM1/c
SNYDER, Dan J., S2/c
SNYDER, Edward, MM3/c
SNYDER, Geo. W., Jr., MM3/c
SOBKE, Arthur, ARM1/c
SOCHALSKI, John B., F1/c
SOKOLA, John, SK2/c
SOLANO, Iaidro, CSTA
SOLOMON, Ruble J., CM3/c
SOLON, Clifford S., ARM3/c
SOMERO, Emil J., MM3/c
SOMMER, Sidney, S1/c
SOMMERS, Wm. P., S1/c
SOMMERFELD, Walter Ruben, S2/c
SOMMERVILLE, Louis H., AMM2/c
SONNIER, Ulysses, AMM2/c
SOQUIST, Reynold, ACRMA
SOREM, Lennard L., AM1/c
SORENSEN, Jas. F., EM3/c
SORTUN, Einar O., GM3/c
SOTO, Mike V., S1/c
SOUTHER, Ernest Otto, M2/c
SOUZA, Alfred, MM1/c
SOWA, Jos. H., S1/c
SOWDER, Wm. J., SM2/c
SOWELL, Don R., PhM2/c
SOWELL, James Walker, MM1/c
SOZA, Baudelio, F1/c
SOZZI, Jos., AMM3/c
SPADER, Ernest, HA1/c
SPAETH, John R., MoMM2/c
SPANGENBERGER, Carl C., Jr., S2/c
SPANGLER, Edwin L., Jr., ARM2/c
SPARKMAN, Eldon E., CPhMa
SPARKMAN, Howard S., Jr., F2/c
SPARKS, Jack D., S2/c
SPASSEFF, Paul P., RM2/c
SPEARING, Geo. L. J., Jr, AP1/c
SPEER, Wm. J., TM2/c
SPEIGHT, General, StM2/c
SPENCER, Geo. R., MM1/c
SPENCER, Wm. J., WT2/c
SPERRING, Chas. E., WT2/c
SPERRY, Don E., PhM3/c
SPERRY, Jas. F., S2/c

CASUALTIES

SPICER, Fred J., S1/c
SPICER, Wm. M., S1/c
SPIEGEL, Earl, MM2/c
SPIER, Obra Gerald, S1/c
SPIERER, Elwood R., S1/c
SPIESS, Norman J., PhM3/c
SPIETH, Robt. S., PhM2/c
SPILKER, Edw. H. J., ARM3/c
SPILLANE, Chas. W., Cox.
SPINK, Chas. W., GM1/c
SPINK, Paul W., SF2/c
SPINKS, Robt. D., S2/c
SPISHOK, John, WT1/c
SPITZBERG, Saml, S1/c
SPRADLEY, Jas. W., S2/c
SPRIMONT, Clarence H., MoMM3/c
SPRINGER, Fred W., WT3/c
SPRINGSTEEN, Chester A., S1/c
SPURLOCK, Jake, Ck3/c
SQUIRES, Raymond J., S2/c
STAATS, David Elias, AM2/c
STACK, Johnie Franklin, S1/c
STADDON, Kennith E., PhM3/c
STAFFORD, Jas. P., Jr., SF2/c
STAGGS, Jack H., GM3/c
STALLINGS, Robt. M., F1/c
STALTER, Milo C., HA1/c
STAMBAUGH, Wm. A., CYA
STAMBOUGH, Archie F., F2/c
STANCIU, Victor D., PhM2/c
STANCIL, Harold L., AMM1/c
STANDEFER, John Y., PhM3/c
STANFIELD, Henry A., EM2/c
STANGL, Reinhardt J., F1/c
STANIORSKI, Leonard, MM2/c
STANLEY, Jas., S1/c
STANLEY, Jas. D., M3/c
STANLEY, Jason, GM2/c
STANSBERRY, Gilbert J., S2/c
STANTON, Ervin Warren, S2/c
STAPLES, Clinton V., MM3/c
STARKOVICH, Rudy, M3/c
STARN, Clayton, Jr., AOM3/c
STATON, Jas. C., RM3/c
STAUBACH, Chas., CEMP
STAY, Robt. E., S2/c
STAYMATES, Albert H., S2/c
STEBURG, Frank A., CMMA
STECYK, Edw., PhM3/c
STEELE, Lynn E., AMM2/c
STEELMAN, Benj. S., PhM3/c
STEEN, Albert J., CM1/c
STEENBERG, Francis L., BM1/c
STEFAN, Robt. W., S1/c
STEHMAN, Donald, MM3/c

STEIN, John H., ARM2/c
STEINKAMP, Fredk. E., S1/c
STELLA, Robt. J., F1/c
STEMEN, John I., S1/c
STENSON, Owen P., AOM1/c
STEPHENS, Edgar N., PhM1/c
STEPHENS, Jas. G., F2/c
STEPHENS, Lorenzo J., StM2/c
STEPHENSON, Jas. W., MM2/c
STEPP, Billie, S2/c
STERN, George Morris, S1/c
STEVE, John, CRMA
STEVENS, Douglas W., S1/c
STEVENS, Jas. J., CPhMA
STEVENS, Parker A., MM2/c
STEVENS, Russell L., S1/c
STEVENS, Wm. G., Jr., AM1/c
STEWART, Chas. R., PhM2/c
STEWART, Geo. H., AOM2/c
STEWART, James W., SF3/c
STEWART, John H., S2/c
STEWART, Melvin C., S2/c
STEWART, Russell C., PhM3/c
STEWART, Wayne H., AOM3/c
STEWART, Wm. R., WT2/c
STEYER, Rich. C., S1/c
ST. GEORGE, Jos. D., S1/c
ST. JOHN, Francis T., Y1/c
STICH, Leroy E., Ptr2/c
STICKLER, Elmer W., S1/c
STICKMAN, Wm. F., CMMP
STILLE, James F., Jr., AMM1/c
STILLWAGON, Douglas E., S2/c
STINGER, Allen K., AOM3/c
STINSON, Arthur W., F2/c
STIPEK, Gustave J., CCMA
STOKES, Airst L., StM2/c
STOLZENBURG, Vaughan C. F., MM3/c
STONE, Allen R., Cox.
STONE, Harold R., M1/c
STONEHOCKER, Buford J., COMMA
STONEMAN, Clinton E., ART2/c
STONEY, Alvin H., BM2/c
STOOKEY, Byron E., MM3/c
STORK, Edward A., S1/c
STORM, Francis J., ARM1/c
STOROST, Roy E., S1/c
STORY, Argus W., Jr., AOM3/c
STOTTS, Aulton D., EM3/c
STOUFFER, Elvin E., ARM2/c
STOUT, Chas. B., PhM3/c
STOUT, Roy C., Jr., SC2/c
STOVALL, William Coy, CTCP
STOVALL, Wm. E., S2/c
STOVER, Donald E., EM2/c

Strand, Orris M., S1/c
Strang, Chas. L., S2/c
Strasser, Alfred B., CEMP
Strasser, Clarence F., CM2/c
Strasbaugh, Chas. C., Jr., MM3/c
Stratmon, Robt. L., St1/c
Straub, Cyril Edward, SK2/c
Strauch, Adam, CEMP
Strauss, Sam Seymoure, S1/c
Street, Eugene H., MoMM2/c
Strehle, Fred A., SC1/c
Stribling, Wm. J., ARM1/c
Strickland, Thos. L., S2/c
Strickland, Young E., CWTA
Stripling, Gordon, Jr., S2/c
Stroh, Harold, RdM2/c
Strong, Chas. H., S2/c
Strong, Fredk. A., 3rd, CPhMA
Stuart, Walter Edward, MM2/c
Studden, Arthur, MM3/c
Stueve, Emmett G., PhM3/c
Stumpf, Geo. L., Jr., S2/c
Sturrock, Spurgeon S., S2/c
Sturtevant, John F., AMM3/c
Suchomel, John O., BM1/c
Sullivan, Calvin C., S1/c
Sullivan, Bernard, Jr., S1/c
Sullivan, Geo. B., GM3/c
Summerford, Hartley W., MM3/c
Summers, Francis P., AOM1/c
Supinger, Lewis R., GM2/c
Surprenant, Donat R., CWTA
Sutherland, Waldo L., MoMM1/c
Sutton, Eugene F., ARM2/c
Sutton, John T., QM3/c
Suttora, Francis F., AMM2/c
Svec, Archie L., CWTA
Swafford, Jack E., PhM3/c
Swager, Vincent, Jr., S2/c
Swaim, Joyce E., ARM2/c
Swain, Ray B., Cox.
Swalling, Cato H., MM2/c
Swann, Wm. G., MM3/c
Swanson, Walter F., MoMM1/c
Swartz, Carl O., EM2/c
Swartz, Elmer M., F1/c
Swartzwelder, Rich. I., SoM3/c
Sweeney, Wm. M., AOM2/c
Swensen, August John, Jr., S1/c
Swift, Lelean C., S1/c
Swinconos, Peter P., Ptr1/c
Swisher, Howard G., S2/c
Swisher, Maynard, S1/c
Syintsakos, Constantine, S1/c
Sykes, Saml. E., SK2/c

Sylvester, Valleon, CQMA
Szczech, Frank E., BM2/c
Szebeledy, Louis, CPhMP

Taber, Victor C., AMM3/c
Tabor, Jas. E., F1/c
Tagesen, Alvin R., S1/c
Tague, Joseph A., S2/c
Taitano, Luis, Bkr1/c
Take, Roy E., MM2/c
Talbert, James A., StM1/c
Talbot, Harry E., S1/c
Talbot, Jos. E., BM2/c
Talley, Fred, SF1/c
Talley, Kenneth E., BM1/c
Tankersley, Alfred L., PhM3/c
Tanner, Wm. J., S1/c
Taphilias, Geo. F., S1/c
Tapley, Edwin H., PhM2/c
Tarbox, Richard C., S1/c
Taromino, Jos. A., S1/c
Tarvanis, Edward F., AMM2/c
Tascillo, Matteo, Cox.
Tatarek, Anthony P., SC1/c
Tavano, Frank J., S1/c
Taylor, Clair E., BM2/c
Taylor, Clarence I., S1/c
Taylor, Forest L., PhM2/c
Taylor, Henry A., TM2/c
Taylor, Jas., StM1/c
Taylor, Jas. L., S1/c
Taylor, Kenneth W., F1/c
Taylor, Loyd, S2/c
Taylor, Rich., MM3/c
Taylor, Robt. L., FCM2/c
Taylor, Robt. P., AMM2/c
Taylor, Thos. R., StM1/c
Taylor, Warren S., BM2/c
Taylor, Wm. J., Jr., S2/c
Teague, David F., BM2/c
Teague, Jackie L., S1/c
Teague, Jesse Z., S2/c
Teal, Lloyd R., S1/c
Tedder, Wm. H., CMMP
Teitz, Jackson E., MM3/c
Tellier, Leslie W., MM2/c
Templin, Lawrence E., CM3/c
Tenney, Vet E., AOM2/c
Terpstra, Robt. D., S1/c
Terry, Wesley P., ARM1/c
Tessendorf, Sheldon E., F2/c
Tevis, Alvin W., SM3/c
Tharp, Elmer M., MM2/c
Thatcher, Robt. E. H., MM1/c
Thater, Anthony L., BM2/c

CASUALTIES

THEILER, Frank M., MoMM3/c
THOENE, Thos., S1/c
THOMAS, Clyde E., HA2/c
THOMAS, Geo. C., GM2/c
THOMAS, Geo. L., EM2/c
THOMAS, Harrell A., SC3/c
THOMAS, James H., RM2/c
THOMAS, John, CM2/c
THOMAS, John R., MM1/c
THOMAS, Jos. R., GM1/c
THOMAS, Willie D., Ck2/c
THOMPSON, Clyde Carl, Cox.
THOMPSON, Earl S., AMM1/c
THOMPSON, Harry L., GM2/c
THOMPSON, Herbert, S1/c
THOMPSON, John C., GM1/c
THOMPSON, John R., RT1/c
THOMPSON, Laurie T., SF1/c
THOMPSON, Mager A., StM2/c
THOMPSON, Ralph, MMS3/c
THOMPSON, Thos. C., EM1/c
THORLAKSEN, Arthur M., SC2/c
THORNSBURG, Kermit Lee, MM2/c
THORNTON, Brown M., Jr., AMM2/c
THORNTON, Tullie C., S1/c
THRASHER, Edw. G., AMM2/c
THRASHER, Robt. T., TM1/c
THRIFT, Jos. T., Jr., PhM3/c
THURMAN, Irby H., MM3/c
THURMAN, Jos. A., S2/c
THURMOND, Willard A., S1/c
TICE, Wm. L., SC1/c
TILLEY, Owen E., AOM3/c
TILTON, Edw., MM2/c
TINKER, Chas. R., S1/c
TINLING, Henry J., S1/c
TIPPS, Everett S., S2/c
TITSWORTH, Chas. L., AOM3/c
TITZE, Herbert C., HA1/c
TOBEY, Howard S., MM3/c
TOBIN, Harry R., SC3/c
TOBIN, Wm. J., EM2/c
TODD, Donald F., HA1/c
TODD, William Vincent, S1/c
TOLBERT, Early O., S2/c
TOLER, Ollen B., GM2/c
TOMAS, John W., SC3/c
TOMASKOVIC, Cyril S., Cox.
TOMASSI, Eugene P., Cox.
TOMLINSON, Frank E., S1/c
TONEY, Sidney, StM1/c
TONKA, Geo. J., S2/c
TOOKER, Warren E., CM2/c
TOOTHAKER, Frank L., ARM2/c
TOPHAM, Stanley R., RdM2/c
TOPORSKI, Edw., S1/c
TOVES, Frank E., StM3/c
TOWLE, Russell, Cox.
TOWLE, Thos. G., ARM2/c
TOWNLEY, Millard C., FCM1/c
TOWNSEND, Earl S., S2/c
TOWNSEND, John J., Jr., AMM2/c
TOWNSEND, Thos. L., S2/c
TRAMMELL, John L., Jr., EM2/c
TRASK, Paul B., TM2/c
TRAYNOR, Robt. E., AOM2/c
TREADWAY, Ralph W., CCMP
TREGO, Roger V., F1/c
TREMMEL, Louis E., MM1/c
TREVETHAN, Vernon E., MM3/c
TREVISANO, Cosmo, GM2/c
TRIBBEY, Jesse A., MoMM3/c
TRIM, Donald P., Cox.
TRIMBLE, Harold C., S2/c
TRIPLETT, William Frank, S1/c
TROJAN, Matthew, GM3/c
TROOD, Wm. W., PhM2/c
TROSPER, Ollie E., GM1/c
TROWBRIDGE, Raymond E., EM2/c
TROYER, Robt. B., S1/c
TRUDEL, Fredk. C., MM2/c
TRUDEL, Harold A., S2/c
TRUDEL, Venance H., S1/c
TRUJILLO, Dan C., S1/c
TUBBS, Ernest M., ARM3/c
TUBEKIS, Jas. A., S1/c
TUCKER, Harmon B., PhM3/c
TUCKER, Kester L., AOM3/c
TUCKER, Lige L., CEMP
TUCKER, Theo. R., EM1/c
TUNNELL, Chas. H., CM2/c
TURCICH, Chas. J., Y2/c
TURNER, Dan J., S2/c
TURNER, General L., Jr., AOM2/c
TURNER, Geo., StM1/c
TURNER, Kenneth E., PhM2/c
TURNER, Ralph C., AMM1/c
TURNER, Thos. J., Jr., ACRMA
TURNER, Tommy L., S2/c
TURPIN, Frank F., PhM1/c
TUTTLE, Myron P., EM2/c
TUTTLE, Nelson O., Jr., MM2/c
TUTTLE, Thos. E., ARM2/c
TUYN, Rich F., PhM3/c
TWOREK, Henry Thomas, Bkr2/c
TYLER, John L., Jr., GM2/c
TYREE, Lawrence F., PhM2/c
TYSINGER, Raymond L., ACMMA

UBITE, Ernest, StM1/c

UDELL, Merwin F., SM3/c
UHL, Grover E., S1/c
UHRE, Dale V., MoMM2/c
ULBRICH, Robt. E., RM3/c
ULERY, Roy L., MM1/c
ULICKAS, Geo. P., MM2/c
ULLSTROM, John H., S2/c
ULRICH, Robt. L., S2/c
UNDERBAKKE, Bevis A., RdM3/c
UNDERWOOD, Wm. D., S1/c
UNDERWOOD, Wm. R., Jr., TM3/c
UNGER, Robt. W., S1/c
UPCHURCH, John R., CWTA
UPCHURCH, Thos. M., F2/c
URBANEK, Thos., Jr., CM2/c
URBANI, Stephen P., CEMP
URBANSKI, Elmer L., MM2/c
USHER, Orrin J., Ptr2/c
UTTERBERG, Richard W., ARM2/c

VADON, Peter, Jr., F1/c
VALENTE, Peter M., S1/c
VALLANTE, Pasquale, F1/c
VALLES, Roberto, S2/c
VANDERREYDEN, Roy, EM2/c
VANDEVENTER, Frank E., AMM3/c
VAN DEUSEN, Harold P., Cox.
VAN DEUSEN, Robt. J., WT3/c
VAN DIVER, Coy C., Y2/c
VAN DOLAH, Justin S., Jr., AP1/c
VANDRE, Darwin W., S2/c
VAN DYNE, Floyd B., CM3/c
VAN GELDEREN, Buster, BM2/c
VAN GLAHN, Ralph, Jr., AOM3/c
VAN HOOK, Fred D., StM2/c
VAN HOUTEN, Arthur F., S1/c
VAN HOUTEN, Robt. S., MoMM2/c
VAN METER, Wm. T., AOM1/c
VAN RIPER, Ralph A., AMM2/c
VAN WINKLE, Arthur A., S1/c
VAN WINKLE, Jas. A., S2/c
VAUGHN, Robt. A., StM1/c
VAUGHT, Coy C., SK1/c
VAUGHAN, Eugene, S1/c
VAUGHAN, Louis D., ARM3/c
VAUGHN, Clyde E., MM2/c
VEASEL, Wm. R., MM2/c
VEDDER, Grant A., TM1/c
VEGAS, Manuel R., S1/c
VELARDI, Jos. S., F1/c
VELTRI, Frank S., MM1/c
VENDERLY, Donald L., F1/c
VENEGAS, Jess M., S2/c
VENEZIANO, Armando P., S2/c
VENTURA, Frank J., F2/c

VERBITSKY, Jas. E., F1/c
VERIGAN, Geo. D., F2/c
VERKUILEN, Ronald W., PhM2/c
VESMAS, Julius, GM1/c
VICKERS, Lawrence V., BM2/c
VICKNAIR, Lionel C., Jr., S2/c
VICKNAIR, Warren J., Jr., EM2/c
VICSIK, John, F1/c
VIEIRA, Gilbert, S2/c
VIEIRA, Joaquim, Jr., S1/c
VIERLING, Wm. E., MoMM1/c
VILLA, Peter A., AMM1/c
VILLETT, Normand, S2/c
VINCENT, Ivan R., S1/c
VINCENT, Oland M., PhM2/c
VINES, John E., PhM2/c
VINING, Thos. R., Jr., RM3/c
VIRDEN, Calvin C., F2/c
VISE, Wm. G., HA1/c
VISNICH, Geo., SM2/c
VITOLO, Geo. F., BM2/c
VLASICH, Peter L., CCMP
VOELKER, Delmer O., S2/c
VOGEL, Jos. L., MM3/c
VOIGT, Ferdinand M., F1/c
VOLK, Wendelin J., Cox.
VOLKER, Chas. J., CBMP
VOLKER, Raymond E., S1/c
VOROS, Frank A., S1/c
VOSS, Lucien L., SPM2/c
VOTAW, Herman V., PhM1/c
VOYLES, Vernon W., MM3/c
VYDFOL, Fred A., MM1/c

WACHTER, Marvin C., MM2/c
WACHUNAS, Chas. S., EM3/c
WACKERMAN, Wm. W., Jr., S1/c
WADDELL, Robt., StM1/c
WADE, Jack W., S2/c
WADE, Hollis Dean, S1/c
WADE, Wilton W., AS
WADOSKY, Andrew A., ARM2/c
WAGENKNECHT, Robt. B., AOM2/c
WAGERS, Sherman C., Cox.
WAGNER, Arthur D., SoM2/c
WAGNER, Earle J., MoMM2/c
WAGNER, Eugene, F1/c
WAGNER, Robt. E., AMM2/c
WAGONER, Jas. E., AOM2/c
WAITE, Eugene F., S1/c
WAJERT, Frank J., S1/c
WALCH, Geo. J., Cox.
WALDEN, Chas. O., S2/c
WALDEN, John G., Jr., AMM3/c
WALKER, Andre P., PhM3/c

CASUALTIES

WALKER, Clarence J., ARM2/c
WALKER, Ernest E., S1/c
WALKER, Frank C., GM1/c
WALKER, J. Frank, Y1/c
WALKER, Jack D., BM2/c
WALKER, Jas. B., Jr., S1/c
WALKER, Jas. H., Jr., AMM3/c
WALKER, Paul A., S2/c
WALKER, Paul B., S2/c
WALKER, Raymond L., SM2/c
WALKER, Robt. P., HA1/c
WALKER, Robt. T., HA1/c
WALKUP, John P., S2/c
WALL, John F., AMM1/c
WALL, Jos. P., ARM2/c
WALL, Lamonte A., MM2/c
WALL, Theo., S2/c
WALLACE, Elmer E., S1/c
WALLACE, Francis H., SM3/c
WALLACE, Jos. T., TM3/c
WALLACE, Percy H., S1/c
WALLACE, Wm. C., S1/c
WALLER, James, S2/c
WALLER, Joe T., S1/c
WALLS, Wm. H., S2/c
WALMSLEY, Jos. V., PhM3/c
WALSH, David S., M1/c
WALSH, Edw. K., MoMM2/c
WALSH, Norman, F2/c
WALSH, Wm. T., F1/c
WALTER, Arlen A., S1/c
WALTER, Warner J., MM2/c
WALTERS, David J., CM1/c
WALTERS, Jas. T., SK3/c
WALTERS, Wendell M., MoMM2/c
WALTERS, Wm. N., S1/c
WALTON, Dallas Marril, Cox.
WALTON, Rupert W., S2/c
WANDA, Jos. E., SF1/c
WARCISKIE, Edward P., AMM1/c
WARD, Alonzo G., EM3/c
WARD, Francis I., CMMA
WARD, John E., Jr., S1/c
WARD, Martin J., S1/c
WARD, Wm. A., MoMM1/c
WARE, Fred E., S2/c
WARMBRODT, Fredk. L., PhM3/c
WARMOTH, Walter O., Jr., ARM1/c
WARNER, Stanley L., MoMM2/c
WARREN, Chester E., RM2/c
WARREN, Geo. A., S2/c
WARREN, Hubert, EM2/c
WARREN, Raymond S., Jr., GM2/c
WASSUM, Joseph Cox, F1/c
WASZKIEWICZ, Lawrence J., S1/c

WATERMAN, Lee, F1/c
WATERS, Norman E., AOM1/c
WATKINS, Geo. L., StM1/c
WATKINS, William Merle, AMM1/c
WATSON, Albert G., MoMM1/c
WATSON, Earl E., S2/c
WATT, Robt. N., F1/c
WATTS, Edwin A., QM1/c
WAWRZONEK, Louis J., PhM1/c
WAYMACK, Wayne L., ARM2/c
WAYNICK, Delbert L., S2/c
WEAVER, Albert A., S1/c
WEAVER, Bruce E., S1/c
WEAVER, Jas. K., EM2/c
WEAVER, Jeff, StM1/c
WEAVER, Marlin A., S2/c
WEBB, Donald R., HA1/c
WEBB, Edw. P., Jr., SC1/c
WEBB, Eugene U., MM3/c
WEBB, Ray J., S2/c
WEBB, Thos. L., Cox.
WEBB, Wm. G., MM2/c
WEBBER, Edw. C., CEMP
WEBER, John G., MM1/c
WEBER, Reese C., Jr., S1/c
WEBER, Robt. H., BM2/c
WEBSTER, Harry L., Prt1/c
WEBSTER, Marion F., CEMP
WEBSTER, Morris D., PhM3/c
WEBSTER, Sidney M., Jr., M3/c
WEDEKING, Jas. L., FC3/c
WEEKS, Billy B., StM2/c
WEEKS, Chester S., WT2/c
WEGNER, Herman A., EM2/c
WEHNER, Wm. G., MM3/c
WEIDE, Edw. L., MM3/c
WEIDENER, Albert G., SF2/c
WEIGAND, Alfred J., Jr., AMM3/c
WEIGAND, Ralph J., S1/c
WEIGAND, Walter R., SoM1/c
WEINGARTZ, Lawrence W., S1/c
WEIS, Walter J., MoMM1/c
WEISS, John Jos., Jr., RdM3/c
WEISS, Lester H., MM1/c
WEITALA, Jalmer E., SC3/c
WELBAUM, Quentin R., AOM3/c
WELCH, Grant D., S2/c
WELCH, Jas. S., AOM2/c
WELCH, Roy B., AMM3/c
WELKE, Artman F., F1/c
WELLMAN, Donald Wiltsie, AMM2/c
WELLS, Arthur, Jr., PhM1/c
WELLS, Chas. E., AMM1/c
WELLS, Conway Clarence, CMoMMA
WELLS, Donald Allen, S1/c

WELLS, Paul R., SK3/c
WELLS, Rupert A., MM3/c
WELLS, Wm. A., EM2/c
WELTZ, Arthur J., SF1/c
WENDEL, Lewis F., S1/c
WENDROFF, Robt., HA1/c
WENK, Henry T., Jr., GM3/c
WENTHE, Claude L., MM3/c
WENTWORTH, Dale E., SM1/c
WERGERS, Geo. T., S2/c
WERNER, John F., ARM2/c
WERNER, Robt. C., S2/c
WERSEBE, Dan J., WT2/c
WEST, Bryce L., S2/c
WEST, Clayton C., F1/c
WEST, Earnest, ACOMP
WEST, John J., MM2/c
WEST, Philip L., F1/c
WESTERHUIS, Louis Joseph, S1/c
WESTFALL, Howard V., S2/c
WESTFALL, Robt. W., MM1/c
WESTON, Robert Leonard, F3/c
WETHERALD, Thos. R., MM1/c
WETZEL, Louis C., AMM3/c
WHALEN, Eugene H., S2/c
WHALEY, Leonard F., BM2/c
WHEELER, Eric M., S1/c
WHEELER, Lanois M., ARM2/c
WHEELER, Robt. J., PhM2/c
WHITACRE, Melvin F., MM3/c
WHITAKER, Melvin L., S1/c
WHITBY, Stanley N., ARM2/c
WHITE, Clifford C., Jr., TM2/c
WHITE, Edw. B., S2/c
WHITE, Ferguson B., QM2/c
WHITE, Fred H., S2/c
WHITE, Jas. R., S2/c
WHITE, Jesse L., S2/c
WHITE, John W., StM2/c
WHITE, Lawrence M., GM3/c
WHITE, Merel L., S2/c
WHITE, Ralph A., CSFP
WHITE, Robt. L., MM3/c
WHITE, Stewart C., Jr., ARM3/c
WHITE, Thos. A., S1/c
WHITE, Walter E., F1/c
WHITEFIELD, Gerald D., S2/c
WHITEHEAD, Irvin L., EM1/c
WHITESELL, Ernest G., S2/c
WHITLEY, Jay O., Cox.
WHITLOCK, Damon L., CEMA
WHITMARSH, Donald A., MoMM1/c
WHITNEY, Basil E., AOM1/c
WHITNEY, Clyde O., S2/c
WHITNEY, Warren B., CM1/c
WHITTED, Raymond C., AOM3/c
WHITTED, Walter T., MoMM2/c
WHITTLE, Theo. E., CM1/c
WICK, Harvey C., AMM2/c
WICKERS, Robt. E., S2/c
WICKERSHAM, Jas. F., MM2/c
WICKLIFFE, Leland E., S2/c
WICKSTROM, Gustof A., WT3/c
WIDENER, Vergil D., Mus2/c
WIECHMANN, Harry A., CSFA
WIEGAND, Robt. E., SoM3/c
WIERSCHING, Vernon T., MM3/c
WILCZYNSKI, Tadeusz B., S2/c
WILDER, Paul, WT1/c
WILDER, Robt. A., S1/c
WILDING, Robt. F., AerM2/c
WILES, Adrian C., RM3/c
WILKINSON, Claud A., MM2/c
WILKINSON, Edwin E., S1/c
WILKINSON, Thos. W., GM3/c
WILLARD, Glenn R., S1/c
WILLCUTT, Boyd B., MM3/c
WILLEKE, Howard O., CM1/c
WILLERTON, Robt. P., Y2/c
WILLIAMS, Bert E., MM3/c
WILLIAMS, Billy D., HA1/c
WILLIAMS, Charles Errett, AOM3/c
WILLIAMS, Chas., FC1/c
WILLIAMS, Dewey, CEMP
WILLIAMS, Eligie P., ARM1/c
WILLIAMS, Fred H., StM1/c
WILLIAMS, Harold E., AOM2/c
WILLIAMS, Harold R., MM2/c
WILLIAMS, Harry L., AMM3/c
WILLIAMS, Haskell V., SF2/c
WILLIAMS, Horace V., Jr., MM3/c
WILLIAMS, Howard, SF1/c
WILLIAMS, Jas. H., ARM2/c
WILLIAMS, John., S2/c
WILLIAMS, John R., Jr., S2/c
WILLIAMS, Junior R., S2/c
WILLIAMS, Lyman L., F1/c
WILLIAMS, Lynn H., MM1/c
WILLIAMS, Odie E., Jr., AMM1/c
WILLIAMS, Robt. B., Jr., ARM3/c
WILLIAMS, Robt. T., SC2/c
WILLIAMS, Roy E., Y1/c
WILLIAMS, Roy W., TM3/c
WILLIAMS, Washington, S2/c
WILLIAMS, Wayne Rupert, SF2/c
WILLIAMS, Willie, StM1/c
WILLIAMS, Wm. F., StM1/c
WILLIAMS, Wm. K., RM3/c
WILLIS, Fleet F., BM2/c
WILLIS, Joe, StM3/c

CASUALTIES

WILLIS, Lowell F., PhM3/c
WILLIS, Robt. E., MoMM3/c
WILLIS, Robt. T., S2/c
WILLOWS, Ronald G., S1/c
WILLSON, Bill, S2/c
WILSON, Bertrand Miron, ACRMA
WILSON, Carl L., S2/c
WILSON, Charles Eugene, S2/c
WILSON, Chas. A., RT1/c
WILSON, Chas. J., S2/c
WILSON, Eldon L., F2/c
WILSON, Harold R., Bkr2/c
WILSON, Jas. A., PhM3/c
WILSON, John D., S2/c
WILSON, Max, FCO3/c
WILSON, Miller R., F1/c
WILSON, Norman E., MM1/c
WILSON, Robt. E., MM2/c
WILSON, Robt. J., S2/c
WILSON, Walter M., MM3/c
WINDROSSE, Max R., FCM3/c
WINFIELD, Harold William, S1/c
WINFIELD, Jack N., EM2/c
WINGET, Roy E., S2/c
WINIG, Chas. A., FC1/c
WINKLER, Stanley C., QM3/c
WINN, Iley D., ART1/c
WINQUIST, Henry C. A., CMoMMA
WINSOR, Willard I., CYP
WINSOR, Wm. D., GM1/c
WINTER, Theo. L., EM3/c
WINTERS, Herbert R., S2/c
WISE, Robt. A., S1/c
WISE, Wm. M., F1/c
WISEMAN, John A., S2/c
WITT, Ralph Everette, EM1/c
WODZIEN, Edw. C., MoMM3/c
WOELLHOF, Lloyd R., ARM2/c
WOJCIECHOWSKI, Jos. W., S2/c
WOJCIK, Stanley, F1/c
WOJNIAK, Edw. H., EM3/c
WOJTKIELEWICZ, Wm., EM3/c
WOLAK, Johns, Jr., AOM2/c
WOLF, Alex. W., RM3/c
WOLF, Chas. F., GM3/c
WOLF, Jos. A., S2/c
WOLF, Thos. J., AMM2/c
WOLFE, Alfred D., MM1/c
WOLFE, Robt. L., AOM2/c
WOLFF, Warren W., S2/c
WOLLERMAN, Fritz A., GM2/c
WONACOTT, Porter L., F1/c
WONG, Edw. C., MM1/c
WONG, Harry, Bkr3/c
WOOD, Elbert, EM3/c

WOOD, Karl M., ARM3/c
WOOD, Lester O., S2/c
WOOD, Marion A., Cox.
WOOD, Norman E., AOM3/c
WOOD, Russell D., F1/c
WOODARD, Eugene F., F2/c
WOODS, Don E., S1/c
WOODWARD, Alton C., S1/c
WOOLDRIDGE, Robt. M., S1/c
WOOLUM, Wm. E., MM3/c
WORLAND, Manuel F., S1/c
WORSHAM, Chas. E., EM3/c
WRAY, Chas. L., Jr., BM2/c
WRESINSKI, Thaddeus, PM1/c
WRIGHT, Clarence W. M., Y2/c
WRIGHT, Floyd E., S1/c
WRIGHT, Geo. W., S1/c
WRIGHT, Jas. E., StM1/c
WRIGHT, Kenneth M., Cox.
WRIGHT, Marvin B., PhM3/c
WRIGHT, Nathan E., MM3/c
WRIGHT, Wm. J., BM2/c
WURTZ, Kenneth A., F1/c
WYCOFF, Donald E., MoMM2/c
WYLIE, John J., F1/c
WYLIE, Robt. D., MM3/c
WYMORE, Roy C., CM2/c
WYNKOOP, Bennie, S1/c
WYTRYKOWSKI, Henry T., F1/c

YACKABOSKIE, Chester C., S1/c
YADA, Chas. W., S2/c
YAKEY, Donald L., S2/c
YAROSLAVSKI, Jos., S2/c
YAROSZ, Thos., GM3/c
YATES, Edw. D., SF3/c
YEAGER, Stanley L., S2/c
YETTE, Gilbert H., RM1/c
YNIGUES, Donald E., S2/c
YOAKUM, Donaphon A., AOM2/c
YORE, Patrick E., Ptr2/c
YORK, Max L., QM3/c
YOUNG, Chauncey A., WT1/c
YOUNG, Edwin M., S2/c
YOUNG, Everette E., SC3/c
YOUNG, Geo. L., ARM2/c
YOUNG, J. Z., MM2/c
YOUNG, John L., S1/c
YOUNG, John M., SF1/c
YOUNG, John R., S2/c
YOUNG, Kenneth A., S1/c
YOUNG, Kenneth E., TM3/c
YOUNG, Lyle L., AOM2/c
YOUNG, Moses V., CCKA
YOUNG, Raynold B., AMM2/c

Young, Richard C., S1/c
Young, Willie F., MM3/c
Young, Willis E., S2/c
Young, Wm. P., ARM2/c
Youngberg, Albert S., AS
Youngberg, Eugene R., S1/c
Youngblood, Ralph B., S2/c
Youngchild, Robt. P., S1/c
Younger, Robt. A., S2/c
Youngs, Myron E., Ptr3/c
Yung, Herbert M., SF3/c

Zaczek, John S., MoMM2/c
Zaicek, Ralph S., WT2/c
Zaleski, Frank M., S2/c
Zamora, Paul J., S1/c
Zanon, Wm. L., AMM2/c
Zapala, Mitchell J., S1/c
Zaverack, Nelson, S2/c

Zdeb, Orvel P., F1/c
Zechman, David, Cox.
Zehner, Scott P., S1/c
Zeigler, Robt. G., PhM1/c
Zeits, Wm. J., AOM2/c
Zelazny, Leo F., RM3/c
Zemovich, Frank, S1/c
Zernial, Andrew W., Jr., S1/c
Zespy, Jerome A., GM3/c
Ziegenhorn, Gwyen A., S1/c
Zielinski, Robt., Jr., S2/c
Zilm, Norman J., MM2/c
Zimmerman, Henry J., MM1/c
Zintz, Edward L., SC3/c
Zlatnik, Henry F., MM3/c
Zorn, Andrew, Jr., CM3/c
Zunac, John R., F1/c
Zygmont, Walter F., S1/c
Zylks, John W., S2/c

Index

A. W. GRANT, 316, 357, 358, 360-63
ABBOTT, 111, note
ABNER READ, 202, note; 209, 314
Adams, Lieutenant Commander Carlton R., 33, 35
Admiralties, 72, 166-76, 192, 204, 312, * P XXVIII
Aertsen, Lieutenant Gil, 380
Agnew, Commander Dwight M., 128
Ainsworth, Lieutenant Charles G., 150
Ainsworth, Rear Admiral Walden L., 65, 66, 228, 266
Airbases, Japanese, P XI, P XXIX
Aitape, 188, 190, 192, 203, P XXX
ALABAMA, 109, note; 141, note; 161, 197, note; 408, note
ALBACORE, 240, 241, note
ALDERAMIN, P IX
Alexander, Captain Ralph C., 372
Allen, Lieutenant Commander Charles V., 34, 169
Allen, Lieutenant Francis P., Jr., 54
Ames, Lieutenant Commander Oliver, 94
AMMEN, 173, 202, 209
Anderson, Commander Paul R., 41, note
Anderson, Lieutenant (jg) Thomas E., 92
ANDERSON, 111
Andrew, Commander John G., 363, note
Andrews, Chief Yeoman A. H., 57
Angaur, 286, 289, 292, 294, 295, P L, P LII, P LIV
ANTHONY, 64, 70
Apemama, 79, 82, 83, 108, 271, P XIII
APOGON, 99, 160
APPALACHIAN, 122
Armstrong, Commander Henry J., 44, note
Arnold, General Henry H., 306
Arnold, Commander Jackson D., 300
ARTHUR MIDDLETON, 129
ARUNTA (HMAS), 51, note; 202, 209, 316, 357
ASASIO, P XXV
Ashmun, Captain George, 58
ASHTABULA, 321
Aslito airfield, 231, 256, 257
ATAGO, 40, 224, note; 337, 338-41
Atkeson, Commander John C., 410, note
Atkins, Commander Barry T., 355
AUGUSTUS THOMAS, 321
AULICK, 316, 363, note
"Aureole," aerial, P XXIX
Austin, Commander Bernard L., 44, note
Austin, Lieutenant Commander Marshall H., 229
Australia, navy and troops, 12, 13-16, 19, note; 20
AUSTRALIA (HMAS), 51, note; 54, 202, 209, 211, 316, 319
Avery, Lieutenant Clarence F., 157
Ayers, Colonel Russell G. (USA), 131
Ayesa, Lieutenant Benjamin (USCGR), 51
AYLWIN, 132

Babcock, Radioman Ellis C., 247-48, note
BACHE, 170, 202, note; 209, 316, 357
Badger, Rear Admiral Oscar C., 287, 414
BAGLEY, 13, 51, note; 56, 410, note
Baker, Fireman 1/c J. N., 99, 103
Bakutis, Commander Fred E., 353

* P=Plates

Baldridge, Lieutenant Commander Edward F., 295
Balla, Pfc John F. (USMC), 291
Ballentine, Captain John J., 41, note; 59
BALTIMORE, 93, 109, note; 141, note; 150, 197, note; 286, P I
Banta, Lieutenant (jg) Phil, 341
Barber, Lieutenant (jg) R., 196
Barbey, Rear Admiral Daniel E., 17-22, 27, 28, 32, 33, 51, 53, 169, 176, 189, 190, 202, 204, 214, 288, 289, 308, 309, 316 P LIX
Bardshar, Lieutenant Commander Frederick A., 302
Barnard, Lieutenant (jg) ("Barney") 229
Barrowclough, Major General, 65
Bates, Captain Richard W., 145
Battle, going into, 269-70
Battle Ethics, Japanese, 262
Battles. See names of battles
Baughman, Lieutenant Daniel, 23
Baxter, Lieutenant (jg) Denver F., 150, P XXIV
Baylis, Lieutenant (jg) John S., 26
Beachmasters, 21
BEALE, 56, 170, 202, note; 209, 316, 357
Beatty, Captain Frank E., 66
Beckmann, Lieutenant Commander Alcorn G., 39, note; 65
Begor, Lieutenant (Dr.) Fay B., 29
Behrens, Captain William, 329
BELL, 59, 109, note; 141, note; 191, 197, note; 331, note
BELLEAU WOOD, 109, note; 116, 140, note; 141, 158, 179, 247, 253, note; 324, 374
BENHAM, 368
Benitez, Lieutenant Commander Rafael C., 341, 342
Bennett, Lieutenant Commander Carter L., 110
BENNETT, 65, 70
BENNION, 316, 358
Benson, Lieutenant Lloyd G., 204
Bentley, Commander James C., 324, note
Bergin, Commander Charles T., 355
Berkey, Rear Admiral Russell S., 19, note; 54, 170, 172, 202, 203, 209, 213, note; 214, 288, 309, 315, 316, 317, 352, 364
Betio, Battle of, 85-90, P X, P XI, P XII
Beyer, Lieutenant Commander Aaron F., 393
Biak, 202-12, P XXXII
BILOXI, 111, 140, note; 191, 275, 276, 408, note; 414
BIRMINGHAM, 228, 229, 327, 330, note; 331, 371, 372, 373, P XXXIV, P XL, P LXIII
Bismarck Islands and Sea, and Battle of, 26, 71, 75, 78, 79, 166, 167, P III
BLACK, 111, note; 114, note
Blackburn, Commander Tom, 43
Blair, Lieutenant (jg) George M., 43, 150, P XXIV
Blake, Lieutenant Robert H., 54
Blanchard, Commander James W., 240
Blanchard, Lieutenant Commander Theodore, 132
Blandy, Admiral William H. P., 297
Bledsoe, Captain Alfred M., 364
Blick, Captain Robert E., 399
Blitch, Commander Jack, 301
Blood plasma, use of, P XIV, P XLIII
"Bloody Nose Ridge," 292, 293, P LI, P LIII

523

INDEX

Bloom, Motor Machinist's Mate 1/c, 61
Bodler, Lieutenant Commander John R., 94
Bogan, Rear Admiral Gerald F., 323, 368, 369, 381, 405, 408, 413, 415
BOISE, 202, 209, 316, 364
Bolger, Captain Joseph F., 369
Bombardment, naval, 119, 122, 123, 124
Bonins, 166, 201, 221, 229, 235, 275, 276, 298
BOSTON, 109, *note*; 197, *note*; 329, 331, *note*
Boud, Lieutenant Commander Henry B., 289
Bougainville, 37-40, 48, 57, 64, 96, 199, 335
Boulware, Commander Joe W., 293, 358
Bowman, Captain Roscoe L., 93
BOYD, 197, *note*; 331, *note*
Boyington, Major Gregory, 57-58
BRADFORD, 59, 109, *note*; 141, *note*; 145, 197, *note*;
Bradley, Commander Richard B., Jr., 357
Brady, Captain Parke H., 131
BRAINE, 70, 228
Brandt, Ensign Donald C. (USNR), 274
Bratton, AOM Kenneth, P v
Bridges, Lieutenant James E., 143
Briggs, Lieutenant (jg) Sheldon, 116, 123
Brogger, Lieutenant Commander Lloyd C., 50
Brooks, Ensign William C., 384, 387
BROOKS, 34, 169
Browder, Captain Maurice E., 128, 400
Brown, Captain Allen D., 408, *note*
Brown, Lieutenant Carl, 302, 370
Brown, Captain Charles R., 398
Brown, Lieutenant Commander Ellis M., 91
Brown, George, 251, *note*
Brown, Lieutenant George F., 101
Brown, Lieutenant George P., 253, *note*
Brown, Lieutenant (jg), George P., exploits at Battle of the Philippine Sea, and death, 247-48
Brown, Lieutenant Commander William B., 410, *note*
BROWN, 59, 109, *note*; 141, *note*; 197, *note*; 275, 276
BROWNSON, loss of, 56-57
BRYANT, 297, 316, 357, 364
Buchanan, Commander Alfred E. (RAN), 51, *note*; 357
BUCHANAN, 39, *note*; 65, 66, 67, 70
Bulkeley, Lieutenant John, 23, 25
Bullard, 41, *note*; 111, *note*; 114, *note*
BUNKER HILL, 41, 41, *note*; 43, 59, 109, *note*; 141, 141, *note*; 142, 144, 145, 151, 159, 179, 181, 240, 301, 324, 368
Buracker, Captain William H., 128, 370, 371, 372
Burhans, Captain Arthur D., 115
Burial at sea, P xv, P LXXX
Burk, Ensign Joseph W., 62
Burke, Captain Arleigh ("Thirty-one Knot"), 44, 45, *note*; 45-47, 66, 67, 68, 70-72, 193, 300, 378
Burnett, Captain Henry P., 360
Burns, Lieutenant (jg) John A., 196
BURNS, 109, *note*; 112, 141, *note*; 144, 147, 149, 156, 191, 197, *note*; 275, 331, *note*
Burton, Lieutenant William S., 393
Busbey, Captain Leroy W., Jr., 111, *note*; 324, *note*
BUSH, 169, 172, 173, 314

C. K. BRONSON, 109, *note*; 141, *note*; 410, *note*
CABOT, 109, *note*; 141, 141, *note*; 156, 179, 301, 324, 331, 331, *note*; 369, 373, 375
Cain, Lieutenant Commander James R., Jr., 65
Caldwell, Lieutenant (jg) Harry, 341
Calhoun, Ensign Fred, 61, 62
Calhoun, Captain Walter C., 93, 286
CALIFORNIA, 287-88, 312, 316, 321, 360, P LXVII
CALLAGHAN, 410, *note*
CAMBRIA, 114, *note*; 127, 129
Campaigns of the Pacific War, 67, *note*; 332, *note*
Campbell, Lieutenant Earnest G., 54, 169
Campbell, Commander Grafton B., 301
Campbell, Lieutenant (jg) Robert A.,54
CANBERRA, 197, *note*; 327, 330, 331, 331, *note*
CANBERRA (first, HMAS), 329, *note*
Cape Gloucester, 33, 50, 52, 54, 59, 167, P VI
CAPERTON, 109, *note*; 141, *note*; 331, *note*; 410, *note*

Capping enemy column, 358, 358, *note*; P XLVI, P XLVII
Carlson, Lieutenant Colonel Evans, 84
Carmichael, Commander George K., 410, *note*
Carney, Rear Admiral Robert B., 298, 303, 328, 330, 331, 366, 367, 368, 377, 378, P VI
Carolines, 75-98, 138, 154, 161, 162, 176, 177-87, 193, 222, 229, 255, 275, 289, 296-98, P L
Carpender, Rear Admiral Arthur S., 16, *note*; 20
Carr, Gunner's Mate 3/c Paul Henry, 393-95
Carroll, Lieutenant Commander John B., 264
Carroll, Lieutenant Commander Wells W., 94
Carter, Captain Jesse H., 27, 34, 169
Carver, Aviation Radioman 2/c John L., P LXXVIII
Cassady, Captain John H., 39, *note*; 128, 281
Case, Ensign F. D., 362
CASE, 109, *note*; 324, *note*
CASSIN, 324, *note*
CASSIN YOUNG, 197, *note*; 370
Caswell, Commander Gordon L., 93, 111
Caulfield, Commander Cecil T., 299
CAVALLA, 234-35, 240-41
Cemetery, Marine, on Guam, P XLIII
Chamberlin, Major General Stephen (USA), 167
Chamberlin, Major William C. (USMC), 88
Chambers, Commander Thomas E., 51, *note*
Chamorros, 259-60
CHANDLER, 114, *note*; 128
Charan-Kanoa airstrip, 225, 231, P XXXVI
CHARLES AUSBURNE, 44, 45, 66
CHARRETTE, 59, 109, *note*; 141, *note*; 144, 147, 191, 197, *note*; 275, 331, *note*
Chase, Brigadier General William C. (USA), 172, 173
CHAUNCEY, 41, *note*; 111, *note*; 114, *note*
Cheek, Captain Marion ("Mike"), 367
Chennault, Major General Claire L., 279, 307
CHESTER, 111, *note*; 323, *note*
CHICKASAW, 313
CHIKUMA, 224, *note*; 338, 392, 396, 415, 418
China, 297-82, 306-07
CHITOSE, 223, *note*; 345, 407
CHOYODA, 223, *note*; 345, 407, 410
CHOKAI, 224, *note*; 338, 392, 397, 418, 418, *note*
Christiansen, Lieutenant Frank M., 115
Church service before battle, P LVIII
Citation, Unit, Presidential, 174
Claggett, Lieutenant Commander Bladen D., 147, *note*; 339, 341
Clarey, Commander Bernard A., and his "Crushers," 420
Clark, Captain Guy W., 39, *note*
Clark, Rear Admiral Joseph J. ("Jocko"), 95, 116, 229, 232, 235, 275
CLAXTON, 44, 45, 46, 316, 363, *note*
CLEVELAND, 66
Clothing, soiling of, in the Japanese navy, 278-79
Coast Guard, P VII, P XXVII, P XXXIV, P L
Cochran, Commander Joe B., 56, 170, 202, *note*
Coe, Commander Benjamin, 297
Coffee, Commander Doyle M., 169, 357
COGSWELL, 109, *note*; 141, *note*; 275, 276, 331, *note*; 410, *note*
Cole, Lieutenant (jg) James G., 196
Coleman, Lieutenant Thad T., Jr., P XXII
Collins, Captain J. A. (RAN), 51, *note*
COLORADO, 86, 110, 128, 132, 273
COLUMBIA, 66, 316, 364
Coney, Captain Charles E., 202, 304, 306, 314, 315, 350-51, P XLVIII
Congressional Medal of Honor, 31, 85, 96, 101, 292
Conley, Commander Thomas F., Jr., 81
Connaway, Commander Fred, 99
CONNOR, 59, 109, *note*; 141, *note*; 191, 197, *note*
Conolly, Rear Admiral Richard L., 114, 121, 122, 124, 266, 316, P XLI
CONVERSE, 44-47, 66, 69, 197, *note*
"Convoy College," 420
Conwell, Lieutenant Commander Lester C., 41, *note*
CONY, 316, 363, *note*
CONYNGHAM, 27, 28, 32, 33, 34, 51, 52, 53

INDEX

525

Cook, Lieutenant George C., 99
Cook, Commander Lawrence B., 357, 363
Cooley, Captain Thomas R., 408, *note*
Cooper, Commander Joshua W., 358
Copeland, Lieutenant Commander Robert W., 394
Copeman, Commander Thomas H., 59
CORAL SEA, 93
Corey, Commander Howard G., 34, 357
Corn, Captain William A., 117, 128
CORREGIDOR, 93
Cory, Lieutenant George L., 31
COTTEN, 109, *note*; 141, *note;* 410, *note*
Coward, Captain Jesse, 352, 355, 356
COWELL, 59, 109, *note*; 141, *note*; 197, *note*; 331, *note*
COWPENS, 95, 109, *note*; 141, 141, *note*; 149, 179, 244, 301, 324, 331, *note*
Cox, Commander William R., 355
Craig, Lieutenant Albert E., 31
Craighill, Lieutenant Commander Richard S., 34, 169
CRAVEN, 109, *note*
Crawford, Captain David S., 382
Crawford, Captain John G., 408, *note*
Crenshaw, Lieutenant (jg) James R., Jr., 247
Crissy, Lieutenant William J. E., 362
Cromwell, Captain John P., story of, 99-103
Crowe, Major Jim (USMC), 88
Crutchley, Rear Admiral V. A. C. (RN), 13-16, 19, 19, *note*; 51, 54, 202, 203, 208-11
Cruzen, Captain Richard H., 382, 418
CUMMINGS, 109, *note*; 324, *note*
Curts, Captain Maurice E., 364
Cushing, Jim, 185-87

DACE, 338-44, 369, 420
DAILEY, 351
DALY, 56, 170, 202, *note*; 209, 316, 357
DANCE, 147, *note*
DARTER, 151, 338-44, 369, 420
DASHIELL, 87, 88
Davao, 75, 183, 184, 203, 205, 208, 299
Davis, Rear Admiral Glenn B., 197, *note*
Davison, Rear Admiral Ralph E., 298, 323, 326, 353, *note*; 366, 368, 369, 373, 381, 405
Dean, Captain C. W. (USCG), 127
Dechaineaux, Captain E. V. (RAN), 51, *note*
Decker, Lieutenant Commander Arthur, 141, 143, 159
del Valle, Brigadier General Pedro, P XLI
Demetropolis, Commander George, 64
Denegre, Lieutenant Thomas B., Jr., 242
DENNIS, 388, 389, 393, 398
DENVER, 289, 297, 316, 321, 364
Deutermann, Commander Harold T., 275, 410, *note*
de Zayas, Lieutenant Colonel Hector D. (USMC), P XLIII
Diary of a dead Japanese at Eniwetok, 133-37
DICKERSON, 65
Dickey, Captain Fred C., 413
Dillard, Lieutenant Rowland W., 30
Dillon, Captain Wallace M., 128
Distinguished Service Cross, 172
Divers, P LV, P LVI
Dodge, Lieutenant Commander Harry B., 110
Dodsworth, Lieutenant William, 341
Doe, Brigadier General J. A. (USA), 203
Doi, Commander Yasumi, 37-38
DORTCH, 109, *note*; 141, *note*; 410, *note*
Dow, Captain Leonard ("Ham"), 367
Dowdle, Lieutenant John J., 195-96
Downing, Lieutenant Commander Arthur L., P LXXVIII
Doyle, Captain Austin K., 413
Drake, Captain Waldo, P XXVII
Draper, Lieutenant Commander William F., paintings, P XXXVI, P XLI, P XLII, P XLIX
DRAYTON, 34, 51, *note*; 56, 169
Driscoll, Boatswain's Mate 2/c, Robert, P LXXIX
Dry, Lieutenant Commander Melvin H., 110
Dublon Island, Truk, P XXIV

DuBose, Rear Admiral Laurence T., 111, 191, 275, 276, 299, 327, 330, 331, 409-10, 411, 412
Dugan, Captain Paul F., 129
Duncan, Lieutenant Commander Charles K., 39, *note*; 41, *note*
Duncan, Captain Jack H., 202, 364
DUNLAP, 109, *note*; 324, *note*
DYSON, 44, 45, 47, 66

Earle, Captain Ralph, Jr., 70
Edson, Colonel Merritt A. (USMC), 85, 90
Eller, Lieutenant Commander Donald T., 112
Ellice Islands, 77, 78, 98, 110
Ellis, Commander William, 405, 406
Emirau, 71, 176, 188
Emrick, Commander Paul E., 41
Engaño, Cape, Plates LXXII to LXXV
Engebi, 127, 128, 135, P XXVI, P XXVII
ENGLAND, 199-201
Eniwetok, 110, 112-14, 124, 126-38, 156, 179, 201, 275, 308, P XXVI, P XXVII
Eniwetok Expeditionary Group, 126
Ensey, Lieutenant Lyttleton B., 87
ENTERPRISE, 96, 97 109, *note*; 116, 140, 141, *note*; 152, 153, 156, 179, 227, 229, 237, 324, 353, 374, 405
Escort carriers, 385, P LXIX
Espe, Captain Carl F., 191, 275
Espiritu Santo, 42, 59, 287
ESSEX, 41, 41, *note*; 109, *note*; 141, 141, *note*; 146, 150, 152, 159, 160, 198, 244, 300, 301, 324, 377, 405, 406, P LXXIII
Ethics of Battle, Japanese, 262
Evans, Captain Ernest E., 388, 396
EVERSOLE, loss of, 321
Ewen, Captain Edward C., 369
Ewing, Ensign Rumsey, 60, 61
Execution of prisoners by Japanese, on Guam, P XLIV
Ezaki, Colonel Yoshio, 174-75

Fahle, Colonel Robert S., 324, *note*
FANNING, 109, *note*; 324, *note*
FANSHAW BAY, 384, 385, 392, 395, 396, 398
FARENHOLT, 39, *note*; 65, 66, 67, 70
Farley, Lieutenant Commander Edward T., 60, 62, 204
Farmer, Lieutenant Noyes D., Jr., 273
Farncomb, Captain H. B. (RAN), 51, *note*
Farrell, Ensign C. C., 196
Fechteler, Rear Admiral William M., 169, 171, 172, 190, 204, 205, 207, 213, 213, *note*; 214, 316
Fels, Lieutenant Commander John R., 127
Fernald, Captain James M., 122
Fiala, Captain Reid P., 228, 355
Fielder, Ensign Wendell Max, 101
Fife, Captain James, 22
Finschhafen, 26, 31, 32-37, 48, 50, 60, 192, 204
Fire control from shore, 120
Fitch, Vice Admiral A. W., P VI
Fitts, Commander William W., 228
Fitzgerald, Commander Philip H., 28
Flaherty, RT 1/c J. M., 361
Flatley, Commander James, 409
Fleck, Commander Thomas M., 207
FLETCHER, 111, 209, 210
FLUSSER, 28, 34, 51, *note*; 52, 54, 169
Flynn, Captain Cornelius W., 13
Foley, Lieutenant Commander Francis J., 39, *note*; 65
Foley, Commander Robert J., 65, *note*; 147, *note*
Foran, Ensign James F., 62
Foristel, Lieutenant (jg) James W., 207
Formosa, 307, 312, 325-32, 336, 345, 346, 353, 354, 417
Forrestal, Secretary James, 122-24, P XVII
Fort, Rear Admiral George H., 293
Fowler, Captain Joseph W., 89
FRANKLIN, 298, 324, 353, *note*; 374, 408
FRANKS, 93, 399, *note*
Frendberg, Lieutenant (jg) A. L., P XVI

INDEX

Freund, Lieutenant Commander Bernard W., 41, *note*
FUJINAMI, 40, 418, 418, *note*
Fukudome, Vice Admiral, 153, 183, 184-87, 325, 326, 336, 353, 374, 377, 402
FULLAM, 65, 70, 289-90
Fuller, Major General Horace, 205
Fuller, Colonel Lewis B. (USMC), 292, P LIV
"Fury in the Pacific" (film), P LII, P LIII
FUSO, 353, 357-60

Galantin, Commander Ignatius J., 420
Gallery, Commander Philip D., 209
GAMBIER BAY, 392-93, 395, 396, P LXIX, P LXX
Gano, Commander Roy A., 44, *note*
Gardner, Captain Mathias B., 116, 153
Gasmata, 33, 50, 56
GATLING, 109, *note*; 141, *note*; 371
GATO, 65, *note*; 147, *note*
Geiger, Major General Roy M., 266, 267, P XLI
Gemmell, ARM 2/c H. B., 195
Gendron, AMM 2/c, 195
Gerner, Lieutenant (jg) William L., 41
Giffen, Rear Admiral Robert C., 145
Gift, Lieutenant Donald P. ("Rip"), P XXXIX
Gilberts, 39, 75-98, 108, 162, 229, P X, P XIII
Gill, Aubrey J., 196
Ginder, Rear Admiral Samuel P., 109, *note*; 126, 128
Gingrich, Captain John E., 123
Glassford, Rear Admiral William A., 12
Glover, Captain Cato D., Jr., 229, 374
Glover, Rear Admiral R. O., 309
Godek, Lieutenant Matt, 341
Going into battle, 269-70
Good, Lieutenant Roman F., 87
Gould, Commander Charles J., 39, *note*
Gould, Commander Frank G., 41, *note*
Gramer, Lieutenant H. C., 330, *note*
Granat, Captain William, 86, 128, 230, 273
Grantham, Commander Elonzo B., Jr., 357-58
GRAYSON, 39, *note*; 331, *note*
Green, Lieutenant Maurice F., 391
Green, Commander Thomas C., 30
"Green Dragons," P II
Green Island, 64, 65, *note*; 188, P VI
Greenacre, Commander Alvord J., 175
Greenup, Commander Francis A., 353
Greytak, Commander John J., 41, *note*
GRIDLEY, 93, 109, *note*; 264
Griggs, Commander Gale E., 209
Griner, Major General George W., Jr., 258
Gritta, Captain Paul B. (USA), 107
Gruebel, R. W., 196
Guadalcanal, 6, 16, 18, 64, 75, 237, 255, 379
Guam, 126, 156, 159, 160, 162, 209, 220, 225, 228, 264-70, 288, 290, 296, Plates XLI to XLV
GUEST, 65, 70
Gwynne, Lieutenant Frederick W., 95-96

Habecker, Commander Frederic S., 320, 357
HAGGARD, 120, 131, 399, *note*
Haggart, Captain Robert S., 122, 128
Hagie, Ensign Bradford, 238
HAGURO, 224, *note*; 338, 392, 395, 397, 399, *note*; 417
HAILEY, 131, 132, 399, *note*
Hains, Commander Hamilton, 199
Hale, Lieutenant Commander Fletcher, 363, *note*
HALFORD, 70, 316, 357, 364
Hall, Commander Finley E., 95
Hall, Captain Grover B. H., 96
Halmaheras (Moluccas), 207, 211, 215, 221, 285, 288, 289, P XLVIII
Halsey, Admiral William F., Jr., 21, 38-39, 40, 48, 67, 71, 76, 199-200, 285, 296-98, 302-04, 306, 309, 311, 317, 318, 321, 322-32, 347, 348, 354, 366-401
  Dirty Trick Department, 366-67
  message to fleet, 416
Halsey, Lieutenant (jg) William F., III, 39
Hamachek, Lieutenant (jg) Russell E., 26

Hamberger, Commander De Witt C. E., 44, *note*
Hammill, Lieutenant Hunt, 361
HANCOCK, 324, 413
Hanks, Lieutenant (jg) Ralph, 95
Hannekin, Colonel Herman H. (USMC), 292
Hansen, Commander Henry O., 39, *note*
Hansen, Lieutenant Commander Samuel, 393
Hanson, Rear Admiral Edward W., 197, *note*
Happel, Pfc Junior F. (USCG), P LX
Hara, Vice Admiral, 155, 197
Harranek, J., 196
Hardy, Commander Robert J., 357
Harrill, Rear Admiral William K., 229, 232, 235
Harris, Commander David A., 120
Harris, Lieutenant Commander Francis, 50
Harris, Colonel Harold D. (USMC), 292
Harrison, Radioman 2/c William Henry, 207
Hart, Colonel Franklin A., 122
Hartley, Captain Henry, 323, *note*
HARUNA, 222, 223, *note*; 248, 338, 375, 387
HARUSAME, 154, *note*; 208, 209
Haskins, Commander Enrique D., 369
Hathaway, Commander Amos T., 389, 396
Hauck, Lieutenant Commander Philip F., 65
Hawkins, Lieutenant William D., 87-88
HAYATAKA-class, 247, P XLVIII
Hayler, Rear Admiral Robert W., 65, 289, 297, 364
HEALY, 109, *note*; 141, *note*; 410, *note*
Hean, Commander James H., 242
HEERMAN, 128, 388-90, 396, 398
Heffernan, Captain John B., 360
Hellcats, P XXII
Henderson, Captain George R., 39, *note*
HENLEY, and loss of, 13, 33-36
HENRY T. ALLEN (*ex* PRESIDENT JEFFERSON), 20
Henshaw, Lieutenant Marvin J. (USA), 171, 172
Hering, Lieutenant Commander Walter H., 410, *note*
Herrmann, Captain Ernest E., 329
Herron, Commander Edwin W., 56
Hertel, WT 3/c W. G., 361
HEYWOOD L. EDWARDS, 293-94, 316, 358
Hickman, Chief Radioman Reuben F., 150, P XXIV
HICKOX, 109, *note*; 141, *note*
Higgins, Ensign Thomas P., 91
High, Commander Paul L., 297, 357
Hill, Rear Admiral Harry H., 79, 81, 85, 86, 114, 114, *note*; 115, 126-29, 133, 196, 230, 266
Hill, ARM 2/c R. E., 196
HIYO, 223, *note*; 248, 253, *note*
HOEL, and loss of, 93, 130, 388-91, 395, 398
Hoerner, Captain Herbert ("Jack"), 367
Hoffman, Captain Harry D., 66
Holden, Captain Carl F., 140, *note*; 145, 408, *note*
Hollandia, 16, 28, 33, 177, 179, 188-92, 304, 306, 308, 309, 312, 313, P XXX, P XXXI
Holmes, Chief Commissary Steward L. M., 361
Holt, Lieutenant Commander Philip C., 207
HONOLULU, 65, 66, 292, 316, 320-21, P LVIII
HOOVER, Rear Admiral John H., 85, 108, 111, 119
HORNET, 179, 181, 229, 300, 301, 303, 324, 413
Hoskins, Captain John M., 372, 372, *note*
Hough, Major Frank O. (USMCR), *The Island War*, 259, 293, 322, *note*
HOUSTON (first; lost), 329, *note*
HOUSTON (second), 327, 329, 330, 330-31, *note*; 331
Howitt, Lieutenant E. M. (RANVR), 60
Hubbard, Commander Miles H., 363, *note*
Hudson, Lieutenant Leonard H., 355
Hudson, Captain Lester J., 39, *note*
HUDSON, 65, 70
HUGHES, 93, 111
Humboldt Bay, 190, 191, 203, 205, 209, 308
HUMPHREYS, 50, 51, 169
Hundt, Captain Lester T., 59, 158
HUNT, 109, *note*; 141, *note*
Hunter, Captain Lunsford L., 84, 117
Hurff, Captain Jack E., 410
Hurst, Major Hunter (USMC), 292, P LII
Hurt, Captain Samuel H., 111, 129, 359, 364
Hustvedt, Rear Admiral Olaf M., 144, 197, *note*

INDEX

Hutchins, Seaman 1/c Johnnie David, 30–31
Hutchins, Commander Thomas B. III, 202, *note*
HUTCHINS, 56, 170, 202, *note*; 209, 316, 357
HYUGA, 346, 402, 404, 411, 420

Icenhower, Commander Joseph B., 420, 421
IDAHO, 110
ILLUSTRIOUS (HMS), 281, 282, P XLVI
INDEPENDENCE, 41, 41, *note*; 89, 301, 324, 369, 374, 375, 381, 404, 405
INDIANA, 109, *note*; 197, *note*; 240
INDIANAPOLIS, 79, 128, 131, 132, 224, 227, 228, 232, 233
Indians, Sioux, use at the Admiralties, 176
Ingersoll, Captain Stuart H., 237
INGERSOLL, 109, *note*; 141, *note*; 275, 276, 331, *note*; 410, *note*
Inglis, Captain Thomas B., 228, 331, 371–73
Inland Sea, 330, *note*; 345
INTREPID, 109, *note*; 141, 141, *note*; 143, 146, 148, 151–53, 156, 157, 301, 324, 369, 373, 375, 405
IOWA, 109, *note*; 141, *note*; 144, 145, 147, 148, 197, *note*; 408, *note*; 414
Irwin, Commander William D., 83
ISE, 346, 404, 411, 420, P LXXII, P LXXIV, P LXXV
Isley, Lieutenant Commander Robert H., Jr., 95, 227
Island War, The, by Major Frank O. Hough (USMCR), 259, 293, 322, *note*
ISUZU, 91, 98, 346, 407
Iwo Jima, 223, 298
IZARD, 109, *note*; 141, *note*; 144, 147, 191, 197, *note*; 275, 276

Jaluit, 108, 156, P XXIII
James, Lieutenant Richard E., 273
Jamison, Captain John W., 21
Jarman, Major General Sanford (USA), 258
Jarrell, Commander Albert E., 209
JEAN NICOLET, barbarity to crew by Japanese, 280–81
Jennings, Commander Carter B., 355
Jennings, Captain Ralph E., 229
Jerome, Colonel Clayton C. (USMC), 322, *note*
Jeter, Captain Thomas P., 240
"Jimas," 229, 233
JOHN C. BUTLER, 388, 393
Johnson, Captain Douglas P., 384
Johnson, Captain Einar R., 128, 228
Johnson, Captain Felix, P XXXI
Johnson, Commander Francis J., 410, *note*
Johnson, Captain Rudolph L., 41, *note*
Johnson, Captain William D., Jr., 128, 400
JOHNSTON, 132, 388, 390, 395, 396–98
Jones, Captain Carl H., 86
Jones, Commander Carlton B., 415
Jones, Lieutenant Earl, 341
Jones, Lieutenant (jg) Ed, 341
Jones, Captain James L. (USMC), 83, 115, 271
Jones, John Paul, 60, 62
Jones, Colonel Louis R., 122
Joy, Rear Admiral Charles T., 267, 331, *note*
Just, Lieutenant Commander Fred W., 199

Kaitner, Commander William E., 59
KALININ BAY, 392, 395, 398, 401, P LXIX
Kamikazes (suicide fliers), 206, 252, 319–21, 352, 401, P LXXVI
Kane, Captain Joseph L., 400
Kanze, Lieutenant (jg) Robert F., 195–96
Karpe, Commander Eugene S., 59
Kato, Captain Kenkichi, 376
KATORI, 145, 146, 147, 154, *note*
Kavieng, 36, 38, 58, 59, 64, 67–72, 176
Keefe, Lieutenant (jg) Joseph F., 55
Keliher, Captain Thomas J., Jr., 240
Kelley, Lieutenant Gerard W. (USA), 84
Kelly, Lieutenant Robert B., 351
Kelly, Commander William D., 65, 289
Kenney, Lieutenant General George C., 189, 204, 308
Kenny, Commander William T., 128

Kernan, Gunner A. B., 97
Ketcham, Captain Dixwell, 128
Ketchum, Lieutenant Commander Gerald L., 27
Kibbe, Commander Richard L., 408
KIDD, 41, *note*; 111, *note*; 114, *note*
KILLEN, 316, 357
Kimmins, Commander Anthony (RN), 122
King, Admiral Ernest J., 153, 220, 306, 369, P XXXVII
Kinkaid, Vice Admiral Thomas C., 19, *note*; 50, *note*; 76, 167, 172, 188, 189, 204, 209, 308, 311–14, 321, 347, 350, 351, 365, 369, 381, 382, 391, 405, 407, 413, 414, 418, 421–22
Kintberger, Commander Leon, 391
KINU, 207, 208
KITKUN BAY, 387, 392, 400, P LXX, P LXXI
Klahn, Lieutenant (jg) Dale C., 281, P XLVII
KNAPP, 109, *note*; 141, *note*; 275, 276, 331, *note*; 410, *note*
Knight, Commander A. V. (RANR), 50
Koenig, Lieutenant Commander Joseph W., 93
Koga, Admiral Mineichi, 7, 8, 110, 126, 139, 154, 177–87, 191, 220, 325, 374
Kolcsynski, Seaman 1/c, 281
KONGO, 223, *note*; 338, 375, 387, 388, 390, P XXXVIII
Koreans, 260, P XIII
Kossler, Commander Herman J., 234–35, 240–41
Krueger, Lieutenant General Walter, 59, 167, 188, 192, 204, 308, 319
KUMANO, 224, *note*; 338, 391, 397, 415, 415, *note*; 418
Kurita, Admiral Keno, 37, 38, 40, 44, 154, 177–80, 223, 223, *note*; 335–38, 344–45, 349, 354, 369, 373–77, 381, 384, 387, 388, 395, 398, 400, 402, 405, 413–24
Kuzume, Colonel, 206, 212
Kwajalein, 77, 78, 91, 98, 104, 106–25, 139, 156, Plates XVII to XX
KYOSHIMO, 375, P LXV

Lae, and Lae-Salamaua area, 12, 13, 25–32, 37, 204, Plates III to V
"LAKACOOKIE," 354–55
Lake, Lieutenant Commander Richard C., 341, *note*
LAMSON, 28, 34, 51, 51, *note*; 52, 56, 57
Laney, Lieutenant (jg) Willis G., 148
LANG, 109, *note*; 141, *note*
LANGLEY, 109, *note*; 128, 179, 194, 244, 301, 324, 377, 411
Laning, Commander Caleb B., 170, 202, *note*; 357
LANSDOWNE, 39, *note*; 65–67
LARDNER, 39, *note*; 65–67
Leahy, Admiral William D., 306, P I
Leary, Vice Admiral Herbert F., 12, 16, *note*
Lee, Rear Admiral Willis A., Jr., ("Ching"), 98, 197, 197, *note*; 234, 235, 240, 332, 379–80, 405, 408, 408, *note*
Lehrbas, Colonel Lloyd, P XXXI
Lenahan, ARM 2/c J. J., 196
LEUTZE, 316, 358
Lewis, Soundman George A., 91
Lewis, Lieutenant John R., 54
LEWIS HANCOCK, 109, *note*; 141, *note*; 414
LEXINGTON, 95, 96, 98, 179, 181, 194, 229, 233, 238, 250, 300, 301, 324, 368, 369, 377, 404, 408, 409, 410, P XVI
Leyte, and Battle for Gulf of Leyte, 19, *note*; 27, 102, 252, 299, 303–04, 306, 308, 309–11, 312, 314, 315, 316–21, 322–32, 347–423, Plates LVII to LXII, P LXV, P LXXIV, P LXXVII, P LXXX
Lidstone, Commander Nicholas A., 93
Lindsay, Lieutenant William N., Jr., 295
LISCOME BAY, and loss of, 92–94, 117
Liste, Lieutenant Rudolph F., 321
Litch, Captain Ernest W., 229, 377
"Little Beavers," 44, *note*; 68, P VII
Lobit, Lieutenant Colonel W. E. (USA), 173
Lockwood, Vice Admiral, 200, 420
Logie, Colonel Marc J. (USA), 118
LONG, 173, 174
Loomis, Commander Sam C., Jr., 273–75

INDEX

Los Negros, 166, 167, 169, 170, 174, P xxviii
Loud, Commander Wayne R., 224, 309
LOUISVILLE, 111, 128, 132, 197, *note*; 316, 321, 350, 358, 359, 364
Lucas, Sergeant Jim (USMC), 88
Luedemann, Lieutenant (jg) Carl F., 247
Lynch, Seabee R. A., P xxviii
Lynch, Lieutenant Commander Richard B., 82
Lynch, Ensign Robert F., 22-23
Lyon, Lieutenant Bethuel B. V., Jr., 362
Lyttle, Captain George, 287

MacArthur, General Douglas, 8, 12, 13, 18, 23, 48, 67, 71, 76, 166-72, 177, 179, 181, 183, 186, 188, 285, 286, 288, 303, 304, 305, 306, 309, 311-15, 318, 350-51 P I, P xxxi, P xlviii, P lix
"MacArthur's Navy," 20, 308
MacDonald, Lieutenant P. M., 98
MACDONOUGH, 132, 194, 227
Mahaffey, Lieutenant John K., Jr., 295
MAHAN, 27, 28, 34, 51, *note*; 52, 54, 169, 171
Maher, Commander Joseph B., 56-57
MAIKAZE, 147, 154, *note*
Majuro, 109, 114, 114, *note*; 115, 126, 140, 141, 191, 193, 198, 222-24, 271, P xxvi
Makin, 77, 79, 84, 91, 93, 104, 108, 117, P xiii
Malcolm, Lieutenant (jg) Ian D., 355
Maloelap, 91, 108, 111
Manila Bay, attack on, 300-03
Manus, 166, 175, 200, 202, 308, 368
Marcus Island, 198, P III
Marek, Pfc Harry J. (USMC), 83
Marianas, 78, 124, 126, 154, 156-62, 166, 177, 183, 198, 201, 211, 219-82, 287, 333, P xxxiii, P xlv
"Marianas Turkey Shoot," P xxxvii, P xlviii
Marines, 18, 54, 55, 57-58, 59, 71, 289
at Angaur, P L, P liv; Betio airstrip, P x, P xi, P xii; Cape Gloucester, 54-55, P vi; Empress Augusta Bay, 38-40; Engebi, P xxvii; Eniwetok, P xxvii; Guadalcanal, 55; Guam, P xlii, P xliii; Kwajalein, P xviii, P xix; Namur, P xvii; Peleliu, Plates li to liv; Saipan, 255, P xxxiv, P xxxv: Tarawa, P xiii, P xiv, P xv; Tinian, P xl; Truk, P xxiii
dive bombers, 322, *note*
Negro unit at Peleliu, 293
Samoan, P vii
Marix, Lieutenant Commander George E., 321
Marshall, General George C., 306
Marshalls, 59, 75-98, 106, 108, 141, 156, 162, 222, 229, 255, P xvii, P xviii, P xxvi
Martin, Captain Charles F., 290, 360
Martin, Brigadier General Clarence, 62
Martin, Captain Harold M., 374
Martin, Captain William I., 153, 225-27
Martineau, Lieutenant Commander David L., 121
MARYLAND, 86, 110, 291, 312, 316, 360, P lxvii
Mass aboard a transport, P x
MASSACHUSETTS, 109, *note*; 141, *note*; 150, 197, *note*; 408, *note*
Masters, Chief Motor Machinist's Mate J. J., Jr., 25
Mathier, Lieutenant (Dr.) Akin, 106
Matsuura, Commander Goro, 78, 91
Maurer, Commander John H., 420
MAURY, 93, 109, *note*
MAYA, 40, 102, 224, *note*; 338, 342
Mayer, Captain Andrew D., 228
McCain, Vice Admiral John S., 288, 301, 323, 326, 331, 366, 368, 369, 407, 413, 414, 415
MCCALL, 109, *note*; 264
McCampbell, Commander David, 370, 405, 406, 407, 409
McCann, Captain Allan R., 408, *note*
McClintock, Commander David H., 339-41, 343-44
McCollum, Captain Arthur H., 382
McConnell, Captain Robert P., 95
MCCORD, 128, 132
McCornock, Commander Samuel A., 169
McCoy, Pfc William A. (USMC), P xlv
McCrea, Captain John L., 145
MCDERMUT, 355, 356

McGinnis, Commander Robert D., 111
McGurl, Captain Daniel Michael, 111, 191, 408, *note*
McIlhenny, Commander Harry H., 28, 35
McKenna, Captain Francis J., 400
McKinney, Commander Eugene B., 134, *note*
McLaren, Commander Earle K., 65
McLean, Captain Ephraim R., 127
McLean, Commander John B., 87, 88
McManes, Captain Kenmore M., 209, 210, 357
McNeil, Lieutenant (jg) (Dr.) John J., 362
McWhinnie, Lieutenant Commander Charles J., 65
MEADE, 91
Meadors, Lieutenant William W., 390
Mecleary, Captain Frank, 287
Meola, Commander Vincent J., 324, *note*
Merchant ships, Japanese, lost at Truk, 154, *note*
Merrill, Rear Admiral Aaron S., 38-39, 66
MIAMI, 408, *note*; 414
Michael, Captain Stanley J., 111, *note*; 331, 369
Midway, Battle of, 6, 252
Mille, 91, 95, 108, 115
Miller, Captain Charles C., 410
Miller, Commander Daniel B., 371
Miller, Lieutenant Commander Dwight L., 415
Miller, Lieutenant Commander Lewis R., 111
Miller, Commander Norman H. ("Bus"), P lv
Miller, 109, *note*; 197, *note*; 331, *note*
Milley, Chief Quartermaster John P., 396
Milne Bay, 13, 16, 21, 27, 33, 51, 214
MILWAUKEE, 127
Mindanao, 285, 299, 303, 306, 318, 322, 347
Minelaying, aerial, 181
Minesweepers, 294-96
MINNEAPOLIS, 141, *note*; 144, 145, 197, *note*; 240, 316, 364
MISSISSIPPI, 84, 93, 110, 117, 118, 119, 139, 312, 316, 360, P lxvii
MISSOURI, "chow line," P viii
Mitchell, Major General Ralph J. (USMC), 57
Mitscher, Admiral Marc A., 67, 70, 72, 109, 110, 126, 140, 144, 156, 157, 161, 177, 178, 180, 188, 191-94, 206, 222, 224, 225, 228, 233-37, 242, 245, 249-50, 255, 266, 273, 275, 285, 298-300, 302, 303, 368, 369, 377, 378, 379, 381, 404, 405, 406, 408, 409, P xxxviii
message of commendation by the Admiral, 161-62
MOBILE, 111, 140, *note*; 157, 161, 191, 275, 276, 327, 331, *note*; 410, 411
MOGAMI, 40, 224, *note*; 353, 356, 357, 358, 363, 364, 364, *note*; P lxv
Molumphy, Commander George G., 110
Momote airdrome, 169-72
MONSSEN, 355, 356
MONTEREY, 59, 109, *note*; 141, 141, *note*; 158, 179, 237, 324, 327
Montgomery, Rear Admiral Alfred E., 40, 89, 98, 109, *note*; 152, 158, 198, 235
Moody, Rear Admiral Clement (RN), 281
Moore, Commander Allen W., 363, *note*
Moore, Lieutenant Commander Ray, 353
Moore, Captain W. E., P xli
Mora, Coxswain F. P., 57
Morgan, Commander Charles C., 65, 309
Morotai, 286, 288-89, 303, 304, 308, P xlviii
Morris, Commander Robert L., 59
MORRIS, 93, 111
Morrisey, Lieutenant (jg) Thomas J., 55
MORRISON, 299, 371
Morton, Commander Robert C., 170, 202, *note*; 357
Motes, Lieutenant Commander Jesse, 93
Motion picture, "Fury in the Pacific," P lii, P liii
Moulton, Captain Horace ("Doug"), 367, 377, 378
MOUNT OLYMPUS, 391
Mountbatten, Admiral Lord Louis, 282, P xlvii
Moyers, Lieutenant H. H. ("Hank"), 246
Mudge, Major General Verne D. (USA) 322, *note*
Mueller, Major General Paul J. (USA), 294
MUGFORD, 34, 51, *note*; 56, 57
Mullaney, Commander Baron J., 202, 209
MULLANY, 173, 202, 209
Mullinix, Captain Allen P., 323, *note*

INDEX

Mullinix, Admiral Henry W., 92
Mumma, Commander Morton C., 25
Munholland, Commander John, 91
Munroe, Lieutenant Commander Frank A., Jr., 24
Munroe, Lieutenant Commander J. S., 213, note
MUNSEE, 330, note; 331, note
Murphy, Captain Vincent R., 408, note
MUSASHI, 154, 177, 180, 211, 223, note; 336, 338, 373-76, P LXV
MYOKO, 224, note; 338, 373, 375
Myhre, Commander Floyd B. T., 39, note; 65

NAGANAMI, 42, 338
Nagano, Fleet Admiral Osami, 7, 70, 276-77
NAGATO, 223, note; 338, 375, 387, 389, 399
Nagumo, Vice Admiral Chuichi, 221, note; 261-62
Nakajima, Commander Chitataka, 178, 179, 181
Namur, 109, 114, 121, 122, 123, 124, 125, P XVII
Napton, Captain John R., Jr., (USMC), P VII
NASHVILLE, 54, 169, 170, 174, 175, 202, 208, 304, 306, 312, 313, 314-18, 350-51, P XXXI, P XLVIII
NASSAU, 111, note; 114, note
NATOMA BAY, 111, note; 114, note
Naval Academy mural, P XLI
Navy Construction Battalion ("Seabees"), 173-74, 176
Neale, Commander Edgar T., 24
Negro Marines at Peleliu, 293, P LIII
Nelson, Lieutenant Charles W., 247
Nelson, Lieutenant George I., 30, 207
Nelson, Lieutenant Robert S., 196
Neutralization Group and Units, 111, note
New Britain, 13, 35, 48-53, 76, 167
New Guinea, 9-17, 20, 22, 24, 27, 28-36, 48, 76, 104, 126, 162, 166, 167, 176, 177, 183, 188, 190, 201, 202-15, 222, 228, 285, 286, P II, P IV, P XXX, P XXXII
New Ireland, 13, 64, 68, 69, 116, 167
NEW JERSEY, 109, note; 140, 140, note; 144-47, 156, 197, note; 297, 323, 366, 368, 369, 407, 408, note; 414
NEW MEXICO, 84, 93, 94, 110, 267
NEW ORLEANS, 141, note; 197, note; 410
Newcomb, Lieutenant H., P V
NEWCOMB, 316, 357, 360, 362
Newell, Lieutenant Robert T., Jr., 106
Newsome, Lieutenant Robert F., 389
Nicholas, Lieutenant Lloyd, 153
Nichols, Captain Charles A. Godfrey (RAN), 364
Nicoll, Lieutenant Commander Delancey, 94
Nimitz, Admiral Chester W., 40, 76, 97, 98, 108, 115, 124, 126, 128, 131, 160, 176, 183, 188, 198, 201, 220, 221, 234, 266, 269, 277, 285, 286, 302-04, 306, 322, 324-25, 333, 369, 408, P I, P XVI, P XXXVII
Nisewander, Commander Terrell A., 357, 361
Nishimura, Admiral Shoji, 336, 337, 354-58, 363, 364, 376, 414, 419
Nishino, Commander, 356, 357, 358, 363
Noble, Captain Albert G., 54
NORTH CAROLINA, 109, note; 141, note; 196, 197, note
NOSHIRO, 40, 91, 224, note; 338, 387, 415
NOWAKE, 154, note; 415, 418

OAKLAND, 109, note; 140, note; 275
O'Connor, Lieutenant Commander Desmond K., 106
Oftsie, Captain Ralph A., 41, note; 146, 276
O'Hare, Lieutenant Commander Edward H. ("Butch"), 96, 97, 238, 239
Ohmae, Captain Toshikazu, 404, 420
Oil, lack of, Japanese, 335
O'Kane, Lieutenant Commander Richard H., 147, note; 195, P XXV
Okinawa, 244, 312, 323-25, 368, 421
Oldendorf, Rear Admiral Jesse B., 197, 197, note; 228, 289, 290, 309, 312, 313, 347, 350, 352, 354, 356, 358, 358, note; 359, 360, 363, 364, 364, note; 391, 407, 424
Olsen, Captain S. A. (USCG), 129
Olson, Lieutenant Louis C., 313

O'Mara, Kid, 409
Omark, Lieutenant (jg) Warren R., 247-48
O'Neill, Soundman J. C., Jr., 361
Onishi, Admiral, 352, 374
Operation Catchpole, P XXVI
Operation Cherry Tree, P XXXIII
Operation Flintlock, 59, 104-25, P XVII
Operation Galvanic, 79, 97, 98, P XIII
Operation KON, 222
Operation SHO, Number One, 333, 336, 337, 416-17
Operation TO, 198
ORACLE, 114, note; 127
Osler, Lieutenant Commander Paul G., 39, note; 41, note
Osmena, Sergio, P LIX
O'Sullivan, Colonel Curtis D. (USA), 118
OVERTON, 106, 107
OWEN, 109, note; 141, note; 197, note; 415
Owens, Commander Seymour, 273
OYODO, 346, 408, 411
Ozawa, Vice Admiral Jisaburo, 37, 40, 139, 177, 178, 183, 222, 223, 223, note; 236-37, 240, 241, 244-54, 335, 336, 337, 345, 347, 374, 376, 402-12, 416, 419, 420

PT's, 22, 23-25, 31-32, 59-62, 214-15, P II, P IX
Pace, Lieutenant Commander John E., 393
Painting of Charan-Kanoa, P XXXVI
Paintings by Draper, P XLI, P XLII, P XLIX
Palaus, 68, 69, 126, 154, 177-87, 191, 200-01, 203, 205, 211, 222, 275, 287, 285, 288, 290, 291-94, 308, 311, 323, 325, 329, P XLIX, P L, P LII, P LIII, P LIV
Parker, Commander Charles W., 59
Parker, MM 1/c, 362
Parker, Captain Wayne A., 87
Parry Island, 127, 128, 129, 132, 133
Paseler, Ensign Bill, 340
Patrick, Brigadier General Edwin D. (USA), 213
Patten, Captain Stanley F., 116
Peleliu, 286, 288, 289, 291-94, 329, Plates XLIX, to LIV
Pendleton, Lieutenant Commander Walton B., 199
PENNSYLVANIA, 110, 117, 128, 129, 132, 290, 316 321, 360, P LXVII
PENSACOLA, 111, note; 323, note
PERKINS, 27, 28, 32
Perkins, Commander William B., 147, note
Perry, Captain John, 247, 374
Perry, Commodore Matthew C., 323
PERRY, loss of, 294-95
Petersen, Captain Wallis F., 70
Peterson, Lieutenant William E., 32
PETROF BAY, 400
Petross, Commander Lynn C., 59
PHELPS, 121, 127
Philippine Sea, Battle of, 244-54, P XXXIX
Philippines, 12, 20, 183, 184, 207, 285, 286, 299-305, 307, P LXXIX
Phillips, Lieutenant Commander John L., Jr., 96, 97
Phillips, Commander Richard H., 51, note; 356
PHOENIX, 54, 169, 170, 174, 175, 202, 209, 316, 364
Pie-eating contest, P IX
Pierce, Lieutenant Herbert R., Jr., 87
Pingley, Lieutenant Commander John F., 330, note
Platz, Gunner George H., 247-48, and note
Plunkett, Pfc Ralph L. (USMC), P XLV
Polar Circuit, 200-01
Ponape, 110, 126, 156, 193, 197, P XXIX
PORTLAND, 114, note; 115, 128, 131, 132, 197, note; 316, 364
Powell, Lieutenant Commander William T., Jr., 128
Powers, Vice Admiral Sir Arthur J. (RN), 281
Pownall, Rear Admiral Charles A., 95, 98
Pratt, Lieutenant Richard R., 65
Prayer before battle, P LVIII
PREBLE, 111, note; 295
PRESIDENT JEFFERSON. See HENRY T. ALLEN
Presidential Unit Citation, 174
Price, Major General C. F. B (USMC), P VII
Price, Gunnery Officer Walter, 340-41

INDEX

Price, Commander Walter H., 299, 371
PRICHETT, 197, note; 299, 326
Pride, Captain Alfred M., 116
PRINCETON, 39, 40, 41, note; 42, 109, note; 128, 179, 301, 324, 353, 370-73, 377, P LXII, P LXIII, P LXIV
PRINCETON (new), 372, note
PRINGLE, 64, 70
Prisoners, execution by Japanese, P XLIV
Pullen, Lieutenant Weston C., 354

Rabaul, 13, 16, 25-28, 33, 35, 36, 37-47, 48, 56, 64, 66, 67, 69-72, 79, 91, 176, 335, P III, P V
Radar, 28, 32, 43, 45, 46, 54, 65, 68, 89, 95, 96, 98, 101, 106, 107, 146, 151-52, 153, 157, 194, 209, 210, 234, 242, 242, note; 253, 276, 300, 315, 339, 357, 360
Radford, Admiral Arthur W., 96
Radio Tokyo, 329
Raffman, Lieutenant (jg) Relly I., 149
Ragsdale, Admiral Van H., 128
Ramey, Commander John W., 194, 227
Rand, Lieutenant (jg) Arthur G., Jr., 242
Rangers, United States, 333
Ray, Captain Herbert J., 360
RAYMOND, 388, 393
Recovery units and teams, 145, 149-51, 194-96, 273-75
Redfield, Captain Herman J., 360
Reeves, Rear Admiral John W., Jr., 109, note; 140, note; 141, 156, 182, 229, 235, 297
Refueling at sea, P XXVIII
REID, 28, 34, 35, 36, 51, 51, note; 52, 169, 171, 205
Reid, Lieutenant Sam, 341
REMEY, 228, 355, 356
RENO, 371, 372
Reynolds, Commander Luther K., 44, note
RICHARD P. LEARY, 316, 320, 357, 360
Richardson, Commander Alvin F., 371
Richardson, Major Iliff D., 185-87, 351
Rickets, Motor Machinist's Mate 2/c Edward F., 100, 103
Rickey, Seaman 2/c Nathaniel, 35
RIGEL, 21, 214
Ridgway, Lieutenant Augustin K., 29
Riera, Commander R. Emmet, 353
Riggs, Captain Ralph S., 240, 408, note
Riker, Commander Monro M., 111
RINGGOLD, 79, 81, 82, 85, 87, 88
Risser, Lieutenant Commander Robert D., 232
Rittenhouse, Commander Ellis Brooks, 93, 111
Roach, Commander John P., 420
Robbins, Commander Berton A., Jr., 358
Roberts, Captain John S., 202, 364
Roberts, Captain Ralph H., 65
ROBINSON, 293, 316, 357, 364
Roby, Commander John J., 41, note
Roche, Lieutenant Albert I., 54
Roi, 91, 98, 109, 112, 114, 121, 122, 125
Rolf, Lieutenant (jg) Robert W., 29
Roosevelt, Franklin Delano, at Pacific conference, 286, P I
Roosevelt, Mrs. Franklin Delano, P VII
ROSS, 297, 313, 316
Rourke, John Paul, 101
"Rover Boys," 121
Rowe, Lieutenant Commander (Dr.) John B., 94
Royal, Rear Admiral Forrest B., 316
Ruddock, Rear Admiral Theodore D., Jr., 150, 273, 290, 359
Ruff, Commander Lawrence E., 232
Rummel, Lieutenant William K., 118
Rupertus, Major General William H. (USMC), 54, 59, 292, P LIV
Rutter, Lieutenant Robert, 397
Ryukyo Islands, 200, 307

SAGE, 114, note; 127
Saidor, action at, 62-63
SAILFISH (ex SQUALUS), 25, 101-03
ST. LO, 392; loss of, 400, 401

ST. LOUIS, 65, 66
Saipan, 126, 152, 159, 160, 183, 220, 222-25, 228-43, Plates XXXIII to XXXVII
attack on, story by Captain Martin, 225-27
Chamorros, 259-60
dismissal of Major General Ralph C. Smith, 258-59
Japanese commanders, 221, note
Japanese explanations, 260-61
Koreans on, 260
losses at, 267, note
suicide charge of Japanese; cost to Americans and enemy, 263
Saito, Lieutenant General Yoshigo, 220, note; 260-63
Sala, Commander Roland (Dr.) 372
Salamaua and Salamaua-Lae area, 12, 13, 25-28, 31, P III
SALT LAKE CITY, 111, note; 323, note
Samar, 299, 309, 311, 312, 365, 366-83, 413
Sample, Captain William D., 229
Sampson, Commander Robert R., 173
SAMUEL B. ROBERTS, 388, 389, 393, 398
Samuels, Lieutenant Jerome M., 169
San Bernardino Strait, 336, 337, 345, 347, 365, 380, 381, 382, 384-401, 414, 417, 422
SAN DIEGO, 39, 41, note; 109, note; 141, note
SAN FRANCISCO, 141, note; 197, note
SAN JACINTO, 198, 324, 374, P LXXII
SAN JUAN, 39, 41, note; 109, note
SANDS, 50, 51, 169, 297
SANGAMON, 128, 400, P LXXVII
Sansapor, P XXXII
SANTA FE, 81, 82, 111, 140, note; 191, 275, 276, 299, 327, 330, note; 410, 411, 412
SARATOGA, 39, 40, 41, 41, note; 42, 109, note; 128, 281, P V, P XLVI, P XLVII
Scammell, Lieutenant (jg) Scott, 195
Schatz, Lieutenant Commander Otto C., Jr., 39, note; 65
Schlemmer, Machinist George S., 152
Schmidt, Major General Harry (USMC), 114, 121, 124, 255
Schneider, Lieutenant Commander Frederick H., Jr., 363, note
Schoeffel, Captain Malcolm F., 95
Schoeni, Commander Walter P., 99
Schreiber, Commander Earl T., 371
Schwab, Lieutenant Commander Ernest L., 340
Schwartz, Lieutenant Commander Frank D., 50, 169
Scott, Commander J. A., 103, 180
Scott, Lieutenant Commander James II, 199
Scribner, Lieutenant Gilbert H., Jr., 92
Scruggs, Captain Richard M., 204, 206-07, 317
Scull, Commander Gifford, 410, note
SCULPIN, 99-103
Seabees, 173-74, 176
SEARAVEN, 99, 110, 127, 145, 149, 151, 160
Searcy, Lieutenant John M., 274
Seeadler Harbor, 166, 170, 174, 175, 202, 308, 312
Seibert, Major General Franklin C. (USA), 214
Selleck, RM 1/c W. M., 362
Settle, Captain Thomas G. W., 128, 364
SHAW, 51, note; 52, 56, 57
Shea, Lieutenant Edward C., 66
Shea, Commander William H., Jr., 410, note
Shelby, Lieutenant Commander Edward E., 110, 147, note
Shepard, Captain Andrew G., 66
Sherman, Rear Admiral Frederick C., 39, 41, 58-59, 109, note; 112, 114, 141, 141, note; 158, 299, 301, 323, 353, 368-71, 375, 377, 381, 402, 405
Sherman, Lieutenant Commander Philip K., 39, note; 41, note
SHIGURE, 154, note; 208, 353, 356, 357, 363, 364, 419
Shima, Vice Admiral K., 330, note; 354, 355, 363, 364
Shimanouchi, Rear Admiral Momochio, 207, 208
Shionoya, Warrant Officer, diary, 133-37
Ships, Japanese, lost at Truk, 154, note

Ships sunk in Battle for Leyte Gulf, 422-23
Shoemaker, Captain James M., 374
SHOKAKU, 223, *note*; 240-41, P XXXIX
Shoup, Colonel David (USMC), 85, 88, 90
SHROPSHIRE (HMAS), 51, *note*; 54, 56, 202, 315, 316, 364
Shumaker, Captain Samuel R., 197, *note*
Sibuyan Sea and Island, 378, 381, 404, P LXVIII
SIGOURNEY, 70, 316, 363, *note*
Silber, Lieutenant Commander Sam L., 142, 159, 160
Silverthorn, Colonel M. H., P XLI
Simpson, Captain Rodger W., 67
SKATE, 134, *note*; 147, 147, *note*
SKIPJACK, 110, 160
Skon, Ensign W. A. ("Ardy"), 96
Skorupski, Lieutenant Ed, 343
Slaughter, Lt. Comdr. John S., 363, *note*
Slightom, Lieutenant (jg) John D., 247
Slocum, Captain Harry B., 240, 364
Slot, the, 22, 37, 65, 71
Small, Rear Admiral Ernest G., 111, 111, *note*; 114
Smith, Rear Admiral Allan E., 323, *note*
Smith, Carol (USCG), P LX
Smith, Commander Daniel, 374, 405, 406, 411
Smith, ARM 2/c David H., 273
Smith, Harold P., P XXVII
Smith, Major General Holland M. (USMC), 71, 84, 110, 124, 266, P XXXVI
  dismissal of Major General Ralph C. Smith, 258-59
Smith, Commander J. McD., 65
Smith Lieutenant Commander James T., 27
Smith, Major General Julian (USMC), 85, 86, 90
Smith, Captain Page, P XLVII
Smith, Second Lieutenant Paul C., 268
Smith, Major General Ralph C. (USA), 84, 256
  dismissal by Major General H. M. Smith, 258-59
Smith, Commander Thurmond, 169
SMITH, 27, 28, 34, 35, 36, 51, *note*; 52, 169
Smoot, Captain Roland N., 357-58
Snowden, Commander Ernest M., 238
Soerabaja, 281-82, P XLVII
Solomons, 6, 7, 12, 13, 16, 17, 20, 21, 22, 27, 39, 48, 57, 64, 66-67, 70, 72, 76, 79, 124, 139, 166, 287, 353, 380
SONOMA, 30, 32, 33, 34, 207, 321
SOUTH DAKOTA, 109, *note*; 112, 141, *note*; 197, *note*; 240, 408, *note*
Spanagel, Captain Herman A., 54
Speck, Commander Robert H., 299
SPENCE, 44-47, 66, 69
Spencer, Captain Douglas A., 327, 410
Sprague, Rear Admiral Clifton F. A. ("Cliff"), 240, 382-85, 388, 392, 393, 395, 397, 399, 400, 413, 417, 418
Sprague, Rear Admiral Thomas L., 146, 288, 309, 313, 347, 385, 399
Spruance, Admiral Raymond A., 76-78, 79, 85, 97, 99, 108, 124, 126, 140, 140, *note*; 144-48, 156, 224, 225, 229, 232-34, 236, 241, 245, 252, 266, 285
"Spruance haircut," P XXI
SQUALUS. *See* SAILFISH
STACK, 39, *note*; 41, *note*; 109, *note*; 141, *note*
STANLY, 66, 68
Stark, Lieutenant Commander William W., 169
Stassen, Commander Harold E., 58, 367
Stebbins, Lieutenant Commander Edgar E., 160
Stedman, Lieutenant Charles H., 320
Steffanides, Commander E. E., Jr., 420
Stephan, Lieutenant Commander Charles R., 39, *note*; 65
STEPHEN POTTER, 109, *note*; 141, *note*; 197, *note*; 331, *note*; 368
STERETT, 39, *note*; 41, *note*; 109, *note*; 141, *note*
Stevenson, Lieutenant Commander William A., 147, *note*
Stich, Commander Francis S., 203
Stilwell, General Joseph, 306
STINGRAY, 273-75

STOCKTON, 169, 172, 173
Stout, Commander Herald F., 44, *note*
Stovall, Commander William S., Jr., 151
Strean, Commander Bernard M. ("Smoke"), 245-46
Strother, Chief Electrician's Mate, 340
Struble, Rear Admiral A. D., 316
Stump, Rear Admiral Felix, 385, 399, 416
Subic Bay, and attack on, 300-03
Submarines, 60, 199-201
Suicide fliers, Japanese. *See* Kamikazes
Sullivan, Captain Dennis J., 400
SULLIVANS, THE. *See* THE SULLIVANS
SUNFISH, 110, 147, *note*; 160
Surigao Strait, and Battle of, 311, 316, 336, 345, 347-65, 414, 419, 422, P LXVI, P LXVII, P LXVIII
SUWANNEE, 128, 400, P LXXI, P LXXVI
SUZUYA, 224, *note*; 338, 397, 418
Swaim, Ph M 1/c W. H., 361
Swift, Lieutenant Henry M. S., 60
Swift, Major General Innis P., 167

Tablas Strait, 373, 415, P LXXVIII
Tacloban, 311, 315, 316, 318-19, 345, 400, 414, 418, P LIX, P LX, P LXI
TACTICIAN (HMS), 281, P XLVII
TAIHO, 223, 223, *note*; 241, *note*; sinking of, 240
TAKAO, 40, 224, *note*; 338
Talauds, 303, 306
TAMA, 46, 407, 421
Tana Merah Bay, P XXX
TANG, 147, *note*; 160, 194-95, P XXV
Tapotchau, Mount, 231, 255, 261
Tarawa, 77-79, 81, 85, 104, 108, 115, 117, 118, 192, 285, 290, 292, P X, P XIV, P XV, P XVI
Tate, Lieutenant (jg) Benjamin C., 247-48
Tawi Tawi, 211, 222, 223, 229
Taylor, Captain Herbert Watson, Jr., 93, 313-14
TePas, Lieutenant Paul E., 148
Tedder, Commander Fondville L., 131, 202, *note*
Tennent, Commander John G., III, 111
TENNESSEE, 110, 122, 128, 129, 132, 228, 230-32, 287-88, 312, 316, 360, P LXVII
TERUTSUKI-class, P LXXII
THE SULLIVANS, 109, *note*; 141, *note*; 197, *note*; 331, *note*
Theiss, Commodore P. S., 230
Thebaud, Rear Admiral Leo H., 197, *note*
Theobald, Lieutenant Commander Robert A., Jr., 27, 169
Thomas, Torpedoman, 101
Thomas, Commander William D., 93, 131, 390
Thompson, AOM 2/c H. A., 196
Thompson, Lieutenant Commander Harry L., Jr., 128
Thompson, Commander Wells, 209
THORN, 316, 363, *note*
Thornwall, Commander Charles A., 200
"Thundermug, The," P LV
Thurber, Captain Harry R. ("Ray"), 44, *note*; 292, 320
Tidball, Lieutenant (jg) James M., 28
Tillar, Ensign Thomas Cato (USNR), 303-04
Tiner, Lieutenant Emmett L., 107
Tinian, 126, 157, 160, 220, 225, 228, 271-73, P XXXIII, P XL
Todd, Pharmacist's Mate Paul A., 100, 103
Todd, Captain Tarleton P., 410, *note*
Togo, Admiral, 358
Tojo, Hideko, 70, 276
Tokyo Express, 208
Tokyo Rose, 330
TONE, 224, *note*; 338, 392, 396, 397, 399, *note*; 417
Torpedo boats. *See* PT's
Torrey, Lieutenant Commander Philip, Jr., 146, 159
Toyoda, Admiral Soenu, 208, 221-23, 233, 244, 313, 325, 333-46, 364, 376
Transports, P LXVI
TRATHEN, 131, 202, *note*; 209
Tribble, Commander John C., Jr., (US Coast and Geodetic Survey), 115

INDEX

Trincomalee, P XLVI, P XLVII
Truk, 8, 37, 40, 42, 43, 67-70 76-79, 91, 99, 101, 103, 104, 110, 124, 126, 129, 134, 138-55, 177, 179, 193-201, P XXIII, P XXIV, P XXV
Tsushima Strait, Battle of, 358, *note*
Tsutjimura, Rear Admiral, 221, *note*
Tulagi, 13, 287
TUNNY, 103, 180, 182
Turner, Rear Admiral Richmond Kelly, 84, 110, 114, 116, 117, 230, 232-33, 235, 266, P XXXIX
Tweed, Radioman 1/c George R., 264
Typhoons, 322-23

Ulithi, 182, 233, 275, 286, 288, 290, 296, 297, 298, 323, 327, 331, *note*; 368, 369, 379
Underwater Demolition Teams, P LV, P LVI
Unit Citation, Presidential, 174
Uranowich, Chief Signalman, 57

Valenzio, Photographer 1/c, P v
VanMater, Commander Blinn, 64
VanMetre, Commander Merle, 299
Van Ness, Ship's Carpenter, 281
Vanous, Commander William W., 175
Veasey, Commander Alexander C., 410
Vella Lavella, 57
Vieweg, Captain Walter V., 392
VINCENNES, 408, *note*; 414
Visayan Sea and Visayas, 223, 318, 347, P LXXVIII
Visser, Commander Richard G., 56, 170
Vitiaz Strait and Battle of, 24, 26, 32, 35, 51, 60, 62, 189
Vogeley, Lieutenant Commander Theodore R., 169
Vraciu, Lieutenant Alexander, 238-40, P XXXIX

Wakde, 188, 191, 202-11, P XXXII
Wake Island, 77, 126, 198, P IV
Walker, Lieutenant John Denley, 246, 247
Walker, Colonel John T. (USMC), 129, 251-52
Wallace, ARM 3/c S. E., 41
Ward, Commander James H., 27
Ward, Lieutenant Commander Norwell G., 110
Ward, Lieutenant Commander R. E. M., 101
Wardroom, dining in, P IX
Warlick, Captain William W., 408, *note*
WARRAMUNGA (HMAS), 51, *note*; 173, 202, 209, 316
WASATCH, 288, 312, 314, 351, 381, 391
Washing machine at Kwajalein, P XXI
WASHINGTON, 109, *note*; 408, *note*
WASP, 198, 240, 301, 324, 327, 413
Watson, Brigadier General T. E. (USMC), 126, 127, 255
Webster, Lieutenant Gordon J. (RNZNR), 87
Weed, Lieutenant Edwin G., 274
Wegforth, Captain John F., 377
Well, Ensign Wilbur B. ("Spider"), 240
Weller, Captain Oscar A., 413
WELLES, 169, 316, 363, *note*
Welte, Lieutenant Commander Cecil R., 324, *note*
Wendorf, Ensign E. G., 250
WEST VIRGINIA, 312, 316, 359-60, P LXVII
WESTRALIA, 20, 50, 51, 52

Wewak, 16, 28, 33, 188, 189, 191
Weyler, Rear Admiral G. L., 352, 363
Wheeler, Captain Charles Julian, 111, 191
Wheeler, Lieutenant Commander Rexford V., Jr., 173
White, Lieutenant Howard A. (USCGR), 57
White, Lieutenant (jg) Norman, 95
WHITE PLAINS, 392, 400, P LXXI
Whitehead, Captain Richard F., 131, 309
Whitney, Captain John Perry, 386, 395
WICHITA, 109, *note*; 141, *note*; 197, *note*; 327, 330, *note*; 331, *note*; 410, 411
Wieber, Captain Carlos W., 377
Wiley, Captain Herbert V., 360
Wilkinson, Lieutenant Eugene P., 340
Wilkinson, Vice Admiral Theodore S., 65, 285, 296, 304, 208, 309, 312, 314, 316, 391
Willey, Commander Robert S., 324, *note*
Williams, Radio Gunner, 225, 226
Williams, Commander Henry, Jr., 202
Williams, Commander Paul D., 324, *note*
Williamson, Lieutenant Commander John A., 199
Wilson, Captain Earl J. (USMC), 86, 89
Wilson, Commander Edmond F., 169
Wilson, Captain Ralph ("Rollo"), 367
WILSON, 39, *note*; 41, *note*; 109, *note*; 141, *note*
Wiltsie, Captain Irving D., 94
Winn, Commander Walter C., 295
Winston, Lieutenant Commander Philip W., 410, *note*
Winston, Commander Robert A., 240
Winters, Commander Hugh, 377, 408-09, 410
Wolsieffer, Commander Frederick, 203
Wood, Lieutenant Commander Ernest W., Jr., 302
Woodlark, 21, 22, 24, 27, 214, 317
WOODWORTH, 39, *note*; 65-67
Wordell, Commander Malcolm, 411
Wotje, 108, 111, 111, *note*; 114
Wright, Captain Jerauld, 111, 191, 410

YAHAGI, 223, *note*; 338, 375, 387, 389
Yamamoto, Captain, 185, 186
Yamamoto, Admiral Isoruku, 6, 7
YAMASHIRO, 353, 356, 357, P LXV
Yamashita, General, 319
Yamata, Rear Admiral, 124
YAMATO, 134, *note*; 211, 223, *note*; 336, 338, 344, 374-76, 387, 389, 399, 401, 416, 417, P LXXVIII
Yap, 178, 182, 233, 275, 296, 304, 306, 308, 309, 316, 368
YORKTOWN, 95, 109, 116, 140, *note*; 141, 142, 151, 152, 159, 179, 229, 247, P XXVIII
Young, Lieutenant Commander Andrew L., Jr., 93
Young, Lieutenant John A., Jr., 320
Young, Commander Robert C., 410, *note*
Younger, Soundman Junior, 342

Zacharias, Captain Ellis M., 84, 267
Zinn, Lieutenant Franklyn K., 127
ZUIHO, 102, 223, *note*; 345, 407, 409, *note*; 411, P LXXIV
ZUIKAKU, 223, *note*; 241, 248, 345, 406-07, 408, 409, 419, P LXXIII, P LXXV